New England Literary Culture

Cambridge Studies in American Literature and Culture

Editor

Albert Gelpi, Stanford University

Advisory Board

Nina Baym, University of Illinois, Champaign–Urbana
Sacvan Bercovitch, Harvard University
Richard Bridgman, University of California, Berkeley
David Levin, University of Virginia
Joel Porte, Harvard University
Mike Weaver, Oxford University

New England Literary Culture

From Revolution Through Renaissance

LAWRENCE BUELL
Oberlin College

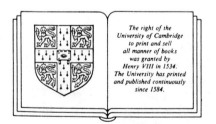

The right of the
University of Cambridge
to print and sell
all manner of books
was granted by
Henry VIII in 1534.
The University has printed
and published continuously
since 1584.

CAMBRIDGE UNIVERSITY PRESS

CAMBRIDGE

NEW YORK PORT CHESTER

MELBOURNE SYDNEY

Published by the Press Syndicate of the University of Cambridge
The Pitt Building, Trumpington Street, Cambridge CB2 1RP
32 East 57th Street, New York, NY 10022, USA
10 Stamford Road, Oakleigh, Melbourne 3166, Australia

© Cambridge University Press 1986

First published 1986
Reprinted 1987 (twice)
First paperback edition 1989

Printed in the United States of America

Library of Congress Cataloging in Publication Data
Buell, Lawrence.
New England literary culture from revolution
through renaissance.
(Cambridge studies in American literature and culture)
Bibliography: p.
Includes index.
1. American literature – New England – History and
criticism.   2. New England – Civilization.   3. New
England in literature.   4. Puritans – New England.
I. Title.   II. Series.
PS243.B84   1986   810'.9'974   85-14893

British Library Cataloguing in Publication Data
Buell, Lawrence
New England literary culture from revolution
through renaissance. – (Cambridge studies in
American literature and culture)
1. American literature – New England – 19th
century – History and criticism
I. Title
810.9'974   PS234

ISBN 0 521 30206 4 hard covers
ISBN 0 521 37801 X paperback

For Denise and Deirdre

Contents

vii

Acknowledgments

A book of this scope could not have been written without help from many sources. So far as scholarly assistance is concerned, I want to express special thanks to a number of colleagues who commented on drafts of portions of the typescript or provided other guidance and support: Nina Baym, Lauren Berlant, Robert Caserio, Michael Colacurcio, W. Patrick Day, Robert Ferguson, Robert Gross, Walter Harding, Gary Kornblith, Carol Lasser, Christie Lerch, Robert Longsworth, James McIntosh, John McWilliams, Joel Myerson, Leonard Neufeldt, John Olmsted, Robert Pierce, David Porter, David Robinson, Daniel Shea, Teresa Toulouse, Harlan Wilson, Sandra Zagarell, and Grover Zinn. Frederick Buell helped me at several points to understand where my thoughts were moving before I understood myself. To the superb students whom it has been my good fortune to teach year after year at Oberlin College, I am grateful for helping to keep me intellectually challenged and at least relatively open-minded into my middle years. To the intellectual ambience of Oberlin College I am indebted for prompting me to stretch my mind beyond my original discipline as well as within it and for evidence that the ideal small communities imaged in New England literature have a basis in fact.

In a more tangible sense, Oberlin College has helped me with two paid leaves of absence, with several research grants, and with secretarial support from three heroic typists: Jan Dahl, Thelma Kime, and Sandy Peacock. I am also grateful for a Senior Research Fellowship provided by the National Endowment for the Humanities, during which time much of this book was drafted.

Versions of a few sections were previously published in three essays. To Garland Publishing, Inc., I am grateful for permission to republish parts of Chapter 4 that appeared originally in *American Literature: The New England Heritage* (1981), edited by James Nagel and Richard Astro; to the University of Texas Press, for permission to reuse in Chapters 10 and 11 portions of an article on Hawthorne and Stowe that appeared in Volume 25, Number 1, of *Texas Studies in Literature and Language* (1983); and to the University of Notre Dame, for the opportunity to deliver the first version of Chapter 7 at a summer conference, the contributions to which were subsequently published in the spring 1983 issue of *Notre Dame English Journal*.

The two short excerpts from Elizabeth Stoddard's correspondence that appear in Chapter 16 are quoted by permission of the Houghton Library, Harvard University, and the American Antiquarian Society, Worcester (Richard Henry Stoddard Papers).

Finally, for support beyond anything I can describe, I thank all the members of my family, especially my wife, Kim, and the two young scholars to whom this book is dedicated, my daughters, who have grown up as it has grown up, and who have seen to it that I was saved from excesses of ivory towerism.

Abbreviations of Frequently Cited Works

DAB   *Dictionary of American Biography.* Ed. Allen Johnson and Dumas
Malone. 20 vols. and index, 1928–37. 6 suppls., 1944–81.

DL   *The Letters of Emily Dickinson.* Ed. Thomas H. Johnson and
Theodora Ward. 3 vols. Cambridge, Mass.: Harvard Univ.
Press, 1958.

DP   *The Poems of Emily Dickinson.* Ed. Thomas H. Johnson. 3 vols.
Cambridge, Mass.: Harvard Univ. Press, 1955. *Cited by poem
number.*

DT   Dwight, Timothy. *Travels in New-England and New-York.* Ed.
Barbara Miller Solomon. 4 vols. Cambridge, Mass.: Harvard
Univ. Press, 1969.

EW   *The Collected Works of Ralph Waldo Emerson,* vols. 1–3. Ed.
Alfred Ferguson, Robert Spiller, Joseph Slater et al. Cambridge,
Mass.: Harvard Univ. Press, 1971–83.
The Complete Writings of Ralph Waldo Emerson, vols. 3–12. Ed.
Edward W. Emerson. Boston: Houghton Mifflin, 1903–4.

HW   *The Centenary Edition of the Works of Nathaniel Hawthorne.* Ed.
William Charvat, Roy Harvey Pearce, Claude M. Simpson et al.
16 vols. to date. Columbus: Ohio State Univ. Press, 1962–.

JMN   *The Journals and Miscellaneous Notebooks of Ralph Waldo Emerson.*
Ed. William H. Gilman et al. 16 vols. Cambridge, Mass.: Harvard Univ. Press, 1960–82.

LL   *The Letters of Henry Wadsworth Longfellow.* Ed. Andrew Hilen. 6
vols. Cambridge, Mass.: Harvard Univ. Press, 1967–82.

LoW   Lowell, James Russell. *The Works of James Russell Lowell.* 10 vols.
Boston: Houghton Mifflin, 1892.

LW   Longfellow, Henry Wadsworth. *Complete Writings.* Ed. Horace
Scudder. 11 vols. Boston: Houghton Mifflin: 1904.

MOW   *"The Morgesons" and Other Writings, Published and Unpublished, by Elizabeth Stoddard.* Ed. Lawrence Buell and Sandra A. Zagarell. Philadelphia: Univ. of Pennsylvania Press, 1984.

TJ   *The Journal of Henry D. Thoreau.* Ed. Bradford Torrey and Francis H. Allen. 14 vols. Boston: Houghton Mifflin, 1906. Where superseded by Thoreau's *Journal,* vols. 1–2, 1837–48, ed. John C. Broderick et al. (Princeton: Princeton Univ. Press, 1981–4), the latter text is cited instead.

Wa   Thoreau, Henry D. *Walden.* Ed. J. Lyndon Shanley. Princeton: Princeton Univ. Press, 1971.

WW   *The Works of John Greenleaf Whittier.* 7 vols. Boston: Houghton Mifflin, 1892–4.

PART I

Four Overviews

I

Theoretical Premises

> One cannot do theoretical research without having the courage to put forward a theory, and, therefore, an elementary model as a guide for subsequent discourse; all theoretical research must however have the courage to specify its own contradictions, and should make them obvious where they are not apparent.
>
> Umberto Eco, *A Theory of Semiotics* (1976)

> We do what we can, & then make a theory to prove our performance the best.
>
> Ralph Waldo Emerson, *Journals and Miscellaneous Notebooks* (1834)

This book is a study of New England literature during the years when it developed from an amateur pastime to its peak of distinction, the so-called New England Renaissance of about 1830–60. I shall explore the foundations, the unfolding, and the literary results of this great change, giving special attention to major writers – Emerson, Thoreau, Hawthorne, Stowe, and Dickinson particularly – but surveying them in relation to a host of other figures and to the conventions, values, and institutions that shaped their work in common. I hope in the process to contribute to the understanding of the authors and genres discussed, of the ideology of provincialism in general and the New England strain in particular, the phenomenon of literary emergence, and the ongoing attempt to chart a course for American literary history.

The following chapters approach New England letters from two complementary vantage points. Parts I and II, starting with Chapter 2, concentrate on aspects of the regional literary experience that were nationally representative in the Emersonian sense of exhibiting in highlighted form trends that were visible throughout American literary culture: the rise of authorship as a profession (Chapter 2); the literary ethos that arose from the interplay of professional with amateur writing and the impact of

3

Neoclassical and Romantic styles upon preexisting aesthetic values (Chapters 3–4); and the form and ideology of three important genres (Chapters 5–7) that flourished under those conditions, genres practiced throughout the country, although New England writers stood preeminent. Parts III and IV take up the more region-specific issues of the codification of the New England self-image into a myth of Puritan antecedence (Chapters 8–11) and an iconography of place (Chapters 12–16). The contrast in focus between the book's two halves is meant to suggest both that regional particularity is not the sole or even the chief feature of period writing and that the literary expression of regional self-consciousness was an important corollary of the institutionalization of letters described in Part I.

The fact that New England literary culture was neither wholly self-generated nor unique makes clear-cut demarcation of the territory impossible. In this study, "New England literature" means primarily the creative writing (including nonfictional prose) produced by several hundred major and minor authors (most of them listed in the table at the end of the Appendix) who either grew up in the six New England states between 1770 and 1865 or lived the greater part of their working lives there. Secondarily the phrase refers to the work of outlanders like Cooper and Melville who, through serendipity or contagion, showed at times a New England orientation. Some readers may question the inclusion of such work, but in the long run any shortcoming, I think, lies in the opposite problem: that intensive concentration on literary events within the region has kept me from showing the full extent of cultural solidarity between New and Old England and the full extent of the diffusion of New England influences throughout America.

A few words about the two initial chapters, and then we are under way. Both are introductions of different kinds. The present chapter outlines my conception of literary history, with special reference to New England writing of the period under review, against the background of recent literary theory. In this it is intended to remedy a chronic shortcoming of Anglo-American literary historiography to date, refusal to examine its own implicit theoretical positions; and, in the process, to provide some comfort for those fellow workers in my vineyard inclined to view the late explosion of literary theory only as a monolithic, hostile force threatening our extinction as a species. By the same token, I realize that some readers, rightly expecting to find a work of literary history rather than of literary theory, may find their access to the rest of the book blocked by Chapter 1. If so, they are hereby invited to proceed directly to Chapter 2 or 3, depending on their familiarity with the subject.

Chapter 2 provides a short narrative of the growth of New England literary institutions, a kind of Brooksian *Flowering of New England* in miniature. It is designed especially to introduce the period's writers, pertinent intellectual movements, and literary economics to the nonspecialist, although some of the material therein will be unfamiliar even to the experienced. Those already well versed in early national and antebellum literary history may wish to peruse Chapter 2 more quickly, in order to come to terms at once with the more probing discussions that follow.

I

No informed practitioner of literary history can fail to be aware of working in a genre whose premises are vaguely understood and variously evaluated by colleagues of different critical persuasions. This makes it incumbent on individual scholars to explain their goals and methods and to respond in some way to the common misperception that literary history is a bankrupt enterprise. For literary history today is indeed at a curious impasse. Its demise, like that of Puritanism, has been proclaimed for some time, yet, like the Puritan spirit, it has managed to persist, in vigorous if mutated form. "We are all disenchanted," writes Geoffrey Hartman, "with those picaresque adventures in pseudo-causality which go under the name of literary history, those handbooks with footnotes which claim to sing of the whole but load every rift with glue."[1] Quite so; yet those handbooks continue to be inflicted on students from coast to coast. "Considerations of the actual and historical existence of writers are a waste of time from a critical viewpoint," writes Paul de Man, and one must agree, insofar as "critical viewpoint" means viewing history *sub specie textualis*.[2] Yet the discredited project continues, not just at the level of humdrum compendiums but also at the level of advanced research. Feminist revisionary scholarship, for instance, is justly credited with having refined our thinking about the meaning and production of nineteenth-century literary texts, yet such works as Ann Douglas's *Feminization of American Culture,* Nina Baym's *Women's Fiction,* and Mary Kelley's *Private Woman, Public Stage* derive much of their force from the assumption that biographical and historical evidence matters.[3]

Controversy over whether the study of literature in extraliterary context is irrelevant or philosophically disreputable is, of course, longstanding, yet since the early 1970s it has reached a new peak of epistemological crisis, owing, I think, to two very different, although related, factors. One is the direction of American literary theory. Traditional literary history was first called into question and the development of superior models impeded by the new criticism's distinction between literary and nonliterary domains and its isolation of the supposedly autonomous artifact as the privileged object of study. No matter whether real-life new critics actually continued to engage in old-fashioned historiography. The crucial point was that their theory conceived of literary history as a series of discrete texts grouped together according to the principle of unfolding formal and generic norms. That left the would-be historian without a means of connecting literary microcosm with social macrocosm, and thereby without a way of providing a full account of literary development, which, as Wellek and Warren granted, is a "complex process" caused partly by "social, intellectual, and all other cultural changes."[4] In a more sophisticated form, the same problem besets literary semiotics, which, together with its younger relative, deconstructionism, has become new-critical formalism's most powerful competitor in American literary theory. Semiology initially seems to provide a more solid basis for literary history by breaking down the parochial distinction between literary and nonliterary discourse and by recognizing the culturally conditioned nature of both. Yet because it is based on the paradigm of culture as communications system, semiology tends to approach literature and its social context synchronically, as one conflated field of discourse governed by norms whose envisaged unity or internal rifts are of greater interest than their historical development, and to regard "external" reality itself as text or artifact. Study of the relationship between literary text and historical and biographical context continues to be sidelined, but for the opposite reason: Whereas under new criticism the problem is that one cannot see beyond the realm of the literary into that of the extrinsic, under semiology the problem is that there no longer seems to be any extrinsic domain as such. We are enveloped in a macrosystem of codes and acts of signification from which there is no escape to history, because it *is* history. As Umberto Eco puts it, with unintentional grimness, "Every attempt to establish what the referent of a sign is forces us to define the referent in terms of an abstract entity which moreover is only a cultural convention."[5]

It should be added at once that both the new critics and newer literary theorists have continued to maintain a certain interest in the historiographical project that they have questioned. Wellek and Warren end their *Theory of Literature,* the new criticism's *summa theologica,* with a call for the elaboration of a "new ideal of literary history"; Hartman repeats this gesture in *Beyond Formalism;* Jonathan Culler expresses the hope that "one source of energy for criticism in the coming years may be the reinvention of literary history."[6] Yet from where they stand, the project necessarily seems a "desperately vast undertaking," as de Man says[7] – one that seems to involve vast inferential leaps to conjectures that are not of central interest anyway, given the overriding commitment either to verbal icon or to the phenomenon of textuality as the main object of study. From this perspective, to the extent that literary history seems possible at all, it presents itself either as a kind of erotics of reading, which one frankly delivers as fictive improvisation (e.g., Hartman's *Criticism in the Wilderness*) or else as a hermeneutic like Harold Bloom's, whose playful convolutions keep it so provisional and darksome as to amount almost to a confession of arbitrariness.

The second challenge to the traditional historical narrative of literary development as a weave of aesthetic, biographical, and sociohistorical factors is even more threatening, because it comes from within. Through its resourcefulness and proliferation, literary-historical inquiry has called its own solidity into question. Doubtless, the most important reason why, for example, no full-scale scholarly history of American literature was undertaken between 1948 and 1984 is the sheer logistical problem of sorting out the huge and increasingly diverse body of scholarship.[8] So many avenues of possible inquiry were opened as to make the story that in our Parringtonian innocence once looked so clear seem like the "Garden of Forking Paths" of Borges' Ts'ui Pên, in which each action leads to every possible outcome. Take the way in which feminist revisionism has put all discourse under the sign of gender. This issue having been broached, earlier studies once regarded as definitive seem to dissolve into rhetoric and the whole past to become a battleground. Likewise the shift from old-style new-critical single-text analysis to new-style analysis of interpretive convention may have been brought about by the dissonance among the "objective" close readings produced under the former regime. These provide both the ground for Jonathan Culler's call for a moratorium on interpretation ("One thing we do not need is more interpretations of literary works") and the data base for his studies of reading competence.[9]

That limits to empirical study of literary history have been demonstrated both in theory and in practice does not, however, undermine the value of the enterprise. The absolute of relativism is no truer than its mirror opposite, the naive objectivism that assumes the possibility of approaching one's subject without cultural bias. As Clifford Geertz says of anthropology, the fact that "cultural analysis is intrinsically incomplete" does not support the argument that, since "complete objectivity is impossible in these matters, . . . one might as well let one's sentiments run loose. . . . That is like saying that as a perfectly aseptic environment is impossible, one might as well conduct surgery in a sewer."[10] To cite just one case in point, the American literary scholar of the past generation whose work has probably suffered the least obsolescence is William Charvat, who specialized in the study of how the economics of publishing affected authorial behavior and literary development, tracking down statistics on royalties and examining publishers' cost books. Without Charvat we would know a good deal less about what the literary choices made by Hawthorne, Longfellow, and Melville signify.[11] Whether the same can be said of most critical analyses of their work is questionable. That the benefits of a rigorous empiricism are not to be underestimated seems still more obvious from the current scene in the neighboring discipline of historiography. Equally intensive methodological ferment in this field has pushed it in the opposite direction from literary studies, as social and, in particular, economic historians have made major gains in their advocacy of quantitative approaches to replace what they regard as the critical impressionism of old-school political and intellectual history. The diagnosis of the predecessor's shortcomings is similar; the recommended cure is very different.[12] Whereas in literary studies Continental literary theory has ushered in an age of speculation, in historiography cliometrics has led to a new positivism. That very divergence makes it all the more crucial to listen to the claims of both, especially if one happens to be a student of American Studies, an enterprise built on an uneasy marriage of history and literature now in imminent danger of divorce. Cliometrics challenges both old- and new-fashioned literary study, both past and present, at some of its most vulnerable points, such as its tendency to limit attention to a handful of major works in each age – the aesthetic equivalent of the concentration, in traditional historiography, on the behavior of dominant elites that is one of recent social history's primary objects of attack. In my appendix, "Vital Statistics," I respond to that challenge by applying quantitative methods to the study of the careers of 276 New England writers, in order to reinforce and extend my account of the social history of period authorship given in the balance of this book.

Such exercises, however, also show the limits of their own applicability. They show at once that literary history can yield objectively true stories (such as "proliferation of new-critical close readings helped to stimulate Jonathan Culler's studies of reading competence"). Yet by their intensified methodological self-consciousness they also show that literary history will continue to be an interpretive project, one that involves transposing percepts from one medium or framework into another and, consequently, the production of culture-bound textualizations of the thing described, subject to restatement in the light of new principles or evidence. The situation for literary historians seems to be the same as Geertz says it is for ethnographers: Their scholarly constructs, being interpretations, are therefore "fictions . . . in the sense that they are 'something made,'" although not thereby "false, unfactual, or merely 'as if' thought experiments."[13]

The great value of this statement is its straightforward recognition of the interdependence of subjective envisionment and objective research. Among theorists of literary history, a counterpart is Hans Robert Jauss, whose "aesthetics of reception" (*Rezeptionsästhetik*) is a self-styled synthesis of Marxist and formalist elements. Jauss describes the continuity of literary tradition and history as a "dialectic of question and answer that is always kept going . . . from the present interest."[14] Literary history results from the interaction of two "horizons of expectation": (1) the critic's, which is shaped by a cultural context that includes the residue of earlier interpretations, and (2) that of the culture in and for which the work was written, which Jauss sees as providing a standard against which to measure the work's originality. Through this interaction, a kind of compact is arrived at between objective and subjective domains, so that the literary scholar can say, with social historian Natalie Zemon Davis, "What I offer you here is in part my own invention, but held tightly in check by the voices of the past."[15]

Jauss's theory is questionable in several respects: It tends to presuppose that the object of historical study is the individual classic; that the work's original deviation from critical orthodoxy is the chief measure of its quality; that the study of contemporary responses to major works is the best way of getting at a period's literary assumptions; that the possibility of perennially valid questions and answers can be ruled out; and that the course of history is dependent upon the process of reception – an impression that has led Marxist critics to criticize Jauss's system as a rarefied form of bourgeois consumerism.[16] Yet I take him as having at least prepared the way for a satisfactory formulation of the dialogical relationship between the student and the object of study, the dimensions of subjectivity and objectivity inherent in that relation, and the elements of individual uniqueness and public representativeness in both work horizon and reader horizon. His formulation takes account of the inevitable myopia and present-mindedness of literary study at any point in history without denying either its capacity to draw meaningful conclusions or the status of history as an extratextual field with which researchers can come into relation, albeit self-interestedly.

But to establish the grounds on which literary history is possible is only the beginning of the job. The analytical framework itself remains to be specified. One reason, surely, why Geertz's semiological theory of reading cultures is much more relaxed in its acknowledgment of the limits of what scholarship can accomplish than Jauss's painstakingly circumspect seven theses on how to do literary history is the fact that the ethnographic procedures on which Geertz reflects have been more rigorously articulated and have won a much broader consensus than those of literary historiography, Jaussian or otherwise. The latter (at least in the English-speaking world) continues to be practiced with much less methodological forethought – without, for example, one's having taken a seminar on how to do it or having absorbed more than a smattering of the main models and theoretical discussions. That the question of whether the whole enterprise is possible has been seriously entertained is doubtless not so much because the questioners believe it impossible under any circumstances as because we have reflected insufficiently on how literary history should be done. Hence the need for those who would practice it to spell out their notions of form, scope, and method.

Hence, too, any mature conception of the structure of literary history must draw not simply on formalist and empiricist scholarship but also on Marxist investigations. The Marxist tradition, indeed, has generated the closest approximations to date of a satisfactory model to replace the unselfconscious names–dates–movements–trends approach of old-style impressionist historicism. Literary Marxism, once it gets past the pigeonholing stage of reducing literary narratives to rudimentary allegories, shows signs of furnishing a program at once more cohesive than old-style literary history and more successful than formalism and semiotics in accounting for how social forces condition literary language and the production of texts. That is because Marxist theory envisages language not merely as a relational system that conditions discourse, and thereby threatens to collapse social reality back into text, but also as "articulated social *presence*," itself the creature of the social reality it textualizes.[17] In the hands of comparatively nondoctrinaire practitioners such as Raymond Williams, Pierre Macherey, or (sometimes) Georg Lukács and Frederic Jameson, Marxist literary historiography becomes powerfully responsive both to the old, persistent, and I think entirely justifiable desire for a coherent, self-consistent vision of history that writer and scholar can glimpse and further through their respective forms of literary praxis and also to the new-fashioned awareness of the necessarily mediated character of all historical knowledge. Jameson, for instance, reassures us that "if interpretation in terms of expressive causality or of allegorical master narratives remains a constant temptation, this is because such master narratives have inscribed themselves in the texts as well as in our thinking about them"; they reflect "our collective fantasies about history and reality," which, in turn, represent the inscription of the "absent cause," history itself, upon the collective unconscious.[18] This semioticized version of Marxist hermeneutics promises all that the bourgeois scholar nurtured in the gospel of textual intrinsics could hope for by way of a broader vista: a Pisgah glimpse of a promised land of coherent historical movement and structure, a land rightly closed to us by the mediations of text and consciousness (if the prophet told us we could enter it, we would chide him for wishful thinking) but reassuringly *there*. Jameson's vision, despite its pretentious rhetoric, goes a step farther than Jauss in suggesting how we may venture to approach the truth of history, whatever that truth may be, and beckons us on to formulate our instruments of analysis in the knowledge that they are bound in a sense to be collective fantasies yet can become carriers and promoters of knowledge for all that.

II

Altogether there seem to be at least four major types of instruments, corresponding to the ways in which literary history takes shape. Literary history may be seen as structured in terms of epochs, canons, matrices of institutionalized controls reflecting an interplay of intrinsic and extrinsic forces, and temporal sequences. Any work of literary history makes at least implicit claims about all of these modes of structuration. No historian can avoid bias or distortion in the process; yet none can avoid believing (and with good reason) that these are actual ordering principles, even if their operation cannot be specified beyond a certain point. The question is not whether they really constitute literary-historical structures but how and to what extent those structures operate. I want, therefore, to comment briefly on each as regards the present study. To a considerable extent, my views are ad hoc, arising as much from a pragmatic sense of how to present my subject to advantage as from a theory of how literary history should be written. I admit this with some embarrassment (relieved by knowing that I have company) but not because I fear that any theoretical spottiness necessarily invalidates my presentation. Any future attempts to articulate models for doing literary history will have to conclude that to some extent circumstances alter cases and will have to take shape through critiques of other partial formulations like mine.

1. *Periodization.* Periodization is a necessary evil of all historical study. Anything short of universal history must periodize, yet boundaries and degree of internal coherence are notoriously hard to specify. "Nothing would be more false," writes Michel Foucault, "than to see in the analysis of discursive formations an attempt at totalitarian periodization, whereby from a certain moment and for a certain time, everyone would think in the same way, in spite of surface differences, say the same thing, through a polymorphous vocabulary, and produce a sort of great discourse that one could travel over in any direction."[19] Yet when Foucault himself turns to the writing of his own "archaeologies," he constantly periodizes in ways that look slipshod in light of his theory. He is not alone.

Both contextual and aesthetic rubrics are often used as the basis of periodization in literary history, though Wellek and Warren are surely right in arguing that the former are justified only insofar as they have implications for the latter.[20] Both types of classification are used in this book. At times I refer to political boundaries (the Revolution and the Civil War); in Chapter 1 I subdivide the field into five "generations," but elsewhere I shall for the most part utilize only two period designations, the more conventional "early national" (sometimes "Federalist") era and the "antebellum" era, the approximate dividing point being around 1815, the end of America's second war of independence. The aesthetic justification for this two-part scheme is that it corresponds to the succession from Neoclassical to Romantic hegemony in New England literary culture. Hegemony does not mean unanimity however, and in fact one of the aims of this book is to point up the limitations of dichotomizing among Neoclassical, Romantic, and Realist insofar as they apply to New England literary thought and practice. Particularly in Chapters 12 and 16, when discussing the interrelation of Romantic and Realist regional prose, my use of these time-honored period designations is intended to raise questions about the rigidity of scholarly convention in the process of invoking it. Of course, the very act of invocation perpetuates the impression of distinct epochs of taste, whereas there are some features of the literary scene for which the whole question of the pertinence or impertinence of these period categories is irrelevant: hymnology, for instance. My way of compensating for this has been to start by presenting the story of regional development largely from the standpoint of emerging literary professionalism rather than of shifts in literary taste. This, indeed, is the single most basic theme in terms of which the years under review are seen as unified: the rise of regional literary development. The Revolution makes an appropriate starting point not because it marks a change in literary mode – on the contrary, it falls about midway in the history of New England Neoclassicism – but because it forced regional literary culture to begin anew in several senses. It threw the literary society of the region's intellectual capital, Boston, into disarray; it made necessary the reconception of New England and other regional cultures as part of a national whole; and it made inevitable, through the achievement of political independence, an evolution toward a fully articulated system of literary institutions that had been lacking in colonial times. The Civil War – a more porous divider for this study, which in Part IV ranges as far forward as the early 1900s – marks the approximate point beyond which the energy of the New England Renaissance began to abate, although the region's literary prestige continued for many years thereafter.

2. *Defining the literary field: canon and selectivity.* "Literature," in my notion of it, comprises potentially all written and oral utterances, insofar as anything made out of words can be treated as a literary artifact, although I would characterize individual utterances as literary in proportion to their capacity to provoke responses to them as verbal constructs, above and beyond their perceived function as means of communication.[21]

A decade ago, in reaction to the overwhelming concentration of the new criticism on poetry, prose fiction, and drama, I felt obliged to argue on behalf of a literary approach to writing outside the conspicuously fictive genres. Today my position will seem noncontroversial, even tame. Much more critical attention is now paid to nonfictional prose, and the influence of structuralism and its progeny has led many to question whether, as de Man puts it, all writing should not be seen as part of the empire of the literary: "What [modern critics] call anthropology, linguistics, psychoanalysis is nothing but literature reappearing, like the Hydra's head, in the very spot where it had supposedly been suppressed."[22] I would not go that far. First, I am not any more comfortable than de Man turns out to be with the total obliteration of the boundary between that which knows itself as fictive and that which cannot avoid fiction in the process of attempting to tell the truth, although borderline cases like Nietzschean aphorism, Camusian parable, and Lacanian psychoanalysis weaken that boundary. Nor would I agree with de Man's apparent assumption that what these modes of writing share is simply fictionality. That may be the single most important linking motif, but also of great importance, and all the greater given the tendency of current literary theory to suppress the point, is the transfictional dimension of fictive works, particularly their didactic and referential aspects. Without question, the choice of a fictive form (e.g., a didactic poem rather than a homily, or a historical novel rather than a history) constitutes in itself an act of resistance to the didactic or the referential in a strict sense. But that does not imply an abandonment or rejection of the extrinsic domain. On the contrary, "Fictions," as Jeffrey Sammons notes, "would be wholly incomprehensible if they did not refer constantly to phenomena of external experience."[23] On this point, I align myself with the "silent majority" of critics whom George Levine drolly pictures as "angrily staring through the bars of this prison house of language into which they have been thrown for an indeterminate sentence on fictitious charges, with no sign of parole."[24] One of the great values of studying nonfictional and fictional forms together – historiography and historical romance, for example – is that the relationship is not uni-directional: Comparing them can make us more aware not only of the fictionalizing tendencies of the one but also of the historicizing tendencies of the other.

   This bi-directionalness seems an especially crucial aspect of periods of literary emergence such as the one surveyed here, in which belles lettres were moving toward, yet still far from attaining, their present degree of autonomy. In such a situation, compounded, as we shall see, by certain factors peculiar to the American scene, literature is under great pressure to remain socially responsible while simultaneously it is encouraged by promptings from both within and without to develop itself independently. Thus the aesthetic impulse starts to flourish but, in the process, becomes displaced into nonfictional forms (as would-be writers continue to fulfill their literary impulses through law and divinity, for example) and into fictive forms like those of Hawthorne's tales, which reflect the struggle between pure invention and the sense that moral law and historical fact provide the only safe and proper grounds for mental exercise. Indeed, one of the most crucial points I have to make about New England literary culture is that it takes shape according to the logic of this two-way pull.

This study, then, will swim vigorously with the tide of fashion in approaching "nonliterary" modes of discourse such as theology and historiography as fictionalized modes, yet it will also distinguish between these and more avowedly fictive constructs, and it will approach both as textualizations not only of cultural values but ultimately also of social reality.

Owing partly to its fence-straddling notion of how fictive, nonfictional, and extraliterary spheres interrelate, this study has been written with several distinct notions of canon in mind. On one level, the book may be read selectively as a reinterpretation, through explication and contextual commentary, of the work of literary figures regarded by consensus as major. I have taken for granted from the start that any literary history of the era would have to reckon carefully with the work of Emerson, Thoreau, Hawthorne, and Dickinson (to name only the four who seem most important to me). To this extent, the book follows a great figures – great classics approach to literary history, seeing it as taking shape in terms of what seem to be its peaks of achievement. At the opposite extreme, however, I have also invoked an exceptionally broad definition of canon, as in the Appendix, a collective profile of several hundred literary careers. There and elsewhere I argue that the achievement of the few figures on whom scholarship usually concentrates (the "canon" in the conventional sense) cannot be understood without reference to a much more inclusive group.

My researches in the latter, in turn, have led me to conclude that a number of neglected figures deserve much closer scrutiny, not just in order to make background generalizations about the greats but also to appreciate them as artists in their own right. Thus my study also participates in the work of canonical revision initiated by feminist and ethnic studies.[25] For example, I assign Harriet Beecher Stowe, still stigmatized by many as ephemeral, a major figure's role and single out for extended discussion in Chapter 16 Elizabeth Stoddard, hitherto overlooked even by most specialists in women's literature yet in my judgment "the most strikingly original voice in the mid-nineteenth-century American novel after Melville and Hawthorne" (*MOW*, p.xi).* These are but the two

---

* Works frequently cited will be abbreviated. See the list of abbreviations that immediately precedes Part I.

most visible examples in a series of resuscitations that includes also William Joseph Snelling, Ellen Hooper, Eliza Townsend, Tabitha Tenney, St. John Honeywood, Stephen Burroughs, and Peter Oliver, among others. Would that there were room for more.

I have not tried, however, to achieve either a total and proportionate coverage of works that consensus has seemed justly to regard as great or a systematic job of canonical revision. That is because both these priorities have been balanced against a third and ultimately overriding goal of mapping the coordinates of literary culture. Hence my discussions of individual authors and works are, in the long run, exemplary. That means shortchanging a number of works and authors worthwhile from an aesthetic standpoint in favor of less distinguished examples. Any such disproportionateness from the standpoint of literary intrinsics will, I hope, justify itself by what it manages to disclose about the norms within and against which the period's classics necessarily took shape.

For some, of course, any attempt to discuss notable literary achievement in terms of cultural representativeness will seem tendentious. This view is by no means limited to old-style new critics. R. S. Crane, the patriarch of Chicago pluralism, also opined that the literary historian's central mission was to examine texts "with a view to the new state of affairs brought about by the work's appearance," a dictum that recalls T. S. Eliot's notion of how the "really new work" alters the whole Platonic order of literary history.[26] Crane's project would presumably feature the history and structure of those special moments, and Jaussian *Rezeptionsästhetik,* as we saw, seems to extend the same way of thinking. Americanists have been especially ready to define the American literary achievement in terms of a select number of talents who have put themselves at odds with mainstream middle-class culture and to identify American literary distinctiveness with stylistic or visionary uniqueness. One or both of these distinctions underlies, for instance, Roy Harvey Pearce's characterization of the American poetic tradition as "antinomian"; Michael Bell's sharp differentiation between a half-dozen highly self-conscious American romancers and their run-of-the-mill colleagues; Ann Douglas' contrast between the sentimentalization of mid-nineteenth-century culture and the resistance of Fuller and Melville; and Leo Marx's contrast between middle-class acquiescence to technological progress and the complex pastoralism of the major writers.[27] I myself am enough of a Romantic at heart not to balk too much at the association of excellence with independent-mindedness, yet I would argue that this approach makes best sense when it recognizes the symbiosis of respectability and deviance – when it recognizes (as Tocqueville did) that the reverse side of republican individualism is conformity, and that the latter, as well as the former, has been quite thoroughly internalized by most major

American writers. I like to think of my own research as marked, for better or for worse, by a dogged persistence in keeping that relationship in the forefront of its vision as an aspect and qualification of the uniqueness of any original artifact. Just as my earlier study of Transcendentalism argued that Transcendentalist individualism was built on the more moderate premises of the Unitarianism it ultimately reacted against, so here the individuality of New England's greatest literary achievements is shown as having been made possible through their partial assimilation of cultural norms, which helped provide the creative irritants that produced the scattering of pearls across the oyster bed.

3. *The organization of the literary field: some institutional controls*. Claudio Guillén is surely right in claiming that the "history of literature . . . is characterized not so much by the operation of full systems as by a tendency toward system or structuration."[28] That appraisal reflects not only an acknowledgment of the perceiver's limits but also the fact that literature takes shape as innumerable discrete utterances that only by inference can be seen as affiliated or sequential. Hence R. S. Crane's affirmation that there may be "as many different schools of literary history as there are schools of literary criticism – or . . . schools of historical interpretation."[29] But within this welter of possibilities we may hope to specify the more promising modes of interrelation. Any complete list would certainly include the matrices that I am especially interested in tracking: the generic, the ideological, and the socioeconomic. These might be considered as interdependent controls, operating in such a way as to constrain but not wholly to dictate aesthetic choice.

Genre is the principle of literary organization on which this study relies most heavily. For some, that will be grounds for suspecting it, inasmuch as genre study today is at a sort of crossroads. It flourishes with unprecedented vigor, yet those who engage in it often do so self-deprecatingly, aware that "numerous contemporary critics and theorists consider received generic classifications discredited" and anxious to propitiate that opinion, even though the effect of their work is to reaffirm the more traditional view that genre is the "core of the theoretical endeavor called poetics."[30] The reason for this self-division is surely that the concept of genre, like that of period, is indispensable yet easily misused. If we think of genres as a hierarchy of fixed forms, each individual work belonging to one and only one such category, then naturally we shall reject the notion of genre as an anachronistic ossification.[31] If, on the other hand, we think of genres more flexibly as clusters of stylistic and thematic traits that a number of works hold more or less in common and that change irregularly over the course of time, then the concept of genre seems much more fruitful. At all events, it *is* indispensable, for both writer and scholar. Writers "always need relevant generic models and directions of departure," as Alistair Fowler points out. "At the very least, they have to know which rules are worth breaking."[32] For the literary scholar, "Genre serves as the place where the individual work enters into a complex network of relations with other works."[33] It abstracts us away from the individual text, but in such a manner as to make possible a clearer understanding both of its typicality and of its idiosyncrasy within the larger literary field.

In this study, therefore, I have discussed individual works in large part within the context of a series of overlapping generic patterns, using the latter as my main protagonists, so to speak. This approach has the obvious disadvantage of limiting discussion of aesthetic hybrids like *Walden* to one or two generic planes, a problem not particularly noticeable in the case of obscure works but manifest when the work happens to be a classic that has been subjected to innumerable readings from diverse standpoints. Yet I think we may hope to gain some sense of a work's overall complexity and individuation by studying how it differentiates itself from even a single generic model, so long as we do not insist that is the only model.

Another advantage to studying literature at the generic level is that genres, as clusters of conventions, provide better keys to the ideology of a literary culture than individual texts studied seriatim. This brings me ⌈IN A SERIES⌉ to the second of my matrices. As Emerson once said of the facts of natural history, so with literary genres. Consider them formalistically, and they remain "barren like a single sex. But marry [natural history] to human ✓ history, and it is full of life" (*EW* 1:19). So too for the cultural historian, for whom the ultimate interest in genres lies in their status as indices of ideological orientations affecting literary choice. I take as axiomatic the propositions of Marxist aesthetics that "aesthetic form is to be conceived of as ideological"[34] and that the "artistic process . . . should be regarded as a form of *ideological praxis*," but I gloss the term *ideology* in the neutral sense of "implicit value system" rather than in the pejorative sense of "false consciousness." The business of the student of literary culture is, as Macherey puts it, to dismantle the literary object "in order to be able to reconstruct it *in the image* of its meaning, to make it denote directly what it had expressed obliquely."[35] Individual texts, generic fashions, and pe- ✓ riod modalities are all, so to speak, concentric structures that function as vehicles of ideological orientations that to a considerable extent constrain the individual work to take the shape it does.

What sorts of orientation? These cannot, as I see it, be encompassed by a materialist explanation alone, although that is certainly part of the picture. Although in Chapters 2 through 4 I attach considerable importance to class and class consciousness as influences on authorship, I do not continue on this same level as resolutely as I might. At the end of Chapter 3, for instance, when discussing the stance of self-conscious observation that Emersonian and Hawthornian personae habitually take toward their subjects, I do so mainly by reference to author-speaker ambivalence toward moral and intellectual orthodoxy, rather than, as Carolyn Porter does in her ground-breaking study *Seeing and Being,* by interpreting the mode of observing consciousness as symptomatic of a reified vision shaped by rising industrial capitalism.[36] Although Porter's analysis is fruitful, I myself have generally stuck to charting the moral, theological, and ethnic dimensions of the texts and genres I discuss. I have done so because I believe that these dimensions comprise realities of social experience whose "demystification" belittles their importance not only as private mental events and catalysts for literary expression but also as determiners of history. Consider the popular impact of *Uncle Tom's Cabin.* To ascribe this to the book's status as a sanctification of bourgeois domesticity, seen in turn as an artifact of the emerging capitalist order, does indeed get at the particularity of Stowe's translation of evangelical religious values into nineteenth-century terms. But such a diagnosis strips that translation of the very aspect of its ideology that gave it an irresistible authority of sanctification for its Yankee admirers.

Naturally my sensitivity on this point reflects biases of my own. Personal values, familiarity, and force of scholarly habit have made me give more credence to religious and moral motives as determinants of New England culture than might a reader who had not, like myself, been steeped in the literature of the Unitarian and Transcendentalist controversies. Whereas a poststructuralist would wish to make the problematics of signification the center of any study of Emerson, Hawthorne, Dickinson, and Thoreau, I discuss that problematics not primarily for its own sake but as a symptomatic reaction to the breakdown of moral and theological consensus. Whereas a materialist scholar would want to discuss that conceptual breakdown as a symptom of technological and social change and its social impact, appealing to such texts as Hawthorne's Bunyanesque satire "The Celestial Railroad," I would appeal to the same text to make the point that the New England imagination of the period habitually articulated itself in moral and religious categories.

Yet I by no means deny that the seemingly autonomous operation of the moral or visionary imagination is in part socioeconomically determined. On the contrary, I have tried to be on the lookout for such absent causes, as in my discussion of the village ideal (Chapters 12 through 14), a phenomenon that cannot be understood without taking note of the fact that it tends to exclude the emblems of urbanization that were largely responsible for giving rise to the pastoralizing vision in the first place. In the same spirit is my treatment of the structure of the literary profession, in Chapters 2 and 3, and in the Appendix, which not only concede but

proclaim that New England's literary development was influenced by socioeconomic givens. Emerson could not have become a prophet of
cosmic optimism unless the role had paid well enough; it paid well
enough because enough Americans were attuned to a gospel of moderate
progressivism; and they were attuned to that gospel in large part because
of the nation's remarkable economic growth, of which the rise of a full-
blown literary industry was a conspicuous example. But I argue as well
that the same social conditions that directed authorial choice, and thereby
in a sense prove the validity of a materialist analysis, reinforced in authors
of the era an antimaterialist ethos – forced upon them, indeed, a conception of their proper role and proper themes so dignified and exalted as to
make even some of the more strait-laced literati feel unwashed at times.
Writers were socialized, that is, in such a way as to activate the moral
imagination, to give it the status of an autonomous rhetorical and thematic force, and this in turn converted it into a history-shaping influence,
as in Stowe's case. To "unmask" that autonomy as a social reflex of the
bourgeois era is useful in pointing to a hidden relationship but reductive
insofar as it keeps one from acknowledging (1) that the result was to turn
the moral imagination and its individual spokespersons into history-
making change agents, and (2) that the deepest significance of the "reflex"
may lie not in the dependence of human thought on material precondi-
tions but in its refusal to allow its ideals to be formed in the image of such
determinants. Point 2 is admittedly a faith statement, but point 1, as regards New England writing during the first century of American nationhood, seems amply justified by the verdict of history as well as by the
manifest content of the texts themselves.

I should add that I do not see economic, ideological, generic, or any
other such determinants as absolutely dictating the form or agenda of
particular literary works. One must, for one thing, regard the ideological
dimension of literature as in some sense a creation of discourse rather
than vice versa. As Macherey notes, form is itself "capable of independent transformations, or of an inertia, which bends the path of ideological history."[37] An instructive case in point is the ironic bind imposed on
those early American literati who felt constrained to spout literary nationalism in borrowed forms, despite their sense of the forms' inappro-
priateness to the American scene. They were refuted by their media, and
knew it. They knew that they were fated to remain colonials until they
could discover a voice of their own. In this case, we see form as inertia,
constraining ideology. Conversely, the larger sequence of which that moment was one stage – the sequence of submission to a discourse perceived
as alien, followed by increasingly successful attempts (such as Emerson's,
discussed in Chapter 6) to reground that discourse in the true nature of
things – this sequence is a case of discourse positively redirecting ideol-

ogy, as well as vice versa, discourse itself being shaped by Jacksonian ideology. These Emersonian and other experiments also illustrate another important and increasingly muddled aspect of the relationship between text and literary institutions: the role of authorial initiative. I see nothing to be gained by the structuralist-semiotic reduction of the author to a function or nodal point in a field of forces, except for the value that such apocalyptic pronouncements have in underscoring the fact that authors are as apt to be manipulated by the conventions they use as vice versa.[38] That is certainly so – but to study an age of literary emergence and differentiation is also to be made aware, right away, that authorial originality, authorial resistance to convention, and power of authorial initiative are potentially just as formidable realities of literary history as the conditioning influences of genre, ideology, and marketplace. No literary history should attempt to reduce a Dickinson or a Whitman either to an altogether independent agent or to a mere cultural symptom.

4. *The movement of literary history.* Insofar as its fundamental units are individual texts and oeuvres, literary history reduces itself to narrative sequence far less easily than, say, the Battle of Gettysburg or the abolitionist movement. Each work is a new beginning as well as a continuation; genre and period concepts imply stasis more than change; literary movements and coteries may flourish in chronological succession without having anything to do with one another. Such considerations militate against relying too much on a narrative approach, and they have kept me from trying to emulate the charming raconteurship of Van Wyck Brooks's *Flowering of New England,* except for preliminary-overview purposes in Chapter 2.

Nevertheless, literary history does clearly unfold through time. It does yield true stories, even though these usually cannot be told without a good deal of interpolation and readjustment. This book is, on one level, an anthology of such tales: the odyssey of Scripture-based poesis, the rise and decay of the literary village, and so forth. Linking them, moreover, are broader sequential movements. Of these the most obvious is the story of the increasing volume, solidification, and diversity-amid-centralization of the New England literary scene. This story comes close to being a straight-line narrative in the grand manner of nineteenth-century realism. Because modern life is always moving from simple to complex, very likely most epochs of Western literature since the Middle Ages would disclose a similar pattern, but mine, I think, is more spectacular than most. A related movement is the shift from the artist conceived as public citizen toward the artist as private visionary or entrepreneur, who seeks an individual and sometimes even a countercultural voice but longs also for the imprimatur of the old consensus and proves it by continuing to play moral monitor even when assuming postures of irreverence. This too is hardly a unique tale; it is implicit in the transition from Neoclassical to Romantic hegemony everywhere; but here again the drama is heightened because in nineteenth-century America the professionalization of letters, the rise of Romanticism, and the democratization of political power happened with striking suddenness and simultaneity.

Third, and related to the first two movements, is the literary invention of New England as a cultural unit and focal point within the national whole, undertaken partly out of local patriotism, partly in antagonism to it, partly in the uneasy sense that what one was depicting either was fast passing out of existence or had never existed at all. Insofar as New England writing of our period becomes mimetic, that is its major project, and it is interestingly in tension with the first two trends. They called a developed literature of the New England experience into being but ensured, at the same time, that programmatic regionalism, or any other ism, would become impossible in the free market of the imagination except as one term of a dialogue between the impulse to conventionalize and the impulse to exercise poetic license. It was inevitable, during a period of rapid national literary development, for writers to seize on whatever images they could find that seemed culturally expressive and construct instant traditions out of them. In this way Pilgrimism became a cult and rallying cry, as we shall see in Chapter 8. But given the energy and newness of national letters, it was equally predictable that the icons would be handled idiosyncratically by some and debunkingly by others, even before the paint on them had dried. Hence, in reviewing the various themes discussed in Parts II through IV, the reader of this book will repeatedly note a pattern of constructive, stabilizing, tradition-building, and sustaining forces contending against forces of skepticism, erosion, and dispersal. The cozy Our Towns of New England imagination continually threaten to metamorphose into gothic prisons or comic backwaters.

These vicissitudes are both period-specific (reflecting the clash between rising literary hopes and regional ego, as New England's place in the expanding republic became conspicuously smaller) and also endemic to regional literary culture generally. One gets at the essence of literary subcultures not simply by listing all their dominant images and letting it go at that but by approaching each in the expectation that one is going to find not a stable configuration but a battlefield. That is because the ideology of a cultural province is constructed in the face of external challenge to its resistance to amalgamating itself fully with the national mainstream and in the face of self-doubt resulting from split allegiances and the nagging sense that attachment to province, however appealing, is somehow backward or unworthy.

The fact that provincial literary expression and ideology are beset with intimations of insubstantiality is very likely an important reason why studies of American culture regions are today somewhat unfashionable outside the fields of economics and geography and the company of the literary faithful who, for whatever reason, are precommitted to some chosen province. After all, is it not tenuous to insist on the importance of subcultural identification in an emergent, complex nation-state? Is not the phenomenon vestigial at best, doomed to die out, if it has not done so already? These questions should not daunt the inquirer. For one thing, the answer to the second question is an unequivocal no. Just as the globalization of international issues has, if anything, intensified nationalism rather than the reverse, so ethnic and regional provincialism, in America and elsewhere, has thrived in the face of nationalization. Furthermore, the element of tenuousness presents a great opportunity for those who face it squarely and do not try to sweep it under the rug, fearing to endanger the clarity of their arguments. In the questions it raises about its own premises, American provincial consciousness reveals itself not as epiphenomenal to American literary history but as paradigmatic, for a similar dialectic has been inherent in the notion of American literature from the start, obsessed as it and its historians have been with proclaiming and defining a distinctiveness that they fear may not – and may never – exist commensurately with their longing for it. Perhaps that is the deepest sense in which it may be affirmed that to conquer the nation, one must attack through its provinces. It is high time we began the assault.

2

A Narrative Overview of New England's Literary Development

The very *donnée* of the piece could be given, the subject formulated: the great adventure of a society reaching out into the apparent void for the amenities, the consummations, after having earnestly gathered in so many of the preparations and necessities.

Henry James, *The American Scene* (1907)

Then was exhibited all the richness of a rhetoric which we have never seen rivalled in this country.

Ralph Waldo Emerson, "Historic Notes of
Life and Letters in New England" (1867)

The story of New England letters between the Revolution and the Civil War reads in many ways like a straightforward narrative of growth and improvement.[1] At the start, we find literature composed by a small number of genteel amateurs in Connecticut and eastern Massachusetts, all minor figures by any high standard, confining themselves to poetry and nonfictional prose. In fiction and drama, hardly anything had yet appeared, and nothing memorable. New England's major towns, mostly scattered along the Atlantic Coast from Portland to New Haven, had newspapers that local scribblers used as outlets but no literary magazines and no publishing industry as such. Circulation of books and pamphlets was for the most part local.

By 1865 the situation had changed dramatically. Spread throughout every New England state, although concentrated especially in the Boston area, were hundreds of practicing creative writers, some of whom even earned their living from literature. The best had produced work in every genre (except drama) that today is recognized as excellent. Literary institutions were solidly in place. Boston led the nation in quality of literary publishing, if not in volume, headed by the firm of Ticknor and Fields, whose stable of authors included Emerson, Thoreau, Hawthorne,

23

Holmes, Longfellow, Lowell, Stowe, and Whittier. The *Atlantic Monthly*, started in 1857, had become almost at once a regional literary voice of high distinction in which the rising generation sought to publish alongside the eminences just named. Most New England towns of any consequence had at least one lyceum, sponsoring public lectures, readings, and debates. This was an increasingly significant source of income for regional writers. The academic communities and larger towns also had clubs or informal networks of social and intellectual interchange that supplied literary professionals and amateurs with at least a local cross-fertilization. The most imposing of these was Boston's Saturday Club, to which all the *Atlantic* luminaries belonged.

Risking some oversimplification, we may distinguish for overview purposes five "generations," or stages, to this unfolding: the Revolutionary era writers, who reached intellectual maturity by the mid-1780s or before; the Federalist era writers, who developed their mature styles roughly between 1790 and the War of 1812; and three generations of New England Romantics, who hit their stride, respectively, about 1815 to 1835 (the era of Washington Allston, William Cullen Bryant, and the senior Richard Henry Dana); 1830 to 1850 (Emerson, Hawthorne, and Longfellow); and 1845 to 1865 (Lowell, Thoreau, and Dickinson).

I

The first generation's leading writers were the elder Connecticut Wits – John Trumbull, Joel Barlow, Timothy Dwight, and David Humphreys.[2] They formed its only important literary coterie, and even at that it might be more accurate to call them a group of comparatively autonomous operators, whose similarity of background (Connecticut Valley culture, Yale College) and collaborations in the 1770s and 1780s were accentuated in retrospect as a result of their successors' greater interdependence and the Wits' own consciousness of being at the threshold of national literature. The rising glory of American culture, the *translatio studii* or supposed transfer of the seat of learning and letters from Old World to New, was a mutual enthusiasm for them during the Revolutionary years, celebrated in several Augustan-style "progress pieces," of which Barlow's visionary epic *The Columbiad* (1807) was the belated summa. Otherwise their paths tended to diverge. Trumbull, mainly a satirist of provincial manners, quickly turned most of his energies to the law. Dwight became a champion of Edwardsean Calvinism and a pastoral myth of a presecularized agrarian New England in tract, tome, and song, as he moved through a parish ministry to the presidency of Yale. Humphreys became a successful textile manufacturer of meager literary output. Barlow, to the dismay of the rest, became a Jeffersonian deist and Jacobin, living much of his later life abroad in a series of business and government posts.

One important common trait, however, was the convergence of literary and civic leadership. That all four writers were socially prominent and politically influential was no coincidence. During these years, New England's literati of even minor consequence tended to be from the educated elite. The gradations of status among them – Barlow the farmer's son versus Dwight, the scion of a leading Northampton family – may help to explain the eventual antiestablishmentarianism of the first relative to the second; but the differences in caste were largely erased by the Yale education that led both to literature and pointed each toward becoming a prominent public servant in his own way.

Much the same is true of the next generation also.[3] Virtually all of the important literary people continued to be college graduates or the equivalent, with scattered exceptions, such as the self-taught Universalist minister Elhanan Winchester, author of the much reprinted millennial epic *The Process and Empire of Christ* (1793), and David Hitchcock, the Berkshire shoemaker-poet, who vainly tried to stave off poverty during the early 1800s by writing Neoclassical verses that reflected the high Federalism and high Calvinism of his social betters. But there were now more writers and more literary enterprises. The Boston literary scene, in particular, had started to come alive after being severely disrupted by the war. During the Revolutionary era, New England's metropolis had had in its vicinity only two long-term residents who wrote literary works of enduring interest: Mercy Otis Warren, of Plymouth, author of patriotic satirical dramas; and the African-born poet Phillis Wheatley, the one non-gentry figure in late eighteenth-century New England whose works are read seriously as literature today. By 1790, however, Boston had begun to resume its place as the region's intellectual center. Local antiquarians, led by Congregational minister Jeremy Belknap – author of a lively satirical-allegorical narrative of American settlement (*The Foresters*, 1792) – were in the process of founding the first of many state and local historical societies in a century-long, nationwide movement spearheaded by New Englanders. The region's first notable literary periodical had been founded, the *Massachusetts Magazine* (1789–96), featuring poetry and fiction that imitated such pre-Romantic models as "Della Crusca," Laurence Sterne, and the Oriental tale. A law student, William Hill Brown, had written *The Power of Sympathy* (1789), a Richardsonian roman à clef, billed by its publisher as the "first American novel." It was not, but it marked the start of intensive exploitation of the novel by regional authors. Author-actress Susanna Rowson, who had started writing in Britain during the 1780s, had just arrived in Boston to become the area's leading Richardsonian. Hannah Foster would soon follow with *The Coquette* (1797), and Royall Tyler (*The Algerine Captive*, 1797) and Tabitha Tenney (*Female Quixoticism*, 1801) would produce sprightly adaptations of eighteenth-century picaresque. In 1800, a wealthy Maine widow, Sarah Keating Wood, would begin her career as New England's most prolific writer of Radcliffean gothic fiction with *Julia and the Illuminated Baron*.[4]

Meanwhile, the theater in New England made impressive headway during the 1790s against the forces of moralism that were to leave their imprint on New England writing throughout the nineteenth century.[5] By the early 1800s, the Boston stage had influenced the lives of many New Englanders of literary bent. Brown wrote a play for it before his premature death. Rowson wrote several and acted as well. Some of the most serious Harvard students, like Joseph Stevens Buckminster, later a patron saint of Unitarianism, attended performances when they could, despite the college's nominal prohibition. A less serious Harvardian like Robert Treat Paine, Jr., alienated his eminent father by marrying an actress and deviating repeatedly from more respectable careers in journalism and law into acting and other forms of theater haunting. Such was the local interest in theater that a magazine partially specializing in it flourished briefly at Boston (*Polyanthos*, 1805–7, 1812–14). One index of the drama's quick acceptance by the post-revolutionary intellectual elite was that a larger fraction of its writers wrote for the stage (either plays or poetic fore and after pieces) than wrote prose fiction, which seems to have made more rapid gains among popular audiences.[6] It was ominous, however, that the first New England (and American) play of quality, Tyler's *The Contrast* (1787), was written and produced at New York. When, shortly thereafter, Tyler changed his residence from Boston to Vermont, he turned increasingly to closet drama. In the more cosmopolitan towns, theater had become well established by 1800 – in Providence and Portland especially – yet New England never began to rival New York as a center for American drama.

Tyler's relocation to Brattleboro was symptomatic of a dispersal of literary activity and institutions throughout New England during the Federalist era. In 1790, Tyler's wife remembered, Vermont was "considered the outskirts of creation by many, and [an area] where all the rogues and runaways congregated."[7] This situation soon began to change. By the mid-1790s, Vermont had a (short-lived) "literary magazine" (the *Rural Magazine: or, Vermont Repository*, 1795–6) and a handful of aspiring minor poets, two of whom besides Tyler had real promise: Josias Lyndon Arnold, son of the man who persuaded Vermont to ratify the Constitution, and Thomas G. Fessenden, son of the Congregational minister at Walpole, just across the Connecticut River. The first died early and the second soon moved on, yet by 1820 the state had produced future University of Vermont president James Marsh, Coleridge's leading American interpreter; minister-poet Carlos Wilcox, who might have fulfilled his ambition to write the great American religious poem had he lived beyond his early thirties; historical romancer Judge Daniel Pierce Thompson; and attorney-newspaperman-poet John G. Saxe, whose comic verse made him a midcentury lyceum favorite. Although Vermont never got near the point of challenging Boston for literary primacy, by the early nineteenth century its image as infested by ring-tailed roarers like Ethan Allen (himself a literary man in his own way) had begun to fade.

Such diffusion of talent, through resettlement and local nurture, combined with the traditional localism of New England village life, led for a time to decentralization of literary activity. The major works of the Revolutionary generation had generally been printed in Boston, Hartford, and New Haven. Although these continued to be the region's main publishing centers (especially the first two), a good deal of the interesting literature printed between 1790 and 1820 appeared elsewhere, in Portland, Portsmouth, Worcester, even Exeter, Leominster, and Litchfield. Particularly striking was the case of Walpole, New Hampshire, which, for a fraction of the 1790s, became the site of the region's best literary publishing, thanks to Joseph Dennie, the "American Addison." Having moved to Walpole from Boston "under the pretence of practicing law," Dennie found a congenial knot of Federalist gentlemen to relieve the tedium of rusticity. When he took over the town newspaper in 1796, his energy and contacts enabled him to make it, almost immediately, the best literary periodical of its moment. In this paper, which Dennie rebaptized the *Farmer's Weekly Museum,* was published much of the work of the second generation of literary talent from Massachusetts and upper New England: not only Tyler, Paine, and Fessenden but also the playwright, essayist, and editor David Everett; journalist and poet Charles Prentiss; the waggish poet-schoolmaster William Biglow; the poet and essayist Isaac Story; and the minister-satirist John S. J. Gardiner. Concurrently Dennie issued from the same press his *Lay Preacher* (1796), the best periodical essay series between Franklin's and Irving's; Tyler's *Algerine Captive;* and the miscellaneous anthology *The Spirit of the "Farmer's Weekly Museum"* (1801), in which his leading authors were all represented.[8]

But Walpole, New Hampshire, was a sandy foundation for a literary empire. Cosmopolite Dennie chafed at its social limitations. His Toryism offended some; his dandified manners scandalized others. But the chief problem was economic. Dennie's printer went through several bankruptcies, involving Dennie in serious losses, owing partly to primitive marketing methods. (Bostonians, Dennie noted, could not "supply themselves with a book" like Tyler's that "slumbers in a stall at Walpole.")[9] In 1801 Dennie sold out and moved to Philadelphia, then America's biggest, wealthiest, most sophisticated city, entrenching himself as editor of the *Port Folio,* which he quickly made America's first stable and remunerative literary periodical.

In this Dennie reenacted a pattern of literary-entrepreneurial expatriation from New England that Benjamin Franklin had begun, one that was followed by several of Dennie's younger acquaintances and that became almost a ritual for a substantial fraction of the next three generations. All of the evidence suggests that New England far exceeded other regions in per capita production and consumption of literature, but for a combination of reasons – one of which was the decentralization of publishing in New England until the mid-1800s, and the lack of the large and efficient distribution networks that the New York and Philadelphia publishers had developed much earlier in the century – New England also produced a disproportionate share of literary expatriates.[10] Thus the region was bled of literary talent, yet the emigrants compensated for their desertion by assuming positions of literary leadership from New York to Charleston to Cincinnati to San Francisco. Without perhaps fully intending it, these expatriates helped to shape national literature in a New England mold. Rufus Griswold, a Baptist ministerial dropout from Vermont, was in good part responsible through his anthologies of American poetry for perpetuating the impression of New England's leadership in verse.[11] Horace Greeley, another Vermonter, and William Cullen Bryant from the Berkshires, infused New York journalism with New England moral tone. Sarah Hale, Catherine Sedgwick, and Caroline Gilman based their influential brand of conservative feminism on New England's model of the domestically multicompetent but educated and morally self-reliant woman, the heart of the didactic thrust of the women's magazines and woman's fiction that they helped inspire.[12]

Walpole's speedy rise and fall as a literary center was not entirely typical of the cultural vicissitudes of New England communities of the era. During the second and third generations, literary-intellectual circles of greater stability coalesced in a number of larger towns, especially Hartford, New Haven, Litchfield, Providence, and Portland, as well as Boston and its vicinity. These circles tended to begin either as extensions of the social interchange of the more intellectually curious among the local gentry or, in college towns, as extracurricular spinoffs of student life. But although the circles were ongoing, usually their years of splendor were brief. Two vignettes should convey the picture well.

Take first the case of Litchfield, in northwestern Connecticut,[13] where the first notable collection of *American Poems* (1793) was printed by native son Elihu Hubbard Smith, a second-generation Connecticut Wit, possibly with the aid of his friend Charles Brockden Brown, the proofs of whose novels Smith later helped read and correct. This event was fortuitous, since Smith was sojourning in Litchfield for a short visit before escaping with relief to his medical practice and his Friendly Club of kindred spirits in New York City. Yet Litchfield had prepared Smith for his editorial task through its genuine if limited cultural resources (such as its

early willingness to countenance theatrical performances and Smith's father's well-stocked library). By 1820, Litchfield had become, at least to a
sympathetic eye, "not only one of the most elevated features in the physical conformation of Connecticut, but one of the focal points of literature
and civilization,"[14] owing to the presence of such Federalist luminaries as
judge and legal scholar Tapping Reeve, head of America's leading law
school (1784–1833), which attracted from throughout the United States
such future men of distinction as John C. Calhoun and Horace Mann.
The two sons of attorney James Gould, Reeve's assistant and successor,
were also about to attempt literary careers. The future novelist John
Pierce Brace was head teacher in his aunt Sarah Pierce's nationally famous
academy for young women and the much admired writing instructor of
Harriet Beecher Stowe, whose father, Lyman Beecher, a leader in evangelical circles, was minister at Litchfield for sixteen years. By the late
1830s, however, all of these people had died or decamped, and Litchfield
became permanently memorialized through Beecher family memoir and
fiction mainly as the quaint site of old-time Puritan virtue now, alas, out
of fashion, and of obsolete theological controversies now happily forgotten.

Portland, Maine, on the other hand, became more solidly established
as a literary center and lasted as such for a longer time.[15] By the second
decade of the century, it had a lively theater; two Congregational ministers of some literary note; two rival newspapers receptive to local literary
talent (especially the Federalist Portland *Gazette,* where Longfellow
printed his first poem); and a knot of young professionals who liked to
write. The more senior of these included attorney Nathaniel Deering,
author of bad dramas and delightful comic tales, and journalist-humorist
Seba Smith (creator of the Down East letters of Major Jack Downing),
who set up as a schoolmaster in Portland after graduating from Bowdoin
in 1818. Other literary Portlandites, native or imported, included Smith's
wife Elizabeth Oakes Smith, a future poet and feminist lecturer of note;
the two Longfellow and the two Mellen brothers, all four aspiring poets
and sons of prominent local lawyers; novelist John Neal, back home in
1827 after a decade of wandering; Ann Stephens, writer of regional
sketches and domestic fiction, as well as the first dime novel; Isaac Mc-
Lellan, later to become the bard of American sporting life; and a future
best-selling novelist, Joseph Holt Ingraham. During the later 1820s and
1830s, the Portlandites launched several significant projects that featured
each other's work: Neal's weekly newspaper, the *Yankee* (1828–9); Stephens's *Portland Magazine* (1834–6); and *The Portland Sketch Book* (1836),
a gift book also edited by Stephens that included selections from most of
the group just named, as well as from Portland-born Nathaniel Parker
Willis. Collectively, then, Portland bred an impressive array of literary

entrepreneurs, including some of the most popular fiction and poetry writers of their day and several writers who figured importantly in the replacement of the language of polite literary discourse by a more realistic vernacular, Neal and Seba Smith especially. From the record of these contributions and the biographical interlinks among these writers, who were more or less mutually acquainted and tended to keep in touch, one could even argue that the Portland contribution to antebellum New England letters came close to rivaling that of Cambridge or Concord. Yet in Portland itself the center could not hold much beyond the early 1830s. The Longfellows left early; McLellan, the Mellens, the Smiths, and Ann Stephens followed suit; Ingraham went south after a year at Yale. Those who stayed – Deering and Neal – stagnated. Ann Stephens was right in telling Neal that he would have amounted to more if he had settled in New York instead. After the mid-1830s, it became increasingly clear that Portland would be remembered in literary history as little more than a point of origin. Yet the fact that it became such probably depended to a considerable extent upon cross-fertilization among those who later became discontented with the place.

II

Among all New England towns at the start of the nineteenth century, Boston, by far the largest, also had the greatest number of practicing creative writers. But its literary community was slow to coalesce.[16] The most interesting essayist, semifeminist Judith Sargent Murray ("Constantia"), had to bear the stigma of an unfashionable Universalism. Poet Sarah Wentworth Morton ("Philenia") had to contend first with a reputation for un-American frivolity, then with her husband's position as one of the leading Jeffersonians in a Federalist-dominated town. Mercy Otis Warren of Plymouth (b. 1728) was "the old lady" to Joseph Dennie's peers,[17] although her writing career was far from over, and when she took an anti-Federalist stance in her three-volume history of the American Revolution (1805), she was called worse than that. The younger writers did not particularly respect their seniors ("They are all lazy," declared Dennie, and "convene rather to *eat,* than *talk* together")[18] and also had trouble cooperating with each other, falling into foppery (Dennie), alcoholism (Paine and William Biglow), improvidence (John Lathrop), and hidebound asperity (J. S. J. Gardiner).

One cause of such eccentricities may have been that in the relatively liberal climate of eastern Massachusetts the young aspirant's dream of belletristic distinction was less apt to become subordinated to the time-honored notion of literature as an ancillary achievement in the well-bred person's repertoire. Given the embryonic state of literary commercialism, frustration was then inevitable. Consider these facts. (1) Starting in the

1780s, Boston launched more periodicals specializing in creative writing than the rest of New England combined. (2) Until the *Atlantic* (1857), these efforts soon failed. The two best, the *United States Literary Gazette* of the 1820s and the *New England Magazine* of the 1830s, both merged eventually with New York journals, the latter after consuming much of its editor's patrimony. The *Massachusetts Magazine* lasted longer than anything of its kind in America before 1800, but it was less distinguished than Dennie's paper, and it left no successor. By 1800, Bostonians were wondering whether it was true, as Philadelphia alleged, that no literary magazine could survive in Boston – a verdict echoed by Thoreau as late as 1853 (*TJ* 5:506). (3) The high-quality journals that became most solidly institutionalized in New England between 1800 and 1850 were not belletristic but critical quarterlies patterned after the British intellectual and sectarian reviews: the *Monthly Anthology and Boston Review;* the *North American Review;* the *Christian Disciple,* and its successor the *Christian Examiner* (the leading voice of Unitarian Whiggery); the orthodox Congregational *Panoplist, Christian Spectator, New Englander,* and *Bibliotheca Sacra;* the Baptist *Christian Review.* These magazines sometimes included poetry and fiction, but nearly all of it was trash. They were run by circles of well-educated gentlemen, often sympathetic to (properly moral) literature but rarely distinguished writers themselves. Most "literary" organizations – clubs, lyceums, historical societies and the like – comprised a diverse group of professionals or tradesmen seeking recreation and self-improvement. Bona fide aesthetes were either, like Dennie and Paine, driven to the edges (torn between the options of becoming stuffy lawyers or abstemious-living journalists) or else peaceably socialized by the club system, learning to gratify their literary impulses in a watered-down form.

In Boston, this system experienced some strains as a result of the factionalism for which the city was then famous, but by the early 1800s the system was functioning well enough to have created a productive coterie, the Anthology Club, and a periodical published by it (the *Monthly Anthology,* 1803–11) that was to set the tone for Boston's literary elite for more than half a century.[19] The senior members of the club, such as chairman John S. J. Gardiner, were carryovers from less successful projects of the 1780s and 1790s. The younger contingent – Andrews Norton, William Tudor, Alexander Everett, and others – became part of the group that presided over the third-generation establishment, under whose somewhat hesitant aegis the trend toward Romanticism became irreversible. All had strongly conservative instincts, but Norton at least became the American editor of Felicia Hemans, the British Romantic poet who was most admired in America after Wordsworth and Byron; Tudor became the founding editor of the *North American Review* and Everett one of his successors, during the period when the periodical turned decisively toward Romantic values (1830–5); Everett gave Carlyle his most sympathetic Yankee review in the *North American;* Tudor introduced New England readers to Madame de Staël's *Corinne* in the *Anthology.*

The real payoff came only after 1815, however. Until then, literary Boston produced disappointing results compared to the Connecticut Valley. The short-run result of the *Monthly Anthology* was a stuffy, late-Augustan hegemony. Timothy Dwight, who traveled much in New England, once praised Boston as "sufficiently great [in population] to ensure all the benefits of refined society, and yet so small as to leave the character of every man open to the observation of every other."[20] The negative side of this picture appears in one Anthologist's reminiscence that none of the "existing topics of the day were ever introduced," since "parties both in religion and politics were too bitterly opposed to admit of friendly discussions between them."[21] The Anthologists' one great open debate was over the relative merits of Pope and Gray; on life's larger issues they found common denominators where they could and expounded them in their magazine in rigidly doctrinaire ways.[22] Another mark of inbreeding was the encomiums that the Anthologists heaped on their honored dead. Fisher Ames seemed to them America's greatest genius; Joseph Stevens Buckminster, whose chief claim to fame is a timely but rather modest contribution to the rise of biblical criticism, was "one of the most eminent men whom our country has produced."[23] And even had they not been so inbred, little in the way of real creativity could have been expected from a group whose chairman held that the question of who the "best poets, historians, and philosophers of civilized nations" are is a "point indisputably settled."[24]

Late-Augustan Connecticut was hidebound too, but at least it had a tradition of recent literary accomplishment to look back upon. Until the 1820s it looked as if New England's literary leadership might remain in the lower Connecticut Valley, along the Hartford–New Haven axis, where Trumbull, Humphreys, and Dwight resided through most of their careers and where Barlow remained long enough to collaborate with them on *The Anarchiad* (1786–7), a mock-epic pro-Federalist satire against soft money and civil disorder. The fact that all four Wits were politically more prominent than any of their Bostonian counterparts, in New England's most tightly oligarchical state, undoubtedly helped preserve their literary reputations in an age when the civic and aesthetic spheres were considered inseparable. Dwight was "Pope of Connecticut"; Trumbull was a state supreme court justice; Humphreys was the "friend of Washington," dispatched on various errands in the national service. In their shadow gathered a second generation of Hartford-based wits; physicians Lemuel Hopkins, Elihu Hubbard Smith, and Mason F.

Cogswell, the first a holdover from the earlier group; gentleman book-man Richard Alsop; and Theodore Dwight, Timothy's much younger brother, a journalist, lawyer, and politician. Less talented, (except for Hopkins), less influential (except for Dwight), this second generation helped to extend their predecessors' vein of collaborative Federalist satire in prose and verse (e.g., the mock-heroic *Echo* papers, 1791–1805) and dutifully memorialized their elders in anthology and memoir. Much of this material was reprinted elsewhere in New England in periodicals such as the *Farmer's Weekly Museum*.[25]

The combination of literary and moral authority wielded by this two- ✓ generation Connecticut establishment, particularly Timothy Dwight and John Trumbull, was imposing. "Whenever I wanted advice," confessed headstrong Lyman Beecher, "I went to [Dwight] as to a father, and told him everything."[26] Beecher referred, of course, to advice concerning re-ligion, but others were prepared to extend the same deference to Dwight as poet (unaware that Trumbull had been spoofing Dwight's poems for years). For Alsop, he was "majestic Dwight." John Adams could think of "no heroick Poem superior to [*The Conquest*] in any modern language," except *Paradise Lost,* and his son John Quincy Adams was not far behind in admiration. Solyman Brown, one of Dwight's last students at Yale, regarded him as chief among American bards and lamented, at his death, that "his Muse / Shall charm no more, . . . / Nor mends the wayward heart."[27] Today Brown's book of poems is justly remembered only as the object of William Cullen Bryant's milestone review, "American Poetry" ✓ (1818), which, invoking a Wordsworthian standard of unpretentiousness in poetic diction, consigned Brown's doggerel and his Connecticut-centered pantheon of American greats to oblivion with the faintest praise consistent with reviewerly politeness.[28] By 1865, an *Atlantic* essayist re-called the Wits' work as a "profitless employment of labor, unusual in Connecticut."[29] Yet this characteristically Bostonian attempt to rewrite American history in the image of Massachusetts, which began as early as anti-Wit sniping in the *Monthly Anthology,*[30] should not cause us to over-look the closeness of the tie between them and later sensibilities quite different from their own. For instance, Trumbull, whose *McFingal* was their most enduring poem, was the literary mentor of the first Connect-icut Romantics, James A. Hillhouse and Lydia Sigourney; it was said of Sigourney that she would initially "permit none of her poems to be pub-lished which had not been first inspected and revised by Trumbull."[31] Sigourney and Hillhouse, in turn, from their estates in Hartford and New Haven, patronized younger poets of greater ability, like James Gates Per-cival and John Greenleaf Whittier.

For a time, then, it seemed that Connecticut might produce a third generation of poets to maintain the state's traditional preeminence. Hillhouse, Percival, Sigourney, and John G. C. Brainard got a narrow head start on their northeastern contemporaries Washington Allston, Richard Henry Dana, Sr., and William Cullen Bryant. The Connecticut group were the New England pioneers both in the importation of Byronic poetry (Sigourney's imitation of Hemans; Percival's *Prometheus* and "The Suicide"; Hillhouse's biblical drama *Hadad*) and in the exploitation of local landscape and legend that had been anticipated as early as Dwight's *Greenfield Hill* (1794) (Percival's the "Seasons of New England," Brainard's "Matchit Moodus" and "The Shad Spirit"). Brainard was one of the important native influences on the regional poetry of Whittier, who followed him as Hartford newspaper editor and edited his *Literary Remains* (1832) with an affectionate memoir.

Otherwise, however, Connecticut Romanticism had no influence except for Sigourney's inspirational role as a model of literary success for younger women writers. The independently wealthy Hillhouse lapsed into inaction ("He needed the spur of poverty," a friend said);[32] Brainard died young; Percival, who had a double dose of Brainard's impracticality and antipathy to revision, sabotaged his own career through an ungraciousness, vacillation, and inability to outgrow his early Byronics that alienated as influential an array of early backers as any American poet has ever enjoyed. (They included, during the 1820s, the *North American* reviewers, the combined faculties of Harvard and Yale, the New York literati Fitz-Greene Halleck and James Fenimore Cooper, well-placed editors such as Samuel E. Goodrich and William Leete Stone, and Secretary of War John C. Calhoun, who obtained government posts for Percival at West Point and Boston, only to have him resign each almost immediately.) Edward Everett called Percival America's most inspired poet; Whittier pitied the "man who does not love the poetry of Percival";[33] but already Longfellow had admonished an impressionable young friend that Bryant's chaste restraint far outclassed Percival's fulgurous scribble (*LL* 1:143–4). Longfellow underrated Percival's abilities ("The Deserted Wife," to name just one example, shows that Percival was capable of writing very well indeed), but he was correct as to staying power. By the 1860s, Lowell could without fear of reprisal greet the official biography with a review that makes his hatchet job on Thoreau look eulogistic, and another *Atlantic* contributor declared (with a swipe at Sigourney) that "there are no poets known to exist" in Connecticut, "unless it be that well-paid band who write the rhymed puffs of cheap garments and cosmetics."[34]

But by the 1860s, this was uncomfortably close to being right. Though hardly destitute of talent, as we shall see, "from a literary point of view Connecticut was in the trough between two waves,"[35] the era of the Wits and the era of Mark Twain's Gilded Age residency in Hartford. During the 1820s, Hartford and New Haven were distinctly on the wane as centers of publishing and literary activity. A symptomatic change in New Haven was the disbanding of the staidly adventurous *Microscope* (to which Brainard, Percival, and other Yale literati contributed during its brief existence in 1820) and the transfer of its editor, Cornelius Tuthill, to the management of the new *Christian Spectator,* Connecticut Calvinism's reply to the Unitarian *Christian Examiner.*[36] Belles lettres preempted by sectarianism. As for Hartford, Whittier complained to Sigourney in 1833 that Hartford "is by no means a *literary* place, and . . . were it not for yourself it would be only known as the place where a certain *convention* once assembled." The more opportunistic Goodrich, despite strong family and sentimental ties to Connecticut, had already perceived this and long since decamped for Boston, "at that time [1826] notoriously the literary metropolis of the Union – the admitted Athens of America."[37]

This statement shows that he did not leave his Yankee boosterism behind. It is one of those ringing half-truths that explains a good deal about the psychology of the aspiring nineteenth-century literary professional. Goodrich was right about Boston's magnetic image. Always in some sense regarded as New England's intellectual capital, even by hinterlanders like Dwight who disapproved of its liberalism, Boston drew people of literary bent in increasing numbers after 1800. Before then, the number of nonnative Bostonians (like Rowson) who settled there for what might be described as literary reasons seems to have been more or less balanced by Bostonians who migrated elsewhere (Tyler and Dennie). Around 1800, however, the ratio began to change, with the arrival of such leavening influences as Buckminster, Buckingham, David Everett, and T. G. Fessenden. The 1820s was the key decade, bringing Goodrich, Bryant, Percival, Sarah Hale, Bronson Alcott, the Beecher family, actor-playwright-humorist Henry Finn, and numerous others. This trend was in keeping with an overall pattern of country-to-city mobility that, along with immigration, increased Boston's population by a factor of ten from 1790 (18,000) to 1860 (178,000). By 1830, it was becoming clear that Boston would become *the* regional literary center without rival.[38]

The crucial literary institutions were still slow in developing, however. Bryant, Percival, and Hale soon moved on. Before midcentury, no one was able to make a living from creative writing published in the Boston area. (Emerson told Edward Everett Hale that *Representative Men* [1850] was the first book that yielded him any income.) William Charvat makes the point cogently: "Up to 1850, the publishers of the [New York–Philadelphia] axis were the discoverers and interpreters of American literary taste"; "Boston publishers did not even know they had a renaissance on their hands until Ticknor & Fields woke up in the late forties," and when they did, they essentially emulated the marketing and distribution methods that the New York and Philadelphia houses had devised. Boston publishing, then, remained anachronistically and obstinately localized; New England authors who wanted a national hearing were forced, until 1850, to go to the "axis" to get it; the so-called flowering of New England was made possible by entrepreneurs in Philadelphia and New York.[39]

Charvat's hard-nosed argument provides a useful corrective to the romantic picture of a steady crescendo of bustling, Boston-centered activity painted by Van Wyck Brooks in his *Flowering of New England.* It is ironic that the region with the largest quotient of literary talent could not sustain a good literary magazine until after the *Knickerbocker, Graham's,* the *Democratic Review,* and the *Southern Literary Messenger* had flourished for decades farther south. It is ironic that James Munroe of Boston, the American publisher with the nation's most high-powered stable of authors in the 1840s, could not or would not gain them a national hearing. On the other hand, perhaps it is even more remarkable, under the circumstances, that the emigration of literati was no greater. Fewer than one in four of the major antebellum New England authors chose to relocate permanently out of the region (all in New York) during most of their active careers; the others remained based within the region, most of them in eastern Massachusetts.[40] Literary activity in the Boston area did, as Brooks claimed, steadily increase throughout the period, whatever the vicissitudes of American publishing. The leading writers, furthermore, proved on the whole to be staunchly – indeed naively – loyal to New England publishers. Alcott, Channing, Emerson, Parker, and Thoreau relied on Boston-area publishers exclusively, as did Brownson through the 1840s. Except for his *Fable for Critics,* James Russell Lowell's poems were published in Cambridge and Boston, as were those of Holmes, Very, Thoreau, and (with the exception of a volume produced during a Philadelphia sojourn) Whittier as well.[41] Prescott took three of his five major works on the history of the Spanish empire to Harper's of New York, as did Motley for his *Rise of the Dutch Republic* (both men simultaneously publishing in London); but Bancroft and Parkman turned to Little, Brown of Boston to publish their monumental histories of the United States and of the struggle between Britain and France for colonial supremacy. As for antebellum writers of fiction, Hawthorne published only one major book outside of Boston, Stowe only two; and John Neal, after resettling in Portland, published only there or in Boston, except for his three dime novels. There was, in short, a strong centripetal tendency among the region's antebellum writers with respect to publishing as well as residence. That, plus the increasing centralization of significant literary activity around Boston, may help account for the ease with which Ticknor & Fields, with a little charm and financial inducement, were able to corral so many of the region's literary eminences between the mid-1840s and 1860, the turning point being the capture of Longfellow in 1846.[42]

If we were to extend our survey to magazine and anthology publishing, the picture would look more complex, since a number of New England writers printed shorter pieces elsewhere, especially in New York. Yet another version of the same centripetalism would emerge. New York literary life was pervaded by literary migrants from the northeast who, to a considerable extent, helped promote their compatriots' fortunes. In 1860, for instance, the city's leading literary critic, a former Transcendentalist from Massachusetts, on the staff of one of the city's leading newspapers, edited by a Vermonter, was at work with another Massachusetts man in editing the first major American encyclopedia, to be published by a firm founded by another Massachusetts man, who happened also to have the national distribution rights to Webster's speller and dictionary (products of a Connecticut man that had originally been marketed in New England).[43] Some of the lesser expatriate-run magazines – for example, Seba Smith's *Rover* (1843–5) – depended heavily on New England contributions. The number of instances in which New Englanders promoted each other's literary fortunes in New York are altogether so numerous as almost to justify the paranoia of Edgar Allan Poe. Charles Briggs and James Russell Lowell, Rufus Griswold and Maria Gowen Brooks, Horace Greeley and Margaret Fuller – these are a few notable cases.

Literary New England, in short, became more powerful and organized during the nineteenth century, even as it seemed in some senses to be losing a sizable fraction of its creative talent. Through emigration it extended its influence, and at home literary publishing reached a new peak of centralization and of quality, if not quantity, by the time of the Civil War. During this period, northeastern Massachusetts continued, as it had before, to produce roughly half of New England's significant authors, and those who emigrated from New England were replaced by up-country arrivals, corroborating at least halfway Oliver Wendell Holmes's assertion that Boston "drains a large water-shed of [New England's] intellect, and will not itself be drained."[44] The literary flowering of New England was, after all, as Brooks suggested, to a considerable extent the flowering of eastern Massachusetts – although the movement did not end there.

The rise of northeastern Massachusetts to literary preeminence after the middle Atlantic states had taken the lead in all genres is essentially a story of the third, fourth, and fifth generations, though it begins as early as the century's first decade. Important to this process was the role of second- and third-generation intellectuals in launching a local tradition of postgraduate tourism and study in Europe, followed by the attempt to confront their peers back home with the latest trends in Continental thought and to inject some of the rigor of German philological and theological inquiry. The leading cultural intermediaries, so far as the long-range development of New England literature was concerned, were probably Joseph Stevens Buckminster, Edward Everett, George Bancroft, George Ticknor, and Henry Wadsworth Longfellow – the latter four dispatched abroad at one time or another to upgrade their scholarly abilities as preparation for teaching at Harvard. (Longfellow also made an earlier and more extensive tour under Bowdoin auspices.) Harvard did not benefit fully from the contributions of these men, by any means. Bancroft aborted his original plan to study theology and resigned within a year the lowly tutorship in Greek that Harvard gave him in order to found an experimental independent school in Northampton and, eventually, to combine politics and historiography. The other three, sooner or later, also became frustrated with institutional rigidity and overwork and resigned their posts. Yet collectively, through teaching, writing, and personal interchange, they helped revitalize the study of theology, the classics, history, and modern European literature, stimulating cultural comparativism and introducing New Englanders (with mixed feelings) to the "higher criticism" of Scripture – that is, the study of the Bible as a literary and historical document rather than as an inerrant given.[45]

Several additional factors ensured that their work would produce results. One was eastern-seaboard wealth, which financed the trips and the appropriate chairs at Harvard. (Buckminster was assisted by his Brattle Street congregation, the choicest in New England; Everett and Bancroft by Harvard money.) Another was the traditional New England respect for learning. Another was Harvard College itself. Understaffed, under-equipped, and unsophisticated though it was in contrast to Göttingen, Harvard was the region's chief literary breeding ground, attended by more than one-third of all male New England writers of consequence between the Revolution and the Civil War. The key fomentors of the New England Renaissance were either Harvard alumni or closely associated with Harvard influences, though they sometimes reacted against those influences.[46]

A less tangible but even more pervasive background factor was the ethos of liberal, Arminian Congregationalism, whose growth, concurrent with the intensification of evangelical orthodoxy during the Second Awakening (which began in the 1790s), provoked the Unitarian schism of 1815. The Unitarians and the likewise Arminian Episcopalians were the sects with which the great majority of important Massachusetts literary people were at least nominally affiliated during the antebellum years. Eastern Massachusetts was the stronghold of Unitarianism; Harvard was its academic citadel. The five travelers just mentioned were all products of the Arminian-Unitarian establishment.[47] In contrast to the more traditional "Puritanic" brand of Congregationalism that continued to dominate most of the rest of New England during the entire antebellum period and beyond, the Arminian ethos of Unitarianism stressed the formation of Christian character, rather than the experience of conversion, as the key to salvation and regarded the arts positively, as potential instruments of moral improvement, rather than warily as distractions or temptations, drawing less sharp a line than Calvinists did between the domains of sacred and profane, supernatural and natural. The Unitarian ethos was thus not only prepared to countenance free intellectual inquiry and expression but also, at least in theory, to give a much fuller encouragement to them.[48] Thus scholastic theology, throughout the antebellum period, was conducted on a more rigorous level by Calvinists than by Unitarians; but all the best nontheological literary and intellectual magazines were established by Unitarians and other religious liberals, and some of the best literary criticism appeared in the Unitarian reviews. The differences between Unitarian and orthodox aesthetics were not clear-cut; for instance, Calvinism did not necessarily correlate with conservative aesthetic tastes (the *North American Review's* most ardent early champion of Romanticism, Richard Henry Dana, Sr., converted to evangelical orthodoxy);[49] conversely, both parties feared, to different degrees, the supposedly pernicious effects of fiction (although both parties made exceptions for overlapping lists of morally unobjectionable writers from Hannah More through Scott and Dickens). Yet on the whole, it was the Unitarians who welcomed the development of native belles lettres, both for programmatic reasons and for reasons of personal taste, whereas it was the orthodox who were kept a generation or so behind by scruples about the perils of an "unsanctified" literature.

From all of this followed several significant consequences for antebellum New England literary culture. One was that in the production and, even more, in the discussion of literature, aesthetic questions and questions of religious and moral orientation became closely intertwined. Even if writers and reviewers did not work from a specific sectarian bias, they remained acutely concerned with art's moral tendency, much more so than in the age of Joseph Dennie and Robert Treat Paine – although even those would-be Augustan sparks were stuffy enough, in their own way. The growth of native literature and institutions after 1820, throughout the country but especially in New England, was carried on with a degree of public vigilance and authorial self-consciousness about the moral and social responsibility of art that reduced the contrast between the increasing climate of professionalism and the older early national ethos of letters as a patriotic, culturally enriching amateur pursuit.

Second, and also bearing on the question of the autonomy of art, was the extent to which New England's literary development turned out to be shaped by an earlier revival of learning. Massachusetts upgraded its college curriculum and professional training programs (e.g., schools of divinity were established at Harvard and Andover) before it produced creative writing of international stature. The classic school texts (Webster, Morse, and Bingham) preceded the classic works of New England literature. New England writing of the third generation influenced the next less through such belletristic manifestations as Bryant's poetry or Neal's fiction (although these figures were attended to – Neal by Hawthorne, Bryant by Longfellow, for example) than through Edward Everett's lectures on Greek culture, the sermons and literary essays of William Ellery Channing, James Marsh's analytical introduction to Coleridge's *Aids to Reflection,* the post-revolutionary wave of antiquarian historiography begun by Belknap and his circle. To a considerable extent, the literary achievement of the fourth and fifth generations, the New England Renaissance proper, also has a scholarly, theoretical cast. It is a "learned" literature, a literature with a research base – at least by the standards of the day. In Hawthorne's case, this base was historical research; in Stowe's and De Forest's, historical and ethnographic; in Whittier's, folkloric; in Holmes's, medical; in Emerson's, desultory ransacking of world history, literature, and religion; in Thoreau's, regional antiquarianism, the classics, "ethnical scriptures," and natural history; in Fuller's, comparative mythology; in Lowell's, linguistics; in Longfellow's, an absorption of European languages and literatures rarely matched for breadth before or since. It is no accident that New England's most distinguished large-scale collective "literary" enterprises of the fourth and fifth generations were Brahmin historiography (Prescott, Bancroft, Motley, and Parkman) and literary Transcendentalism. If, today, such figures as minister-reformers Orestes Brownson and Theodore Parker still command more attention from American literary scholars than more strictly literary figures such as popular poet Lydia Sigourney or popular novelist Maria Cummins, the answer does not lie simply in such factors as the male-oriented or antipopular cultural tendencies of modern scholarship but also in the particular kind of cultural consciousness-raising promoted by the third generation of literati, which was on the whole more interested in perfecting its epistemology than in perfecting its plots or its iambic pentameter. The kind of literary sophistication that its arbiters encouraged, to borrow Charles Fiedelson's epithet for Emerson, was artistry "in the medium of theory."[50] In this sense Fuller and Elizabeth Peabody were more symptomatic of the New England literary ethos of their day than Sigourney and Cummins, even though the work of the latter more closely approximates our ordinary notion of creative writing.

The popular and highbrow levels of antebellum writing are not so easily separated, however. The sentimental didacticism of the former is by no means the antithesis of the dark allegories of the heart and the essays on the beautiful and the true that we associate with the latter. The New England Renaissance saw a burgeoning of popular as well as serious writing. The third generation is notable not only for its attempts to raise the indigenous standards of intellectual rigor but also for the beginnings of the emergence of a bona fide Grub Street culture, supported by a proliferating middlebrow press, thriving alongside such organs of high culture as the *North American Review* and the *Christian Examiner*. A native market for the subliterary had existed since early colonial times, and since the Revolution it had been on the upswing, as is clear from such indices as the rise of the percentage of popular fiction in late eighteenth-century circulating libraries.[51] Numerous early national authors had made attempts, with varying success, to tap the emerging mass market – the novelists Brown, Rowson, and Foster; Jonathan Plummer, the simpleminded balladmonger from Newburyport whom the eccentric "Lord" Timothy Dexter dressed up in livery; and Connecticut Wit Richard Alsop, who in the last year of his life did former Indian captive John Jewitt the favor of trying to turn his *Journal Kept at Nookta Sound* into a salable commodity.[52]

After the War of 1812, such efforts at producing and purveying subelite literature intensified. The best-known New England productions of the sort are juvenile writing: the Rollo series of Jacob Abbott, the Peter Parley books of Samuel Goodrich, Lucretia Hale's *Peterkin Papers,* the Horatio Alger stories.[53] More important for purposes of our concentration on adult literature, however, were such developments as the rise, after 1825, of literary annuals, miscellaneous and women's magazines of large circulation (which began paying contributors decently in the 1840s) and middlebrow newspapers of literary substance. Take the case of the *New England Galaxy,* which Joseph T. Buckingham, during the period of his editorship (1817–28), made the region's liveliest paper from a literary standpoint.[54] Buckingham, once a poor boy from Connecticut but now on his way to becoming a member in good standing of the Unitarian-Whig establishment, represented both in his personal life and in his editorial policies a link between high and popular culture that attenuated but never collapsed during the years under review. His literary department included, on the one hand, serious writing of considerable skill, mostly contributed by members of the local gentry such as William Austin, the Charlestown lawyer whose "Peter Rugg, the Missing Man" was the best New England gothic tale before Hawthorne's. In the same vein were items printed or reprinted from the works of established authors such as Bryant and Rowson. On the other hand, Buckingham also favored broad, sometimes uproariously farcical pieces in prose and verse by

"Cape Cod Bard" Henry Ellenwood, local schoolmaster Ebenezer Bailey, and others. Byron's *Cain,* Cooper's *The Pilot,* and the completely ephemeral and sensationalized *Witch of New England* were all duly noticed in reviews; and in reprinting from other sources, the *Galaxy* was just as likely to draw banalities from the Vermont *Intelligencer* as to reprint lyrics by Coleridge and Shelley. Just as Buckingham's earlier *Polyanthos* had, in its biographical department, alternated between featuring Boston's leading citizens and noted actors of the day, so the *Galaxy* promoted both popular and elegant literature. That this mixed bag of material was supplied largely by people with college educations is one of many indications that the mass-market literature gaining ground in New England was, in the first instance, largely the creation of gentry scions working together with self-made entrepreneurs such as Buckingham and joining forces, through a sort of downward mobility, with nongentry scribblers like Alonzo Lewis (the "Bard of Lynn"), popular poet Hannah Gould of Newburyport, and hymn writer William B. Tappan to form a literary proletariat that went almost unnoticed by canonical authors and organs of high culture,[55] with rare exceptions like Whittier, who rose from the ranks of the tenth-rate newspaper poets to become, finally, an establishment poet and a Harvard Overseer.

This literary proletariat included some pathetic figures: Sumner Lincoln Fairfield, for example, peripatetic son of a Berkshire doctor, a specialist in poems about classical ruins and apocalypse, who failed at every trade he attempted and became briefly notorious when he accused Bulwer-Lytton of plagiarizing him in *The Last Days of Pompeii*.[56] Fairfield's works and those of most of his peers are of no interest today except to the antiquarian or the pathologist. Those who wish can find the record of their first decade wittily inscribed in William J. Snelling's 1831 Dunciad *Truth, a New Year's Gift for Scribblers,* "now chiefly valuable," wrote Oliver Wendell Holmes in 1885, "as a kind of literary tombstone on which may be read the names of many whose renown has been buried with their bones."[57] Yet the case of Snelling, whom Holmes ungraciously meant to bury also,[58] shows the risks of premature dismissal. Snelling's poem is almost as good as Lowell's *Fable for Critics* but less "interesting," because it concerns itself mostly with forgotten figures – Lewis, Fairfield, Brainard, Percival, George Lunt, "milk-and-water" Mellen, "pond'rous Pickering," "bully butcher Prentice," Harvard dropout Rufus Dawes (who "tells what streamlet wash'd his school-boy chin. – / Pity the booby had not fallen in!"), and "Old Oaken Bucket" Woodworth (Chop wood, O Woodworth, make the anvil ring, / Dig mud, pick oakum, any thing but sing!"). Snelling also wrote some good frontier fiction (*Tales of the Northwest,* 1830) and muckraking criticism (*The Rat-Trap; or, Cogitations of a Convict in the House of Correction,* 1837). But the brash West Pointer turned journalist became persona non grata to the Boston of the 1830s through acerbity, alcoholism, and impoverishment, so that in Holmes's memorial, "poor Snelling, who was not without talent and instruction," becomes paradoxically bracketed as both an exposer and a symptom of the stage of crudity preceding the New England Renaissance proper. Thus Snelling, by the verdict of polite culture, ironically became consigned to the ranks of the burgeoning subliterary that he himself was the first to chart.

Cases such as Snelling's apprise us of the inevitability of oversimplification as we enter the period of the flowering of New England's literary art after 1835. At this point we are faced with a paradox of reputations. The field is becoming increasingly crowded and diverse, yet owing in part to the increased organization and centralization of powerful literary institutions, the canon is getting more selective. Down through the mid-1820s, it becomes progressively harder to tell who the really important New England authors are. The trouble stems partly from scholarly inattention to post-Revolutionary, pre-Romantic literature in New England (a theme to which I shall return in Chapter 4), but partly the trouble is in the nature of the case. After the reputation of the Connecticut Wits began to wane and before Bryant and Catherine Sedgwick were perceived as having begun to set a standard for Yankee poetry and fiction, the field seemed wide open. John Neal saw no reason why he could not be the great American novelist, even though he admitted his shoddy craftsmanship; the semiliterate printer-poet Robert S. Coffin could think of himself as the "Boston bard," while conceding his inability to parse a sentence.[59] Whether Bryant's work was superior to that of Percival and Richard Henry Dana, Sr., was still a matter of debate. But by the Civil War, the regional literary situation had come into a focus that has proved surprisingly enduring. The importance of Emerson, Hawthorne, and Stowe was acclaimed (though justified on different grounds than we would choose); so too that of the Brahmin historians, whose art we still praise, if not their historiography; so too the Schoolroom Poets (Bryant, Longfellow, Whittier, Lowell), whom we value less than the nineteenth century did but still regard as the mainstream of nineteenth-century New England verse. Recognition of some fifth-generation figures, notably Thoreau and Dickinson, took longer. But in general the alert New England reader of 1865 had come rather close to our own conception of who the important New England moderns were, if not to our conception of the reasons why.

That meant, inevitably, the suppression of genuinely interesting material along with much trash. The best productions of early Connecticut Romanticism, for instance. But especially writing of a more popular kind. The best example is Yankee humor in its various branches: the

mock-heroic idyll, the stage Yankee, the Down East epistle, the narrative
of the Yankee trick. Today even most specialists in the period are familiar
with only a fraction of the highly readable work in this vein. They know
about Seba Smith's Jack Downing letters and T. C. Halliburton's Sam
Slick but probably not about Frances Whitcher's *Widow Bedott Papers* or
Ann Stephens' Jonathan Slick. They are much likelier to have looked into
P. T. Barnum's *Life* than into Asa Greene's very amusing *Life and Adventures of Dr. Dodimus Duckworth, A. N. Q.* ("A Notorious Quack") or Nathaniel Deering's hilarious "Mrs. Sykes."[60]

Retrieval of these, however, will probably not displace so much as supplement and somewhat redirect ongoing interest in the literary figures of
the fourth and fifth generations now regarded as "major." Let us turn to
a short survey of them and their emergence, with the full intention of
giving the so-called minor figures their due in later chapters.

III

Let us start by thinking of New England's literary climate at
midcentury as affected most powerfully by a Unitarian-Whig orthodoxy,
emanating chiefly from Boston, that was, however, enriched and complicated by a strong dissenting force that had arisen from within it and by
considerable literary activity that was on the upswing in other quarters
beyond its periphery. The literary aspect of this orthodoxy was a conservative sort of Romanticism first espoused by the Boston literary establishment during the 1820s and 1830s, which commended literature as a
vehicle of moral advancement, approved the hopeful Romantic vision of
human nature's capacity for improvement, prizing reason rather than
emotion as the proper means to that improvement while at the same time
granting a secure place for the latter under the ambiguous heading of
"moral sentiment" and recommending as literary models – after a long,
fond, lingering look backward to the Augustans –[61] Wordsworth in poetry and in fiction Scott. Wordsworth's inspiring didacticism and Scott's
regional historicizing, almost never vulgar and always seemingly on the
side of common decency, civic responsibility, and tolerance, appealed to
their moralistic, patriotic, progressivist but not populist cast of mind.
Among eminent British women writers, they commended especially Felicia Hemans' poetry and Maria Edgeworth's fiction. They advocated the
development of an American literature, while expecting for the most part
that it would take the form of an adaptation of European models rather
than a wholly new idiom. They pointed to Bryant and Sedgwick, both
(happily) Unitarians, as examples of the kind of adaptation they had in
mind.[62]

This aesthetic ideology (though not necessarily the specific models
commended) helped to shape the work of the leading Boston-Cambridge

poets of the fourth and fifth generations – Holmes, Longfellow, and Lowell – whose critical writings, in turn, articulated and transmitted that aesthetic. That is not to represent the three writers as uncomplicated or monolithic. On the contrary, they differed appreciably on some points of doctrine (literary nationalism, for instance), and each had his own private struggles with conventionalism. Longfellow and Lowell had Byronic sides that they repressed with difficulty; Lowell and Holmes were tempted by demons of irreverence, which in Holmes took the form of Augustan mockery and in Lowell a relish for periodic bluff challenges to authority and good breeding. Holmes's *Autocrat of the Breakfast Table* essays and Lowell's *Biglow Papers,* which show each author at his best, both use the fiction of a cantankerous speaker standing aside from a more proper audience and dictating to it, using a more vigorous language than the traditionally polite. Still, these men were also the producers of "Old Ironsides," "The Chambered Nautilus," "Paul Revere's Ride," "The Village Blacksmith," and "The Vision of Sir Launfall" – poets who finally came down on the side of a decorous, ethical, patriotic idealism, just as Bryant did, and with considerable grace and conviction.

Their work was supplemented in this respect by that of the four great Brahmin historians – William Hickling Prescott, George Bancroft, John Lothrop Motley, and Francis Parkman – who (with variations such as Prescott's nostalgia for monarchy, as opposed to Bancroft's populism) presented a saga in which Anglo-Saxon cultural superiority culminated in the establishment of American nationhood, and the New England contribution was considered central. All but one of these seven poets and historians were Harvard graduates, Unitarians, and Whigs. They were acquainted with one another personally as well as by reputation. They were also well acquainted with the editors and regular contributors of the *Christian Examiner* and the *North American Review* (six of them wrote essays for the latter). By both the serious readers of New England and each other they were thought to represent the best in midcentury New England letters. For all of these reasons they can be grouped together, despite such points of friction as Bancroft's role as Democratic machine politician, obnoxious to the rest.[63]

These writers were only the most conspicuous among a larger circle of Boston-Cambridge literati that also included such figures as Andrews Norton's son Charles Eliot Norton; the younger Richard Henry Dana (author of *Two Years before the Mast*); convivial essayist Thomas Gold Appleton; and banker-critic Edwin Percy Whipple, who reviewed the rest with just the right tinge of "objectivity" ("No member of the Saturday Club has ever been more loyally felicitous in characterizing the literary work of his associates").[64]

Basking in this establishment's good opinion but keeping a certain distance from it were Nathaniel Hawthorne and John Greenleaf Whittier. The Salem shipmaster's son whose happiest boyhood years were spent in rural Maine and the Quaker abolitionist from a Haverhill farm did not feel entirely comfortable in the more cosmopolitan world that began to coopt them as early as 1837, when Hawthorne's college classmate Long-fellow wrote a laudatory review of *Twice-Told Tales* for the *North American Review* in which he completely overlooked the gloomy side of Haw-thorne's genius that seemed so plain to Melville.[65] What Longfellow and his cohorts noticed was Hawthorne's exquisitely scrupulous narrative voice (his writings, Fields exuded, "have never soiled the public mind with one unlovely image"). They overestimated (as did Hawthorne him-self) the depth of his desire to overcome his gothic propensities.[66] Or perhaps, without being aware of it, they identified with this struggle, which was really a problem for them also. In effect, Hawthorne put him-self in their camp by stubbornly trying to define himself in terms of the "sunnier" side of his genius, as when he grafted a happy ending onto *The House of the Seven Gables,* or let Whipple become his literary mentor and "improve" the moral of *The Blithedale Romance,* or let the insipid Kenyon and Hilda occupy the field at the end of *The Marble Faun.*

Whittier shared with Hawthorne the engaging tendency to dissolve his antiestablishmentarian impulses into nostalgia or ethical idealism. Thus, despite the fact that he sometimes exhibited a disconcerting extremism (as when he exhorted Longfellow, in 1844, to run for Congress after read-ing his antislavery poems),[67] the Boston-Cambridge literati generally saw him as a sweet and noble soul and as exemplifying the sort of authenti-cally indigenous poetic voice that they (especially Lowell) sometimes as-pired to assume themselves. His lack of artistic polish was explained in the most positive light as an excess of sincerity. Like Hawthorne he was recruited for membership in the Sâturday Club, even though, again like Hawthorne, he avoided its meetings as much as possible.[68]

Placed in at least seeming opposition to the Cambridge-Boston ethos were the Transcendentalists, whose literary center was twenty miles away at Concord, where Emerson, removing in the 1830s, served as the central figure in a literary circle that included Henry Thoreau, the educator-diarist Bronson Alcott, and the minor poet Ellery Channing. At the edge of their circle was former Brook Farmer Hawthorne, during his periods of Concord residency, though he kept as much distance from them as he did from his Boston-Cambridge friends. Into the Emersonian orbit also came, for varying lengths of time, the critic and feminist Margaret Fuller, the poets Jones Very and Christopher Cranch, and a number of liberal-to-radical Unitarian pastors, of whom Theodore Parker was the greatest. Transcendentalism, in fact, really began as a religious movement, an at-tempt to substitute a Romanticized version of the mystical idea that humankind is capable of direct experience of the holy for the Unitarian rationalist view that the truths of religion are arrived at by a process of empirical study and by rational inference from historical and natural evidence.[69] The Transcendentalists' first organized activity, the "Symposium" or Transcendental Club, was originally intended to be for ministers only, though the organizers quickly changed their minds.[70] Those Transcendentalists who, like Emerson, were interested in art found in their ideology a means of intensifying the Unitarian commitment to artistic expression by envisaging the creative process (in Romantic terms) as originating in the experience of divine inspiration. This Romantic conception of the artist was not shared by the entire group. Some Transcendentalist ministers considered it an effete paganization; some Transcendentalist aesthetes thought it too moralistic. But its prominence in Emerson's thinking helped ensure that Transcendentalism's most enduring legacy to American history would be literary.

This contribution was even greater in the realm of theory than in literary achievement proper. Many Transcendentalists wrote verse; but most was blandly platitudinous, and only two poets (Emerson and Very) left a sizable body of memorable work. They rarely attempted drama and fiction.[71] Nonfictional prose was another matter: Emerson and Thoreau developed a challenging, metaphorically and tonally complex, densely packed essay style that other Transcendentalists attempted to a lesser degree (Fuller, Brownson, Parker, and Ellery Channing especially) and that stands as one of the period's major literary accomplishments. More important still, the Emersonian theory of creativity as divination furnished the strongest justification for serious literary effort that American criticism had yet seen, providing an answer to middlebrow complaints about belletristic frivolity by placing the creative endeavor on the most exalted moral plane. This domestication of radical Romantic ideology, imported from Europe chiefly via Coleridge, Carlyle, and Goethe, was as responsible as any exemplification of it for encouraging in such Emersonian disciples as Thoreau and Whitman a dedication to the literary life that was more thoroughgoing than even Emerson's own. In Boston, Prescott, at heart perhaps the most austerely dedicated of all the urban literati in his devotion to craft, felt obliged to hide this high seriousness with a bon vivant's exterior. Thoreau no longer needed to practice such concealments.

The Transcendentalist revolt against Bostonian norms was, however, very much a family quarrel. Transcendentalism began as a reform movement within Unitarianism and was fomented almost entirely by Unitarians of the fourth and fifth literary generations, most of whom kept close social and denominational ties with the Unitarian establishment even during the peak years of controversy (the mid-1830s to mid-1840s) and

worked to change it from within. After 1850, owing to mutual concessions, the breakaway group gradually became reconciled with the mainstream, leading to a semi-Transcendentalization of Unitarianism as a
whole. By 1900, Parker and Emerson, once considered the leading trou-
blemakers, had been canonized, along with their mentor William Ellery
Channing, as pioneer change agents, and more conservative Transcendentalists like Frederic Henry Hedge and James Freeman Clarke had long
been recognized as Unitarian spokespersons. So far as literary history is
concerned, the symbolic turning point was Emerson's enthusiastic
participation in founding the Saturday Club, dominated by Boston-
Cambridge literati. His views on church and faith had become less daring; his social manner had become more relaxed; his lectures were now
more lucid. The Bostonians were also getting used to him: For one thing,
in his deviant way he had always stood at least as staunchly for moral tone
as the most proper among them, and besides, it was impossible to dislike
him personally (he was so gracious and kindly), even when he said outrageous things. As early as the 1840s, the reviews had begun to soften,
partly because they were increasingly assigned to Emerson's friends;[72]
soon Whipple was praising Emerson and imitating his lapidary style;
Longfellow (from the start an avid if sometimes puzzled auditor of his
lectures) put a picture of Emerson in his study; Lowell dedicated a book
to him; eventually Holmes wrote one of the full-dress biographies. To
Lowell, he always remained "Mr. Emerson" or "Dear sir" (as opposed to
"Wendell" or even "Hawthorne"); and Emerson, for all his graciousness,
made it quite clear in his journal that social amity did not extend to unqualified admiration of the Schoolroom Poets as poets.[73] Still the rapprochement was virtually complete.

It did not automatically extend to other Transcendentalists. Alcott and
Thoreau, who observed Emerson's apparent cooptation with (respectively) amusement and scorn, did not follow suit but instead drew closer
to each other in their rusticity. Ellery Channing did the same. We must
differentiate between such birthright Brahmins as Emerson, Clarke, and
music critic John Sullivan Dwight, who comported themselves during
their countercultural phases with enough discretion to leave themselves a
means of reentry, and two other groups who were not so included: those
like Fuller and Ellery Channing, who had the right pedigrees but whose
behavior went too far, and social outsiders such as Brownson (born to a
poor family on the Vermont frontier) and Thoreau (like Emerson a scholarship student at Harvard but less socially credentialed), who could not
accept and were not accorded the usual terms of Cambridge-Boston literary and social exchange.

Starting in the 1830s, with Hawthorne's first great New England tales
and Emerson's *Nature,* as well as the first volume of Bancroft's *History of*

the United States and Prescott's *Ferdinand and Isabella,* the Boston-Concord authors produced over the course of half a century so much of the important literature of the New England Renaissance that insiders and outsiders alike began to refer more than ever to Boston as a synechdoche for all New England. "The literary theories we accepted," remembered the Ohio-born William Dean Howells, "were New England theories, the criticism we valued was New England criticism, or, more strictly speaking, Boston theories, Boston criticism."[74] Van Wyck Brooks's *Flowering of New England* follows the Howellsian line, rarely straying west of the greater Boston area.

Brooks and Howells oversimplified, however, in equating the hegemonic with the total literary result. Although the New England literary establishment became increasingly Boston-centered during the antebellum years, it by no means had a monopoly on creative production, even in its own backyard. The popular romances of Universalist minister's son Maturin Ballou; the humor of journalist Benjamin Penhallow Shillaber's imaginary Mrs. Partington; the plays of actor-manager-dramatist-doctor Joseph Jones; the sentimental fiction of Salemite Maria Cummins – these were homegrown products in which the establishment showed little interest and over which it exercised little control. Furthermore, by midcentury a new sort of regionwide literary dispersal had set in, owing in part to the very success of centralization, and during the next fifty years an increasing percentage of artistically serious new writing was done in such comparative outposts as South Berwick, Maine (Sarah Orne Jewett), and the Isles of Shoals off the New Hampshire coast (Celia Thaxter), where authors could live in comparative retirement yet still be in contact with the publishing and media empires at the Hub or New York, with whose help they could sustain satisfactory networks of epistolary and social interchange.[75]

Up to a point, the increase in high-quality writing done in New England of outside northeastern Massachusetts can be explained in terms of the liberalization of orthodox Congregationalism, about a generation after the Unitarians began aggressively to patronize the arts. As in eastern Massachusetts, the stage was set by the founding of learned institutions (such as Andover Seminary and Amherst College) and intellectual reviews (such as the *Christian Spectator* and the *New Englander*). The key early exemplars tended to be people from the more progressive orthodox strongholds in the Connecticut Valley. These included Harriet Beecher Stowe, whose earliest book (*The Mayflower,* a collection of short miscellaneous pieces) might be taken as marking the first significant stirrings of nineteenth-century orthodox literary culture (1843); her brother Henry Ward Beecher, a pulpit craftsman and sometime novelist; Rose Terry Cooke, of Hartford, whose best regional stories, first appearing in the

1850s, called into question the Stowe-Beecher tendency to idyllicize New
England village life; and Humphreysville cotton manufacturer's son John
DeForest, an even more committed pioneer realist who made his debut
in the 1850s with a history and a serial novel (*Witching Times*, 1856–7) of
Puritan era New England. De Forest's best novel, *Miss Ravenel's Conversion from Secession to Loyalty* (1867), was to proclaim his intellectual origins once more by defining the Yankee orientation in terms of secularized
Puritanism. The greatest of all the Connecticut Valley writers was Emily
Dickinson, in whose poems, as in Stowe's New England fiction, Calvinist categories are repeatedly dismantled yet repeatedly shown as categories of consciousness to which the unmoored soul keeps returning. In
fiction, however, an even more gifted product of late Calvinist culture
than any of the Connecticut Valley novelists was Elizabeth Stoddard of
Mattapoisett, near New Bedford (later to gravitate, like Beecher, to New
York), whose novels and stories astringently probed the tensions between
internalized restraint and banked-up desire in village settings where
"moderate Calvinism" had long since lapsed into formality.[76]

It is tempting to depict these writers and their lesser contemporaries as
having instigated a countermovement in New England letters that shifted
its center of cultural gravity in a westward, and thus more regionally representative, direction. Any such thesis must be carefully qualified, however. First, these authors do not seem as coherent a group as the Boston-
Concord literati. In part this may be because less is known about them.
Except for Dickinson and (more recently) the Beechers, modern literary
scholarship has concentrated overwhelmingly on the hegemonic literary
culture of eastern Massachusetts liberalism. The possibility that we shall
want one day to envisage an equally complex and even more extensive
network of late Calvinist literary culture has begun to emerge from such
studies as Ann Douglas' analysis of the cooperation and rivalry between
female and ministerial authors, Richard Rabinowitz's magisterial dissertation on theological praxis in New England between 1750 and 1850, reconstructions of Dickinson's literary contacts by Richard Sewall and others, and biographies of the peripatetic Beechers (Catherine's career as
writer and educator, Henry Ward's literary and journalistic work, and
Harriet's literary activities in Cincinnati, Brunswick, and Andover).[77] No
further discoveries, however, will alter the fact that orthodox culture was
clearly more decentralized than its liberal opposite. Its original strategy
had been to surround Boston, and the success of that strategy, combined
with internal bickerings among New Haven, Hartford, Andover, Bangor, and other orthodox communities, reinforced the atomization that
geography had made inevitable to start with.

A two-cultures approach to understanding literary organization in
mid-nineteenth-century New England is called further into question by

the increasing interconnection of the Calvinist and liberal branches as the
secularization process ran its course. The cases of Dickinson and Holmes
illustrate the blurring of the lines of division. Dickinson turned for guidance to moderate Transcendentalist Thomas Wentworth Higginson, to
liberal Congregationalist Washington Gladden, to conservative Presbyterian Charles Wadsworth – and finally kept her own counsel. In this she
followed the precedent of admired British models like Charlotte Brontë
and Elizabeth Barrett Browning, for whom piety was also in constant
tension with eclectic free thought. The seemingly prototypical Bostonian
Holmes was the son of a moderate Calvinist minister and on that account
felt a deep rapport with Stowe (which she did not fully share) as another
person who could not get the iron of Calvinism out of her soul no matter
how hard she tried.[78] Again, Emerson and Thoreau, from the safe distance of two generations of Arminian liberalization, looked back senti-
mentally to the ramrod integrity of the Puritan forefathers as a contrast
to contemporary mental and moral flabbiness – a tactic that, ironically,
has since been used against them.[79] The liberal *Atlantic* recruited Stowe as
one of its leading authors in the 1860s; conservative Amherst and Williams invited Emerson to lecture. So, in a certain sense, paraphrasing
Thomas Jefferson's 1801 inauguration speech, it would be fair to say that
they were all Calvinists, and all Arminians.

Two further examples will help to pinpoint both the utility and the
limits of the two-cultures approach. As Charles Feidelson first pointed
out, the Connecticut Congregational minister Horace Bushnell, at midcentury, devised a theory of theological discourse as metaphor that at certain points closely resembles Emerson's theory of language. The similarity was a matter not of direct influence but of the two men having been
indebted to a common source, Coleridge. Coleridge spoke to them in a
similar manner because they were faced, about a generation apart, with a
similar problem within their respective faith communities: the need, as
they saw it, to confront the desiccations of pedantic theologizing with
the truth that theology was inherently a critical fiction.[80] The resemblance between Emerson and Bushnell, combined with their noticeable
lack of contact, testifies both to the separateness of Unitarian and Calvinist culture and also to the importance of theological erosion and European
Romanticism as cultural influences that created a similar sort of literary
ferment throughout New England.

The same can be said of literary reactions to the antislavery crisis by
birthright liberal and conservative religionists. Harriet Beecher Stowe's
appeal to the higher law of conscience in *Uncle Tom's Cabin* is very different from Thoreau's in "Resistance to Civil Government," in the sense that
the latter protest is grounded in a completely individualistic appeal to the
dictates of conscience, the former in an appeal to divine will and the dic-

tates of a superintending Providence that the Arminian-Transcendentalist group would for the most part have regarded as anachronistic. Emersonian Transcendentalism probably had no influence whatsoever on the formation of Stowe's thinking. But in light of that, the affinities between the two (both being religiocentric oppositions to an expedient social conformity in the name of an absolute morality) are the more striking.

In the chapters to come, then, it will be necessary to employ distinctions such as Unitarian versus orthodox, and Unitarian versus Transcendentalist, without giving the impression that they are absolute, since their vicissitudes paralleled and overlapped to a great extent. Furthermore, we need to question not only the coherence and the polarity of such antitheses but also the pertinence of the religiocentric frame of reference itself, although that conceptual framework seems more deeply embedded in the New England imagination of the period than any other. In some contexts, as we shall also see, political distinctions such as Whig versus Democrat or Federalist versus Jeffersonian serve us better. In others, all categories extrinsic to literature are objectionable. Between two poets writing in heroic couplets or Wordsworthian blank verse, the aesthetic resemblance between them as Neoclassicals or Romantics will often outweigh their ideological differences as orthodox or Unitarian. Even where prima facie evidence calling for religiocentric analysis is pretty strong, the results can be grotesque. Take the case of essayist Donald G. Mitchell ("Ik Marvel"). Mitchell can be drafted into the ranks of Connecticut Valley Calvinism-in-decline. He was a Congregational minister's son, a Yale graduate, and a producer of a fairly interesting satirical novel about decadent Puritanism. Emily Dickinson's enjoyment of his *Reveries of a Bachelor* might be taken as collateral evidence of a common post-Puritan restiveness, a common predilection for indulging (within safe limits) a mildly erotic fantasizing as a form of intellectual dissent.[81] Although there is something to this argument, the fact remains that Mitchell's bachelor's reveries and his books on farming, which are his best and most characteristic works, cannot be reduced to the classification post-Puritan unless we are to bring Charles Lamb, Washington Irving, and a good deal of the literature of nineteenth-century American agricultural reform under the same expansive umbrella. Perhaps if Mitchell had written more and better *Doctor Johnses*, he would have been studied more attentively by Americanists than he has been so far. Such is certainly the case with the Tennysonian poet Frederick Goddard Tuckerman, whose sonnets are far better than Jones Very's but who lacks not only Very's striking oddity but his obvious link with the period's main religious currents.

The best illustration of the limits of a religiocentric definition of New England culture is regional realistic fiction. The high-water mark of New England "local colorism," to use the too condescending term by which it is generally called, is really the last third of the nineteenth century, but we shall examine it in some detail in Part IV, since its origins coincide with the rise of Romantic fiction.[82] Produced mostly by writers who lived outside northeastern Massachusetts, set in rural areas in northern and western New England, this body of writing tends by definition (given the geography of regional sectarianism) to be about late Calvinist village life and to be written by cultural insiders. Several of the most important of these – Stowe, Beecher, and Elizabeth Phelps Ward, particularly – were extremely conscious and proud of their evangelical roots, thus reinforcing the impression that regional realism is somehow the product of the Calvinist imagination, even though two of the key early practitioners – Sedgwick and Sylvester Judd (whose *Margaret: A Tale of the Real and Ideal,* 1845, it is the best regional novel before Stowe's) – were Unitarian converts who took a more jaundiced view of backcountry conservatism than most of their successors. Yet the theological dimension of village life is generally and increasingly subordinated to the larger anthropological and narrative purposes of anatomizing village institutions and developing a secular plot, and after the 1850s theological concerns dwindle almost to the vanishing point in the work of younger authors. Mary Wilkins Freeman could still validly call her people Puritans, or children thereof, but she did so with respect to their stubborn and repressed life-style rather than with respect to theology. Altogether, then, although the New England local color movement in a sense represents a literary flowering of formerly Calvinist regions to match the antebellum Renaissance centered in eastern, liberal areas of New England, its sectarian aspect is attenuated, in keeping with the drift of regional culture as a whole.

The fact that local color writing was largely a woman's genre suggests that gender might have been a more significant common bond among its practitioners than either religion or rural themes, an impression reinforced by the correspondence of Jewett, Stowe, Harriet Prescott Spofford, and others. In their work, a more overt emphasis is often placed on female culture than on religious culture; and one might argue, at least on biographical grounds, that the ruralism of these authors was in part related to gender also. Once literary institutions were solidly in place, it was neither necessary nor particularly advantageous for writers to live close to the urban centers unless they aspired to become editors or publishers. These managerial positions remained solidly under male control – another salient feature of the northeastern Massachusetts establishment. The literary establishment was not only urban-based and theologically liberal but also patriarchal. Possibly it did make more room for talented women than its counterparts elsewhere in America. But Margaret Fuller's brief editorship of the *Dial* was the exception; Higginson's patronizing advice to literary aspirants like Dickinson was the rule; and the men-only membership policy of the Saturday Club was symptomatic: The door was shut to poet-lecturer-feminist Julia Ward Howe but open to her domineering spouse. (In this, as in its tendency to suppress controversy, the club system had a muffling as well as an enabling influence on New England culture.) Women might edit gift books and ladies magazines but not *Harper's* or the *Atlantic*. As the data analyzed in the Appendix reveal, nineteenth-century New England women writers were actually more professionalized than their male counterparts. But the structure of the male-dominated literary marketplace was such as to absorb them more easily as contributors than as managers, increasing the incentives (first from the Victorian cult of domesticity, then from the doctrinaire regionalism of the late-century reviews) for them to stay home and write about their immediate surroundings.[83] The story of the rise of New England's institutions of high literary culture is thus inevitably a tale featuring male consolidation of power, including power over canon formation, rather than the female literary culture that accounted for a greater percentage of the literary producers and consumers of the period than a roll call of eminent literary names would suggest.

Ultimately, however, no sweeping generalization will suffice to encapsulate the whole field of regional realism, much less the organization of all of New England literary culture during the years under review. Despite the process of institutional centralization, certain outlying districts remained at least semiautonomous, and some (the Berkshires, especially) even made gains as distinct culture regions.[84] So, in speaking of "New England literary culture," we inevitably overgeneralize from the start. The Arminian tinge of the enclave that created the New England Renaissance establishment did not prevent an upsurge of writing among writers of orthodox background, nor did either development mean that Congregationalists of whatever stamp had a complete monopoly on literary expression (Catholics, Universalists, and Baptists also began to build their own literary networks, for instance);[85] nor did these sectarian efflorescences mean that denominationalism is more than a limited key to the period's literary ideology. Despite male domination of highbrow literary institutions, New England produced growing numbers of important women writers. The fact that most of these increasingly chose not to become Bostonians is suggestive, yet in view of the overall dispersal of authorship throughout the region in the late nineteenth century it is not in itself proof of a dramatic urban-rural split along gender lines.[86]

Such difficulties of classification, frustrating to purists, are of course also a mark of literary success, of a burgeoning literary scene. Without any hedging whatsoever, we may reaffirm that point at least: Both in its institutional development and in its aesthetic results, the story of literary New England between the Revolution and the Civil War was close enough to a rags-to-riches fable for the zeitgeist to evoke that fictional formula from the pen of a Unitarian minister's son, Horatio Alger. By 1865, New England writing had arrived, even though some of its best producers, such as Emerson, were so self-critical that they could not fully believe in their own merits. Indeed, the region would never have it quite so good again, would never in the future have such a large share of the nation's literary talent. For one chapter, that is enough to have shown. We need now to scrutinize the ramifications of that achievement in more detail.

3

Marketplace, Ethos, Practice: The Antebellum Literary Situation

He was so enamoured of the spiritual beauty that he held all actual written poems in very light esteem in the comparison.

Ralph Waldo Emerson, "Thoreau" (1862)

Genius . . . melts many ages into one, and thus effects something permanent, yet still with a similarity of office to that of the more ephemeral writer. A work of genius is but the newspaper of a century, or perchance of a hundred centuries.

Nathaniel Hawthorne, "The Old Manse" (1846)

Chapters 1 and 2 took note of some of the economic and cultural factors that enabled New England's literature to develop. To enable, however, is not in itself to cause. Our charting of these developments only raises anew the question of why they should have culminated so successfully. From the early national standpoint, American literary emergence seemed bafflingly slow; but for us the question should rather be, How could America's classic literary works have been written at a time when the very concept of authorial vocation had hardly begun to crystallize?

This chapter will address the issue of how, at a time when American authors were ostensibly lagging behind their British counterparts, the best of them were able to compose works that today impress many readers not only as great literature but even as in some respects more modern than the masterpieces of Victorian fiction and poetry. My method will be to correlate three levels of literary activity: the socioeconomic level of literary publishing, the ideological level of literary values, and the aesthetic level of the literary artifacts themselves. My paradoxical yet I think defensible argument is that we must understand the achievement of the New England Renaissance as having in good part been prompted by the chief obstacle that it had to confront: the utilitarian, moralistic cast of mainstream culture, which tended to object to the autonomy and even to

56

the legitimacy of art. I shall concentrate in this chapter on antebellum writing, paying special attention to the assimilation of Romantic ideology as a catalytic factor. Chapter 4 will then counterbalance this emphasis by charting the continuities between early national and antebellum letters.

I

The years 1780 to 1860 saw an increasing professionalism at all occupational levels. Booksellers' and other "mechanics" associations began; graduate programs were instituted in medicine, law, and divinity; roles within general occupational categories became more differentiated. In the field of divinity, for instance, charitable organizations and academic theology took control of enterprises formerly conducted by the versatile parish minister.[1] In creative writing we have seen the beginnings of a similar tendency. Although before 1830 none in New England but the independently rich could pursue belles lettres as a primary vocation, by the 1850s Longfellow could earn a living from his poetry, even though he had other sources of support as well; Harriet Beecher Stowe had become her family's chief breadwinner; Emerson was meeting his expenses from literary lecturing. The leading producers of domestic fiction (castigated as a "damned mob of scribbling women" by the envious Hawthorne) were all making very tidy profits. The *Atlantic* was paying poets fifty dollars a page, as opposed to the two dollars offered by the *New England Magazine* in 1835; compensation for literary journalism would triple between 1860 and 1880.[2]

This commercialization of letters led to an increasingly diverse and complicated set of mediations between author and public. Raymond Williams' useful typology of artistic production gives a fuller sense of the changes involved.[3] Williams distinguishes four market situations: the *artisanal* ("the independent producer . . . offers his own work for direct sale"), the *post-artisanal* ("the producer sells his work not directly but to a *distributive* intermediary, who then becomes, in a majority of cases, his factual if often occasional employer"), the *market professional* (the writer negotiates a contract, involving royalties and copyright, with a publisher), and the *corporate professional* (the artist becomes the employee of a literary organization – e.g., a magazine or a newspaper). Simple examples of each phase would be (artisanal) Joel Barlow's trying to sell his poetry by subscription or Joseph Dennie's publishing his own essays in his own newspaper; (post-artisanal) Hawthorne's producing short stories for Samuel Goodrich's gift books; (market professional) Longfellow's negotiating royalty arrangements with Ticknor & Fields; and (corporate professional) Margaret Fuller's literary journalism for the *New York Tribune*. Until at least 1800, the artisanal mode of production was the rule;

market and corporate professionalism did not become possible anywhere in America until the early nineteenth century, but by 1865 the former was the norm and the latter increasingly common. These market changes were not only rapid but also much more complicated, both literally and psychologically, than a straightforward linear succession of discrete stages. Emerson's lecturing, for instance, belongs to phase two, whereas the publication of his essays belongs to phase three; Nathaniel Parker Willis, at different points in his career, tried all four modes of production. Beyond this, more central to our present purposes, was the dissonance in the ideology of authorship that both underlay these changes and was quickened by them.

The fundamental issue had to do with the concept of professionalism itself. During the early national years, New England writing, as we have seen, was dominated by an ethic of genteel amateurism that encouraged sublimation of literary impulses into the socially acceptable forms of cultural patriotism and a bourgeois version of the Old World aristocratic ideal of refined accomplishment. "In no other period in American history," remarks William Charvat, "has our culture been so completely and directly dominated by the professional classes; concomitantly, in no other period has the economically dominant class exhibited such an interest in the arts."[4] He speaks of the years 1810 through 1835, but the generalization might be extended backward indefinitely. Typical of the era were Timothy Dwight, who wrote poetry and literary prose while serving as college instructor, manager of his family's estates, parish minister, and college president; Sarah Wentworth Morton, an affluent Boston matron who created the first American literary treatment of the noble savage (*Ouâbi: or the Virtues of Nature,* 1790); and Charles Sprague, "the banker poet," whose rhetorical set pieces won literary prizes in the 1820s. What is striking is not that such amateurs existed – they still do – but that such were the leading writers of their day.

Collegians who might in a later day have sought to become professional authors often went through a scribbling phase and then settled down to business. Thus jurist Joseph Story published a book of juvenile poems that political adversaries used as a pretext for questioning his stability of character; his son William Wetmore Story later achieved what would seem to have been the father's early aspiration by becoming a sculptor and minor poet. Thus Joseph Stevens Buckminster, gifted with considerable poetic talent and critical sensibility, channeled these into biblical criticism and sermonizing, leaving it to his younger sister Eliza Buckminster Lee to become the family's publishing creative writer in the 1830s and 1840s. Thus when young Longfellow applied in 1824 for a position on the *United States Literary Gazette,* its editor, who might have been expected to applaud Longfellow's literary ambitions, urged him instead to heed his father's advice and become a lawyer.[5]

These elders were being quite practical. New England had thus far seen no exceptions to the rule that conflicts between literary identity and social and professional responsibility led either to the subordination of the first or to disaster. Still fresh in all Bostonians' minds was the case of their first conspicuous literary bohemian, Robert Treat Paine, Jr., who had died impoverished in his father's attic after several times failing to make a go of it in letters. Paine served for his circle as a sort of Federalist Chatterton.

An age in which amateurism is the writer's only viable option might be expected to fashion its literary ideal in those terms. Hence the early republican admiration of a figure like Sir William Jones – barrister, linguist, orientalist scholar, literateur, accomplished in the didactic essay, the discursive treatise, and the patriotic ode.[6]

The ideal, however, was as much compensatory as affirmative. Too many would-be William Joneses were conscious of the limits within which they were forced to operate. Future president John Quincy Adams felt duty-bound to publish poetry "to help remove the 'foul-stain of literary barbarism' from his country," but he also felt bound to remain anonymous, since "no small number of very worthy citizens among us [are] irrevocably convinced that it is impossible at once to be a man of business and a man of rhyme." The poet James G. Percival complained that his literary reputation had ruined his medical practice: "When a person is really ill, he will not send for a poet to cure him."[7] A similar irritation at philistinism, rather than endorsement of the amateur ideal, seems to underlie Emerson's remark, in 1834, that "Webster's speeches seem to be the utmost that the unpoetic West has accomplished or can" (*JMN* 4:297).

Already, however, Emerson himself and other writers were proving this statement wrong by taking advantage of new marketing opportunities such as the rise of the lyceum, which had helped to make practicable Emerson's transition from professional minister to professional man of letters. The vocations both of full-time "serious" artist and full-time "commercial" artist were beginning to loom up as real possibilities for those without independent incomes, and with this came also a new ideological polarization. On the one hand, literary vocation and literary integrity came to be so prized that Thoreau, in revising *Walden,* produced an unprecedented eight drafts, a record previously unapproached even in early New England's most prestigious genre, theology. On the other hand, we find increasingly frank avowals of commercialism, as in the work of miscellaneous writer and ladies' magazine editor Sarah J. Hale. Hale began her career, shortly after being reduced to impecunious widowhood, with a little book of poems that invoked the amateur tradition, disclaiming in its preface all desire for gain. The title, *The Genius of Oblivion* (1823), proved all too apt. But Hale quickly moved into more lucrative genres, justifying her choice in the preface to her successful novel *Northwood* (1827) on the ground that she was her family's sole support.[8]

By 1865, Sir William Jones had been pretty much forgotten; the "configuration of law, literature, and public service" for which he stood was fast being pried apart.[9] Yet the ideal of the writer as omnicompetent man or woman of affairs had by no means lost all its force. Again we may cite Thoreau, who, in an early essay, praised Sir Walter Raleigh as being perhaps the "man of the most general information and universal accomplishment of any in England. Though he excelled greatly in but few departments, yet he reached a more valuable mediocrity in many."[10] Not that valuable mediocrity was precisely what Thoreau himself stood for; yet it seems clear that his insistence on the interdependence of poetics and natural history, of contemplation and action, reflects what he admired in Raleigh. Conversely, even New England's antebellum hack writers liked to represent themselves as having a higher purpose than mere commercialism. For instance, the period's best-selling poet, Lydia Sigourney, although noting that she published in order to help support her parents and compensate for her husband's ailing hardware business, insisted that one of her two chief goals was "to aim at being an instrument of good." (The other was "not to interfere with the discharge of womanly duty.")[11] The same was true of Samuel Goodrich, who high-mindedly pictured himself serving as an apostle of civilization through his Peter Parley books and even had pretensions as a serious artist, publishing, among other works, a volume of Byronic poems and a miscellaneous collection of prose and poetry (*Sketches from a Student's Window*, 1841) in the vein of Irving and Hawthorne.[12]

The continuing lack of clear distinction between literary amateur and professional is nowhere better exemplified than by the reply that Harvard professor and critic C. C. Felton wrote in 1849 to acknowledge a volume of poems by his friend publisher James Fields:

> It has often seemed to me that the position of a man of business, with literary tastes and talents, is one of rare happiness. The union of the two elements of life works out a more manifold experience than either alone, and gives richer materials for thought. While business steadies and utilizes life, the cultivation of letters embellishes and dignifies it. A merely literary life, with few exceptions, is neither happy nor respectable; a merely business life may be very happy and respectable, but it wants the heightening touches of an idealizing imagination. . . . Boston is remarkable for the number of men who unite the two.[13]

Underneath the conventional sweet nothings of the usual thank-you note we detect a more profound set of conventions: the mid-Victorian sage (who also happens to be a fair representative of the highbrow reviewing establishment) affirming the ideal of cultural cohesiveness that binds the whole fraternity of literary gentlemen together, an ideal based on resistance to a specialized professionalism, which is perceived to be emotionally stultifying if not socially dangerous. Felton's pleasure at finding this ideal exemplified by Fields testifies both to its obsolescence (a "rare happiness") and its persistence, at least vestigially. It is equally significant that Felton confers a greater legitimacy on business than on art: Business alone may be prosaic; but it "steadies and utilizes life," whereas a "merely literary life" is usually "neither happy nor respectable." Even allowing for exaggeration in order to please the correspondent, one suspects that Felton and his cohorts considered capitalism less of a threat to the social order than art. Nina Baym notes in her recent study of antebellum novel reviewing that the "first responsibility of the critic" was taken to be to determine "whether a novel is immoral; only after that determination is made may one proceed to examine the work's literary merits and demerits."[14] For some, like Felton, such attempts to use reviewing as a means of social control were undoubtedly based on a sincere conviction that the development of the arts in America ought to be guided by the enlightened elite; for others, the motive was probably the more pragmatic one of wishing to propitiate the Mrs. Grundys (of both genders) among the subscribers. But the rhetorical result was the same.

Thus throughout the years covered by this study, writers and publishers operated in the face of admonitions not to carry literary autonomy too far, not to be socially irresponsible. These they partly internalized and partly resisted. The case of Emerson nicely illustrates the attendant complexities. Emerson is, of course, an outstanding instance of the writer in the process of secession from the ranks of established professionals in order to form a separate caste. His original enthusiasm for the ministry, his first profession, was based upon his confidence in his gift for rhetoric (*JMN* 2:239); his abandonment of the ministry can be seen as the recoil of aspiring literary talent forced to fulfill itself within the limits of the ethic of genteel amateurism and as an attempt to find a way of specializing in expression alone. Once liberated, however, Emerson preferred to define himself in broad terms, as a scholar, and in his studies he cultivated a new amateurism, taking all the arts and sciences as his territory.

Emerson's compromise position is well illustrated by his best-known definition of the scholar as the intellect in the social body that division of labor has fragmented into parts (*EW* 1:53). In developing this image, Emerson first deplores the fragmentation (which has tended to reduce the scholar to a "mere thinker"), then accepts it (by prescribing as the scholar's resources individual contact with nature and books, and as the scholar's duty, self-trust), but ultimately resists the consequences of this solitary individualism by celebrating American cultural independence rather than personal independence, and the scholar's centrality among his fellow citizens rather than his achievement as an end in itself. This makes for a precarious balancing act, as can be seen from the fact that bohemians and Brahmins alike later came to look back to Emerson (each with reservations, to be sure) as a reference point.

Emersonian rhetoric and biography, then, attest both to the endurance of genteel amateurism and to the breakdown of that ideal. Emerson's cheerful participation, after 1850, in activities of the Saturday Club, the Harvard Board of Overseers, and other such embodiments of conservative Boston culture testifies to the continued vitality of a critical mass of literary people who saw themselves as continuous with the business and professional classes, who felt the same sense of solidarity. The continuing breakdown of the ideal is seen in the younger writers who found support in Emerson (often to his discomfort) for anticonventional, risk-taking commitment to their expressive gift at the cost of forfeiting any chance of integration into the ranks of the socially proper. Among them were Thoreau, Ellery Channing, and Emily Dickinson, all of whom cultivated the sense of their differentness and, in their more self-confident moments, positively rejoiced in the thought that their writings were caviar to the general. "Give me a sentence," demands Thoreau, "which no intelligence can understand."[15]

Yet even this war cry implies – and here Emerson's self-division makes increasing sense – not so much total rejection of genteel amateurism as a counterelitism, an exchange of one badge of cultural superiority for another. Like a poststructuralist in a department of new critics, Thoreau is opposing the establishment's discourse with a discourse of his own. Both parties to the debate have their Harvard degrees. The issue here, much as in academia today, is the legitimacy of a new theory, propounded from within the ranks of the educated elite and confronting an old theory felt by its adherents to be axiomatic, hence provoking the response that the challenger is a willfully eccentric and chaos-portending upstart. That is the most fundamental significance of "Transcendentalist rhetoric," the mode of semiunintelligibility practiced by Emerson and Thoreau, in which established theological and philosophical categories (reason, heaven, God) are redefined without footnotes, established conventions of sequential exposition are flouted, and unfamiliar intellectual traditions are appealed to (Confucianism, Hinduism, Neoplatonism, Zoroastrianism). But the participants compete as cultural equals, well bred, well read, with a common commitment to intellectual and moral high seriousness, however differently they define that commitment.[16]

From this account it would seem that Transcendentalist ideology reflects the period's movement toward literary specialization but not the commercialization of letters that made this autonomy possible. Up to a point such indeed seems to have been the case. The literary Transcendentalists resisted depicting art as a commodity, disparaged merely popular writing, and described the writer's vocation in terms of prophecy. Thoreau, in particular, adjusted his life in such a way as to maximize his opportunities for "serious" writing and minimize his dependence on sales. Clearly he sought to achieve the intellectual and literary benefits of specialization; but when it came to turning literature into a business, he had as many reservations as Felton, though they were differently based: Thoreau was more afraid of compromising his standards than of not being able to make a respectable living (or perhaps the former fear expressed the latter in disguise). However that may be, Thoreau's scorn for panderers to popular taste can be read either as admirably high-minded or as a willful blindness to the unusual economic advantages (sufferance and subsidy by family and friends) that permitted him to cultivate unpopularity. The harshest view of the matter, for which there is some basis, would be to type Thoreauvian and Emersonian idealizations of art as prophecy as leisure-class rationalizations made possible by the fact (or illusion, in Emerson's case) that one's survival was not contingent on the verdict of the marketplace. Emerson's genteel preference for thinking that he spoke to a choice group of souls was repeated by Thoreau in intensified form.

Yet, in another sense, even Emersonianism stands for the transition to the commercial. For one thing, the prophetic-didactic view of art was eminently marketable in antebellum America, as Harriet Beecher Stowe proved in *Uncle Tom's Cabin* (1852), the antebellum period's runaway best-seller.[17] As we have seen, writers far more avowedly commercial than Emerson found it to their economic advantage to present themselves as harbingers of moral uplift. Peter Parley on universal history may read like a parody of Emerson on the same subject, but the connection is no less close for all that. Emerson's career as lecturer itself is evidence worth citing. His lyceum manner, though not showy or overtly entertaining, had a breadth of appeal that seems astonishing to those who know him today only through the medium of print. Emerson profited (in all senses of the word) from a lifetime of fascinated study of oratorical styles different from his own. More significant than style, though, is Emerson's behavior: Clearly he did not trek annually through the Midwest during his middle years merely to bring light to the Gentiles. It is reductive, but true, to say that Transcendentalism in his hands became an eminently marketable commodity that (as legions of late-century imitators found) lent itself to mass production. Of course, the commodity was salable only on condition that it disguise its ultimate design on its audience. Self-reliance might be commended as salvific, and it was even acceptable to

commend self-reliance as the way to wealth; but for the lecturer to acknowledge that he was expounding self-reliance in order to make money
was, putting it mildly, to break the dramatic illusion.[18]

II

To recapitulate: We observe two trends in the vocation of authorship in nineteenth-century New England – a movement toward the sense
of a specialized vocation, partially countered by the persistence of a gen-
eralist ideal of cultural coherence, and a movement toward commercialization, partially countered by the persistence of the ideal of art as a form
of cultural service. These crosscurrents produced some fascinating balancing acts, such as one minor poet's debut with both an "Ode to Commerce,"[19] and an "Elegy on the Death of Chatterton,"[19] or Hawthorne's
vacillation between the postures of retiring aesthete and conscientious
civil servant. Perhaps only an antebellum New Englander could have
been both a literary recluse and the intimate friend of an American president.

We move a step closer to confronting the aesthetic implications of such
antinomies by turning from the general issue of vocational autonomy to
the more specific issue of how art during the period is perceived as a
moral vehicle.

Antebellum America inherited from early national aesthetics a polarized view of belles lettres as, on the one hand, trivial (a form of economic
suicide, having no cash value, of secondary importance anyhow to the
practical challenge of nation building) and, on the other hand, the crowning glory of national culture.[20] Versions of this ambivalence can also be
found in Old World criticism during the time of transition from the patronage system to the bourgeois marketplace economy (compare Samuel
Johnson's demystification of writing as a purely commercial activity with
his pursuit of unprecedentedly rigorous critical analysis), but in America
the polarization was aggravated by the lack of a perceptible indigenous
literary tradition and the debate as to what priority art should have in a
developing nation or, indeed, whether artistic accomplishment was
symptomatic of national health or decadence. Well into the nineteenth
century, the literary arts were constantly in the position of defending their
legitimacy from skeptical detractions, some of the most disconcerting of
which came from within their own ranks. (Bryant, at the moment he was
being heralded as a symptom of American poetic emergence, suggested
that poetry was obsolete; Lowell, although ostensibly promoting literary
nationalism, conceded that poets are "not, after all, the most important
productions of a nation," that "we can . . . borrow a great poet when we
want one.")[21] The primary ground of defense, predictably, was to work

from the premise – advanced in all the late eighteenth-century textbooks – that literature is a branch of rhetoric and to justify it on the basis of moral utility, thereby capitalizing on the American prejudice in favor of the practical. Moral principle, pronounced John Quincy Adams, "should be the alpha and omega of all human composition, poetry, or prose, scientific or literary, written or spoken." The boast of one minor poet was that "I never sat down to write when I had not a strong pressure of moral or patriotic sentiment." Joel Barlow, in his preface to *The Columbiad,* was careful to distinguish between his "poetical" or "fictitious" object ("to sooth and satisfy the desponding mind of Columbus") and his "real" object: "to inculcate the love of rational liberty, and to discountenance the deleterious passion for violence and war." "My object," he concluded, "is altogether of a moral and political nature."[22]

In the early nineteenth century, prescriptive didacticism softened somewhat, and the reviewer's key question changed from "Does this book make vice attractive?" to "Does it make virtue beautiful?"[23] Transcendentalist aesthetics went one step further, referring the moral power of great literature to the act of creation (which Emerson, like Coleridge, saw as a quasi-religious experience), rather than to the work's reinforcement or promotion of accepted moral standards. At this point, in theory, an aesthetics completely divorced from morality became possible – Poe's Coleridge-based aesthetic, for example;[24] but in New England this did not happen. Emerson continued to make art subordinate to the moral and religious experience that underlay it and that it, in turn, was seen as designed to provoke in the reader.[25] Amid this one can detect a certain desire to break through the ethical to an untrammeled erotics of free expression ("O celestial Bacchus! drive them mad – " [*EW* 8:70]), but the bacchic impulse is held in check ("The high poetry of the world from the beginning has been ethical [*JMN* 5:476]). Such an aesthetic was bound to leave the finer aesthetic distinctions quickly behind ("How much alike are all sorts of excellence[,] Mr Webster's arguments like Shakspear's plays" [*JMN* 4:315]) and to produce formulations in their own way almost as reductive as those of prescriptive didacticism.

Some Transcendentalist aesthetes, Margaret Fuller especially, considered this position stuffy, and said so.[26] Indeed, throughout the early national and antebellum periods one finds plenty of signs of a not-so-muted protest against programmatic moralism: Robert Treat Paine's vers de société, Henry Finn's joke books of the 1820s and 1830s, and perhaps most spectacularly Royall Tyler's pornographic biblical poem *The Origin of Evil* (1793), in which Eve's eating the apple is represented as fellatio.[27] Why did so shrewd a businessman as Isaiah Thomas, the "father of American book publishing," gamble on *The Power of Sympathy* in 1789?

Certainly not because of its cautionary advice to imprudent young women but because of its sensationalism. As in any era, the nominal standard of aesthetic value (moral benefit) has to be understood as a compromise between prevailing notions of socially acceptable behavior, what the buyer wanted, and what writers desired to produce. The standards of the latter two were, by and large, less high-minded than the first. Nevertheless, the equilibrium achieved by most significant New England writers, including both those today considered classic and those once prominent whose canonical status is now in doubt, was such as to make their work revolve, however erratically, around the axis of ethical idealism.

Two familiar cases in point are Dickinson and Hawthorne. Take first Dickinson's great gnomic satire:

> The Bible is an antique Volume –
> Written by faded Men
> At the suggestion of Holy Spectres –
> Subjects – Bethlehem –
> Eden – the ancient Homestead –
> Satan – The Brigadier –
> Judas – the Great Defaulter –
> David – the Troubadour –
> Sin – a distinguished Precipice
> Others must resist –
> Boys that "believe" are very lonesome –
> Other Boys are "lost" –
> Had but the Tale a warbling Teller –
> All the Boys would come –
> Orpheus' Sermon captivated –
> It did not condemn –
>
> [DP 1545]

Like many of Dickinson's late lyrics, this one issues a Dionysian call in an Appollonian style. It was doubtless intended as a piece of irreverence not merely animated but even playful, having been written as a "Diagnosis of the Bible, by a Boy – " and sent to amuse a collegian nephew housebound by illness (*DL* 3:732); but it is not the utterance of one fully liberated from the grim reductionism it tries to laugh off. Its gnomic method echoes in another key the dryness that it chides. The poem looks through the window of Calvinism at Orpheus playing in the distance. The speaker tries to approximate her subversive prophet to the extent of suggesting what the Bible would be like if read as warbling tale rather than as a conventional sermon, but the table-of-contents approach reduces the Orphic countertelling to a homiletic epitome, so that what results is not so much Orphism as another sermon.

A kindred manifesto, which Dickinson must have appreciated, is the passage in Hawthorne's much discussed preface to *The House of the Seven*

Gables that confronts what are taken to be the moralistic expectations of contemporary readers.

> Many writers lay very great stress upon some definite moral pur-
> pose, at which they profess to aim their works. Not to be deficient, in
> this particular, the Author has provided himself with a moral; – the
> truth, namely, that the wrong-doing of one generation lives into the
> successive ones, and, divesting itself of every temporary advantage, be-
> comes a pure and uncontrollable mischief; – and he would feel it a sin-
> gular gratification, if this Romance might effectually convince mankind
> (or, indeed, any one man) of the folly of tumbling down an avalanche
> of ill-gotten gold, or real estate, on the heads of an unfortunate poster-
> ity. . . . In good faith, however, he is not sufficiently imaginative to
> flatter himself with the slightest hope of this kind. When romances do
> really teach anything, or produce any effective operation, it is usually
> through a far more subtle process than the ostensible one. The Author
> has considered it hardly worth his while, therefore, relentlessly to im-
> pale the story with its moral, as with an iron rod – or rather, as by
> sticking a pin through a butterfly – thus at once depriving it of life, and
> causing it to stiffen in an ungainly and unnatural attitude. A high truth,
> indeed, fairly, finely, and skilfully wrought out, brightening at every
> step, and crowning the final development of a work of fiction, may add
> an artistic glory, but is never any truer, and seldom any more evident,
> at the last page than at the first. [*HW* 2:2–3]

Clearly this passage shows Hawthorne as less than committed to the cruder versions of the shibboleth of art's moral purpose. The basic rhe-torical strategy is to convey the subtler point that moralism in literature does not necessarily either make for good art or improve public morals and to establish a relationship with his reader on that higher ground. The sly humor that characteristically radiates through Hawthorne's prose ("Not to be deficient in this particular . . .") makes one wonder if the writer's profession of conscientious adherence to the convention of fur-nishing a moral is a mere charade, a signal that the discerning reader should read the whole work in the manner recommended by Melville – as a covert subversion of the norms of taste under a pleasant surface cal-culated to lull the superficial philistine. Yet that interpretation will not do. Hawthorne's *American Notebooks,* as every Hawthornian knows, show that moral fables and dilemmas usually supplied the germs of his fictions, a point that the quoted passage obliquely makes when it states the moral and then adds that the moral angle in fiction properly exists as a pervasive, interpenetrating element rather than in the form of a preachy lesson. What Hawthorne objects to is the heavy-handed "Thus we see" interpolation (which he often used himself). This, however, was already quite standard doctrine not only among more enlightened reviewers but even among writers at a more popular level.[28] So the latitude that Hawthorne claims as moral romancer, his assertion of the artist's prerogatives in the face of philistinism, occurs within deference to, indeed proclamation of, the principle of the interdependence of art and morality. Hawthorne's individuality in this area lies neither in his theoretical resistance to overt moralism nor in his actual deployment of moral frameworks, nor even in his sense of the likely impotence of fiction as a didactic instrument (long proclaimed by the detractors of the genre). It lies, rather, in his awareness of the difficulty of refining the moral sensibility so that it can enhance an aesthetic design through subtlety of interpenetration rather than distort it through a too abrupt closure.

Altogether, before 1865 no New England writer of any consequence argued for the position that the moral dimension of art was unimportant. The line between New England and the rest of America is not clear-cut here; in her study of antebellum fiction reviewing, Baym found only one person (Poe) arguing "in principle [that] the morality of the books he wrote about was not his business."[29] New England's position seems rather to have been representative in the Emersonian sense of quintessential, perceiving itself and being perceived by others as unusually principled. One barometer of this is the expatriatism of such literati as N. P. Willis. Willis started his literary career with a series of pious dramatic lyrics on biblical themes written while he was attempting to follow in his father's footsteps by finding a niche in the Boston Congregational journalistic establishment. Initially he wrote, that is, the way a Yale-educated, orthodox Congregational deacon's son ought to write, even though this was at odds with the air of dapper hedonism that he presented in person. When he realized the incongruity, and the paucity of options for him in Boston, Willis escaped to New York and made a highly successful career out of literary gossip.[30]

The American, and in particular the New England, aesthetic during the era of Hawthorne and Dickinson might thus be described in general terms as an aesthetic that presupposed an interdependence of art and morality in which the latter legitimated the former, in an equilibrium that proved somewhat unstable as the moral criterion was challenged by authors and by purchasers but that nevertheless retained its hold. On the one hand, this led to obtuse dogmatics from which not even the most intelligent were exempt; the young George Bancroft for example, asserted (in the *North American Review*) that "there can be no more hideous fault in a literary work than profligacy. Levity is next in order."[31] On the other hand, the very strictness of such boundary drawing stimulated a rich profusion of writing on the margins of conventional moral discourse, such as the passages quoted a moment ago. Their most artful feature is the subtlety with which they problematize the dogmatic structures that gave rise to them by operating in the crevices between outright conformity and outright dissent. Such convolutions of the ethical imagination – arising ironically yet predictably from a cultural climate of deep suspicion toward the arts on moral grounds – provided the single most powerful and pervasive stimulus for the period's major literary achievements.

A closely related phenomenon is the literary response to the mainstream conception of literature's [mimetic] function. As Terence Martin has shown, in the case of early national fiction criticism, reviewers held American literature almost as stringently to the ideal of veracity as to the ideal of morality; and this, in turn, may have had something to do with the American predilection for the romance, which by definition liberated the writer of narrative from the prescribed bondage to actuality.[32] Here again philistinism can be seen as calling into being an aesthetically complex and challenging sort of marginal discourse, again well illustrated by Hawthorne's romances, which (as seen in an even more famous passage from the Preface to *The House of the Seven Gables* than the one I have quoted) advertise themselves both as trivial rambles into cloudland and as a higher form of mimesis (adherence to the "truth of the human heart"). Later in this chapter, and especially in Part III of this book, we shall examine the literary results. At this point, however, I want to press on from the topic of the romance to the more general question of the role of Romanticism in activating the aesthetic syndrome just described.

III

It is probably no accident that Romanticism started to become a major influence in New England at the time when literary professionalism also started to become a viable option. Romanticism was an ethos that reflected and reinforced artists' perception of themselves as a distinct group of specialists needing to establish public legitimacy in a society in which the place of the arts was insecure.[33] By dignifying the creative imagination as a source of quasi-divine authority, Romanticism gave the artist the central position in society and converted the artist's sense of alienation from societal norms from a mark of shame to a badge of honor. At the same time, despite thereby legitimating the artist's wish to deviate from bourgeois norms, the Romantic ethos (at least in its more conservative manifestations – as in Wordsworth, Coleridge, and Carlyle) also appealed to those who, like most antebellum New Englanders, retained a keen sense of social and moral responsibility; for the more conservative forms of visionary Romanticism transmuted the eighteenth-century notion of poetry as a repository of communal wisdom into the idea of the poet as keeper of the collective conscience and prophet of a better society. Romanticism in this sense would indeed seem to have been an ideological formation ideally suited to New England culture, given its traditional emphasis on individual spiritual consciousness and the rights of the individual citizen as central to the vision of the larger social and moral orders. Sacvan Bercovitch has called attention to the similarity between New England Romantic and Puritan thought in this respect. There is a firmly corporate dimension to Emerson's celebration of the self, the sense that speaking one's "latent conviction" is validated only insofar as it becomes "the universal sense" (*EW* 2:27), just as there is in Wordsworth, whose defense for having written an autobiographical epic was that individual experience might turn out to be paradigmatic.[34]

[EXAMPLE THAT SERVES AS A MODEL]

We have not yet, however, gotten to the heart of the significance of the Romantic aesthetic for our writers. This significance lay, finally, not so much in any support that the Romantic ideology gave to the artistic enterprise – although such support was valuable – as in the ideology's own self-division. Anglo-American Romanticism, as a full-blown literary aesthetic, starts with form breaking, as in Wordsworth's objections to Thomas Gray's Latinate dictation. In this, Romanticism differs sharply from Neoclassicism, which sees itself as a process of completion, regularization, and refinement. Romanticism, in contrast, starts with a destructive, ground-clearing impulse that easily moves from the level of mere protest against received forms to the level of an anti-aesthetic impulse of protest against the constraints of art itself. This impulse is manifested in two principal ways: first, in celebrations of the creative process, as opposed to the aesthetic product, the "poetic" being located in the realm of experience rather than in the artifact; and second, in Romantic irony, the systematic breaking of the poetic illusion in order to call attention to it as artifice.[35] In the major phase of British Romanticism, the first type of recoil might, roughly speaking, be seen as characterizing the first generation of Romantic poets and the latter as characterizing the second generation; for Romantic irony is what one is left with once the visionary gleam begins to fade. When the excitement of the idea of visionary immediacy fades, either through loss of belief in it or because the frustrations of the gap betwen envisioned splendor and actual artifact have become too patent, then one is thrown back upon the sense of one's role as self-conscious manipulator. Romantic irony is the fallback position of the artist who might wish to be God, feels this to be impossible, and projects this onto the artifact in a sense humbly, trivializing the work's status as representation yet also arrogantly claiming power over it – perhaps not total control (for the ironist may assume the role of bemused witness to the multiplications of fantasy) but at least a power of observation and appraisal.

DESTRUCTIVE
IMPULSE OF
ROMANTICISM.

TWO IMPULSES OF
ROMANTICISM.

In British Romanticism, the best example of the first type of recoil is Wordsworth's *Pre'ude,* which presents itself as the record of crisis resolution, yet acknowledges the impossibility of reconstructing the growth of an individual mind even as it labors to do so. The best example of the second is Byron's *Don Juan,* in which the growth of the protagonist is framed at each stage by the narrator's declarations that the poem is only a series of ad hoc manipulations. The self-consciousness of the Words- worthian speaker present at the edges of the reading experience becomes the center of Byron's poem, now that the Romantic poet's visionary au- thority (already threatened by Wordsworth's conviction that the vital powers decline as a child grows to adulthood) has attenuated to the van- ishing point.[36]

What is especially interesting about Romanticism in New England is the strength and simultaneity of the two types of Romantic recoil. Con- sider Emerson and Hawthorne, whose work marks the ascendancy of Romanticism in New England. On the one hand, Emerson proclaims a gospel of poesis as shamanism, which, as Harold Bloom remarks, is matched in Britain only by Blake.[37] Yet Emerson's stance by no means implies a high estimate of art as such: Emerson wants only the "poetic gift . . . not rhymes and sonneteering, not bookmaking and bookselling" (*EW* 8:63–4). "Practical" criticism of the kind that Coleridge and Words- worth both engaged in holds very little interest for Emerson. For him there was "higher work for Art than the arts" (*EW* 2:215), both because no artifact ever fully realizes the inspiration behind it and because a merely aesthetic orientation is trivial. The figure of the poet is a hero for him, but literature always bears the prefixional "mere." In his essays, the movement toward prophetic assertion is countered by a tendency to un- dermine his own formulations and to switch nervously from one tone to another. In Hawthorne, who shrinks from overriding programmatic pur- poses and tends, from the time of "Alice Doane's Appeal," to disown his pretensions to being anything more than a storyteller, the self-division takes the form of satire directed toward the daimonism or effeteness of his artist figures and self-ironic representations of his own marginality as artist. Hawthorne oscillates between a vision of the artist as all-powerful magician (e.g., the analogy of mesmerism in the case of Maule, Hol- grave, Westervelt) and a vision of the artist as impotent fool (e.g., the storyteller figure in his early tales). The image of Owen Warland as cre- ator of life in "Artist of the Beautiful" is inseparable from the image of Owen as hapless misfit.

This juxtaposition of the visionary and the ironic strains of Romanti- cism in mutual critique undoubtedly stems in part from the belatedness of American Romanticism.[38] Romanticism did not take root in America until European Romanticism was in decline; it blossomed, for instance, in the wake of Carlylean metafiction (which contributed to the self- consciousness of Emerson's style) and the decay of gothic conventions (which contributed to the self-consciousness of Hawthorne's treatment of the threadbare discovery-of-the-manuscript motif in "The Custom House"). Even when armed with the Coleridgean distinction between reason and understanding, Emerson, with the precedent of Byronism fresh in mind, could never fully indulge the desire to be a Blakean mystic, and so he alternatively praises individualism and speaks patronizingly of his era as the "age of the first person singular" (*JMN* 3:70).

Despite this belatedness, however, antebellum America, and particularly antebellum New England, where aesthetic moralism was especially pronounced, would seem to have been fertile ground for transplantation of a literary ideology that set a high social value on the artist and on the creative process yet deprecated mere artistry. Such an ideology appealed simultaneously to Yankee writers' desire for self-justification and to their distrust of the merely fictive. It led, in turn, to a body of writing that was marked by rare Dionysian moments (Emerson's "transparent eyeball" passage, Dickinson's "Soul's Superior instants," Jones Very's holy sonnets) but was characterized more generally by a tension between the impulse to seize visionary authority and the awareness of the quixoticism of that desire – by a skepticism about art's authority that came both from without (from the general public) and from within. Both Dickinson's poem contrasting Orpheus with the writers of Scripture and Hawthorne's reflections on the romancer's moral responsibility are excellent illustrations.

New England Romantic self-division, however, does not simply have to do with the question either of the authority of art or of what the moral dimension of art should be. Although both of these issues are important they finally are subsumed in a more fundamental question of authority, the question of what reliance, if any, is to be placed on the angle of vision, whether moral or otherwise, from which a writer writes. New England Romantics were, like their great British precursors but even more so, uncomfortable about maintaining fixed moral positions and intellectual schemes, even as they seemed to feel impelled to take fixed positions. Don't imitate me, says Thoreau, because by the time you read this I may have opted for another life-style. With great sententiousness and rigidity he declares his utter elusiveness. Dickinson's sense of the opposition between Orpheus and orthodoxy and Hawthorne's of the opposition between the proper kind of moral romancing and what he takes to be the popular view are efforts to avoid rigidification. In each case, this opposition must be maintained at some potential risk of falling into a rigidity of its own; and in this respect Hawthorne "goes beyond" Dickinson and Thoreau, showing greater awareness of the need to formulate his stance with the flexibility of self-awareness that he has accused the popular view of lacking. The discourse of New England Romanticism is thus most fully elaborated when, as in Hawthorne's preface, it commits itself to serious dispute with a fixed, dogmatic ethical or intellectual stance that is also the internalization of an inner voice, maintaining a certain disengagement from the dialogue owing to awareness of that paradox.

IV

To get a better sense of the literary effects involved, we may consult another pair of examples: two related passages from Emerson's "Spiritual Laws," followed by Hawthorne's description of Young Goodman Brown's return from the forest.

> Nature will not have us fret and fume. She does not like our benevolence or our learning, much better than she likes our frauds and wars. When we come out of the caucus, or the bank, or the Abolition convention, or the Temperance meeting, or the Transcendental club into the fields and woods, she says to us, "So hot? my little Sir." . . .
>
> Not in nature but in man is all the beauty and worth he sees. The world is very empty, and is indebted to this gilding, exalting soul for all its pride. "Earth fills her lap with splendors" *not her own*. The vale of Tempe, Tivoli, and Rome are earth and water in a thousand places, yet how unaffecting!
>
> People are not the better for the sun and moon, the horizon and the trees; as it is not observed that the keepers of Roman galleries or the valets of painters have any elevation of thought, or that librarians are wiser men than others. There are graces in the demeanor of a polished and noble person which are lost upon the eye of a churl. These are like the stars whose light has not yet reached us. [*EW* 2:79, 86]

> The next morning, young Goodman Brown came slowly into the street of Salem village, staring around him like a bewildered man. The good old minister was taking a walk along the grave-yard, to get an appetite for breakfast and meditate his sermon, and bestowed a blessing, as he passed, on Goodman Brown. He shrank from the venerable saint, as if to avoid an anathema. Old Deacon Gookin was at domestic worship, and the holy words of his prayer were heard through the open window. "What God doth the wizard pray to?" quoth Goodman Brown. Goody Cloyse, that excellent old Christian, stood in the early sunshine, at her own lattice, catechising a little girl, who had brought her a pint of morning's milk. Goodman Brown snatched away the child, as from the grasp of the fiend himself. Turning the corner by the meeting-house, he spied the head of Faith, with the pink ribbons, gazing anxiously forth, and bursting into such joy at sight of him, that she skipt along the street, and almost kissed her husband before the whole village. But Goodman Brown looked sternly and sadly into her face, and passed on without a greeting.
>
> Had Goodman Brown fallen asleep in the forest, and only dreamed a wild dream of a witch-meeting?
>
> Be it so, if you will. But alas! it was a dream of evil omen for young

Goodman Brown. A stern, a sad, a darkly meditative, a distrustful, if not a desperate man, did he become, from the night of that fearful dream. [*HW* 10:88–9]

American criticism has been too long accustomed to seeing Emerson and Hawthorne simply as symbolic opposites, representing "light" and "dark" sides of New England Romanticism – the party of hope and the party of irony, the intellectually committed and the intellectually skepti-cal. And these *are* fruitful polarizations in some respects – for example, in dramatizing how *The Blithedale Romance* supplies a corrective to heady Transcendentalist optimism. At first glance, the passages just quoted show a similar contrast. The Emersonian speaker continually tells us what to think; Hawthorne's gazes on the events related with a kind of baffled wonder. But we must beware of hasty polarizations. Emerson and Hawthorne also belong together,[39] as masters of the controlled irony that stems from questioning orthodoxies of their own making or invoking. Emerson's lecture-essay, "The Transcendentalist," is not so distant after all from *The Blithedale Romance,* both being testimonials at once ironic, defensive and heartfelt by disengaged participants in the movement. One of the most valuable results of the application of theory-oriented criticism to American Romantic texts is that it has made the discovery of this kin-ship between Emerson and Hawthorne inevitable, although it has not yet pursued the insight thoroughly.[40] Let us look at how our passages dem-onstrate that kinship.

Both, in the first place, put their subjects rigorously in an ethical/spir-itual context while avoiding the prescriptive dogmaticism that this might have been expected to entail, with the result that their ethical perspectives become difficult to pin down. This is most obvious in the Hawthorne passage. The expected temptation-resistance-triumph scenario (set up earlier by Brown's trip to the woods, his commitment of himself to the devil but final resistance of the "evil one" at the witches' sabbath, after which the whole scene vanishes) is undercut, in the quoted passage, by the insinuation that Brown might only have been hallucinating. The sce-nario is undercut, however, not in such a way as positively to confirm the insinuation but merely to permit the withdrawal of the narrator, whose "Be it so if you will" puts under erasure all previous gestures of narrative authority (such as the reference to Brown's "present evil purpose" in en-tering the forest [*HW* 10:75]). The Emerson passages accomplish a simi-lar reversal without acknowledging it. The statement in the second pas-sage that "people are not the better for the sun and moon" stands in direct contradiction to the let-us-learn-a-lesson-from-nature position of the first passage, which occurs a few pages earlier. The perception of nature as a source of wisdom is now seen to be a false consciousness, a reified displacement of our own powers. By pitting what seem to be two absolutes against each other, Emerson is not, perhaps, being self-contradictory, since the two positions can be harmonized by reading nature, in the second context, as "material earth," with none of the former superadded connotation of "emanation of the world-soul." This is a familiar Emersonian semantic manipulation (all of Emerson's master terms are used in a double sense), and so is the movement within the the the essay from nature-centered to human-centered values. But here Emerson creates with these movements more of a decentering than a harmonizing effect, lulling his readers into thinking that they understand what nature is and then showing that they do not. The correction of the line from Wordsworth's Immortality Ode (which originally reads "Earth fills her lap with pleasures of her own"), denying any and all spirituality to the material world, is the most obvious tipoff that the passage is meant to startle. But still more unsettling is the end of the excerpt, which seems both to return to the envisionment of nature as a source of authority ("the stars whose light has not yet reached us") and to implicate the speaker himself, who has just asserted his authority by correcting our views of nature, in the state of ignorance. Indeed, after meditating further upon the close of the paragraph, the careful reader may wonder if its deepest implication is not, in fact, that the real meaning of the prior claim ("People are not the better for the sun and moon") is "We are too dense to profit from them." If so, the idea would be the same as that startling line in *Nature* "Most persons do not see the sun" (*EW* 1:9), another declaration that contains a literal truth that its phraseology and context tempt us to overlook. Or is that final sentence of the excerpt a completely innocent metaphor? It is, in any event, Emerson's "Be it so if you will" – a reopening of an issue immediately after having seemingly executed a decisive reversal.

The oscillations to which the speakers in Emerson and Hawthorne subject us are all the more provocative because of the mask of insouciance [NONCHALANCE] that both like to assume when delivering their most devastating thrusts ("the good old minister"; "The world is very empty, and indebted to this gilding"). Here, of course, the two writers differ from their more impetuous successors, Melville, Thoreau, and Whitman. Hawthorne's unction and Emerson's briskness are euphemistic celestial railroads tempting the unwary to ignore their many underlying complications, as D. H. Lawrence saw in Hawthorne's case and Jonathan Bishop in Emerson's.[41]

Consider also how the two passages make use of historical frames of reference. Hawthorne's narrative method, including the allegorical framework, provides a recognizable, if not entirely faithful, mimesis of Puritanism. Not entirely faithful, because in Puritan context a young man so anxious to absolve himself of evil would be, at the very least, a caricature of righteousness, if not a downright anachronism (a projection of the Unitarian mind back onto the seventeenth century). Still, the portrait is recognizable in that the allegory of resistance to temptation is Bunyanesque; the specific context recalls the Salem witchcraft delusion and the controversy concerning spectral evidence at the trials; and the rhetoric is quaintly archaized throughout ("Mighty well, Deacon Gookin!"). In fact, as Michael Colacurcio has shown, before writing the story Hawthorne probably immersed himself in the sources as thoroughly as did any historical romancer of his day.[42] The reversal accomplished in the quoted passage amounts, on one level, to a gesture in the direction of dissolving the world that has just been evoked and mimed. Brown's despair ostensibly leaves the community untouched, but insofar as his despair represents a paranoid extreme triggered by communal belief and ritual, his wretchedness also stands for the community's hidden reality. Palpable image dissolves into moral ambiguity, creating an aesthetic distance intensified by the unappetizingness of either alternative. Equally important in dispelling any mimetic illusion is the use of the old-fashioned vocabulary for purposes of mockery. "Old Deacon Gookin was at domestic worship. . . . 'What God doth the wizard pray to?' quoth Goodman Brown." That the deacon is not merely praying but "at domestic worship" and that Brown "quoth" rather than "said" produces a cartoonlike heightening of archaic effect that is the verbal complement of the thematic questions raised about protagonist and community. Both are enclosed in a verbal environment that we see as quaintly distant, despite the pathos of Brown's situation and the universality of the theme of initiation into evil. The story never leaves that environment; it remains historical throughout; but the narrative voice continually makes one conscious of its unreality.

Though neither mimetic nor historical, the Emerson passage, like Hawthorne's, evokes a received intellectual framework whose confines the speaker provisionally accepts (by defining his position in terms of it), only to break it apart. In the second passage the speaker presents himself as the irreverent scholar, appropriating Romantic and Classical imagings of nature's charm, yet in that appropriation emancipating himself by pointing up the naïveté of both types of naturalism, the Wordsworthian and the Arcadian.[43] To see beauty and worth in man, he implies, does not mean a simple ingestion of cultural baggage such as Rome and Wordsworth, any more than it means a simple naturalism. In the same way, the next paragraph invokes an ideal of genteel connoisseurship over against prosaic factotums such as keepers and valets and librarians, yet then threatens to dissolve this civilized vision in the last sentence. This casual scholarliness is comparable to Hawthorne's pretend chronicler's voice.

The tendency of these passages to turn narrative into metafiction and exposition into metacommentary gives them a modern flavor. Since

Charles Feidelson pointed out the connection between modern literary symbolism and American Romantic practice, diagnosing the latter as a mutation from Puritan typologizing, Americanists have learned to think of American Romanticism as a movement "from hermeneutics to symbolism."[44] This diagnosis has been reinforced by students of the impact on American Romantic discourse of the biblical hermeneutics of the higher criticism and echoed by recent critics who, applying recent Continentally generated literary methodologies based on structural linguistics, find antebellum texts moving toward the perception of the arbitrariness of language and literature as a mode of signification and the inevitability of the gap between signifier and signified in the act of signification.[45] *The Scarlet Letter,* for instance, places these very issues at its center through the intricate deployment of the title image, with its obvious self-referentiality.[46] Emerson, likewise, has been advanced by deconsructionist critics as an American Nietzsche who, despite his "logocentrism" (his assumption of a spiritually coherent basis and origin of language) also had the prescience to envisage something resembling the poststructuralist idea of writing – that is, discourse as consisting of the play of chains of metonymic signifiers in an endless text.[47] The most striking and surprising thing about these diagnoses is the suggestion that these artists attained what seems to us a precociously sophisticated state of awareness partly by their resolute antisophistication – their distrust of artifice in the name of nature, truth, morality, or whatnot. Their condition as postcolonials, in an intellectual climate where specialization in art seemed at once imperative and frivolous, forced on them an acute self-consciousness of a type that New England writers, as noted earlier, may have experienced more acutely than their compatriots. This, in turn, provoked a range of artistic responses among the more and the less gifted that at first sight seem mutually exclusive yet turn out to be interrelated: moralistic platitude, dutiful imitation of European models, idiosyncratic aesthetic pioneering. The same conditions that produced Hawthorne produced the reams of redundant filiopietistic memorializations of the Puritan fathers that we shall examine in Chapter 8 (a genre to which Hawthorne himself contributed). The same conditions produced the Emily Dickinson of the pious imitation hymn and the Dickinson of the wicked antihymn, the Emerson of bland Unitarian sermons on self-trust and the Emerson of "Self-Reliance."

Such intermixture of banality and innovation, sometimes within a single passage (as in almost any of Jones Very's better sonnets), is a predictable corollary of the blurring of the lines between high and popular literary ideology. Seeing this, we should resist (or accept only with severe qualification) the tendency of most scholarly study of developed literary culture to concentrate on a limited canon of works that have been accepted as major – an approach that perhaps has a special appeal for American scholars because they so readily assume that high American literature has been countercultural and antibourgeois. Even as the American Studies movement has enriched American literary scholarship by making it more interdisciplinary and by validating the study of so-called subliterary material under the aegis of popular culture, it has reinforced more strictly than has British literary scholarship the notion of a yawning gap between "serious" and "popular" writing. One sees this, for example, in the quickness of students of sentimental American Victorian literature, until very recently, to put it in its place. A symptomatic example would be the stark contrast drawn by Henry Nash Smith, justly revered as the dean of American Studies scholars, between the work of Hawthorne and Melville ("highbrow psychological romance") and Henry Ward Beecher's popular novel *Norwood* (an example, for Smith, of the "paralyzing effect of the genteel cult of ideality"). This formulation understates the degree to which Hawthorne defers to sentimental covention and overlooks the degree to which Beecher engages in a serious project of cultural anthropology.[48] One wonders if this bifurcating tendency has had anything to do with the facts that there is no American equivalent to the *Wellesley Index to Victorian Periodicals* and that the American common reader has not been studied as extensively as the British common reader of the nineteenth century. In any case, the prevailing tendency of American scholarship has been to locate both the merit and the Americanness of American literature in the individualized style and vision of a small number of writers. My own objective is not to go to the opposite extreme but to reach a more balanced perspective. To alter Emerson's adage in "Self-Reliance," I agree that to be a great American writer one must qualify as a nonconformist, but I would also make the Bercovitchian point that this equation of achievement and nonconformity in a text that has given much encouragement to the scholarly tradition that I am trying to revise represents less a solitary counterblast than a personalized elaboration of a consensus view – in this case, the value of individual rights – a view maintained with particular tenacity and long-standingness in New England communities. Hence Emerson's desire to ground the individual in generic man.[49]

Just as the literary effects of writers like Emerson and Hawthorne are usually best understood not as purely idiosyncratic forms of dissent but as dialogues with convention, exhibiting a two-way pull, so more conventional literature, at least during this period when the distinction between the serious and the popular had not yet fully crystallized, is normally best understood not just as serious literature's antagonist or source of provocation but as a counterpart. The more conventional work illuminates norms to which the better works are less strictly bound, while exhibiting in incipient form some of the latter's self-divided or dialogic attitude toward those norms. Our two final examples may help to show this: passages from two best-sellers of the 1850s – *Reveries of a Bachelor,* the semierotic musings of "Ik Marvel" (Donald T. Mitchell), and *The Lamplighter,* a sentimental novel by Maria Cummins that, among best-selling fiction, ran second only to *Uncle Tom's Cabin*. Like the passage from "Young Goodman Brown," the excerpt from *Reveries of a Bachelor* manipulates the speaker in such a way as to confuse the realms of reality and dream. Like the passages from Emerson, the Cummins excerpt opens up the possibility of a reversal of the standards of moral judgment previously established.

Any resemblances along these lines, moreover, are not coincidental, although the likelihood of direct influence is small. Mitchell is working in the same vein of discursive, self-conscious narration that Irving (to whom Mitchell dedicated his sequel, *Dream Life*) introduced to America and that Hawthorne, among New England writers, practiced with great-est subtlety. Cummins is caught up in the same tide of Romantic religion that Emerson expresses with greater refinement but that raises similar paradoxes of authority in both works. But let us look at the passages themselves. The first concludes a meditation in which the speaker has conjured up, out the fire that he is watching, a snug domestic yet erotic vision of an ideal lover-wife, played with it wish-fulfillingly, and then seen it dissolve with the dying of the fire. The second is a significant conversation between the heroine and a man who turns out to be her long-lost father, whom she had thought dead.

> Cares cannot come into the dream-land where I live. They sink with the dying street noise, and vanish with the embers of my fire. Even Ambition, with its hot and shifting flame, is all gone out. The heart in the dimness of the fading fire-glow is all itself. The memory of what good things have come over it in the troubled youth life, bear it up; and hope and faith bear it on. . . . And it mounts higher and higher on these wings of thought; and hope burns stronger and stronger out of the ashes of decaying life, until the sharp edge of the grave seems but a foot-scraper at the wicket of Elysium!
>
> But what is paper; and what are words? Vain things! The soul leaves them behind; the pen staggers like a starveling cripple; and your heart is leaving it a whole length of the life-course behind. The soul's mortal longings . . . are dim now in the light of those infinite longings, which spread over it, soft and holy as day-dawn. Eternity has stretched a cor-ner of its mantle towards you, and the breath of its waving fringe is like a gale of Araby.
>
> A little rumbling, and a last plunge of the cinders within my grate startled me, and dragged back my fancy from my flower chase, beyond the Phlegethon, to the white ashes that were now thick all over the darkened Coals.[50]

"Which, then, shall I trust, – the good, religious men, or the low, profane and abject ones?

"Trust in *goodness,* wherever it be found," answered Gertrude. "But,
O, trust *all,* rather than *none.*"

"Your world, your religion, draws a closer line."

"Call it not *my* world, or *my* religion," said Gertrude. "I know of no
such line. I know of no religion but that of the heart. Christ died for us
all alike, and, since few souls are so sunk in sin that they do not retain
some spark of virtue and truth, who shall say in how many a light will
at last spring up, by aid of which they may find their way to God?"

"You are a good child, and full of hope and charity," said Mr. Phillips, pressing her arm closely to his side. "I will try and have faith
in *you.*" [51]

These passages present quite a contrast to the fine nuancings of Hawthorne and Emerson. Yet it was not merely condescension or anesthesia
of the critical faculties that attracted Dickinson to Mitchell's prose and
interested James Joyce in Cummins so much that he devoted an entire
chapter of *Ulysses* ("Nausicaa") to a parody of Gertrude's character.
Though verbally impoverished, the passages are analogues of the ones by
Emerson and Hawthorne discussed earlier.

The interest of the Mitchell passage lies, like Hawthorne's, mainly in
the way it plays with the question of the reality of what it also seems to
unmask as dream and in the difficulty one has in determining how seriously to take its playfulness. The speaker pursues throughout the chapter
the game of now-I-believe-it, now-I-don't, alternately seeming to invest
his whole soul in his musings and detaching himself from them ("The
pen staggers like a starveling cripple"), to leap from there to an even loft-
ier affirmation ("Eternity," as Presence, as Experience, compared to a
mere literary vision), only to fall back to reality (which, however, is still
the perception of "fancy," tastefully arranged in a neat chiaroscuro of
white ashes and darkened coals). The Absolute is inscribed as a category
yet erased as a reality, entertained as object of desire and banished as wish-
fulfilling dream, producing a continual oscillation between moral intensity and intellectual juggling, the confusion of which is increased by the
montage of "I" and "you," a borderline that Hawthorne himself does not
cross, although Emerson sometimes does. Like them, Mitchell achieves
a considerable sophistication of the speaker, owing to a similar double-
mindedness toward the literary task at hand. Mitchell too can be read
either as a writer seeking to dignify what might otherwise have been perceived merely as trivial (or possibly even improper) fantasies by presenting them as a quasi-religious vision of symbolic import or as a writer
committed to recording the life of the imagination who cannot, for all
that, fully believe in its authenticity.

The Cummins passage seems to have no such elusiveness. It is a prime example of the kind of writing that Hawthorne's preface to *The House of the Seven Gables* seeks to chide and correct. Cummins lays out a simple formulaic antithesis, the effect of which is to give the dialogue a maximum of moral starch and pious gravity. Two features, however, give the passage additional interest for our purposes. the first and less important is the tonal contrast between Phillips and Gertrude – adult urbanity versus naive commitment. Roughly speaking, these are the main components of the more complicated voices of the preceding passages. Cummins' passage, of course, refuses to keep the ambiguity in suspension; it pulls Phillips toward Gertrude, as he meets her more than halfway, in the excerpt's final speech, with an earnestness that begins to match her own, though still with some amused condescension. And before long his mask of detachment evaporates completely, as he unbosoms himself in an impassioned, confessional "I am your father" letter that brings Gertrude instantly flying to his side. On the surface, the Phillips-Gertrude relationship reads like a scribbling woman's accidental retort to Hawthorne: urbane Phillips/Hawthorne, for all his sense of intellectual superiority over the childlike intensity with which he is confronted, is exposed in the act of confessing that Phoebe is his dearest brainchild after all. But this is getting too fanciful. The more significant point about the passage, for our purposes, is that it raises a thematic question, less easily resolved than the narrative itself, as to the proper basis of belief, a question raised by woman's fiction generally – a question that the Cumminses of the antebellum literary world posed in common with Hawthorne and Emerson, though the latter confronted it much more squarely and searchingly, especially in "Young Goodman Brown." Gertrude believes in "goodness," or more precisely in the heart sanctified by Christ. For Phillips, it is *her* goodness, *her* heart. At first sight, the text seems clearly to support Gertrude's vehement refusal to have herself made into an icon – and yet that is exactly what happens. Phillips is absolutely serious, we later find, when he says, "I will try and have faith in *you*." In his confessional letter, he insists that he has lost his "faith in Heaven" and has "no hope in this world, and none, alas! beyond, but in yourself."[52] And through Gertrude's ministrations, Phillips is in fact "redeemed," that is brought back into the human fold. It is intriguing that he is never actually converted. That is more likely an oversight than a strategic omission; yet even so, it seems a revealing lacuna, the text's acknowledgment against itself of how it and its generic sisters are committed to representing as an absolute that to which their explicit value system denies absoluteness.[53] Phillips here stands for the partially enlightened person whose values are not yet properly clarified, yet also in a sense for the ideal reader response, since Gertrude *is* a paragon, however self-effacing – a paragon, indeed, *because* self-effacing. Without its author being fully aware of the fact, the novel has set in motion a dialogue between person-centered and transpersonal values that Hawthorne plays with more subtly in questioning whether Young Goodman Brown should place reliance "in Faith" and that Emerson also creates when he locates authority not in nature but in man and then calls into question human authority too, including his own.

From the standpoint of modern formalist literary aesthetics, the difference in linguistic, thematic, and tonal subtlety between Emerson and Hawthorne, on the one hand, and Mitchell and Cummins, on the other, is supremely important. Cummins lacks the ironic self-consciousnes that we have ascribed to Emerson and Hawthorne, and in Mitchell any such tendency is clogged by the heavy-handedly wistful pathos with which the speaker records his emotional ups and downs. Yet from the standpoint of the literary historian, the analogies between the two pairs are deeply interesting as indices of the intellectual landscape within which the high art of Emerson and Hawthorne grew and flourished, partially in reaction against popular simplifications but partially as a refinement of questions concerning literary and moral authority around which both types of texts revolve but that Hawthorne and Emerson force into the open and treat with a greater degree of awareness. To be sure, the end result of their freethinking was sometimes shocking to the popular taste – as when evangelical heart-religion got reworked into Transcendentalist institutionalism, for instance. We err, however, if we isolate such differences as those features that inevitably mattered most to the major writers and that chiefly enabled them to write. For the great writers as well as for the popular, the notion of art as a vehicle for the moral, philosophical, and religious imagination tended to come first and the problematization of this notion second. The sophistication of the latter idea was made possible by the former commitment, which we must therefore see not just as self-limitation (a Gertrude motive, as it were, tempting every period writer to revert back to the mental level of a schoolchild) but also as a source of creative power. Without evangelical pietism, there would have been no epic-scale diagnosis of American society in *Uncle Tom's Cabin.* Without the earnestness of "Be true!" none of the rich interplay of thematic cross-purposes in *The Scarlet Letter.* Without the transparent eyeball, none of the epistemological gymnastics of *Nature* or the ironies of "Experience."

That is a hard doctrine to impress upon the late twentieth-century mind, which tends to take moral relativism for granted and often equates intellectual and aesthetic maturity with avoidance of commitment. Or perhaps it would be fairer to say that the doctrine is hard to accept not because the horizon of expectations of academia in the 1980s is more thoroughly relativized than that of the classic American writers but because the latter seem to anticipate the former closely enough to tempt us all the more to see the New England Romantics in our image. In any event, herein lies perhaps the main obstacle to historically faithful interpretation. In suggesting the extent to which antebellum writing questioned and subtilized the moral aesthetic, this chapter itself has threatened at times to become an exemplum of that very problem. If so, let this peroration serve as a tardy recognition scene. As modern readers, we may legitimately set store by those aspects of New England's antebellum texts that speak most forcibly to us and may even put them in the forefront of our critiques. To the extent that we wish to think of our knowledge of these texts as historical, however, we must also recognize their grounding in premises that we may not accept or (or so we think) particularly value, such premises as the primacy of the moral imagination. And to the extent that we can suspend our horizon of expectation in this way, we may also find ourselves becoming creatively, if disconcertedly, infiltrated by those same values to which we had been previously resistant.

4

Neoclassical Continuities: The Early National Era and the New England Literary Tradition

> Hail favour'd state! CONNECTICUT! thy name
> Uncouth in song, too long conceal'd from fame;
> If yet thy filial bards the gloom can pierce,
> Shall rise and flourish in immortal verse.
> Inventive genius, imitative pow'rs,
> And, still more precious, common-sense, is ours;
> While knowledge useful, more than science grand,
> In rivulets still o'erspreads the smiling land.
>
> David Humphreys, "A Poem on the Industry of
> the United States of America" (1804)

> Somehow the heroic couplet and the sweeping invocation did not fit
> the praise of the sober New England virtues.
>
> Henry F. May, *The Enlightenment in America* (1976)

Do the years between the Revolution and the Civil War really form a period in New England writing? So far this book has been transmitting mixed signals on the issue. Chapter 2 discussed the entire time span of this study in unitary terms as a movement toward literary self-realization, yet the partial correlations made in Chapter 3 between Romanticism and the rise of professionalism might suggest that we have here two disparate historical and aesthetic segments lumped together.

The notion of a sharp break between an early national or Federalist or Neoclassical period and an antebellum or Romantic period is not merely a scholarly retrospection but is also inherent in the later writers' conception of their historical moment. To antebellum New England authors outside the vicinity of Hartford and New Haven, the Connecticut Wits seemed quite as obsolete as the Puritan poets had seemed to the Wits. As one minor Boston Romantic mused about the legacy of her father's Yale friends, Timothy Dwight and Joel Barlow:

> Numerous copies of the epics of these poets, the Vision of Columbus and the Conquest of Canaan, were arranged upon the study shelves of their friend, probably subscription copies, remaining from year to year in undisturbed quiet. If a child, prompted by curiosity, opened a volume, the unattractive page was restored again to its repose, there to gather the dust of age; but there is no old mortality that can ever consecrate and make venerable poetry that has in itself so little merit.[1]

This chapter is written not primarily to contest this aesthetic judgment (although I shall) but to point out some of the continuities that this characteristically Romantic repression of precursors refuses to acknowledge, continuities not yet widely recognized, and in the process to meditate on the equally interesting topic of why those continuities have not been recognized. I want to start with the second and work back to the first and more important issue, since the inclination to distinguish sharply between early national and antebellum literary eras has been quickened by a too ready acceptance of the Romantics' view that the earlier period is eminently forgettable.

I

Until a generation ago, literary scholars took seriously Emerson's dictum that "from 1790 to 1820 there was not a book, a speech, a conversation, or a thought, in the State [of Massachusetts]" (*JMN* 13:115) – by which Emerson (in the Bay State tradition of overgeneralization) meant the rest of New England as well. This and similar pronouncements led, in American cultural history from Henry Adams through Vernon Louis Parrington, to what Lewis Simpson has called the "myth of New England's intellectual lapse" between the Puritan era and the New England Renaissance.[2] We are still living with the effects of the myth today. The modern resurgence of scholarship on early New England literature has not yet extended to postcolonial writing, despite the appearance of several major studies since the national bicentennial.[3] Since 1970, more than twice as many articles and books have been devoted to Puritan era figures as to the considerably greater number of New England writers who flourished between 1770 and 1820. Yet during these latter years, New England continued to produce by far the greatest number of significant authors of any American culture region, both in absolute terms and relative to its share of the nation's population.[4] Why, then, the lack of critical interest? The most obvious reply is that during that era New England produced no recognized literary classics, unless one counts Benjamin Franklin's *Autobiography,* the work of an adopted Philadelphian started before our terminus a quo and exclusively concerned with pre-Revolutionary events. Nor are there more than a handful of recognized near classics, such as Royall Tyler's *The Contrast,* which popularized the stereotypical stage Yankee, and John Trumbull's *McFingal,* the best of the Revolutionary era verse satires. But that does not seem to be the whole story. Literary scholarship has also been directed away from New England's postcolonial literature by at least two ideological predispositions, which have, in turn, been influential in defining the canon of notable American works.

First, the fact that American literature did not come fully into its own until its Romanticist phase has encouraged the bracketing of early national Neoclassical writing as epiphenomenal.[5] The problem with this view is not so much its major premise as its deduction – although the premise itself looks less convincing when we turn from literature to such other fields as architecture and law. I would concur that Romanticism was more adaptable in the long run to New World conditions than the Neoclassical ideology it superseded.[6] For one thing, Romanticism encouraged literary independence, as opposed to acceptance of European literary modes. Furthermore, by placing a high value on nature and spontaneity (as opposed to the civilized, urban virtues and pleaures), Romanticism converted America's underdevelopment into a national treasure and lent support to the American penchant for contrasting New World simplicity and vast natural resources with Old World crowdedness and decadences. (This vision, however, was itself something of a legacy of Neoclassical celebrations of rural retirement: Pastoralism is the cosmopolitan's recurring daydream.) Again, Romanticism valued individuality of style, the development of an individual voice as opposed to adherence to established standards of taste, and therefore appealed to American antiauthoritarianism. Likewise Romanticism placed a high value on depiction of the isolated individual consciousness as opposed to mundane social interactions; and as a result it was able to draw more deeply than Neoclassicism had done from the depths of New England religious experience, the intense probing into the soul's dark corners that characterized post-Puritan piety well into the nineteenth century. Consequently, the rise of modern Puritan studies and the quest of the American Studies movement to identify native American intellectual traditions made it more or less inevitable that literary scholars would take Perry Miller's seminal essay "From Edwards to Emerson" as a mandate for envisioning an intellectual highroad between Puritanism and Romanticism, along which the Enlightenment appears as a kind of "negative" phase (to use Emerson's epithet for Unitarianism, seconded by Miller despite his ambivalence toward Emerson) in the softening of Reformation piety that was implanted in the 1600s and was to flower into art two hundred years later.[7] In this view, Emerson, Hawthorne, and Dickinson represent the aesthetic payoff of Puritanism. In recent formulations, such as Sacvan Bercovitch's, the Enlightenment phase is given greater legitimacy than in Miller, being seen not as a sort of decadence but in more positive terms, as the point at which the Puritan ethos becomes transformed into national civil religion.[8] This reconception, however, is still too easily accommodated to the view that New England Neoclassicism was either merely a watering down of what preceded or a faint anticipation of what came next. That is, ironically, the unintended conclusion of the most ambitious attempt yet and to establish the period's integrity, Henry F. May's *The Enlightenment in America,* which, for all its sympathy with and understanding of the Enlightenment, gives the final impression of its having been a transient oasis of liberal thought swallowed up by the tide of Second Awakening revivalism.[9]

For literary studies, the result of this emphasis on Puritan and Romantic legacies and their confluence has been a restricted view of what counts in American literary history. Joseph Dennie's work seems less "real" than William Ellery Channing's. A book like *Walden* is canonized not merely because it is an excellent (albeit somewhat labored) piece of prose but also because it strongly reflects Romantic values and their Puritan antecedents. A book like *Female Quixoticism* (1801), Tabitha Tenney's once popular but now forgotten rendition of the theme of the romance-mad young woman in an American context, is a clever, worthwhile novel that may never receive its due, because it is *Walden*'s aesthetic opposite. It is not a work of original genius but an ingenious adaptation of plot motifs derived from European fiction. It delves into its heroine's consciousness only in order to demonstrate how far she deviates from common sense and socially functional behavior; it stresses the importance of conforming to accepted standards of good taste; and it tends to identify the state of nature with the state of stupidity. Though hardly *Walden*'s equal, *Female Quixoticism* deserves more attentive consideration than it has so far received. In addition to being witty and amusing, it is historically significant as a feminist document (inculcating self-reliance and survival skills through counterexample) and, on a more abstract level, as a reflexively self-ironic meditation on the legitimacy of engaging in the act in which the text is engaging: the adaptation of fictive models to the American scene.[10]

Timothy Dwight presents a similar case of critical skewing. Discussions of Dwight's poetry tend to identify his *Greenfield Hill* (an insipid pastoral about the parish where he spent his ministry) as his best poem – at least partly because it foreshadows the personal, concrete, nature-imagey traits of Romantic writing – and to minimize the virtues of what is really his best poem, *The Triumph of Infidelity,* a Calvinist *Dunciad* that pictures American civilization under siege from the Satan-engineered forces of free thought and religious liberalism. Critics have found it hard to warm up to this particular combination of Neoclassical and theological constraint. One all too easily conjures up the picture of an embattled gentleman of what Parrington liked to call the "tie-wig school" fighting innovation with his last gasp.[11]

This image brings us to the second major ideological factor inhibiting appreciation of the literature of the early national period: anti-Federalism. Federalism has been widely represented by historians and literary scholars as a program that accomplished great things during the first steps of nation building but then degenerated into a futile, bigoted reaction against the tide of democratization under Jefferson and Jackson. Revisionary appraisals of Jeffersonianism and Jacksonianism have not altered the image of Federalism much.[12] Admittedly, the Federalist philosophy that the nation should be governed according to the best judgment of its reputable, propertied elite is not very appetizing to present-day Americans. The fact that the great majority of noted New England literati of the early national period were outspoken Federalists who often used literature as a vehicle for reactionary political agitation increases one's reluctance to accept New England writing of the period as an authentic expression of the American mind. Such works as Dwight's *Triumph of Infidelity,* which ridicules folk hero and freethinker Ethan Allan as the "great Clodhopping oracle of man"; or Tyler's *Contrast,* which seems (at least upon first inspection) to present priggish Colonel Manly as a model and ridicule the true-blue Yankee, Jonathan; or Trumbull's *McFingal,* which seems to satirize the Patriots almost as vigorously as the Tories – such works do not seem properly Americanized. They seem to use satire as a means of preserving Old World class distinctions and standards of decorum. Their dependence on Pope, Sheridan, and Butler as literary models reinforces this impression.

The sins of Federalism and Neoclassicism are interrelated. Although the linkage might be questioned on the ground that Neoclassicism is equally typical of Jeffersonian writing, it seems true that Neoclassicism reflected Federalist values more faithfully than Jeffersonian values. Federalism and Neoclassicism both connote respect for tradition, distrust of social change, maintenance of time-tested cultural standards, and commitment to learned rather than popular modes of expression – none of which are commonly thought of as belonging to American literature at its most typical. As long as we accept as axiomatic that the great turning point in American poetry came when "one of the roughs" liberated the genre from the shackles of polite verse, we shall understandably find it hard to see how fastidious heroic couplets denouncing the turbulent lower classes belong in the American canon, no matter how crisp and incisive those couplets may be.

II

Demonstration of ideological bias does not in itself amount to proof that the subject is worth closer scrutiny, except for the sake of some abstract ideal of precision. Beyond that, what claim does Federalist writing have on our attention? One positive argument that I have begun to make and will pursue throughout this book is that the best texts are better than we have realized. This argument on the basis of quality, however, is less pertinent here than at least two other considerations, needed in order to supply a contextual frame for legitimating New England Neoclassicism as more than a series of isolated moments rising somewhat above mediocrity.

The first of these has to do with the authenticity of New England Neoclassicism. The Neoclassical mode cannot simply be written off as a transient fashion symptomatic of American cultural immaturity. It must be understood as genuinely adapted to the needs of late eighteenth- and early nineteenth-century artists and audiences. William Hedges, Lewis Simpson, and other scholars have shown, for example, that the formality and elevation of Neoclassical style were authentic expressions of the Federalist literati's fear of anarchy – a sign of their need to impose restraint and decorum, of their desire to legitimate the new republic by grounding it on the precedents of Greece and Rome, and of their conservatively but genuinely patriotic goal for American literary self-realization – namely the ideal of a native literary establishment that would take its place in an international republic of letters, drawing on a common reservoir of tradition and expertise and rivaling Europe on its own ground.[13] The same point is implied by Richard Bushman's study of colonial satire. Satire, Bushman shows, did not really flourish in New England until the mid-eighteenth century, with the rise of social and political factionalism.[14] By then Butler, Dryden, Pope, Gay, and Swift were dead, well known in America, and even to some extent imitated; but the vogues of *Hudibras* and *The Dunciad* did not start until the native conditions were right for them.

As a further example, showing the fruitfulness of the theory of selective borrowing on even the humblest levels of inspiration, consider the *Miscellaneous Poems* of Jonathan Mitchell Sewall (1801). Sewall's book contains a number of trivial manneristic parrotings of Neoclassical frippery, such as his address "To a Lady Who Fainted on Attempting to Smoke for the Toothache." Yet Sewall often gives his models interestingly New England twists. For example, his poem entitled "On the

Gloomy Prospects of 1776" starts with echoes of Pope's *Essay on Man:* "Canst thou, by searching, the OMNISCIENT find / Or to perfection scan th' ETERNAL MIND?"[15] But Sewall uses this opener as a springboard for a distinctly post-Puritan vision of God chastising his sinful people with the scourge of the redcoats, yet, upon their repentance, purging the invaders from America and ushering in "thy millennium with transcendant bliss." The subtitle says, "Written with allusion to part of √ the 11th chapter of Job." This hint is important. The resignation and acceptance of righteous affliction that Job's story supposedly teaches is a common denominator both of the jeremiad tradition on which Sewall draws for his theme and of Pope's poem, which supplies the literary voice. Although we normally suppose, and with justice, that the sons of the Puritans thought differently from Pope, a deist Catholic, Pope's rhetoric helped Sewall give expression to his un-Augustan jeremiad. What we have here and in many other such cases is a borrowing in the literary realm comparable to the sort of borrowing in the political sphere that led American and British Whigs to draw very divergent inferences from the same body of reading matter and the same constitutional heritage.

This example of Pope's appropriation in the service of a secularized Calvinism responsive to the emphasis on submission to universal law in the *Essay on Man* is not meant to imply that New England writers of the early national period turned to Neoclassical modes exclusively, or even chiefly, as vehicles for expressing their Puritan heritage. More commonly, Neoclassical style seems to have implied a will for freedom from such constraints, either explicitly, as in John Trumbull's satire on the training of ministers, in *The Progress of Dulness* (where the "grave style and goodly phrase, / Safe-handed down from *Cromwell's* days" is lampooned by the narrator in Hudibrastic couplets that themselves may be a politically significant gesture of solidarity with Samuel Butler's anti-Puritanism), or implicitly, as in the Popean universalism of Barlow's epic scope ("One Friendly Genius fires the numerous whole / From glowing Georgia to the frozen pole"), which seems a calculated attempt to transcend the provincial.[16] Altogether, a good deal of the popularity of American Neoclassicism would seem to have been owing to the Revolutionary and post-Revolutionary need to deprovincialize colonial culture. Over against the important perception of students of the Puritan legacy that New England provided the model for the American way needs to be set the perception that Americanization reflected a recoil of the provincial against itself for which Neoclassicism supplied the vocabulary. Thus Barlow, who lost what was left of his boyhood faith between *The Vision of Columbus* (1787) and *The Columbiad* (1807), was able to replace his Miltonic "Seraph" with Hesper (a standard Neoclassical prop) as Columbus' consoler and guide, and through this and other ancillary changes to trans-

pose a New England–style vision of Christian millennialism into an En-
lightenment-style myth of progress. Barlow's Puritan roots undoubtedly
led him partway toward the latter, but the latter liberated him from the
constraints of the former.[17]

To show that early national Neoclassicism was an appropriate ideological vehicle in its day does not, however, prove that it led to anything
other than a cul-de-sac so far as the development of American literary
history as a whole is concerned. Such is the prevailing view. Thus Robert
Arner, after a fine account of how the heroic couplet registers the distinctive sensibility of the Connecticut Wits, concludes elegiacally:

> American poetry has gone its way almost as though the Wits had never
> existed, had never written a line. We come back in the end to Emerson,
> who pioneered on the frontiers of fact and symbol, testing and expand-
> ing the limitations of language, meter, and meaning in a way that ex-
> poses the narrowness of the couplet even if the Wits had been more
> often adept at its use.[18]

We revert, in short, to the familiar sequence of Edwards-to-Emerson-
and-beyond as the backbone of New England literary history, with the
Federalist literati swept back into the dustbin after a brief airing. In order
to make a case for studying them, we must demonstrate continuities between their work and the so-called flowering of New England during the
antebellum era.

✓
SIG. OF
FEDERALISTS.

Such continuities certainly exist, and in sufficient number and importance to make knowledge of literary Federalism indispensable to the student of the New England Renaissance. Even if one never develops a taste
for Trumbull's tetrameters or Dwight's invective, sooner or later one ✓
must acknowledge the importance of Federalist literary culture as a fore-
ground to the achievement of later writers who understandably matter
more to the twentieth-century reader.

Two scholarly strategies of interlinkage are familiar: the related themes
of the rise of literary institutions and the rise of Romanticism. Strategy
one: The Federalist literati inaugurate the process, which, after many
trials and frustrations, is consummated by their antebellum successors.
Strategy two: In early national writing we find a sporadic anticipation of
the later Romanticism within the limits of Neoclassical constraint – for
example, Barlow's epic as a foretaste of Whitman's. Since we played the
first tune in Chapters 2 and 3, let us concentrate here on the topic of
American Neoclassical foreshadowings of Romanticism.

TWO STRATEGIES
FOR JUSTIFYING
THE IMPORTANCE
OF FEDERALIST
WRITING.

All attempts to find an embryonic Romanticism within the Neoclassical may fairly be suspected of [orthogenesis] until proved innocent. When
Kenneth Silverman, describing American culture of the 1780s, stresses
the cult of Wertherism and calls its chief literary exemplar, Joseph Brown
Ladd (a Rhode Islander turned Charlestonian) the "first American ro-

[ALL CULTURES PASS
THROUGH SEQUENTIAL
PERIODS IN SAME
ORDER]

mantic poet," one immediately asks whether the proto-Romantic aspect
has been highlighted in the interest of accommodating the material to the
American literary "norm."[19] Nonetheless, Federalist era writing does anticipate Romantic modes. In English literary history, Neoclassicism leads
into Romanticism by a series of steps so gradual as to seem almost indistinguishable to some;[20] in American writing, the shift in taste is at once
more abrupt and still harder to chart uncontroversially, since the Augustan and pre-Romantic phases coincide more nearly, and the high points
of Neoclassicism and Romanticism are separated by at most two generations instead of a century. Thus we find poet Paul Allen, writing about
1800, by turns approaching Romantic lyricism in "A Night Scene"
("Here on this solitary beach / I muse") and invoking Pope as the model
of a poet who followed nature. Thus arch-Federalist Joseph Dennie, an
Addisonian essayist, welcomed *Lyrical Ballads* enthusiastically – until the
scorn of British reviewers gave him second thoughts. Thus the first true
Greater Romantic Lyric in America ("A Fragment," by Eliza Townsend
of Boston, 1817) was written by a woman who knew the "British classics" thoroughly but may never have read Wordsworth, Coleridge, Shelley, or Keats.[21]

Those inclined to ascribe crypto-Romanticism to American environmental influence can find plenty of evidence. Timothy Dwight's *Travels
in New-England and New-York,* for instance, provides a most affecting and
amusing case of a sober, steady eighteenth-century gentleman trying val-
iantly to confine himself to facts and rational arguments about his native
"country" of New England (to counter the reports of ignorant, malicious
foreign travelers), yet being prompted by a landscape-inspired sense of
wonder to repeated outbursts of Romantic feeling. Dwight apologizes
for indulging in landscape descriptions, which on principle he considers
"indistinct, obscure, and perplexing" (*DT* 1:260), yet he cannot resist.
His reflections on Vermont scenery are typical.

> It is impossible for a person traveling through this cleft of the Green
> Mountains not to experience the most interesting emotions. The un-
> ceasing gaiety of the river and the brilliancy of its fine borders create
> uncommon elasticity of mind, animated thoughts, and sprightly excur-
> sions of fancy; while the rude and desolate aspect of the mountains, the
> huge, misshapen rocks, the precipices, beyond description barren and
> dreary, awaken emotions verging toward melancholy, and mild and ele-
> vated conceptions. Curiosity grows naturally out of astonishment, and
> inquiry of course succeeds wonder. Why, the mind instinctively asks,
> were these huge piles of ruin thus heaped together? What end could
> creative wisdom propose in forming such masses of solid rock? [*DT*
> 2:300]

Dwight's instinctive muting of the personal element, his Neoclassical inhibition against regarding mountains as anything but "horrid" monstros-

ities, should not keep us from recognizing here that the experience behind the rhetoric is close to that of Romantic epiphany – an experience in which the perceiver is brought to a higher plane of awareness through confrontation with nature's inexplicable otherness. Dwight instinctively retreats from mysticism to the rational observer's pose ("inquiry of course succeeds wonder"), but the wonder lingers on:

> In these wild and elevated regions the fancy of the philosopher is much more awake than his intellect. The suggestions of his mind, the very arguments which he uses, and the conclusions on which he fastens, instead of being the sound emanations of logic, are mere effusions of poetry, and need nothing to complete this character except to be written in verse. [*DT* 2:301]

Dwight is finally on the side of the philosophers, discounting "mere effusions" but not without a struggle. Rural New England forced him to the brink of Romantic poetry.

Americanists are too apt, however, to look for moments like these and, having found them, to exaggerate their Romanticist character. In diagnosing the pre-Romantic aspect of Dwight's pastoral, *Greenfield Hill,* we overlook the fact that such topographical verse is actually as much a Neoclassical phenomenon as a reaction against it, the first such poem in British literature being John Denham's *Cooper's Hill* (1642), also widely regarded as the first use of the true heroic couplet in English. Closely scrutinized, the claim for the nearness of Federalist Neoclassicism to New England Renaissance literature can even be reversed into the claim that Neoclassicism never went away. We find mastodons like Edward Everett lingering around until 1865 or after, and a number of writers born after 1800 who might almost have been eighteenth-century writers – for example, Oliver Wendell Holmes (who was fond of likening his life history to that of Samuel Johnson). Indeed, classicism was a dynamic element in the writing of many New England Romantics. Keats's warmest admirer among them, James Russell Lowell, was "brought up in the old superstition that [Pope] was the greatest poet that ever lived," a doctrine he rejected in principle yet internalized to the point of reading every line of Pope carefully at least once and producing the most memorable antebellum Neoclassical verse satire, *A Fable for Critics.*[22] The nonfictional prose style of Hawthorne, to whom the image of Samuel Johnson seemed "almost as vivid . . . as the kindly figure of my own grandfather," reaches back to *The Spectator,* which was the title of his first literary experiment.[23]

HAWTHORNE &
the SPECTATOR

The rubric of "anticipation," then, does not do justice to the complex relation between the earlier and later writing of the time span we are examining. We need also to look for other continuities.

One of the most important of these has to do with the New England Federalists' self-appointed role as arbiters of virtue and taste. The ethos of Neoclassicism encouraged their predisposition to assume a posture of

moral monitorship analogous to that of the Puritan divines before them
and the Transcendentalists and other American poet-prophets thereafter.
The Neoclassical didacticism of Addison, Pope, and Johnson merged
with the heritage of Puritan didacticism to create compounds like the
√ Sewall poem quoted above and, in general, to assist Federalist literati to
envisage their role as lawgivers to their fellow citizens in a way that sets
the stage for the confrontations we later see between American Romantic
writers and the society they prophetically indict and instruct.

In the Federalist literati's execution of their self-appointed monitorship
we find, as the period unfolds, the first stages of the celebrated (although,
as I have argued earlier, overstated) rift between middle-class society and
the writer who stands in loyal, and sometimes not-so-loyal, opposition
as its self-appointed prophet or critic. During the Federalist era, the intellectual and political leadership of New England (and America as a
whole) was coordinated to a degree that intellectuals have been trying to
recapture ever since. As their party lost its hold, Federalist writers became the first group of alienated American intellectuals. The first really
profound statement of the plight of the artist in a republic came, fittingly,
not from Cooper or Poe or Emerson or Hawthorne but from Fisher
Ames, who declared at the turn of the nineteenth century that "it is the
very spirit of democracy . . . to proscribe the aristocracy of talents."[24]
Distaste for Ames's patrician arrogance should not keep one from appreciating how shrewdly he anticipates Tocqueville and Richard Hofstadter
on the subject of American antiintellectualism and how the Federalist literati's growing sense of themselves as an endangered species in a perpetual war against bigots, clods, philistines, and ninnies anticipates the
rebelliousness of writers like Thoreau and Dickinson. Conversely, understanding the Federalist background to Romantic antiestablishmentarianism may help us to envisage the latter not merely as alienated but as also
emanating, much of the time, from civic concern and the writer's desire
to play a significant social role. Linda Kerber, in her excellent book on
Federalist rhetoric, refers to a Federalist-abolitionist "continuum" in
which the "political abolitionism of an earlier generation" (which she sees
as a ploy to advance sectional interests) "was transformed into a human-
itarian abolitionism by sons who took their fathers at their word."[25] She
cites as examples Josiah and Edmund Quincy, John and Wendell Phillips,
and the surrogate father-son relationship of Rufus King and William
Lloyd Garrison. Extending Kerber's point, I suggest that we should think
of a more general continuum linking Federalist intellectuals with the
Transcendentalists and all other New England Romantic reformers who
pictured themselves as commissioned to resist the tyranny of the majority and to raise the communal consciousness to a higher level of cultural
and moral awareness. Listen to how Thoreau's speech on John Brown's
raid echoes Fisher Ames's remarks on the Jeffersonian revolution.

Here is Thoreau:

> We talk about a *representative* government; but what a monster of a government is that where the noblest faculties of the mind, and the *whole* heart, are not *represented*. A semi-human tiger or ox, stalking over the earth, with its heart taken out and the top of its brain shot away. Heroes have fought well on their stumps when their legs were shot off, but I never heard of any good done by such a government as that.[26]

Here is Ames:

> We see ourselves in the full exercise of the forms of election, when the substance is gone. We have some members in Congress with a faithful meanness to represent our servility, and others to represent our nullity in the union; but our vote and influence avail no more, than that of the Isle of Man in the politics of Great Britain. If, then, we have not survived our political liberty, we have lived long enough to see the pillars of its security crumble to powder.[27]

We hear some very similar notes in these two passages: righteous sermonizing in the jeremiad vein; a caustic, mordant gallows humor, reflecting a tendency to see life in terms of extreme outcomes; a sense of belonging to a select vanishing few that are charged to awaken their countrymen from sleep; and above all a vision of the stark discrepancy between the pleasing forms of republican government and the actual perversion of those forms. Both passages also, incidentally, invoke this picture as a way of combating the supposed domination of New England by southern interests. Underlying the rhetoric is an incipient political and cultural separatism that might be interpreted either in a sociological sense (as the centripetal force that tended to draw even resolutely cosmopolitan New England writers, like Barlow with his "Hasty Pudding") or in a more rarefied psychological sense (as a projection of the disaffected intellectual's need to detach himself from the tainted whole).

The resemblances between Ames and Thoreau make increasing sense when we realize that the activist literati in antebellum New England were mostly not Jacksonian Democrats, not lineal Jeffersonians, but were associated at least initially with the Whigs, who were the descendants of Federalism as the party of the region's "natural aristocracy." The prominent New England writers who spoke out about slavery and other public issues during the 1840s and 1850s – Emerson, Thoreau, Lowell, Longfellow, Whittier, and Stowe – were, like Charles Sumner, the politician whom they most admired, generally cool or hostile to Jackson in the 1830s and were members or fellow travelers of the reformist branch of the Whig Party, the so-called Conscience Whigs. The fathers or grandfathers of many of them had been prominent Federalists.

Federalist hauteur could also, of course, lead in due time to conservatism – to the Unitarian establishment that Emerson attacked, to conservative Whiggery, to Brahminism, to campaigns for immigration quotas.[28]

But the persistence of this mentality by no means negates the argument concerning Federalism's radical offshoots; on the contrary, knowing that both stem from a common source should help us to understand better such other nineteenth-century developments as the relationship between the Concord Transcendentalists and the Boston-Cambridge literary set, and the uneasy relationship between both groups and such figures as Walt Whitman and Mark Twain.

SATIRE

One of the chief literary weapons of the disaffected radical or reactionary is satire. Satire was, of course, a hallmark of Anglo-American Neoclassicism.[29] Normally it is not considered a Romantic trait, yet this generalization will not bear close scrutiny. Satire is actually quite prevalent in the work of all of the American Romantics except Whitman, and in him too, if one includes his journalism. A number of antebellum writers – Cooper, Emerson, Thoreau, Dickinson, and Melville, especially – became more satirical as their careers unfolded. Think, for a moment, of antebellum New England literature as defined by the following texts: Emerson's "New England Reformers" and "Historic Notes of Life and Letters in New England"; Thoreau's "Economy," "Resistance to Civil Government," "Slavery in Massachusetts," and "Life Without Principle"; Dickinson's "What Soft – Cherubic Creatures – / These Gentlewomen are – " and "The Bible is an antique Volume"; Whittier's "Ichabod"; Lowell's *Fable for Critics;* Hawthorne's *Blithedale Romance;* Holmes's *Elsie Venner;* and Margaret Fuller's *Woman in the Nineteenth Century.* Focusing on these as a group, we become immediately aware of the persistence, between the early national and the Romantic periods, of New England satire on American shallowness, materialism, and provincialism.

As a specific example, we may return to Timothy Dwight's neglected diatribe, *The Triumph of Infidelity,* in which the fallacy of naive trust in a benign view of Providence and human nature is satirized. Dwight's immediate target is Universalism, the doctrine that all men will finally be saved. This doctrine Dwight regards not only as false but as pernicious, encouraging sin and the speedy perdition of humankind, except for the faithful remnant. Dwight's opposition to Charles Chauncy, whose treatise on universal salvation seems to have inspired the poem, prefigures the tension between Transcendentalist optimism and the reaction to it by Hawthorne and Melville, expressed in works such as "The Celestial Railroad" and *The Confidence-Man.* In both works Satan, or the satanic principle, is shown as (or insinuated to be) the manipulator of bland, euphemistic disguise. Dwight and Melville are particularly similar in the combination of obsessive reiteration and ironic aloofness with which they erode the sugary surface of American optimism. Undoubtedly, part of the reason Dwight is ignored is that he cast his critique in old-fashioned heroic couplets.

Such mannerisms have given Neoclassical style the reputation of specious artificiality since the time when Emerson and his cohorts declared that "Pope and his school wrote poetry fit to put round frosted cake" (*EW* 5:255). Yet it was during the Neoclassical era that provincial manners and colloquial speech began to be taken seriously as literary material. In British literary history the first systematic exploitation of quotidian [EVERYDAY, COMMONPLACE] realism comes in Neoclassical satire, from Ben Jonson through Gay and Swift. Likewise, in New England writing, the best early encapsulations of homespun life and Yankee dialect are drawn in a humorous, patronizing context. Dwight's Ethan Allen, the great clodhopping oracle who "bustled, bruised and swore" in Satan's cause, is a Yankee folk hero not yet taken seriously. Tyler's Jonathan is the rustic Yankee yeoman not yet sentimentalized. The credit for textualizing these popular stereotypes, later turned into literary archetypes, must go to the Federalist gentry.

A particularly instructive example is a verse satire by Yale-educated Federalist lawyer St. John Honeywood, directed at a Republican congressman from Vermont, Matthew Lyon. Lyon was known to Jeffersonians as a martyr of the Sedition Act but to Federalists chiefly as "spitting Mat," the man who spat in the face of fellow congressman Roger Griswold of Connecticut on the floor of the House. Here are excerpts from Honeywood's imaginary congressional speech by Lyon, probably supposed to be sung to the tune of "Yankee Doodle":

> I'm rugged Mat, the democrat,
>   Berate me as you please, Sir;
> True Paddy Whack ne'er turned his back,
>   Or bow'd his head to Caesar.
> *Horum, scorum, rendum, roarum,*
>   *Spittam, spattam, squirto;*
> *Tag, rag, derry, merry, raw head and bloody bones,*
>   *Sing langolee, nobody's hurt, O!*
>
> . . . .
>
> My dam, Sir, was a buxom lass,
>   Her milk was rich and good, Sir;
> No cow that's fed on clover grass
>   Can boast of purer blood, Sir. (Refrain)
>
> My sire he was a strapping buck
>   As ever girl sat eye on;
> What wonder then they had the luck
>   To bring the world a LYON! (Refrain)[30]

This is an unmistakably elitist poem – a quintessential example of Federalism's least attractive prejudices: dislike of non-Anglo-Saxons, the lower classes, and miscellaneous breaches of etiquette that for Honeywood's peers lowers a fellow like Lyon to the bestial level his name implies. Yet the poem is also very close to the roots of popular literary consciousness in its ballad form, its use of the folk hero's boast, and its mimicry of the plain talk and assertive swagger of the man of the people. Honeywood walks a thin line between patrician arrogance and rough-and-tumble horseplay and, in the process, approaches the vernacular spirit later writers embrace more fully. Conversely we must recognize that the sense of looking at common life from above continues to persist: In Thoreau's travelogues and in the genre sketches of Hawthorne and Lowell and even of Stowe and the local colorists, we continue to get the impression of crude specimens of rusticity handled with condescension – of the washed depicting the unwashed. The Federalist writers simply paraded their class consciousness more unabashedly.

To pursue the subject of the "artificiality" of Federalist style one step farther, we can even discover affinities with Romantic style where we would least expect them, namely, in the closed couplet, the most characteristic of Neoclassical prosodic forms. Of course, we instinctively oppose the closed couplet to the more open, fluid style of Emersonian prose, as in the quotation above from Robert Arner. Yet this may be a false dichotomy. Couplet verse and Transcendentalist rhetoric have at least two key traits in common: Both are atomistic methods of construction that put a great premium on the detached saying or image; and both for this reason invite a cerebral, intellectualized reaction, whatever their emotional freight. Benjamin Spencer remarks that in the early national period the "incisive generalization" was regarded as "inherently poetic."[31] True enough. Orators loved such gems as the following tribute to Joseph Warren: "Like Harrington he wrote, – like Cicero he spoke, – like Hampden he lived, – and like Wolfe he died."[32] In such aperçu, and in the homologous style of the verse couplet, we see an anticipation of the effect that Emerson and Thoreau sought in their expository prose. Both types of style, the Transcendentalist and the Federalist, show a fondness for immediate rhetorical effect as opposed to sustained and tightly knit literary wholes, and, at the same time, a respect for learning and intellectual subtlety. The showy classicism of the Federalist literati, with their love of classical allusions and their penchant for unnecessary footnotes, based for the most part on superficial college courses and ⌈desultory⌉ reading, looks backward to Cotton Mather's grab-bag pedantry and forward to Emerson's syncretistic interweavings of odd bits of learning from every source imaginable, likewise dependent on superficial college syllabi and desultory reading. In each case, triumph by aphorism, by appeal to commonsense axioms, and by virtuoso command of book learning that is not recondite but reasonably accessible to the educated layperson is an important rhetorical strategy.[33]

Such strategies are, of course, predictable in a milieu in which literary people feel impelled by personal preference and public responsibility to assume the role of teachers at large and project a sense of themselves as frivolous when, like Hawthorne, they feel uncomfortable in that role. This sense of the public mission of the serious literary artist, which originates in Puritan New England, continues, as we saw in Chapter 3, throughout the antebellum period, although it weakens somewhat by the mid-nineteenth century. In some measure, it underlies all of the continuities described earlier. The most spectacular manifestation of it is apocalypticism. Literature of the early national period, as recent scholarship has pointed out, tends to dwell both on the possibility of millennial or utopian fulfillment and, at the opposite extreme, on total destruction of the world through holocaust or divine wrath.[34] New England writing is particularly rife with such images, sometimes perpetrated simultaneously by the same person. For example, Barlow's *Vision of Columbus,* which presents an optimistic, utopian scenario for world history and America's place in it, was published at the same time as his contribution to *The Anarchiad* (1786–7), a collaborative, dystopian poem by the Connecticut Wits that pictures America as having been destroyed by the forces of civil disorder. We have seen similar ambivalences in the poems by Sewall and Dwight surveyed earlier.

Both possibilities derive from the implicit doubleness of the jeremiad tradition, which, as the disagreement between Perry Miller and Sacvan Bercovitch over its meaning suggests, holds forth prospects of both ultimate fulfillment and ultimate doom for the New English Israel.[35] The epics and mock-epics of the Connecticut Wits effect a secularization of the jeremiad parallel to the process of secularization in the political sphere that began in the mid-eighteenth century when the nation itself became identified with the ideal, sacred goal envisioned by the Puritan divines.[36] In this respect the Wits stand at the head of a dual tradition that persists throughout American secular literature, exemplified on the one side by Emerson, Whitman, Edward Bellamy, and Hart Crane, and on the other side by Cooper (in *The Crater*), Twain, Nathanael West, Allen Ginsberg, and Imamu Amiri Baraka (in his *System of Dante's Hell*).[37] For present purposes it should not be necessary to say more about this dual tradition, except that the American imagination seems to be addicted to envisioning ultimate states of social perfection or annihilation and that the Federalist period, when both possibilities may have seemed more imminent to intellectuals than they ever have since, marks an important state in the unfolding of that tradition.

Finally, we need to understand the metaliterary dimension of New England Romantic texts, stressed in the latter part of Chapter 3, partly in the light of Neoclassical precedent. A corollary of the ironic distance that we have located in both types of writing is the tendency to sabotage dramatic illusion. A literature with a prophetic, apocalyptic bent, for example, is apt to be dissatisfied with simple mimesis and, in its more cool-headed moments, to show a certain amount of self-conscious backing away from its own pretensions.

Two examples, from Trumbull and Hawthorne, will begin to give a sense of Neoclassical and Romantic common ground. First, a glimpse of the Boston town meeting, in *McFingal*:

> Beneath stood voters of all colours,
> Whigs, Tories, orators and bawlers;
> With ev'ry tongue in either faction,
> Prepar'd, like minute-men, for action;
> Where truth and falsehood, wrong and right,
> Drew all their legions out to fight;
> With equal uproar, scarcely rave
> Opposing winds in Aeolus' cave;
> Such dialogues with earnest face,
> Held never Balaam with his ass.[38]

The speaker stands at such a distance from the town meeting that the contending parties appear not merely indistinguishable but phantasmagorical. The debasement of "minute-men" to cover bawlers of all political stripes is the first step in blurring the scene's mimetic clarity. Second, the superimposition on the scene of the abstract frameworks of classical and Judeo-Christian allusion heightens the scene's intensity, only to dissolve it further into indefiniteness through the move from referent to analogue and through the device of arguing for the negative applicability of the allusions ("scarcely," "never") rather than the positive. These effects, plus the tight Hudibrastic grid, convert violent image into playful exercise, the playfulness partly a means of defense against the violence.

Hawthorne's "New Adam and Eve" works similar magic with another popular fervor characteristic of its period, millennarian revivalism. "Let us conceive," says the speaker, "good Father Miller's interpretation of the prophecies to have proved true. The Day of Doom has burst upon the globe, and swept away the whole race of men." The speaker then proceeds to imagine the new primal pair's life-style, "in a mood half-sportive and half-thoughtful" (*HW* 10:247–8). But well before this explicit clue, the condescension of the wording – "Let us conceive" and "good Father Miller" – makes plain the distance of the text from the popular enthusiasm that suggested its fable, and the inevitability that that fable, like *McFingal*'s, will work itself out as a narrative chiefly interesting for its amused reminders of the fabulousness of what is depicted. Like Trumbull, Hawthorne counters the fascination that Father Miller's demotic intensity has for him by dissolving it in an elegant haze of equivocating speculation.

"The New Adam and Eve" goes beyond *McFingal,* crossing the border between fancy and fabulation, by reiterating as it unfolds not only that the events represented are bizarre but also that they are suppositious. Trumbull's approach is, in Wayne Booth's terms, still "stable" irony.[39] Both the object and the basis of the irony are relatively distinct, though not altogether; *McFingal* oscillates between hits at two opposite targets – Squire McFingal, as caricature of the Loyalist gentleman, and (in the quoted passage) the mindless factionalism of which the patriots are at least as guilty as the Tories. Hawthorne, however, destabilizes his irony further through the genial alacrity with which his speaker preempts, as his donnée, the vision of one whom he considers fanatical. *McFingal* comes out solidly for Neoclassical virtues of decorum and restraint, even at the cost of muddying its political commitment to the patriot cause; "The New Adam and Eve" makes an ostensible commitment to populist revivalism (as an example of the saving power of imaginative vision, the context makes clear), while signaling at the same time that this is just a counter in a more elaborate game of the imagination, the seriousness of which for the speaker is impossible to determine. Perhaps the first text might be seen as a Federalist, the second a Jacksonian era response to the perception that the American artist's refined vocabulary is dictated in the first instance by the vox populi. In Trumbull's Federalist aesthetic, the response was an entirely defensive employment of the apparatus of Neoclassical tradition to reduce the unwashed to a lower level of reality. In Hawthorne, good Democrat that he thought he was, the more complex response is to accept the situation in principle but to reserve the right to disown it in practice by reasserting a version of old-style ironic distance. In both cases ambiguity is created by the phenomenon of uneasy confrontation with the prospect of an apocalyptic, world-changing event that the work attempts to seize hold of from a mixture of fascination, acute discomfort, and the desire to assert control over it. This situation reflects both the perils and the aesthetic rewards of the tradition of moral monitorship in early national and antebellum letters.

Putting the last two parallels together, apocalypticism and self-conscious artifice, we might characterize both the early national and the antebellum phases of New England writing as being marked by a visionary self-consciousness that originated as a combination of Augustan-style literary play (cf. Pope's mock epicry, Fielding's prefaces, Sterne's illusion-breaking narratology) and New England–style tension created by the didactic imperative (the burden of the educated elite that dominated regional belles lettres), coexisting uneasily with the writer's increasing sense of impotence or marginalization both as writer and as a member of the elite in a period of social revolution. We cannot prove that this syndrome caused, or even strongly influenced, the paradoxical way in which New England antebellum writers absorbed the visionary and ironic strains of Romanticism discussed in Chapter 3. But the convergence in sensibility, along with the other parallels drawn above, should be enough to make at least a prima facie case for the value of studying early national and antebellum letters as a continuum.

The promise of this approach should be borne out by the next three chapters. In each we examine an important literary mode that flourished throughout the years of our study. Each of these was used at first, by its New England practitioners, as an instrument for guiding and interpreting the collective conscience by didactic expression of public values, rendered in conventionalized forms. Increasingly, however, they were used to express a restive dialogue between the creative imagination and the stylistic and ideological norms to which the writers generally continued in some measure to adhere. Underneath the change of fashion from Neoclassical to Romantic, bringing with it a partial release from the willed standardization that makes early national literature seem to modernist eyes impoverished by contrast to New England Romanticism, we should not fail to recognize these fundamental constants: the will to assume the role of public spokesperson; self-consciousness as to the perceived marginality or effeteness of the artistic sphere; the desire to press a counterclaim for the authority of one's medium by grounding it in such absolutes as truth, nature, and spirit; and – as a consequence of this self-dividedness – a tendency to achieve stylistic and thematic originality through destabilization or subversion of traditional forms of discourse rather than by discarding these forms altogether. Neoclassicism in New England can be seen both as persisting as a constraining force in antebellum writing and also as containing within itself the aesthetic and prophetic elements upon which the antebellum Romantics built.

PART II

Three Representative Genres

5

New England Poetics: Emerson, Dickinson, and Others

Hark! from New England's peaceful shores arise
Ten thousand lyres, whose music sweeps the skies.
  "Peter Pindar, Jr.," *Parnassus in Philadelphia* (1854)

[Nature] appoints us to keep within the sharp boundaries of form as the
condition of our strength.
           Ralph Waldo Emerson, "The Superlative" (1882)

Of the three major fictive genres, poetry alone was held in anything like
high regard throughout our period. The writing of poems was respectable to an extent that the writing of prose fiction and stage plays definitely
was not. Today it seems odd that the more mimetic genres were held
suspect by an age of aesthetic utilitarianism in favor of the form now
usually considered as having the least social impact. Undoubtedly, cultural inertia had much to do with this anomaly: Poetry had a traditional
prestige the other genres lacked, as a polite accomplishment sanctioned
by Milton, Pope, and (later) Wordsworth as an instrument of instruction
and ennoblement. In any event, poetry was written throughout the
American colonies from an early date and was institutionalized as a regular feature of the publishing scene well before the Revolution, whereas
fiction and drama emerged much more slowly, not achieving similar legitimacy until well into the nineteenth century.

    The premodern poetry of New England presents to the literary histo-
rian the paradox of an inconsequential superiority – "superiority" since
by any standard American poetry between the Revolution and the centennial was dominated by New Englanders. Except for Philip Freneau
and Edgar Allan Poe, America produced no important poet before 1855
who was not of New England extraction. Yet also "inconsequential," because the achievement of all the New England poets except Emily Dick-

105

inson today seems at best a foreshadowing, at worst a dead end, in light of the prevailing notion of American poetic development. American poetic distinctiveness is generally seen as consisting, stylistically, in formal experimentation, especially in Whitman's break from traditional prosody and Pound's instigation of literary modernism, and in the quest for an American idiom to replace traditional poetic diction. Ideologically, American poetic distinctiveness has been seen as consisting in its anti-nomian or Adamic impulse to resist mainstream cultural values (Roy Harvey Pearce); its preoccupation with the domains of the natural and the eternal, as opposed to the secular and the temporal (Hyatt H. Waggoner), and its "Orphic" dialectic between the imperatives of untrammeled freedom and necessity (Harold Bloom).[1] Although these theories collide at certain points, they broadly reinforce one another to create a composite portrait of the truly American bard as a solitary entrepreneur of mystical bent who writes in an idiosyncratic and – preferably – vernacular voice, with less adherence than British poets to the accentual-syllabic tradition.[2] The result of such theorizing has been to enshrine Whitman, the most iconoclastic and charismatic of national bards, as the "archetypal American poet"[3] and to relegate the great bulk of premodern New England poetry to the sidelines.

To be sure, Emerson is normally seen as having begotten Whitman – a deed so portentous that in some expositions Emerson rather than Whitman becomes the key reference point.[4] Emily Dickinson, not in the "Whitman tradition" yet certainly an example of the experimentation that this tradition has supposedly made normative in American poetry, is customarily seen both as a coeval symptom of American poetic emergence and as a parallel instance of Emersonian begetting, although recent feminist scholarship has tended to put those two claims at odds.[5] Finally, it is common to reach back behind Emerson to find the roots of American poetic distinctiveness in Puritan thought, particularly in the posture of the solitary but self-appointedly representative ego seeking, in an act of both piety and self-assertion, to interpret the mystical design of the universe.[6] Such foregrounding privileges the literary history of New England above that of other regions as *the* American matrix from which *the* American poetic tradition ultimately arose, but only insofar as it foreshadows the modernism of style and urge for transcendence of formalism that are seen as quintessential to American poetry. F. O. Matthiessen's refusal to see merit in Emerson's poetry, apart from a "few herbs and apples," is repeated by Harold Bloom's identification of "Bacchus" as virtually the sole instance of untrammeled Orphism in Emerson's verse. In most overviews of American poetry, Longfellow and Bryant barely exist; they are checkpoints to be passed by as quickly as possible, unless one is bound to a format requiring "coverage."[7]

Without going to the opposite extreme of arguing for Whittier's superiority to Whitman, I seek to complicate the prevailing views of American poetic distinctiveness by taking a fresh look at the aesthetics of New
England poetry between the Revolution and the Civil War, approaching
this material in two ways that depart from the usual scholarly procedures.
First, in the spirit of the previous chapter, the differences between Neoclassical and Romantic texts, although acknowledged, are minimized, the
primary emphasis being on the definition of poetic strategies common –
although not necessarily unique – to the period as a whole. Second, and
still more controversially, the experimentalism of Emerson and Dickinson is seen as being not so much a dissent from the poetic norms created
by mainstream poetry as a creative elaboration of those norms. In particular, I interpret the achievement of Dickinson, the greatest of the premodern New England poets, as well as that of her lesser contemporaries,
in terms of each other rather than in opposition to each other – without,
I hope, underestimating Dickinson's originality. Section I will define this
method; Section II will put it to use.

My analysis will center, for the most part, on familiar texts. The fig-
ures anthologized in George Whicher's *Poetry of the New England Renais-
sance* (1950) include most of those I consider significant: Joel Barlow,
William Cullen Bryant, Ralph Waldo Emerson, Henry Wadsworth Long-
fellow, John Greenleaf Whittier, Oliver Wendell Holmes, Jones Very,
Christopher Cranch, Henry David Thoreau, William Ellery Channing II,
James Russell Lowell, Henry Howard Brownell, Frederick Goddard
Tuckerman, and Emily Dickinson. To them I should add a number of
Neoclassical poets (John Trumbull, Timothy Dwight, Royall Tyler, and
Robert Treat Paine, for starters), and, among antebellum figures, James
Gates Percival, Richard Henry Dana, Sr., Frances Osgood, and Maria G.
Brooks, as well as several others (mentioned in this or other chapters)
who occasionally produced notable work. Canonical expansion, how-
ever, is in itself less important to me here than the reappraisal of a canon
previously defined.

I

Among earlier overviews of premodern New England poetry,
one of the most helpful is the first section of Bernard B. Duffey's *Poetry
in America.* Duffey's theory of American poetry from the antebellum era
through World War I is based on the polarity of "fictions of coherence"
and "fictions of incoherence." For Duffey, the "coherence" refers to the
collective achievement of five key New England figures – Bryant, Emerson, Longfellow, Holmes, and Whittier – and the cultural system that
their work expressed (the work, in other words, of the conservative
Schoolroom or Fireside poets, plus Emerson and minus Lowell – the lat-

ter somewhat arbitrarily excluded). For the poet of coherence, as opposed to the more open style of a "poet of incoherence" such as Whitman, the artifact was a simulacrum and vehicle for what is finally – after all doubts and hesitations have been aired or suppressed – a secure and communally applicable vision, a vision inherently religiocentric. For the poet of coherence, religion functioned as a "parent imagination whose own history seemed to attest the communal reality of subjectively conceived truth" and thereby held forth the possibility of a rapprochement between poetic inspiration and communal understanding.[8]

Duffey's formulation is useful as a nonjudgmental sketch of the cultural controls under which New England Romantic poetry operated and of the average aesthetic results. His account could easily be extended backward, with a few modifications, to encompass the Connecticut Wits as well. By and large, New England poetry, as written throughout the years under review, is a poetry written in traditional verse forms, grounding its utterance in some kind of spiritual or ethical vision, spoken either by an impersonal, authoritative authorial voice or by a lyric voice that becomes the means of dramatizing an ethical stance; a poetry in which images tend to be converted into moral exempla, in which passion is generally sublimated into piety or abstraction or, if directly expressed, is expressed in such a way as to make plain the risks of its own excess. Whether cognitive or sentimental, it is prevailingly a regulated poetry of moral statement, written in regulated accentual-syllabic verse. Thus the first major New England Romantic, William Cullen Bryant, follows the late, rather than the early, Wordsworth by favoring speakers who keep personal references to a minimum; by almost never picturing the speaker in conversational interaction with another person (Bryant prefers apostrophe to an inert landscape or to an absent object of rhetorical address); and by framing his greatest poems with homiletic abstractions:[9]

> To him who in the love of Nature holds
> Communion with her visible forms, she speaks
> A various language.
>   ["Thanatopsis," lines 1–3]

The depersonalization ("To him"), reliance on abstraction ("visible forms"), and polysyllabic diction are ceremonializing carryovers from eighteenth-century rhetoric designed to metamorphose the anxiety about death that is embedded in the poem into a communication that soothes and uplifts and thereby becomes personally reassuring and socially useful. The poem flirts with a nihilistic view of death subversive of the values of Bryant's audience, a view that we know, from its recurrence and inconsistency of treatment in his poetry, tempted Bryant greatly.[10] Unlike Whitman, however, Bryant "conquers" not by opening himself up to the experience of the great mother but through the distancing effect of a controlled and elegant serenity.

From Bryant's transitional position, we may look backward and forward and observe similar effects. Looking forward, to the height of New England Romanticism, we find the Transcendentalist poet Jones Very's divine madness expressing itself, paradoxically, in Shakespearean sonnets. Although Emerson expressed skepticism about Very's credentials as mystic on the ground of his bad grammar and spelling ("Cannot the spirit parse & spell?"),[11] what is even more striking about Very's inspiration, under the circumstances, is its strict and predictable regularity:

> 'T is a new life; thoughts move not as they did
> With slow uncertain steps across my mind;
> In thronging haste fast pressing on they bid
> The portals open to the viewless wind
> That comes not save when in the dust is laid
> The crown of pride that gilds each mortal brow,
> And from before man's vision melting fade
> The heavens and earth; their walls are falling now.
> Fast crowding on, each thought asks utterance strong;
> Storm-lifted waves swift rushing to the shore,
> On from the sea they send their shouts along,
> Back through the cave-worn rocks their thunders roar;
> And I a child of God by Christ made free
> Start from death's slumbers to Eternity.[12]

Three ABAB quatrains and a couplet, each quatrain constituting an autonomous meaning unit that at the same time neatly moves into the next, building toward the climax (lines 9–12), whose significance is summarized in the last two lines. The experience of the holy? Up to a point, yes, but structured by, and encased in, a familiar theory of conversion morphology that the poem purposes not to enact as experience but to proclaim as doctrine, with the experience as the exemplum. Very's metaphors are sometimes innovative, his message often outrageously so (as when he impersonates the Holy Spirit: "I come the rushing wind that shook the place / Where those once sat who spake with tongues of fire").[13] But even at such moments, Very's antinomianism is mediated by scriptural and doctrinal formulas and by prosodic decorum.

Looking backward, we find a counterpart in the Hudibrastic verve of late eighteenth-century satire. Here is John Trumbull's Popean fantasia of young ladies' artillery at a ball, from *The Progress of Dulness*, Part III:

> So once, in fear of Indian beating,
> Our grandsires bore their guns to meeting,
> Each man equipp'd on sunday morn,
> With psalm-book, shot and powder-horn;

And look'd in form, as all must grant,
Like th' antient, true church militant;
Or fierce, like modern deep Divines,
Who fight with quills, like porcupines.[14]

It is hard to know just how to take this, given that a degree of scoffing at Puritan rigidity was *au fait* among New England Augustans yet considered objectionable when it went very far. It is interesting, though speculative, to read the passage as a potshot against the mentality of those whose criticisms of Part I ("Tom Brainless," a satire on the training of provincial clergy) goaded Trumbull into a defensive preface and a shift to less controversial targets such as female vanity. Especially if so – but even if not – the passage makes a good third exhibit of subversive impulses regulated into serviceable moral utterance. The impact of the put-downs of holy zeal, both ancient and modern, is blunted by their lightsomeness and their function as ancillary elaboration of the theme of foppery. Even as he accomplishes this self-protective trivialization, however, Trumbull also gives his text intellectual-ethical starch, raising it above mere mimesis of ephemera to an implied statement of moral and historical equivalence.

These cuttings from the intertext of Neoclassical-Romantic New England poetry will have begun to illustrate the nature of what Duffey labels "the coherence." They do not, perhaps, add up to a powerful case for studying it closely, except for antiquarian reasons. On the contrary, such poetry seems more notable for what it does not do than for what it does: for its failure of nerve and its need to reduce to formula, to avoid the full implications of its own train of thought. This very issue, indeed, is the bête noire of the burgeoning scholarship on Emerson's poetry, treated at length in three monographs during the past decade.[15] Emerson's verse will make a good springboard for us, because it is the only more or less conventional verse from Trumbull to Longfellow whose pretensions to aesthetic achievement present-day scholars have agreed to take seriously.

EMERSON

Though ranging in tone from the laudatory to the dismissive, the recent scholarship concurs that Emerson's best poetry is in his prose, that his verse is a diminished achievement compared to his aesthetic ideals, reflecting with honorable exceptions either a bondage to traditional poetic forms (David Porter) or a midlife retreat from Transcendentalist assertiveness to wary stoicism (R. A. Yoder).[16] The stylistic limitation of Emerson's verse is seen not so much in its prosodic ineptitude, relative to, say, Longfellow's skill, as in its failure to break through to a more modernist aesthetic. This scholarly verdict is corroborated by Emerson himself. His criticism positively requires us to be disappointed in his poetry. He wished to "write such rhymes as shall not suggest a restraint, but contrawise the wildest freedom" (*JMN* 7:219), and in his essays lyrically describes the effect he had in mind ("The melodies of the poet ascend, and leap, and pierce into the deeps of infinite time" [*EW* 3:14]). But his own poems scarcely begin to enter that promised land. By his own criteria, as Albert Gelpi has said, he is at best a "teetotaling Bacchus, . . . too fastidious and remote to be a full-blooded and abandoned Dionysian."[17] His favorite verse form, the tetrameter couplet, seemingly leads to a caricature of the bipolar mode of vision that enriches his essays, which ruminate magically on the play and reconciliation of opposites and on the analogy and antithesis between the realms of nature and spirit. In Emerson's prose, one experiences these mental operations as plentitude; in his poems, they are apt to be felt as impoverishment.

> Silent rushes the swift Lord
> Through ruined systems still restored,
> Broadsowing, bleak and void to bless,
> Plants with worlds the wilderness;
> Waters with tears of ancient sorrow
> Apples of Eden ripe to-morrow.
> House and tenant go to ground,
> Lost in God, in Godhead found.
>   [*EW* 9:158]

> There is no virtue which is final; all are initial. The virtues of society are vices of the saint. The terror of reform is the discovery that we must cast away our virtues, or what we have always esteemed such, into the same pit that has consumed our grosser vices. [*EW* 2:187]

These two passages (the conclusion to "Threnody" and an excerpt from "Circles") are exercises in aphoristic reiteration and antithesis in which the prose sentence is equivalent to the poetic line unit or couplet: for example,

> There is no virtue which is final
> all are initial.
> The virtues of society
> are the vices of the saint.

But the verse lacks the rhythmic variety and linguistic density of the prose (note the redundancy of "rushes" and "swift," "bleak and void"), so that quite apart from the additional contrast in respect to orthodoxy of sentiment, the verse reads like mere rationalization. "The simply balanced couplings," as Porter says, "programmatically misrepresent the intractable density of experience."[18] Here and elsewhere Emerson seems to have been seduced by an antiquated notion that couplet rhyme corresponds to the universal order of things.[19]

To hold this unequivocally against the poem, however, would be an unfair denial of its donnée. For the poem (an elegy for Emerson's son) seeks precisely to move from the intractable density of experience into [DIFFICULT TO MOLD, SIMBOON] the realm of the ideal. If this is the poem's limitation, it is also the chief source of interest. Although the quoted lines are prosodically and syntactically humdrum, the passage is nonetheless of the greatest psychological interest (and complexity) as a working out of the need to displace the particulars of actuality with a consoling abstraction that will balance the father's desire for a personalized, parenting God image against the seer's rigorous refusal to see the divine as anything other than an inherent cosmic principle (a "sublime It," as Emerson once said), which in turn was likely a projection of Emerson's impulse to depersonalize relationships of all sorts. Even the resultant myth per se is not so simple as it seems, the flat assertiveness of the finale being qualified by the ambiguity of passive versus active (the "swift Lord" blesses like a patriarchal figure but is also passively "restored," like an indwelling principle of natural order) and by the status of these lines as dramatic projection (the voice of the "deep Heart"). In this context, the apparently procrustean syntax and prosody should be seen not simply as superimposed formulas but as part of a dramatic attempt to give meaning to experience by ritualizing, despite an awareness of the difficulty of finding anything meaningful in it.

"Threnody" haters, mindful of the contrast to more full-blooded Romantic elegies like Whitman's "When Lilacs Last in the Dooryard Bloom'd," may read the previous paragraph as an apology for euphemism. Is not, after all, the retreat to idealizing abstraction the quintessence of what was wrong with mid-nineteenth-century New England verse? Well, yes and no. Yes, it can lead to a deadening of the creative faculties, and, like any cultural given, it places a limit on what those faculties can hope to accomplish. Yet it also makes possible some types of creative achievement that might not otherwise have come into being.

In order to appreciate this fully, we need to turn to Emily Dickinson, the only New England premodern whose poetry needs no defense. However much or little she may have been influenced by Emerson, it is clear that she too favors an epigrammatic mode of expression in which the couplet is the primary unit of meaning and images are intellectualized into abstractions.[20] Her poetic "scenes," as Robert Weisbuch points out, provide typically not a mimesis so much as an analogy of experience; not "my life and environment in November" but the "lower meters of the Year" (*DP* 1115); not "my fearful anticipation of death" but a hypothetical scenario of having been cut off from life by an intrusive fly or of death personified as a gentleman caller (*DP* 465, 712).[21] The "habitual motion" of her revisions, and indeed of her whole poetic career, is, as David Porter shows, a process of "abstracting away from perceived reality," sometimes to the point of unintelligibility.[22] "Acres of Masts" becomes "Dome of Abyss" (*DP* 291); "in her Castle above them" becomes "in the Crescent above them" (*DP* 216), and so forth. A poem about a hummingbird be-

comes a poem about disoriented perceptions occasioned by a hummingbird. Here is the first version:

> Within my Garden, rides a Bird
> Upon a single Wheel –
> Whose spokes a dizzy Music make
> As 'twere a traveling Mill –
>
> He never stops, but slackens
> Above the Ripest Rose –
> Partakes without alighting
> And praises as he goes,
>
> Till every spice is tasted –
> And then his Fairy Gig
> Reels in remoter atmospheres –
> And I rejoin my Dog,
>
> and He and I, perplex us
> If positive, 'twere we –
> Or bore the Garden in the Brain
> This Curiosity –
>
> But He, the best Logician,
> Refers my clumsy eye –
> To just vibrating Blossoms!
> An Exquisite Reply!
>
> [DP 500, ca. 1862]

Here is the second version:

> A Route of Evanescence
> With a revolving Wheel –
> A Resonance of Emerald –
> A Rush of Cochineal –
> And every Blossom on the Bush
> Adjusts its tumbled Head –
> The mail from Tunis, probably,
> An easy Morning's Ride –
>
> [DP 1463, ca. 1879]

The second version clearly pleased Dickinson: She sent it to at least five
correspondents, including her "preceptor," Thomas Wentworth Higginson. Gone is the skeletal narrative; gone is the dramatic situation, the
trace of any originating event; gone is the dog; gone is the lyric speaker.
What was formerly a poem about the response of speaker to bird is converted into a riddle poem that in effect makes the theme of the first (the
perplexity and slow realization caused by the hummingbird's dartings)
the central and only subject. The revisionary process echoes, perhaps coincidentally, Dickinson's biographical withdrawal. In a famous oblique

response to Higginson's request to know her better personally, Dickinson praised the epistolary medium over personal intercourse: "A Letter always feels to me like immortality because it is the mind alone without corporeal friend" (DL 2:460). This could have been a description of her philosophy of revision.

Dickinson's increasing obliquity, whereby ego and experience become displaced by algebraic abstraction, is very close to the trait most often held against Emerson and accounts for how a poem with so characteristically Dickinsonian a phrase as "to comprehend a nectar" could have been mistaken for his.[23] This phrase simply improves on Emerson by combining the method of abstraction ("plants with *worlds*") with metonymy ("bleak and void to *bless*") to achieve the composite effect of "comprehend." The devices of metonymy and abstraction are in either case the keys to the verbal art here. It is true only in a relative sense to say that Emerson's poetic style is "deprived of life" whereas Dickinson makes literary capital out of her deprivations. Both, in fact, are strategies of "impoverishment," although Emerson's is less interesting, being less totally resourceful and less heterodox.

Dickinson's obliquity has been variously explained on contextual grounds. The two best lines of speculation, perhaps, are the feminist and the religiocentric. A brief discussion will set the stage for a further exegesis of Dickinson's relation to Emerson – and their contemporaries.

Feminist critics have been inclined to read Dickinson's indirectness as part of an "aesthetics of renunciation," the mode of self-effacing assertiveness that represented the superior nineteenth-century woman poet's mingled accommodation and defiance of the constraints placed on women writers by the patriarchal culture they inhabited.[24] From this perspective, the poetics of Whitman and Dickinson, who are inevitably paired as the two giants of nineteenth-century American protomodernism, appear to be characteristic male and female reaction formations, he leaning toward a naked and total disclosure, she toward an armored and total self-concealment.[25] According to the older way of explaining Dickinson's sensibility in terms of her theological culture, the gap that increasingly opens up between the referent and the riddlesome, abstract discourse is symptomatic of her ambivalence toward the system of values in which she was nurtured, which she drew upon for metaphors and perhaps yearned to accept but ultimately could not. Both lines of explanation can be illustrated by Dickinson's "bridal" poems, in which she claims the "Right of the White Election" (DP 528). Sandra Gilbert and Susan Gubar see these poems as a verbal enactment of the role that Dickinson assumes in life, the role of sequestered Victorian angel, a role that amounted at once to ritual submission to patriarchal dictate and, by the same token, to a position from which she could feel authorized to exercise her poetic powers with impunity. From the religiocentric perspective, Dickinson's bridal role was a means of overcoming the guilt impressed upon her by the Calvinist system that she could not accept, through a strategy of asserting her innocence and spiritual authority in emblems reserved for the elect. The two lines of speculation ultimately conflict, not only over the question of whether Dickinson was more interested in her soul's fate or her situation as a woman but also over the status of her poetry as covert confession, feminist criticism tending to read the poems expressively rather than thematically. The explanations share, however, a reading of Dickinson as a poet driven into hiding by an ambivalence toward cultural norms that prompted her to adopt a reserved, elliptical, indirect mode of expression. Each line of explanation represents her (convincingly, to my mind) as appropriating the terms of an orthodoxy identified as masculine to construct her own "anti-allegory" (Robert Weisbuch's useful term) in which her sense of the gap between signifier and signified becomes the basis for decentered use of key words and images (such as "bride" and "white") as the x's and y's of an algebra of her own. Freed from the prison of referentiality, she could then "use metaphoric language without anxiety."[26] Well, *almost* freed. Dickinson's recentering project still involves a sort of bondage to the frames of reference that she undermines. The awareness of logocentrism, as Jacques Derrida points out, does not in itself permit escape. On the contrary, as its deconstructors we are also its legatees and, in a sense, its prisoners.[27]

The special interest of this analysis of Dickinson's situation, for our present purposes, is its applicability as a key to the situation of premodern New England poetry in general, men's as well as women's. This claim will initially sound strange, since we are accustomed to conceiving of the Schoolroom Poets as Dickinson's intellectual opposites. That is partly true, but by no means altogether so. We know that Dickinson cheerfully read Longfellow and Lowell. More important, the other poets of our period, not only the Emersons but also the more capable of the middlebrow poets, seem to have been stimulated by equivalents of the two conditions that Dickinson scholars have seen as prompting her unique achievements.[28]

Consider first the easier case of the convention that poems shall reinforce religious and moral order. This stipulation imposed a grid on experience that regularly produced, not just in Dickinson but in all poets of any ability, a tension between the bent of private passion and the norms that one was expected to accept and to use one's art to uphold. We know that Longfellow, like Tennyson, struggled for a long time with Wertheresque tendencies before he was able to regulate his pulse as a matter of course to the platitudes of "Psalm of Life," one of Victorian America's favorite American lyrics:

Tell me not, in mournful numbers,
  Life is but an empty dream! –
For the soul is dead that slumbers,
  And things are not what they seem.

Life is real! Life is earnest!
  And the grave is not its goal;
Dust thou art, to dust returnest,
  Was not spoken of the soul.
                [*LW* 1:19]

And so on. This hymn is certainly much inferior to Dickinson's brand of hymnody: Its language is insipid; its tone, relentlessly univocal. But note the parallels. Each poet proceeds by a strategy of displacement of experience by abstraction, and in each case the displacement involves rejection of "orthodoxy." Longfellow's poem is significantly subtitled "What the Heart of the Young Man Said to the Psalmist." As such it too is an irreverent response to authority. Beyond that, bringing the two poets even closer, the response is really a disguised appropriation of authority as a vehicle for externalizing what we know to have been Longfellow's own doubts and thus presenting what began as inner drama as a kind of doctrinal controversy between youth and authority. The New Englanders reversed Yeats's famous dictum: Their poetry was made by turning the quarrel with themselves into rhetoric.

In Longfellow's case, the debate is of course a setup. He could count on his readers to side with the youth's view (hence the poem's antiauthoritarianism is only nominal). Yet the point in question was not a nonissue. In fact, the question of the importance of life relative to the afterlife was a major point of dispute – between Unitarian and orthodox Congregationalists, for example – and from this vantage point Longfellow, the son of an officer of the American Unitarian Association, begins to look like an embattled Unitarian advocate. Above and beyond any sectarian squabble, Longfellow's poem can be seen as a timely effort to allay the widespread malaise felt by the more serious-minded in a rapidly secularizing country where the demands of "life" seemed increasingly central when measured by the yardstick of one's pious ancestors.

Longfellow's swerve away from experience to abstraction is executed for the sake of bonding speaker to reader in a creedal affirmation that will be clear and publicly acceptable, and in this sense Longfellow remains Dickinson's opposite. We need simply recognize a continuum. The middle ground is held by such poets as the Transcendentalists Very and Emerson, who write in the awareness of entertaining unpalatable dissents from orthodoxy and use art as much for provocation as for communication. Very's impersonations of divinity, thinly disguised as dramatic monologues, are a male equivalent of Dickinson's claims to transcendence in such poems as "Title divine – wife is mine!" (*DP* 1072)

That Dickinson's ambivalence toward religious and moral orthodoxy shares something with the other poets of the period is relatively easy to show. Her status as serious woman artist, in what Suzanne Juhasz describes as the double bind of being required to keep silent yet impelled to speak out, would seem to differentiate her more sharply.[29] Here, however, we must take account of the analogous if less severe double bind imposed upon all poets – indeed all serious creative writers – during the period. The American writer's position, as described in the preceding two chapters, was comparable to the predicament that feminist scholars have perceived in Dickinson and her sisters. The American writer was both marginalized and pedestalized – both useless (as measured by the materialistic scale of priorities in a developing nation) and, at the same time, a national necessity (as the symptom of complete cultural emergence). The writer was charged with the responsibility of finding an American voice for a still colonialized culture not disposed to recognize or value that voice – a problem especially oppressive for the poet, given the fact that the British poetic tradition was more imposing than that of the novel. The American writer was charged with the mission of developing his or her talent from a position of social marginality that was supposed, nonetheless, to express itself not as bohemianism but, rather, as an articulation of national values. The New England writer was further enjoined to express the dictates of individual conscience but, somehow in the process, to reinforce the communal consensus – an uneasy double mandate even in Puritan times and rendered more uneasy with the advent of Romanticism.[30]

"Psalm of Life" shows signs of such stresses. As a call to the strenuous, achieving life, this poem accepts the terms of the conventional valuation of business over art, repudiating what the poet would perhaps rather have written ("mournful numbers") and yet also achieving a sort of control over philistinism by its seizure of the position of articulator, of trumpet, of Scripture – of having rewritten a chapter of the Bible for nineteenth-century America.[31] Longfellow defers, denies himself, and triumphs through didacticism.

But we have lingered too long on a mediocre poem. A better example of such defensive-aggressive seizure of control is Emerson's poem "The Problem." This poem is a kind of public justification of the speaker's refusal to be a clergyman – the self-unfrocked Emerson's apologia.

> I like a church; I like a cowl;
> I love a prophet of the soul,
> And on my heart monastic aisles

> Fall like sweet strains, or pensive smiles;
> Yet not for all his faith can see
> Would I that cowled churchman be.
>
> [EW 9:6]

The poem starts and ends with this same assertion, the central part consisting of a series of reflections designed to make sense of the paradox by demonstrating in effect that Christianity affords only one manifestation of the world soul whose workings the speaker prefers to contemplate in their totality. But note how carefully the dissenting, individualistic element is kept in check. Unlike "Threnody," "The Problem" does not seek to resolve itself. On the contrary, matters are complicated by the fact that after what appears to be a full explanation supplied by the main body, the poem ends simply by repeating the initial formulation of the problem, as if the speaker were still back at square one.[32] Emerson refuses to draw the "logical" conclusion – that the poet's vision is more comprehensive than the priest's. Such a denouement would seem logical, given the main argument. Yet the text refuses to proclaim the QED of the poet's triumph. This silence seems all the odder because the speaker has caricatured his opposition by imaging the preacher in what, for Emerson's post-Puritan audience, would have seemed outrageously medieval terms: "monastic," a "cowled churchman." Yet the silence and the medievalization actually go together. Both are symptoms of a reluctance to attack too directly, because the clerical alternative still holds the speaker's imagination. So he engages not the direct object of his fascination but a more vulnerable surrogate; he claims no victory; and in fact he winds up presenting the poetic vision of the world soul as an ecumenicalization of the bibliocentric view he has seemingly put behind him:

> Ever the fiery Pentecost
> Girds with one flame the countless host,
> Trances the heart through chanting choirs
> And through the priest the mind inspires.
>
> [EW 9:8]

In this summation, the action of the Neoplatonic world soul is partially refamiliarized in Christian terms as a "pentecost" mediated by choir and clerisy.[33] In claiming poetic independence in the name of a nonsectarian spirit, the speaker establishes himself as its priest. Emerson takes greater risks than Longfellow (e.g., the pantheistic "Out from the heart of nature rolled / The burdens of the Bible old"), but the poet is allowed to fulfill himself – as usual for Emerson – only as priest. He who knows himself to be marginal (like Emerson, in his dissent from professional and theological orthodoxy) protects himself from adversaries both without and within by putting on the armor of respectability.

The double bind imposed on Emerson and Longfellow – (1) Be independent, but (2) Conform – is clearly not so severe as the one that feminist critics have discerned in the period's women writers, nor do Emerson and Longfellow approach the degree of originality within traditional prosody with which Dickinson exploits her medium. Like her work, however, the Emerson and Longfellow poems turn out to be provocatively complicated forms of interplay between two types of discourse: the language of the socially proper, and the language of the disaffected sensibility that must, however, fulfill itself by speaking in the first mode in such a way as to assert control over it. Viewed thus, with Dickinson's more spectacular and conflicted brand of mingled deviance and deference in mind, conservative New England poetics starts to look like a more complex affair than we ordinarily suppose. In the next section I shall try to elaborate this proposition by charting four specific aesthetically fruitful strategies typical of that poetics, continuing the method of juxtaposing Dickinson with her New England contemporaries and precursors.

II

The first and simplest of these four strategies might be called the romance of repression. Dickinson's poetry shows a perennial interest in the idea of disciplined renunciation, either for its pathos ("Renunciation – is a piercing Virtue –" [*DP* 745]) or for its grandeur ("The Soul's Superior instants / Occur to Her – alone –" [*DP* 306]). In either case, the implied self-image is that of infinite passion concealed beneath innocuous surface:

> On my volcano grows the Grass
> A meditative spot –
> An acre for a Bird to choose
> Would be the General thought –
>
> How red the Fire rocks below –
> How insecure the sod
> Did I disclose
> Would populate with awe my solitude.
> [*DP* 1677]

Adrienne Rich is undoubtedly right in referring Dickinson's motif of "Vesuvius at Home" (*DP* 1705) to her confinement as woman of genius.[34] But the motif also happens to be the common property of New England tradition. A version of it is already a staple, at the start of the period, in the anxiety registered by Neoclassical poetry at the prospect of a loss of mastery over personal and social passion.[35] Those prone to such excess were no exceptions, and Robert Treat Paine's sprightly Harvard Phi Beta Kappa poem of 1797, *The Ruling Passion,* makes a good exhibit here:

Like Egypt's gods, man's various passions sway;
Some prowl the earth, and some ascend the day;
This charms the fancy, that the palate feasts:
A motley Pantheon of birds and beasts!
Were the wild brood, who dwell in glade and brake,
Some kindred character of man to take;
In the base jackall's, or gay leopard's mien,
The servile pimp, or gay coquette, were seen;
The patient camel, long inured to dine
But once a fortnight, would a poet shine;
The stag, a cit, with antlered brows content;
The rake, a pointer, always on the scent;
The snake, a statesman; and the wit, a gnat;
The ass, an alderman; the scold, a cat.
. . . .

Life is a print-shop, where the eye may trace
A different outline, marked in every face;
From chiefs, who laurels reap in fields of blood,
Down to the hind, who tills those fields for food;
. . . .

From ink's retailers, perched in garret high,
Cobwebbed around with many a mouldy lie;
Down to the pauper's brat, who, luckless wight!
Deep in the cellar first received the light;
And, all impelled, as various passions move,
To write, to starve, to conquer, or to love![36]

Paine's geniality, and his readiness to include his own type in the menagerie, make this excerpt more interesting than the usual Federalist depictions of the potential for chaos in human nature and the body politic. Paine relishes the panorama he bestializes and seeks to regulate by reducing it to intellectual and prosodic order. The paradox heightens as Paine goes on to anatomize the various figures in his bestiary, ending with a sketch of the poet in propria persona ("Lured by [Poesy's] charms, I left, in passioned hope, / My Watt's Logick for the page of Pope" [p. 185]), followed by a lament for the lack of patronage of the arts in young America. "Ruling passion" now becomes laudable spirit of enterprise, and the poem is transformed ingenuously into an advertising gimmick. The poem, then, turns out to be an indulgence and defense of the excess that it purports to regulate through its strictures, an indulgence that is legitimated not so much by the direct pitch for sympathy near the end but by the strategy of regulation, its riotous, exuberant panorama rendered in austere syntax and prosody. The fun of the piece consists in ventilating one's high-spiritedness under the guise of preserving law and order.

Once the Romantic movement starts to lyricize New England poetry, the need for regulation seems less axiomatic, the question of how passion is to fulfill itself within the givens of restraint becomes more urgent, and the better poems on this theme become more complex. If New England never produced a Byron, it was not for lack of responsiveness even to the forbiddenness of the allure,[37] as the following remarkable untitled poem by Ellen Hooper suggests:

> Better a sin which purposed wrong to none
> Than this still wintry coldness at the heart,
> A penance might be borne for evil done
> And tears of grief and love might ease the smart.
> But this self-satisfied and cold respect
> To virtue which must be its own reward,
> Heaven keep us through this danger still alive,
> Lead us not into greatness, heart-abhorred –
>
> Oh God, who framed this stern New-England land,
> Its clear cold waters, and its clear, cold soul,
> Thou givest tropic climes and youthful hearts
> Thou weighest spirits and dost all control –
> Teach me to wait for all – to bear the fault
> That most I hate because it is my own,
> And if I fail through foul conceit of good,
> Let me sin deep so I may cast no stone.[38]

To this Romantic sensibility, the restraints invoked by the Federalist poets as a necessary corrective have become so stultifyingly internalized as to create the reverse problem. Self-shackled by its pattern of two symmetrical stanzas of measured blank verse, the poem cries for release from formula – though at the same time rather pathetically clinging to its prison bars: The speaker requires immediate release, yet prays for patience; she shrinks from "virtue" and "greatness" but also from imagining more than an innocuous satanism ("a sin which purposed wrong to none"). These provocative self-divisions are such as to make one wager that the author, a minor Transcendentalist, is unlikely to become another Whitman (the poet of evil as well as good); yet they forecast the even more conflicted approach that Dickinson uses in her poems of renunciation:

> I cannot live with You –
> It would be Life –
> And Life is over there –
> Behind the Shelf
>
> . . . .
>
> Nor could I rise – with You –
> Because Your Face

Would put out Jesus' –
That New Grace

. . . .

And were You – saved –
And I – condemned to be
Where You were not –
That self – were Hell to Me –

So We must meet apart –
You there – I – here –
With just the Door ajar
That Oceans are – and Prayer –
And that White Sustenance –
Despair –

[*DP* 649]

As in Hooper and Paine, the strategy is to declare allegiance to the passion one represses. To say that life with the beloved must be declined because it would be the opposite of the orthodox definition of life (immortality, "Behind the Shelf") is already to have blasphemed. What separates Dickinson from the other two is the speaker's recognition of the impossibility of the stance on which she insists. The speaker follows through the renunciation act to the end, aware all the time that she is ineligible for the payoff. She will not rise with the beloved; she cannot be saved; so the "white sustenance" of nunhood equals despair, not heavenly bridal. Or, such bridal *is* despair. Like Hooper, Dickinson uses the Transcendentalist method of taking as the coordinates of one's argument the Platonized terms of received orthodoxy (e.g., heaven and hell as states of the soul rather than as supernatural realms) but inverts this method more thoroughly.[39] Hooper would like to believe that sin done for the sake of self-reliance would not be sin after all but only sin in quotation marks. Dickinson makes clear that such an escape is impossible so long as one remains theologocentric. Or, to be more exact, because her speaker's extrication from the norms through her capacity for detached understanding of her terms of confinement is more complete than Hooper's, her sense of entrapment is more total.

In these poems by Hooper and Dickinson, the mental set that Duffey calls "the coherence" can be seen as having served as a creative irritant of a high order by reason of its very constrictedness. That is not to say, however, that in order to qualify as interesting, the romance of repression needs to become self-consciously religious or philosophical. Such is by no means the case with some of its most interesting exemplars, of whom the most accomplished is Frederick Goddard Tuckerman.

His heart was in his garden; but his brain
Wandered at will among the fiery stars.

Bards, heroes, prophets, Homers, Hamilcars,
With many angels stood, his eye to gain;
The devils, too, were his familiars:
And yet the cunning florist held his eyes
Close to the ground, a tulip bulb his prize,
And talked of tan and bonedust, cutworms, grubs,
As though all Nature held no higher strain;
Or, if he spoke of art, he made the theme
Flow through boxborders, turf, and flower tubs
Or, like a garden engine's, steered the stream,
Now sprouted rainbows to the silent skies,
Now kept it flat and raked the walls and shrubs.[40]

This masterful sonnet by the "other" nineteenth-century literary recluse of the Connecticut Valley is an ars poetica. "If he spoke of art," it was, as here, generally through such "innocuous" metaphors as gardening. The florist-sonneteer tends his prosody as he tends his boxbushes. Through self-restriction, elected, we surmise, through some mixture of taste and self-therapy, the gardener establishes the boundaries within which he can feel safe – Dickinson fashion – to reveal to the reader, if not to his neighbors, the inner life that blossoms gorgeously and grotesquely under this kind of nurture: his devils, angels, "bards, heroes, prophets, Homers, Hamilcars." Tuckerman is less easy to integrate into generalizations about the "New England mind" than Dickinson, whose poetry is more doctrinal and whose withdrawal into reclusiveness less easily reducible to the theory of a particular life trauma; but the Tuckerman pattern of passion repressed by the dual constraints of prosodic austerity and some internalized code of values, yet at the same time expressing itself all the more poignantly through that act of repression, puts him decisively in the regional mainstream.[41]

A second and related strategy used in many of the better poems of "the coherence" might be called the theme of the absent center. A good example is Whittier's "Telling the Bees," a narrative in fourteen balladlike stanzas in which the speaker slowly and deliberately describes his return after a month's absence to the farm of his beloved to hear the hired girl telling the bees of a death in the house (to keep them, according to local superstition, from leaving):

Then I said to myself, "My Mary weeps
    For the dead to-day:
Haply her blind old grandsire sleeps
    The fret and the pain of his age away."

But her dog whined low; on the doorway sill,
    With cane to his chin,
The old man sat; and the chore-girl still
    Sung to the bees stealing out and in.

> And the song she was singing ever since
>   In my ear sounds on: –
> "Stay at home, pretty bees, fly not hence!
> "Mistress Mary is dead and gone!"
>
> [*WW* 1:188]

End of poem. What raises it above sentimentality is that the experience the poem is really about is never disclosed. The speaker's tone is scrupulously reportorial, lingering in the preceding stanzas almost intolerably on all the preliminary details, risking the same sort of parody that Lewis Carroll made of Wordsworth's "Resolution and Independence." The impact of the death on the speaker is barely hinted at, and then only by the indirection "in my ear sounds on," which tells us that the narrative as a whole – in its odd quietness – registers the impact. The speaker tells his slowly unfolding story because he has to. But because of the way he tells it, the poem leaves us guessing whether his method of retrospection leading only to the threshold of the realization implies that he has not yet fully come to terms with what has happened to him, that he cannot bear to confront the experience again now that it is over, or some other alternative. What does the hired girl feel as she chants to the bees? Just as mysterious, for all its naïveté, is the speaker's chant to us.

The obvious link between the romance of repression and the poem of the absent center is fear of experience, such as seems, incidentally, to have characterized the real-life Whittier's behavior with the many women who were sexually attracted to him.[42] (Might the flesh-and-blood Whittier have been actually somewhat relieved by the death of his love?) A number of his New England contemporaries, including Whittier himself, write about the experience of not being able to bear too much reality. "I cannot rid the thought nor hold it close," says Tuckerman's speaker about the image of a mysterious man in "an upper chamber in a darkened house," clearly a self-image of some kind – the madman in the attic, as it were. Do not read to me "from the grand old masters," says the speaker of Longfellow's "The Day Is Done." I'm tired. Read from some humbler poet that will soothe me. "Rock me to sleep, mother, – rock me to sleep!" cries the speaker of Elizabeth Akers Allen's poem: "Make me a child again just for to-night!" Never let it be said, however, that such regressiveness, perhaps justly regarded as the great stigma of genteel traditionalism, failed to make great poetry. If the case of Whittier is not convincing, try Dickinson's

> Before I got my eye put out
> I liked as well to see –
> As other Creatures, that have Eyes
> And know no other way –
>
> But were it told to me – Today –
> That I might have the sky

For mine – I tell you that my Heart
Would split, for size of me –

The Meadows – mine –
The Mountains – mine –
All Forests – Stintless Stars –
As much of Noon as I could take
Between my finite eyes –

The Motions of the Dipping Birds –
The Morning's Amber Road –
For mine – to look at when I liked –
The News would strike me dead –

So safer – Guess – with just my soul
Upon the Window pane –
Where other Creatures put their eyes –
Incautious – of the Sun –

[DP 327]

This poem starts where Whittier's leaves off, in that it is about something like the same emotional condition in which Whittier's narrative is told. A nameless trauma (the absent center) has prompted a retreat from direct participation in the world of the senses. What saves the poem from the impression of a Longfellow or Allen-like failure of nerve is the aggressiveness of the retreat that it announces. The poem recalls Dickinson's answer to Higginson's query as to whether she found her sheltered life boring: "I never thought of conceiving that I could ever have the slightest approach to such a want in all future time" (DL 2:474). The juxtaposition of that level of commitment with the equally strong and antithetical sense of loss differentiates the poem from the standard permutations of the retreat from experience. The retreat, as dramatized here, is neither facile nor accepted simply as retreat.

This and a number of other poems of the absent center could be seen as arising from a specifically feminist consciousness. Take the following lyric by Frances Osgood:

A cold, calm star look'd out of heaven,
   And smiled upon a tranquil lake,
Where, pure as angel's dream at even,
   A Lily lay but half awake.

The flower felt that fatal smile
   And lowlier bow'd her conscious head;
"Why does he gaze on me the while?"
   The light, deluded Lily said.

Poor dreaming flower! – too soon beguiled,
   She cast nor thought nor look elsewhere,
Else she had known the star but smiled
   To see himself reflected there.

A number of Osgood's better poems (which are better than most scholars realize) present, as here, a speaker contemplating with demure sarcasm a less cautious sister's vulnerability to love.[43] They are poems about passion from which the passion has been withheld. In this way, more obtrusively than in Dickinson, they become feminist fables, poems whose coolness in no sense amounts to simple evasion but to necessary self-defense. A defense, interestingly, that involves the productive reuse of the tactics of the exploiter. The speaker makes herself cold like the masculine star, but hers is the cold light of awareness rather than the sterility of narcissism. Here Osgood goes farther than Dickinson, who never ceases to be fascinated by the metaphor of the *solsequim,* the daisy charmed by the sun.

ABSENT-CENTER

Yet the absent-center poem has nothing inevitably to do with sexual politics. More often it involves the more general strategy of contemplating or rationalizing the elusiveness or loss of some ideal from a present position of spiritual barrenness. Such is the case with a number of Emerson's major poems: "Blight," "Forerunners," "Days," "Terminus" – even "Brahma," to an extent. So too Christopher Cranch's "Enosis" ("We are columns left alone, / Of a temple once complete") and Longfellow's "Mezzo Cammin," his rigorous self-appraisal at age thirty-five. So, too, many of Dickinson's "poems of aftermath," which some of her best critics see as her most distinctive mode, where the poem (as in the case discussed above) takes rise from the state that follows a peak experience, pleasurable or painful, rather than the experience of the experience.[44]

The phenomenon of an absent center arising from the sense of aftermath or fulfillment not yet reached might seem to be a distinctively Romantic phenomenon, as Romantic as Wordsworth's Immortality Ode (the Romantic poem of aftermath par excellence, in the eyes of Victorian Anglo-America) or Blake's *Marriage of Heaven and Hell* (the first great British Romantic poem of anticipation). The Romantic tendency to see fulfillment either as something vanished or as something yet to be grasped has, however, an indigenous parallel in the rhetoric of the jeremiad, which represents the present moment as a nadir of iniquity, seeing the spiritual golden age both as prior and as prospective. Even secularized sophisticates reverted throughout our period, in crisis situations, to what might loosely be called a typological equation of past and future utopias set in contrast to an empty or unworthy present. Toward the end of our period, we see this especially in the resurgent neopilgrimism of New England abolitionist rhetoric such as Lowell's Yankee version of Tennyson's "Locksley Hall":

> New occasions teach new duties; Time makes ancient good uncouth;
> They must upward still, and onward, who would keep abreast of
>   Truth;
> Lo, before us gleam her camp-fires! we ourselves must Pilgrims be,

Launch our Mayflower, and steer boldly through the desperate winter
 sea,
Nor attempt the Future's portal with the Past's blood-rusted key.

[*LoW* 7:184]

A curious but typical doublethink: The present stands indicted for its
bondage to the past, yet it may save itself by building a utopia based on a
vision from the past.

The rhetoric of the 1850s, as we saw from the comparison of Thoreau
and Ames in Chapter 4, has a precedent in early national fears of republican degeneracy, which also invoke a heroic past as a future pattern for
an erring present. Among poetic examples of the late eighteenth century,
certainly the most engaging, if not the most typical, is Joel Barlow's
Hasty Pudding. This mini–mock-epic celebration of the recipe, and rituals
of consumption, of a favorite New England dish is only superficially an
apolitical catharsis of expatriate nostalgia.[45] As the dedication indicates,
"A simplicity in diet, whether it be considered with reference to the happiness of individuals or the prosperity of a nation, is of more consequence
than we are apt to imagine." Hence the poem's "programmatic" purpose:
to combat the "vicious habits" of oversophisticated appetite with the
standards of pristine, rural New England, symbolized by the hasty pudding, which Barlow claims is rightly named and rightly made there as in
no other region. The poem becomes increasingly a celebration of lost   HASTY PUDDING
Yankee farm life, culminating in a seriocomic apostrophe to the family
cow ("How oft thy teats these pious hands have prest!"). Although the
experience that ostensibly gave rise to the poem was the speaker's delight
at having unexpectedly found his favorite dish in Savoy after having "long
in vain" "wandered up and down," the poem as it actually takes shape is
an attempt to revive a culture of the past as a model for the culture of the
future, an attempt that the speaker simultaneously believes in and recognizes the quixoticism of through the mock-heroics, which are, among
other things, the speaker's way of making public his awareness of the
idiosyncrasy of his personal attachment to his subject.[46] The device of
invoking a remembered happiness to fill a present emptiness later becomes a staple of Romantic regionalism in all genres, the poetic high-
water mark being Whittier's *Snow-Bound*. This "idyll" is the comic opposite of the Whittier poem with which I began this section, a poem in
which the lost past seems retrievable after all. Yet *Snow-Bound,* too, is
really a poem of the absent center, in which the enclosure of the household as a snug unit by the threatening yet protective storm turns out to
be not just a pleasant memory but also an implied metaphor for the white
magic of the poem itself, which holds up "these Flemish pictures of old
days" as a way to warm one's fireside against the storm of time, "the
restless sands' incessant fall" (*WW* 2:139, 158). Again the strategy of

using the literal level of memory as a shield against the inner blankness is employed.[47]

Probably the most common form taken by the impulse to idealize that underlies both Whittier poems is the procedure, ultimately based on the seventeenth-century meditative lyric, of moving in a two- or three-stage sequence from a concrete, present dramatic situation to a consolatory or at least conclusive ethical reflection. This is our third motif. It is too well known to need extensive definition. The poet sees a flower blooming in the woods, wonders why that fragrance is being wasted on the desert air, realizes that "beauty is its own excuse for being" (Emerson's "The Rhodora"). The poet sees a bird in flight and from its instinctive sureness concludes that "in the long way that I must tread alone," God "will lead my steps aright" (Bryant, "To a Waterfowl"). The poet calls his beloved's attention to a "busy fly . . . only born to die" and converts it into an emblem of the frivolity that she should avoid by ceasing to flirt and solemnizing their relation in wedlock (Dwight's "A Song"). Image, idea. Image, idea. Image, idea. The basic game is the game of correspondential vision in the service of coherence. Every time the poet finds meaning in the flower, everyone's trust in an orderly cosmos is reinforced. Many skillful but undistinguished period poems consist of such tours de force, like the three just cited. Such poems fall under George Orwell's rubric of "good bad poetry" – "a graceful movement to the obvious."[48] The game allows, however, for more complicated permutations. One is to replicate the complexity of the situation on the level of the ethical statement, so that one's closure avoids closure. For example, Dickinson's

> A spider sewed at Night
> Without a Light
> Upon an Arc of White.
>
> If Ruff it was of Dame
> Or Shroud of Gnome
> Himself himself inform.
>
> Of Immortality
> His Strategy
> Was Physiognomy.
>   [DP 1138]

The issue, as usual, is the meaning of the image. The meaning, as usual (cf. Bryant and Dwight) has to do with immortality. (Dickinson was entirely typical of her age in regarding this as "the Flood subject," DL 2:454.) The spider's action, as usual for a Protestant meditation on the insect kingdom, is an exemplum that teaches something about immortality. Even the chief lesson seemingly taught is predictable enough: divine inscrutability. One reading, at any rate, would be that the juxtaposition of stanzas two and three suggests that the spider's nondisclosure of intent ("Himself himself inform") is symbolic ("physiognomy") of the divine design – which would be to say nothing more than that God moves in a mysterious way his wonders to perform. What is not so usual is that the poem refuses to demystify that mysteriousness by rendering the proposition explicitly or by allowing it to stand as the only possible inference. An equally plausible interpretation would be that the spider's assiduous sewing in the dark images the strategy that the soul must employ in order to attain immortality. And this, in turn, raises the unanswered question of whether, under the terms of this poem, immortality is discovered or constructed. Dickinson thereby doubles the metaphor in the manner of its unfolding, as Oliver Wendell Holmes failed to do in his better-known poem about unceasing spiritual progress toward a mysterious end, "The Chambered Nautilus." The neatness of Holmes's allegory of the soul as shell-voyager, and especially the sculpted peroration of the last stanza ("Build thee more stately mansions, O my soul"), makes a self-contradiction as blatant as the "O daring joy, but safe!" at the end of Whitman's "Passage to India."[49] On the other hand, the same explicit structuring is used to good effect in Longfellow's "Seaweed," which equates what is washed up on the beach with the "fragment of a song" culled by the poet from the storms of experience and preserved in books "like hoarded / Household words" (*LW* 1:292). Here a doggedly symmetrical "as . . . so" formula (four self-contained stanzas apiece) opens up the poem by underscoring the irony of the packaging process being described. The poem makes the same acknowledgment as Emerson's "The Poet": Poetry was written before time was, and when we try to record it, all we set down is fragments. Emerson's essay registers this through fragmented rhetoric; Longfellow's poems, through a style that calls attention to the futility of their own attempt to present the fragmentary as a whole. Longfellow might even be credited with a certain Melvillian cat-and-mouse surreptitiousness here, with using the domestic simile of hoarded household words to suggest to the more discerning reader an awareness of the futility of the way in which Fireside Poets are read: Their poems are lovingly reduced to quotable mottoes to be woven into samplers, but the poets themselves realize how skimpy these fragments really are.

The other principal way in which poets of the period raise the image-to-idea game above the level of facile exercise is to dramatize the movement as a labored process, in which the "anagogical redirection of feelings"[50] from experience to creedal formula is accomplished only with great difficulty. Take, for example, the once anthologized poem "Incomprehensibility of God" (1824), by the obscure Boston poet Eliza Townsend, an awkward but interesting proto-Romantic.[51] "Incomprehensibility" might be described as the closest thing on record to a Unitarian de profundis. Its method, like that of its scriptural sources (Job and the psalms of lamentation), is to scan the creation in the passionate hope of finding not merely God's handiwork but God himself. Alas, everything the speaker sees is "*Thine*, not *Thee*." At the climax, she longs for death rather than more frustration:

> No human eye may look on Thee and live?
> *Welcome the penalty! Let that come now,*
> Which, soon or late, must come. For light like this
> Who would not dare to die?

But with this catharsis her rage abates, and she recoils from her presumption with an abruptness that is also very psalmlike ("Peace! my proud aim," etc.), embracing the good Arminian resolve to "tend / E'en to the perfecting thyself" instead of chasing after the infinite unknowable. The strength of the poem, such as it is, lies in having made these final pieties, which are entirely conventional, seem as hard-won as possible, so that the poem speaks to both the need for submission and the need for heresy.

This I take also to be one of the secrets of the popularity of the period's most successful poet after Longfellow, Lydia Sigourney, the "sweet singer of Hartford," a more interesting writer than one would suppose from the standard critical practice of invoking her (with some justice) as an epitome of religious sentimentalism and stylistic meretriciousness. Nina Baym has made it impossible for us any longer to dismiss out of hand what used to be called the "sentimental novel." Sooner or later we shall have to make a similar accommodation for sentimental poetry.[52] A number of Sigourney's poems start, in any case, with a disturbing and emotionally charged image that cries out for rationalization and moves from this tortuously toward a reassuring close.

> Death walketh in the forest. ["Death among the Trees"]

> This is the parting place; this narrow house,
> With its turf roof and marble door, where none
> Have entered and returned. ["The Tomb"]

> Why is the green earth broken? ["Death of a Young Wife"]

To a modern taste a more engaging effort in this vein is the less pretentious "To a Shred of Linen."[53] The poet-housewife is scandalized to discover a scrap of cloth left behind after cleaning and also immensely relieved

> That no neat lady, train'd in ancient times
> Of pudding-making, and of sampler-work

is at hand to admonish her, "*This comes of reading books,*" or "some spruce beau" to say, "*This comes of writing poetry.*" The rest of the poem represents a sort of playful atonement for the speaker's domestic misdemeanor. "Well – well – / Come forth – offender!" she admonishes the telltale scrap,

> hast thou aught to say?
> Canst thou by merry thought, or quaint conceit,
> Repay this risk, that I have run for thee?

There follows a fantasy of the history of the scrap, from its original state as flax, to its conversion into domestic product, to its recycling into literary article – with a digression about New England housewifery along the way. The latter is not really so digressive, actually, because the aim of the fantasy is to synthesize poetry and housekeeping, to show that at least on the literary level the speaker has perfect control over all her scraps. "Go down / Into the paper-mill," she orders the shred in the last stanza,

> and from its jaws,
> Stainless and smooth, emerge. – Happy shall be
> The renovation, if on thy fair page
> Wisdom and truth, their hallow'd lineaments
> Trace for posterity.

Disorder into order, scrap into cloth at last. The frugal housewife has used up the last shred.

Poems like Townsend's and Sigourney's are intellectual melodramas that flirt with chaos on their way to resolution. The process of anagogic displacement is complicated further when the image turns out to mean the opposite of what one would predict, as in Longfellow's "Snowflakes," where the "Silent, and soft, and slow" descent of the snow turns out to signify the "secret of despair" (*LW* 3:69), or when the poem refuses to complete its dialectic, as in Dickinson's "I heard a Fly buzz – when I died" (*DP* 465), which ends with the speaker's failure of vision as her mourners await the arrival of the "King."

These examples suggest the fourth and last strategy that I shall discuss here. The opposite of the third, it consists in the unraveling of a premature closure. Lowell's "After the Burial," for instance, is about the speaker's refusal to be consoled by his interlocutor's pious bromides after the death of his beloved.

> That little shoe in the corner,
> So worn and wrinkled and brown,
> With its emptiness confutes you,
> And argues your wisdom down.
> [*LoW* 9:216]

So ends one of the few American poems that Emily Dickinson singled out for praise (*DL* 2:649), on the kind of note with which Sigourney would have begun and from which she would have moved toward an affirmation that did away with despair. Like Lowell, and unlike his usual

self, is Bryant's "Hymn to Death," a strikingly dissonant, two-part affair
that begins in Bryant's most orotund style ("I am come, / Not with re-
proaches / . . . I am come to speak / Thy praises") but interrupts itself
partway with the shocking news of his father's death:

> Alas, I little thought that the stern power
> Whose fearful praise I sang, would try me thus
> Before the strain was ended.

The poem now switches from celebration to lament, disclaiming its original assurance:

> Shuddering I look
> On what is written, yet I blot not out
> The desultory numbers; let them stand,
> The record of an idle revery.[54]

Anticlimactic? Heavy-handed? Yes, but also daring. Bryant turns the elegy on its head and boldly unmasks the process of idealizing defensiveness to which elegies generically fall prey. The undercutting process is
more devastating than in Lowell's poem, where the inconsolability has a
cocky, holier-than-thou ring to it – perhaps the reason for George Arms's
uncharacteristic acerbity toward it in his study of the Schoolroom
Poets.[55]

The New England lyric of anticlosure, like the other patterns that we
have been exploring, goes back at least as far as the early republic, to
Federalist satire of Jeffersonianism like Royall Tyler's "Ode Composed
for the Fourth of July" as celebrated in "some country towns in Massachusetts, and Rye in Newhampshire":

> Squeak the fife, and beat the drum,
> INDEPENDENCE DAY has come!!
> Let the roasting pig be bled.
> Quick twist off the cockerel's head.
> . . . .
> Sambo, play and dance with quality;
> This is the day of blest Equality.
> Father and *Mother* are but men,
> And Sambo – is a Citizen.[56]

The ritual of patriotic celebration is seen as a bogus mode of unity, leading instead to disorder and violence, as the result of the blurring of distinctions of race, sex, and caste.

Romantic poems of unraveling like those by Bryant and Lowell extend
Tyler in no longer attaching value to the order or orthodoxy that their
poems undermine. One of the most arresting cases, awkward though it
is, is Emerson's poem "The Sphinx."[57] Here is the skeletal plot: The

sphinx wonders when someone will guess her riddle ("The meaning of man," *EW* 9:20); a poet steps forth and gives an answer, which turns out to be "correct" Emersonian doctrine; but the sphinx, at first seemingly daunted, reprimands the poet and escapes, thereby implying that the riddle remains to be guessed, and turning the poem itself into a riddle. The answer to that riddle seems to be that a merely doctrinal reply will not do. "Take thy quest through nature," the sphinx admonishes the poet. The person "who telleth one of my meanings / Is master of all I am" *(EW* 9:24–5). The poem reverses the expectation established by centuries of image-idea poems, saying in effect that formula falsifies: Those final stanzas in which poets sum up the meaning of a pond or forest or dandelion or cricket do not in fact complete a poem but empty it. The sphinx escapes. Emerson thus atones for his sins of slickness in "The Rhodora" and – even more egregiously – in "Each and All."[58]

In Dickinson, as always, the pattern that we are tracing is best developed. She is just as aware of the precariousness of doctrinal structures as Emerson, but she feels the problems and possibilities of her position more keenly because she sees those structures both as all-important and as bankrupt. Hence the finely calibrated disintegration scenario of

> This World is not Conclusion.
> A Species stands beyond –
> Invisible, as Music –
> But positive, as Sound –
> It beckons, and it baffles –
> Philosophy – don't know –
> And through a Riddle, at the last –
> Sagacity, must go –
> To guess it, puzzles scholars –
> To gain it, Men have borne
> Contempt of Generations
> And Crucifixion, shown –
> Faith slips – and laughs, and rallies –
> Blushes, if any see –
> Plucks at a twig of Evidence –
> And asks a Vane, the way –
> Much Gesture, from the Pulpit –
> Strong Hallelujahs roll –
> Narcotics cannot still the Tooth
> That nibbles at the soul –
>
> [*DP* 501]

The method of this poem is to subject to gradual erosion the faith stance of lines 1 through 4, admitting first that "philosophy – don't know"; then that public opinion weighs against it, that faith itself sometimes slips, and finally that the "tooth" of doubt is a constant. The affirmation of faith becomes a confession of skepticism, quickened by the need for the faith that eludes her.

III

From the preceding discussion, selective as it necessarily has been, we can extract a composite portrait of the New England muse, recognizing, of course, that any such generalizations take us only so far into personal idiosyncrasies. New England premodern poetry moves in the direction of repression, regulation, and intellectualization, forging structures that are at most slight variations on inheritances from the English accentual-syllabic repertoire, though in some cases long assimilated by regional folk culture (e.g., the ballad stanza of common measure in hymnody). Except when fulfilling culturally sanctioned rituals such as worship and grieving, New England premodern poems tend to avoid becoming exclamatory or expansive, leaning rather toward understatement and laconic compression. They habitually engage in doctrinal codification, or at least pretend to. Except for some experiments with regional dialect, the language of premodern New England poetry is literary rather than colloquial. The linguistic innovations of Emerson and Dickinson are mostly results of sophisticated metaphorical displacements, rather than vernacularization.

The special interest of such poems to a modern reader arises most often from their resistance to the closure toward which they are driven intellectually, emotionally, and aesthetically, and, in particular, from the strategic use, both stylistical and thematical, of ellipsis (repression of the dilemma) and irony (exploitation of the dilemma) to suggest the perception of this self-dividedness. In the heart of the New England poet is an obtuse, dogged, moralizing figure like the neighbor in Frost's "Mending Wall." This figure always conditions the poet's behavior, to a greater or lesser degree. There is no escaping him. The question is always whether the poet will be able to maintain enough distance from the alter ego to avoid an abrupt reductionism. When the poet does, the result can be a marvelously intricate job of self-enclosure that teaches us that the neighbor is not the personification of aesthetic deadness that we thought – not the dead weight keeping the poet back from becoming Walt Whitman – but in fact a muse in his own right. Frost's persona, for instance, makes poetic capital from a kind of imitation of his neighbor's wall-building recessiveness. He accomplishes this through a desultory, adage-strewn ("Spring is the mischief in me"), ironically condescending discourse that is all the while kept secret from his neighbor, and indeed even from himself, in that it bespeaks a suppressed petulance greater than he concedes. The poem, rather than the wall building, is the building of the wall.[59]

To what extent is it justifiable to speak of a New England tradition in poetry? The situation seems to be as follows. (1) Most of the poets discussed in this chapter were familiar with the work of a number of the others. The majority were associated with one or more regionally based coteries of the period: Trumbull, Dwight, and Barlow with the Connecticut Wits; Paine with a loosely knit turn-of-the-century group of Federalist writers that included Sarah Wentworth Morton, Charles Prentiss, and John Lathrop; Emerson, Very, and Hooper with the Transcendentalists; Longfellow, Lowell, and Holmes with the Boston-Cambridge literary elite of which they formed part of the nucleus, along with (eventually) Emerson; Sigourney with a literary circle that she gathered in Hartford, including among others the young John Greenleaf Whittier, who in his turn was well acquainted with most of the Cambridge group and with clusters of Quaker and abolitionist poets; Osgood with a circle of Providence poets that included Sarah Helen Whitman, Anne Lynch (Botta), Albert G. Greene, and others, and with a much larger circle of New York literati. Even Emily Dickinson, not only through her reading but also through contacts with Samuel Bowles, Josiah Gilbert Holland, and Thomas Wentworth Higginson, kept herself informed about the contemporary literary scene. (2) On the other hand, in no case was any New England poet *the* primary demonstrable influence on another's work. In no case was there anything like the Emerson-Whitman relationship, with the exception of Emerson's influence on Thoreau and Ellery Channing. On the contrary, all the major figures of the period were nurtured more on European models than on American, and the same holds true for all subsequent New England poets, at least through the time of Frost. The omnivorous reading habits of Longfellow and Emerson are simply more spectacular instances of the general assumption that the aspiring poet should not limit attention to "one particular sort of excellence" but "study the beauties of all."[60] (3) Nevertheless, by the late nineteenth century, if not before, a New England poetic "voice" or tradition had been created. One confirmation of this is John C. Kemp's important study of Frost's regionalism, which shows how in Frost's case the assumption of a New England voice was an acquired role that the Californian nonfarmer arrived at only after having tried out other models. Frost was an admirer of Poe and a fin-de-siècle aesthete well before he was an Emersonian.[61] His success at regional impersonation shows that by the turn of the twentieth century, New England had projected a poetic voice that could be recognized, imitated, truckled to (as in Frost's essay on Emerson), adapted, and extended.

How important to American letters is the poetic we have surveyed? R. A. Yoder, at the conclusion of his book on Emerson's poetry, distinguishes two Emersonian traditions: the line through Whitman, "invoking the myth of the whole, cosmic man," and a "second, more restrictive Emersonian line" of "dramatic or situational lyric" that, like Emerson's verse, as opposed to his prose, tries to find possibility within limitation. Under this rubric Yoder includes Dickinson, Robinson, and Frost – as well as Stevens and Ammons, whom Bloom preempts as Whitmanians.[62] Yoder, it seems to me, is in effect adumbrating the poetic that has been discussed in this chapter, a poetic of which Emerson and Dickinson are the most original exemplars and transmitters but not, as we have seen, the only practitioners. Waiving Stevens and Ammons as borderline cases (although if I had scope enough I would support Yoder here), one can still readily find a great number of notable recent American poets far more assimilable to the New England aesthetic than to the Whitmanian: Robert Francis, Philip Booth, Elizabeth Bishop, Richard Eberhart, William Stafford, even anti-Emersonian Yvor Winters. Tastes differ wildly, but I suppose most readers will find at least one or two poets in this list whom they consider truly important.

A minimalist defense of the legacy of premodern New England poetry would rest on the retort of Flannery O'Connor's antievangelist Hazel Motes to his landlady, who is shocked at his having blinded himself and wrapped barbed wire around his chest. "It's not natural," she protests. "It's something that people have quit doing – like boiling in oil or being a saint or walling up cats." Haze replies: "They ain't quit doing it as long as I'm doing it."[63] One then cites almost any poem by Robert Francis, and the argument is over.[64] A more sturdy defense would be to go on to raise the question of whether a laconic ethical idealism in tight prosodic structures from a village or pastoral standpoint is not as genuinely American a mode of expression even now as an expansive, imagistic-catalog, urban panorama in free verse. For Frank O'Hara, no; for Wendell Berry, on his Kentucky farm, yes. For Theodore Roethke, caught between the greenhouse and the far field, the question is moot. This single chapter has not, of course, been able to explore the issue exhaustively; but I hope to have shown that it is an issue worth reckoning with. I have tried to do this by exploring some of the best generic achievements of the New England poetic, and especially by representing Emily Dickinson as the instance that shows its full capabilities, rather than by following the usual approach of holding her up as proof of her contemporaries' sterility. Assuming that she still speaks to us, so, however faintly, must they.

6

New England Oratory from Everett to Emerson

[The] orations of Webster and Everett are destined to become the classics of all posterity, and receive like veneration.

James Spear Loring, *The Hundred Boston Orators* (1852)

What is called eloquence in the forum is commonly found to be rhetoric in the study.

Henry David Thoreau, *Walden* (1854)

The preceding chapter described premodern New England verse as a "poetry of regulated moral statement." The next two chapters should further help to explain why.

One reason was that the era between the Revolution and the Civil War was the self-styled "golden age of American oratory."[1] The prestige of oratory overshadowed that of poetry, not to mention fiction and drama, and resulted in the persistence, well into the Romantic period, of the Neoclassical tendency to define belles lettres as a branch of rhetoric.[2]

I

Oratory, as F. O. Matthiessen observes, was the "one branch of literature in which America . . . had a formed tradition" by the turn of the nineteenth century.[3] The early national sense of literary inferiority did not extend to the area of public speaking. Samuel L. Knapp, in the first extended survey of American literary culture (1829), boasted that in a half century the nation had generated more "distinguished orators and rhetoricians" than Athens had produced in a thousand years.[4] Even more sober witnesses generally agreed that whatever the state of American literature might be, American oratory was something to brag about.[5]

Both the quantity and the quality of oratorical performance were especially notable in New England, owing partly to the Congregational tradition, which set a high value upon an educated ministry and upon the sermon as the centerpiece of the worship service, and partly to the quasi-democratic structure of local government, which encouraged public expression – at least by the elite. New England ministers, in particular, did not hesitate to affirm that New England pulpit eloquence was equal or superior to that of Britain.[6] Predictably, the American lyceum movement began in New England and achieved its greatest successes there and in the states to the west that had the highest proportions of New England settlers.[7] From New England also emanated the first American textbooks on the art of speaking, notably Caleb Bingham's *Columbian Orator* (1797), which taught Frederick Douglass both to read and to understand his right to freedom.[8] Throughout our period, instruction and practice in public speaking occupied a much more important part of the curriculum than today. "No country on earth has ever laboured harder to make orators than our own," wrote Knapp, and he may have been right.[9] The style of most of the writers we examine in this book was first formed – or mal-formed – by innumerable school and college exhibitions.

From this context arose the young Emerson's three greatest American literary heroes – Edward Everett, William Ellery Channing, and Daniel Webster – and a phalanx of other New Englanders who won local and sometimes national literary reputations primarily on the ground of their speaking ability. In public affairs, these included men like Federalist congressmen Fisher Ames and Harrison Gray Otis ("From his cradle, as from Plato's, swarmed the Hyblean bees, and left the honeys of eloquence on his tongue"), Cotton Whig Rufus Choate, and Conscience Whig (later Republican) Charles Sumner. Examples from the ministry were genteel proto-Unitarian Joseph Stevens Buckminster, orthodox Congregationalist Edward Payson (after whom more nineteenth-century American authors were named than any other preacher), the more liberal Congregationalists Lyman Beecher and his son Henry Ward Beecher, and the Transcendentalist reformers William Henry Channing and Theodore Parker. From the same context emerged, at one or two removes, literary classics like Emerson's essays, Thoreau's *Walden* and reform papers, which were for the most part first delivered as lectures.

Like portrait painting and architecture, oratory was an art that thrived in early America because it was perceived as socially functional. First, it met certain religious and political needs, especially in New England, needs that rose incrementally during the next half century owing to the proliferation of sects, revivalism, local governments, and public rituals for bolstering civic pride. Election and Independence days, commencement ceremonies, the anniversary of the Pilgrims' landing – none of these could be properly celebrated without at least one showpiece oration. Second, the Neoclassical ideology that dominated early national aesthetics set an exceptionally high value on the art of public address. American

Enlightenment intellectuals were conditioned to view oratory not just as a graceful accomplishment but as a vital sign of the health of the Republic. "By the eternal constitution of things," declared John Quincy Adams, in America's first formal treatise on rhetoric, "it was ordained, that liberty should be the parent of eloquence; that eloquence should be the last stay and support of liberty; that with her she is ever destined to live, to flourish, and to die."[10] Adams's notion of an indissoluble connection between freedom and oratory might have been influenced by personal experience, but it was also based solidly on deductions from ancient history previously made by such approved British Neoclassical rhetoricians as Hugh Blair, who correlated the rise of oratory with the rise of the Greek city-states and the decline of Roman oratory with the collapse of the Roman republic.[11]

Here, then, was a literary form of which even a philistine must approve – that even a severe critic of America's literary attainments must see as a field of immediate promise. It was sanctioned by classical tradition, yet also inherently American. Oratory is altogether the example par excellence of how Neoclassicism helped to give rise to an American literary aesthetic even while seeming to discourage indigenous self-expression. The example of the younger Adams is instructive. His principles of rhetoric were modeled closely, even slavishly, on classical theory ("A subject, which has exhausted the genius of Aristotle, Cicero, and Quinctilian [sic]," he wrote, "can neither require nor admit much additional illustration"); yet Adams also encouraged American literary autonomy by the emphasis that he placed on the link between oratory and liberty and by calling specific attention to special opportunities for the American orator in the pulpit (only a New Englander could have seen it as the "throne of modern eloquence") and in commemorative oratory, largely neglected in Britain.[12]

Of particular fascination to the period was the supposed power of oratory. "It is historical fact," the young Emerson noted, "that when Demosthenes was about to plead in a cause, multitudes flocked from the remotest corners of Greece to the Forum at Athens" (JMN 2:9). Because Emerson himself felt a "passionate love for the strains of Eloquence," he was hopeful about his chances for success in the ministry, despite a withering sense of inferiority in other respects (JMN 2:238–40). He continued to be a lifelong connoisseur of eloquence, particularly of kinds different from his own, and he wrote two lecture-essays on the subject, defining eloquence before all else in terms of power, power that has at its aim to "alter in a pair of hours, perhaps in a half hour's discourse, the convictions and habits of years" (EW 7:64). This view was entirely traditional. The Columbian Orator makes the same point several times over: "An Alexander and a Cesar could conquer a world; but to overcome the passions, to subdue the wills, and to command at pleasure the inclinations of men, can be effected only by the all-powerful charms of enrapturing eloquence."[13] Benjamin Franklin had told with wry humor the story of being swept up by George Whitefield's mesmeric power; our period tended to speak of such experiences in tones of high seriousness. It relished such stories as the anecdote of proper young George Ticknor being so excited by Daniel Webster's bicentennial oration at Plymouth that "I thought my temples would burst with the gush of blood."[14] Gossipy compendiums like James Spear Loring's *Hundred Boston Orators* and William Buell Sprague's *Annals of the American Pulpit* (1857–69) testify to a widespread interest throughout the period in anecdotes of American eloquence.

This interest continued despite an awareness that the myth of eloquence was overstated. During the debates of the Continental Congress, John Adams complained, business got bogged down in rhetoric: "Every man upon every question must show his oratory, his criticism, his political abilities."[15] Writing partly with himself in mind as an example of the consequences of this rush to oratory, Adams later remarked in his *Autobiography* that the careers of Washington, Franklin, and Jefferson were "enough to shew that Silence and reserve in public are more Efficacious than Argumentation or Oratory."[16] Ironically, Adams himself was remembered by New Englanders as the person who swayed the Congress toward independence by the force of his oratory. One of Daniel Webster's best-known oratorical triumphs was his imaginative re-creation of Adams' never recorded speech. This feat was, in fact, the centerpiece of Webster's public eulogy on Adams and Jefferson. In it Webster for the most part made a conscientious effort to render Adams' downright style and to avoid bombast.[17] Yet Adams' own account of the occasion makes clear that it was more prosaic. Careful, reiterated reasoning, it seems, was what carried the day, rather than eloquence. Adams' son displayed the same practical wisdom when, following Blair, he noted that the modern lawyer has less opportunity to display his eloquence than the ancients because he must address points of law rather than the passions of the judges.[18]

Yet Webster's wishful reconstruction was not merely a preenactment of modern movie-style courtroom dramas; for there were enough public crises to sustain the myth of oratorical power right down through the Civil War. For New Englanders, two favorite examples, in addition to the ones just given, were the 1796 congressional speech by Fisher Ames in support of Jay's Treaty – so powerful that an opposition member allegedly moved adjournment so that the house could recover from the experience – and the close of the Dartmouth College case, argued by Webster before the Supreme Court on behalf of the Federalist former administration that sought to oust the state-mandated Jeffersonian regime that had displaced it. (It is symptomatic of the Federalist control of the organs of elite culture in early national New England that both of these instances were Federalist triumphs.) In the Dartmouth case, Webster was said to have ensured victory by making an emotional plea on behalf of his alma mater: "It is, Sir, . . . a small College. And yet, *there are those who love it.*"

At this point Webster broke down, according to his friend Rufus Choate, leaving Chief Justice Marshall with his "tall and gaunt figure bent over as if to catch the slightest whisper, the deep furrows of his cheek expanded with emotion, and eyes suffused with tears." Whereupon Webster recovered himself and "fixing his keen eye on the Chief Justice, said, in that deep tone with which he sometimes thrilled the heart of an audience":

> "Sir, I know not how others may feel," (glancing at the opponents of the College before him,) "but, for myself, when I see my Alma Mater surrounded, like Caesar in the senate-house, by those who are reiterating stab upon stab, I would not, for this right hand, have her turn to me, and say, *Et tu quoque mi fili! And thou too, my son!*" [19]

This is a story to be relished in any age, but especially in a period that believed in decisive moments more than we do today. That appears to have been true both in government and in religion. In religion, Second Awakening revivalism and genteel refractions such as the Transcendentalist movement fostered a belief in instant spiritual transformations. In law and politics, the number of landmark decisions and the perceived threat of institutional chaos were greater during the nation's formative period than today. Add to this the small size and relative social unity of the federal, regional, or local governing elites, as well as the comparatively high number of classically educated politicians throughout the period, and the admiration for oratorical prowess becomes understandable even without recourse to the fact (also germane) that the period was by our standards a media-starved era. No reasonable discounting on the score of exaggeration can erase the peculiarity, to a modern ear, of John Adams' declaration that when Fisher Ames gave his treaty speech, "There was not a dry eye . . . in the house, except [those of] some of the jackasses who had occasioned the necessity of the oratory," or of the report that oratory often brought the younger Adams to tears. [20] Such reactions among the most sophisticated help to provide a context for the period's narrow-minded objections to the seductive appeal of drama and fiction. The puzzling vehemence of these objections make better sense if we think of them as authentic gestures of self-protection akin to the liberal religionists' horror at the effects of revivalism. Even passable oratory and bad drama could make a striking impression on highly cultivated people of the day. [21]

The myth of oratorical power, then, heightened though it was, reflected both a greater aesthetic susceptibility to eloquence than obtains today and also a not entirely groundless hope, or fear, that a single individual might be able to engineer a major social change through sheer rhetorical force.

II

Approaching that rhetoric itself with this myth of its power in mind, the modern reader is likely to be disappointed to find a very few oases amid a desert of grandiloquence. Perusing the excerpts in James Spear Loring's *Hundred Boston Orators,* one soon comes to expect this kind of rant:

> The demon of party spirit has pervaded even to the penetralia, and subverted the altars of the Penates, while, enthroned on the ruins, he triumphs in domestic discord. . . . History points to her sanguine leaf, the mournful memory of party rage. See Marius' spear reeking with gore! Behold, expiring breath lingers on Sylla's blade![22]

The tortuousness here arises partly from the exigencies of the situation (a Jeffersonian trying to reprove a Federalist audience without being too pointed), but that hardly makes the diction more appealing.

The best-known – though seldom read – exemplum of the sins of the early American oratorical tradition, as inculcated by Adams and other well-meaning preceptors, is the interminable harangue that Edward Everett made at Gettysburg just before Lincoln presented his masterfully laconic Gettysburg Address. Everett begins:

> Standing beneath this serene sky, overlooking these broad fields now reposing from the labors of the waning year, the mighty Alleghanies dimly towering before us, the graves of our brethren beneath our feet, it is with hesitation that I raise my poor voice to break the eloquent silence of God and Nature. But the duty to which you have called me must be performed; – grant me, I pray you, your indulgence and your sympathy.
>
> It was appointed by law in Athens, that the obsequies of the citizens who fell in battle should be performed at the public expense.[23]

The elaborate periodic syntax, the mania for modifiers, and the classical contexting make an extreme contrast with Lincoln's pithiness. Everett was speaking a dead language.

The contrast between them seems most obviously a contrast between generations and between college-trained and down-home eloquence, yet it also reflects a difference in rhetorical modes recognized as equally legitimate in traditional rhetorical theory. Blair, following French rhetoricians, called them the *style periodique* (Everett's mode) and the *style coupé,* in which the "sense is formed into short interdependent propositions."[24]

Blair recommended a mixture of the two in every composition. Although Cicero, the great exemplar of the periodic style, was the oratorical hero of the Federalists' greatest speechifier, Fisher Ames, Ames's own rhetoric, as shown in the sample quoted in Chapter 4, was known rather for the "terseness, strength, and vivacity of the short sentence, than the dignity of the full and flowing period. . . . for sententious brevity, for antithesis and point." These traits, a later observer noted, also typified the style of the commentator John Thornton Kirkland, Harvard president and one of Emerson's undergraduate mentors.[25]

These characterizations of Ames and Kirkland's style apply, of course, to Emerson's own rhetoric. It is common to think of Emerson's literary maturity in terms of a movement from artificiality to authenticity, marked by the rejection of Neoclassical affectation that Everett's work epitomized and by the rejection of the formulas of Unitarian preaching. That is true, but the two kinds of rejections cut across one another. The rejection of Everett was a rejection of Ciceronianism (*JMN* 8:268–70). But the discipline of Unitarian sermonizing encouraged a plain, pointed style, compared to which Emerson's later style looks, in its own way, ornamental. For rhetorical if not for ideological reasons, the young Emerson's practical experience as a preacher must in itself have contributed to his eventual disenchantment with Everett's platform manner. As I have shown elsewhere, Arminian ministers took the lead, around the turn of the nineteenth century, in converting the highly formalized Congregational sermon into a freer form, doing away with the traditional three-part structure that involved the disciplined pursuit of a Bible-based doctrine through a series of logical steps backed up by proof texts. Unitarian sermons thus became inspirational essays following no prescribed form.[26] This could and did lead to vapid displays of floral rhetoric; but in the preaching of the minister whom Emerson admired most, William Ellery Channing, it led to a style as austere as an old-fashioned meetinghouse. Here, for instance, is Channing on the subject of contemporary religion and preaching:

> Religion ought to be dispensed in accommodation to [the] spirit and character of our age. Men desire excitement, and religion must be communicated in a more exciting form. . . . It must not be exhibited in the dry, pedantic devisions of a scholastic theology; nor must it be set forth and tricked out in the light drapery of an artificial rhetoric, in prettiness of style, in measured sentences, with an insipid floridness, and in the form of elegantly feeble essays. No; it must come from the soul in the language of earnest conviction and strong feeling. Men will not now be trifled with.[27]

Channing's nominal springboard for this passage is the welcome shift in poetic taste from Augustan to Romantic; his subtext is the need for Uni-

[margin handwritten note:] SHIFT TO FREER FORMS IN CONGECATIONAL SERMONS.

tarians to stay competitive with the evangelicals by providing less tinsel and more punch. Channing himself is too scholastic quite to imitate the thing he would describe ("ought to be dispensed in accommodation to" is very formal phrasing); but he leans in that direction by favoring short, reiterative declarative clauses to convey a sense of urgency, with an almost total avoidance of ornamental metaphor and allusion. Word pairings and adjectives of intensification are his only embellishments. The most convoluted sentence in the passage quoted is used to parody the measured prettiness it describes ("tricked out in the light drapery," etc.). Channing's rhetoric relies for success almost exclusively on the succinct and vehement repetition of general principles. This mode of speaking was very much in keeping with Unitarianism's conception of its message as the pristine Gospel of Christ, stripped of all Calvinist encrustations. Purification in doctrine was related to purification of utterance.[28]

Emerson profited from Channing's example without becoming an imitator for long. As a preacher, he lacked Channing's intensity but cultivated a similar directness. As a lecturer and essayist, he became far less direct, favoring metaphor and imagery and paradox and deliberate discontinuity. He did this both for reasons of personal taste and on the principle that truth is most nearly conveyed not through propositional statement but through its embodiment in images, as well as in response to the demands of his lay public for more intellectual gymnastics than in a normal sermon. At the same time, Emerson's staple remained the pungent, compressed, detached aphorism. Emerson, in other words, indulged a chastened version of the elegance that he had once admired in Everett, within the limits of the *style coupé*.

Other orators of Emerson's generation who were touched by Channing's influence developed in varied ways. George Ripley emulated Channing's simplicity and emphasis of statement but with a more sedate, academic penchant for close-knit argument.[29] Theodore Parker shared Emerson's taste for imagery and allusion but carried Channing's forthrightness to a much more colloquial level, as in the following passage (from the 1850s) in which he depicts the "practical atheism" of those who abet slavery.

> Mr. New England is greedy for money; Mr. South Carolina greedy for slaves. Mr. New England steals men in Africa, or in Massachusetts, and sells them to his brother, Mr. South Carolina, getting great pay. You say to both of these, "This is very wrong; it is inhuman, it is wicked." But the atheists say, "What do we know about right and wrong?" "I only know," says Mr. New England, "it brings me money." "I only know it brings me slaves," says Mr. South Carolina. "All we want is money and slaves." You can have nothing further to say to these two gentlemen.[30]

The simple syntax and the device of the Bunyanesque-Dickensian allegorical dialogue make this sound like a children's story. Parker is partly playing a favorite role of his, that of the homespun critic of oversophistication; partly catering to the lowest common denominator of his large, mixed, transient, and urban congregation; partly pitching his sermon below the level even of an unsophisticated adult audience in order to dramatize the stupidity of both parties to the debate. Channing and Emerson would not have done this; but Channing helped to make it possible, and Emerson would have understood.

In Charles Sumner, on the other hand, a Parkeresque tendency to hammer home basic truths coexists with an Everett-like grandiloquence.[31] To speak in the grand manner, in a style peppered with redundant allusions, was second nature to Sumner. This is evident from his first important public speech, a July 4 oration (1845) entitled "The True Grandeur of Nations," which culls literary, legal, and historical examples from practically every European culture, in order to show that international warfare is an indefensible crime. Under one heading he alludes to the Emperor Constantine, the Archbishop de Retz, Cicero, Benjamin Franklin, Tacitus, the *Iliad*, the *Odyssey, Macbeth,* Voltaire, the Bible, Coleridge, and Raphael. The oration is altogether the most resplendent performance in the whole history of Federalist–Conscience Whig pacifist rhetoric that starts with Channing's antiwar sermons in the 18-teens and culminates in Thoreau's protest against the Mexican War in "Resistance to Civil Government." It is interesting that although even the old-school memorialist James S. Loring criticized Sumner for his "exuberance of classical allusions,"[32] Emerson never seems to have considered accusing Sumner of rhetorical decadence as he did Everett ("a mere dangler & ornamental person" [*JMN* 9:380]). Rather, Sumner was a "noble head, so comely and so wise," to be classed among the greatest orators in history (*EW* 11:250–51). So far as Emerson and other antebellum abolitionists were concerned, Sumner's ornamentalism was quite functional. It gave their values an effective public expression.

Nowhere is this better illustrated than in the part of Sumner's Senate speech entitled "The Crime against Kansas" (1856) that provoked the historic assault by Preston Brooks, a kinsman of the target of his verbal aggression, thereby pushing North and South one step closer to armed conflict.

> The Senator from South Carolina has read many books of chivalry, and believes himself a chivalrous knight, with sentiments of honor and courage. Of course he has chosen a mistress to whom he has made his vows, and who, though ugly to others, is always lovely to him, – though polluted in the sight of the world, is chaste in his sight: I mean the harlot Slavery. For her his tongue is always profuse in words. Let

her be impeached in character, or any proposition be made to shut her
out from the extension of her wantonness, and no extravagance of manner or hardihood of assertion is then too great for this Senator. The
frenzy of Don Quixote in behalf of his wench Dulcinea del Toboso is
all surpassed.[33]

On and on the metaphor continues, linking Senator Butler's quixotism
with the threat of secession and working in Stephen Douglas as Butler's
Sancho Panza. Readers may quarrel, as they did then, over whether this
passage is inspired or fanatical; but few would deny that it is an elegant
piece of invective. It could have been managed only by someone steeped
in classical rhetoric and used to working with elaborate literary allusions.
Sumner does not always have these under control, but the intensity with
which most of the speech is written enables him to bring off most of his
effects. Sardonic hyperbole, to which Sumner was much given, at least in
this case perfectly expresses inner conviction. "I would go further, if language could further go," he affirms, defending the extremism of his use
of the term *crime*.[34] The speech as a whole is a landmark of antebellum
New England eloquence, far greater in historical importance than the
abolitionist orations that surpass it from a literary standpoint (e.g., Thoreau's first defense of John Brown, and Emerson's first speech against the
Fugitive Slave Law) and not too far behind them in literary quality at that.
Particularly imposing are Sumner's refutation of the charge of fanaticism
(evoking the precedents of Luther, Hampden, Milton, Russell, Sidney)
and his cornucopia of lurid analogues for the crime against Kansas (en-
slavement, piracy, satanism, reptilian insinuation, the Massacre of St.
Bartholomew).

Sumner was, however, the last orator of the old school to command
the respect of New England's intellectual avant-garde. Although the
florid manner of that school became a permanent part of the American
literary tradition through the agency of Walt Whitman, the main trend in
Yankee eloquence, amid such countercurrents as Emerson's movement
away from Channingesque simplicity, was from a copious ceremonial
rhetoric to a plainer style. John Quincy Adams felt obliged to lecture
Harvard students in detail on each of the six parts of the classical oration.
Even though Adams himself believed (with Aristotle) that the only necessary parts were the proposition and the proof, he followed Cicero "because it has been prescribed to me."[35] No such prescription hamstrung
his successor, Edward Tyrell Channing. Channing's *Lectures on Rhetoric
and Oratory* say almost nothing about form and continually emphasize
that modern oratory must differ from ancient oratory and take its shape
from the circumstances at hand. Thinking, for instance, of lyceum lecturing and other types of demonstrative oratory, Channing stresses that
"there must be a popular tone to the address, an adaptation to various

minds, so that all shall be moved."[36] Channing by no means encouraged his students to express themselves colloquially or even originally, as students of Thoreau's college essays have been quick to point out, but at least he recognized that language is a continually changing thing, even as he conservatively advised students to avoid slang and model their expression on the great works of English literature.[37]

On balance, then, like his more eminent brother, Edward Channing encouraged the movement away from stilted rhetoric. He did this particularly in his remarks about preaching, which (like a good Unitarian) he characterized as similar in basic method and purpose to secular oratory, being "intended to affect human conduct." His instructions are open-ended and pragmatic: "The only thing required is, that the preaching be impressive; and to make it so, we must withhold no outward help which belongs to so great a public ministration."[38] His orthodox brethren followed the same path, although at a certain distance. During the early nineteenth century, the Calvinist rhetoric professors at rival Andover Seminary busied themselves with codifying an elaborate set of rules governing homiletics. This process culminated in a 600-page summa by Austin Phelps, spouse and father of the two Elizabeth Phelpses.[39] This academic drift toward Alexandrine intricacy, however, was already being countered by practicing ministers. The speeches of Lyman Beecher, a blacksmith's son and a veteran of Second Awakening revivals, were far more idiomatic than those of his mentor Timothy Dwight, and Henry Ward Beecher's style was more colloquial than that of his father, just as Parker's was more so than Channing's. "Above all other men," the younger Beecher told his Yale divinity students, "the preacher should avoid what may be called a literary style, as distinguished from a natural one. . . . Never be grandiloquent when you want to drive home a searching truth. Don't whip with a switch that has the leaves on, if you want to tingle. A good fireman will send the water through as short and straight hose as he can."[40] Beecher and Parker represent denominational extremes, but also the denominational drift. And their churches, along with the Episcopalian, were by far the most "learned" ones in the region.

III

The speeches of New England's greatest antebellum orator, Daniel Webster, illustrate the transitional character of antebellum eloquence. Like Everett, Webster was schooled in the grand style, and he was equally facile when it came to adorning or strategically obscuring a point with classical allusion, as when, in a lecture at the Boston Mechanics' Institution, he sagely referred to the Doric architecture of the Roman sewers, or when he justified the Compromise of 1850 by reference to Greek and Roman acceptance of slavery.[41] But Webster was even better known for plainness and point. "All his words tell," wrote Emerson, "& his rhetoric is perfect, so homely, so fit, so strong" (*JMN* 10:393). Emerson looked upon Webster as a kind of natural force – "so much a piece of Nature & to be admired like an oak or an elephant" (*JMN* 10:394). Until he became disillusioned with Webster over the slavery issue, Emerson liked to collect Websterisms that showed his rootedness in nature, such as "You cannot keep out of politics more than you can keep out of frost" (*JMN* 5:63–4).

Today we may at least begin to get a sense of what Emerson saw in Webster by comparing a passage from Webster's first oration on the Bunker Hill Monument (1825) with Everett's oration at the site of the Battle of Lexington (1835). The latter was a performance that Emerson liked, but it made him realize for the first time that Everett was becoming a feeble echo of Webster (*JMN* 5:32–3; 8:326). The comparison shows it. Here is Everett addressing the surviving veterans:

> Sixty years have passed away; – two full returns of the period assigned by the common consent of mankind to one of our transitory generations. I behold around me a few – alas! how few! – of those who heard the dismal voice of the alarm-bell, on the nineteenth of April, 1775, and the sharp, angry hiss of the death volleys from the hostile lines. Venerable men! we gaze upon you with respectful emotion. You have reached an age allotted to the smallest portion of our race, and your gray hairs, under any circumstances, would be entitled to our homage. As the survivors of the militia of Lexington, who, on the nineteenth of April, 1775, were enrolled in defence of the rights of America, and obeyed the alarm which called you to protect them, we regard you as objects at once of admiration and gratitude.[42]

Now Webster:

> Venerable men! you have come down to us from a former generation. Heaven has bounteously lengthened out your lives, that you might behold this joyous day. You are now where you stood fifty years ago, this very hour, with your brothers and your neighbors, shoulder to shoulder, in the strife for your country. Behold, how altered! The same heavens are indeed over your heads; the same ocean rolls at your feet; but all else how changed! You hear now no roar of hostile cannon, you see no mixed volumes of smoke rising from burning Charlestown. The ground strowed with the dead and the dying; the impetuous charge, the steady and successful repulse; the loud call to repeated assault; the summoning of all that is manly to repeated resistance; a thousand bosoms freely and fearlessly bared in an instant to whatever of terror there may be in war and death; – all these you have witnessed, but you witness them no more. All is peace.[43]

These parallel passages take one a good way toward appreciating the shades of distinction in period oratory. Webster is not Lincoln, but neither is he Everett. Webster is by no means above bombast and cliché ("shoulder to shoulder, in the strife for your country"), but he is a much more vivid scene painter than Everett. Everett is sketchy, redundant, abstract. Webster's timing is better, as in the gradual buildup of short phrases to an elegant climax in the penultimate sentence. He also roots the passage more solidly in the present: this day, these heavens, these oceans. Everett's way of dramatizing the contrast between the past and the present is to linger bathetically over the gray hairs of the broken-down old relics; Webster gives them dignity by stressing the bounteous peace that has followed the war and seeing them as enjoying the gratitude of the community, rather than as mere objects of gratitude. Altogether Webster's language, though fulsome by today's standards, is far more succinct than Everett's. These contrasts, as Webster-watchers saw, had a lot to do with the fact that he began his career as a small-town lawyer, whereas Everett began his as a society preacher and Harvard professor.[44]

Webster's ceremonial orations were, moreover, orotund compared to his usual speeches as legislator and his pleas as lawyer. The famous excerpts (such as the peroration to his best-selling 1830 Senate speech, ending "Liberty *and* Union, now and forever, one and inseparable!") give a somewhat misleading impression. E. P. Whipple rightly described Webster's mature style as "plain, terse, clear, forcible; and rising from the level of lucid statement and argument into passages of superlative eloquence only when his whole nature is stirred by some grand sentiment."[45] For Theodore Parker, likewise, Webster's strength was that "he could make a statement better than any man in America."[46] This is well illustrated by Webster's notorious Senate speech of March 7, 1850, which permanently alienated the antislavery vote. With unusual painstakingness, Webster devotes the bulk of the speech to a reconstruction of the historical background of the sectional crisis, the historical consistency of his own views on slavery, and the reasons why he now supports a strengthened Fugitive Slave Law and the allowing of slavery in the Mexican territories.

> We must view things as they are. Slavery does exist in the United States. It did exist in the States before the adoption of the Constitution, and at that time [Webster liked the legalistic tightness of the "does" and "did," "before" and "at" formulas]. It will be found, Sir, if we will carry ourselves by historical research back to that day, and ascertain by authentic records still existing among us, [Webster also loved such Burkean appeals to the weight of precedent] that there was then no diversity of opinion between the North and the South upon the subject of slavery. It will be found that both parts of the country held it equally an evil.

Hence the decision to ban the African slave trade within twenty years, a decision, Webster carefully notes, that was opposed by some Southerners, including the father of the Constitution, James Madison. Why?

> You observe, Sir, that the term *slave*, or *slavery*, is not used in the Constitution. The Constitution does not require that "fugitive slaves" shall be delivered up. It requires that persons held to service in one State, and escaping into another, shall be delivered up. Mr. Madison opposed the introduction of the term *slave*, or *slavery*, into the Constitution; for he said that he did not wish to see it recognized by the Constitution of the United States of America that there could be property in men.[47]

The tone of infinite deliberation, combined here with the tactic of apparently throwing full support to the side opposite the one he will eventually advocate, is typical of Webster's rhetorical prudence and reflective of his self-image as national unifier. These devices are extended, owing to the occasion. Webster is about to flout his most vocal constituents, so he edges as gingerly yet authoritatively as possible down that path. At the end of the speech, he rises to a fervent peroration on the need for union, but the speech as a whole, like these excerpts, conveys (typically) the impression of a wide-sweeping mind keeping its formidable energies under careful restraint.

Webster's rhetoric, like Channing's, influenced his hearers in diverse ways. On the one hand, the relative plainness of his style helped woo the young Emerson and other admirers away from such models as Everett and encouraged them to cultivate a more "natural" style. On the other hand, Webster's combination of temporizing and dogmatic legalism also inspired in opponents – the middle-aged Emerson and other reform orators – a new rhetoric of extremism. Webster's attitude of clipped hauteur toward abolitionist societies ("I do not think them useful") was countered by abuse ("Webster the disgraced and bankrupt chief of a broken and ruined party"); and his measured legalism, by incendiary appeals to the higher law ("Is virtue constitutional, or vice?")[48] More basic than either of these outcomes, however, was Webster's significance as a media event – as a perpetrator of eloquence that inspired the kind of rhetorical analysis that Whipple did in essays and Emerson in journal entries and the kind of counterexamples just quoted from Wendell Phillips and Thoreau. Webster would not have attained such prominence, of course, had he not been a shrewd politician backed by strong mercantile interests. To paraphrase the Websterian adage that Emerson wrote down, you cannot keep politics out of an explanation of Webster's reputation as orator, although the influence was reciprocal. Yet so great was the literary world's inclination to picture him and other spell-binding contemporaries as primarily speakers that their oratorical power seemed to take on a life of its own, detach itself from the context of realpolitik that allowed it to flourish, and loom up as the autonomous expression of some hypostasized Nature or inherent quality of character – thereby perpetuating the myth of eloquence in an age of print. "Wave after wave his eloquence flows on, / Sublime, resistless in its mighty force," writes one of the innumerable bad poets who elegized Webster's death.[49] The tendency when characterizing Webster as orator was, as here, to mysticize his eloquence by understating the degree to which one's sense of it as eloquence depended upon prior agreement with his opinions.[50]

Emerson struggles mightily with this problem in his second address on the Fugitive Slave Law, written after the death of Webster, whom he memorializes in the speech. Emerson carefully distinguishes Webster from "vulgar politicians," chiefly on the ground that "his countenance, his figure, and his manners were all in so grand a style, that he was, without effort, as superior to his most eminent rivals as they were to the humblest" (*EW* 11:220–1). Emerson remembers especially Webster's Bunker Hill address. Webster was "so thoroughly simple and wise in his rhetoric; he saw through his matter, hugged his fact so close, went to the principle or essential, and never indulged in a weak flourish" (*EW* 11:222). Yet, concludes Emerson, "There is not a single general remark, not an observation on life and manners, not an aphorism that can pass into literature from his writings" (*EW* 11:224). Emerson is not necessarily wrong here, but he is elliptical to the point of capriciousness. First, he suppresses the fact that he himself was for many years a collector of Webster's sayings, one of which Emerson had been quoting for several years in his lecture on "Eloquence" (ironically, the adage that "the curse of this country is eloquent men" [*EW* 7:75]). Second, Emerson hides (probably from himself as much as from his audience) the full extent to which his tribute-followed-by-critique of Webster's oratorical style is, in fact, a critique of Webster's politics. Emerson agreed with Webster before; he disagrees with him now. To diagnose Webster's failing, therefore, as "sterility of thought, the want of generalization in his speeches" that kept the rhetoric from becoming lastingly memorable (*EW* 11:223–4) is wrongheaded – but hardly unique. It looks backward to the way in which Federalist historians liked to memorialize Fisher Ames (as standing for an absolute of eloquence, rather than for party politics), and it looks forward to the already burgeoning tradition of American responsiveness to political figures on aesthetic grounds that in modern times have made us uncertain whether Kennedy's defeat of Nixon, or Reagan's defeat of Carter, was the result of platform or of platform manner.

The age of Webster marked a turning point in the disengagement, within the field of oratory, of the dimensions of aesthetics and advocacy, in keeping with the growing autonomy of the aesthetic domain noted in Chapter 3. Until the nineteenth century, American oratory developed largely as an aspect of theological or political praxis. This situation began to change with the development of oratory as a discipline in the school and college curriculum and with the proliferation of such secular rituals as Fourth of July orations. (Webster's first publication was just such an address, which he had delivered in 1800 at the age of eighteen.) The situation changed decisively as a consequence of the lyceum movement, a network of locally generated lecturing societies that first developed in New England during the late 1820s (inspired by British example) and soon spread throughout the region. As historian Donald Scott points out, one of the premises of the lyceum as an institution was that the "lecture was an oratorical form deliberately and carefully separated from all partisan and sectarian discourse."[51] That this was not entirely true is demonstrated by Josiah G. Holland's 1865 reminiscence of the lyceum, which makes the same point as Scott's article yet immediately contradicts itself by declaring that the "popular lecture . . . has been the devoted, consistent, never tiring champion of universal liberty" – that is, antislavery.[52] That was not true either, but it was true enough of rhetoric in the 1850s to show that the lyceum was more than just a forum for value-free inquiry. The key point for our purposes, however, is that Holland, like Emerson, was kept by his ideology from acknowledging the full extent to which the lyceum was more than just a performance medium.

Altogether, the individual performers tended to operate under the following ground rules. On the one hand, they inevitably injected their personal commitments to some degree. Politicians like Webster and Everett were in demand as lyceum speakers; Webster himself was president of the Boston Lyceum for a decade, and it was as natural for him to promote Whiggery from the platform as for Lucy Stone to promote feminism, Beecher morality, and Emerson Transcendentalism. On the other hand, as Emerson found to his relief after turning from the parish ministry to the lecture circuit, the lyceum lecturer did speak, and was expected to speak, as a free agent, not as an institutional mouthpiece. Thus Wendell Phillips' most common and sought-after lyceum piece was "The Lost Arts," although he also lectured against slavery.[53] By the same token, although the lyceum was nominally devoted to the diffusion of knowledge – a kind of nineteenth-century equivalent to educational television – it came closer than any previous institutionalization of oratory to defining itself as a form of art and entertainment.[54] A sample of the standard fare are the eighteen items sponsored by the Salem Lyceum in 1853–4: a concert by the Mendelssohn Quintette Club, and speeches by George Sumner on "France," Emerson on "American Character," George B. Cheever on "Reading with Reference to Mental Culture," W. H. Hurlbut on "Cuba and the Cubans," William R. Alger on "Peter the Great," John P. Hale on the "Last Gladiatorial Exhibition at Rome," Octavius B. Frothingham on "Europe," George W. Curtis on "Young America," Henry Ward Beecher on "Ministrations of the Beautiful," Theodore Parker on "The Function of the Beautiful in Human Development," Bayard Taylor on "The Arabs," Henry W. Bellows on "New England Festivals," Anson Burlingame on "The Valley of the Mississippi," David A. Wasson on "Independence of Character," a Prof. Guyot on "Distribution of the Races," and Phillips on "The Lost Arts."[55] It is unusual but not unique that ten of the seventeen talks were given by men of ministerial background. The all-male cast is typical of the antebellum period, when prejudice against women lecturers was strong.[56] The emphasis on history, geography, and aesthetics is also typical, presumably reflecting not only audience interest but also the desire to remain comparatively apolitical.

IV

We need now to ask, more specifically, what impact the cult of oratory had on New England writing in general.

First, and most fundamentally, it was a means of employment. Between 1830, when large-scale lyceum activity had just begun, and the close of our period, a higher percentage of American writers (at least in New England) depended on oral performance as a major source of income than at any time since – although the college lecture circuit and the flow of creative writers into academia may have begun to narrow the contrast between then and now. At least one-third of all the antebellum male authors surveyed in the Appendix and one-half of all major authors regardless of sex were professional oral performers as a secondary, if not a primary, line of work. Bronson Alcott and Margaret Fuller were public "conversationalists."[57] Channing, Beecher, Brownson, Emerson, and Parker were all ministers, at least for a significant period, and the latter four were lyceum lecturers also. Longfellow and Lowell were academic lecturers, and Lowell was a lyceum performer as well. So was Holmes. Very tried all three media: teaching, preaching, and the lyceum. Thoreau, though not always a successful public performer, delivered his best discourses from the platform. Bancroft and Bryant were not professional speakers, but political speechifying was part of their role as activists. So too with Whittier, who, like Holmes, became a lyceum performer in his middle years. The cult of oratory, then, not only betokened but furthered the development of literary expression as a specialized field of endeavor.

The relationship between public speaking and a writer's literary style and philosophy is, of necessity, somewhat speculative, yet several generalizations may be ventured. First, despite the shifts in taste, pedagogy, and practice that we have noted, the persistence of public speaking as an art and, increasingly, as a means of livelihood helped ensure the continuance of classicism into the Romantic era. For instance, Park Benjamin, who as a college versifier had favored Wordsworthian nature meditation, found that as a platform poet in the late 1840s and 1850s he achieved his best successes with satirical verses in pentameter couplets as in "The Age of Gold."[58] Pope paid off in hard cash. The conservatism of the audience's taste conditioned that of the performer, or perhaps it would be more accurate to say that the Neoclassical aesthetic was more functional than its detractors claimed: The crispness of heroic couplet satire was prosodically and intellectually more invigorating in performance than low-key, serpentine Wordsworthian blank verse. In any event, pentameter couplets remained the preferred medium for platform verse long after the Civil War. On a more ideological level, the oratorical tradition may have helped curb the Romantic tendency toward privatism. Emerson, for example, normally writes about the poet with the sense of the poet as a communicator: a sayer, an announcer, a liberator, a lawgiver. This may help account for his fascination with the Welsh bards as poetic models – they were rhetors as well as lyrists – and for his notion of the poet as a "representative" who "apprises us not of his wealth, but of the commonwealth." The poet is pictured as standing out "among partial men," partly because Emerson considers the poet as a socially responsible, socially accountable being (*EW* 3:4). In this Emerson reflects the Neoclassical notion of the writer as transmitter of public values and promoter of civic virtue.

In Thoreau's case, the public dimension of oratory might seem to have had the opposite effect, as when he establishes his persona in *Walden* with great self-consciousness:

> I should not obtrude my affairs so much on the notice of my readers if very particular inquiries had not been made by my townsmen concerning my mode of life. [*Wa* 3]

The lyceum, where the first version of *Walden* was delivered, would seem to have had the effect of provoking in this speaker a greater sense of separateness – yet the awareness that he is speaking to an audience that asked for it is also self-validating. And it may have affected the tenor of *Walden* pretty drastically. Left entirely to himself, Thoreau might have composed a reminiscence, maybe nothing more than a glorified log book like many of the entries in his later journal. (That, significantly, is one direction in which Thoreau moved when expanding *Walden* beyond the lecture stage: He added a lot of data to the second half.) Faced with an audience, the speaker is prompted to enrich the chronicle with apologia, homily, and (to put us in our places) also whimsy and mythification.[59]

But even as the institutionalization of oratory retarded the erosion of Neoclassical values in some important ways, its single most important contribution – the lyceum's, particularly – was to provoke a metamorphosis of genteel rhetorical norms during the antebellum period, to help ensure that Webster rather than Everett would be looked back upon as the superior stylistic model, until even Webster would eventually come to seem orotund. At the risk of tunnel vision, I shall continue to focus on the Concord Transcendentalists, and especially on Emerson, the New Englander whose public addresses loom largest as an enduring literary achievement.

Taylor Stoehr's excellent study of the Concord group points out that they liked to affect a kind of antieloquence.[60] The *Columbian Orator* had called gesture the "second part of pronunciation," noting that "he, who claps his hand to his sword, throws us into a greater panic than one who only threatens to kill us."[61] Emerson, Thoreau, and Alcott disdained such trickery. They avoided physical gesture, avoided colorful but distracting costume (such as Bayard Taylor's shiek outfit), avoided for the most part the extremes of emotion, and relied simply on sincerity of character and modulations of voice (Emerson's was said to be particularly effective).[62] Emersonian self-reliance led them to reduce the classic precepts of oratory almost to the sole injunction that the basis of true eloquence is personal integrity and to repress the counterinjunction that the orator's first job is to conciliate the audience.

Thoreau's shyness made him carry this doctrine to an extreme. He confessed to feeling demeaned by trying to "interest my audience."

> I am disappointed to find that most that I am and value myself for is lost, or worse than lost, on my audience. . . . I should suit them better if I suited myself less. . . . I would rather that my audience come to me than that I should go to them . . . *i.e.,* I would rather write books than lectures. [*TJ* 7:79]

Hence Thoreau's lectures often failed.[63] Emerson, however, coming to the lyceum with more experience as a public speaker and after the comparative straitjacket of the pulpit, found the new forum liberating. His literary standards were almost as high as Thoreau's, but his temperament led him to take a more relaxed, less adversarial view of lecturing: "Speak with the vulgar, think with the wise" (*EW* 12:286). This principle helped to shape what Emerson liked to call his "doctrine of leasts," meaning that the greatest laws are visible in the tiniest phenomena (*EW* 4:114). "'Tis the vulgar great who come dizened with gold and jewels. Real kings hide away their crowns in their wardrobes, and affect a plain and poor exterior. . . . Jesus is born in a barn, and his twelve peers are fishermen" (*EW* 7:175–6). This principle underlies the first two of Emerson's three rules of rhetoric in "Art and Criticism" (*EW* 12:282–99): the "low style" and "compression."[64] In other words, be succinct and use direct, idiomatic statements that go to the heart of things: "The lowest classifying words outvalue arguments; as upstart, dab, cockney, prig, granny, lubber, puppy, peacock" (*EW* 12:287).

Emerson did not absolutely need the lyceum to teach him this. He could have derived it from the study of some of his favorite authors, such as Montaigne, or simply from listening to the speech of Concord farmers. But he might not have learned his lesson so well had he not faced the challenge of having to captivate audiences of an increasingly heterogeneous sort during thirty years of lecturing. A good measure of the impact of the lyceum on Emerson's prose style is his revision of passages from journal to lecture to essay, even after he had outgrown his youthful Neoclassical floridity.

> Your neighbor is an audacious morose ruffian: people fear & hate him. What entitles me to his civility? He has little sons & daughters who are getting along into the dame's classes at our little school. Thus nature contrives to intenerate her granite & felspar & keep the balance true, takes the boar out & puts the lamb in. [*JMN* 7:95 (1838)]

> Your neighbor is an audacious, morose ruffian; a bad citizen; a dash of the pirate in him: people fear and hate him. What has made him civil? Nature sends him a troop of pretty sons and daughters who are getting along in the dame's classes at the village school; and to win regard for them he has smoothed his grim scowl. Thus nature contrives to intenerate her granite and felspar, – takes the boar out, and puts the lamb in, and keeps her balance true. [1839][65]

> Is a man too strong and fierce for society, and by temper and position a bad citizen, – a morose ruffian, with a dash of the pirate in him; – nature sends him a troop of pretty sons and daughters who are getting along in the dame's classes at the village school, and love and fear for them smooths his grim scowl to courtesy. Thus she contrives to intenerate the granite and felspar, takes the boar out and puts the lamb in, and keeps her balance true. [*EW* 2:58 (1841)]

The journal passage is, on the whole, polite discourse. The lecture deformalizes: "a dash of the pirate"; "What has made him civil?" instead of the stilted "What entitles me to his civility?"; "a troop of pretty sons and daughters." The essay, in condensing (the opening clause comes from an earlier part of the lecture paragraph), reformalizes somewhat as befits the difference between platform and print: "a dash of the pirate" is made more grammatical through subordination, and the brisk rhetorical question disappears. But compared to the journal, the final version remains casual. The journal shows that Emerson had already begun to practice the low style and compression ("takes the boar out & puts the lamb in"); the revisions show how the medium of the lecture enabled him to become truer to those principles.

Emerson thus moved his style a notch closer to New England speech. During the Federalist era, Timothy Dwight slightingly characterized the "*Boston style*" ("a phrase proverbially used throughout a considerable part of this country," i.e., New England, "to denote a florid, pompous manner of writing" [*DT* 1:368]), an application in the rhetorical sphere of Dwight's New Light hobbyhorse that eastern Massachusetts had lapsed from the good old New England way. Emerson would have sympathized. He wrote of the average New Englander's style of storytelling: "What hesitation and reserve in his narrative! He tells with difficulty some particulars, and gets as fast as he can to the result, and, though he cannot describe, hopes to suggest the whole scene" (*EW* 7:68). This serves rather well for a description of Emerson's own platform style, as Bronson Alcott noted:

> In speaking he pleases, practising a sort of hesitancy between the readings of his paragraphs, as of the spring of locks or choice of keys at the showing of cabinet specimens; seems sensitive at the delay sometimes, and the negligency, as it were, of another – as anxious as we are to get sight of each as it comes forth from the separate drawers, yet hesitating till the gem is out and flittering, so glad to see and admire . . .[66]

Alcott gives here a good sense of how Emerson was able to make the deliberate avoidance of eloquence into an effective platform manner. The orator as Yankee.

But it is simplistic to describe the development of Emerson's mature style as a process of vernacularization. That is not precisely what Emerson wanted. In the passage quoted earlier, the phrase "a troop of pretty sons and daughters" sits next to "Thus nature contrives to intenerate," which stays unchanged through the two revisions. What Emerson was after was rather a "dash of the pirate" to add salt to his civility – or, more exactly, a sense of different modes of discourse rubbing against each other.

The full implications of such diversification in language levels have not, perhaps, been realized. To grasp them, it is helpful to resort to the critical vocabulary of M. M. Bakhtin, who studied similar effects in Roman and Renaissance narrative. Bakhtin observes how, during these periods, through "carnivalization" (i.e., the use of festive, parodic forms from folk culture as counterpoint to the solemnity of dominant myths and rituals) and *polyglossia* (interplay of different languages – e.g., the classical and the vernacular in the Middle Ages and Renaissance), consciousness is freed from the "tyranny of its own language and its own myth of language." Greek literature was comparatively monoglossic (comparatively, because "one's own language is never a single language"); "Roman literary consciousness," from the start, was "bilingual," the "Latin literary word" viewing itself *through the eyes* of the Greek word." Hence the "Roman *stylized,* and not without a certain cold sense of alienation from his own language." This bilingualism, interacting with a third linguistic strand of indigenous vernacular, made possible a "maximal distance between language itself and the world of themes and objects." This, in turn, made possible the rise of parody (carnivalization) to "new ideological heights."[67]

Bakhtin's sketch of *polyglossia* and its effects points up some important aspects of writing during our period. Like Bakhtin's ancient Rome, postcolonial American letters was a product of cultural imperialism marked by an increasingly active interplay between a normative and monoglossic Neoclassicism and the impulse to Americanize literary discourse in accordance with usage either conservatively (through the slight adjustments in vocabulary proposed by Noah Webster) or radically (through basing literature on folk speech). Some writers and critics even tried to Indianize American letters by imitating native American rhetoric (Longfellow's *Hiawatha* being the culmination of a half century of unsuccessful experiments). To an extent, these developments derive from British Romanticism, which also (see the *locus romanticus,* Wordsworth's preface to *Lyrical Ballads*) challenged monoglossic hegemony in the name of a more authentic common speech. But in America, as a postcolonial nation more culturally diverse than the mother country, the question of literary language was more complicated and the response more disparate, ranging from a longer and more tenacious adherence to Neoclassicm, on the one hand, to a more extreme colloquialization than one finds anywhere in the mother country except in Scotland and the novels of Dickens. Everett illustrates the former extreme; the imitation folk speech of Lowell's *Biglow Papers,* the latter. In between we find styles like Webster's and Emerson's that strike some balance between the polite and the popular. Some fascinating dissonances in taste and expression resulted from such juxtapositions. "Perhaps the 'Lycidas' was his favorite short poem," remarked Ellery Channing of Henry Thoreau; "at least I have heard it most often from his mouth; but he knew the Robin Hood Ballads remarkably well."[68]

Much of the interest in Thoreau's and Emerson's work as prose stylists arises from the sense of such dissonances. Whereas Webster stood for the reduction of Latinate floridity to Doric plainness, Transcendentalist rhetoric (as Channing's observation suggests) stood for a more open confrontation or interplay between genteel and vernacular discourse, an interplay in which the latter was the privileged element (associated with nature, as opposed to artifice), although more as a way of preventing stuffiness than as the stylistic norm. Emerson praised Montaigne's *Essays* as the "language of conversation transferred to a book," words so "vascular and alive" that they would bleed if you cut them; but he acknowledged that Montaigne exhibited a "biblical plainness coupled with a most uncanonical levity," although the "offence is superficial" (*EW* 4:168, 165). But Emerson was too straightlaced to bear much Rabelesian carnivalization and committed, in the long run, to developing the linguistic and thematic vein of "strong common sense" as a corrective to, and concretization of, an idealizing rhetoric and vision. "Cannot Montaigne & Shakspeare consist with Plato & Jesus?" he exclaims, in a moment of frustration, after he has tried "correcting old discourses" so as to make them more earthy but found that he has edited out more of the high-mindedness than he intended (*JMN* 7:253).

Emerson's vacillation should not be regarded merely in an ironic light, because it helped make creative achievement possible, not only for Emerson but also for his less scholastic younger contemporaries. These examples tell the story:

> I reason, Earth is short –
> And Anguish – absolute –
> And many hurt,
> But, what of that?
> [*DP* 301]

> Magnifying and applying come I,
> Outbidding at the start the old cautious hucksters,
> Taking myself the exact dimensions of Jehovah,
> Lithographing Kronos, Zeus his son, and Hercules his grandson,
> . . . .
> Accepting the rough deific sketches to fill out better in myself,
>   bestowing them freely on each man and woman I see.
> [Whitman, "Song of Myself," lines 1026–9, 1036–7]

For nowadays, the whale-fishery furnishes an asylum for many romantic, melancholy, and absent-minded young men, disgusted with the carking cares of earth, and seeking sentiment in tar and blubber. Childe Harold not unfrequently perches himself upon the mast-head of some luckless disappointed whaleship, and in moody phrase ejaculates: –
Roll on, thou deep and dark blue ocean, roll!
Ten thousand blubber-hunters sweep over thee in vain.
[Melville, "The Mast-head," *Moby-Dick*]

In none of these cases can we describe the style merely as a reduction of a formal, traditional discourse to an earthier plane. All of these passages are polyglossic juxtapositions dependent for their effects upon a continuing interplay between contrasting stylistic levels. In the first, by Dickinson, the homiletic abstraction of the first two lines is called into question by the colloquialization of the last two but is not dispensed with. (The poem's three stanzas raise the same question three times.) In the second, Whitman's "outbidding" denotes the replacement of old-fashioned, ponderous sermonic-scriptural language with hucksterese but also the retention of the older framework, which is needed to give his advertisements for himself solemnity and divine sanction, as well as the thrill of irreverence. In the third, Melville's purpose is ostensibly to puncture bloated Byronism with whaleman's lingo ("nowadays," "seeking sentiment in tar and blubber"); but Ishmael cannot avoid assimilating, in the process, the vocabulary he seeks to discredit any more than Melville wants to purge his book of Romanticism and metaphysics, so that the final linguistic and thematic result, as in Whitman, is a collage of the demotic and the high-falutin' ("not unfrequently perches himself") that both jars and exhila-rates. The linguistic accomplishment of the American Renaissance, like that of the English Renaissance its writers all admired, was not simply the result of their discovery of a more vigorously direct idiom than Neo-classical rhetoric had encouraged but, more fundamentally, the result of a sharpened awareness, in consequence, of the effects to be gained from the employment of contrasting planes of discourse – an awareness, we saw in Chapter 4, already present in Federalist writers like Tyler and Honeywood but complicated during the Romantic era.

One further passage from Emerson will enable us to clinch this point. The passage comes as part of a pullback qualification following a tribute to Shakespeare.

> Shakspeare would have sufficed for the culture of a nation for vast pe-riods. The Chinese have got on so long with their solitary Confucius and Mencius; the Arabs with their Mahomet; the Scandinavians with their Snorre Sturleson; and if the English island had been larger and the Straits of Dover wider, to keep it at pleasure a little out of the imbroglio of Europe, they might have managed to feed on Shakspeare for some ages yet; as the camel in the desert is fed by his humps, in long absence from food. [*EW* 12:295]

This is late Emerson (from the 1859 lecture "Art and Criticism"). Com-pared to the twice-revised passage about the boorish neighbor, it lacks the invigorating juxtaposition of speech levels. Emerson's youthful rhet-oric was stiltedly genteel; the later Emerson's rhetoric was too often a monotonous sort of polite cracker-barrel. In this swing we see the limi-tation of Emersonian *polyglossia:* It is an unstable compound, the move-ment toward the low style leading finally to a rhetorical deflation that is the obverse of Whitman's movement toward artifice in his later poetry. Nor is the deflation simply rhetorical. The weakness of the passage quoted arises more fundamentally from an analogous shrinkage of vi-sion, a slick complacency, a too easy assumption that this casual sketch will serve as a comprehensive overview that needs no further probing. The bibliographic razzle-dazzle in the form of offhand chitchat ("The Chinese have got on so long with their solitary Confucius.") is a perfect example of what Emerson elsewhere decried as the "American superfi-cialness" (*EW* 10:342). The passage fails, then, to achieve a true juxtapo-sition of cultural contexts, just as it fails to achieve a true juxtaposition of vocabularies. At the same time, from the ruins of Emerson's linguistic and cultural project, we can discern what was truly dynamic and revolutionary in it. Emerson's theory of discourse privileges British literary tradition (Shakespeare) yet distances itself from that tradition by valorizing Shakespeare (as the context of the passage establishes) as a vernacular rather than literary artist and by making clear the tradition's ethnocentricity. Emerson imagines a discourse that encloses the British within itself as part of a syncretistic assimilation of disparate cultural voices and values, a discourse that will simultaneously preserve and decenter by making Anglo-American letters more global, a discourse that is forever disrupting the literary order by moving in the direction of a lower style (the "key to every country" being "command of the language of the common people," *EW* 12:285) and forever challenging the cultural order by acknowledging the need to transcend its Anglo- and Euro-centrism. The urbanity of tone that miscarries here by coming across as smugness should also be read more sympathetically as an awareness of the artificiality of all cultures and texts. Emerson acquired this insight as part of his literary maturity, having been forced, by the conditions of oral performance, to recognize the difficulty of extricating his personal voice from intertextual bondage. "Here I am writing a ΦBK poem," he journalizes in 1834, "free to say what I choose & it looks to me as if it would scarce express thought of mine but be a sort of fata Morgana reflecting the images of Byron, Shakspear, & the newspapers" (*JMN* 4:315). On this occasion he succumbed to heroic couplets; but as his sense of the gap between "literary" and "natural" modes of expression became more acute, his resistance increased, as did his ability to make literary capital of the gap between modes of discourse.

Emerson's program, as I have described it, was of course not just a digest of gleanings from his adventures as public speaker. That was only one of the stimuli driving him not just to linguistic experimentation but to a thoroughgoing revaluation derived from all aspects of his experience of the most basic Western values. We shall see this very plainly in the next chapter when we examine the Transcendentalist critique of Protestant theology, which used comparative religion as a weapon – one of Emerson's contributions to American intellectual history. Yet we should not underrate the influence of the oratorical media of which Emerson availed himself in shaping that critique. Consider, for example, his mature belief that no subject can be grasped except through inspired sallies from diverse angles. Emersonians are familiar with the stylistic and thematic marks of this conviction, which Barbara Packer captures beautifully in observing how *Nature* tempts one to

> . . . adopt the analytic license of textual criticism and ascribe some parts of the book to *SR* (a pious "supernatural rationalist" who assembles a collection of exempla designed to prove the wisdom of God from evidences of design in the creation), others to *A* (a furious antinomian who

proposes an "infernal" or Blakean reading of these same exempla), and others still to R (the redactor – a shadowy figure, dispassionate and self-effacing, who attempts to reconcile the work of his predecessors by an exercise of hermeneutic ingenuity).[69]

This comment should be set next to Bronson Alcott's remarks, quoted above, on Emerson's platform style. Packer here responds to the notoriously abrupt shifts in perspective that are one concomitant of Emerson's atomistic prose, shifts designed in part, as she notes, to inject what Bakhtin calls a "polyphonic" dimension (a dialogue of different perspectives) into the exposition.[70] Alcott shows how discontinuity not only in text but also in modulation of voice was played by Emerson for all it was worth as a platform tactic. To be sure, this was not just a method but was grounded in Emerson's considered beliefs about knowledge and personality, grounded in the conviction that "every body leads two or three lives, has two or three consciousnesses which he nimbly alternates" (JMN 5:64) and in the conviction that "nothing is secure but life, transition, the energizing spirit" that expresses itself differently moment by moment (EW 2:189). But these convictions were themselves conditioned by the method of utterance. They were conditioned, in the first instance, by the practice of composing by agglutinations of journal entries, and in the second instance by the lecture format, in which the incisiveness of the part counted for more in relation to the whole than in the reading experience. Emerson could have found no forum better adapted than the lyceum to reinforce his penchant for a rhetoric of local effects loosely arranged under an umbrella concept, since in lectures stimulation and consciousness-raising, rather than methodical exposition, were the main objectives.

The institutionalization of oratory as a powerful genre in New England and as Emerson's primary medium of "publication" undoubtedly had something to do, finally, with the self-dividedness of his tendency to devalue the literary. Because Emerson instinctively tended to define literary effect in terms of prophetic eloquence, he tended as a critic to exhibit an exaggerated version of the usual Romantic tension between the desire to pinpoint literature's enduring, universal moments and the sense of its immediate obsolescence. Both extremes imply a respect for voice and a distrust of text. If Emerson shows sometimes a strikingly poststructuralist sense of the rhetoricity of discourse and the textuality of thought, it is partly because he was so attuned – as a Yankee subjected to British-influenced classical education, then armed with Wordsworth's manifesto on poetic diction, and admonished by the mixed responses of the audiences before whom he spoke – to the difficulty of following through on his commitment to speak charismatically to the uninitiated. As the frustrated journal entry from 1834 suggests, Emerson's awareness of intertextuality resulted from his logocentrism – a perspective that he wryly assumed in his awareness of the impossibility of his glowing vision of a literature of Living Words that would electrify audiences with the force of a Webster, an Everett, or a Channing.[71]

In varying degrees, the same can be said of Emerson's major contemporaries. The three passages from Dickinson, Whitman, and Melville quoted a moment ago all take shape as a response to a rhetoric of declamation that the authors have partly absorbed. Thoreau's *Walden* bills itself as an attempt to "say something" to "you . . . who are said to live in New England"(*Wa* 4), Hawthorne's *Twice-Told Tales* as an attempt to "open an intercourse with the world" (*HW* 9:6), Stowe's *Uncle Tom's Cabin* as a report of "sayings . . . word for word as heard by [the author] herself, or reported to her."[72] It would be mistaken to claim more than a limited influence for oratory as a specific literary model informing the period's canonical literature generally. For some authors, Whitman especially, it was clearly more important than for others: for Thoreau more than Hawthorne, for Whitman more than either. But to the extent that it was an influence, their Romanticist tendency to disparage the "merely literary" and to see it as a trap for the unwary writer was reinforced.

V

One is tempted to identify the 1860s as a turning point in the history of American oratory, after which it began to decline – and to conclude that that was just as well. The modern literary critic is apt to think of the impact of oratory on literature as baleful rather than benign (with honorable exceptions such as Emerson). ("The truth is," says the best study on the subject, "that Americans of the early nineteenth century were conditioned to an extravagance of style both in prose and poetry which modern taste condemns as outrageously 'rhetorical,'" owing to the relegation of literature to the role of rhetoric's handmaiden.)[73] Signs of change were now apparent: The late nineteenth century produced no Daniel Websters; in Congress the critical phase of deliberations shifted from speechifying to committee meetings, as the size and agenda of both houses more than doubled during the nineteenth century; and classical learning (which had supplied the original ideological basis for the cult of oratory) began to lose its prestige, indeed to be seen increasingly as anti-American.[74]

This, however, was only part of the picture. In fact, classical learning remained vigorous, if embattled. The Jacksonian era, which ensured its CLASSICAL eventual decline, also saw a landmark reaffirmation of the value of the LEARNING classics to higher education that ensured they would retain a prominent PERSISTED IN place in college curricula for the rest of the century.[75] Even Transcenden- HIGHER EDUCATION talist eclecticism, which strove to be global in scope, remained to a great extent classically based, as we see from Thoreau's veneration of Homer (in the "Reading" chapter of *Walden*) and Margaret Fuller's use of classical mythology in *Woman in the Nineteenth Century*. At the Saturday Club in the 1860s, when Oliver Wendell Holmes punned in Latin about the change in presidencies at Harvard, it was Emerson who recorded the joke for posterity.[76] Nor was the golden age of oratory over. On the contrary, even though congressional oratory was in decline, even though antislavery agitation had ceased, the late nineteenth century was the apogee of the public lecture movement, of women's rights and temperance campaigning, and even (despite or perhaps because of Gilded Age secularism) of homiletic eloquence – the culmination of the era of the so-called pulpit princes such as the younger Beecher, Phillips Brooks, and William A. Taylor.[77] Nor is it true that the continuance of flourishing traditions of public address was altogether dependent on the vestiges of classicism. Quite the contrary applies, for instance, to the frontier humor style of some lyceum performers – Berkshire-born Josh Billings, for example, or Artemas Ward, or Connecticut adoptee Mark Twain, who started to become a prominent figure on the lecture circuit in the 1860s.

On the other hand, it is not entirely fair to see the platform style of these men as a symptom of the release of America from the straitjacket of classical rhetoric and to indict classicism for prolonging American literary delinquency. Emerson's career shows that this is a half truth. He was handicapped by his Harvard training (the capstone of a whole boyhood of indoctrination into Brahmin gentility) in the sense that it kept him from ever reaching either of two kinds of authenticity much prized by Americanists. He could never speak like a real "native type" such as Major Jack Downing or a Davy Crockett (never mind the fact that they themselves were essentially fabrications), and he could never opt wholly for the thoroughgoing devotion to literary art that we moderns have been taught to see as the mark of artistic integrity. Yet it seems clear that in neither of these cases is the virtue all on one side. Emerson's classical education not only helped make him a speaker but also put him in a unique position to develop the polyglossic style described in section IV of this chapter. Again, the fact that he was a rhetor long before he thought seriously of becoming a Romantic artist helped him to retain a strong sense of the place of the performer and the performance in the larger body social or politic. The ethos of the rhetor could lead to the subordination of the individual to the formulaic, but the ethos of artistic integrity had its pitfalls too: It could lead to the jejune narcissism of an Ellery Channing. Indeed, it may be that the accomplishments of the New England Renaissance are to be ascribed in good part to its writers' position at the necessarily brief and transient moment of having to choose between the public way of the rhetor and the more privatistic way of the literary artist.

"A man must rise alternately on the horses of his private and his public nature" (*EW* 6:47). That Emersonian aphorism, yanked out of context, may be a good summation of both the liminal status of period rhetoric (moving between the poles of a rule-based, publically shared ritual discourse and a more original, "natural" style) and the aesthetic value of the much maligned oratorical mode (not a dying horse to be jumped from but part of a precarious but invigorating circus act of cross-leaping).

As Emerson's career also suggests, the substantive issue around which explicit debate over these alternative social and rhetorical stances tended most often to revolve was the issue of religion. The erosion of consensual religious values helped ensure the demise of the ideological underpinnings upon which the ethos of the rhetor had been built, although since this shift was only initiated, not completed, during the period, religious literature, like oratory, benefited in the short run from the climate of ferment. In the next chapter we shall trace this process through.

7

Literary Scripturism

The religion of one age is the literary entertainment of the next.
Ralph Waldo Emerson, "Character" (1866)

If there is anything in art that can take the place of religion, we should like to see it.
Josiah Gilbert Holland, *Every-Day Topics,* 2nd series (1882)

That American thought before 1865 was markedly religiocentric is a scholarly commonplace. Such was especially true of New England, owing to the Puritan imprint, which Enlightenment rationalism did not erase.[1] Indeed, since the Reformation no region of the English-speaking world has probably come closer to producing a body of writing that bears out Northrop Frye's dictum that the Bible is the master text to which all Western literature may ultimately be referred.[2] To affirm this is not necessarily to insist that religious motives were the sole or the primary determiners of human behavior even in the most pristine era of New England's settlement. Revisionist historians have argued with some cogency that the documents on which intellectual history à la Perry Miller has based its theologically oriented reconstructions of the New England mind are a "rarefied form of cognitive speculation conducted by the members of a specially trained elite"[3] that understate the importance of other motivating factors, social and economic, even for the elite itself.[4] This argument, however, though valuable as a corrective, is even less satisfactory as a comprehensive formulation of Puritan thought. "Compared with Americans of the 18th or the 19th century," Daniel Boorstin commonsensically remarks, "the Puritans surely were theology-minded."[5] The same can be said of the contrast between the 1850s and today. In order for an *Uncle Tom's Cabin* to be the national best-seller of the 1980s, its diagnosis of American social ills would need considerable secularization, unless students of contemporary religious preferences

166

have grossly underestimated the evangelical presence.[6] Particularly in the formulation of the "American way" for public purposes, including programs for the development of national letters, Christian ideology was the central animating, formative element down through the Civil War and Julia Ward Howe's unionist paean "The Battle Hymn of the Republic."[7]

Christian ideology was so pervasive, indeed, that a single chapter cannot possibly explore all its literary ramifications. For convenience's sake, we shall concentrate on the single and most central topic of the use of Scripture as a structural and thematic model for New England writers, broadening our rubric a bit to admit Herman Melville, in line with the ancient if debatable practice of appropriating him as an exhibit of certain New England traits.

I

Between the Revolution and the Civil War, the relationship between New England writing and New England piety became increasingly complicated. The period saw a proliferation of literature using biblical themes and models that, however, took place within the context of a softening of theological rigor and in some ways accelerated that process though in other ways seeming to reverse it. As we began to see in Chapter 2, the institutionalization of American belles lettres was accompanied and facilitated by a shift in biblical studies, led by New England scholars, from something like universal agreement among professing Christians that the canonical Scriptures were inspired, historically accurate writings to something like the present state of controversy, in which the traditional view had to contend against varying shades of liberalization, including the claim that the Bible was no more inspired than any other document.[8] Recent scholarship has shown that these two trends interrelate as follows. First, the erosion of the Bible's privileged status acted as a literary stimulus insofar as it prompted creative writers to think of secular literature as a legitimate and even rival means of conveying spiritual experience. During the Romantic period especially, the distinction between sacred and secular writing was not just blurred but sometimes even inverted by such claims as the argument that Scripture is only a form of poesis, hence dependent for its authority on inspired vision, which artists have in greatest measure. Consequently, a number of Anglo-American writers, starting with Blake in England and Emerson in America, took the position that the poet has the right, indeed the duty, to reconstruct mythology for himself and his era.[9] In the second place, the decline of scriptural authority was symptomatic of a general softening of dogmatic structures, particularly in mainline Protestant sects, that had the effect of pushing homiletics and apologetics themselves in a more literary direction, away from the systematic presentation of doctrine and toward impressionistic appeals to intuition and experience. One notable trend in Protestant preaching, for example, was the changing ratio of doctrinal exposition to elaboration of narrative and descriptive elements, as we move from the sermons of the disciples of Jonathan Edwards to the sermons of Lyman Beecher, in the next generation, to the sermons of Beecher's son Henry Ward and the other late nineteenth-century "pulpit princes." The new style partly just represented a pragmatic accommodation to what audiences seemed to demand, but partly it marked a deeper change in theological outlook, faith increasingly being defined in experiential as opposed to creedal terms.[10]

The net effect of these changes was, at least superficially, to interlink the domains of religious and belletristic enterprise more closely. Secular literature acquired greater spiritual legitimacy as the propagation of religion came to be seen as dependent upon verbal artistry and as the record of revelation itself was seen to be a verbal artifact. Thus the young Emerson's Calvinist Aunt Mary, ever suspicious of newfangledness, could begin to conquer her distaste for her nephew's short-lived daydream of reviving the drama in a chastened form fit for New England by reminding herself of Eichhorn's theory that the Revelation of St. John itself was expressed in dramatic form (*JMN* 2:375). Thus by 1850 one of the leaders of the liberal wing of Congregational orthodoxy could go so far as to assert (though not with impunity) that "poets . . . are the true metaphysicians."[11] The interpenetration of religion and literature also had its risks, however, in that the erasure of the old line of distinction between sacred and secular writing bespoke and also furthered an association of spirituality with the process of perception or expression, as opposed to the content of Scripture or doctrinal codification thereof. Ultimately this drift toward subjectification threatened to deprive the would-be believer of any objective referent for the "religious sentiment" and indeed of any secure criteria for determining whether a given utterance, scriptural or secular, was or was not inspired. This is the Trojan horse of the higher criticism. "The pleasures of interpretation," as Frank Kermode observes, "are henceforth linked to loss and disappointment."[12] The emergence of this awareness is one of the most important ways in which antebellum New England literary thought seems modern, for hermeneutics – both biblical and literary – still wrestles with the same problem today.

II

One of the best ways to get an insider's grasp of the trends just sketched is to observe the changing and increasingly diverse ways in which Scripture itself was adapted for literary purposes during the century following the Revolution. A convenient starting point is a 1772 Yale commencement address, *On The History, Eloquence, and Poetry of the*

Bible, given by M.A. candidate Timothy Dwight. Impetuously young Dwight proclaims his oration a significant first. "No person," he says, "hath ever attempted to entertain this assembly by displaying" the Bible as a piece of "fine writing," apart from "its purity and holiness, which by no means need a panegyric." Since tributes to classical art are commonplace, shall we, asks Dwight, remain "blind to Eloquence more elegant than Cicero, more grand than *Demosthenes*; or to Poetry more correct and tender than *Virgil*"?[13] Clearly not. Dwight proceeds to fill the gap by showing the superiority of the Bible to the literature of the Greeks and Romans in every genre.

The general tactic of reading the Bible as a compendium or model of the classical genres was not new; Milton, himself following earlier Renaissance practice, had done so in using Job as a model for *Paradise Regained.*[14] But in conservative New England, Dwight's oration was unprecedented as a sustained exercise in specialized examination of biblical rhetoric, as distinct from truth content. In this strategy, Dwight unwittingly followed English biblical scholar Robert Lowth's ground-breaking lectures *De Poesi Sacrae Hebraeorum* (1753), the first (and for many years the only systematic) analysis of Old Testament poetics, and anticipated Hugh Blair's *Lectures on Rhetoric and Belles Lettres* (1783), the most influential late eighteenth- and early nineteenth-century textbook in its field, which approvingly summarized Lowth's findings.

Dwight, Lowth, and Blair – all Protestant divines – of course intended as the climax of their comparisons to present the Bible as beyond comparison; yet in their isolation of the stylistic element and in their sustained comparison of sacred and secular rhetoric, they encouraged the relativization of Scripture. An instructive example is Lowth's account of the process by which Hebrew poets drew on local associations for imagery, which they then converted into metaphor.[15] This exercise in cultural geography was simply an application of the most up-to-date theory of literary creation, associationist aesthetics. Yet by representing Scripture as environmentally determined, this line of analysis could be and eventually was construed either as casting doubt on the purity of Old Testament inspiration or as lending support to the view that latter-day poets might be equally inspired.

The more immediate and anticipated consequence of the literary approach was the exploitation of the Bible as a literary model to a greater extent than it had ever been. Dwight advocated the literary representation of scriptural episodes, and he tried to follow his own advice in a series of poetic reworkings of biblical narratives.[16] Here, of course, he simply followed Puritan precedent. Although in theory the Puritans held that God's altar needed no polishing, from the earliest times verse paraphrase of biblical narrative and psalmody had been considered respectable; the most popular of all Puritan poems, Michael Wigglesworth's *Day of Doom*, was an extrapolation from biblical vignettes of the Last Judgment; Isaac Watts's translations of the Psalms were classics of Puritan hymnody; and the most monumental New England Puritan work, Cotton Mather's *Magnalia Christi Americana*, might be described as a vast historical fiction consisting of variations on the theme of Exodus. Yet there had been very little in New England by way of embellished retelling of biblical narratives, beyond verse paraphrase, for the sake of literary effect as distinct from didactic edification; and Dwight may be credited with ushering in a new era for New England authors in the literary appropriation of Scripture in the freedom with which he used his sources and the degree of conscious stylization he gave to his materials. We see this best in his most ambitious poem, *The Conquest of Canaan* (1785), America's first full-scale Miltonic epic, based on the Book of Joshua.[17] As the preface states, Dwight freely altered chronology and characterization in the interest of preserving the three dramatic unities, not hesitating to invent characters and events when it suited him.[18] These embellishments were not so much pure fantasy, however, as a series of aesthetic and thematic compromises with the source that permitted maximal dramatic effect (by epic standards) and thematic elaboration within an overall narrative design still recognizably scriptural. Book 10 for instance, provides a visionary panorama in imitation of *Paradise Lost*, Books 11 and 12. Dwight has Joshua view the future course of Jewish history, the coming of Jesus, the rise of Christianity, the settlement and growth of America, and the end of the world. Although no such vision was, of course, vouchsafed the biblical Joshua, the device reflects a variety of prophetic passages in the Old Testament and in a more general sense a traditional Christian belief in typological continuities of sacred history from old dispensation to new, down to the present and beyond.

Notwithstanding the many readjustments and interpolations, then, *The Conquest of Canaan* is still best described as a gigantic elaboration of Joshua, Chapters 7 through 11. Significantly, Dwight refused to countenance the obvious reading of his poem as an allegory of the Revolutionary War, with George Washington (to whom the work is dedicated) as the hero – even though Dwight repeatedly compares biblical and revolutionary events.[19] He was doubtless sincere in objecting to any interpretation that would make the poem's ultimate referent anything but Scripture itself. To the extent that the poem does reflect current events, they take on meaning through their resemblance to their scriptural antecedents, rather than vice versa. Dwight's thinking does not reflect at the conscious level the "great reversal" described by Hans Frei – namely, the shift away from the early Reformation, precritical mentality of fitting one's own frame of reference into the biblical frame to the later, critical mentality that begins by posing the question of whether the biblical narratives really stand up as history according to our standards of probability.[20]

Yet certainly the shift has begun to take place on an intuitive level. Dwight has claimed the license of making improvements in the story for the sake of dramatic effect; he has claimed, that is, a liberty in the realm of aesthetics that he later vigorously sought to deny in the realm of biblical criticism to liberal adversaries whom he accused of wilfully reading as figurative, or bracketing as spurious, texts that seemed to undermine their position.[21] Ironically, Dwight's own embellishments inevitably assume the status of revisionary readings of Joshua. A simple case would be his handling of the exposure of the Israelite thief who defies the Lord's ban on taking booty from Jericho and thereby causes a military setback. In the original, God gives meticulous directions to the puzzled Joshua as to why the battle was lost, how to detect the traitor, and how to execute him. In Dwight this speech is (uncharacteristically) much shorter, and Jehovah's conclusion more vague: "Stones shall his house destroy, and flames devour." In the source, Joshua sentences the traitor curtly and indignantly. Dwight's Joshua is indignant too, but we are assured that normally "his feeling mind / To crimes was gentle, and to misery kind."[22] The overall effect is to soften and humanize considerably, while preserving a degree of relentlessness that approximates Old Testament and military epic decorums.

Dwight's purpose in making these changes was undoubtedly as innocent as that of Hannah More, in her contemporaneous *Sacred Dramas* (1782), whose Jewish characters, she realized, might speak too much like Christians, yet "I was more anxious in consulting the advantage of my youthful readers by leading them on to higher religious views, than in securing to myself the reputation of critical exactness."[23] Furthermore, Dwight had a precedent in Puritan typological exegesis, which worked from the premise that the old dispensation was to be read in light of the new.[24] It was anachronistic to have Moses, in a flashback rerun of his parting words in Deuteronomy, exclaim prophetically, "Jesus descends; the filial GOD is born" (2:680), but it was typologically apt. Dwight always stands, however, at the border beyond which reverence for biblical authority shades into independent, creative recasting for the sake of embellishment, resulting in displacement of text by fiction. The strategy of euphemism, in time, crystallizes into the settled position that the Bible is too obscure or crude for the taste of contemporary readers (especially the young). Typology, in time, becomes unmoored from its traditional and consensual basis and becomes a part of the artist's repertoire of metaphor.[25]

Dwight's basic approach, then, is to rework both letter and spirit within an aesthetic and theological framework that at the same time, in an elastic way, still defers to the authority of the original narrative. This modestly innovative conservatism holds for most of the Bible-based literature produced between the Revolution and the Civil War. These cut across a variety of genres, the most ambitious being biblical epic and its prose successor the biblical novel, the commonest being pulpit retellings of Bible stories and the short narrative lyric on a biblical episode, which is the direct descendant of the old-fashioned biblical paraphrase.

In this latter vein, ignored by most scholars yet noteworthy as a barometer of nineteenth-century taste, one of the most popular practitioners was the young Nathaniel Parker Willis. Willis' "Hagar in the Wilderness," "Lazarus and Mary," "Jephthah's Daughter," and other such pieces, written before he forsook his boyhood Calvinism for a lucrative career as New York journalist, were "said long to have remained among the favourite edifications of devout old persons in New England."[26] Willis, like most of his fellow laborers in the field, specialized in portrayals of domestic pathos, thereby illustrating the sentimentalization of evangelical piety between Dwight's day and the late 1820s.[27] Willis' version of the Abraham and Isaac story, for instance, puts chief emphasis on Isaac's touchingly innocent sportiveness as he gambols along to the scene of the sacrifice. "Every tree," says the speaker,

> And fragrant shrub was a new hiding-place;
> And he would crouch till the old man came by,
> Then bound before him with his childish laugh,
> Stealing a look behind him playfully,
> To see if he had made his father smile.[28]

In this way the poem slowly works up to a climax of extreme tearjerkiness, in which, after the angel's intervention, Abraham falls on his face and weeps. One wonders what Kierkegaard's reaction would have been.

Some samples of the genre are more interesting to a modern eye. Lydia Sigourney's evocation of the Last Supper, in her poem of that title, becomes provocative when the persona, after surveying the disciples, lingers on Judas and suddenly fears that she may be as much of a betrayer of the Lord as he: When "I feel the breathing of those holy men," she says, "I see how deep / Sin in the soul may lurk."[29] She now applies to herself the curses that she has just leveled at Judas; breaking the dramatic illusion, she calls attention to her unworthiness and inability to trace the scene. What started as description becomes introspection ("Lord! – is it I?") – but only for a moment; for the poem is abruptly brought to a close with a formulaic prayer. Another striking but imperfect performance, Henry Knight's re-creation of "God in the Garden" commanding Adam's obedience, has a strikingly Blakean ring:

My word is Fate. On Me creation hangs.
Heaven's sapphire pavements, and the searing bars
Of Hell's dire access – they by Me were fram'd.
Around me throng Cherubick hosts of love.
Now, man, attend – 'tis Deity commands.[30]

The problem here, however, is that as one reads on, one fears that the dramatic irony is entirely unintentional – that this is another case of God the Father reasoning like a school divine.

For controlled irony, one turns to a work like the following lyric by Emily Dickinson, who was presumably responding to the mawkishness of Willis and company when she wrote *her* little poem on Abraham:

Abraham to kill him
Was distinctly told –
Isaac was an Urchin –
Abraham was old –

Not a hesitation –
Abraham complied –
Flattered by Obeisance
Tyranny demurred –

Isaac – to his children
Lived to tell the tale –
Moral – with a Mastiff
Manners may prevail.
[*DP* 1317][31]

We note that Dickinson and Willis both exploit the same sense of horror at the prospect of loving father sacrificing trusting son. For both poets the family bond is the sacred center from which the rest of the scene is viewed. Both have come a long way from Dwight's zestful if tempered rendering of Jehovah's implacable decrees. Willis, however, accepts the scriptural assumption that it is right for Abraham to do as he is told, whereas Dickinson resists this, undercutting the Willis approach further by substituting for his sentimentality a laconic grimness. Yet at the same time, Dickinson's approach also involves a closer return to the text than his, in that she discards the pretty elaboration of imagery, incident, and emotional texture that is standard fare for the whole genre in favor of a much sparser, summarizing style that is not so much an imitation as a kind of mocking echo of the comparatively toneless objectivity of the original Genesis narrative. Altogether Dickinson binds herself to that narrative in accepting, at least for present purposes, its main contours as the aesthetic and historical givens within which she will operate. So she still falls within what I have called the conservative approach to scriptural embellishment, even though the effect of her piece is to undermine the premises of the approach.

III

Dickinson rarely attempts anything resembling straightforward biblical narrative, however, even though her poetry is suffused with scriptural references, nor did any of the best antebellum New England poets.[32] Indeed the only distinguished large-scale attempt of the sort in the English-speaking world was Byron's verse drama *Cain*.[33] The following poem is far more typical of Dickinson's practice in that fraction of her canon that makes use of biblical scenarios:

> Just so – Jesus raps –
> He – does'nt weary –
> Last – at the Knocker –
> And first – at the Bell.
> Then – on divinest tiptoe – standing –
> Might He but spy the lady's soul –
> When He – retires –
> Chilled – or weary –
> It will be ample time for – me –
> Patient – upon the steps – *until* then –
> Heart! I am knocking – low at thee.
>   [*DP* 317]

This poem begins by seeming to envisage Rev. 3:20 as mininarrative ("Behold, I stand at the door, and knock: if any man hear my voice, and open the door, I will come in to him, and will sup with him, and he with me"). The first six lines, taken in themselves, represent a simple extension of the Willis-Sigourney type of biblical scene painting, except for the unusual homeliness of "tiptoe" and "spy." The poem then shifts over to the other, primary New Testament knocking reference: "Ask, and it shall be given you; seek, and ye shall find; knock, and it shall be opened unto you" (Matt. 7:7). But the effect of the collage, ironically, is to pull the poem away from its biblical context. Because narrative continuity is broken, and because the two biblical passages cut in opposite directions, the last five lines reorient the poem around the dilemma posed by the image of Jesus wooing the lady giving way to the image of the speaker knocking at the heart's door. Two very different inferences might be drawn from this sequence. We could read it as an irreverent assertion that Jesus' attempted ministration to the lady is nothing more than a simile for the deeper, more persevering care shown by the speaker for the "heart" (a synechdoche for the auditor, presumably); or we could read the poem as an anguished semiconfession (especially if one envisages the lady as the speaker herself), suggesting how the coy, perverse refusal of Jesus' offer

– out of smugness, perhaps ("It will be ample time for – me") – puts a person in the position of suppliant, alienated from one's own heart.[34]

The poem, in short, like many of Dickinson's, is finally about an enigmatic crisis adumbrated by the speaker, rather than about the biblical passages themselves, but the passages supply the conceptual frame within which the crisis is to be pondered. The poem thereby exemplifies a second general literary approach toward biblical narrative during our period, according to which the scriptural antecedent continues to be structurally central but is made subservient to some other thematic principle, usually in such a way as to raise questions about the authority of Scripture even while acknowledging its emotional force. Dickinson's poems of this type, as a rule, either dramatize doubt directly ("It always felt to me – a wrong / To that Old Moses – done – / To let him see – the Canaan – / Without the entering" [DP 597]) or imply that the Bible is meaningful only when subjectified ("One Crucifixion is recorded – only – / . . . And yet – / There's newer – nearer Crucifixion / Than That –" [DP 553]).

Such strategies, unsurprisingly, figure earliest in New England literature in writing by Unitarians, who among all the leading Protestant sects were the first to interest themselves actively in the higher criticism. Let us look at two such examples. The first is the only American biblical poem of the era to achieve, so far as I know, both critical and financial success: "The Airs of Palestine" (1816), written by a future Unitarian minister, John Pierpont, for delivery at a benefit performance of sacred music. In some quarters it earned him the reputation of being America's leading bard, although W. J. Snelling was more on target when he called Pierpont "prime parson, but poor poet." The *Airs* is an 800-line, loosely assembled whirlwind tour through a series of Old and New Testament musical highlights (the trumpets of Jericho, David's lyre, the angels' song to the shepherds at Bethlehem, etc.), followed by a series of pastoral sketches of music in the North and South American wilderness, the Scottish highlands, and other places in the Western world designed to illustrate the spread of Christianity. The unifying principle is an equation between music and spirit. To music, exclaims Pierpont, "religion owes her holiest flame." Music is pictured as "the Power that all obey"; "the throne of heaven" is not "above her spell," / Nor yet beneath it is the host of hell."[35] The nascent pantheism in these lines is pretty insipid: Pierpont is really not doing much more than playing stock metaphorical games with the biblical motif of music as integral part of ritual and celestial procedure. Furthermore, the poem's structure, far from being innovative, derives from a variety of eighteenth-century models: topographical poetry, the progress poem, and the visionary panorama poem (like Book 10 of *The Conquest of Canaan*). Pierpont's biblical impressionism, in other words, in itself carries no distinct implication of heterodoxy. Yet in giving the spirit as music metaphor priority over narrative causality, Pierpont was helping to start the tendency to collapse religion into the ecumenical myth of the Oversoul later expounded by Emerson and Thoreau.[36]

A more self-consciously revisionist effort than Pierpont's, though not at all of the mystical sort, is *Julian: or Scenes in Judaea* (1841), the last of three novels about the ancient world during the early Christian era by another Unitarian minister, William Ware.[37] This text is America's first significant attempt at dealing in prose fiction with the life of Jesus. Julian, the hero, is a romanized Jew in the process of finding his ethnic identity. He joins the Jewish nationalist movement in Palestine and is strongly drawn toward Jesus, but ultimately rejects him because Jesus is not a political messiah. This is doubly ironic because, like the Christians, Julian longs for spiritual renewal and the purgation of corruption and formalism from the church establishment. But Ware deliberately avoids a heavy-handed denunciation of Julian as apostate, judging him indirectly by leaving us with a view of him as a disappointed man afflicted by spiritual dryness, rather like T. S. Eliot's Magi.

Julian has been appraised, with some justice, as a timid anticipation of the biggest antebellum biblical best-seller, *Prince of the House of David* (1855), by the more evangelical minister-novelist Joseph Holt Ingraham.[38] Both are epistolary novels purporting to give eyewitness accounts of the life and times of Jesus; but Ingraham focuses squarely and fervently on the central figure of Jesus, whereas Ware keeps Jesus mostly in the background, concentrating Walter Scott-like on depicting the observer figure. From this it is easy to conclude simply that Ware was too inhibited or unimaginative to do what Ingraham later did. Actually, however, the two texts aim at different goals: Ingraham's goal is an embellished retelling in the Dwight tradition, designed to dramatize the life of Jesus as a story of irresistible power; Ware's is apparently to create a narrative in the liberal-revisionist vein that dramatizes the difficulties in the way of accepting Jesus, stressing the cultural gap between Jesus and even the most sympathetic of onlookers among the privileged and the sophisticated.[39] Ware makes this point tellingly by the comparative obliquity with which he treats most of the gospel events to which he alludes – the teachings, the miracles, the Passion, the Resurrection. The reader sees these from a distance, mainly through the reports of those outside the Christian movement.

This narrative approach clearly has theological implications. It suggests, first, Ware's appreciation of the alienness of the Christian revelation to the traditional Jewish mind. Beyond this, it suggests the difficulty that the most earnest and enlightened people in any age might have in accepting as redeemer someone who inverts their preconceptions and stands for

a kingdom not of this world. The narrative method also perhaps reflects
Ware's own ambivalence toward the Gospels, given his commitment, as
a liberal Unitarian scholar, to the method of rational-empirical inquiry.
Unitarian intellectuals were earnest Christians whose forte, however,
consisted in casting doubt on orthodox claims for the Bible's trustwor-
thiness as a historical record by interpreting Old and New Testaments as
culture-bound documents and by explaining supernatural events other
than the gospel miracles as psychological projection. In this view, the
gospel narratives assumed an even more central importance in the canon
than ever before, as the one place where the Bible's authority as the source
of a truly inspired ethics could be securely established; yet to establish its
textual authenticity and meaning seemed now so much more arduous a
task than ever before in the history of American Protestantism as to put
the Gospels at a greater distance even from those who wished to believe.[40]
The structure of Ware's *Julian* mirrors this paradox of the importance of
the historical Jesus as against the difficulty of access.

IV

Once the relativization process well under way in Ware becomes
complete, then biblical narrative loses its privileged status as focal point
and becomes, as Theodore Parker put it, as human a document as Newton's *Principia,* the Vedas, and the Koran.[41] It becomes, in other words,
one among many mythical frames of reference that may potentially be
used as analogues to clarify, complicate, exalt, or satirize the mundane.
The literary work no longer centers on events in ancient Judaea or Canaan
or a vignette of Jesus knocking at the door. The center of gravity may
become, for example, a present-day retreat to Walden Pond, which is
viewed not only as a reenactment of pioneer and Puritan questing but in
terms of Christian asceticism ("Higher Laws"), Homeric epic ("Reading"),
or Oriental (Persian, Hindu, Confucian) models of contemplation and
spiritual discipline. Or the subject may be the voyage of a Nantucket
whaler, to be understood not only in terms of such Judeo-Christian antecedents as Ishmael's wanderings, the testing of Job, and Jonah's and
Ahab's resistance of Jehovah but also in terms of numerous other mythological analogues ranging from Egyptian to Polynesian. The multiplic-
ity of these analogous yet disparate frames of reference reinforces the paradoxical impression, created in each case, of the intimacy and yet at the
same time the strangeness of the interfusion of mundane particulars (like
the minutiae of whaling) with the mystery of myth.

In Melville's novel, as the different mythological strands compete with
each other for our attention they make the text more luminous, through
their diversity of implication, yet at the same time threaten to cancel each
other out; and the whole idea of a nineteenth-century whaling voyage as

a sacred narrative is both enhanced by the narrator's amazing resourcefulness in converting tar-and-blubber details into metaphor and called into question by the density of those details, as well as by the comic extravagance of much of the metaphor building. The mythic dimension of the text is thus made imaginatively potent but epistemologically dubious.

This duality reflects not only the legacy of the higher criticism but also that of the older skeptical-rationalist tradition, known to American readers at a much earlier date from such sources as Pierre Bayle (whose *Dictionary* was used by Melville), Voltaire (to whom Dwight had ironically dedicated his *Triumph of Infidelity*), David Hume (the fearsome "Goliath" of skepticism, to the young Emerson's imagination), Thomas Paine, and Constantin Volney (whose *Ruins of Empire* was translated by Joel Barlow and Thomas Jefferson). These writers espoused a debunking version of comparative mythology that had the effect of reducing Christianity to superstition, an approach that was in part an anticipation of, in part a counterpoint to, the tendency of the higher criticism, which, in diagnosing biblical narrative as mythology, usually at least purported to treat it in an affirmative light as the creative product of religious consciousness. These writers, who for generations had been denounced by the New England intellectual establishment, did not even now become respectable; but their point of view came to be taken more seriously.[42]

Let us look more closely at the literary consequences of the post-Christian, comparatist approach to biblical models through the example of *Moby-Dick,* which arguably warrants preemption in a study of New England literature on solider grounds than the dubious genealogical-geographical arguments that Melville was "New Englandish" by virtue of paternal ancestry, maternal creed (Calvinist, albeit Dutch), literary affiliations (Hawthorne), and sometime residence (the Berkshires). Like Harriet Beecher Stowe's *Uncle Tom's Cabin,* with which *Moby-Dick* has much in common,[43] Melville's masterpiece is on one level a book about the presumptions of New England cultural imperialism, part of the exposé being the New Englander's discovery of what it means to live in the larger world. Like *Uncle Tom's Cabin, Moby-Dick* may be taken as a document in the history of New England's extraordinary transcontinental and international diaspora, which in Stowe's version sent Vermonters south to become slaveholders and overseers (all the chief exhibits in the novel are people from Vermont) and in Melville's version equipped the Yankee-owned American whaling industry with its officers, the rest of the world supplying the brawn for the crew. Crucial to each plot is the pattern of holding up a nonwhite center of values in juxtaposition to the New England ethos – Uncle Tom and Queequeg. But whereas Tom essentially just mirrors in idealized form the Christian virtues that the dominant culture values in principle, Queequeg is deployed in a more complicated way, both underscoring the gap between cannibal and Christian and raising a question as to who is who. This is one of many ways in which Melville moves, in *Moby-Dick*, toward an ambivalent, comparatist framework in which all myths, and yet no myths, seem to be keys to meaning.

This effect is created in *Moby-Dick* most fundamentally by the highly self-conscious way Melville goes about citing texts and creating his own. Devices such as the prefatory "extracts" and the classification of whales as types of books keep reminding us – to an extent that the texts discussed earlier in this chapter do not – that the text at hand is an exercise in reading and writing.[44] To apply this to Melville's use of the Bible, consider how the Jonah story is dealt with in its two primary occurrences: Father Mapple's sermon (Chapter 5), and Chapter 83, "Jonah Historically Regarded."[45] These two chapters imitate and comment upon complementary styles of theological discourse. This is obvious in the latter case, one of Melville's funniest pseudoscholarly tours de force, in which Ishmael pretends to defend the historical reliability of the Jonah story, using the style of the old-fashioned exegetical commentary (still very much alive in Melville's day)[46] against the criticism of a skeptical old salt. The narrator resorts to a series of increasingly ridiculous arguments to uphold biblical inerrancy. The irony is less obvious in the chapter on Mapple's sermon, which imitates contemporary folk preaching with such force and apparent naïveté as to convince even some of Melville's best critics that it "states the ethical standards against which the fates of Ahab, Ishmael, and the rest are subsequently measured."[47] The text, however, has already called Mapple's moral authority into question through sly insinuations as to the theatricality of his pulpit style, and it does so again in the following chapter, which depicts Ishmael's abrupt and cheerful apostasy to idol worship. Not evangelical preaching but the "soothing savage" redeems Ishmael's heart after all. Later on in the narrative, when we see that some of Mapple's statements might actually be construed as lending support to Ahab ("Woe to him who seeks to pour oil upon the waters when God has brewed them into a gale!"), the sermon's claims to authoritativeness are further undermined.[48] Both Jonah chapters, then, turn out to be acts of ventriloquism perpetrated ironically, readings of Scripture by two types of biblical literalists whose faith in the Jonah narrative, rather like Dwight's *Conquest of Canaan,* leads to an imaginative reconstruction that the careful reader sees as defective.

Yet the matter does not rest here, at the point where the philosophes would have stopped, because the two chapters rub against each other in the reading experience. In "Jonah Historically Regarded" the learned apologist is so transparently unconvincing as to reduce Jonah's story to absurdity, whereas Mapple's sermon operates on a level of pathos and power that commands us to take the analogy seriously, whatever we think of Mapple. Melville's approach, then, involves remythologizing as well as demolition. Traditional theology is exposed as phantasmal, but in spectral form it still haunts the narrative. The story of Jonah is both a sham and, at the same time, deeply meaningful. This wavering doubtless has much to do with the metaliterary character of *Moby-Dick,* since Melville's approach dooms him to be forever engaged in the acts of reading and writing, in establishing and dismantling his myths.

In antebellum biblical criticism, there is, predictably, no precise counterpart to Melville, no out-and-out comparative mythologist. Even Transcendentalist enfant terrible Theodore Parker, at least in his public statements, stopped short of David Freidrich Strauss's *Das Leben Jesu,* the culmination of early German myth criticism.[49] This collective caution was probably caused not so much by the dearth of skeptical people as by the fact that American biblical scholarship was closely tied to denominationalism. Yet in the work of the more sophisticated scholars, particularly the Unitarian liberals, we find at least some anticipation of Melville. In each case, we find the narrator-critic engaged in a laborious quest to distinguish truth from deception, made complicated by the working assumption that what is literally false or misleading might be at least figuratively valid.

A good illustration of this analogy is the exegesis of Jesus' temptation in the wilderness (Matt. 4:1–11) by Andrews Norton, Emerson's chief adversary in the "Miracles Controversy" of the 1830s and the Unitarians' leading New Testament scholar.[50] Norton starts from the position that the passage is genuine (not an interpolation) yet cannot be taken literally. What then? The obvious solution would be to read it as allegorical psychodrama, with Satan as "moral evil hypostasized." This, however, Norton finds unsatisfactory because, among other reasons, the conception of Jesus as genuinely tempted is "wholly incongruous with his character," and, as a Unitarian, Norton cannot accept that Jesus, a being "inferior" to God, was in any sense capable of performing a miracle that God himself did not will in the first instance. Norton likewise rejects several other hypotheses. The text makes sense, Norton concludes, only if we first approach it as a garbled report of what was originally a discourse by Jesus on the nature of his messiahship. Norton's conjectural reconstruction is that the temptation narrative was originally offered by Jesus as a parable retorting to the disciples' false expectations of him as a secular chieftain, according to the popular view. Norton imagines something like the following exchange as the origin of the temptation narrative:

> And they said, When wilt thou manifest thyself in thy kingdom and be exalted, thou and thy followers?
> And he spoke a parable to them, saying, The Son of Man was in the

wilderness, praying to God and fasting; and Satan came to him to tempt him, and said, Lo! thou art hungry! since thou art the Son of God . . . , command these stones to become loaves of bread.[51]

For Norton, this conjecture solves the problem nicely.

Norton's and Melville's approaches to Matthew and Jonah are similar. For both, the biblical narrative is powerful, but absurd in a literal sense. Both display a relish for undermining the claim of inerrancy and for pointing up the credulity and superstitiousness of previous commentators and of the biblical authors themselves. In both cases, however, there is an underlying commitment to reworking the narrative in such a way as to make it usable. And in both cases, the solution involves the creation of an original narrative that presents itself as the literal level to which the text – now conceived as legendary – refers. It is ironic that Norton, years later, in effect answers Emerson's call at the end of his Divinity School Address (which Norton thought blasphemous) for some inspired person to come forth and rewrite Scripture to give it more "epical integrity" (EW 1:92).

In contrast to Melville, Norton is always working toward closure, approaching the Bible as historical cryptogram. Norton is confident of being able to clear up all obscurities through careful ratiocination. His notion of myth is more reductively negative than Melville's. Although the quoted passage catches Norton in the act of remythification, in principle myth, in Norton's rationalist framework, is tantamount to misrepresentation. The narrative that Norton invents has no luminousness for him; it is simply a demonstration of the truth he thinks he has induced from the empirical evidence. Melville, in contrast, approaches biblical (and non-Christian) myth, at least up to a point, as a vehicle of symbolic expression, interpreting literal events in terms of partial but tenuous linkages between Ishmael's mysteriously motivated sea journey and Jonah's flight from Joppa, between the God-defiance of Jonah and of Ahab, between Tashtego's deliverance from the whale's head and Jonah's; and perhaps also between the relentlessness of Ahab after his traumatic first encounter with Moby Dick and Jonah's rigidity after assuming the prophetic role following his deliverance from the whale.[52] The result is a patchwork biblical symbolism that looks on the surface like Puritan typology, although it is stripped of the assumption of coherence in which typology is grounded.[53]

V

Moby-Dick might thus be seen not only as an analysis and revision of the story of Jonah and other sacred narratives now reconceived as myth but also as a kind of sacred narrative itself, generating, for example, an original myth of the whale (albeit from the residue of earlier myths).

On this level the romance reflects the period's most radical conception of the literary appropriation of Scripture: the Emersonian view that writing, literally as well as etymologically, should *be* Scripture, that the poet's proper job is to write the ultimate Bible that has never yet been written: "'Tis high time we should have a bible that should be no provincial record, but should open the history of the planet, and bind all tendencies and dwarf all the Epics & philosophies we have (*JMN* 8:438)."[54] This position is based on Emerson's belief that all extant religious systems and records thereof are intertranslatable expressions of the same divine spirit; that the individual has direct access to that spirit, which exists within him; and that the individual, on this most fundamental level, is not idiosyncratic but universal, so that a discourse completely purged of idiosyncrasy is at least conceivable, if only as an asymptotic limit. This conceptual framework, as Emerson intimates in "History," is in theory both all-inclusive ("There is nothing but is related to us, nothing that does not interest us"; everything in the realm of the Not-me belongs in the new Bible) and yet at the same time built upon the assumption of the centrality of the privileged individual observer ("If the whole of history is in one man, it is all to be explained from individual experience.")[55]

It was from within this framework that Emerson issued his call, at the end of the Divinity School Address, for the "new Teacher" to complete the "fragmentary" "Hebrew and Greek Scriptures."

As for the kind of scripture that Emerson had in mind, the primary models seem to have been, in ascending order of importance, belletristic poesis of the sublimer kind (e.g., *Paradise Lost*); sacred literature in the Judeo-Christian and other traditions; and most especially the mystical notion, derived from Swedenborgianism and other Christian and Platonic sources, of the book of nature, of nature conceived as a vast symbolic text, the purer complement of the humanly composed Book of Revelation, which Emerson regarded as by definition comparatively imperfect.[56] "If adequately executed," the representation of the correspondences between nature and spirit "would be the poem of the world, in which all history and science would play an essential part," Emerson says with reference to Swedenborg, whose oeuvre Emerson reluctantly dismisses as too dogmatic (*EW* 4:120). Emerson's other definitions of poetic form and of his own vocation as poet are likewise centered upon the idea of perception of mystical correspondence.[57]

The idea of the writer as prophet commissioned to write the ultimate scripture-poem of the universe was immensely stimulating for those authors of the next generation affected by Emerson. It underlies Thoreau's Scripture-centered program of reading in the early 1840s; the pervasiveness of biblical references in *Walden*, which he greatly increased during the process of revision; his aspiration to make and record his acts with such "deliberateness" as to invest them with a cosmic significance approximating that of the staff carved by the artist of Kouroo, which, when consummated in the fulness of time, became transformed "into the fairest of all the creations of Brahma."[58] It underlies Whitman's assumption of a prophetic or demiurgical role as the speaker of *Leaves of Grass*: his hope that it would be the "New Bible"; its encyclopedic scope, encompassing even "mossy scabs of the worm fence"; its psalmic intonations.[59] It even tinged with a bit of inebriation Emily Dickinson's more cautious muse.[60] "Every man that writes is writing a new Bible; or a new Apocrypha; to last for a week or a thousand years," wrote Carlyle in 1832. He was not attempting to describe New England literature, but unwittingly he summed up its most cherished dream.[61]

Yet the new Bible did not get written, unless one counts *The Book of Mormon*. Although unquestionably a heady and energizing ideal, the prophetic-bardic model of the writer led in fact mostly to fragmentary results: Alcott's Orphic Sayings, Thoreau's collections of "Ethnical Scriptures," and, on a somewhat larger scale, Whitman's catalogues. The only complete literary works of the period that can qualify as scripture in any strict sense of the term are the "inspired" poems of Jones Very, like this one, in which the speaker is Christ himself:

> This is the rock where I my church will build
> Harder than flint its sure foundations are
> . . . .
> Knock and thou too shall enter in
> I hold the keys and who but me can bind?

In another, "Thy Brother's Blood," the speaker is a prophet figure standing enraged, Amos-like, for absolutism:

> I have no Brother, – they who meet me now
> Offer a hand with their own wills defiled
> . . . .
> Go wash the hand that still betrays thy guilt;
> Before the spirit's gaze what stain can hide?[62]

As the first example shows, however, Very's "original" scripturism is always in danger of lapsing into mere biblical ventriloquism. Perhaps that was inevitable. To set out to write Scripture was to put oneself in the bind of aiming at a truly "original relation to the universe" (*EW* 1:7) and at the same time to acknowledge that one was following a model, whether univocally Christocentric as in Very, or pluralistic as in Thoreau, Whitman, and Melville.

Literary scripturism, then, was a vastly exciting project doomed, by definition, to failure. Small wonder that Emerson looked in vain for his ideal poet. His own essays and poems on the theme increasingly acknowledge this. They consist mainly either of prospective descriptions of the ultimate poem or poet to come or of meditations about the gap between inspiration and utterance. The gap became increasingly formidable from "Self-Reliance," to "Experience," to "Illusions," until it seemed that Emerson's project had become the charting of the phenomenal envelope of illusions in which we are trapped rather than the experience of transcendence that frees us.[63] That is not quite the whole story, since Emerson's discontinuous, aphoristic rhetoric might be described as rhetoric of transcendence, each new perception a new circle effacing the last, obliterating contexts, obliterating all limits. That is Emerson's great hope in "Circles," for instance. Furthermore, as Thomas McFarland says of Romantic fragmentariness in general, "The logic of incompleteness is . . . the logic of infinity": The fragmentary utterances of Emersonian man speaking as fitfully inspired God-in-ruins imply through their very fragmentariness a magnificent totality somewhere over yonder.[64] Finally, and most important, the dream of writing as scripture keeps one going. It allows one to believe that I am born to victory even if I am defeated every time, that my bark will sink to another sea. So Emersonian irony, as is clear from his theory of the comic as residing in the sense of a botched perception of the whole (*EW* 8:155–74), is understandable only in terms of its commitment to the model of writer as prophet and of literature as Scripture. But this aspiration usually manifests itself as an ironic dialogue between intimation and actuality. So with Thoreau. So with Dickinson. So with *Moby-Dick*'s treatment of the "symbolic" character of the whale, which in some ways the text suggests is nothing more than an inscription written onto him not only by Ahab but also by the narrator, who, with disarming candor, explicitly classifies whales as books and admits, by conceding the defectiveness of his taxonomy, the impossibility of the enterprise. The attempt to write the gospel of the whale threatens to become a confession and enactment of the inability to achieve anything beyond the act of writing itself.[65]

The intimation that the quest for a new Scripture must inevitably end in the mere writing of books without end perhaps first starts to dawn as one becomes aware of the inevitable obsolescence of Scripture as conceived in Romantic terms. "The quality of the imagination is to flow, and not to freeze," says Emerson (*EW* 3:34), in the process of criticizing Swedenborg's visions for excessive rigidity and thereby qualifying his own earlier association (in *Nature*) of fixed spiritual properties with particular natural facts. Thus the inspiration of one moment is qualified by that of the next; thus the Walden experience, which it took Thoreau a decade to write up, can never be canonical because it is a past stage of being, perhaps no longer expressive of its author's needs, not to mention another's. Thus Romantic Scripture is from the start an impossibility because its authority resides only in the moment of utterance. The ironies multiply when one realizes that one is seldom, in any case, inspired – or, if inspired, capable of utterance; and they become overwhelming when one starts to wonder (with Melville) whether the rationalists might after all have been right that there is no such experience as inspiration – only its counterfeit.

VI

Looking back over the ground covered in this chapter, we see that the literary liberation of the Bible was made possible, in its first stages, by an unwitting collaboration between theistic writers who contributed the bulk of the period's Bible-based literature and the rise of a historicocritical method of analysis that often resonated disconcertingly with rationalist skepticism. This led to a comparative mythological approach to Scripture that sometimes moved in the direction of debunking it as fabrication but sometimes led to an emphasis on the luminous meaningfulness of its symbolism or even to a campaign for literature as scripture.

It would seem, then, that Bible-based literature cannot go beyond quotation, paraphrase, and translation, and maybe not even that far, without putting the writer – voluntarily or not – in the position of rewriting Scripture and thus setting up the individual imagination in a sort of rivalship. And when this happens, sooner or later a conscious process of critical examination is bound to ensue, the end result of which will be to produce writers who explicitly assert the priority of their own imaging over the original, either in frustration (as they recognize the possibility of solipsism) or in affirmation (as they assert the possibility of an original relation to the universe.) At this point, faith in the authority of the original text, assuming that it existed to start with, is transferred to faith in the literary process, and piety merges with aestheticism.

At least in the short run, the results of this merger were invigorating, not only for literature but also for biblical criticism. In *Moby-Dick* a good example of the latter is how Melville's ambivalence toward Ahab as heroic madman goes beyond the usual contemporary readings of the biblical Ahab as exemplum of the evil tyrant and thereby anticipates the late nineteenth-century hypothesis (now accepted) that the Ahab stories in 1 Kings reflect a conflation of pro-Ahab and anti-Ahab commentators.[66] But the synthesis was unstable. It was probably no accident that the drift of Melville's career, from *Typee* to *The Confidence-Man*, was from narrative to metanarrative, with plot (mythos) eventually becoming swallowed up by the narrative consciousness. Melville's ambivalence toward storytelling as such grew in proportion with, if not as a function of, his epistemological uncertainty: The figure of the confidence man had a literary as well as a theological component to its symbolism.

As usual, Dickinson formulated the problem most succinctly, if obscurely:

> A Word made Flesh is seldom
> And tremblingly partook
> Nor then perhaps reported
> But have I not mistook
> Each one of us has tasted
> With ecstasies of stealth
> The very food debated
> To our specific strength –
>
> A Word that breathes distinctly
> Has not the power to die
> Cohesive as the Spirit
> It may expire if He –
> "Made Flesh and dwelt among us"
> Could condescension be
> Like this consent of Language
> This loved Philology.
>
> [*DP* 1651]

Each of us, says the first octave, has personally experienced "a Word made Flesh" – a living Word – meaning, I take it, some kind of literary communication (poetic or epistolary) that struck us with a power and authority like that ascribed to the Logos in John 1:1–14.[67] The second octave, however, suggests that the meaningfulness of this experience is contingent on the actual relationship between word and Logos that has been metaphorically asserted.[68] The living Word, though immortal in itself, depends for its "expiration" on the truth of the Incarnation in the Christian as well as the linguistic sense – depends, that is, upon the promise of eternal life implicit in the "condescension" of Christ-Logos in becoming flesh. "Expire" here seems to combine the familiar modern sense of "death" with the now obsolete sense of "breathe out" or "emit," thereby suggesting the allied concepts of eucharistic transformation and dispersal of the Word through consumption of the host and the Incarnation-death-Resurrection cycle that the Eucharist symbolizes in an extended sense. Without this divine antitype, the experience of word-made-fleshness remains a merely personal one, the eucharistic metaphor being crucial to the glorification of the process of verbal transmission. To paraphrase another poem, which emphasizes the dilemma rather than the splendid possibility of transcendence, the abdication of belief makes the experience smaller (*DP* 1551).

The poem resists this conclusion, of course, by thrusting the metaphorical vehicle forward with such feeling at the end: "Like this consent of Language / This loved Philology." That sounds like a pledge of allegiance to the philological. The "Word made Flesh" that really inhabits the speaker's life is not the Incarnation of Jesus but the incarnation of the human word in the luminous, intersubjective fantasy that the speaker has enjoyed in secret. So in a sense the poem does affirm a religion of language, whereby the Incarnation itself is introduced in the manner of a somewhat dry and scholarly analogue. But writing's worshiper depends on that analogue to validate her emotion. Since she doubts the possibility of this higher communion, all she is finally left with is the compelling but insubstantial metaphor of language as miraculously alive. Thus the poem shields itself from recognizing, yet acknowledges all the same, that secular philology remains on the merely emotive level unless authorized by sacred philology.

VII

Altogether, two stages in the disappearance of belief might be distinguished: the first marked by the increasing anxiety that the spirit in which one wishes to believe may not exist, the second marked by the increasing sense that the religious framework no longer commands any appeal even metaphorically. The latter did not become even a possibility in New England culture until much later. Dickinson and her major contemporaries operate at varying points along the first stage, sometimes vacillating wildly (like Dickinson) from work to work and even passage to passage. Their imagination remains in most cases at least loosely bibliocentric, despite the centrifugal impulses some display. When Hawthorne writes of his ancient colleagues that they were "seated, like Matthew, at the receipt of customs, but not very liable to be summoned thence, like him, for apostolic errands" (*HW* 1:7), we see the prophetic handwriting on the wall. To use the evangelist's occupation as grist for one's witticism is a sure sign that biblicism is lapsing into decadence but also that it remains very much alive as a frame of reference, as the subsequent romance of the scarlet letter makes clear.[69] Altogether, a good deal of what is most challenging and memorable in the literature of New England between 1770 and 1860 arises from the interplay, often within the same work, between the voices of the believer, the seeker, the skeptic, and the virtuoso. This interplay becomes increasingly complex, self-conscious, and (as non-Christian mythography is introduced) broad-ranging, proof of the Thoreauvian maxim that "decayed literature makes the richest of all soils" (*TJ* 3:353).

Nowhere is this more evident than in the case of the most spectacular product of the religious imagination in antebellum New England, Harriet Beecher Stowe's *Uncle Tom's Cabin,* a fitting text with which to end this chapter. The commercial success of this novel, which outsold its nearest rivals in popular fiction by a margin of three to one,[70] warns us again not to envisage the stages of literary scripturism as a simple linear sequence. Such writers as Melville, Thoreau, and Dickinson represent the literary avant-garde but not the net cultural outcome of the religious tendencies of the period. On the level of popular culture, religious behavior arguably moved in a direction precisely opposite to that of the secularization process that I have charted. Historians of American religion have shown, for example, that evangelicalism and church membership dramatically increased during the early nineteenth century, at the very time when the higher criticism was taking hold in elite circles.[71] *Uncle Tom's Cabin* is even more saturated with evangelical sentiment than *The Conquest of Canaan,* with which we began this chapter, and the contrast in this regard between Stowe and Dwight's major Neoclassical contemporaries – Trumbull, Barlow, and Dennie, for instance – is so dramatic as to suggest that the present chapter ought to be reconceived in terms of a movement from early skepticism or indifferentism to faith, rather than vice versa.[72]

But although Stowe thus reminds us that the Willis approach to Abraham strengthened its hold on New England culture even as Dickinsonian skepticism gained ground, her writing is equally valuable as an exhibit of the ferment within the precincts of orthodoxy itself that, in the long run, pushed Christian evangelicalism into phases two and three, even while appealing to and seeming to promote old-fashioned, Bible-centered Christianity. Up to a point, *Uncle Tom's Cabin* is a traditional jeremiad. It assaults institutionalized religion, as Puritan fast-day sermons did, by invoking against it the vision of a true and purified holy commonwealth, arguing from a review of the signs of the times that its spiritual pathology can be cured only by religious revival. But the book finally calls for something closer to revolution than to restoration, insofar as it finds the true sources of spiritual renewal and authority on society's margins – in women, children, and blacks – and insofar as the religion of the heart that such people exemplify for Stowe represents a challenge to the patriarchal theological establishment. Stowe was by no means the sole or first voice in the movement toward the "domestication of theology,"[73] whereby the stern, masculine God of justice was modified into a feminized God of mercy, and the glittering but remote abstraction of heaven was redefined in terms of the warm, intimate image of home. But Stowe might at least be credited with having produced "the *summa theologica* of nineteenth-century America's religion of domesticity."[74]

The boldness of her prophetic imagination is shown most strikingly in her treatment of Scripture, which she reverenced but which, like every good feminist and antislavery advocate, she knew she also had to challenge. And she did not take the easy route of haggling over the Pauline passages that counsel acquiescence to slavery as the law of the land or admonish women to keep silent in church. "This novel," as Jane Tomp-kins says, "does not simply quote the Bible, it rewrites the Bible."[75] Stowe is led, for example, to create the first fictional Christ figure in American literature, [76] in the person of Uncle Tom, whom she carefully feminizes as a "Victorian heroine: pious, domestic, self-sacrificing, emotionally uninhibited in response to people and ethical questions."[77] As in the New Testament, a book of Acts follows the passion narrative. Tom's very literal crucifixion leads causally to his young master George Shelby's conversion to abolitionism and symbolically to the evangelization of Africa by the surviving black characters. They then start to carry out the millennial vision intimated long before of Africa's future rise to greatness as the race most likely to develop Christian virtues to perfection (owing to its characteristic traits of trustingness and humility). Thus Stowe brings about the triple triumph of Christianity, Africa, and the feminine, and with this the humbling of American spiritual pride, not only through the book-long indictment of slavery but through her neat reversal of the ideology of American manifest destiny – the debased residue of the Puritan and Revolutionary conception of American chosenness.

Like any author, Stowe must have been unaware of some of her book's ideological implications. In conceiving the plight and destiny of women and blacks as interrelated examples of the Christian idea that the humble shall be exalted, Stowe made it easy to conceal from herself the full extent of her ambivalence toward blacks (whom she could not comfortably accept as fellow American citizens) and toward the rights of women (whom she sees, conservatively, as influencing society through moral suasion rather than through the political process). At least the novel shows no recognition that its proposed solutions would, if implemented, leave any legitimate unmet need or demand out of account. The text exhibits a comparable blindness, I think, in its handling of biblical analogies. Despite her conviction that *Uncle Tom's Cabin* was divinely inspired, Stowe probably would have insisted just as strongly that it was not an attempt to rewrite the Bible as Dwight insisted that his *Conquest* was. Uncle Tom is certainly meant to be "The Martyr" (the title of the chapter recording his death), not "the Christ." For both Tom and the narrator, the distinction is obvious. But the text cannot keep from crossing the line, importing, with some variations, the biblical motifs of the drink presented to the crucified man, the dialogue with the two thieves (Tom saves both, not just one), and the two-day interval between the Passion and the "Resurrection" event of George's transformation by Tom's example after receiving his last words. These collages of gospel and vernacular events blur the distinction between type and antitype, a blurring more consistent than Stowe may have realized with the text's overall insistence that faith is validated only through decisive moral action.

Stowe's redirection of theology to the end of social mimesis and protest was thus both a symptom of theological decay and of creative theological revival. Her father, by humanizing Edwardsean theology, had both softened its rigors and extended its influence. Stowe practiced a similar – indeed (as Ann Douglas points out) competing – form of revivalism. In *Uncle Tom's Cabin,* as in Emerson's Divinity School Address, the theory and practice of religion tend to boil down to a single imperative: People must do what "they feel right."[78] "Dogmatism resting on sentiment": That summation of Theodore Parker's message by one late nineteenth-century church historian sums up even better Stowe's feminized evangelical Christianity.[79] But the boiling-down process remained emotionally powerful – as the reception of *Uncle Tom* shows – so long as entrenched orthodoxies remained with which to do battle, either without or within. In such a climate, religious literature, which almost by definition complements, if it does not oppose, theological discourse by relying on affective appeal rather than cognition, is bound to flourish. And in mid-nineteenth-century America, as Stowe found, to her amazement, it flourished sufficiently to help ensure the transformation of civil strife into holy war.

Reinventing Puritanism: The New England Historical Imagination

8

The Concept of Puritan Ancestry

No ancestry in the world is half so illustrious, as the Puritan founders of New England.
> Nathaniel Appleton Haven, "Early Settlers of New Hampshire" (1841)

Yesterday is the enemy of Today.
> Ralph Waldo Emerson, "The Protest" (1839)

The more radical the rejection of anything that came before, the greater the dependence on the past.
> Paul de Man, *Blindness and Insight* (1971)

From our survey of the broader contours of the New England imagination we turn now to its regionally oriented aspects, its historical literature and its literature of place. These, by and large, exhibit the same primary traits so far identified: a concentration on poetry and prose, as opposed to drama; a strong rhetorical and didactic element, frequently offset by aesthetic distancing; a tendency to achieve originality by working disruptively within conventionalized patterns; a fondness for playing the formal off against the vernacular; and a markedly Protestant ideology. With these as instruments, New England writers re-created their region as a literary artifact. In this chapter we begin examination of the key ingredient, the myth of Puritan antecedence.

As we shall see, it was during our period that America's stereotypes about the Puritans fully crystallized and began to exert a fascination for creative writers that still runs strong today. The notion of America's Puritan legacy, in both its Jekyll and its Hyde aspects, is the legacy of the writers we are about to survey.

A haunting meditative poem by the local colorist Celia Thaxter may help us to anticipate the challenges of the task at hand.[1] It starts:

193

> Crushing the scarlet strawberries in the grass,
> I kneel to read the slanting stone.

The scene: "In Kittery Churchyard" – Thaxter's title. The marker: for "Mary, wife of Charles Chauncy, died April 23, 1758, in the 24th year of her age" – Thaxter's epigraph. The speaker reacts immediately and sympathetically:

>   Alas!
> How sharp a sorrow speaks! A hundred years
> And more have vanished . . .
> Since here was laid, upon an April day,
> Sweet Mary Chauncy in the grave away.

She indulges this emotion at length by imagining the pathos of the husband's grief. But then the beauty of the present day breaks in on her, and her fantasy shifts to imagining Chauncy's recovery from sorrow:

> The storm and stress of strong and piercing pain
> Yielding at last, and he grew calm again,
> Doubtless he found another mate before
> He followed Mary to the happy shore!

As the slight ironic bite of the last couplet suggests, however, Thaxter has no truck with easy resolutions. The ending makes this clear:

> But none the less his grief appeals to me
> Who sit and listen to the singing sea
> This matchless summer day, beside the stone
> He made to echo with his bitter moan,
> And in my eyes I feel the foolish tears
> For buried sorrow, dead a hundred years!

The speaker here pays tribute to old mortality but rather against her will. As a woman, she partly resists the compulsion to identify with the widower's easily consoled grief; and, more important, she dislikes in herself the weakness of becoming fixated on a century-old event ("buried dead a hundred years"), especially on such a nice day.

The speaker's reluctant and self-conscious avowal of emotional identification with what she rationally knows is an alien other whose nearness she has fantasized makes a good monitory image with which to begin discussion of New England historical mythography. It reminds us of the ever widening gap between our period's writers and the Puritans with whom or against whom they aligned themselves, whether or not they acknowledged that gap. It further suggests that the extremes of hostility and filiopietism that the Puritans provoked in their descendants were equally symptomatic of the historical distance between the eras and of the necessity of bridging that distance through projective myth, whether such myth making took the form of well-documented and elegant critical

[handwritten margin note: [IMMODERATE REVERENCE FOR FOREBEARS OR TRADITION.]]

fictions or, as here, sheer daydreaming. Finally, Thaxter's poem reminds the modern interpreter of the perils of taking any verbal artifact about the past as evidence of a decisive, permanent impress of history on the mind of the individual or the collective. For the average New Englander of our period who thought at all about the matter, the sense of Puritan origins was probably more a mood inspired by special occasions than a constant, indwelling magnetic force. We insist on more at the risk of falling into absurdity. That, however, is not to trivialize the subject. Some moods of our own conjuring can affect behavior powerfully, as Thaxter's poem also attests, and as the remarkable vogue of historiography in the early republic demonstrates many times over.

I

The first century of American nationhood was, indeed, a history-conscious age. "Never before or since," affirms one of the best books on the subject, "has history occupied such a vital place in the thinking of the American people as during the first half of the nineteenth century."[2] The American Revolution provided the first impetus, inspiring a spate of attempts to record its history in such a way as to achieve an intellectual consolidation of the political gains of independence.[3] Starting in the 1790s, the historical-society movement took root in the northeast and spread throughout the country.[4] Historical topics became standard magazine fare; historical oratory reached epidemic proportions. Local, state, national, European, and world history all became fields of widespread investigation. In each decade from 1790 to 1830, historical works, including historical fiction, accounted for a quarter or more of America's best-sellers, climbing to a peak of more than 85 percent in the 1820s.[5]

Amid this upsurge of historicizing, New England kept the dominant position it had held during the colonial era, when it had generated in the "providential histories" from William Bradford through Jonathan Edwards the only genuine tradition in colonial historiography.[6] Almost half of the historical societies founded in America between 1790 and 1830 were New England–based or devoted to the memorialization of the New England past.[7] Half of the historians whom the *Dictionary of American Biography* lists as having flourished between 1800 and 1860 were New Englanders,[8] most of whom displayed a special interest in their own region. "Definitive" histories of five of the six New England states were written, beginning with Jeremy Belknap's *History of New-Hampshire* (1784–92), the best (like Belknap's) distinguished for their day, and none yet quite superseded.[9] John Gorham Palfrey began the most comprehensive regional history ever attempted, his five-volume *History of New England* (1858–90), and two other Massachusetts historians, George Bancroft and Richard Hildreth, produced the best among many comprehensive histories of the United States. Prescott's histories of the Spanish empire, Motley's of the Dutch Republic, and Parkman's of the struggle between Britain and France for control of North America gave New England, and particularly Massachusetts, primacy in other branches of Euramerican history as well.

The New England output of fictive works on historical themes was equally prolific. This started a generation or so after the boom in historiography, America following the pattern of Enlightenment Britain, which saw the rise of historiography both as a field of research and as a field of literary accomplishment (e.g., in Hume and Gibbon) but little in the way of important historical poetry, fiction, and drama until Sir Walter Scott. (On the eve of Scott's *Waverley,* one Boston reviewer was so rash as to declare that the historical novel was a played-out form.)[10] But in the four decades after 1815, New Englanders produced some one hundred book-length literary works on New England historical themes alone and countless shorter pieces. These included the best fiction of Hawthorne and Stowe; some of Longfellow's and Whittier's most popular poems; and the antebellum theater's most successful colonial melodrama, John A. Stone's prize-winning *Metamora: or the Last of the Wampanoags* (1829), one of many period idealizations of the Puritans' greatest Indian adversary, King Philip.

So far as the field of American history was concerned, New England's leadership was not just a function of the more developed state of the discipline there or the region's unusual wealth of historical documents, important though these factors were. Also crucial was the place that had been prepared for the Pilgrims and Puritans in the emergent American civil religion, thanks to the conventions of providential history, to the ideological campaigns of the Revolutionary era, and in particular to the efforts led by New England pamphleteers to invoke the Puritan hegira as a type and precedent of latter-day tribulations wrought by British encroachments and as justification for resisting them. The first glimmerings of revolutionary ferment during the 1760s suggested it; the early histories of the Revolution confirmed it; Bancroft's *History of the United States* (1834–74) codified it: the founding fathers of American ideology were those New England sectaries who brought to Plymouth and Massachusetts Bay the sense of divine chosenness and the germ of the ideas of patriotic resistance to tyranny and of a "new order of human freedom."[11] American values became to a large extent a nationalized version of what was once the ideology of the tribe that had become dominant in the New England region. In consequence, the Puritan phase of New England history, of which New Englanders were the primary custodians and interpreters, became invested with a special mystique as the key source of what was distinctively American. During our period, the priority of New England's contribution to American identity by no means went unchallenged – from partisans of Virginia, for example. But in the long run the legend of America's Pilgrim-Puritan pedigree won out over the claims of less conspicuous victims of persecution, such as the South Carolina Huguenots or the Pennsylvania Quakers, or less high-minded founders, such as the more avowedly opportunistic colonists of Virginia. Nations, like people, will tend to think of themselves as well as they can. New England, on balance, seemed to furnish an ennobling self-image, and that, combined with effective promotion of the image (partly through New England's control of literary institutions), ensured its perpetuation.[12]

The next few chapters examine the mystique of Pilgrim-Puritan origins as a literary construct. The first step will be a more exact definition of that mystique, including some of its salient self-contradictions. That will set the stage for a discussion, in Chapter 9, of the principal locus of controversy among Puritanism's interpreters. That, in turn, will prepare us for a more intensive look at fictive treatments of Puritan history in Chapters 10 and 11.

Concentration on portrayals of the New England past has the disadvantage of keeping us from doing justice to the diverse achievements of the New England historical muse. Three of the region's greatest historians, Prescott, Motley, and Parkman, will be treated only in passing here. On the positive side, concentration will permit us to reflect at length on how period writers singled out, at least for literary purposes, New England's Puritan roots as the principal ingredient of regional identity. The Puritans, as one scholar observes, did not, in fact, "constitute the entire population of early New England, but they [obtained] something like a monopoly on publicity,"[13] so that by the mid-nineteenth century "New Englander" and "child of the Puritans" had become nearly synonymous.

II

A mid-nineteenth-century antiquarian once remarked that the public impression of the "glory of our Puritan fathers" was not formed so much through "our formal and elaborate histories" as through "our Plymouth Rock and Fourth of July orations, our town and church centennials, and our New England festivals, now observed in the chief cities of the land."[14] He was right. For the quintessence of filiopietistic mythography, the best place to turn is to the orations delivered on Forefathers' Day (December 22), the anniversary of the Pilgrims' landing. First celebrated on the eve of the Revolution as a low-key political protest, Forefathers' Day was observed during the early national period at intervals in Plymouth (starting in 1769), Boston (1797), and New York (1805) but really came into its own at the Plymouth bicentennial (1820), at which Daniel Webster delivered the first of his great patriotic orations. The next three decades saw a proliferation of New England Societies as far south as New Orleans and as far west as San Francisco, and a corresponding proliferation of oratory.[15]

Most Forefathers' Day speeches undertook not just to celebrate the Pilgrims' landing but the entire epic of New England history. The settlement of Plymouth was seen as the first in a providentially appointed series of events leading to the founding of Massachusetts Bay and the other New England colonies. Ordinarily no distinction was made between Pilgrim and Puritan, separatist and nonseparatist.[16] This breadth of scope and glossing over of differences was partly a matter of principle, partly a pragmatic deference to the etiquette of the occasion, whose most basic purpose was ritual affirmation of a corporate New England identity.

Following the Puritan historians, nineteenth-century orators agreed (especially those of clerical background) that the primary if not the exclusive purpose of New England colonization was spiritual: to escape persecution and to perfect the work of the Reformation. "Our fathers," Horace Bushnell insisted, had no "political objects in view . . . their end was religion, simply and only religion."[17] The orators liked to stress New England's uniqueness in this respect, sometimes at the expense of other colonies. "The planting of North America upon merely mercenary motives and selfish principles had been attempted once and again, and had failed," affirmed Leonard Bacon, glossing over the settlement of Virginia. "Our fathers and predecessors came under the influence of higher motives." Indeed, declared Webster, there was nothing like it in the history of the world.[18]

Although religion might have been the primary motive for New England settlement, it was also important that many of the founders were "republicans in principle," even though it is questionable whether they would have emigrated "merely from their dislike of the political systems of Europe." Puritans and Pilgrims showed democratic tendencies from the start, in their rejection of intermediaries between God and the individual, in their opposition to prelatical and political tyranny, in their formation of churches whose "members were the source of all power." Thus they applied to ecclesiastical organizations principles that "if introduced into civil government, would produce a pure democracy." These tendencies were manifested also in the relative equality of wealth in New England and the structure of local government, according to which power and responsibility were much more diffused than in the mother country. Therefore, although the "idea of the sovereignty of the people never presented itself to their minds," nonetheless, "from the beginning, the inevitable current of events swept towards democratic institutions, and . . . with the elements that were at work, none other were possible." Thus it could be said with justice that the "free nature of our institutions," as Daniel Webster put it, "have come down to us from the Rock of Plymouth."[19]

This naturally was cause for much self-congratulation. It showed, said Webster's nephew, that the "peculiarities of American character – our distinctive national features – are New England." Other sections, conceded Massachusetts congressman Robert Winthrop, might have produced great heroes also, but "not more does the fame of Washington surpass that of every other public character" in the history of the world "than the New England Colony, in its origin and its influences, its objects and its results, excels" Washington's native province of Virginia. Charles Wentworth Upham, historian of Salem witchcraft, approvingly quoted the vision that his brother-in-law Oliver Wendell Holmes had imputed to the Pilgrims: "The continent is ours!" Even the nonjingoistic Emerson could assert in the "language of coldest history" that "Boston, the capital of the Fathers, . . . was appointed in the destiny of nations to lead the civilization of North America."[20]

In addition to the two most fundamental themes of Protestant piety and civil liberty, the orators identified sundry other New England traits that had since become key influences in American society. The most important of these were industry and related qualities (thrift, common sense, practicality, adaptability) and the comprehensive commitment to education, evidenced in Harvard's early founding, the development of free schools, and New England's high literacy rate.

Most orators rejoiced that these legacies endured, although some cautioned, jeremiad-fashion, that there had been a slippage in piety and morals. As befitted the occasion, orators liked to stress New England's cultural solidarity over time, the (increasingly precarious) "facts" that nineteenth-century New Englanders were overwhelmingly of Pilgrim-Puritan stock, that "there is scarcely a principle of government or civil polity" in contemporary New England "but may be traced back through slight variations to a deep spring-head at Plymouth."[21]

The strong emphasis placed by the orators upon the binding continuity of Pilgrim-Puritan tradition sounds very Whiggish, and it is no accident that all of the men I have quoted were Whigs. Prosperous merchants of Whig persuasion dominated the New England societies at New York and Plymouth where these speeches were delivered; and insofar as voices like Webster's were widely influential, the rhetoric of pilgrimism might be looked at as a Whig artifact.[22] Yet Democrats of New England extraction were also ready to claim kinship with the founders. Local Jeffersonians objected, for example, to the first celebrations of Forefathers' Day in Boston not on the ground that it should not be celebrated but because they held that the forefathers' memory had been sullied by the perversion of the ceremony into a Federalist promotional event.[23] All of the New England societies had at least a sprinkling of Democrats; in some they predominated; and their commemorative rhetoric was hard to distinguish from that of the Whigs.[24] It was, furthermore, a Democratic politician, George Bancroft, who with slight modifications gave the spirit of the orators its most memorable codification in his *History of the United States.*

Although it is hardly true that Bancroft's contemporary position in the field was "as unshaken as that of Herodotus among the Greeks,"[25] his version of American history was indeed more widely taken as authoritative than any other. The conservative Whigs to whom his politics seemed traitorous and repellent ironically preferred his rendition to the anti-Romantic (and on the whole more responsible) interpretation of his nearest competitor, the Conscience Whig historian Richard Hildreth.[26] Bancroft put the orators' vision into a larger Euramerican context. The Reformation, for Bancroft, essentially represented the spirit of liberty, as against the feudal system dominated by the hierarchies of church and monarchy. "The reform in religion was the seed-plot of democratic revolutions."[27] Calvinism was the most dynamic and politically progressive of the early forms of Protestantism, and among Calvinists the Puritans were the most free from "credulity" and deference to priestcraft. Puritanism in the New World led inevitably, therefore, to protorepublican institutions such as government by the whole body of freemen and the planting of villages that were little democracies in themselves. The revolutions of 1688 and 1776 were consummations of the original Reformation spirit, in which it was natural that New England should lead the colonies.[28]

Bancroft gave special emphasis to the Anglo-Saxon origins of the Reformation spirit that led to Puritanism. His history was generally anti-French and anti-Catholic, despite token praise for Lord Baltimore's tolerationism and the efforts of Jesuit missionaries in Canada. In contrast, Bancroft saw the "Germanic race" as distinguished for its "love of personal independence" and regarded this as both the ideological and genealogical origin of most of the colonists.[29] This Anglo-Saxonism, David Levin points out, was an early example of the increasing emphasis placed by nineteenth-century New England historians on America's Teutonic roots. Although the antebellum historians never penetrated to the "theoretical source of the assumption, they all believed that the essential libertarian gene was Teutonic."[30] This assumption shows up in a wide variety of other contexts, such as the interpenetration of abolitionism and racism in the writings of such antislavery advocates as Harriet Beecher Stowe and Theodore Parker.[31]

In certain particulars, Bancroft the Democrat differed from the Whig orators quoted above. He praised, for example, the average New England citizen of the seventeenth century at the expense of the Puritan establishment, blaming the persecutions of Quakers and witches on the ministers and magistrates and insisting that the people themselves "never attempted to torture or terrify men into orthodoxy."[32] Yet the lines of distinction between Bancroft and the Whig memorialists were continually blurred by their mutual fondness for indulging the vision of a progressively unfolding national destiny and by Bancroft's endorsement of the idea that Puritan New England was the republic in embryo. That Bancroft strategically played down the party element in his history is made clear by comparing it to his political speeches, such as the demagogic July 4, 1836, *Oration Delivered Before the Democracy of Springfield*. Here Bancroft conflates Whiggery and Toryism and identifies the spirit of New England as specifically Jeffersonian.[33] His *History of the United States* is far more irenic. Altogether it is clear that the *North American Review*'s consistent praise of Bancroft was based upon more than his personal friendship with some of the reviewers. The differences among them were more than compensated for by the bonds of patriotism and filiopietism. Even on the potentially divisive subject of the meaning of the Revolution, their divergences were slight. As Sacvan Bercovitch points out, New Englanders in general tended to play down the revolutionary connotations of the Revolution by identifying the great migration as the key formative national event. Actual "independence was not the spoils of violence, but the harvest of Puritanism."[34]

The two epochs were thus linked indissolubly together by a century of rhetoric. "O Pilgrim Ark of Liberty!" effused Julia Ward Howe. "Will there be, as long as the name of America shall last," asked Edward Everett, "a father that will not take his children on his knee, and recount to them the events of the twenty-second of December, the nineteenth of April, the seventeenth of June, and the fourth of July?"[35] Intermediate events in New England history, such as the Confederation of 1643 and the rebellion against Governor Andros in 1689, were also seen as characteristic expressions of the founders' spirit that foreshadowed the later emergence of the republic. Thus the Puritan's habit of seeing history in typological terms as fulfillment of biblical prophecy was perpetuated, with the creation of the republic identified as the millennial fulfillment toward which the preceding crises pointed.

III

So much for the consensus legend of New England and America's Pilgrim-Puritan origins. But did audiences really believe it? Did the orators themselves? Toward the end of his study of the Cavalier myth, William R. Taylor suggests that probably "few, if any, Southerners, no matter what they said, really believed in the Cavalier – only in the need for him."[36] The New England Puritan is a more empirically verifiable figure, yet New England historians face a similar problem of double-think. Take the familiar case of Emerson, whose first significant publication, his 1835 *Historical Discourse* delivered at Concord's bicentennial, was a somewhat restrained contribution to filiopietistic oratory. It ends as follows:

> I feel some unwillingness to quit the remembrance of the past. . . . Fortunate and favored this town has been, in having received so large an infusion of the spirit of both of those periods [the era of first settlement and the era of revolution]. . . . And so long as a spark of this faith survives among the children's children so long shall the name of Concord be honest and venerable. [*EW* 11:85–6]

Very well. Yet all students of American literature know how Emerson's next publication, *Nature,* started:

> Our age is retrospective. It builds the sepulchres of the fathers. It writes biographies, histories, and criticism. The foregoing generations beheld God and nature face to face; we through their eyes. Why should not we also enjoy an original relation to the universe? [*EW* 1:7]

The second passage seems to recoil from the first. Had Emerson, then, merely been playing the somewhat forced role of good citizen and local booster, which he now disowns in his impatience with the claustrophobia of village conservatism? There is some evidence of that. When asked to join in the bicentennial, Emerson's private reaction was "Why notice it? Centuries pass unnoticed" (*JMN* 5:55). Yet that he also had a deep filial attachment to Concord and its historical mystique is equally clear from his manner of recording his move there in the previous year: "Hail to the quiet fields of my fathers! Not wholly unattended by supernatural friendship & favor let me come hither"[37] – though he adds: "Henceforth I design not to utter any speech, poem, or book that is not entirely & peculiarly my own work" (*JMN* 4:335). A return to historical and genealogical roots paradoxically, but understandably, suggests the idea of a fresh start. In the journal the associations are harmonious; in the juxtaposition of the two published passages, they clash. The birth of New England was a luminous and superintending idea for Emerson, but what made it so was the sense of the pristine, which might also prompt him to direct attacks on the conservative historicism that Pilgrimism could produce. By the same token, even the radical program for an "original relation" is grounded in the precedent of the founders. *Nature* is not demanding that we become children merely of the future but that we recapture the unmediated vision of the "foregoing generations." Transcendentalism is not antinomian but based on solid precedent. Again, the position is illogical (how can a recapturing, a "we also" mode of aspiration, be "original"?) but understandable. Having celebrated the memory of his ancestors' firstness, Emerson wants the feel of that firstness too.

Emerson is thus led to differentiate sharply between Puritanism as empirical phenomenon and Puritanism as symbol. When he writes that "Calvinism suited Ptolemaism" (*JMN* 4:26) or states that "it is not in the power of God to make a communication of his will to a Calvinist. For to every inward revelation he holds up his silly book" (*JMN* 8:379), Emerson refers to the obstinacy of the literal institution. When he affirms that the "great-hearted Puritans have left no posterity" (*EW* 11:131) or asks "What is to replace for us the piety of that race?" (*EW* 1:135), he invokes the founders as a symbol of the ideal in order to fill a present emptiness. As the essay, "History," shows, he valued history, at least in his Transcendentalist phase, less for its own sake than for its exemplary character. This was a mysticized version of the Enlightenment view of history as philosophy teaching by example.[38] History is the record of the universal mind, of which each individual is an epitome; therefore the study of history may be rewarding because the attentive mind will always be finding situations applicable to it, but by the same token history is in a sense superfluous, because "all the facts of history preexist in the mind as laws."[39] The study of history can help to activate our dormant mental powers, but in a sense we know all we need to already.

This antihistorical strain might seem to make Emersonian Transcendentalism an unhelpfully extreme instance of the inconsistency of attitudes toward history in our period. At first sight, it seems to have little in common with the antiquarianism of a Prescott, who declined an invitation to write a history of the Mexican War on the ground that "I had rather not meddle with heroes who have not been under ground two centuries at least."[40] There is an affinity, nonetheless. The Brahmin historians, as David Levin observes, "looked on the Past from the highest station reached in human progress" – they too were post-Enlightenment Romantics.[41] Even those who, like Prescott and Parkman, found certain features of past epochs more congenial than their own nonetheless approached the colonial and European past as inferior stages of civilization and conceptualized their history in terms of a clash between reactionary and progressive forces, using the standards of the enlightened present (characterized by religious liberalism and republican institutions) as models for the latter.[42] Bancroft, in particular, unhesitatingly judged past epochs according to the principle that the "last system of philosophy is the best, for it includes every one that went before" and depicted the process of modern history as a progressive unfolding of the divine will, more fully realized in the present than any other.[43] Emerson, for his part, moved rather quickly to a similar evolutionary conception of history after *Essays, First Series*.[44]

Altogether it is quite clear that the legend of the founding fathers was something less pristine than a spontaneous effusion of cherished values unselfconsciously imbibed by the Puritans' descendants from ancestral springs. Let us review the complicating factors briefly.

First, as we have seen, filiopietistic rhetoric involved conscious adaptation for various motives – ranging from Bancroftian opportunism to Emersonian civic duty – to various occasions. Perhaps the most striking case on record is that of Robert Treat Paine, who, when Boston's opposition to the theater was overcome, rejoiced that the "Vandal spirit of puritanism is prostrate in New-England," yet at a Forefathers' Day celebration a few years later delivered a ringing poetic tribute (to the "patriarchal stock" who landed on the "consecrated rock") that is said to have introduced the term *Pilgrim* into popular usage.[45]

Second, public recognition of the basic facts of early New England history seems not to have been nearly so great during the Federalist era as after the historical and oratorical institutions were set in place in the early 1800s. Paine, in his *Federal Orrery,* felt obliged when printing a 1794 Forefathers' Day ode to footnote "yon wave-beaten rock" and, for a Washington's Birthday poem two months later, to remind readers that the "first settlers of New England arrived at Plymouth in the winter."[46] It seems, then, that in the 1790s, if not the 1820s, there were some quite well-educated people who were not up on the red-letter days rattled off by Everett in the 1824 oration quoted a moment ago. Though Pilgrimism was already a motif in early national rhetoric, New England Neoclassicism was also liable to repress or satirize provincial ancestors to a much greater extent than we would suppose, judging from Bancroft and the orators. Their legend-building campaign, which peaked in the 1820s and 1830s, was more a resuscitation than a perpetuation of filial feeling toward the region's primal ancestors.

Third, the legend of Pilgrim-Puritan origins was patently reductive. New Hampshire and Maine had not been settled in the first instance by idealists seeking religious and civil liberty; Vermont had been a spillover frontier haven for less successful and more venturesome New Englanders; Rhode Island had been settled by refugees from Massachusetts Bay persecution, in a pattern that state historians (and Bancroft) liked to hold up as more faithful to the ideals of civil and religious freedom than Massachusetts.[47] The consensus myth was all too clearly a Massachusetts-centered myth (see the snippet from Emerson's oration cited earlier in this chapter), a myth some outlanders found it convenient to appropriate in order to dignify their colony's history but that all conscientious state historians knew the limitations of and that some – especially Rhode Islanders – keenly resented.

Fourth, many New England intellectuals, including some historians, are on record as having found New England history drab. George Richards Minot, whiling away his leisure hours by continuing Thomas

Hutchinson's history of Massachusetts Bay (unaware that Hutchinson himself had already done the job better) persuaded himself that his data gathering was of "general utility," even though "it is evident that a more brilliant and productive space of time might have been selected."[48] James Russell Lowell, ever ready to appeal to the sacred memory of the fathers in times of political crisis, was at other times vocal on the opposite side. "There is very little poetry in American history," he writes in an 1859 review of a tedious history of New England. "It is a record of advances in material prosperity, and scarce anything more. The only lumps of pure ore are the *Idea* which the Pilgrims were possessed with and its gradual incarnation in events and institutions. Beyond this all is barren."[49] The next year, Lowell was prepared to go even farther:

> The Puritans left us a fine estate in conscience, energy, and respect for learning; but they disinherited us of the past. Not a single stage-property of poetry did they bring with them but the good old Devil, with his graminivorous attributes, and even he could not stand the climate. Neither hoof nor tail of him has been seen for a century. He is as dead as the goat-footed Pan, whom he succeeded, and we tenderly regret him.[50]

Lowell here inverts the orators' claims about the luminousness of the Puritan inheritance and sheds crocodile tears over the "demise" of a creed in which a majority of New Englanders – if not a majority of the *Atlantic*'s readers – probably still believed. Lowell's irreverence in his capacity as editorial arbiter of the *Atlantic* suggests a fairly widespread awareness among his class that the myth of Puritan-Pilgrim sanctity was a bit of a pose.

Fifth, as we can infer from the testier outbursts of Paine, Emerson, and others, <u>many New Englanders found the memory of the Pilgrim-Puritan fathers embarrassing</u>. The Quaker and witchcraft persecutions, for example, were blots on the escutcheon that were hard to explain away. Some did not care to palliate them. "Let not an unqualified, undiscriminating admiration of the Puritans . . . be considered an exclusive test of one's love for his native New England," wrote an exasperated reviewer of one of the orations that I have quoted. "We know many a son of New England, yielding to none in pride and love for their father-land, who will never submit to such a test."[51] Many of the orators labored under this problem. In 1850, for example, Daniel Webster, having recently seen fit to place the interests of sectional harmony above the antislavery sentiments of New England, found the Pilgrim heritage, which he had invoked against slave holding in 1820, now much harder to swallow, since the Pilgrims' ideology seemed based on moral and theological absolutes conceived as "binding on all, by the authority of the word of God." Webster was reduced to meeting this with the common but shaky argument

that toleration of diversity is "not inconsistent with the great and fundamental principles of religion" and that therefore we are entitled to see
ourselves as simultaneously one with the founders and more flexible than
they.[52] The whole speech is a conspicuous example of the strategic use of
fulsome tributes as a means of disguising embarrassment at having been
forced to praise principles antagonistic to one's own. Had Webster been
candid, he would have repeated Hawthorne's now famous declaration in
"Main-Street," published the year before: "Let us thank God for having
given us such ancestors; and let each successive generation thank him, not
less fervently, for being one step further from them in the march of ages"
(*HW* 11:68).

Finally, quite apart from any reservations they might have felt about
the founders' principles, the more discerning New Englanders were
aware that the "march of ages" had placed them at such a distance from
early colonial culture that any evocation of the founders was at best a stab
at recuperation. "I find on seeing a painting of our village as it appeared
a hundred years ago," Thoreau muses, "that I had not thought the sun
shone in those days – or that men lived in broad day light then" (*TJ*
1:417). This comment registers the inevitable feeling of strangeness
caused by the gap between then and now that Forefathers' Day orators
either repressed by insisting on continuity or implicitly confirmed by
presenting the founders' era (unlike Thoreau) as more luminous than
ours, which threatens to be engulfed in darkness. (Thoreau used that tactic too, of course, when he praised John Brown as the last Puritan.)[53] We
do well to remember that antebellum New Englanders were separated
from their seventeenth-century ancestors by a time span almost twice as
long as that which separates them from us.

IV

Having noted all of these barriers that interfered with a spontaneous filiopietism in New England between the Revolution and the Civil
War, one naturally wonders anew how public interest in New England
origins could have made headway during these years, which were also the
very era when such forces as urbanization, industrializations, and immigration were pushing New England culture from pastoralism to modernism at a faster rate than ever before or since. One obvious explanation is
that the impression of [evanescence] itself stimulated attempts at restoration. Harriet Beecher Stowe and Henry Ward Beecher, for example, pro-
fessedly wished to chronicle the "primitive" phases of New England village life that they thought they had known in the "pre-railroad times,"
precisely because they saw it being wiped out.[54] Second, as we have seen,
the Pilgrim-Puritan ethos had a broad national appeal owing to its flattering representation of the ideals of American settlement. Third, this ethos

[DISAPPEAR LIKE VAPOR]

was especially prized by New Englanders, not just for the usual reason of local patriotism but also because of New England's sense, at least among many of the region's elite, of a loss in national influence between the Revolution and the Civil War. The demise of the Federalist party, the War of 1812, westward expansion, the extension of slavery to the territories, the strengthening of the Fugitive Slave Law, the failure of the Whig Party at the presidential level, New England's declining percentage in the national population – this succession of developments was not, by any means, bemoaned by all New Englanders; but in toto it represented a blow to the regional ego, which in every case constituted the main power base of the losing party. To be able to conceive of America as at least symbolically Puritan was, under these circumstances, some consolation.

So far as literary history is concerned, two additional factors deserve special notice. One was the rise of Second Awakening evangelicalism. Evangelical conservatives took advantage of growing historical nostalgia by using the Pilgrim-Puritan mystique as the cornerstone of jeremiads against liberal lapses, claiming themselves to be the "proper and legitimate representatives" of New England's founders, as Lyman Beecher said in explanation of why the new, orthodox Congregationalist monthly he had just founded in Boston (1828) was to be called *The Spirit of the Pilgrims*.[55] One of the first full-dress orations before the New England Society of New York, in fact, turned into a diatribe against Unitarianism. Offended Unitarians in the audience issued a rejoinder in which, among other things, they made it plain that they considered themselves just as legitimate heirs of the Pilgrims as the clerical orator.[56] To a considerable extent, the hidden agenda of early nineteenth-century Puritan historiography and literature became the fight between Calvinists and Arminians over the meaning and authority of the Puritan past. This is by no means to say that the period's historians turned to history writing solely or even mainly for propagandistic reasons, but only that in the ideological dimension from which no intellectual inquiry, however disinterested, is ever free, the religious element was most crucial – and in some cases designedly so. The next chapter will take a detailed look at the stakes and issues in this debate.

The second factor in the continued appeal of the Pilgrim-Puritan myth was the vogue of historical romance provoked by Sir Walter Scott's *Waverley* novels (1814–29). These were almost immediately seized upon by critics and creative writers not only throughout America but throughout the entire Euramerican world as a model for literary nationalism, that is, for recording the history of national experience in fictive form.[57] New Englanders stressed their special applicability to New England history. If Scott had succeeded in dramatizing the Covenanters, how much more promising as literary material must be the "fortunes of those sterner puritans . . . who, with a boldness of adventure, under which the spirit of chivalry itself would have quailed, . . . crossed a trackless ocean."[58] Scott's work was an especially happy discovery for Arminian intellectuals because it seemed to justify the liberal line on both fiction and history. Scott's combination of sophisticated entertainment and moral soundness seemed to confirm that the novel could be a powerful instrument of good; his manner of emplotting Presbyterian and Highlander resistance against British centralization resonated better with liberal ambivalence toward the Puritan founders as noble extremists whose memory should be honored without too literal an attempt at revival than it did with the hagiographical tendencies of nineteenth-century evangelical orthodoxy. For example, Rufus Choate, in his 1833 oration at Salem calling for a series of New England Waverley novels that would vivify the *"old Puritan character,"* which in every respect was an "extraordinary mental and moral phenomenon," clearly had in mind a feat of taxidermy, not a resurrection. This mentality was the opposite of that displayed by the Reverend Leonard Withington's *Puritan Morals Defended,* a sermon delivered in the same town the year before, at the dedication of the former Salem Theater as an orthodox Congregational meetinghouse. Withington (who, during a youthful apprenticeship as Joseph T. Buckingham's printer's devil, had, ironically, been a compulsive theatergoer) rejoiced at this sign of reconversion of the town to Puritan ways. He acknowledged what Choate presupposed – that in the public eye "Puritanism resembles one of the buried statues of antiquity . . . found in the ruins of some temple"; yet he argued that there was substantial continuity in creed and in "system of manners" between the believers of 1620 and those of 1832.[59] In reading Scott on the Covenanters, the Unitarians tended to see compassionate evenhandedness, whereas the orthodox saw prejudice, and distortion of the historical record.[60] Historical romance about early New England became largely a Unitarian preserve, whether chiefly because religious liberals had fewer scruples than the orthodox about writing fiction or because Scott's key structural device of balancing an obsolescently rigid but heroic culture against a modern, pragmatic, middle-class culture fitted with their view of the Puritan past.[61]

Scott's further contribution was to effect a fruitful confusion of the categories of history and fiction. Even in the eighteenth century, the boundary had been indistinct. It was common for fictions to attempt to palm themselves off as true histories; conversely, as Leo Braudy has shown in the cases of Hume, Fielding, and Gibbon, the narrative consciousness in fictional and rationalist histories made use of comparable strategies of unification.[62] In Neoclassical New England, however, the two narrative modes seemed to be headed on divergent courses. The novel initially developed through heavily mannered, stylized subgenres such as picaresque, Radcliffean gothic, and sentimental fiction, whereas historiography seemed to divest itself of fictive design by moving from a providential to an empirical framework of analysis.[63] The best New England historian of this period, Jeremy Belknap, was by temperament a compiler rather than an ideologue, and his most admired predecessor was the annalist Thomas Prince.[64] Scott helped retard the divorce of historiography and fiction by inventing a popular narrative form that impressed many contemporaries as more truly historical than most history books and that brought period historiography and fiction into a closer relationship. On the one hand, Scott's historical romances helped to prompt writers of fiction to engage in serious historical research that, as Michael Colacurcio has shown in Hawthorne's case, was capable of great sophistication.[65] On the other hand, Scott influenced such historians as Prescott, Bancroft, Motley, and Parkman to write histories with a strong narrative line, using similar stylistic and structural devices, most notably Scott's culture-conflict formula. They looked on the dramatization of history as an essential part of doing history and tended increasingly to define the "literary" element of historiography not as embellishment but as the key to its success as history, substantively as well as aesthetically. Part of the historian's total responsibility was to bring history alive; in addition, the production of a history that was purely narrative (i.e., from which overt moral or philosophical analysis à la Voltaire or Gibbon had been expunged) tended to be seen as a guarantee of objectivity.[66]

This mentality led to some interesting mystifications, not exclusively confined to writers of this period, as recent metahistorians have pointed out in calling attention to the ideological dimension of narrative form in modern as well as nineteenth-century historical writing.[67] Every thinking person was, to be sure, well aware of the difference between fictional and historiographical narrative. Reviewers compared fictions to fictions and histories to histories.[68] On principle, however, New England intellectuals blurred the distinction between history and fiction by stressing the creative writer's responsibility to depict social reality and the historian's obligation to bring history to life. Both of these positions were, in effect, attempts to reverse the tendency of these kinds of narrative to become too highly specialized and, therefore, unappealing to the larger reading public. That was becoming harder as the standards for research and adherence to original documents became more exacting (the Romantic historians priding themselves on being thorough archivalists) and as the fictive genres became more autonomous and institutionalized. Thanks to the achievements of mixed genres such as historical romance and Romantic narrative history, the further specialization of disciplines was retarded until after the Civil War. Meanwhile the intellectual community was faced with the paradox of both recognizing and denying the presence of two radically opposed evaluations of narrative. In fiction, narrative skill was in a sense automatically held suspect as a potential instrument of self-deception unless kept properly in check. But when it came to historiography, great faith was placed in narrative skill as the decisive factor in bringing history to life.

Here was a situation that could lead to the extremes of critical naïveté and narrative subtlety. The amateur antiquarian Rufus Choate and the professional romancer Nathaniel Hawthorne make a convenient pair of examples. Running throughout Choate's call for New England Waverley novels is a simplemindedly-invoked metaphor of historical romance as visual show:

> [Historical romances] cause a crowded but exact and express image of the age and society of which they treat to pass before you as you see Moscow or Jerusalem or Mexico in a showman's box. They introduce genuine specimens, – real living men and women of every class and calling in society, as it was then constituted, and make them talk and act in character. You see their dress, their armor, and their weapons of war. . . . Time and space are thus annihilated by the power of genius. Instead of reading about a past age, you live in it.[69]

Choate knows that it is all a show but denies any element of deception or distortion. This denial is indeed crucial to his whole stance. His enthusiasm is predicated on the faith that historical romances "introduce genuine specimens, – real living men and women." Choate's scenario sounds a lot like the familiar panoramic scenes that Hawthorne, who might actually have been listening to Choate's oration, produced in such tales as "The May-Pole of Merry Mount," which handles the question of narrative historicity with much greater canniness. After sketching the roisterers and the historical background of the antagonism between Pilgrim-Puritan and the infant colony at Merry Mount, the tale says, "After these authentic passages from history, we return to the nuptials of the Lord and Lady of the May" (*HW* 9:62). What appears to be a naively awkward transition is actually packed with innuendo. The naïveté is a device, like the device of the showman-narrator in "Main-Street," to break the dramatic illusion and expose the "authentic passage" as fictional construction in retrospect (yet at the same time to freeze it on a different mimetic plane from the Edward-Edith plot). The story's deliberately ill-timed endorsement of the middlebrow Choate line on historical fiction exposes the simplemindedness of that mentality while still acknowledging that some sort of tie does, or ought to, exist between historical reality and fictional representation. Choate wants his fiction without acknowledging its fictionality; Hawthorne wants to assert the impossibility of nonfictional fiction without altogether sacrificing the referential aspect, without which he too would have trouble believing in his enterprise.

These types of doublethink are related at least indirectly to those of the Forefathers' Day orations. Hawthorne on Merry Mount and Choate on the domestication of Waverley both betray the awareness that modern representations of early colonial history must involve acts of communal autohypnosis. Choate faces this squarely and with gusto. One reason for preferring historical romance to history, he affirms, is that "much of what history relates . . . chills, shames, and disgusts us," whereas the romancer can pick and choose, recording the "useful truth . . . only" and "leaving all the rest to putrefy or be burned."[70] Historical romance, then, records all the history that's fit to print. Its selective censorship only makes it more quintessential as history and does not invalidate it, any more than the standard nineteenth-century practice of "improving" the style of one's manuscript sources was considered as invalidating one's historiography. This could be an apology for all Forefathers' Day orations en masse (a genre to which Choate contributed). Hawthorne, in "The May-Pole of Merry Mount," recognizes with characteristically greater sophistication the mirror image of the same phenomenon when he represents the Puritans as "most dismal wretches, who said their prayers before daylight, and then wrought in the forest or the cornfield, till evening made it prayer time again" (*HW* 9:60). No careful reader will want to take this as Hawthorne's serious, considered judgment on Puritanism or even as a simple reflection of the speaker's momentary sympathy with the Merry Mounters, although the sentence is timed so as to capitalize on that sympathy. Its function is rather to implant the caricature that a modern, secularized age might be inclined to see as Puritanism and work from that to a more complicated final image in which Puritanism is associated with something like adult reality, and Merry Mountism (including reflex anti-Puritanism) now seems a childish indulgence that the mature person has outgrown, although of course the narrator subordinates the pleasure principle with a pang of regret and insulates us from the full weight of this transformation by urbanely fashioning his allegorical couple and their rite out of papier-mâché. If this reading is correct, "fiction" (the plot and its outcome) winds up correcting the "authentic passages from history," which are based on the easy polarization of gaiety and morbidness ("jollity and gloom were contending for an empire"), without yielding to the opposite extreme. In any case, the tale clearly recognizes the impulse to reduce history to stereotypes by starting its portrayal of Puritanism with what we instantly suspect, and later are shown, is an egregiously reductive image.[71]

Both the benign censorship recommended by Choate and the complicated image manipulation practiced by Hawthorne imply what the orators conceal: that Puritan history was a controversial field. That undoubtedly enhanced its popularity as a literary subject. Even the sketchiest comparisons between literary and historical records soon make one aware of the extreme selectivity of antebellum fictive historicizing. At the start of the Scott vogue, one *North American* reviewer proposed a threefold agenda for American romance: "the times just succeeding the first settlement," "the aera of the Indian wars," and the Revolution.[72] This list is as interesting for what it omits as for what it includes. Voyages of discovery; mercantile development; the life-style of traders, trappers, and fishermen; the rhythms of early agricultural life; the growth of cities and civic institutions like colleges, ministerial associations, and government structures; the experiences of New Englanders who migrated to other colonies or repatriated to Europe – these topics held little interest for the reviewer and also, as it turned out, for the writers themselves. Their work tended in fact to center on the three phases of colonial history prescribed by the critic. And of these, by far the best work was done on the first phase, the institutionalization of Puritanism. New England's role in the Revolution inspired some memorable poems, of which Emerson's "Concord Hymn" and Longfellow's "Paul Revere's Ride" are best known, and one or two creditable romances, such as Cooper's *Lionel Lincoln* and Daniel P. Thompson's *Green Mountain Boys*. But the quality was thin compared to the literary treatments of Puritanism by Hawthorne, Stowe, Longfellow, Whittier, and lesser figures to be discussed later in Part III. Indian themes were also given frequent but mediocre treatment. They tended to be subsumed under treatments of Puritanism, as in Gideon Hollister's silly *Mount Hope; or Philip, King of the Wampanoags* (in which the titular hero gets completely upstaged by a swashbuckling love and adventure story involving settlers) or Cooper's unjustly neglected *The Wept of Wish-ton-Wish* – a better novel than any of the Leatherstocking tales – in which the depiction of family and community life on the Puritan frontier is excellent but the subplot involving the Indian chief Miantanomoh is a well-meant sentimental distraction. When Indian life is made the central subject of a work, the result is invariably a pasteboard caricature of noble savages or bestial villains; when the Revolution is made the central subject, the result is melodrama, with such rare exceptions as Hawthorne's "My Kinsman, Major Molineux." The "absence" of the Revolution as a literary event in American history is perhaps due less to bourgeois suppression of American revolutionary origins (although famous tales like "Molineux" and Rip Van Winkle's twenty-year sleep through the years of strife support that interpretation) than to the fact that the many attempts at portrayal have been too programmatically simplistic to make it into the American literary canon. For antebellum New Englanders, the patriots were much closer to being unequivocally right in their struggle against Britain than the Puritans were in their struggles against Indians and heretics. The persecution of Loyalists was less troubling than the persecution of witches.[73]

The Puritans, in short, supplied a creative irritant superior to that of the other themes most obviously suggested by the example of Scott. The theme of Puritanism was all the more challenging as a subject because of its cultural proximity in spite of its chronological remoteness. The aborigines of New England were virtually extinct; no longer did Britain threaten to control America, at least politically; but the question of how and whether the Puritan tradition ought to be sustained or revived was still a live issue for nineteenth-century New Englanders and was becoming livelier with evangelical resurgence and the rise of religious pluralism.

This continuing but increasingly diverse religiocentrism helped to guarantee that most antebellum literary portrayals of the Puritan era would stress the religiocentrism of Puritan culture – would be, in other words, literary equivalents of Perry Miller or Alan Heimert, rather than of John Demos or Kenneth Lockridge. This prioritization was partly responsible for the fact that in our century the Miller approach to Puritan history preceded the recent revisionist emphasis on the secular life and institutions of nonelites. As we turn, then, to an examination in Chapter 9 of the way New England historiography between the Revolution and the Civil War was colored and shaped by sectarian disputes over the meaning of the past, we shall not only be preparing the way for further discussion of period literature but also sketching in an intermediate step in the history of historical interpretation from the Puritan chroniclers to contemporary academic scholarship.

9

The Politics of Historiography

> Historical writing has always been an instrument of party warfare.
>
> Michael Kraus, *The Writing of American History* (1953)

> There are plenty of people in our day who know, or seem to know, just what our Puritan fathers would be, were they to live in this age of the world. . . . But it very much lessens the value of such knowledge to find hardly any two exactly agreed about it; and, especially, to find that each one's own peculiar notions of morals and religion and theology are just the notions which he is sure those fathers would now adopt and teach.
>
> Joseph S. Clark, *A Historical Sketch of the Congregational Churches in Massachusetts* (1858)

Between the Revolution and the Civil War, historiography about Puritanism was spearheaded by New England Protestants of Puritan descent and particularly by those affiliated with one of the lineal descendants of the Puritan Congregational church. These historians, ranging from amateur fumblers to serious researchers whose work set the contemporary standard of scholarly rigor, assembled, preserved, and at times mutilated an immense amount of data still assiduously mined today; provided the key sources for the historical portions of period oratory and historical literature; and set or at least anticipated the agenda of later historical inquiry and the basic ideological perspectives that have governed modern scholarship on Puritanism.

Most of this early work now looks shallow and repetitious. But it is rarely dull. It is enlivened by perpetual conflict between filiopietistic and critical instincts and in particular by its appropriation as an instrument of sectarian warfare – if "sectarian" is not too restrictive a term for controversies that in fact extended across the whole range of communal values and life-style. This chapter will try to give an insider's view of the storm center of that conflict, some grasp of which is crucial to a full understanding of the historical literature of the period.

I

The storm center was the dispute between Arminian-Unitarian and orthodox Congregationalists (including both moderate Calvinists and the more conservative New Divinity faction of Edwards and Hopkins) over the facts, meaning, and authority of the New England past, a dispute that was a logical extension of the two parties' disagreements over doctrinal questions, and a prime illustration of the point that apparently minor squabbles often have major repercussions. Broadly speaking, the liberals took the position that creeds, doctrines, ecclesiastical polity, and Scripture were products of their original historical eras not literally binding on contemporary worshipers if reason and the advancing state of knowledge seemed to dictate otherwise. The conservatives sought to align themselves with the spirit of Reformation Calvinism, the literal dictates of Scripture, and the Westminster Confession and Catechism. Underlying this disagreement was the liberals' fundamental conviction that the heart and test of piety is moral conduct, a present-minded outlook conducive to historical and ethical relativism (although Unitarians would have denied this), as against the orthodox conviction that the heart and test of piety is the conversion of the sinner from depravity to grace, an absolutist outlook that conduces to the view that doctrinal systems remain the same from age to age (although the orthodox would have conceded that their forefathers might need correcting on some points).[1]

Broadly speaking, the trend in New England historiography during the colonial period had been from orthodox to latitudinarian, from partisanship to qualified objectivity, resulting in a critical, rationalist appraisal of Puritanism. In the early national period, this trend was epitomized by the work of Jeremy Belknap, who was both the best regional historian of his day and also the most active organizer of historical institutions, being the prime instigator of the Massachusetts Historical Society and of Forefathers' Day celebrations in Boston.[2] Belknap was at once a lover of colonial history and an increasingly outspoken critic of Puritan rigidity and its modern avatars. He started his parish ministry as a theological conservative, taking the Edwardsean New Divinity position against the Half Way Covenant (which permitted, for instance, baptism of nonmembers' children), and he was always considered an evangelical minister. But he came by midlife to question whether he could conscientiously assent even to the most liberal of creeds and found himself powerfully drawn to Charles Chauncy's doctrine of universal salvation, which had frightened Timothy Dwight into the philippics of *The*

Triumph of Infidelity. "Although some gentlemen stigmatize me with the name of a *'Latitudinarian,'*" he wrote, "if I err, I had rather err on the side of catholicism than of bigotry."[3] He admired the founders' "fortitude and perseverance" but deplored the "folly and incompetency of [the] sanguinary laws" that they enacted against heretics and argued that their image of the Indians was grossly prejudiced.[4] Equipped with a droll sense of humor and a gift for gentle satire, Belknap relished Laurence Sterne's ministerial persona Yorick, tactfully but firmly evaluated his clerical predecessors by urbane rationalist criteria, and rejoiced that he lived in an enlightened age. This outlook was shared by the knot of collegial antiquarians of whom he became the leader when he moved to Boston in 1787: ministers John Eliot and James Freeman, attorneys James Sullivan and George Richards Minot, physician William Baylies, and others who formed the nucleus of the infant Massachusetts Historical Society. This little group of committed if complacent literati resumed the work, begun by Loyalist historian Thomas Hutchinson, of rewriting state and local history in the image of their liberal rationalism.[5]

These antiquarians, however, hardly spoke for all of New England. Their tranquillity was disrupted almost at once by the arrival of Yale-trained, outspokenly Calvinist Jedidiah Morse. In 1789 Morse became the Congregational minister at nearby Charlestown, owing in good part to behind-the-scenes efforts by Belknap, who liked him personally despite their theological differences and had decided that the "father of American geography," as Morse came to be called, would make a valuable acquisition.[6] Morse's *American Geography* (1789) was indeed an important pioneer text, attempting, for example, the first formal classification of American culture regions, among which Morse paid special attention to New England's history and traits.[7] In the process, however, he also gave much offense with peremptory claims about the recent decline of old-line piety in New England and his elevation of the virtues of his native Connecticut above those of her neighbors, most notably the "unhappy state" of Rhode Island.[8]

Morse's judgmentalism drew a sharp retort from James Freeman, minister of King's Chapel, Boston, America's first Unitarian church. Morse had previously chided Freeman for publishing an expurgated edition of the hymns of Isaac Watts; now Freeman retorted in kind. His anonymous pamphlet, *Remarks on the American Universal Geography* (1793), indicted Morse on twenty-one counts of ignorance, inaccuracy, plagiarism, and bigotry.[9] Most significant for our purposes was Freeman's response to Morse's claim that the "degeneracy of the congregational churches from that order, fellowship, and harmony, in discipline, doctrines, and friendly advice and assistance in ecclesiastical matters, which formerly subsisted among them, is a matter of deep regret to many, not to say most people of that denomination." On the contrary, writes Freeman, "at no period has christian charity prevailed, more than at present." True, the "congregational churches do not agree in *doctrines*" as they did "before the age of Edwards and Mayhew," but this is not to be deplored as the decline of piety but rather celebrated as the rise of the "spirit of free inquiry and zeal for truth." Morse's revised edition, Freeman granted, was an improvement, but not enough. Morse had excised the offending statement just quoted but continued to insist that there was "much danger" that New England would "liberalize away all true religion."[10]

The Morse–Freeman dispute sets forth, more than two decades before the American Unitarian movement officially began, what later became the key point of debate between Unitarian and orthodox Congregationalists regarding New England history. Was that history to be seen as a process of evolution from worthy but defective original principles toward greater purification and enlightenment, or was it to be seen as an increasingly embattled attempt on the part of the faithful to maintain what was alleged to be the pristine piety of the founders? In practice the debate became more subtle than this, because the Orthodox were ready to admit that the Puritans had sometimes been limited by the prejudices of their age, while the liberals, in their statements about the founders, departed markedly from filiopietism only when reprobating doctrinal narrowness. Thus the orthodox William Allen curtly described Ann Hutchinson, in his *Biographical Dictionary,* as an "artful woman, who occasioned much difficulty" for the Puritan magistrates, whereas the liberal William Emerson, though also siding with the "moderate party," could "hardly help dropping a tear of compassion over the intolerance of the age, and the hardship attending the case of this female fanatick," banished for "doing nothing more" than exercising the "rights of conscience and the liberty of private judgment" for which the forefathers supposedly stood.[11] Orthodox historians were quicker to show respect for the Puritan establishment and to see issues from its standpoint; liberal historians declared a semiindependence from its authority through their urbanity and their sympathy, however patronizing, with the heretic. Indeed some heretics were looked upon by some liberals as more truly their ancestors than the pillars of the Puritan commonwealth. The elevation of Roger Williams to American sainthood as New England's true apostle of "soul liberty" was the result of a fortuitous confluence of Rhode Island boosterism and Unitarian historians like Bancroft, who sought both to bury traditional Calvinism and to make Puritanism relevant to their own day by redefining the Puritan heritage as the source of the libertarian spirit that the Puritans themselves would have disowned.[12]

II

√   One of the best touchstones for differentiating between Arminian and orthodox approaches to Puritan history is the treatment of Cotton Mather. To trace the vicissitudes of Mather's reputation during our
period will give us a good taste of its controversial flavor.

David Levin has written perceptively about the "hazing" to which
Cotton Mather has been subjected by American historians from the nineteenth century through Samuel Eliot Morison and Perry Miller. With the
aid of such revisionary scholarship, we are today in a better position than
ever before to reevaluate the history of Mather's reputation dispassion-
ately.[13] The hazing of Cotton Mather is a legacy of the Unitarian controversy. The Unitarians latched onto Mather as a scapegoat through whom
to assail all that they disliked in the Puritan tradition: superstitiousness,
officiousness, self-righteousness, hypocrisy – and modern anti-Matherite
scholars have followed their lead.

Condemnation of Mather was not the liberals' first posture. Until the
1820s, liberal antiquarians were inclined to look indulgently upon Mather
as an amusing curiosity. "I wish you was here," writes Belknap to his
favorite correspondent, "to laugh with me at Dr. Mather's 'Wonders of
the Invisible World.'" The *North American Review,* in its early days, recommended "a fair perusal" of the *Magnalia* as "an achievement not to be
slighted." To some extent, this attitude persisted throughout the period.
James Russell Lowell summed it up in 1860 when he said of the *Magnalia
Christi Americana* that "with all his faults, that conceited old pedant con-
trived to make one of the most entertaining books ever written on this
side the water."[14]

This complacency was jolted, however, by the rise of militant orthodoxy. The more extreme orthodox apologists seemed to demand a total
return to the principles of seventeenth-century Puritanism, as when the
Reverend Thomas Robbins defended the adoption of the "laws of Moses
. . . together with the civil precepts which are found in other parts of the
Scriptures" as the proper basis of civil polity not only for the forefathers
but for "all civilized nations." This was the antithesis of Belknap's condescension toward the "Jewish theocracy" of the founders.[15] The ground-
swell of pro-Puritan sentiment threatened to bring back to life, with a
new air of authority, dodoes like Cotton Mather whom the liberals had
fancied extinct. Robbins was in fact preparing a new edition of the *Magnalia* (1820). Accordingly, Unitarian references to Mather take on a new
animosity during the 1820s. To start with, in case anyone still had any
doubt about the matter, James Savage disposed of Mather's pretensions as
a historian in his monumental edition of John Winthrop's *Journal,* a book
familiar to Hawthorne and a number of other creative writers on histor-

ical themes. Savage never loses a chance to convey the message that Mather had "published more errours of carelessness than any other writer on the history of New England."[16]

Beyond Mather's sins as a historian, two other aspects of his career became prime targets of liberal criticism: his part in the Salem witchcraft delusion, and the zeal with which he opposed the group of Bostonians that disputed his father's leadership at Harvard and founded the Brattle Street Church. Charles Wentworth Upham, in his *Lectures on Witchcraft* (1831), the then definitive treatment of the Salem episode, accused Mather of using the witchcraft delusion as a means of promoting a religious revival that would "increase his own influence over an infatuated people." Upham suspected that Mather was "instrumental in causing the delusion in Salem; at any rate he took a leading part in conducting it," and when it had subsided he tried to rekindle public anxiety in Boston.[17] Mather's culpability was immediately made the chief topic of a laudatory review of the *Lectures* in the *Christian Examiner* by another Unitarian minister, Francis Parkman, father of the historian. Parkman supplemented Upham's charges with tidbits from Mather's as yet unpublished diary, disclosing a "miserable vanity coupled with jealousy, thinking most extravagantly of self, and not less mean and unreasonable in distrusting others."[18]

Josiah Quincy's bicentennial *History of Harvard University* (1840) picked up where Upham and Parkman had left off. Quincy agreed that Mather was the "chief cause, agent, believer, and justifier" of the witchcraft delusion and argued that Increase Mather was also responsible for "producing and prolonging that excitement." Quincy's main concern, however, was to expose the self-interestedness of the Mathers' attempts to keep Harvard College and the Boston churches under conservative Congregational control. The Mathers, in this drama, are cast as the forces of reaction, whereas the Brattles and Governor Leverett are the forces of light. The Harvard tradition, Quincy argues, had been characterized by "freedom from sectarian influence." Thus the first two presidents of Harvard were "known unbelievers in points of religious faith to which the Congregational clergy of that time rigidly adhered"; college officers from the start condemned excessive evangelicalism; the university's first motto was simply *Veritas* and only under Increase Mather became *Christo et Ecclesiae*. It almost seems as if Quincy wishes to argue that Puritanism, at Puritan-founded Harvard, was really somehow contrary to the true Harvard spirit. Not surprisingly, Quincy took a positive view of Mather-opposed ecclesiastical reforms such as the founding of the Fourth Congregational Church (Brattle Street Church) in Boston, which Quincy calls the "first-fruit of that religious liberty, which the charter of William and Mary introduced into Massachusetts."[19]

Orthodox antiquarians did not sit idly by while a Puritan saint was being besmirched. They generally agreed that Mather was pedantic and credulous, that he had shown bad judgment in his conduct during the witchcraft delusion. But they were much more respectful toward him, commending his "unequalled industry," "vast learning," "unfeigned piety," and "most disinterested and expansive benevolence," whereas liberals saw him as foolish and malevolent.[20] Josiah Quincy was thus promptly raked over the coals by the Calvinist *American Biblical Repository* in two of those meticulous, interminable, logic-chopping reviews in which the orthodox habitually demonstrated greater stamina, if not greater brilliance, than their Unitarian adversaries. One, Enoch Pond's "Examination of Certain Points of New England History, as Exhibited by President Quincy in His History of Harvard University, and by Other Unitarian Writers," contained a lengthy defense of Cotton Mather's character. A few years later, Pond supplemented his remarks in a biography of Increase Mather, staking out a position that was upheld by subsequent orthodox commentators.[21]

Pond absolved father and son from all charges of having fomented the witchcraft delusion of 1692, arguing, on the contrary, that they served as moderating influences and showed throughout an attitude of compassionate concern for proper justice rather than a persecuting spirit. Pond was perhaps the first historian to point out the extent to which the case against Cotton Mather rests on the partisan testimony of Robert Calef. Pond and his Orthodox colleagues admitted that Mather was taken in by the delusion but denied that his credulity was in any way atypical of the era.[22] As for the Mathers' attempts to keep Boston and Harvard orthodox, orthodox observers naturally viewed them not as signs of personal ambition but as heroic efforts to "prevent that declension which was evidently approaching." As Pond observed, the main reason why the Mathers "received so much harder treatment, at the hands of President Quincy," than their almost-as-orthodox opponents was that the Mathers were "called, in divine Providence, to stand in the breach, when those innovations on New England usages *commenced,* which have since resulted in the utter apostasy of so many of the churches of the Pilgrims" – for example, the requirement of a public profession of faith by candidates for church membership, specifically omitted from the regulations of Brattle Street Church.[23]

Despite – or because of – his bias, Pond astutely grasped the key issue in the dispute over the meaning of Cotton Mather. Mather was a convenient symbol for both Unitarians and Calvinists because of the resemblances between some of the key events in his career and the more recent events of the Unitarian schism. Like the Calvinists of 1805 and after, Mather had fought the battle for orthodox control of Harvard and had lost.[24] Like them, he had helped to establish a rival institution on conservative principles (Yale in 1701, Andover Seminary in 1808). Like the nineteenth-century orthodox, Mather had been charged with bigotry and superstition and priestcraft. For the Unitarians, Cotton Mather, like Jedidiah Morse, epitomized arrogant sacerdotalism; for the orthodox, as with Morse's own image of himself, Mather was an early martyr to Arminian sneakiness. Unitarians particularly liked to parade the witchcraft delusion as the lamentable example par excellence of the lack of rational theology and to draw a direct line between Mather's participation in that delusion and his obsession with particular providences and signs of divine favor and disfavor toward himself and his family. Above all, Mather, as the putative mastermind of the hysteria of 1692, satisfied the Unitarian need to find a skeleton in the Puritan closet that would show beyond power of refutation the essentially pathological nature of Calvinism without frustrating the Unitarians' equally powerful need to venerate the Puritan founders. Thus Edward Everett Hale, trying to retort to a hostile exposé of Puritanism, cited Cotton Mather as the prime example of the degeneration of second- and third-generation New England, comparing this process with the degeneration of culture on the American frontier.[25]

The Unitarians, in other words, agreed with orthodox complaints about the declension of New England piety. But Unitarians, taking late seventeenth-century Puritan jeremiads at their word, placed the declensionary period at an earlier date, and they interpreted the decline as a positive symptom, on balance – as the passing of theocratic rigidity, which in itself represented a narrowing of focus from the more humane and creative vision of the first founders. The moral of Cotton Mather, for the Unitarians, was that by 1700 it was high time for the medieval night of ossified Calvinism to give way to the golden dawn of Reason. The orthodox naturally considered this an insulting caricature. Whatever Mather's weaknesses, they fundamentally admired his rigorous piety, shared his belief in particular providences, and denied that he was in any sense an unworthy heir of the founders.[26]

Historical imaging, like any other, is never done purely on principle but is also governed by the immediate circumstance. Quincy's extreme anti-Matherism was no doubt dictated in part by his sense of obligation to defend the Unitarian hegemony at Harvard. In other circumstances, etiquette called for greater charity. In W. B. O. Peabody's life of Mather, written for Jared Sparks's Library of American Biography, for example, the liberals' whipping boy was, Unitarian reviewers noted, "more favorably estimated than has of late been common" (i.e., among Unitarians).[27] To be sure, Peabody went through the familiar litany in depicting Mather as credulous, "self-exalting," "notoriously wanting" in "good sense and sound judgment." But he also stressed Mather's positive virtues as a conscientious father and dedicated philanthropist and tried to exculpate him from the charge of Machiavellian scheming at Salem.[28] As in a short account that Peabody wrote for the *Knickerbocker,* the "Diary of Cotton Mather," the biography tempers the Unitarian case against Mather by a partial return to the earlier, more good-humored liberal image of him as a stylist whose works remind one of Jeremy Taylor, "not so much by their richness," to be sure, as by their "oddness of illustration, which makes us wonder by what sort of intellectual process they could have connected it with the subject at hand." Although the *Magnalia* has justly "fallen into disrepute with those who read for instruction," "its quaintness recommends it to those who read for amusement."[29]

As a biographer, Peabody was required to play fair. As Mather's successor in the pulpit of Boston's Second Church and as official parish historian, Chandler Robbins was obliged to bend over backward. Robbins devoted the longest single section of his history to a sympathetic reappraisal of Mather, than whom "few historical characters are less understood," arguing that the "protruberance of a few eccentricities has thrown all the elements of his character into false perspective." Robbins' Mather, though not quite a paragon, is an exemplary husband and father ("in the domestic relations, his character shines with a mild and beautiful lustre"), praiseworthy for his ideas about early education ("as judicious as they were in advance of his age"), his charitable activities ("There is hardly a branch of philanthropic enterprise, into which his interest and exertions did not spread"), and his comparative tolerance of other views despite occasional outbreaks of bigotry ("He was more liberal and tolerant in regard to religious opinions and sects than the majority of divines of his own day and school").[30] Altogether this was a forebear of whom even a Unitarian might approve.

Robbins' portrait is unique within the Unitarian community. His colleagues suspected that it was motivated by duty as much as conviction, and they were probably right.[31] Still, its attempt at fair-mindedness, like Peabody's, should also be seen as an authentic reflection of the comparative flexibility of the Unitarian line and also as a precedent for James Russell Lowell's offer to open the pages of the *North American Review* to a sixty-page attack on the treatment of Mather in Upham's monumental *Salem Witchcraft* (1869), which Lowell had favorably reviewed. This was, indeed, a landmark work of local social history, still of great value today, although marked by the judgmentalism toward Mather of the earlier, popular *Lectures on Witchcraft.*

Upham's critic was William Poole, later the compiler of *Poole's Index,* a Connecticut native and Yale graduate then serving (rather surprisingly) as librarian of the Boston Athenaeum, one of the bulwarks of the Harvard-Arminian establishment. Without overtly pushing any theological position of his own, Poole confined himself to a devastating exposé of Upham's selective use of source material and his pretensions to read Mather's mind. "Mr. Upham," Poole sneers, "is never at a loss to know what Mr. Mather 'contemplated' on any occasion, – what 'he longed for,' – what 'he would have been glad to have,' – what 'he looked upon with secret pleasure,' – and what 'he was secretly and cunningly endeavoring' to do." The same intense concern for the alleged witchcraft cases that Upham uses to "prove" Mather's design of agitating and manipulating public opinion, Poole uses to "prove" that Mather's conduct was consistently "marked with kindness, patience, and Christian charity."[32] Whereas Upham had supported his charges by a worst-construction approach to Mather, Poole supported his, as might be expected, by a worst-construction approach to Mather's critic Robert Calef, whose character as a witness Poole impugns.

This and other loopholes left room for a lengthy rejoinder from Upham.[33] The precise degree to which Mather can be blamed for his conduct still remains a matter of debate. For our purposes, the key point about the Upham–Poole exchange is that for the first time since the inception of the Unitarian movement, the opposing interpretations of the most notorious episode in Mather's career were debated – though heatedly – for the most part through a close examination of the available records and without resort to sectarian mud-slinging. Furthermore, the "orthodox" side did at least as well as the "Unitarian" in the liberal stronghold. When the *Memorial History of Boston* was commissioned (1881), Poole was asked to do the chapter on witchcraft.[34] This did not silence the Uphamites, however. Brooks Adams and Henry Cabot Lodge continued to advance the anti-Mather line, against which Poole animadverted in trenchant reviews, while the orthodox asked rhetorically: "Is it not high time that the historical slanders on the character and influence of the clergy of New England be given a death-blow?"[35] A tricentennial history of Salem (1935) still referred to "Cotton Mather's militant advocacy" of the witchcraft prosecutions.[36] Poole had seen that Mather received a hearing, but Mather's adversaries remained in control of the field. Their position was consolidated in the mid-twentieth century by the greatest intellectual historian America has known. Perry Miller exonerated Mather from the charge of superstitious belief in the validity of spectral evidence but only in order to double damn him on the score of hypocrisy and self-servingness. "He tried," writes Miller, "to make those killings legitimate when he knew they were murders by dressing them in the paraphernalia of the federal doctrine [i.e., covenant theology]. . . . He tried it even though he knew that the covenant remedy of confession had become a farce." So, Miller adds with characteristic salt, Robert Calef tied the right can to the right tail, and "through the pages of this volume it shall rattle and bang." Miller, like Upham, is never at a loss to know what Cotton Mather contemplated. His image of Mather has understandably been disputed, but whether the revisionists can make the monster human remains to be seen.[37]

III

The great Cotton Mather debate was only one skirmish in a much broader arena of controversy between liberal and conservative Congregational historians. Throughout the first four decades of the nineteenth century, the debate escalated dramatically. After the Freeman-Morse exchange, the next round was the composition of two full-scale histories of New England, the first by Hannah Adams, whose work was underwritten by a group of liberal Bostonians, and the second by Morse and another conservative divine, Elijah Parish. Adams' *Summary History of New England* (1799) was lauded by the anti-Calvinist *Monthly Anthology and Boston Review*. The *Anthology* blasted the Morse-Parish *Compendious History of New England* (1804), accusing the authors of plagiarizing Adams and of trying to bully her into not abridging her work for textbook use, as she later did.[38] This led to a nasty public spat, complicated by Morse's role in the fight for control of Harvard in 1805. Although the Morse-Parish text outsold Adams', Morse claimed that his reputation was damaged by the episode and appealed his case to an "impartial" committee of three lawyers, who returned an inconclusive verdict.[39]

The controversy over the two histories was fought much more on the basis of politics and personalities than on their relative merits. Their substantive differences, however, are also noteworthy. Adams is predictably less sympathetic than Morse and Parish toward Puritan attempts to ensure religious uniformity. Both books excuse Puritan persecution of Quakers by appealing to the general intolerance of the age, but Adams stresses that "to us, who live in an enlightened age, where the principles of religious toleration are clearly understood, the conduct of the early settlers of New-England must appear truly astonishing," whereas Morse and Parish blame the Quakers as "enemies to government, unless administered by Quakers." Adams celebrates the founding of Rhode Island; Morse and Parish pass by the event dryly. Adams commends the Plymouth Pilgrims for being less rigid in their principles than those of Massachusetts Bay; Morse and Parish make no such distinction. This becomes another standard contrast in party historiography. The elevation of Pilgrim spirit above Puritan spirit tends to be made by liberals in search of evidence of broad-mindedness in early New England or in search of a means of being anti-Puritan without being antifilial.[40]

Adams, as well as Morse and Parish, sees New England as divinely favored; but for Adams the secular history of the region is considerably more important than for Morse and Parish. The early founding of Harvard signifies for Adams chiefly the forefathers' concern to promote knowledge and schooling; for Morse and Parish, the goal was to ensure a learned ministry. The seventeenth century takes up less than 40 percent of Adams's history, as against 75 percent of Morse and Parish's. Adams leaves the impression that New England has evolved well beyond its Puritan stage and is now in the act of advancing, under the republic, to "scenes of future grandeur." Morse and Parish, on the other hand, seek to persuade their readers to "admire, then love, then imitate the shining virtues of their pious forefathers." They insist – astonishingly, to anyone but a Connecticut Valley Congregationalist – that the Saybrook Platform of 1708 should still be considered the "discipline and orthodoxy of New England." They close with a jeremiad on the need to preserve the ancient spirit of New England in an impious age.[41]

A further step in the institutionalization of the rivalry between Arminian and Calvinist historians was the appearance, in 1808, of two dictionaries of American biography, one by the orthodox William Allen, president of Bowdoin College in Hawthorne's day, and the other by John Eliot, a Boston minister and friend of Belknap's who specialized in reviews of early Americana for the *Monthly Anthology*. A glance at the entries for Cotton Mather, Jonathan Edwards, and Charles Chauncy will show the predictable differences in emphasis, outlook, and tone: Allen is ponderous, encyclopedic, reverent, and picky; Eliot is breezy, anecdotal, urbane. Unfortunately for the liberals, Allen's dictionary was far more accurate and comprehensive. It went through three editions to Eliot's one.[42]

Meanwhile, the orthodox, aroused by Morse, had established a Calvinist journal, the *Panoplist,* to neutralize the *Anthology*. Since both magazines were staunchly pro-Federalist and anti-French, vying with each other in the praise of George Washington and Fisher Ames, their theological disagreements were all the more conspicuous. Both gave considerable space to historical articles purporting to clarify episodes from the regional past by reading them in the light of orthodox or liberal principles. The *Panoplist,* for instance, obliquely expressed displeasure with the incumbent of Brattle Street Church, Joseph Stevens Buckminster, by running a biography of a predecessor who was an "able and zealous advocate for the distinguishing doctrines of the gospel."[43] The *Anthology*'s historiography, however, was on balance far more impressive, because the magazine's conductors, as liberal intellectuals intending to produce a miscellaneous literary journal rather than a sectarian organ, were much more committed to antiquarianism for its own sake. One of the *Anthology*'s most notable features, inspired by Buckminster, was a series of "retrospective reviews" of early American works, including a number of histories, from John Smith's *Generall Historie of Virginia, New-England, and the Summer Isles* to Ezra Stiles' history of the regicide judges. These reviews, however, though mostly written with intent to be fair, invariably reflected Arminian norms. In the tradition of liberal patronage of Rhode Island, John Callender's *Historical Discourse* on that state was warmly praised. Nathaniel Ward's *Simple Cobbler of Aggawam* was criticized for overzealousness (of the "firmest and most deadly sort") though commended as a "curious specimen of the wit and talents of an eccentric genius." Readers were warned that Daniel Neal's *History of New England* was too pro-Puritan. Thomas Morton of Merry Mount was chided for dissoluteness and cynicism yet also judged indulgently as an amusing raconteur and as a victim of Puritan intolerance.[44]

After 1806, when the *Panoplist* was founded, Arminian and orthodox Congregationalists became increasingly armed with an ever more elaborate array of media through which to wage their sectarian battles, including the battle over the interpretation of provincial history. It would be tedious, though possible, to give a minute account of these disputes. A satisfactory impression may be gained from the cases already noted. Pro-Unitarian works such as Quincy's *History of Harvard* were ripped apart by the orthodox press, and vice versa; the insufficiently pietistic treatment of the Puritan fathers in the *Library of American Biography,* edited by Unitarian minister and Harvard professor (later president) Jared Sparks, was countered by the orthodox series of Massachusetts Sabbath School biographies. Generally speaking, the key historiographical breakthroughs – the beginnings of the historical society movement, the elevation of history to a major division in the *Anthology,* the publication of historical society collections, the launching of Sparks's American biography series, the tightening of scholarly and literary standards in historical writing – were Unitarian initiatives to which the orthodox responded by imitating Unitarian improvements in research technology but countering Unitarian propaganda and trying to do it one better by more meticulous attention to historical detail and theological nicety.

By midcentury, intradenominational warfare had begun to subside, as orthodoxy started to liberalize, Unitarianism moved in a temporarily more conservative direction in recoil from the Transcendentalist menace, and Congregationalists of all stripes began to perceive that the rise of the Baptists, Methodists, and Catholics, not to mention the "nothingarians," had created a permanent state of denominational pluralism, whether they liked it or not. Several major histories sufficiently temperate, sophisticated, and well documented came to elicit praise from both the major contesting parties. Among these projects, the two most notable were both by Unitarians: George Bancroft's *History of the United States* and John Gorham Palfrey's *History of New England.* Bancroft and Palfrey succeeded not just because of their unprecedentedly thorough research and scope (both devote considerable space, for instance, to transatlantic antecedents and relations) but because each made significant concessions to orthodox values while at the same time retaining an essentially liberal angle of vision. Bancroft's approach was to extol Calvinism, on the one hand (as the harvest of the Reformation), and the secularization of piety on the other (the Puritan spirit as the shaper of republican character and institutions). This involved some dubious juggling, as when he tried to exhibit Jonathan Edwards as America's first philosopher of progress.[45] But the net result was an interpretation well calculated to satisfy New Englanders: He was able simultaneously to exalt the Puritans, to preach a progressivist theory of history, and to establish the centrality of New England in the history of the republic. He was careful to gloss over or omit the most divisive episodes in the history of early New England Congregationalism: the Half Way Covenant, the Great Awakening, the silent rise of Arminianism, and the Old Light – New Light division among orthodox Congregationalists during the eighteenth century.

Palfrey succeeded by adhering for the most part to a documentary approach and by siding, when he passed judgment, almost always with the Puritan establishment. Though conceding in his introduction that his religious beliefs would have excommunicated him from Massachusetts Bay, Palfrey also emphasized his reverence for the founders' memory, and he proved it by defending the expulsion of Roger Williams (whom Bancroft idolized) and by sounding even more anti-Quaker than Morse and Parish (though deploring Quaker executions). Palfrey's justification of the Puritans, however, is on administrative rather than theological grounds. Suppression of disruptive influence was necessary, he contends, not to maintain orthodoxy but to preserve the security of the infant commonwealth.[46] In this way Palfrey avoids compromising his own principles.

Palfrey's history has a distinctly Whiggish flavor as compared to Bancroft's, identifying the rise and prosperity of New England with the development of its social and political structures rather than with the unfolding of the great idea of liberty. Palfrey agrees with Bancroft, however, on the two most fundamental ideological points: that "civilized New England is the child of English Puritanism" and that Puritanism tends to lead to civil liberty.[47]

The histories of Bancroft and Palfrey, like the relatively dignified exchange between Poole and Upham, betoken a partial transcendence of sectarian bias on the part of Congregational historians generally. Even Morse and Parish revised their history so as to make later versions less pugnaciously Calvinist.[48] Not that anything resembling full consensus or objectivity was attained. Both in their general argument and in detail,

Bancroft and Palfrey effected, insofar as their work was received as standard, a kind of qualified Unitarian hegemony in historical scholarship. Both, in their basic lines of argument, associated progress with secularization. Neither came up to the conservative standard of filiopietism. Both, for example, took versions of the standard Unitarian line against Cotton Mather's behavior at Salem, although for different reasons.[49] Quite apart from the cases of Palfrey and Bancroft, furthermore, any tendencies toward a consensus view of Puritanism achieved in Congregational historiography were at least partially offset by the rise of a small but important group of writers practicing history in dissent from both the orthodox and the Arminian brand of filiopietism.

IV

The dissenting tradition in early national historiography starts with such first-generation products as Samuel Peters' *History of Connecticut* (1781) and Isaac Backus' *History of New-England, with Particular Reference to the Denomination of Christians Called Baptists* (1777–96). Neither made a great impression on the Congregational scholarly mainstream, at least in the short run. Peters, a Loyalist minister from Connecticut who had emigrated to England, was dismissed, with some justice, as a rascally slanderer of his native state and as a satirist rather than a historian.[50] The lack of establishment interest in Backus, an eminent Baptist minister,[51] was probably due to the fact that Congregationalists in general did not take Baptists seriously until the nineteenth century. Backus' *History*, however, though awkward and uneven, seems in retrospect an important piece of scholarly pioneering. He combines lumpish documentary with penetrating analysis of the rise of the Baptists and the record of Congregationalist discrimination against other sects after escaping from persecution themselves. As a Calvinist, Backus does not wish to disassociate Baptists from the Puritan tradition; rather, his approach is to argue for the primacy of the Baptist strain. Its "faith and practice," as he puts it, "come the nearest to that of the first planters of New England, of any churches now in the land, excepting in the single article of sprinkling infants."[52] In this line of argument, Backus anticipates the argumentative strategy of other post-Puritan sectaries, who also sometimes sought denominational self-justification by the ploy of arguing that their way was the closest to the polity or the "essential spirit" of the founders.[53]

The nineteenth century saw the disestablishment of Congregationalism throughout New England and its reduction to the status of a minority sect. The ratio of Massachusetts Congregational churches to all others, which was more than 2:1 in 1800, had diminished to roughly 2:3 by 1858.[54] The change would have looked still more pronounced were it not for the divisions of Congregational churches that resulted from the

Unitarian controversy. Dissenting interpretations of New England history increased accordingly. One well-known example is the work of Orestes Brownson, the former Unitarian and Transcendentalist minister-reformer who converted to Catholicism in 1842 and then became its leading apologist in New England. Until his conversion, Brownson espoused a Bancroftian theory of history with a proto-Marxist twist; afterward he inverted the theory, characterizing the supposed progress of New England religious thought from Puritanism to Unitarian liberalism and beyond as a decline, the sign of Protestantism's inevitable lapse into fragmentation and atheism.[55]

More disturbing to the establishment, however, than Brownson, whom it wrote off as a boorish, turncoat propagandist for a socially marginal church, was the more ambitious dissection of New England history as decay undertaken by Boston attorney Peter Oliver in *The Puritan Commonwealth* (1856), a withering appraisal of early Massachusetts polity from an Anglican, Royalist perspective. This anomaly is a neglected masterpiece of antebellum historiography, easily as sophisticated from a literary standpoint as Prescott's best work, although its obsessive polemics are the antithesis of his narrative pictorialism. Oliver argues that the Puritans betrayed the good faith of "King Charles the Martyr" and the "kindness and indulgence" of his son ("like that of a father to his wayward children") by illegally using a charter intended for business purposes alone as the basis of a political regime.[56] The Massachusetts Bay Colony was therefore founded on fraud, and England's eventual annulment of the charter was well warranted. The true foundation of civil liberty in New England was laid, Oliver argues (out-Bancrofting Bancroft), "*in spite of* the elders and magistrates," when the freemen began to resist the ruling oligarchy. And the freemen, he adds (drawing back abruptly from the democratic line), "were not struggling for humanity, but only for self."[57]

Oliver castigates the Puritans as vindictive persecutors. Their persecutions were less justifiable than the Anglicans', he claims, because Puritanism lacked the authority of an established church to curb the deviance to which Puritanism inevitably gave rise through its emphasis on the right of private judgment. The record of Puritan intolerance Oliver therefore interprets both as evidence of Puritanism's instability ("always ready to crumble into a dozen sects") and as evidence of hypocrisy ("though its elders loved to engage in 'theological logomachies' among themselves, they were always ready for a friendly reconciliation over the ruins of a rival fanaticism").[58] The Puritans' Indian policy was even more reprehensible, a betrayal of the missionary hopes of their royal sponsor. "The spirit of a false faith," observes Oliver wickedly, "taught the Puritan Pilgrims that heathen blood and lands are lawful motives, as well as lawful spoils, of Christian warfare." Granted, "there was no inborn love of cruelty among them," but that only made matters worse.

> To slaughter an Indian was a painful religious exercise, as much as to spend a day in bodily abstinence. For this reason, the Puritan soldiers were pitiless. The negation of works in their religion also coöperated to promote injustice in their policy; and where violence was not a Puritan rite, it was but too often a right of Puritanism. Thus, between the two, the aborigines were wholly sacrificed; and a system of religion, which confessedly had an eye to the things of Caesar as well as to those of Heaven, in the short space of fifty years swept from New England one hundred thousand human beings.[59]

Even Oliver's antagonists had to admit that he wrote brilliant prose. Indeed no historian of Puritanism before or since, except for Perry Miller, comes close to matching Oliver's elegant hauteur. His mordant incisiveness leaves a far more powerful impression on a twentieth-century reader than either Bancroft's bombast or Palfrey's dehydrated periods. *The Puritan Commonwealth* is also carefully (if selectively) documented and meticulously argued, making formidable use of Oliver's legal expertise.

Of course Oliver's militant Anglicanism made him an easy target. The response to Oliver by the Unitarians, sharpened no doubt by the increasing competition they were getting from the Episcopal church as the choice ecclesiastical haven for the region's liberal elite, shows the limits to which they were prepared to go in undercutting the extreme filiopietism of Calvinist historians and helps put in perspective the intradenominational feuds already discussed. A clear signal is conveyed by the *North American's* review of Oliver, penned by one of the most rabidly anti-Matherite Unitarian ministers, George E. Ellis. "All men of sense," Ellis concedes, recognize that the "praise of the Puritans" "has been carried so far as to become a grievance." But although he has "long anticipated a book such as this," he is shocked by the result. Its "spirit . . . is a very bad one"; Oliver's "diseases of fancy mark him almost as a monomaniac." Ellis is doubly shocked that a "descendant of the Puritans" could write such a thing – though, on second thought, it might have been expected from the scion of a prominent Loyalist family.[60]

In short, the Unitarians, like the Puritans in Oliver's image of them, were also prepared to bury their theological logomachies when faced with a rival fanaticism. Cotton Mather might be hazed, but not John Winthrop, whom Unitarians and orthodox alike agreed in revering as the George Washington of Massachusetts.[61]

Even more controversial than Oliver, because more ambitious and more objective, was the work of a maverick Unitarian, Richard Hildreth, whose six-volume *History of the United States* (1849–51) rivaled Bancroft's as the leading work in the field. Like Oliver, Hildreth set out in avowed opposition to filiopietism.

Of centennial sermons and Fourth-of-July orations, whether pro-
fessedly such or in the guise of history, there are more than enough. It
is due to our fathers and ourselves, it is due to truth and philosophy, to
present for once, on the historic stage, the founders of our American
nation unbedaubed with patriotic rouge.

A sardonic astringency marks Hildreth's style throughout. Whereas Bancroft describes the rapture of Walter Raleigh's men at discovering the lush
vegetation of the North Carolina seacoast, Hildreth observes that the
"vigorous vegetation of these sandy islands . . . concealed the poverty of
the soil." Compared to Bancroft, Hildreth's description of the Revolutionary War, as one reviewer put it, is as "cold-blooded . . . as if the
writer had been engaged with an account of a long struggle between two
tribes of savages in the heart of Africa."[62] The same Olympian aloofness
characterizes Hildreth's treatment of the supposedly heroic age of New
England history. Although he consistently sides with the colonists
against the Crown and thus demonstrates a nominal patriotism, Hildreth
is quick to expose instances of self-interested, ludicrous, and discreditable
behavior. He notes with relish that the Puritans had to place limits on the
extent of public devotions in order to keep from crippling secular business. He emphasizes New England's complicity in the slave trade "at the
very birth" of its commerce. He continually exposes conflicts of interest
among the New England colonies over border disputes, jurisdictional
questions, and the like. He takes aim at Bancroft's heroes – Roger Williams, for example – noting Williams's hostility toward the Quakers
(which Bancroft denied) and his acceptance of a ten-year-old Indian boy
as one of the spoils of King Philip's War.[63]

Hildreth's *History* received curiously mixed reviews. The two main
complaints were contradictory: It was said to be only a dry "narrative of
public events . . . without any attempt to generalize them or deduce from
them the broader lessons of experience," but it was also described as
being systematically biased – a charge that implied a strong thesis.[64] Actually, both complaints were valid, up to a point. Organizationally, Hildreth's *History* is weaker than Bancroft's, containing much more sheer
chronicle in proportion to interpretation, since Hildreth is considerably
less interested in overt philosophizing and colorful portraiture, though
quite capable of both. Yet his *History* was by no means a throwback to
the annalism of Thomas Prince and Abiel Holmes. It was informed
throughout by a consistent though complex point of view, namely that
of the hardheaded social critic with a keen sense of social justice but at the
same time a lively awareness of human capacity for self-interested behavior and a dislike of theory divorced from practice. Hildreth, as a Conscience Whig, was disposed both to criticize political and religious estab-
lishments and at the same time to see social and economic determinants
as the key shapers of institutions, in contrast to Bancroft's Romanticist

emphasis on great ideas and representative men. The pageantry of Revolutionary War battles, the canonization of Roger Williams, the idealization of Puritanism as the cradle of democracy were all so much tinsel to Hildreth. As his defenders, like Upham's opponent W. F. Poole, often pointed out, Hildreth was a man ahead of his time in his avoidance of gush and in his commitment to a more empirical study of history than the Brahmin Romantics practiced.[65] By the same token, he limited himself by his reaction against their brand of narrative history. Even more than Oliver's, Hildreth's history suffers from its intent to serve as a corrective, the problem of focus being caused in part by its tendency to proceed by reacting against received notions rather than by building up an independent synthesis.

Hildreth is said to have been crushed by the hostile reception of his *History*.[66] Certainly he became a disappointed man. The supposed failure of the book, however, has been exaggerated. Though commercially less successful than Bancroft's, it was reissued six times within thirty years of its initial printing. Even when it first appeared, the reception was by no means uniformly hostile, at least in the North. Though some disparaged it (notably the *North American* and *Democratic* reviews – an unholy alliance), the intellectual organs of the Baptists and the Universalists considered it the best American history ever written; a leading Congregational journal anticipated that it would become the "*standard* history of our colonial and revolutionary existence"; Transcendentalist Theodore Parker praised it warmly; and even the more cautious review in the *Christian Examiner*, by Oliver's nemesis George Ellis, averred that "Mr. Hildreth has done enough to secure for himself a distinguished place in his chosen department of literature."[67] In view of this broad support, however, the primary reservation expressed from within Hildreth's own ethnic group of Unitarian Whigs is all the more notable: His history was less patriotic, less pietistic than it should have been. Even if Hildreth could not positively be accused of infidelity, he was, the *North American Review* admonished, shockingly unenthusiastic about the "worth and dignity of the motives which brought our Puritan fathers to these shores." For insufficient filiopietism, the Unitarians were ready to chastise not only an outsider but each other as well – although the painful duty was made easier for this reviewer by Hildreth's objectionable abolitionism.[68]

V

Having seen all this, we must now ask what bearing it has on the study of more strictly belletristic works, apart from the real but obvious value of reminding us that history (like other branches of nonfictional prose) also belongs in the category of literature. In the first place, an understanding of the terms of historical debate and their denominational and cultural underpinnings during our period is a prerequisite to under-standing the symbolic import of the rather limited repertoire of events, personae, and terminology deployed in the period's fictions of Puritan history. The examples given contrasting Adams with Morse and Parish, Emerson with Allen, Quincy with Pond, and so forth, begin to open up the possibility of a comprehensive ethnographic reading of antebellum New England literary texts in terms of a common but disparately envi-sioned semiotic code. To return to the example of Cotton Mather, when we open our Hawthorne and read in *Grandfather's Chair,* Hawthorne's his-tory of Massachusetts for children, that Cotton Mather was the "chief agent of the mischief" in Salem, or when we read at the climax of "Alice Doane's Appeal" the description of Mather as the devil's "good friend" ("representative of all the hateful features of his time; the one blood-thirsty man, in whom were concentrated those vices of spirit and errors of opinion, that suffices to madden the whole surrounding multitude"), we discern that Hawthorne, at least for the nonce, is writing from within the Arminian-Unitarian vision of Puritanism.[69] Conversely, when we read in Harriet Beecher Stowe's semiautobiographical novel *Poganuc People* of the heroine's delight when her minister-father brought home Robbins' spanking-new edition of the *Magnalia* ("What wonderful stories these! and stories, too, about her own country, stories that made her feel that the very ground she trod on was consecrated by some special dealing of God's providence"), we realize that we are in the opposite camp. For Stowe, Mather turns out to bear somewhat the same relation to Jonathan Edwards that in the Unitarian mind John Winthrop bore to Mather.[70] Stowe, that is, invokes Edwards as her stern Puritan archetype, by con-trast to whom Mather looks broad-minded. That is an idiosyncratic reading – the reading of an orthodox Congregationalist in the process of turning Episcopalian – rather than an orthodox reading per se; but it is unquestionably *an* orthodox reading and, what is more, a reading in the Connecticut Valley, New Divinity tradition of orthodoxy. In Chapter 11, in which Hawthorne and Stowe are discussed in depth, we shall get a fuller sense of what such contrasts signify.

Second, reading period historiography gives us a better idea of what was meant in Chapter 8 by the characterization of antebellum belletristic writing about Puritanism as predominantly a Unitarian achievement. The most searching of the three detailed studies of New England histor-ical romance conventions, Michael Bell's *Hawthorne and the Historical Ro-mance of New England,* bears this out, even though it does not discuss nineteenth-century sectarianism. "The great theme of the Matter of New England," Bell notes, is the "conflict within Puritanism itself between the forces of tyranny and the forces of liberty." This thematic emphasis throws the spotlight on the key instances of persecution in Puritan history, the witchcraft hysteria of 1692 being the single favorite exemplum. The general tendency in the romances is to melodramatize such instances of persecution by imaging the sufferers as opposers of intolerance. Puritanism, however, is rarely depicted as a monolith. The characteristic ideological orientation of the romances toward it is ambivalence rather than rejection. This is illustrated, for example, by such subthemes as the adaptation of the jeremiad myth of second- and third-generation decline into hypocrisy, formalism, and bigotry (which allows the romancer to celebrate the heroism of the founders but also to see Puritanism as needing to be saved from the consequences of rigidification) and the theme of female revolt against patriarchal authority. The romancers favored young female rebels (among whom Hawthorne's Hester is a desentimentalized variation), Bell suggests, because male rebellion would have been too overt a challenge to authority. "The female rebel, on the other hand, avoids overt revolution," and as a result is more successful: Her revolt is shown as bringing about the easing of oligarchic and peer restraints even as she is absorbed peaceably into the Puritan system by marriage to the most attractive available man.[71] This explanation overlooks more obvious reasons for featuring heroines, such as the desire to appeal to the predominantly female readership of novels, but Bell is unquestionably right about the ideological implications of the aesthetic choice of featuring strong women characters in Puritan romances.

The ambivalence toward Puritanism that Bell discerns in the New England romance and that also pervades antebellum fictions of Puritanism in other genres is precisely like that exhibited by the liberal historians. This is no accident, since Unitarians were the leading producers of such works. Take two of the first significant New England historical romances, Lydia Child's *Hobomok* (1824) and Catherine Sedgwick's *Hope Leslie* (1827). The career of Sedgwick's title character reflects a myth of confinement by Puritan bigotry that Sedgwick had previously twice played out in contemporary settings and that reflected her own life situation as an embattled religious liberal in a Berkshire milieu dominated by reactionary Calvinism.[72] Nurtured permissively on the frontier, so that she has grown up in a spirit of Wordsworthian natural piety and without the usual degree of internalized self-denial and hostility toward intellectual and ethnic outsiders, Hope is abruptly plunked down into a proper Bostonian household (the Winthrops') and forced to pass the test of minute surveillance. In a series of melodramatic adventures, Hope tries her patrons' patience, risks ostracism and even death, but finally wins their respect so fully that the reader is clearly not supposed to raise the question as to whether she will wither after her storybook marriage into the establishment. Child's *Hobomok*, the first and probably the only antebellum fiction to give any kind of support for miscegenation (which Child

openly endorsed in her American history for children,)[73] pits heroine
Mary Conant against her tyrannically rigid father, who forbids her to
marry her Episcopalian suitor. On the rebound, she becomes the squaw
of a friendly Indian admirer, Hobomok, and even has a child by him – a
far more disastrous outcome than the senior Conant would have dreamed
of. When her former lover returns, however, Hobomok generously (and
all too conveniently) gives her up and leaves the scene. In the end, Mary
becomes reconciled with her now repentant father. Her son, the "little
Hobomok," even becomes a "peculiar favorite" of his ("partly from consciousness of blame, and partly from a mixed feeling of compassion and
affection"). The first marriage is easily annulled and a happy ending follows. Mary's compassionate steadfastness, like Hope's, has proved to be
the sustaining principle of coherence in the world of the romance.[74]

   More striking than these works by Unitarians is the persistence of the
same conventions, once established, in the writing of the handful of theologically more conservative romancers. For example, the last of the three
Tales of the Puritans (1831), by Delia Bacon, daughter and sister of Orthodox divines, takes its impetus from the Hobomok-like situation of the
town minister's daughter forbidden by her parents to consort with a Canadian Catholic, whom, after various adventures, she marries. Hints of
his future conversion hardly make much difference to the plot dynamics.
Likewise, Baptist minister Joseph Banvard's Priscilla . . . An Historic Tale
of the Puritans and the Baptists (1853) has the heroine duly undergo a Puritan-style conversion but later works up to the familiar Unitarian-style
melodrama of heretics persecuted by establishment bigotry, leading to a
happy escape to Rhode Island in the end. Harriet Beecher Stowe's historical fictions also are built, as we shall see, upon the pattern of the female
protagonist who critiques entrenched theocracy by the power of her temperament, if not through an overt challenge. Altogether the only fiction
of Puritanism known to me that stays resolutely Calvinist from start to
finish is The Fawn of the Pale Faces (1853), by Stowe's old Litchfield
teacher John P. Brace, who, significantly, says in his introduction that he
"trusts that the grave charge of want of 'Orthodoxy,' which was made by
certain fastidious critics against his first work, will not be repeated
against this."[75] That former work, the more interesting Tales of the Devils
(1847), is a bizarre visionary allegory about the unsuccessful temptation,
by the spirit of Ernest Maltravers (a newly dead and damned scoundrel
named after a Bulwer-Lytton hero), of his bastard son Robert, a somewhat implausibly ideal figure whose life turns out to be a smashingly
successful Horatio Alger story, despite his devil-father's efforts. The
Fawn of the Pale Faces is also about the testing of a young man, Edward
Dudley, who through various trials of self-discipline (including temporary renunciation of his love for his sweetheart) grows into a rather re-

pressed and stereotypically Puritan stalwart, for which he is rewarded with his sweetheart after all. The book, however, is confused about this process, both affirming the rightness and nobility of self-discipline and conceding that the process of self-discipline has left Edward a less responsive partner than his wife would wish.

Altogether it would seem that either the conventions of romance prevented conservative authors from speaking their convictions (note the necessity, in melodramatic love plots, of casting stern elders as blocking figures) or else the creative process triggered in the sensibility of these writers a partial liberation from creedal restraints. In any case, when orthodox writers ventured into the charmed world of romance, they did so at peril to their orthodoxy.

Another aspect of the Arminian outlook more compatible than that of orthodox Calvinism with historical fictionalizing was the greater extent to which Arminianism was committed to a present-minded value system that it more or less knowingly imposed on the past. All historiography becomes increasingly like romance as it starts to turn polemical, but the Unitarian polemical project was more conducive to romance to start with. It authorized imaginative transformation of the past in the present interest more openly than orthodoxy did, and it had the further advantage of being built upon the paradox of mingled reverence for and repudiation of ancestors. For such paradoxes are, or so modern literary scholars believe, the sine qua non of an advanced literary taste. Unitarian historical ideology, then, was more amenable to effective fictionalization because it entailed a more elegant critical fiction of the Puritan past to start with.

This last statement would doubtless have nettled nineteenth-century liberal antiquarians. Yet most would have granted that they saw Puritanism at a greater aesthetic remove than the orthodox did and that they did not see themselves as Puritan cohorts with the same literalness. The orthodox were not bona fide old-line Puritans either (there had already been considerable mutations of polity and doctrinal waterings-down within their ranks as well); indeed they themselves confessed to feeling tragically removed from the founders' era, to being anxious and perhaps inadequate progeny in an age of secularization. But their comparative sense of the subject of the forefathers as "sacred ground" ("too poetical for poetry, too romantic for romance") inhibited the free play of imagination. It required that the literary result "come up to the previous conceptions of their readers" – that is, that it toe the party line.[76]

At the same time, any hard-and-fast distinction between Arminian and Calvinist imaging of the Puritans based on the contrast between the "fictional" and the "antifictional" is simplistic, since for both parties the "history" of New England resolved itself into the mediation of a structured narrative that the latter-day reader was asked to accept as the reality of the Puritan experience.

> The crisis had now arrived, when the existence or the extermination of the infant colony was to be determined: When they were to triumph in peace, or perish in the hands of merciless savages. Rome staked less in the war with the Sabines, and Sparta at Thermopylae, than was now hazarded by this feeble colony, on the event of battle.[77]

This is from the account of the Pequod War in an orthodox history of New England settlement. The rhetoric is, of course, indistinguishable from that of narrative fiction. The "historical" account is an emplotment of a myth of crisis identical in structure with Hawthorne's "Jollity and gloom were contending for an empire" in "The May-Pole of Merry Mount," however different the ideology. For both Calvinist and Arminian, early New England history was a saga with a moral involving a series of more or less mutually agreed-upon episodes. The quarrel was not about the structure but about the moral – not about the narrativization of the past as a series of interrelated crisis stories but about the question of how the saga was to be interpreted and replicated. The orthodox rightly sensed that the translation of the saga into the vocabulary of historical fiction tended to produce, from their standpoint, a profanation, whereas the liberals rightly sensed that such a translation tended to fit their programmatic goals. But the dual tendencies (remarked in the last chapter) for antebellum historical fictions to be validated on the basis of their grounding in fact and for narrative to be seen as the proper mode of achieving historical objectification kept both orthodox and liberal writers from clear-cut differentiation, either in theory or in practice, between history and narrative as such.

Finally, a word about the literary significance of the dissenting versions of New England history outside the divided stream of Congregational tradition. The dissenting versions were rarely used as sources by antebellum producers of fictionalized history (some of whom, as we shall see, did little homework). These histories, however, represent a centrifugal tendency within the field of historiography parallel to developments within literary narrative. Hildreth's attempt to depose Romantic pictorialism, for instance, is related to the shift in literary narrative fashion from Romantic to realistic modes, a shift to which Hildreth, in a small way, contributed by his imitation slave narrative, *The Slave: or, Memoirs of Archy Moore* (1836). Brownson's emphatic anti-puritanism and Oliver's defense of Thomas Morton represent potentialities that a number of creative writers, in the freer form of the historical romance, attempted to explore or indulge.[78] Antebellum fictionalizations of Puritan history, considered as interpretations of that history, likewise tend to carry the revisionary impulse far enough to place themselves on the borderline between the filiopietistic consensus of Congregational antiquarianism of both stamps and the more radical critiques of the dissenting historians. In the next two chapters we shall examine this literature in more detail.

10

Fictionalizing Puritan History:
Some Problems and Approaches

As we may by now be tired of hearing, language, in representing reality, most forcefully demonstrates reality's absence.
George Levine, *The Realistic Imagination* (1981)

When art emerges from the self-awareness of a social group and communicates to those outside it, certainly knowledge of a form of consciousness, of experience, of self-understanding different from our own is transmitted. . . . . It is important, however, to be clear about what we are learning, what kind of truth is refracted in this way. It is a communication of subjectives and appearances, not of analytic understanding, for which fiction can be no more than evidence.
Jeffrey Sammons, *Literary Sociology and Practical Criticism* (1977)

In this chapter and the next, we turn from historical accounts of the Puritan past to a more direct study of belletristic portrayals. As we do, the task of understanding the historical dimension of period thinking becomes trickier than ever. If self-styled works of history often seem more like the reflections of fancy than of fact, the relationship between a piece of creative writing and its historical referent is even more elusive. A work of history is already a textualization of the original phenomena. A work of historical fiction is, then, a combination of retextualized source material and artistic elaboration (mediated by literary convention, of course). Small wonder that theories of historical fiction do not agree as to whether such writing can meaningfully be defined in terms of the sort of historical knowledge it furnishes.[1] Small wonder that Hawthorne's best critics hold antithetical views of the importance of history as a stimulus to his art. For Michael Colacurcio, Hawthorne's writing shows a profound grasp of Puritan history and ideas; "Young Goodman Brown," "The Minister's Black Veil," and *The Scarlet Letter* exhibit an understanding as deep as any nineteenth-century New Englander possessed of the central issues of the Salem witchcraft delusion, the Great Awakening, and the Antinomian

239

controversy, although these texts are not simply "about" those episodes. Nina Baym, on the other hand, distinguishing between Hawthorne's historical writing and his fictional use of history, sees the latter simply as one among various devices that he adapted from the repertoire of contemporary narrative technique for expressing thematic preoccupations by no means special to Puritanism.[2] The disparity between the two verdicts is anticipated by the conflicting testimony of period romancers themselves, one presenting her work "as [not] being in any degree an historical narrative, or a relation of real events," another claiming to provide a "description, a living picture, of the times of our forefathers."[3]

Chapters 10 and 11 examine the problematics of historical representation by New England belles lettres in more detail than was possible in the brief discussions toward the end of Chapters 8 and 9. I shall not try to resolve earlier critical disagreements into a single view to be applied to all historical fictions, because it seems to me that the disagreements reflect ambiguities inherent in the nature of the case. For example, historical literature necessarily involves an admixture of fabrication and truth telling, of historical consciousness and present-mindedness; most historical literature is spotty on the level of chronicle and analysis, yet, at its best, is able to render character and consciousness more sensitively than most historical monographs. This chapter explores how these ambiguities are built into the fictions of Puritanism by examining the effect of four influences on the writers' thinking about Puritanism: genre, life experience, historical research, and programmatic purpose. The operation of these will be illustrated, respectively, by a short account of the assimilation of Walter Scott's approach to romance as a model for Puritan fictions, by the autobiographical historicizing of Eliza Buckminster Lee, by the history-based fiction of Josiah Gilbert Holland, and by the thematic design imposed on New England materials in Henry Wadsworth Longfellow's neglected trilogy, *Christus*. Chapter 11 then examines at much greater length the achievement of the region's two greatest writers of historical fiction, Hawthorne and Stowe.

I

As we have already begun to see, the state of received theory and practice of historical romance on the eve of the first serious American experiments guaranteed confusion and disharmony over the question of the historicity of historical literature. The problem was imported with the first texts and reviews of Scott's work and was further complicated here. As modern scholarship attests, Scott's fiction can be claimed either as one of the high points of Romantic fiction (from which perspective one views it as historicized gothic) or as one of the chief precursors of Victorian realism (from which standpoint its representational density seems more important than its Romantic elements).[4] Scott himself helped provoke this conflict of interpretations because he rightly held both that his novels portrayed historical reality and that they were not minutely historical: They did not, for instance, exactly render archaic language, for fear that "universality" would be sacrificed. His justification of this mixed mode – namely, that the constants of human nature from age to age outweigh differences in period culture – reflects the fact that Scott relied to a large degree on intuitive projection to give animation and shape to his materials.[5] Although Scott would not have endorsed Emerson's Transcendentalist theory of history, he would have assented to Emerson's declaration that "I have not so near access to Luther's mind through his works as through my own mind when I meditate upon his historical position" (*JMN* 4:348). It is fair to say both that Scott's historical fiction has a documentary basis (although he was apt to rely more on memory than on research)[6] and that moving back into history was for Scott a form of imaginative liberation. Indeed, "History releases Scott into romance," as George Levine observes, precisely "because it anchors him firmly in fact," inasmuch as "history in Scott testifies to the *fact* of the marvelous and mysterious."[7]

Historical fiction, then, was to provide an illusion of mimesis that legitimated it as realistic yet at the same time was not simply a mimesis and indeed owed some of its mimetic power to projection onto the past of romantic fantasy and present-minded ideology – defined at the conscious level, to be sure, as authorial perception of the constants of human nature. In practice this meant that any representation that did not grossly violate the reader's previous understanding of the era in question might be commended as historical if the artist displayed enough pictorial adeptness. Meticulous research was in principle a desideratum but less important to literary success than imaginative power and the audience's ideological orientation.

In New England, the question of the mimetic status of fictions about history became further muddled. One such complication arose from the utilitarian cast of American critical thought, concerned as it was about the supposed duplicity of the imagination in substituting false and seductive images of reality for reality itself.[8] This meant, when historical fictionalizing was adduced as a counterexample, a strategic forgetting of the fictional element. Thus Andrew Peabody, conditioned to equate fiction with distortion, argued that Scott "can hardly be called a writer of fiction," since "his great art consists in so adjusting the minute incidents of history . . . to bring out in high relief the picture of the times."[9] Verbal clues such as "hardly" and "adjusting" show, of course, that Peabody (like Rufus Choate, cited in Chapter 8) knew very well that Scott's romances were not entirely factual, a point made in what at first seems an antithetical declaration by a fellow Boston reviewer that Scott's reputation "is built upon his works of fancy." But this writer likewise goes on to identify the historicity of Scott's works of fancy as the primary source of their interest and charm.[10]

The inconsistency of critical pronouncements is reflected in the variety of mimetic levels on which period writers wrote historical fictions concerning the Puritans. On the one hand, we find romances that do little more, by way of touching base with history, than invoke the Puritan era as a symbolic backdrop against which to lay out a melodrama, pitting individual against society, that belongs to no particular realm of time except the realm of romance. Catherine Sedgwick's *Hope Leslie,* noted in Chapter 9, and Eliza Lee's *Naomi,* discussed later in this chapter, are works of this kind, works that rerun the Cinderella plot that Sedgwick has previously introduced into American writing as the archetype for woman's fiction. At the opposite pole, we find works laid out on a patiently documentary or pseudodocumentary basis, like John Greenleaf Whittier's *Margaret Smith's Journal,* which purports to be the observations of a young Englishwoman visiting her Puritan relatives in seventeenth-century Massachusetts. The book has a plot of sorts, unified by the device of contrasting love affairs, but the heart of it is Margaret's chatty, miscellaneous ramblings about Puritan people and topics. A number of the leading figures of the day are trotted across the pages. Margaret hears old Nathaniel Ward tell stories about former times, whereupon young Benjamin Tompson (a "gay witty man, full of a fine conceit of himself") pipes up with the preface to his *New Englands Crisis.* She meets a "pert, talkative lad, a son of Mr. Increase Mather, who . . . hath the reputation of good scholarship and lively wit," some samples of which are appended (*WW* 5:106, 128). Altogether, the diary device becomes a means of deploying Whittier's storehouse of historical anecdotes in a manner consistent with his didactic purposes. (He sees to it that Margaret attains a proper sympathy with heretics, Indians, and accused witches without going so far as to alienate her Puritan relatives.) "Every line is true," effused one reviewer; "every color and shade a copy from the reality."[11] Well, hardly. In fact, Margaret is little more than a variation on the type that Hope and Naomi also exemplify: the enlightened female outsider who functions as critic of provincial rigidity, risks getting into trouble for her outspokenness, but escapes unscathed.[12] But one sees the basis for the reviewer's reaction: Whittier has presented his narrative in a gossipy, unpretentious, low-key, desultory manner that provides the illusion of an intimate glimpse of daily life in Puritan times.[13]

The contrast between Whittier's documentary realism and the historicized melodrama of a Sedgwick is a predictable result of the diffusion of the influence of a major literary innovator, a result all the more predictable given that both outcomes are possibilities inherent in Scott to start with and reinforced by broader traditions of romance and realism that concurrently influenced antebellum writing. It may also be, however, that the period's conception of the Puritan era itself helped to ensure that ✓ the Realistic and the Romanticist dimensions of Scott's art developed not simply in coordination but also at cross-purposes with each other.

This possibility is certainly suggested by such a work as the epic poem *Whatcheer* (1832), by Rhode Island judge Job Durfee, which chronicles Roger Williams' wintertime exodus from Massachusetts with so minute a fidelity to fact that a local schoolmarm used it as her principal source for a child's biography of the state's founder. When Durfee has the faithful Indian guide describe the lay of the land ahead, we immediately perceive that we are being given a geography lesson.

> Dark rolling Seekonk does their realm divide
>   From Pokanoket, Massasoit's reign,
> Thence sweeping down the bay, their forests wide
>   Spread their dark foliage to the billowy main.

Here and throughout, Durfee provides scrupulous footnotes for references to people, places, and events. Scott's device of scholarly documentation is carried to the nth degree. The passion for minute exactness is amusingly at odds with the elevation of tone ("I sing of trials stern, and sufferings great, / Which FATHER WILLIAMS in his exile bore") whereby Durfee seeks to turn Williams' flight into a symbolic exodus from Egypt to Canaan in the tradition of *exemplum fidei*.[14] What makes the poem not simply pedestrian but absurd is the contradiction in mimetic levels that arises from having evoked the realm of transcendent myth within the rigid limits of prosaic literalism. Durfee wants, like Scott, to associate the past with romantic grandeur, but he is bowed down by the weight of too much history instead of being imaginatively liberated by it.

Perhaps the same could have happened to any lawyer-antiquarian who turned his hand abruptly to creative writing without the long immersion in legend collecting and literary balladeering that preceded the Waverley novels. Yet Durfee's aesthetically self-limiting concern for the facticity of his fable seems also to be a characteristically Yankee susceptibility, reminiscent of the question raised by contemporary authors and reviewers as to whether a national past so recent, so mundane, so fully recorded could supply an adequate stimulus to the literary imagination. Notwithstanding the oratorical glorifications of Pilgrimism constantly ringing in their ears, antebellum New Englanders had a harder time than Scott envisaging their region's past as an era of romance. This may have something to do with the copresence of disparate mimetic levels in New England historical fiction, documentary sometimes rubbing provocatively or uneasily against melodrama or mythification, as when Hawthorne opens *The Scarlet Letter* with a historical account of prison building followed by an allegorical rose image. This procedure amounts to an implication both that the era depicted marks the beginning of the continuum of our prosaic time and that it belongs in some premodern arcadia. The chapter seems unsure as to whether to opt for a chronicle style of historicizing or a poeticized legend in the manner of Edmund Spenser.

Underlying this hesitancy is an important divergence from Scott's myth of the historical process and from his conception of the relationship between past and present eras. The divergence is suggested very pointedly by Hawthorne's rewriting of a passage from Scott in which the contrast between past and present mentalities is summed up in the language of heraldry.

> The wrath of our ancestors . . . was colored *gules;* it broke forth in acts of open and sanguinary violence against the objects of its fury. Our malignant feelings, which must seek gratification through more indirect channels, and undermine the obstacles which they cannot openly bear down, may be rather said to be tinctured *sable.* But the deep-ruling impulse is the same in both cases; and the proud peer, who can now only ruin his neighbor according to law, by protracted suits, is the genuine descendant of the baron who wrapped the castle of his competitor in flames.[15]

The corresponding passage in Hawthorne, of course, is the coda to *The Scarlet Letter,* in which the narrator (like the figure of Old Mortality in another Scott novel) observes the "semblance of an engraved escutcheon" on the single gravestone that serves both for Hester Prynne and Arthur Dimmesdale:

> It bore a device, a herald's wording of which might serve for the motto and brief description of our now concluded legend; so sombre is it, and relieved only by one ever-glowing point of light gloomier than the shadow: – "ON A FIELD, SABLE, THE LETTER A, GULES." [*HW* 1:264]

For Scott, the past stands for both the fascination and the horror of a more untrammeled expression of the passions that we moderns subdue. In Hawthorne and the New England romance generally, this symbolic relationship is reversed. It is the ancestors, like Colonel Pyncheon and the Puritan elders in *The Scarlet Letter,* who ruin their adversaries by relentless application of law. "Sable" stands for "us" in Scott, for "them" in Hawthorne. The "gules," the spontaneous manifestations of impulse, are associated in New England romance with the rebel protagonists, typically modern heroines in Quaker garb, who are projected back onto history as refreshing contrasts to the grayness of the Puritan establishment. In this respect James Fenimore Cooper's juxtaposition of a vanishing romantic Indian culture with the legalistic culture of Anglo-American settlement is much more in the Scott tradition. The contrast between old and present-day New England could not be so easily formulated in terms of the feudal and romantic versus the bourgeois and prosaic. Puritan history provided an "escape into a romantic past" more in the sense that it afforded opportunity for dramatizing archetypal conflict between symbolic opposites such as liberty and tyranny than in the sense that Puritan culture itself seemed inherently romantic, like that of the Scottish Highlanders in the Waverley novels. Scott's Covenanters stand for exciting, disturbing anarchy; Puritans, in New England historical literature, generally stand for tight civic organization. If the Puritan era was the heroic age of regional history, it also stood for the reality principle: for Endicott's forcibly ushering the flower children of Merry Mount into responsible adulthood. Antebellum writers sometimes looked at this "fact" positively (as the triumph of law and order), sometimes negatively (as the triumph of bigotry or anti-aesthetic philistinism). But in either case it was hard to associate those sober old-time worthies with Scott's freer world of romance.[16]

At the same time, the literary reinventors of Puritanism also found evidence in New England history of Scott's contrasts between then and now. Pointing to the hierarchical state of Puritan society, they could draw a watered-down version of the feudal-bourgeois contrast. Pointing to the simpler political and economic institutions of preindustrial colonial life, they could represent Puritanism in at least staidly pastoral terms. ("Sweet was the air and soft; and slowly the smoke from the chimneys / Rose over roofs of thatch," sings Longfellow in *The Courtship of Miles Standish* [*LW* 2:337]). Pointing to such extreme manifestations of Puritan superstitiousness and bigotry as the Salem witchcraft delusion and the Quaker persecutions, they could invoke the old Scott contrast between colorful but disturbing ancestors prone to outbreaks of primal violence and a more rationally regulated present. Indeed one of the ironies of nineteenth-century fictional portrayals of Puritanism is that they tended to put at the center the more grotesque manifestations of Puritanism, defining the epoch and its institutions in terms of extreme instances, so that the project of memorializing the New England past for which Rufus Choate and others so energetically campaigned became, in the long run, more of a rattling of the skeletons in the closet.

New England historical fictionalizers were thus pulled two ways, drawn to conceiving of the relationship between regional past and present in Scott-like terms yet also to deviation from his myth of epochal contrast. Take, for instance, *The House of the Seven Gables,* a book that has trouble making up its mind as to whether society changes or stays the same. Up to a point, it preserves Scott's formula, envisaging the movement from seventeenth to nineteenth century as a movement from the age of wizardry to the age of science, from social hierarchism toward a greater egalitarianism, from prejudice to common sense. The text also, however, inverts the Scott formula by identifying the future rather than the past as the realm of romantic possibility. This, of course, is still to preserve a myth of epochal change. Yet the swerve away from Scott implies also a different conception of the relationship between epochs, imagining it as a continuum of Puritan-founded institutions that form the basis of the present social structure and its inequities. (Even here Hawthorne does not break from Scott so much as draw out the implication of Scott's claim that the "deep-ruling impulse is the same in both cases.") At this point the text seems to change from a standard Arminian story of emancipation from Puritanism to a critique of the filiopietistic celebrations of institutional continuity that formed the conservative side of the Arminian epic of New England history. Hence the notorious problem of the book's denouement.[17] The establishment of the modern Judge Pyncheon as the reincarnation of the Puritan Colonel Pyncheon amounts to a claim that the power structure is ongoing, and this threatens to undermine the credibility of the text's belated suggestion that a new order of things has come about and to expose the storybook ending as based on nothing more substantial than a change of ownership. Equally notable, for present purposes, are the mimetic vacillations that accompany this thematic ambivalence. The emphasis on the modern avatar of the Maule-Pyncheon feud threatens to turn the historical aspect of the book into a papier-maché fantasy backdrop for a realistic novel manqué. As in Durfee's *Whatcheer,* the result is a curious mixture of mimetic modes: Puritanism as fantasia set against Puritanism as solid social fact – the difference being that Hawthorne recognizes, and at least fitfully exploits, the inconsistency: "How can we elevate our history of retribution for the sin of long ago," the narrator mock-laments, "when, as one of our most prominent figures, we are compelled to introduce – not a young and lovely woman, nor even the stately remains of beauty . . . but a gaunt, sallow, rusty-jointed maiden[?]" (*HW* 2:41). The seeming resistance of New England history to conventionally romantic treatment becomes at least potentially the opportunity for metaromance.

Altogether, the ambiguity of Scott's own style of mimesis, the ambiguity of critical pronouncements about the mimetic norms of historical fictions, and the inconsistency displayed by new England writers as to whether the Puritan past should be conceived as belonging to the realm of romantic otherness or as continuous with quotidian reality make it difficult to generalize about the mimetic norms of Puritan fictions. To the extent that New Englanders were conditioned by critical theory to prize veracity and conditioned by the sense of the past (imbibed from filiopietistic platitudes or a sardonic inversion thereof) to see Puritanism as integral with their own historical reality, Scott's example tended to reinforce the ideal of mimetic fidelity, and with that a protorealistic aesthetic. Yet this same sense of historical proximity could, in a romantic melodrama, trigger the urge to dissolve Puritan society into a stereotypical antagonistic force (Sedgwick) or coexist side by side with grandiose mythicizing (Durfee). Likewise, the acceptance of a Waverley-style contrast between premodern and modern epochs did not necessarily lead to a less mimetic approach to the past (Whittier), although it did supply a kind of authorization for romantic heightening (Hawthorne), either for the purpose of licensing one's fancy or as a way of strategically banishing Puritanism to the dark ages (Hawthorne, Sedgwick).

Literary representations of New England history varied further in accordance with individual authors' personal encounters with Puritanism and its vestiges; their historiographical interests; and their programmatic aims – to name the most important determiners of how the conventions of historical representation were brought to bear from work to work. Let us now look at three popular writers whose careers afford good illustrations of each of these motivating factors.

II

Exhibit A is Eliza Buckminster Lee, author of several books about the New England past, including *Naomi* (1848), a romance about the Quaker persecutions in Boston at the start of the Restoration.[18] The special interest of Lee's career, for our purposes, is its approximation to that of the domestic heroine, Puritan-style. Her books about New England culture present an interesting case of the interplay between life story and literary convention and provide one sort of explanation for the anachronistic quality of her "historical" romance, which might be read as answering the same question that Palfrey plays with in the introduction to his *History of New England:* How would someone like me have fared at the hands of the Puritans?

Like her apparent literary model, Catherine Sedgwick, Lee came from a gentry-class Congregationalist family that made its escape to Unitarianism after she had grown to adulthood. Lee's elder brother, Boston minister Joseph Stevens Buckminster, was, together with William Ellery Channing, the leading intellectual influence on the early stages of that movement. Her father, also Joseph (1751–1812), was a minister of the moderate Calvinist stamp, who, after a short period as a very minor Connecticut Wit, presided during the rest of his career over the choicest congregation in New Hampshire, Portsmouth's First Church. Lee's childhood was not altogether happy. Dr. Buckminster's income, like that of almost all late eighteenth-century Congregational clergymen, was small; and as one of the oldest and apparently the healthiest among a family of seven, Lee was forced to play nursemaid to an invalid stepmother and act as a substitute mother to her younger siblings, while her admired brother was given the chance for higher education at Exeter and Harvard. Lee had no chance of economic or intellectual fulfillment until she was almost forty and safely married to a well-to-do Boston merchant.

The recollection of a constricted childhood surfaces between the lines of her generally dutiful *Memoirs* of her father and brother, and more pointedly in the semiautobiographical *Sketches of a New-England Village,* which includes a number of scenes later adapted for the *Memoirs.* The well-meaning but stiffish minister-father, a distant relation of Jonathan Edwards; the sickly stepmother whose death temporarily drove her husband to distraction; the Piscataqua setting; Old Hannah, the faithful family retainer; the visits of the country cousins to maternal relatives near Boston – this and other autobiographical material appear, with a good deal of fantasy intermingled. The nature of the heightening is significant. Lee inevitably stresses the rusticity and the quaintness of the persona's girlhood environment relative to her own. The location is a "remote" rural village, not the comparatively urbane seaport Portsmouth, although the topography matches it closely; the period of residence is "nearly the last half of the [eighteenth] century" (Lee was born about 1788); the manse (one of those "old fashioned houses . . . fast disappearing from our country") is "stained here and there with spots of moss and decay," the doorstep worn "by the weary feet of many pilgrims." The church community is dominated by old men who resemble Scott's Covenanters. "Puritanism, like the common air, was breathed in our village." Would that it had been, for the sake of Dr. Buckminster, who had chronic trouble collecting his salary from his recalcitrant flock. But in Lee's memory/fabrication the never-never land of her late eighteenth-century New Hampshire was a monolith of austere piety and civic virtue, blighting to a young girl's spirit for a reason quite different from the secularism for which postcolonial New England's seacoast towns were famous:

> It is impossible for me to describe the deep melancholy that took possession of my mind at this early age, when the darkness of twilight and evening gathered over the ocean. The darkness seemed to come up from some mysterious region beyond, where thought was lost, and despair dwelt.

"The New England past" has been reinvented for literary purposes as internalized Calvinist gloom.[19]

In Lee's *Memoirs* of the Buckminster men, the theme of the sensitive soul's struggle against Calvinism is replayed in the form of the dispute between father and son over the younger Joseph's increasing commitment to liberal theology. After earnestly trying to dissuade him from the vocation to which his mother had consecrated him on her deathbed ("You had better be a porter on the wharf than a preacher with such views"), the senior Buckminster gave in and even consented to preach the son's ordination sermon at the ultraliberal Brattle Street Church in Boston. But the father was never fully reconciled to his son's heterodoxy. Lee presents both men sympathetically, as noble souls whose mutual love kept them intimate even when they disagreed; but she leaves no doubt as to her own position. The conflict is between the father's "old-fashioned idea" of ministerial vocation and Joseph's "more liberal view." Joseph, Jr., is the first of an exciting new breed of preachers; the father belongs to an older world. This contrast between worlds is melodramatized by such devices as the vignette of Joseph, Jr., preaching his first sermon in his venerable step-grandfather's meetinghouse in Old York, Maine, one of the "most ancient and primitive in the country," its pews "dark with age," its ceiling beams rough-hewn. Brattle Street's civilized liberalism is a "healthful development from the deep roots of the tree of life"; Calvinism is pathological. When Lee relates her father's conversion experience, with obvious distaste, she argues that his conviction of his own sinfulness was the first eruption of a "form of nervous disease which followed him at intervals . . . through the whole of his life," namely, "melancholy apprehensions about the religious state of his friends, and of his own religious condition and safety."[20] Lee alternates thereafter between characterizing her father as a prisoner of Puritan strictness and melancholia and trying to show that his heart was more genial than his creed.

Lee's writings about New England, then, begin to take on the character of an autobiographically motivated attempt to replicate and further, in the literary sphere, the liberation from the dark night of Puritanism that she sees as the meaning of her family odyssey. *Naomi* is in keeping with this program.

Written while Lee was gathering materials for the *Memoirs, Naomi* evokes the nightmare extreme of the Puritan shadow that by comparison merely tinges her other two New England books. The title character is an orphaned nineteen-year-old with Quaker sympathies who arrives from England, virtuous and well bred, to live with her orthodox but hypocritical merchant stepfather, who goes over his accounts on Sunday while pretending to read his Bible. The stepfather wants her out of the way so that he can get control of her estate; the magistrates prosecute her for helping a Quaker woman (her old nurse) escape whipping; the ministers persecute her because she holds the inner light more sacred than the Bible. After a lengthy imprisonment, Naomi is given twenty-four hours to leave the colony, in the dead of winter. Of course she succeeds, and we learn that two years later she and the hero, a like-minded young Harvard graduate, are happily reunited as Quaker settlers of New Jersey.

Despite the picturesque ending, Naomi is not much closer to actual Quakerism than she is to Puritanism. As Bell notes, Lee is at pains to distinguish her from the "ignorant," "vulgar," "illiterate" sectaries.[21] Quakerism attracts Naomi for the same reason that it attracts Bancroft – its valuation of natural piety above religious forms and dogma. "Although she differed altogether from the Orthodox church," Naomi "held nothing in common with the Quakers of that day but the essential principle of their faith, the belief of the inward voice of truth in the soul." Otherwise she finds most of them in appallingly bad taste. In short, Quakerism is a stick with which to beat the Puritans. By the same token, Lee is careful to stop short of antinomianism, though Naomi is continually likened to Ann Hutchinson. The inquisition by the elders is a distinct echo of Hutchinson's trial, but when asked if she believes herself to be in a state of grace, Naomi gives a very different answer: "If I am not, God can give me grace; and if I am, he can keep me in it."[22] Altogether, Naomi is the domestic novel heroine as Channing Unitarian projected back upon the seventeenth century.

In all three works discussed, the gap between enlightened present and Puritan past is heightened by exaggerating the quaint or gothic elements of the latter. In *Naomi,* the remote past, of which the recent past is both a diluted version and the model from which the quintessential horrors of 1660 are extrapolated, is most strikingly juxtaposed with the enlightened present through melodramatic heightening and the use of the anachronistically modern liberal-minded outsider as heroine and center of consciousness. Taken together, the three works dramatize the problem of how simultaneously to declare independence from and acknowledge kinship with a tradition that one has not grown beyond as much as one would like to think. In the two nonfictional works, the *Memoirs* and the *Sketches,* the tradition is bracketed more or less successfully; in *Naomi* it comes back with a dreamlike intensity.

III

The Puritan romance written by Emily Dickinson's friend the editor and literary wheelhorse Josiah Gilbert Holland is also built on the familiar conflict of liberalism and rigidity, but with some notable variations. For one thing, Holland was by no means as free-thinking as the adopted Bostonian Lee. "Conceived and suckled in Calvinist piety" of the Connecticut Valley village milieu in whose image Lee recast her childhood for *Sketches,* Holland, as his best biographer says, "remained priggish and prudish to the end of his days," a "paragon of all the copybook virtues." (What Holland liked best about *The Scarlet Letter* was that its conclusion had made the moral explicit.)[23] More significant for our purposes, however, is the difference in how he constructed *The Bay-Path*

(1857), a fictionalized treatment of the early years of his town, Spring-field, Massachusetts, whose history Holland had just finished writing in his two-volume *History of Western Massachusetts* (1855). Whereas the his-torical dimension of Lee's Puritan romance was more indebted to family history than to her study of seventeenth-century materials, Holland's was much closer to being a gap-filling interpolation of source material that he had studied in a more or less systematic way.[24]

The novel's central figure is William Pynchon, Springfield's founder, leading citizen, and chief magistrate, a man shown as too wise to believe that Puritan institutions are always right but too socially responsible to shirk the task of trying to make them work as humanely as possible. Hol-land's thematic design, surprisingly well executed for a first novel by a journalist of limited education who later yielded to the temptation to manufacture banalities, is to show the difficulty that even a worthy group of individuals have in maintaining mutual harmony and cohesiveness, owing to human failings, problems in communication, and the imper-sonality of even the most rudimentary political system. Despite being a conscientious and compassionate judge, Pynchon cannot prevent his salty plebeian friend John Woodcock from being punished, with an ex-orbitant fine and imprisonment, for intemperate criticism of the local minister, George Moxon. Despite Pynchon's friendship with Moxon, he cannot prevent the credulous preacher from inciting the community to cry witchcraft against Woodcock's unstable daughter Mary (a sometime ward of the Pynchon family), who is thereby driven to madness. These discouragements are instrumental in bringing Pynchon's dissent from Puritanism to the surface in the form of a heretical treatise on the Atone-ment, the Puritan oligarchy's reaction to which drives him (like Lee's Na-omi) back to England.

The Bay-Path follows rather closely the course of events described in Holland's *History of Western Massachusetts*. The *History* was a popular work that he wrote for amusement and to promote the fortunes of the Springfield *Republican* (of which he was assistant editor and part owner), yet impressive enough to earn him membership in the Massachusetts Historical Society and a citation in the *Harvard Guide to American History*. *The Bay-Path* might be described as a critical fiction aimed at completing a jigsaw puzzle for which the *History* itself had been able to provide only skeletal fragments in the form of facts concerning the lives of early Springfield settlers. These were the major pieces: (1) Certain suggestive episodes in Pynchon's life; his early decision to lead a group of settlers from Roxbury, near Boston, to the wilds of Massachusetts; his unusually mild distribution of justice, by Puritan standards; his publication, in late middle age, of a liberal interpretation of the Atonement, denying that God would have been so unjust as to subject Jesus, an innocent being, to the torments of hell; his temporary recantation under public pressure; and his eventual return to England, where he reaffirmed his position. (2) The unsuccessful prosecution of Hugh Parsons and his wife, Mary, for witch-craft, following an epidemic of communal hysteria in which the local minister (like Samuel Parris of Salem Village in 1692) took a leading part as accuser because of the affliction of his two children. (3) Mary Parsons' infanticide, sufferings, and death. (4) Preacher Moxon's return to Europe in Pynchon's company, apparently as a disappointed man. (5) The adventures of local troublemaker John Woodcock, a pioneer who helped build Springfield's first house but disappeared from the settlement after figur-ing in several litigations. (6) The noble stature of Pynchon's daughter Mary and her husband Elizur Holyoke, who, along with other worthy members of the Pynchon clan, remained to lead and develop the planta-tion after her father's departure.

In the process of weaving these data into a fictive synthesis, Holland made some alterations of fact (e.g., merging the Parsons and Woodcock families) and of interpretation, assimilating history to romance conven-tion. Moxon becomes a stock image of the credulous, vindictive, mean-spirited, self-serving parson, resembling the Unitarian caricature of Cot-ton Mather. The relationship between Woodcock and Pynchon looks suspiciously like that of Natty Bumppo and Judge Temple in Cooper's *The Pioneers,* although Holland is much more on the side of law and or-der. Such instances testify to the inevitable deformation of historical data when transmuted into fiction, even when the fabricator has been steeped in that material and attuned to a historiographical mode. Most striking, perhaps, is the extent to which *The Bay-Path* follows the familiar Puritan-romance convention of a plot constructed around the theme of the per-secution of deviance. To a degree, this emphasis does correspond to Hol-land's ideological position along the mid-nineteenth-century theological spectrum. Holland's mature values and the directional movement of his career make him an exemplum of the cautious, belated liberalization of Connecticut Valley Orthodoxy that followed a generation or so in the wake of the Unitarian movement, under the aegis of such people as Hol-land's friend and sometime minister Noah Porter and the Reverend Henry Ward Beecher, to whom Holland dedicated one of his early books.[25] But from *The Bay-Path* alone it is much harder to tell that Hol-land was a pillar of the theological culture against which Eliza Lee reacted than when we consult the full record of his life and writings. The conven-tions of historical romance, as we saw in the last chapter and shall see in the next, seemed to produce in conservative New England authors a cer-tain suspension of critical judgment, so that the novels came out sounding strangely liberal. Or perhaps a better way of putting it would be to say that the romance permitted them to indulge their own skepticism about the intellectual limits to which, on sober second thought, they remained solidly committed. For, notwithstanding his indulgence of heresy and deviance, Holland does still take a tack markedly different from Lee's in defining as the heart of his conflict not the melodramatic struggle between establishment and deviant, insider and outsider, but the struggle within the establishment itself, between its leaders and within its chief. It is almost as if Hawthorne had made Dimmesdale the clearly dominant character in *The Scarlet Letter* and relegated Hester to an ancillary role. For Holland, as for Harriet Beecher Stowe, the question is whether an essentially worthwhile social order can be fine-tuned enough to remain viable, to avoid excessive legalism and rigidity – not whether Puritanism should be scrapped. Hence the agony of the organization man is given more of an airing than the agony of the dissenter.

Not only is *The Bay-Path* obviously a fictionalization of history; the historical interpretation with which Holland began was itself a critical fiction. Other historical evidence, for example, suggests that Holland's local patriotism may have caused him to idealize Pynchon. He did not, at any rate, take much account of an alternative image of Pynchon (from witnesses who may themselves have been biased) as a canny, aggressive fur trader quick to resent political and economic rivalry, intent on consolidating his power in the region of the upper Connecticut. Yet when all necessary deductions are made on the score of wish-fulfilling fantasy, it remains that *The Bay-Path* is, in the main, a reasonably responsible and workmanlike exercise in historical inference – a speculative answer to the question "What is the significance of the simultaneous prosecution of Pynchon for heresy and of the Parsonses for witchcraft?" Holland's answer to the first part of the question is that Pynchon was an independent thinker with the public-spiritedness and also the good fortune to suppress and channel his dissent until he could no longer stand the growing rigidity of the Massachusetts Bay Colony. Pynchon's quick departure from Roxbury and his subsequent quarrels with authorities in nearby Connecticut seemed to Holland to prefigure Pynchon's more esoteric theological heresy and to establish a symbolic tie between him and social outsiders. ("I knew there was some of the same stuff in you that there was in me," Woodcock tells Pynchon, "and I knew it was a kind of stuff that always leaked out of a man 'fore he died.")[26] Heresy and witchcraft are related symptoms of intolerance: the deviance of the aristocracy, and the deviance of the working class. Pynchon's humiliation by the General Court, which, along with the Boston clergy, temporarily browbeat him into recantation, is paralleled with the trials of Woodcock's daughter and son-in-law, the couple accused of witchcraft. However much Holland plays fast and loose with the documentary evidence, the result is a coherent and fairly astute exercise in the historical sociology of deviance.[27]

IV

Henry Wadsworth Longfellow presents a third approach to historical fictionalizing to set beside those of Lee and Holland. Longfellow's
eclecticism has generally kept readers from appreciating the extent of his
considerable interest in New England as a literary subject.[28] His first publication was in fact a poem about Lovewell's Fight; he later wrote several
Irvingesque prose pieces about New England manners, of which his
novel *Kavanagh* is a sort of culmination and valedictory; among his better-known works, *Evangeline* and *The Courtship of Miles Standish* render
episodes from colonial times in competent if soporific hexameters. And,
as is much less well known, Longfellow also produced in late life a work
that appraised Puritanism on a far broader scale than any other belletristic
contribution of the period – not that vastness equates with quality, of
course. The work in question is *The New England Tragedies* (1868), the
third part of his *Christus* (1872), a trilogy of poetic dramas that also includes *The Divine Tragedy* (1871) – a rendering of the life of Jesus – and
The Golden Legend (1851), which retells the story of a medieval prince
whose disease could be cured only through the willing self-sacrifice of a
maiden. (The story ends happily when the prince rejects the temptation
of forfeiting her life for his and marries her instead.) The two *New England Tragedies* concern the Quaker persecutions and Salem witchcraft,
respectively. "John Endicott," set like *Naomi* in the early 1660s, shows the
ministers and magistrates, led by Endicott and John Norton, trying with
increasingly rigorous measures to silence the heresy, personified especially by Wenlock Christison (a fortuitously symbolic name) and his
daughter Edith. Edith has been whipped and Christison is about to die
when the king's missive of reprieve arrives. In the last scene, the judgment against the Puritans is further carried out as the deaths of Norton
and two leading judges are reported and we see Endicott himself die,
overcome by humiliation and a growing sense of guilt. Meanwhile,
Longfellow has prepared for this turnabout by emphasizing the popular
revulsion against the persecutions, dramatized in part by the invention of
an unhistorical John Endicott, Jr., who rebels against his father and be-
friends the Quakers.

In "Giles Corey of the Salem Farms," Longfellow repeats the pattern
of common people victimized by overzealous prosecution of supposed
spiritual truancy. Again the prosecuting forces are dramatized by two
representative figures (Hathorne the magistrate and Cotton Mather the
minister); again the play focuses on one case (the Coreys); again the plot
culminates in courtroom drama. Here, however, the tragedy deepens.
There is no reprieve, and the whole community, not just the oligarchy,
was responsible for the delusion. The virtuous Coreys are victimized by
malicious neighbors.

The New England Tragedies has never aroused much scholarly interest, nor has *Christus* as a whole, apart from *The Golden Legend*. The best critical study of Longfellow, Newton Arvin's, disdains the trilogy as dull and disunified.[29] This modern astringency, for once, is in keeping with the nineteenth-century consensus. *The New England Tragedies* sold briskly at first, but its critical reception was lukewarm, even among Longfellow's friends. The trilogy was issued in a very modest edition (512 copies apiece), which was scantly reviewed.[30] *The Golden Legend* had done very well, but that was two decades before.

The reasons for the indifference are not hard to detect: The trilogy is a very long work in a genre long since unfashionable: religious closet drama. The ambitiousness and complexity of the themes are more interesting than the style. Furthermore the work is somber – even more so than *The Scarlet Letter*. This tended to distress nineteenth-century readers[31] without winning over modern critics, who seem to have had a hard time believing that after decades of willed cheeriness and carefully modulated melancholy Longfellow could really have succumbed to the melancholy side of his nature in a major opus. Arvin, for one, dismisses the ending because he misreads the epilogue as expressing a "kind of Tennysonian trust that 'somehow' all is well."[32]

The low valuation of *Christus* is ironic, because Longfellow intended it as the crowning achievement of his literary life. This was his long-deferred attempt to rival *The Divine Comedy*. He carried the design in his head for more than thirty years. In 1841, it first occurred to him to attempt a "long and elaborate poem by the holy name of CHRIST; the theme of which would be the various aspects of Christendom in the Apostolic, Middle, and Modern Ages" (*LW* 5:3). The next year he sketched out the design, coincidentally with the writing of his Dantesque sonnet "Mezzo Cammin," where he declares the hope that he will complete a great work, even though "half of my life is gone" (*LW* 1:260).

> CHRISTUS, a dramatic poem, in three parts:
> Part First. The time of Christ (Hope).
> Part Second. The Middle Ages (Faith).
> Part Third. The Present (Charity). [*LW* 5:5]

In other words, Longfellow begins, unlike Lee and Holland, with an abstract conception of Christian history; only after many years of reflection was he led to the subject of Puritanism as his modern exemplum.

Longfellow did not work constantly on his design, by any means. He concentrated on it at intervals and the rest of the time kept it in the back of his mind as a grand, solacing dream, in compensation for rueful guilt at dissipating his energy on other things. His first serious approach to planning dates from late 1849. Correcting proof for a volume of minor poems, he writes in his journal:

> And now I long to try a loftier strain, the sublimer Song whose broken melodies have for so many years breathed through my soul in the better hours of life, and which I trust and believe will ere long unite themselves into a symphony not all unworthy the sublime theme, but furnishing "some equivalent expression for the trouble and wrath of life, for its sorrow and its mystery."[33]

Over the next sixteen months he completed *The Golden Legend*. Then came a five-year hiatus. In 1856–8 he drafted and revised the first of the New England tragedies, pausing along the way to do *The Courtship of Miles Standish*. He then let "John Endicott" sit for another decade, rewrote it (changing it from prose to poetry) in 1867–8, and almost immediately added "Giles Corey." By December 1870 he had begun *The Divine Tragedy*, which soon took "entire possession of me, so that I can think of nothing else."[34] In 1872 he inserted the transitional interludes and finale, emphasizing as he did so that "this is an old, old design, twenty years old and more, and only now completed. In a certain sense one part explains and requires the others" (*LL* 5:514; cf. p. 473).

The message of the trilogy is the imperativeness of love. It is enforced by having the last scene of *The Divine Tragedy* dominated by Christus' question to Peter, "Lovest thou me?" It is reinforced by Abbot Joachim's prelude to *The Golden Legend:* "Love is the Holy Ghost within; / Hate the unpardonable sin!" (*LW* 5:165). Love is what redeems Prince Henry from his selfish consent to Elsie's death. And in the prologue to "John Endicott" we are told, in an echo of Abbot Joachim, which in turn echoes 1 Cor. 13:13, that the play teaches

> The tolerance of opinion and of speech,
> Hope, Faith, and Charity remain, – these three,
> And greatest of them all is Charity.
>
> [*LW* 5:358]

Limp biblical paraphrase like this reminds us of Emerson's dismissal of *In Memoriam* as the "commonplaces of condolence among good unitarians in the first week of mourning" (*JMN* 11:322). But the latent burden of the trilogy is more complex than its manifest slogans. The real theme is the failure of the ideal of charity to realize and sustain itself more than fitfully. The ideal triumphs in Henry's redemption, but it fails in Part 3, set in the modern era. The interlude between Parts 2 and 3 is spoken by an enraged Martin Luther, who, in contrast to gentle Joachim, thunders down curses on pope, priests, and Erasmus. The world of Puritan Boston and Salem is his legacy. Here love is frustrated and powerless. The conflict between the Puritans and the Quakers alienates the two Endicotts from each other, causing them anguish. The son's rebelliousness is motivated largely by his love for the beautiful Quaker Edith. But this is not to be another Henry and Elsie affair. Edith flatly rejects him as a suitor, demanding a disinterestedness of which he is incapable. The drama ends with Endicott, Sr., crying "Absalom!" and the romantic subplot unfulfilled. In "Giles Corey," the witchcraft issue so completely alienates kindly but credulous old Giles from his skeptical, hard-headed young wife Martha that ultimately he testifies against her in court. When they rally to each other, it is too late; both are condemned. In the epilogue, St. John, the apostle of love, who has been wandering the earth for centuries (in fulfillment of Jesus' hint, John 21:22, that John would tarry until the Second Coming), acknowledges, "Instead of Love there is hate; / And still I must wander and wait." Avoiding prophecy, avoiding all facile cosmic optimism, he concludes simply with the precept that one's acts are more important than one's creed: "Not he that repeateth the name, / But he that doeth the will!" (*LW* 5:525, 527).

As this parting shot indicates, Longfellow's triptych is ostensibly very much a Unitarian tragedy. In the Unitarian view, the revelation of Jesus was genuine, but its meaning has been obscured by subsequent theological overlay. In the poem, this process begins as soon as Jesus departs. The epilogue to *The Divine Tragedy* has the apostles piously reciting the Apostles Creed in antiphon. This is both a fervent affirmation of Jesus' impact on them and also an ironic translation of his living presence into formula. What happens later bears this out. Longfellow simply did not believe that the just should live by faith, if faith meant speculative belief or visionary enthusiasm as opposed to virtuous action animated by love. This is evident not only in the schisms produced by mere opinion in the two *New England Tragedies* but also in *The Golden Legend*. Elsie's noble spirit of self-sacrifice is given a morbid turn by a vision of Christ beckoning her to die. Her father (and the reader) immediately recognize this for what it is, a temptation analogous to the temptation of Jesus, dramatized in *The Divine Tragedy*. Lucifer's presence throughout the drama reminds us of this. Lucifer in Longfellow represents not so much metaphysical evil as the denial of human love. He disappears when Henry and Elsie direct their love toward each other instead of toward the sacrificial rite. Thus between the first and second parts of the trilogy increasing emphasis is put on the extraneous and delusive quality of supernatural belief as opposed to Christian action. Parallels between the first and third parts reinforce this. In "Giles Corey," for instance, there is an ironic replay of Jesus' exorcism of the Gadarine lunatic's devils by casting them into swine. Giles Corey's cattle, like the biblical pigs, mysteriously dash into the river. But the Salemites who see this event as evidence of Martha's witchery are deceived; it is only the deviltry of Corey's hired man, John Gloyd.

The tragic part of Longfellow's Unitarian vision arises from the awareness of the extent to which supernatural beliefs can be projections of the believer's self-interest or neurosis. Longfellow pursues this commonplace much more relentlessly than many of his liberal contemporaries. Instead of seeing the Reformation, Bancroft-fashion, as a step toward the elimination of popish superstition, the text sees it as giving rise to fanatical extremes less attractive than the holistic orthodoxy that it displaced. In the world of *Christus* as a whole, *The Golden Legend* finally becomes an idyll sandwiched in between visions of a harsh reality in which martyrdom appears to be the only option for the virtuous. And even martyrdom is not particularly attractive. In short, Longfellow meant just what he said when he predicted, in his journal, that *Christus* would seek "some equivalent expression for the trouble and wrath of life." His approach in *Christus*, especially in *The New England Tragedies*, is usefully contrasted with his more famous rendition of Puritan life in *The Courtship of Miles Standish*, which he intended as a "kind of Puritan pastoral."[35] The poem achieves this goal through a comic plot in which an idealized John and Priscilla arrive at the predictable marriage after overcoming the temporary complication of Standish's involvement. Standish is the most interesting figure, however. His character is subordinated to comic convention too, when he joins the wedding party at the end and reaffirms his friendship with Alden. But before that he must purge his hostility through Indian fighting – Longfellow's rather facile explanation for Standish's sanguinary militarism. Instead of killing Alden, Standish brings back a sachem's head. The poem here shows a muted appreciation of the somber side of Puritanism. In the third part of *Christus,* however, this aspect dominates, and the result makes better imaginative sense. When "John Endicott" defeats conventional love expectations by having Edith tell John, Jr., to purify his mind and stop thinking about her, the text is truer to its vision of its subject than *The Courtship of Miles Standish,* because it acknowledges that the emotional deformations upon which the Puritan system is built make domestic tranquillity impossible. In effect, *The New England Tragedies* presses the Unitarian critique of the twistedness of the sectarian mind so far that there is no place for the usual liberal turnaround (through counteremphasis on human capacity for reason and self-improvement) within the design of the trilogy. History is not progressive here; it moves from crucifixion to crucifixion. The trilogy remains Arminian in its evaluation of Christian history, but the history it records would seem to refute the Arminian theory of history. The compositional process seems in this case, as in Holland's, to have produced a text that stands partially in tension with what its author thought he believed.

 The New England Tragedies is hardly an unqualified success. The language is flat; the imagery, often hackneyed; the scenes, choppy. The characters talk like ventriloquist's dummies. But conceptually it is ambitious, even elegant. If Lee's work represents Puritan romance as autobiograph-

ical refraction and Holland's Puritan romance as historiographical reconstruction, Longfellow's exemplifies Puritan romance as metahistorical
cosmic design. Longfellow treats Puritan history on the same grand scale
as the providential historians did – as a crucial chapter in the great work
of redemption, though inverting their vision and that of their modern
successor, Bancroft. Longfellow replaces the image of a New England –
guided America concretizing Reformation ideals with the image of the
ironic shrinkage of Christian hope exemplified by the failure of charity
under Puritanism. In the process, he confronts without oversimplification all of the key motifs generated by the period's historical and literary
reinventions of Puritanism. Concerning the question of whether history
tells a story of religious decline or religious progress, he makes the contrast between the older and the younger Endicott suggest that the father
is less Christian, but more admirable in his staunchness, than his sentimental son. Concerning the issue of whether oligarchy or popular superstition was mainly responsible for the excesses of Puritanism, Longfellow
makes the villainy stem from the first in "John Endicott" and from the
second in "Giles Corey." Concerning the harshness of the Puritan order,
Longfellow habitually juxtaposes images of rigor and mercy. In the first
play, the leading minister, Norton, is a fanatic who is played off against
the senior Endicott, who – unlike the grim figure of Hawthorne's tales –
would prefer to avoid the shedding of more blood. In "Giles Corey," the
magistrate, Hathorne, is the fanatic, whereas Cotton Mather (thanks to
Longfellow's consultation of W. F. Poole) is the comparative liberal who
is reluctantly drawn into the prosecutions.[36] Longfellow thus prevents a
single-minded readerly reaction against the authorities. He is less successful in avoiding sentimentalization of their victims: By the logic of the
rest of the trilogy, for example, "John Endicott" ought to have shown
Edith and her father as deluded by their martyr complexes, but this is not
done. "Giles Corey" manages better by presenting Giles and Martha as a
homely provincial farming couple, capable of petulance and fits of temper that later undo them. Arvin complains about how Longfellow's concentration of focus makes the witchcraft delusion "seem smaller, more
narrowly localized, and less feverish than it really was," yet that is precisely the play's strength. In avoiding the sensationalism of works such as
his friend John Neal's *Rachel Dyer,* which was part of his background
reading, Longfellow was better able to show how discord existed to start
with in a simple, apparently placid farming community.[37] The aesthetic
result is not impressive enough to raise the *New England Tragedies* or
Christus to a fully canonical level, but it should entitle Longfellow to a
place in the great American tradition of honorable literary failures.

The cases of Lee, Holland, and Longfellow attest to the interplay between
experiential, historiographical, and ideological factors in the literary re-

construction of the New England past. Historical data, biographical background, ideological formations such as Arminianism and Orthodoxy – all help to shape these texts and are reshaped, in turn, by the process of textualization, which expresses authorial vision in a conventional vocabulary sometimes bemusingly at odds with the author's biographical record. It is clear that nineteenth-century texts give us images of Puritanism abstracted from their prototypes, images, moreover, whose family resemblance is a function as much of literary convention as of their grounding in a common historical nexus and even at that are sufficiently diverse to suggest that we ought rather to think in terms of Puritanisms in the plural, so far as the antebellum imagination is concerned. This latter point becomes even more evident when we turn to the two authors who produced the richest vein of Puritan reminiscences and whose work reflects, even more pronouncedly than does the contrast between Lee and Holland, the presuppositions of the distinct yet overlapping subcultures that produced the competing ideologies of Puritan history outlined in Chapter 9.

II

Hawthorne and Stowe as Rival Interpreters of New England Puritanism

> Man was mercifully made with the power of ignoring what he believes.
> It is all that makes existence in a life like this tolerable.
>
> Harriet Beecher Stowe, *Oldtown Folks* (1869)

> [Holgrave] had that sense, or inward prophecy – which a young man
> had better never have been born, than not to have, and a mature man
> had better die at once, than utterly to relinquish – that we are not
> doomed to creep on forever in the old, bad way, but that, this very
> now, there are the harbingers abroad of a golden era, to be accom-
> plished in his own lifetime.
>
> Nathaniel Hawthorne, *The House of the Seven Gables* (1851)

Nathaniel Hawthorne and Harriet Beecher Stowe are by far the most ambitious and distinguished literary chroniclers of New England history.
Both dedicated the bulk of their creative energies for a score, more or
less, of their most productive years to the fictionalization of the New
England past. Stowe wrote four major books on the subject: *The Minister's Wooing* (1859), *The Pearl of Orr's Island* (1862), *Oldtown Folks* (1869),
and *Poganuc People* (1878). Hawthorne produced a number of superb tales
and two full-length romances, as well as a child's history of Massachusetts, *Grandfather's Chair* (1841). The two authors make an instructive
matched pair. Both rely heavily on the conventions of historical fictionalizing with which we are becoming familiar; yet they differ in preferred
subject matter, mode of portrayal (Hawthorne's style being closer to that
of gothic romance, Stowe's to Victorian realism), and ideological orientation (Hawthorne working out of the literary culture of the hegemonic
regional center; Stowe, from that of the evangelical-dominated periphery).

For the sake of convenience, I shall focus especially on a pair of texts, √
Hawthorne's *Scarlet Letter* and Stowe's *Minister's Wooing* but shall move

outward from these, as the situation warrants, in order to take in the authors' writings as a whole.

I

For both Hawthorne and Stowe, there is an era of the New England past that especially resonates and to which they persistently return. For Hawthorne, it is the century following the first settlement of Massachusetts; for Stowe, the half century after the Revolution or, in theological terms, the two generations following Jonathan Edwards, who in Stowe's literary universe has a mythic founding-father status comparable to John Winthrop's in *The Scarlet Letter*. In this we see the first sign of the main cultural difference between the two writers. Hawthorne, like most other antebellum historicizers, identifies Puritanism chiefly with the doctrines and polity of the founders of the Massachusetts Bay Colony and the early settlements formed by dispersals from there to the Connecticut Valley. Stowe, however, thrusts the epic of seventeenth-century settlement into the background for the sake of concentrating on the later, and to her more decisive, revolution wrought by Edwards, who in the dominant seventeenth century–oriented story of Puritanism barely appears at all. In this respect Stowe is a far more original and path-breaking New England historical fictionist. Indeed, we might credit her with having achieved a sort of breakthrough for literary Calvinism, which, in the persons of Josiah Gilbert Holland and Joseph Banvard and Stowe's old instructor John Pierce Brace, we have seen being dragged to the left while attempting a conservative recasting of what was essentially a Unitarian-set scenario of resistance to Puritan rigidity.

Yet Hawthorne's and Stowe's apparently very different spheres of concentration also have a good deal in common. They represent similar stages in the development of the parent strain of Puritan culture and its Edwardsean filiation. Both writers are preoccupied with anatomizing the features of an age of consolidation that followed the key inaugural events of the epoch: with appraising, both sympathetically and satirically, the social rituals that sustained community and constrained individual deviance yet at the same time provoked it; and such consequences of institutionalization within a holy commonwealth as hypocrisy, secularization of piety, isolation of the clergy into a priestly caste, and the tensions arising from the conflict between the feeling that the younger generation is unworthy of its forebears and the desire to liberate it from the dead hand of the past. These themes Stowe, like Hawthorne, treats with a mixture of fascination qualified by relief at Puritanism's subsequent decline. The work of both writers, then, like that of most contemporary historical fictionalizers, is suffused with ambivalence toward Puritan repressiveness.

We see this especially in the character configurations of our central MINISTERS
texts. Near the center of each is a minister, the figure who, of course, ✓
preeminently embodied Puritan values in nineteenth-century eyes: Arthur Dimmesdale and Samuel Hopkins. Each is based partially on a life
model, and each text elaborates with a good deal of historical sophistication upon the controversies in which those two ministers become em-
broiled: the Antinomian controversy in *The Scarlet Letter* and the contro- ✓
versial Hopkinsian notion of disinterested benevolence as the test of
conversion in *The Minister's Wooing*.[1] Each pastor is shown as exceptional
within his field yet as limited by its assumptions. Each thereby represents
in different measure both the grandeur and the pathology of the old-time
New England divine. Dimmesdale has eloquence and sensibility, by
means of which he not only charms his congregation but also creates,
even for an unsympathetic reader, at the very least a spectacle of impressive talent gone awry. Hopkins has a rocklike integrity that prompts him
to denounce slavery at the cost of losing his richest parishioner. Yet both
ministers are also strange, gothic creatures subjected to the narrator's periodic mockery: bookish, introverted, self-flagellating, cerebral, inept –
living indoor existences and inhabiting private fantasy worlds. Hopkins
has to be tugged to get him to come to meals, like Swift's Laputans.
Both, finally, are shown as insecure and self-divided beings, in sharp contrast to their public images. This insecurity is ascribed chiefly to temperament, but in a larger sense it is designed to illustrate Puritanism's potential, as the nineteenth century saw it, for pushing its devotees to the
extremes of morbidity and despair.

The ministers, then, have several similar thematic functions. They represent the Puritan ethos in extreme form. As such they are both the heroes and the victims of their milieus. Likewise they are both means of
satirizing the community at large, which is, by comparison, trivial-
minded; yet, on another level, they are themselves the prime targets of
satire inasmuch as their communities are presented as more commonsensical and less extreme than they.

A second parallel, the complement of the first, is the use of young WOMEN
women protagonists, Hester Prynne and Mary Scudder. Both characters PROTAGONISTS
are also loosely based on historical models, each linked to the minister in
a kind of love relationship and contrasted with him as being more practical, better developed emotionally, and intuitively wiser and shrewder.
Hester and Mary thus become instruments for critiquing Puritan theological and social order. Through its treatment of Hester, Boston indicts
itself; and in a more general sense her emerging antinomianism is contrasted with the community's legalism to pose a moral dilemma that
Hawthorne never resolves, although his critics have often tried to resolve
it for him. Likewise Mary Scudder's natural inclination to marry hand-

some young sailor James Marvyn contrasts with her mother's conventional aspirations for her (a match with the minister), just as Mary's spontaneous piety contrasts with Hopkins' theological scheme. The central device in both books, then, is to take an undogmatic, intuitively perceptive, liberal female sensibility and set it against a more traditional, dated, culture-bound, male sensibility.

In neither case is this symbolic relationship one of simple polarity, however. Dimmesdale is powerfully attracted to Hester's heresy of putting their love above all else; Hester, at least nominally, imitates Dimmesdale's submission to the rites of the community in the epilogue. In Stowe's novel Mary and Hopkins are bound together as soul mates, if not as spouses, through parallel gestures of self-sacrifice near the end (her willingness to give up her old love in order to fulfill her pledge to marry Hopkins; his willingness to give her up to the man she wants), which are shown to be practical applications of Hopkinsian disinterested benevolence. Thus the denouement of *The Minister's Wooing* can be described as a victory not just of the clichés of sentimental comedy but also of the ultimate values of the faith-community purged of their ugly aspects. These ambiguities of relationship and outcome epitomize each author's overall ambivalence toward Puritanism.

Like the general scenario of focusing ambivalently on the institutionalization of Puritanism, the structural and thematic configurations just noted are not unique to Stowe and Hawthorne. Versions of most can be found many times in the works of their lesser contemporaries. Take the device of counterpointing the sensible, undogmatic young woman with the rigid minister who warps others and himself with his dogma.[2] In Holland's *The Bay-Path,* Mary Pynchon is played off against the Reverend Moxon in this manner, as is Eliza Lee's Naomi against the Boston clergy. The relationships between Mary and Hopkins and between Hester and Dimmesdale represent variations on this theme and bespeak a flowing with the tide of popular Romantic and American thought, which routinely preferred natural-born intuition above intellectual systems; with the tide of popular literary taste, accustomed (as we saw in the case of *The Lamplighter,* at the end of Chapter 3) to seeing apparently ignorant and powerless young women spiritually outdo men; and with the gender stereotypes and sexual politics underlying these patterns. Stowe's deployments of Eva and Uncle Tom as evangelists are warm-ups for the upstaging of Hopkins by Mary and by the Marvyns' black servant Candace, who brings gospel comfort to her mistress after Hopkins' theories have brought only despair. All of this is by way of qualification of what I shall have to say about Hawthorne and Stowe as exceptional cases. Their individuality of perspective, their distinctiveness from each other, their ability in general to penetrate and formulate historical reality are all circumscribed by intertextual and cultural constraints that sometimes, as in Holland and Longfellow, threaten to make them speak in voices not their own. Their historical fictions are projects of a limitedly individualistic kind, whose special achievements consist in their ability to refine, enhance, alter, and question the collective vision and vocabulary of the New England historical imagination.

My way of trying to give a sense of this combination of personal and collective envisionment will be to present Stowe and Hawthorne as maverick representatives of Calvinist and Arminian culture, which nurtured the two chief traditions of Puritan historicizing discussed in Chapter 9. In Stowe's case, the pertinence of this approach will seem obvious to anyone familiar with the rudiments of her life and work. In Hawthorne's case it will seem stranger, despite my having pointed out that the conventions of historical fictionalizing about seventeenth-century New England within which he worked were Unitarian artifacts; for most readers are still accustomed to thinking of him in Melvillian terms, either as a latter-day Puritan or as a non-Puritan obsessed with Puritanism – as one who either really was or, at least, pretended to be haunted by his patriarchal ancestors. This view is not wrong, exactly; but in characterizing Hawthorne's art as a dialogue with Puritanism, it tends to overlook the intervening cultural gap that separated him from it. Hawthorne is, in fact, a prime case of how the picture of New England's literary history becomes oversimplified when we skip quickly from the Puritans to the Romantics. The notion of Hawthorne as attempting to strike a truce with Puritan influences is actually much more applicable to Stowe. Hawthorne had to project himself back into the Puritan frame of mind across a wider historical chasm, although he was aided by the residues of Puritan culture around him.[3] We begin to see this when we look closely at the major stylistic and thematic differences between the two writers.

Among these, the most basic are the chronological nearness and, more important, the felt vitality of Stowe's Puritan era as against Hawthorne's. Both writers point up the archaic quality of period manners and the distance between then and now, but for Stowe the tie is much more intimate. We are reminded that Mrs. Scudder's old-fashioned kitchen is probably like our grandmother's, which we perhaps recall. The bygone and the perennial in New England culture are interwoven, as by the mixture of tenses in the following passage: "The rigid theological discipline of New England is fitted to produce rather strength and purity than enjoyment. It was not fitted to make a sensitive and thoughtful nature happy."[4] The "is" in the first sentence gives the lie to Stowe's attempt to prove Hopkinsianism anachronistic. Partly she wants to; partly she does not. At the close, continuity is stressed by having Mary and James become Hopkins' parishioners; their marriage symbolizes the humanization of the New

England way, but they stay within the fold. James's conversion must be duly undergone and approved before the union can take place. *The Scarlet Letter,* by contrast, finds happiness possible only in Europe, and Hawthorne shows no sense of the Puritan past as having any bearing on the present except as an incubus. Elsewhere he entertains a more progressive view of history, paying lip service, for instance, to the Bancroftian cliché that the Revolution was a flowering of the Puritan spirit; but he is nowhere near Stowe's enthusiastic conception of old-time New England as the "seed-bed" of all that is best in modern America.[5] For every orthodoxly patriotic affirmation in Hawthorne, we find at least one ironic disassociation.[6] Hawthorne may appeal to tradition as an antidote to wild-eyed Transcendentalism, but the New England past as such he does not portray as an idyllic pastoral state, as Stowe often does, but rather as grim, melancholy and austere.

These differences in the sense of what the past was like and in one's relation to it are underscored by such stylistic contrasts as Stowe's pro-torealistic evocations of parlor conversation in contrast to Hawthorne's use of symbolic tableaux and deliberately archaic language. Hawthorne's Puritan urchins speak like this: "Behold, verily, there is the woman of the scarlet letter; and, of a truth, moreover, there is the likeness of the scarlet letter running along by her side! Come, therefore, and let us fling mud at them!" (*HW* 1:102). Stowe avoids such stylized diction, except in the case of Hopkins, who talks like a theological tract. His "conversation" in fact consists in good part of passages lifted from his published works. This, however, is done to dramatize his remoteness from the "real" world of the novel, not its remoteness from ours. Stowe's people, indeed, sometimes seem too bustlingly colloquial to be properly old-fashioned, whereas Hawthorne's Puritans seem by comparison often too remote to contemplate, except externally. His narrators present themselves as striving self-consciously to breathe life into those quaint old wooden figures. From his first tales to his last, from "Alice Doane's Appeal" to "Main-Street," Hawthorne's fictional treatments of Puritanism are apt to be as much about the problem and process of reconstructing the Puritan era as they are dramatizations of it. The seriocomic account of the discovery of Surveyor Pue's bundle in the Custom House reanimates a dying gothic convention with precisely this metafictional aim in mind; and interspersed throughout the romance proper are then-versus-now contrasts such as the capsule portrait of Mr. Wilson ("He looked like the darkly engraved portraits which we see prefixed to old volumes of sermons," *HW* 1:65), reminding us that the world being described really exists beyond our fingertips and must be retrieved painstakingly and imperfectly from printed sources. Stowe's narrators, on the other hand, though also conscious of a historical distance between themselves and their subjects,

express no self-conscious reservations as to whether the past can be re-
captured or as to whether they might be engaging in misrepresentation
or conjecture. They are apparently confident of their ability to give a full
and accurate mimesis.

The two obvious explanations for the contrasts just noted are that
Hawthorne's Puritan era is simply more distant and that the two writers
are, in any case, working on different mimetic levels. To some readers
these explanations will suffice. Yet for a complete understanding of the
case, a little further exploration is, I think, necessary. To begin with, it is
notable that the two authors' orientations toward their imagined worlds
correlate with a difference in life experiences. Stowe's fictional historicizing is much more demonstrably family romance than Hawthorne's.
Hawthorne was an interested gatherer of genealogical information about
his Puritan ancestors, and he plays with the ideas of having personally to
atone for their misdeeds and of standing under indictment by them for
being a mere storyteller. But his evocation of such links with the past is
always done with a degree of aesthetic distance that suggests tour de
force, though it might also have some of the underlying psychological
import claimed by Frederick Crews in *Sins of the Fathers*.[7] The function
of Stowe's fiction as veiled autobiography and as a means of coping with
personal problems is much more transparent.[8] On the superficial level,
what she writes about her province of the regional past is often based on
direct experience or family tradition – especially her late novel, *Poganuc
People* (1878), about growing up in a Connecticut town during the era of
disestablishment, in which the heroine is essentially herself. On a deeper
level, several of her novels, as Charles Foster has shown, dramatize actual
life crises, among them *The Minister's Wooing,* in which the protracted
agonizing over the question of whether James Marvyn has died unregenerate replicates a trial that Stowe had just undergone as a mother and had
earlier been party to after the death of her sister's fiancé in a scenario
closely paralleled here.[9] Stowe evaluates her father's theology, which was
what had caused her to experience both ordeals as cataclysmic, through
Hopkins, who, among all of Lyman Beecher's mentors, expounded Calvinism in its sternest form. This enables Stowe to engage in the double
game of exorcising the harsher points of that theology while avoiding
filial impiety and affirming the essential nobility and humanitarianism
underlying Hopkins's creed.

Stowe, then, grew out of the environment that she depicted in her New ✓
England fiction. For Hawthorne, immersion in Puritanism was more of
an acquired taste. ("As for his Puritanism," remarked a younger cousin,
"he never had any.")[10] Stowe grew up thinking of herself as a child of the
covenant, whereas Hawthorne, to the extent that he can be said to have
identified with Puritanism at all, seems to have done so not as a condi-

tioned response but because he found in it, after reaching adulthood, a useful means of externalizing the "experience of radical solitude" that he had discovered within himself.[11] This is not to say that Hawthorne was entirely sheltered from social contact with conservative religionists. On the contrary, as a child he lived for periods of time with his pious and evangelical Manning aunts, whose hectoring both irritated and amused him; but the nature of any Calvinist influence from that quarter and from his Manning uncles, who personified to a degree the capitalistic aspect of Puritan energy,[12] was at most like the inoculation that Emerson received from his Aunt Mary, who awed him as a child but in the retrospect of his maturer thought took on the appearance of a unique anachronism (the one genuine Puritan of his intimate acquaintance), likelier for purposes of symbolism and anecdote than as a bona fide life model.[13] Even if one grants a closer psychological bonding to the past than this – even if one grants, for example, the psychobiographical argument that Hawthorne's choice of subject manner was in some sense grounded in a filial or moral imperative to come to terms with his ancestors and their values[14] – it is clear that the choice entailed more of a consciously self-imposed program of research and meditation than it did for Stowe. No doubt this is partly why Stowe expresses no Hawthornian reservations about her fictional subject as dreamlike, as cut off from present-day actualities. For her, the material *was* reality to a greater extent than it was for Hawthorne, notwithstanding that it was a reality that technological and social change and intellectual liberalization were in the process of making obsolete.

The two writers' treatments of Puritan community make an illuminating contrast. In Hawthorne's book, community is primarily seen as a monolithic entity functioning as a symbolic backdrop against which is played out the drama of the inner lives of individual figures more or less alienated from the community. For Stowe, the life of the community is of greater intrinsic interest; and the social dimension of a main character's life is on the same level of importance and reality as his or her inner life. When Dimmesdale returns from the forest, for instance, he meets three parishioners who are obviously of no importance to the romance except as representing different kinds of temptation. In a Stowe novel, such characters would also remain formulaic, but they would also likely be named, given brief histories and characteristic gestures and speech patterns, and dramatized more fully in relation to the main characters and the life of the town.

This difference in the sense of intimacy with, or distance from, the Puritan community is very much in keeping with the split between Arminian and orthodox intellectuals over the meaning of the Puritan legacy. As we saw in Chapter 9, the orthodox view was that the Puritans still represented the best models of piety and conduct for the 1800s, whereas

the Arminian view was that the Puritans were admirable human specimens for their era, beyond which, however, modern society had fortunately long since evolved. Nineteenth-century religious conservatives rejoiced to envision themselves as an integral part of an ongoing Puritan
family. For the liberal intellectuals with whom Hawthorne associated, all
such celebrations were carefully qualified by the sense of relief that Puritanism had ceased to be a live option after the early 1700s, owing in good
part to the spread of Arminian ideas. For liberal thinkers, indeed, the
term *Puritanism* had limited reference to the eighteenth century. The
"theocracy" that Stowe depicted was what came to be called in orthodox
circles "*the* New England theology" – the Edwardsean tradition of Bellamy, Hopkins, Dwight, Emmons, Taylor, Beecher, and Park. In the
Arminian-Unitarian cultural experience, however, this theocracy was
little more than a vaguely defined antagonistic force[15] that belatedly became a direct threat when old-line moderate conservatives joined forces
with the stricter Edwardseans, who previously had had little visibility in
the urban coastal enclaves that were the liberal strongholds.[16] Thus for
Stowe, the moderate Edwardsean minister's daughter from Litchfield,
Connecticut, Puritanism primarily meant the "strict Bible-based ethos of
my parents and their neighbors," whereas for Hawthorne, the shipmaster's son from a parish in Salem that turned Unitarian during his boyhood, Puritanism primarily meant the "quaint, rigid views that prevailed
most strongly in New England during early colonial times." Hawthorne
came to take Puritanism more seriously than that but continued to see it
mainly as a seventeenth-century phenomenon. In *Grandfather's Chair,*
eighteenth-century history is mainly military history, and the last and
virtually the only eighteenth-century Puritan hero is Samuel Adams. In
placing the decline of the Puritan spirit in the early eighteenth century,
Hawthorne was solidly in line with Unitarian historiographical practice.
This sharply contrasts with Stowe, for whom Puritan theology, in keeping with the Connecticut Valley outlook in which she was nurtured, primarily meant Edwardseanism and for whom the decline of Puritanism
thus did not seem really to begin until the early national era, and hardly
even then until the revolution in transportation.

Of course, it will not do to call Hawthorne a Unitarian and Stowe an
Edwardsean and let it go at that, even though Stowe was technically an
evangelical Congregationalist until her conversion to Episcopalianism
and Hawthorne was a nominal Unitarian married to a quasi Transcendentalist. *The Minister's Wooing* argues that Hopkinsian disinterested benevolence and the traditional conception of conversion experience need
translation into more humanistic terms; so Stowe is at most post-
Edwardsean. Likewise Hawthorne was hardly hand in glove with Henry
Ware, Jr., and Ezra Stiles Gannett. Like Emerson, Hawthorne criticized

Unitarianism for its coldness, wrote off Concord minister Barzillai Frost (Emerson's model of the bad preacher, in the Divinity School Address) as a well-meaning dodo, and wistfully compared the energetic spirit of pristine Puritanism to the flaccidness of its liberal successor.[17] Moreover, unlike Emerson, Hawthorne maintained a lively awareness of the "evil in every human heart," which, as Melville realized, went considerably beyond the usual qualifications of contemporary Arminian ministers (*HW* 8:29). So Hawthorne needs to be pictured as in at least partial recoil from Unitarianism. But it is well to bear in mind each author's intellectual point of departure within New England theological culture. In Stowe's case the theological orientation needs no further belaboring. In Hawthorne's case a few additional remarks are in order, since it is more customary to see him as post-Puritan than as post-Unitarian.

Hawthorne *was,* to be sure, post-Puritan. So were almost all other New England Unitarians, both genealogically and intellectually. To see Hawthorne in more particularized terms, however, as a dissident within Massachusetts liberalism, helps us to address more precisely the vexed questions of the extent and nature of Hawthorne's interest in Puritan history and theology. The evidence at first sight does not add up. "Ethan Brand" seems to presuppose – or at least to test out – a Calvinist conception of human nature; that at least is its imaginative center, if not its ultimate intellectual allegiance. "The Great Stone Face," in the same collection, seems almost an Arminian parable of moral perfection attained through right conduct. Again, the evidence of Hawthorne's fiction, as Michael Colacurcio has shown, suggests that for a birthright liberal he had an extraordinarily astute grasp of the theological and legal issues central to such Puritan era crises as the Antinomian Controversy (to which he adverted no less than four times in his published work)[18] and the Salem witchcraft delusion. Yet when one turns to his notebooks and his correspondence, one finds scant commentary on Puritan history and theology, most of it anecdotal (e.g., cases of moral delinquency from the Gosport, New Hampshire, church records) or descriptive squibs ("Dress of an old woman, 1656"). Notebook references to witches dwell on their sensational, spooky aspects; the overt theological references are generally offhanded ("Five points of Theology – Five Points at New York") (*HW* 8:544–51, 256, 227). By far the most extensive notebook exercise in typological thinking is a series of idyllic Concord entries of 1842 in which Hawthorne fancies himself and his bride as Adam and Eve in Eden – passages that are Transcendentalist rather than Calvinist, and written within half a year of the piece that most demonstrably follows a Puritan literary model, "The Celestial Railroad," which prompted a rave review from New England's leading Calvinist periodical.[19] These discrepancies threaten at first sight to expose Hawthorne as a chameleonlike, if not

intellectually dishonest, thinker and to support Nina Baym's argument ✓
that Hawthorne was only superficially interested in Puritanism.[20]

The data seem more coherent, however, if we picture Hawthorne as
experientially removed from Puritanism as a social phenomenon (hence
the persona of the notebooks: the mainly secular-minded collector of anecdotes, historical and genealogical trivia, and moral-allegorical situations); too much the enlightened liberal to interpret religious supernaturalism except as projection, yet sufficiently interested in local history and
in the demonic aspect of human experience to become at intervals a careful explorer of the Puritan mind and a careful user of Puritan concepts
and rhetoric as vehicles of expression. Such a hypothesis also helps make
sense of some troublesome cruxes in Hawthorne's major work, such as
why Goodman Brown seems completely unaware of the possibility that
he is a fallen and not merely a tempted being (his innocence at the start of
the tale is of a distinctively Arminian kind); or why the conclusion to *The
House of the Seven Gables* breaks so quickly from the thematic principle of
imputed sin that has ostensibly governed preceding events, thereby suggesting the Arminian-humanistic position that the doctrine of imputation
is a human construct that can be countered by right conduct in the present;[21] or why Pearl's devilishness vanishes as soon as the Victorian ideal
of family unity is affirmed in public at the end of *The Scarlet Letter*.

Altogether it would appear that Baym's conception of a de-
Puritanized, modern Hawthorne is not so much at odds with the Cola-
curcian image of a Hawthorne thoroughly steeped in Puritan sources as
might be thought. The two interpretations do reflect extremes in Hawthorne that are logically inconsistent. Their copresence, however, makes
experiential sense in light of his historical situation. Both versions of
Hawthorne rightly presuppose an initial posture of intellectual detachment from his artistic materials, and from that basic starting point the
notion of a de-Puritanized Hawthorne and a re-Puritanized Hawthorne
to a considerable degree go hand in hand. For example, Hawthorne
would understandably have been driven all the more to systematic *study*
of Ann Hutchinson as a result of having formed his conception of the
"female antinomian type" from observations of a certain sort of contemporary woman, rather than from having assimilated the doctrine and history of antinomianism as part of his religious training – and the former is
indeed the way he approaches Hutchinson in his first pass at the subject
in "Mrs. Hutchinson": as an antecedent of the modern emancipated
woman. Conversely, in notebook jottings relating to stories eventually
written about hypocrisy and secret sin in a Puritan context, it seems entirely predictable that a person of the background I have described would
show an initial interest in such topics that was moral-universal rather than
historiographical or theological in a technical sense. Nor was this syn-

drome unique to Hawthorne: Both the liberalism of perspective and the penchant for antiquarian investigation were common among writers in the Scott tradition, and in Scott himself.

II

With the foregoing in mind let us turn back to our two main texts and pursue more searchingly the question of what is to be gained from envisioning them as products of Arminian and Calvinist culture. Both, as noted earlier, reflect important chapters in the history of Puritan thought. *The Minister's Wooing* explores and critiques the most radical and divisive article of Samuel Hopkins' theology, the doctrine of disinterested benevolence – or, vulgarly expressed, the idea that the test of regeneration is the willingness to be damned for the glory of God. *The Scarlet Letter* obliquely reflects the Antinomian Controversy: its personalities (Hester echoing Ann Hutchinson, Dimmesdale suggesting a collage of John Cotton and his son, a convicted adulterer); its issues, seen especially in the handling of Hester's sexuality and emerging philosophic individualism; and even its rhetoric, the bastard child being a common post-Reformation metaphor for theological heresy and used by the Puritans in this case. These topics are dealt with by Stowe and Hawthorne, however, in distinctive ways that correspond to cultural differences between the two writers. The most basic difference is that Stowe's handling of the theological issues is more overt. She gives a direct exposition of the doctrine in question and the concept of divine sovereignty underlying it. In Hawthorne's text, such references are left almost entirely implicit. (The most searching review of Hawthorne's historical sources prior to 1972 claimed that Hester and Dimmesdale had no real-life antecedents.)[22] In general, Stowe's characters, even the less educated, think and talk in a more specialized theological vocabulary than Hawthorne's do. The parlor conversation, in Chapter 4 of Stowe's novel, between Hopkins and two of his parishioners over the relative merits of Arminianism and New Divinity has no counterpart in Hawthorne's fiction. This does not mean that Stowe was more interested in theology than Hawthorne; on the contrary, she often treats it with dry irony, as mere hairsplitting. The point is rather that Hawthorne chose to concentrate more exclusively on the psychological and moral dimensions of his subject and present them mainly in nontechnical language. Thus Hawthorne explicitly indicates his awareness of the Puritan heresy-as-bastard metaphor,[23] yet ostensibly he dramatizes the Hester-Pearl-Dimmesdale triangle as a psychological, moral, sexual, and familial crisis rather than a matter of heresy.

Hawthorne's comparative avoidance of an explicit theological vocabulary is very much in the vein of liberal thought. For the Unitarians, the categories of seventeenth-century Covenant theology were largely fictive to begin with; both in discussing the past and in engaging their contemporary opponents, the strategy of Unitarian controversialists was either to argue that Calvinist categories were specious or to reduce them to moral universals. George Bancroft's *History of the United States* does precisely the latter when it defines Calvinism primarily as the germ of the spirit of liberty. Hawthorne's emphasis reflects this tradition. For Stowe, rather like the early opponents of Unitarianism who insisted on the necessity of preaching the "distinguishing doctrines" of the gospel, a greater nominalism was required in order to be true to the underlying realities, which, from the liberal viewpoint, were obscured by such literalism.

To illustrate through a pair of key examples: Crucial to both novels are ✓ the related questions of what constitutes assurance of salvation and, in particular, what is the spiritual condition of the male lover. In Stowe, the specific issues are whether Hopkins has defined the morphology of conversion too rigidly, thereby excluding some worthy souls and driving others to despair, and whether James Marvyn, in particular, has been saved or doomed. Hawthorne, in his characterization of Dimmesdale, explores the limitations both of visible sanctity as a test of one's salvation and the implications of the antinomian position, according to which sinful works (e.g., adultery) would not necessarily argue against one's being in a state of grace. Through Dimmesdale's case history, then, Hawthorne probes the alternatives between which the historical Cotton was caught.[24]

The manner of dramatization varies considerably between the two texts, however. In Stowe's work the merits of Hopkins' scheme of "unconditional submission" is explicitly discussed between Mary and Mrs. Marvyn, explicitly rebutted by Mary in a letter to Hopkins; and a looser, modern-evangelical model of conversion is explicitly urged by the Marvyns' servant Candace, enacted by James, and duly reported in a letter to Mary that reads rather like a testimonial from a nineteenth-century evangelical magazine. Hawthorne presents theological issues rather as problems in moral conduct: What part should Dimmesdale play in relation to Hester? Should he confess the adultery in public? Should he and Hester run away together? In *The Minister's Wooing*, there is no question as to whether in Stowe's eyes James Marvyn's receipt of grace is a crucial and triumphant experience. In Hawthorne's novel, the sense of the reality of the supernatural realm to which the implicit Puritan categories refer is sufficiently attenuated as to cause many readers to wonder whether Dimmesdale's final "salvation" is only another form of solipsistic self-indulgence,[25] distracting him from his responsibility to Hester – whether, far from being the "triumphant ignominy" that he calls it (*HW* 1:257), the last scaffold scene simply completes the earlier ironic portrait of Dimmesdale as a "true religionist, with the reverential sentiment largely developed, and an order of mind that impelled itself powerfully along the track of a creed, and wore its passage continually deeper with the lapse of time" (*HW* 1:123). I am inclined to think that a wholly ironic reading of the scene is a modernist distortion yet that Hawthorne has opened the door to it by using earlier references to the supernatural mainly as symptoms of psychological projection but then having Dimmesdale at the end define his problem more as one of his relationship to God than as one of dereliction in his duties to Hester and their child.[26]

A more precise sense of Hawthorne's and Stowe's positions as mavericks within their respective traditions can be gained from their treatment of their heroines, Hester and Mary. Hawthorne's very choice of a heroine whose prototype is Hutchinson is the first clue that the romance belongs in the liberal tradition of antebellum historical meditation, since Hutchinson was invariably treated more attentively in liberal historiography (which tended to see her as a martyr to Puritan bigotry) than by orthodox writers (who tended to see her as a menace to Puritan authority).[27] In general, as we have noted, nineteenth-century interest in heresiarchs varied proportionately with the liberalism of the commentator. *The Scarlet Letter* goes on, however, to deviate strikingly from this pattern when, in the second half of the book, the narrator seems, at least provisionally, to endorse a Calvinist conception of human nature and to represent Puritan social ritual as psychologically necessary (to normalize Pearl and liberate Dimmesdale) and perhaps even as morally right. Thus the handling of Hester in the denouement, as Michael Bell points out, might be thought of as a critique of the motif, in antebellum New England romance, of the admirable woman who defies the Puritan establishment. Hawthorne's characterization points up the essential duplicity and simplemindedness of such stereotypical "good" heroines, who are identified with a sentimentalized "nature" purged of its subversive aspects.[28] Furthermore, as Colacurcio implies in characterizing Hester as standing partway between Hutchinson and Margaret Fuller, Hawthorne's heroine could also be viewed as a critique of a more radical, Transcendentalist individualism. Hutchinson was seen by some Transcendentalists as the ancestress of the movement, and the romance can be seen as reacting through the portrayal of Hester to specific Transcendentalist positions, as in her preaching to Dimmesdale in the forest the tenets of higher-lawism ("What we did had a consecration of its own"), self-reliance ("Heaven would show mercy, hadst thou but the strength to take advantage of it"), and rejection of the past as model ("The past is gone! Wherefore should we linger upon it now?").[29] Until midpoint, despite innuendos to the contrary, Hawthorne mainly manipulates reader response so as to encourage us to see Hester as more sinned against than sinning. To most readers today (and even to some in 1850), Hester initially seems fallen only in a technical sense, the adultery seems more a social crime than a symptom of depravity, and the community's behavior seems more criminal than hers. This moral ratio is then questioned, if not reversed, in the second half of the book. Consequently, the romance becomes an examination of the claims of an Arminian or a Transcendentalist model of human nature in terms of the example of a Puritan martyr, rather than an analysis of the martyrdom case pure and simple.[30]

Turning now to Stowe's Mary Scudder, we at first seem to find a replication of the stock romance heroine and the genre's shallow Arminian assumptions. Here and elsewhere Stowe seems to delight in inventing New England girls so pure that they seem, like herself as a child, to have received grace without undergoing the trials of old-fashioned conversion. The two-dimensionality of her portrayal seems all the more anachronistic when Hopkins, far from protesting Mary's objections to his salvationist scheme, readily accepts her spirituality as greater than his own. The presence of a character perilously like a nineteenth-century sentimentalist formula threatens to compromise the integrity of Stowe's historicism; and, from a purely mimetic standpoint, it does. Yet Stowe tries also to prevent us from seeing Mary just as a transplant from a de-Calvinized era. Mary is no mere apostle of natural piety. On the contrary, she falls into a particular tradition within the ranks of Congregational orthodoxy, a tradition of female saints who walk with the Lord from infancy. Stowe's immediate model was her own mother; the prototype was Jonathan Edwards's wife Sarah Pierrepoint, Edwards's supposed description of whom (beginning ."They say there is a young lady who is beloved of that Great Being") was famous in orthodox circles throughout the nineteenth century and is quoted in several of Stowe's works.[31] In short, although the figure of Mary reflects a popular antebellum stereotype, it is also carefully anchored to Puritan precedent and is used in such a way as to convert the novel into an exemplum of humanization within the Edwardsean tradition.[32] Mary is not so much Hopkins' theological antagonist as the embodiment of what is spiritually vital in Hopkinsianism. She is the Muse who inspires him to write his *Treatise on the Millennium;* her influence is the main reason her husband eventually becomes a pillar of Hopkins's church. Mary, in other words, is used as an instrument for revising and reaffirming a still viable tradition.

III

I could go on to note other telltale signs that differentiate the two texts as products of liberal versus orthodox imagination, such as the contrast in ministerial style between Hopkins, whose particular brand of social ineptness calls to mind the rustic, unpolished Calvinist preacher depicted by Stowe in several other works, as against Dimmesdale, who belongs in the line of refined, effete, supersensitive, tubercular young divines who in the nineteenth century were especially linked with liberal sainthood.[33] Rather than continue multiplying distinctions, however, it is better to move on to other implications of the contrast.

First, we should not picture the two writers as consistently aware of themselves as postliberal or postorthodox, nor should we expect that their literary treatments of Puritanism can be explained fully in terms of that difference. Take, for instance, their use of Puritan typological thinking. Although Hawthorne was culturally farther removed from intellectual circles committed to the theological premises underlying typology, his writing reflects that tradition to at least as great an extent as Stowe's, although somewhat differently.[34] Stowe's text relies on typology as a structural principle in a more fundamental sense than Hawthorne's. Hopkins' courtship of Mary is seriocomically related to the interpretation of the Canticles as a foreshadowing of the consummation of Christ's marriage with the church and the soul at the end of time. In this sense, if the union of maiden and minister were to take place, it would mean that the End Times have come: a preenactment on the personal and parish level of Hopkins' grand Mary-inspired vision of the millennium. The book's support for Mary's resistance to the union, which would (as a friend puts it) be tantamount to her taking the veil, constitutes a revisionary reading of the original figure, an argument that the spousal consummation may not be healthy either for the human spirit or the earthly community as a whole. In this way Stowe, by adapting the Puritans' own vocabulary, elaborates her basic idea that the Puritan scenario for the great work of redemption needs readjustment.[35]

Hawthorne's rhetoric is less Bible-based than Stowe's, and in his typological recastings, he is much more interested in representative figures or Christian allegorical symbols (e.g., the infant Pearl as a "forcible type" of Hester's "moral agony") than in the exegetical figures most distinctive to Puritan tradition, which connect historical events in a prophecy-fulfillment pattern (e.g., Dimmesdale's sense of his congregation's view of him as the new Enoch).[36] "Type," in Hawthorne's vocabulary, as for most antebellum writers, usually means nothing more specific than "allegorical image," and even when Hawthorne unmistakably uses a Puritan type, one must bear in mind that his figurative strategies are likely to have been equally if not more informed by non–New England sources such as Spenser's *Faerie Queene* or Bunyan's *Pilgrim's Progress* (the latter being the one Puritan book that he is known to have encouraged his children to read). Yet Hawthorne shows an awareness of the typology of New England's mission that is fully equal to Stowe's. The most familiar proof texts here would be "Endicott and the Red Cross" and "The Grey Champion," both of whose title figures, as well as their ritualistic acts of defiance, are presented as types of the spirit of revolution.[37] To be sure, in most such cases, including the two just named, Hawthorne's typologizing has at least a covertly deconstructive aspect.[38] In *The Scarlet Letter* we see this in the ironic suggestion that Dimmesdale's prophetic election sermon was inspired by sexual yearning.[39] In the Hawthorne canon as a whole, *Grandfather's Chair* is the most elaborate case. Hawthorne here turns his vignettes of key moments in Massachusetts history, recast from Bancroft's history and other sources, for the most part into exempla of persecution, intolerance, suffering, and violence that dismay rather than edify his juvenile auditors, relying on the child's-text convention of innocent wonder as both a mitigation and a cover-up for the absence of conventional filiopietism. Yet Hawthorne's style, overall, is more steeped than Stowe's in typological *discourse:* figurative scriptural analogies (Hester as Madonna or Whore of Babylon) and allegorical readings of events (the interpretations of the *A* in the sky as a particular providence) that rest on Puritan precedent and lend themselves to full-blown typological schemes, although Hawthorne's approach – as always in his mature work – is to problematize them.

Consequently we must not infer that the comparative distance from the Puritanism that Hawthorne's works depict made him a less astute deployer of Puritan categories. On the contrary, as the example of figuration shows, that same distance allowed him to use Puritanism masterfully as a vocabulary. Approaching the allegorical cast of Puritan thinking with the characteristic self-consciousness of the more sophisticated classes in the age of insurgent Pilgrimism, Hawthorne was in a better position than Stowe to perceive from the start the arbitrariness of allegorization and the "analogy between the form of allegory and the form of obsessive-compulsive behavior."[40] Seeing this way allowed Hawthorne to explore the obsessiveness of Puritan behavior, to envisage Puritanism as an avatar or quintessence of a universal human susceptibility in this regard and to make his mimesis on either level double back in self-reflexive awareness of the disrelation of romance conventions to reality and the arbitrariness of signification in general, so that his narratives become fables of signification at the same time as they work themselves out as fables of Puritanism.[41] Hawthorne's status as outsider, then, paradoxically helps bring him near his Puritans even as it confirms his distance from them and helps make him a more searching anthropologist in some respects than Stowe. Stowe can envisage the institutional church and the structure of New England theology as artifices, but she stops short of considering the possibility (broached by the narrator's treatment of Dimmesdale's election sermon) that the typology of New England's mission might be subject to the same interpretation. Hawthorne, because of the self-consciousness that historical distance and meditation on the warping effects of allegorization and the romance mode have reinforced in him, is forced to stand at a greater remove from his Puritan subjects, so that he and we begin to question whether the text is really grounded in history at all. Yet by the same token he is enabled by his historical and aesthetic alienation to expose the alienating and alienated qualities of the Puritan vision.

But rather than play Stowe and Hawthorne off against each other, it would be fairer to say that their different angles of vision enabled them to illuminate different aspects of Puritanism. Stowe provides us with a far more extensive mimesis of the social reality of the fictional worlds she portrays. Hawthorne is unwilling, probably unable, to give animation to social surfaces the way she does in recounting "theological tea" or the etiquette of wedding-dress making in the old times. (Indeed, for him to do so would be a violation of his sense of the gap that separates him from these rituals.) Hawthorne's substitutes for such scenes are his stiffish emblematic processions or set-piece meditations such as the chapter on the prison door, which, through their formalization, confess that they are not photographic imagings but literary analogues of Puritan rituals. Yet when it comes to the portrayal of the inner stresses and self-deceptions caused by hypocrisy, by the inability to accept grace, and by the uncertainty as to whether one is to be saved, Hawthorne seems closer to his subject. Both writers are well aware of these dimensions of Puritan experience. But Stowe, with occasional exceptions such as her treatment of Mrs. Marvyn's despair over her son's supposed death, treats the heart's interior perfunctorily and schematically, as contrasted with Hawthorne's anatomy of Dimmesdale – abstract and putative as it is. In these differing emphases, Hawthorne comes closer to capturing the nuances of such psychological records as the agonized diaries of Thomas Shepard and Michael Wigglesworth, whereas Stowe looks forward to recent historiographical emphasis on the social structures and external lives of the Puritans. Stowe thus became a model for later realistic portrayals, in regional fiction, of the textures of daily New England life, rituals, and folkways, whereas Hawthorne, for whom Puritan attitudes had greater reality than their institutional correlatives, became the key transmitter to posterity of Puritanism's psychological and semiological aspects.

This basic contrast between Hawthorne and Stowe – and at the same time the impossibility of insisting on any such contrast as an absolute – is confirmed by their later work, after *The Scarlet Letter* and *The Minister's Wooing*. With respect to their use of the New England past as fictional subject, their careers move in opposite directions. *The Scarlet Letter* is the culmination of Hawthorne's attempt to realize Puritanism in fiction, after which he turns toward present-day settings. The close of *The House of the Seven Gables* marks the transition. By the time he wrote *The Blithedale Romance*, as James McIntosh tellingly puts it, Hawthorne is treating "the authority of New England culture, which had both oppressed and stimulated him during his early years as a writer, as curiously irrelevant."[42] For Stowe, on the other hand, *The Minister's Wooing* is the start of a fictional retreat from confrontation of contemporary issues that Hawthorne belatedly engages in *The Blithedale Romance* back to the past of her childhood and her parents' lives. As she does, she increasingly suspends her critical judgment and gives way to nostalgia, although she continues to use the convention of the disengaged narrator and the escape-from-orthodoxy plot even in her most sentimentalized piece of historicizing, *Poganuc People* (1878). "As I get old," Stowe confessed to Oliver Wendell Holmes, "I do love to think of those quiet, simple times when there was not a poor person in the parish, and the changing glories of the year were the only spectacle."[43] Stowe's sense of the break between her times and the old times was overridden by the strength and charm of her memories of that bygone era. Hawthorne's near abandonment of the New England past suggests the opposite. On the other hand, Hawthorne became even more of a literary Calvinist as he moved away from the depiction of Puritanism per se. The trope of the fall is important in all four of his major romances, but in contrast to the first two, where the symbolic fall takes place before the narrative starts and the narrative proper concentrates on the work of redemption, in the later two the matter of the romance is really the fall itself – the corruption of utopian hopes in *The Blithedale Romance* and of the natural man in *The Marble Faun*. Hence the exultation of one Calvinist reader of *The Marble Faun* ("Our old Puritanic theology on the subject [of sin] is there, without abatement or apology") and the dismay of another ("He dwells so much upon gloomy wrongs, and portrays the horrors of remorse, without showing its only legitimate relief, – hope of pardon through an atoning Saviour").[44] In some ways, then, Hawthorne came to out-Puritan even the Orthodox, who were gravitating like Stowe toward a milder faith. Hawthorne's neo-orthodoxy, if that is the right label, can thus be seen as a sort of rebuke not just to Arminian-Transcendentalist optimism but to the whole drift of mainline Protestant thought, although as the second Calvinist reader just quoted partly discerns, it is also identifiably the rebuke of a disaffected liberal uncomfortable with the whole framework of supernaturalism and thus unable to image redemption, at least in his romances, except in the form of human (female) innocents like Phoebe, Priscilla, and Hilda.

The careers of Hawthorne and Stowe, in short, corroborate what was said in Chapter 2 about the limits, as well as the value, of the "two-cultures" approach to New England literary history. Much can be gained from seeing these authors in relation to their respective roots in East Coast liberalism and Connecticut Valley conservatism, but the distinctions quickly start to blur and crisscross. This happens in part because of the decline, noted in Chapter 9, of vigilant custodial attentiveness to the niceties of discrimination among competing sectarian traditions. Stowe and Hawthorne both disassociate themselves from such hawkish rigor from the start. With this (collective) lapse of rigor it became possible for Stowe to reminisce affectionately about Calvinism's glacial age, for Hawthorne to reinvent Calvinism in terms of secularized moral equivalents, and for both to achieve a bipartisan appeal. By the same token, this change in intellectual climate betokened the general decay of the New England historical imagination as a critical instrument. The later careers of both writers show this as well. The tendency in Hawthorne's work for history to disappear and for Puritanism to endure only in thematized form and the tendency in Stowe to settle cozily back into the past both amount to tacit concessions that Puritan history is tangential to present-day concerns. The golden age of Pilgrimist oratory, inaugurated by Daniel Webster, was drawing to a close, and with it the golden age of Puritan fictionalizing, which drew its energy from critical dialogue with oratorical platitude and the yeast of sectarianism. As the modern avatars of Puritanism crumbled, as even diehard Hopkinsians softened into ecumenicism and the old, past-haunted families like the Pyncheons became increasingly isolated anachronisms, Puritan history lost its force as a burning issue and became more thoroughly tied into benign consensus rituals – though still lively enough to be capable of reanimation by an incisive or original mind, as its treatment by H. L. Mencken, Perry Miller, and Arthur Miller in their various ways attest.[45] That is part of the explanation for the obsolescence of Stowe's literary renditions of Puritanism as opposed to Hawthorne's, hers being tied so closely to the literal referent, his more thoroughly transforming Puritan categories into techniques that could be transported across regional and temporal lines. But Puritan obsolescence aside, the exploitation of New England culture generally, as a literary subject, was still very much on the upswing in 1865. Of this larger project, the works that we have been examining in this section were but a portion. In the next chapters we shall look at the rest of that story.

PART IV

New England as a Country
of the Imagination:
The Spirit of Place

The Cultural Landscape in
Regional Poetry and Prose

I call it rich without compunction, despite its several poverties. . . .
When you wander about in Arcadia you ask as few questions as possible.

Henry James, *The American Scene* (1907)

Here, in these shades, these deep seclusions hid
Beneath the whisp'ring leaves and o'er our moors
A ragged independence lives at ease,
Wearing those good adornments of the race,
Such as pure air, warm suns, and builds the Hero
Urban pens describe.

Ellery Channing, *Near Home* (1858)

The literary reinvention of Puritanism was only part of the more far-
reaching project of articulating all of New England culture and its institutions in literary form. This larger project preceded and outlasted the
vogue of historical writing, at its height between 1820 and 1850. This
chapter and the next four will examine some characteristic ways in which
New England writing codified the regional sense of place.

Here, as before, the Revolutionary era supplies a somewhat arbitrary
yet justifiable starting point. It is arbitrary in the sense that the New England landscape and ethos had already been mapped in some detail by
early explorers, by Puritan historians, and by diarists and travelers like
Samuel Sewall and Sarah Kemble Knight. It is justifiable, however, in
that post-Revolutionary literary nationalist aesthetics tended temporarily
to suppress and erase old-style colonial attachments and to create at least
the illusion that any future regionalism would have to build itself anew.
"Writers of the late eighteenth century," observes Cecelia Tichi, "were
eager to transcend the confines of New England history and to include
other regions, especially the South, in their affirmations of America re-
born to national redemption in liberty." Hence the attraction, for Joel

283

Barlow and others, of the symbol of Columbus, who "was not associated with any specific region and so could attach to all."[1]

This tendency to minimize the regional for the sake of a programmatic nationalism, which influenced even so lococentric a person as Timothy Dwight, was further reinforced by Neoclassical aesthetics, which, as we saw in Chapter 4, tended to satirize provincialism in the name of cosmopolitan intellectual and aesthetic standards, even though this also involved a sort of recuperation of the provincial through the detail with which it was exposed to satire. Neoclassical internationalism, furthermore, was both an effect and a cause of a more far-reaching early American self-consciousness about attempts to poetize local materials.

> 'Tis hard to rhyme
> About a little and unnoticed stream,
> That few have heard of

confesses a New England poet of the 1820s as he gamely attempts to immortalize his native river.[2] This is far from Alexander Pope's easy assurance that Windsor's "green Retreats" are "at once the Monarch's and the Muse's Seats."[3] This American poet, John G. C. Brainard, labored under the compound handicap of obscure materials and a genre made popular through its application of the more storied British countryside, a genre, moreover, that in its traditional eighteenth-century form called for a rather quick leap from local detail to generalized meditation. All of this conspired to keep Brainard's literary landscape on the level of tepid generic abstraction.

Nevertheless, over the long run the forces that initially blocked the development of a regionally oriented literature helped to produce it. Eighteenth-century programmatic topophilia concretizes into Romantic particularism; programmatic literary nationalism takes shape in large part as the expression of America's constituent subcultures. The symbolic culmination of this process during our period was the work of Thoreau, of whom Larzer Ziff has rightly said that "no American writer so tried the proposition that to be thoroughly rooted in region was to discover the source of universality."[4] At the same time, as the case of Thoreau also shows, regional literary consciousness necessarily operated in the knowledge of its own self-limitation. This induced in its practitioners a wide range of uneasy tones, from deferential apology to self-congratulatory pushiness, and helped to ensure that the most enduring literary reconstructions of regional experience would be in ironic modes such as the ones treated in Chapters 15 and 16.

The process of development can be illustrated in miniature by the genre to which the poetical excerpts just quoted all belong: the topographical or locodescriptive poem, a loosely knit work of indeterminate length (usually one hundred to five hundred lines), describing the prospect of a mountain, a river, an estate, a town, a region, a journey, embellished with historical, legendary, moralistic, and sometimes also personal reflections.[5] The best-known examples from British literature, all familiar to early national writers, were John Denham's *Cooper's Hill,* Pope's *Windsor Forest,* and Oliver Goldsmith's *Deserted Village.* Inherently miscellaneous in structure, such poems tended to become padded and superficial, but at best they conveyed a pleasantly kaleidoscopic impression of the landscape and its nuances, woven (like nature itself, in the Neoclassical view) into a pleasing *concordia discors.*[6]

Such poems were very popular in postcolonial America. The genre was both easy to imitate and consonant with the American poet's conception of how to proclaim America's cultural resources. Goldsmith's poem, in particular, gave rise to a whole subgenre of New World counter-Goldsmith idylls designed to portray whither the emigrants from his depopulated "sweet Auburn" had fled. Philip Freneau invented it ("The American Village," 1772); others who followed suit included Timothy Dwight ("The Flourishing Village," Part 2 of *Greenfield Hill*); Goldsmith's Nova Scotian namesake and nephew (*The Rising Village*); Maine governor Enoch Lincoln (*The Village*); Massachusetts minister Samuel Deane the younger (*The Populous Village*); and journalist Charles W. Denison, whose "American Village" (1845) is one of the last of the old-school examples. These poems are all affectionate retorts to Goldsmith, after whose Auburn at least nine American towns were named. His lost ideal of the stable, holistic, benignly paternalistic community of honest rustics, now broken up by the British enclosure laws, was pictured as having been reconstituted under more solid auspices in America, where "Every farmer reigns a little king," protected by "Laws, that on nature and on reason rest / Long-tried, and sanctioned by Religion's test."[7] Particularly exciting to New World bards was the quickness with which these communities had arisen out of nowhere. As Dwight wrote elsewhere, there was "something far more delightful in contemplating the diffusion of enterprise and industry over an immense forest" than in the most exotic romance (*DT* 2:212).

Apart from the attractions of this particular theme, topographical poetry was well calculated to appeal to the American muse for the sake of its instructive qualities, its combination of the descriptive and the didactic. A case in point is Sarah Wentworth Morton's *Beacon Hill* (1797), conspicuous as an example of New England (and specifically Bostonian) ethnocentrism striving dutifully to become national by jumping from a glimpse of the Battle of Bunker Hill to a comprehensive historical and geographical survey of the entire thirteen colonies uniting under Washington in revolutionary struggle. The poem opens by claiming a special status for itself as the production of "the HISTORIC MUSE," not "vain

fiction" like "the tales of *Ilion,* and the *Latian* war." "What though no Genius, with enchanting power, / Charm the coy MUSES from their classic
bower," when it is the "ray of TRUTH" that inspires "*Columbia's native
minstrel?*"[8] This poem also shows up the nagging insecurity of early
American topographical poetry, which feels compelled to measure itself
against its antecedents, sometimes abjectly, as in Brainard, but more
often with bluster, as here. Thus Dwight boasts that the view from his
seat at Greenfield Hill is

> Etherial! Matchless! such as Albion's sons,
> Could Albion's isle an equal prospect boast,

would have

> tun'd to rapture, and o'er Cooper's hill,
> And Windsor's beauteous forest, high uprais'd,
> And sent on fame's light wing to every clime

– thereby conceding that despite the superiority of his prospect, his poem
was not likely to rival his great British precursors' either in quality or in
circulation.[9]

In time, however, American topographical poets learned how to make
literary capital even out of those points that had caused them insecurity.
In Emerson's "Muskatequid," for example, the very insignificance of the
Concord River landscape is made the cause of celebration:

> Because I was content with these poor fields,
> Low, open meads, slender and sluggish streams,
> And found a home in haunts which others scorned,
> The partial wood-gods overpaid my love
>   [*EW* 9:141]

and granted him the gift to penetrate the inner meanings of the quiet
landscape then described. His submission to lack of sublimity is rewarded
by a total rapport with the genius loci. Whittier's "Last Walk in Autumn"
follows the same strategy in reverse, moving from a fairly full composition of place to doctrinal inference:

> O'er the bare woods, whose outstretched hands
>   Plead with the leaden heavens in vain,
>   I see, beyond the valley lands,
>   The sea's long level dim with rain,
>   Around me all things, stark and dumb,
>   Seem praying for the snows to come,
> And, for the summer bloom and greenness gone,
> With winter's sunset lights and dazzling morn atone.
>   [*WW* 2:37]

Instead of immediately asserting its perceptual credentials and then doing
its best to substantiate, this poem relies on the sensitivity of its evocation

of New England's bleak November to justify the claim that although New England is no Florence, the austerity of the landscape is a positive moral, if not aesthetic, advantage:

> Better with naked nerve to bear
> The needles of this goading air,
> Than, in the lap of sensual ease, forego
> The godlike power to do, the godlike power to know.
>
> [*WW* 2:43]

Except for the severity of its monastic overtones, Emerson's and Whittier's celebration of the sparse or stark cannot be called a uniquely New England-ish adaptation of the British topographical tradition. Emerson and Whittier closely follow Wordsworth, who also prides himself on the ordinariness of his poetic materials. Major epiphanies are inspired by encounters with an obscure leech gatherer or an unknown woman carrying water in a broken pitcher. Wordsworth finds nothing about the source of his beloved River Duddon "for hope to build upon," "No sign of hoar Antiquity's esteem," but then proceeds to find much personal and philosophic significance. Emerson and Whittier, in other words, participate in the general Romanticist inversion of the values of public and private, mainstream and marginal, an inversion that can be traced farther back to earlier topographical poems such as John Dyer's "Grongar Hill" (1726, 1761), "whose silent shade," where "sweetly-musing Quiet dwells," is seen as the abode of the "modest Muses."[10] The most ungenerous view of the originality of "Musketaquid" and "The Last Walk in Autumn" would be to type them as derivative Romantic mutations of a motif inherent from the start of topographical poetry. A more charitable verdict would be to credit the New Englanders, by reason of their sensitivity to the spareness of their landscape (a combination of provincial diffidence and hard-headed awareness of the rigors of the environment), with having brought to a sort of consummation the Romantic quest to find poetry in spots previously overlooked.

Meanwhile, the region's topographical poets were also, in the spirit of Morton and Dwight, attempting with some success to overcome the handicap of obscurity in another way, which recalls the campaign described in Chapter 8 to promote public awareness of the Puritan heritage, namely, by poetizations of landscapes that infused them with an aura of legend and history. Thus Dwight devoted major sections of his *Greenfield Hill* to reminiscences of the Puritan conquest of the Pequods and the British burning of Fairfield during the Revolution (the closeness of the analogy between these events escaped his literal-minded muse). Thus the Indian legends associated with various places were exploited in poems such as Bryant's "Monument Mountain" and Whittier's "Mogg Megone," comprising a genre that has a fictional complement in tales such as Hawthorne's "Great Carbuncle." To invest the regional landscape with such associations was an uphill battle; as Whittier complained, "our modern Yankee sees / Nor omens, spells, nor mysteries" (*WW* 1:25). Yet by 1860, Frederick Goddard Tuckerman could look without any manifest affection at a western Massachusetts landscape and see

> faces, forms and phantoms, numbered not,
> Gather and pass like mist upon the breeze,
> Jading the eye with uncouth images:
> Women with muskets, children dropping shot
> By fields half harvested or left in fear
> Of Indian inroad, or the Hessian near;
> Disaster, poverty, and dire disease.
> Or from the burning village, through the trees
> I see the smoke in reddening volumes roll
> The Indian file in shadowy silence pass
> While the last man sets up the trampled grass,
> The Tory priest declaiming, fierce and fat,
> The Shay's man with the green branch in his hat,
> Or silent sagamore, Shaug or Wassahoale.[11]

Through skillful montage and unobtrusive but significant detail ("the last man sets up the trampled grass"), this poem communicates the sense of a richly layered history, with the years of white settlement (from frontier to Revolution to Shay's Rebellion) quietly blending in with the earlier, longer, vaguer era of the "silent sagamore" whom the whites had displaced. A past as resonant as Denham's or Pope's had emerged in New England landscape poetry.

So fully had it emerged, indeed, as already to have given rise to its own sorts of stereotyping. We see this especially in the topographical verse written for the centennials of towns, churches, and local associations of various sorts. Writing it became, by the end of our period, a literary industry fully as extensive, and fully as ritualized, as the Forefathers' Day orations discussed in Chapter 8. By midcentury, no local centennial celebration was deemed complete without its appropriate hymn, ode, ballad, or discursive poem. Many of these poems were in the topographical vein and adhered to a standard format. They would begin with some recognition of the site and the occasion: "Here, on this storied shore, within the sound / Of these old voiceful waters, have we met / To spend a profitable hour" – or the like. The auditors would be reminded of the lapse of time since the town or institution began ("One hundred times hath Winter, drear and chill, / In his snow blanket wrapped this sleeping hill!") and of the "great changes" time had wrought – though also of the continuity between past and present. In the process, the audience would be impressed with the fact that "this is consecrated ground we tread!" and reminded that we should "mark the way wherein our fathers trod." Sundry notable events and personages would be enumerated, sometimes with a touch of humor (always qualified by reverence), with an emphasis on the development from wilderness to civilization, in the case of the town centennial poems. The poem would conclude with some gesture of reconsecration to the spot ("Dear native town!"; "Land of my birth, thou *art* a holy land!"; "Home! Home – most sacred spot of all the earth"). For the sake of balance, it might along the way be conceded that "Thou are not faultless – no, nor free from stain," especially if the poet no longer resided there. But in general, the picture would be resoundingly affirmative, optimistic about the future and showing pride in communal progress to date.[12]

The quotations are a fair index of the general quality. Almost all of these occasional pieces have, understandably, vanished into oblivion. The one canonical remnant is Emerson's 1837 "Concord Hymn," one of the few, ironically, that is farsighted enough to predict its own oblivion in its look forward to the infinite future. This commemoration of the Concord battle monument contains in its four tight quatrains most of the motifs just noted: the grounding in place ("On this green bank, by this soft stream"); the description of contrast and continuity between then and now; the enumeration of the fathers' exploits, with a touch of wryness ("embattled farmers"); and the gesture of ongoing filial piety ("We set today a votive stone") (*EW* 9:158–59). One reason why this poem survives, aside from its being a minor work by a major author, is the masterful succinctness with which each stanza gives particular, local detail a sense of infinite extension. The farmers "fired the shot heard round the world"; "Time the ruined bridge has swept / Down the dark stream which seaward creeps": the stream being both the Concord River and the stream of time. Those Concordians knew how to interconnect the local and the cosmic.

As the range of works so far noted suggests, New England's topographically oriented poetry between the Revolution and the Civil War is too heterogeneous to be subsumed within a single verse tradition, however much it may have been influenced in its early stages by the model of British locodescriptive verse from Denham through Goldsmith. The poems already cited include a hymn (Emerson), a sonnet (Tuckerman), and a meditative lyric (Whittier), as well as more traditional descriptive meanderings in heroic couplet and blank verse. We also find a wide variety of subgroupings according to theme. Two have so far been defined in some detail: the counter-Goldsmith and the centennial poem. Other such categories, each with its own conventions, include symbolic tree poems (to be discussed in Chapter 13), river poems, estate poems, and poems of the season.

All of these formal and topical permutations are New World variants of British models, sometimes innovative, sometimes not. New England estate poems – for example, James A. Hillhouse's "Sachem's Wood," Henry Knight's "Wicomb-Spring," and Ellery Channing's "Hillside" (from *The Wanderer*) – are dreary reiterations of Old World formulas. New England river poems have more verve. "No country on the globe is better watered than New England," affirmed geographer Jedidiah Morse.[13] Whether or not he was right, the poets of New England do give that impression. Of the landscape verse selected for Henry Wadsworth Longfellow's anthology of New England poems of places (*Poems of America: New England*, 1878), river poems were the largest category. The Housatonic, the Passumsick, the Nashaway were all transmuted into song. The Concord fared best, thanks to Transcendentalist eloquence; but the Connecticut figured most prominently, owing to its length and to the redundant pertinacity of the late Puritan muse. Had we the time, it would be worth experimenting to see if we could detect in the scores of extant poems to the "Dark-Rolling Connecticut" ("sweetest stream that poet ever sung") an encapsulation of Emily Dickinson's world, because in them the river has a way of turning into a synechdoche for Connecticut Valley culture – "the generous offspring of a simple land," as Lydia Sigourney put it. The basic routine, in any event, is predictable enough: the panoramic view of the river from source to mouth; the catalog of settlements; the admission that other rivers surpass it in fame or size, balanced by an insistence on its beauty and importance to the region and to the poet's solace; glimpses of the river at different seasons; and its constancy through time, despite its also being a metaphor *of* time.[14]

More arresting than these stereotypical ploys is the imagery of New England seasonal verse. Comparing their climate to that of the motherland, New Englanders were especially conscious of their impressive autumn and protracted winter. Autumn, in particular, was the season that seemed to bear a special New England imprint. It was definitely not Keats's "Season of mists and mellow fruitfulness" but a time, for better or worse, of sharp visual and moral contrasts. On the positive side, the literary nationalist could stress the splendor of the frost-wrought fall colors, so much more striking than the "dull colors of an English autumnal foliage." But generally writers also saw the skull beneath the skin. "We cannot forget, if we could, that this beautiful magnificence of the forests is but the livery of death," intones one Maine author. Here and elsewhere one finds autumn beauty diagnosed in terms of the most feared New England disease ("the hectic cheek / Of a consumptive girl who ere her time, / In some gay anguish half renews her prime") and the idea of Indian summer, associated not with its picturesque colors but with extermination of the red man.[15] One Dickinson poem metaphorically pictures the autumn landscape as bleeding to death (*DP* 656). From this vantage point, autumn is "like a man / Whose head is in his prime turned gray"; the leaves are "types of our mortality"; nature "Weaves the shroud which dreary Winter presses / Sadly down upon those withered faces, / Which were lately Nature's blooming graces." For the British poet, autumn is, until the end, still "vigorous," its "yellow lustre gilds the world"; for Thoreau, November is when "a man will eat his heart, if in any month" (*TJ* 4:405). Robert Lowell, a century later, timed it right when he set Jonathan Edwards' perception of the spider as a symbol of mortality in the month of "gnarled November."[16]

The correlation of last things – natural, human, eschatological – is, of course, hardly peculiar to the New England muse. More distinctive is the sharpness of juxtaposition between the splendor and the decay (cf. Wallace Stevens' "The maidens . . . stray impassioned in the littering leaves")[17] and the tendency to stress the scene's bleak rigor with a prophetic intensity that almost manages to turn bleakness back into its opposite. Whittier's "Last Walk in Autumn" works that way. So does the following, very differently styled Dickinson lyric, written in her most abstract and gnomic style:

> The murmuring of Bees, has ceased
> But murmuring of some
> Posterior, prophetic,
> Has simultaneous come.
> The lower metres of the Year
> When Nature's laugh is done
> The Revelations of the Book
> Whose Genesis was June.
> Appropriate Creatures to her change
> The Typic Mother sends
> As Accent fades to interval
> With separating Friends
> Till what we speculate, has been
> And thoughts we will not show
> More intimate with us become
> Than Persons, that we know.
>   [*DP* 1115]

Of the various ways in which this haunting poem could be read, one would be as a stylization of the experience of late autumnal emptiness (nature's sounds ceasing, metaphorized as friends departing), an emptiness "prophetic" of death and the End Times, but charged also with expectation, as the speaker anticipates some cosmic payoff – if not the final Revelation, then at least revelation of one's hidden thoughts, to which at last one is able to listen. To the extent that the poem's code language has an environmental ground, it is probably similar to that of Thoreau's late autumnal withdrawal into his cabin, though Dickinson more pointedly suggests here the inner spaces that open up from the fading of summer stimuli. The housebound recluse was in a better position to muse at leisure on the New England perception of autumn's withdrawal of external life supports as an intellectual process, over and above its naturalistic aspects.

The sparseness of a late New England autumn, on which Thoreau, Whittier, Dickinson, and others all insisted in their several ways, may have resonated to such a degree because it epitomized a feature of the region that New England writers, despite their boosterism, were repeatedly constrained to admit might be its chief literary-ecological trait: its resistance to poetic appropriation.

> O for a pencil rapid as the light
> To paint the glories bursting on the sight!
> Making the plain New England landscape seem
> The unfamiliar scenery of a dream

cries the speaker in a poem by Christopher Cranch, as he sees a picturesque sunset – disclosing, by the outburst, frustration with the dullness of the landscape as it usually is. "In a New England hand the lyre must beat / With brave emotions," warns Ellery Channing,

> when the cutting sleet
> Doth the bare traveller in the fields half blind,

although fortunately all is not lost because

> freezing to the trees congeals a rind,
> Next day more brilliant than the Arab skies,
> Or plumes from gorgeous birds of Paradise.

The challenge of retrieving poetry from a landscape that often seemed as refractory to art as it was to tillage was the great burden, and the great opportunity, for the topographical muse of New England. In their gloomier moments, her poets felt faced, like upland farmers, with the prospect of starvation and the lure of emigration to a sublimer or more storied realm. Wallace Stevens' fascination with Florida and the Caribbean is entirely typical here. Those who stayed home, like Thoreau and Dickinson, felt driven to compensate through imaginary travels to the Ganges, Chimborazo, Tunis, and other exotic places. At best, however, they could congratulate themselves on having made poetic riches out of seemingly unpromising raw material. Stevens, than whom no New England poet was ever more conscious of his local austeries, captured the syndrome better than he perhaps intended when he wrote

> In a world of universal poverty
> The philosophers alone will be fat
> Against the autumn winds
> In an autumn that will be perpetual.[18]

The immediate reference is to the battening of the speculative imagination in the wake of the collapse of the dogmatic religion, but in the poem's larger context impoverishment of landscape and impoverishment of doctrine are intertwined. Alienation from traditional ideology, which in Part III we saw was a vital if often covert element in antebellum New England historicizing, also accounts for part of the emphasis of physiographic harshness in the landscape poems cited earlier. Channing, for instance, sees the land as "cold and flinty," partly because it is inhabited by a "plain strong race" that he praises for stolidness rather than for cordiality (despite some game attempts at the latter), because he feels somewhat alienated from the communal values.[19] The impetus behind the poem is the urge to convert the impression of poverty at all levels into a speculative synthesis that can fill the affective void of which the speaker is guiltily conscious for both personal and patriotic reasons. Geography, manners, and doctrine are all reciprocals.

The New England topographical muse, then, turns out to be a complicated affair. Though strongly derivative of British models and often conscious of such, it is also mindful of starting, culturally, from scratch – a self-division probably endemic to provincial cultures everywhere. Its local loyalties often lead to patriotic exaggerations, which also seem, however, to be attempts to avoid facing the "fact" of ecological and cultural impoverishment. Literary cliché, then, needs at times to be read as strategic defense rather than as simple imitation. Impoverishment, however, is sometimes squarely faced as a "reality" and even flaunted for the flattering image it suggests of Yankee moral, economic, and literary hardihood. Once aware of this, we become sensitized to the whole project of New England landscape poetics as ideological construct, to whose fictive nature the more sophisticated writers (like the critics of consensus historiography) sometimes call attention, although the trenchancy with which Stevens does this would have been considered bad form by our poets, who, even as they tip us off as to the artifice of their enterprise, also ingenuously seek to impress on us the accuracy of their portrayals.

Landscape poems were by no means the only vehicle used by New England writers to invoke the genius loci. To an even greater extent, they cultivated a variety of overlapping prose genres. These at first developed more slowly than descriptive verse from their utilitarian antecedents, but the long-range results were more impressive, and the remaining chapters in Part IV will concentrate almost entirely on them. At this point, a brief overview will be helpful.[20]

At the start of our period, New England writers had at their disposal a number of nonfictional prose models for codifying the regional experience, apart from narrative and annalistic history. Chief among these were the traveler's account, imitated by Dwight in his four-volume *Travels* (discussed in Chapter 14); the natural-history essay or treatise, which formed a regular part of the regional histories of Belknap, Williams, Williamson, and others; and autobiographical narrative, which in subgenres such as the Indian captivity story sometimes became more descriptive than autobiographical.[21] All of these genres were originally utilitarian rather than aesthetic forms, but the eighteenth century saw the production of a number of more "literary" examples (e.g., Benjamin Franklin's *Autobiography*, William Bartram's *Travels,* and Gilbert White's *Natural History of Selbourne*) that helped make possible further, more poetic adaptations of these models by later writers like Thoreau.

Probably the single most important American prose work in teaching native writers to exploit regional material for literary purposes was Washington Irving's *Sketch-Book* (1819–20), a loosely connected series of descriptive pieces, interweaving essay and fiction (with a few poems thrown in), in tones ranging from affection to musing reminiscence to light irony and satire. Irving's settings were mostly British, but his overall approach and his two American tales greatly interested New Englanders. Longfellow, Hawthorne, and Whittier, for example, all considered writing works that would do for their region what "Rip Van Winkle" and "The Legend of Sleepy Hollow" had begun to do for the Dutch country of New York. Hawthorne's *Twice-Told Tales* and Whittier's *Supernaturalism of New England* reflect this plan, although Hawthorne's scope is broader and Whittier's more restricted – an amateur monograph on the state of regional superstition.[22] Another important contemporary influence on New England writers, owing in part to the region's township-oriented sense of place (to be discussed in the next chapter) was the sketches of local English life and manners in Mary Russell Mitford's *Our Village* (1824–32), which provided a more documentary model than Irving's of the blend of essay and anecdotalism, especially (but not exclusively) attractive to women writers.[23] Owing to the precedents of Irving and Mitford, from the 1820s on a standard item in the repertoire of antebellum literary magazines and annuals was the short local tale or sketch on topics such as are indicated by these titles: "A Legend of Monhegan," "Our Village Post-Office," "A Connecticut Christmas Eve," "Sebago Pond," "Our Village Pastor," "Our Village Poet," and "Recollections of the Village of———." The *New England Magazine* (1831–5) was particularly rich in such contributions: Whittier, Longfellow, Hawthorne, and John Neal all wrote such pieces for it.

A number of antebellum writers produced book-length collections of this kind. Lewis Mansfield's *Up-Country Letters* (1852), relished by Hawthorne, was a series of epistolary sketches of the customs and rituals of a Connecticut family transplanted to New York State. Lydia Sigourney's

Sketch of Connecticut, Forty Years Since (1824), like Eliza Lee's *Sketches of a New-England Village* (1838), discussed in Chapter 10, was a semifictionalization of childhood experiences, the evangelical-filiopietistic opposite of Lee's Unitarian revisionism, loosely organized, like Lee's *Sketches,* as a series of glimpses of the people and institutions of a local community (Norwich, Connecticut). Such works could either shade over into episodic novels (e.g., George Lunt's *Eastford; or, Household Sketches* [1855], where anatomy of village institutions coexists uneasily with a romance plot) or into monographs (Jacob Abbott's topical essays on *New England, and Her Institutions* [1835]). The usual result was some sort of compromise, well exemplified by the most monumental literary anatomy of traditional New England customs, Harriet Beecher Stowe's *Oldtown Folks* (1869). *Oldtown Folks* is a piece of amateur historical sociology analyzing the economic, social, and spiritual life of a late eighteenth-century New England village, with special attention to stratification, marginalization, and the indoctrination of the young. Anticipating the more imaginative scholarly town histories of today, such as Robert Gross's *Minutemen and Their World,* Stowe provides an array of thumbnail biographies of Oldtown dramatis personae and interweaves these with depictions of such community rituals as the Sunday worship service, fireside chats, funerals, tithing, school attendance, and the like. All of this is basically a synthetic collage of her Litchfield memories and her husband Calvin's yarn spinning about old Natick, Massachusetts, mediated by desultory reading and by what had already become conventional formulas for codifying the experience of village life. Yet the book is also the skeletal bildungsroman of its observer-narrator Horace Holyoke, to whose personal development the text intermittently keeps returning.

Texts like *Oldtown Folks,* insofar as they develop an ongoing plot, also ✓ belong to a tradition of attempts at <u>the great American novel</u>, New England style, attempts originally inspired by some of the same models that produced the social anatomies of Victorian fiction: Edgeworth and Scott at first (along with the "sentimental" residue of the former and the "gothic" residue of the latter), then Dickens and (for women writers, chiefly) the Brontës. The native strain begins with Catherine Maria Sedg- *SEDGWICK.* wick's novella *A New-England Tale* (1822), really more an exposé than an exposition of provincial village culture, too heavily committed to a Cinderella plot (virtuous heroine enthralled by wicked guardian aunt) and anti-Calvinist satire (Calvinism being the root of that same aunt's depravity) to accomplish much by way of regional mimesis. Sedgwick's second book, *Redwood* (1824), also leans on the device of a melodramatic, family-centered plot but undertakes a much more ambitious social analysis by bringing together a group of figures who comprise in microcosm the contrasts between New England, the Middle Atlantic States, and the

South, in a Lake Champlain area setting where the healthful domestic economy of a New England–style household is played off against that of a deviant, "fanatical" community, the Shakers.[24] A few years later, Sarah Hale, in *Northwood: or, Life North and South* (1827), carried Sedgwick's comparatism to greater depth with the help of the dubious plot device of having a New Hampshire country squire donate one of his sons, the hero, for adoption by his childless Carolinian in-laws. From the comparatist but still essentially Yankee perspective thereby created, Hale anatomized New England character and institutions from both an insider's and an outsider's angle of vision.[25] This design is facilitated by the return of the native, who must reacculturate himself by slow degrees. The novel includes some splendid set pieces, including one of the first and best among countless Thanksgiving Day dinner scenes in New England writing, and one of its most memorable renderings of a village social. Thanks to Sedgwick, Hale, and their contemporary John Neal (see his *Down-Easters*, 1833), the stage was set for younger writers to produce more sophisticated results. The most important novelists among these, in addition to Hawthorne and Stowe, were Sylvester Judd, author of *Margaret: A Tale of the Real and the Ideal* (1845), whose superb genre sketches and authentic use of dialect led Margaret Fuller and James Russell Lowell to acclaim this work as the first truly Yankee novel[26] and Elizabeth Stoddard, whose fiction of the 1860s, in which Hawthornian provincial gothic merges with Victorian realism, will be discussed in Chapter 16.

The staple of regional prose, however, continued to be the short sketch or tale. Hawthorne was always more secure in it than in the full-length romance, except for *The Scarlet Letter;* the plots of Hale, Judd, and Stowe were less impressive than the sums of their parts. The major local colorists of the mid- and late nineteenth century – Rose Terry Cooke, Sarah Orne Jewett, Mary Wilkins Freeman, and Rowland Robinson being the greatest – were writers of microanalyses rather than major synthetic overviews.

Even from what little has been said so far, it is clear that to represent regional prose fairly one must use conventional distinctions of genre and period with caution. The division between fictional and nonfictional prose is very indistinct here. To be sure, one can almost always make a rough classification. Take the opening lines of two installments in a newspaper series by John Neal on Yankee customs: (1) "I intend, without confining myself to time – place or connexion, to say something about New England as it was"; and (2) "It was a general opinion, that my breeches were spoilt, when I upset the dye pot."[27] The first announces itself as essay; the second, as tale. Yet the two modes overlap: The second piece is billed as an essay describing "husking," whereas the first threatens to turn into a story about the persona as a young boy. Such fluidity is to be expected from a milieu that valued the didactic, the utilitarian, and the exposition of native culture. This combination of aesthetic priorities gave support to the incorporation of an "authentic" documentary base into any fictionalized treatment of regional materials, even as it ensured that "documentary" accounts would be subject to a certain amount of fictionalization.

This interpenetration of fictive and referential elements in the literature of place also calls into question the conventional distinction between Romantic and Realistic eras. Although it is loosely accurate to label Dwight's textualization of landscape Neoclassical, Hawthorne's Romantic, and Freeman's Realistic, the boundaries are fuzzy. It is well to remind ourselves that just as Scott was the father both of historical romance and Victorian realism, so Sedgwick was the inaugurator both of the New England romantic tale and of New England local colorism.

New England regional prose, like topographical poetry, quickly generated an extensive repertoire of character types (pastors, schoolmasters, yankee peddlers, and other tricksters, jacks-of-all-trades, and ne'er-do-wells), customs (Thanksgiving, church going, huskings, commencement celebrations), and local legendry. These all have factual or at least folkloric origins, but to read the literature of place in extenso is to become quickly aware of the standardization and selectivity with which cultural bias and intertextuality derealized the "authentic" materials in the process of transmuting them into literary prose. Why were deacons so often eccentric or downright repulsive? Why is the theme of improvement in agricultural technology almost wholly absent from these regional sketches and tales? Why are bodily functions rarely mentioned? Why are there so many cases of reclusive spinsterhood? In every case the answer has to do not only with the facts of social history but also with the constraints of ideology and literary convention. The female hermit of Jewett's Shell-heap Island, in *The Country of the Pointed Firs,* reverberates backward to hundreds of domestic tales, back from there to Romantic lyrical balladry, and back from there to pre- or sub-literary folk narrative. As Warner Berthoff observes of American local colorism in general, regional mimesis "points toward an imaginative sociology that is at once objective and visionary."[28]

From the examples just given one might infer that the process of production and reading of these somewhat ritualized texts must be a rather cut-and-dried affair. Just spot the motifs, consult the motif index, and the interpretation proceeds according to formula. Nothing could be further from the truth, at least for the reader who can get beyond the stage of perceiving repetition as a simple Xeroxing process. The presence of ritualization is actually in a sense liberating, for the variety-within-standardization that it permits (the permutations being endless) and for the implication of a larger import that the act of ritualization makes. To take an easy example: In any substantial account of New England manners during our period, depiction of a Congregational worship service was a must. This device, of course, is used to dramatize provincial religiocentrism. The obsessive reiteration of this device in the literature becomes most suggestive. Its typically reverential use in *Northwood* is one of many ways in which the rhythms of New England village life are solemnized and raised from the realm of time to the level of eternal recurrence. In Judd's *Margaret,* it is used satirically: Young, rustic Margaret gawks at the preacher "perched in what looked like a high box," sits down in the section meant for blacks, immediately gets bored, and leaves. The droll and slapdash tone makes the satire seem all the more pointed in contrast to the portentousness of the usual "worship service chapter."[29] In Stowe, churchgoing scenes can be imposing, cozy, stultifying, or vaguely absurd, depending on context, and the effect in each instance is heightened for the reader who is aware of the almost inevitable prominence of worship tableaux as indices of New England ideology. In *The Minister's Wooing,* Stowe grants the Reverend Samuel Hopkins his finest hour by reinventing his tract against slavery as an eloquent homiletic performance delivered before an awed community (even though the text has previously acknowledged that he was a dry preacher with a tiny flock). Chapter 5 of *Oldtown Folks* nominally insists on the communal importance of the worship service while recording it through the eyes of a boy who finds it rather oppressive. The device of scanning and classifying parishioners, used elsewhere in Stowe and in the tradition generally to confirm the sense of the occasion's social import, here threatens despite dutiful protestations to the contrary, to turn into an image of spiritual bankruptcy. The most detailed and amusing vignette, significantly, is of a great-uncle who unconsciously but habitually disrupts the solemnity of the proceedings.

The richness of descriptive and symbolic texture in the best regional prose from Sedgwick and Hale to Judd and Stowe to Jewett and Freeman is apt to provoke the response that the documentary element is much stronger than the narrative design and thereby to put the two aspects of the work in conflict. "Beneath her tireless didacticism, one discovers a durable core of realistic observation," says a typical verdict on Stowe – implying that the sociological element is sophisticated but the plot childish.[30] There is a sound basis for this reaction: Often the plot of the regional sketch or novel does boil down to a simple affirmation or inversion of romance formulas. Yet the rind-core metaphor implies a too easy separation of parts. The situation can be illustrated by a characteristic story by Rose Terry Cooke, "'Tenty Scran,'" a biographical-anthropological study of a New England spinster from birth through orphanhood to old age. The story's strength is in its genre scenes, in the ease with which it seems, in its episodic pursuit of Tenty's career, to comprehend the community's social rituals in minutest detail.

> She went to church on Sundays in a clean calico frock and a white cape, sat in the singers' seat and uplifted her voice in Lenox and Mear, Wells and Bethesda, shared her fennel with the children in the gallery, looked out the text in her Bible, and always thought Parson Goodyear's sermon was intended for her good, and took it in accordingly.[31]

Thus the text sums up twenty years of Tenty's churchgoing in a way that suggests the narrator knows such cases thoroughly without being so entrapped in them as to lose analytical detachment. The story is also notable as one of the first (1860) to defeat the Cinderella expectation of the woman's fiction era: Tenty loses her heart to scapegrace Ned Parker, but when she gets wind of his return after twenty years of wandering she finds that she has quite recovered from the affair; and when he appears, a "coarse, red-faced, stout, sailor-like man, with a wooden leg," drinking, smoking, chewing, and cursing, she refuses him in disgust. This reversal of expectation, however, is done in the interest of another sort of sentimentalism: the presentation of Tenty as moral exemplum of virtuous frugality. She is idealized from start to finish. From early childhood, she had "her father's firm and sunny character"; her last recorded act is to spend almost all her savings to maintain worthless, alcoholic, dying Ned (anonymously, of course) in the comfort he never deserved. So, in the end, the narrator's self-proclaimed commitment to "stubborn facts" in resisting the temptation to make her heroine beautiful turns out to be so much sand in the reader's face, tied as the text is to idealizing on the moral plane.[32] "Realistic" context and wish-fulfilling fable seem to be set at odds, despite the pretense of subverting a traditional, more blatantly wish-fulfilling plot.

Yet the moral-exemplum approach to plot building here is really the corollary of the story's type of realism. We are apt to miss this point by exaggerating the extent to which local color realism strives for facticity through an objective mode of presentation. "Sarah Jewett's most distinctive quality lies in her ability to enmesh the actual touch of the countryside"; "Mary Wilkins Freeman is our most truthful recorder in fiction of New England village life"[33] – these appraisals are not wrong, but in their praise of the most salient technical aspect of regional realism they misrepresent as a process of photoduplication what is actually a process of objectification or externalization of a previously assimilated set of norms and ideals picked up not only from observation and experience but also from earlier literary models (both indigenous and foreign): Goldsmith and Mitford, Irving and Stowe, and others. Plot and setting in regional prose are both really complementary projections of a myth of provincial life conceived in "'Tenty Scran,'" quite typically, as appealingly humble, obscure, and dull, in the eyes of the world. "Nothing happened in Deerfield; so nothing happened to 'Tenty Scran.'"[34] Her career is the temporal coordinate of the same reality of which the portrayal of village mores (and Tenty's habitual routine) is the spatial coordinate. Plot and setting project the same concept of village life. The element of documentary realism, which, as noted above, becomes strongly ritualized in regional prose, rests, despite first appearances, just as much on a process of mythic abstraction as the much more obvious fable of the plot. The equivalence is broadly true not just of Cooke's stories but also of the more overtly romanticized sketches by earlier writers (such as Stowe and Lunt) and of the more unequivocally dark pastoral that follows (such as Freeman's), although the precise admixture of mythicizing abstraction varies.

As our discussion of topographical poetry has suggested, Cooke's recourse to the theme of "nothing" is hardly accidental. Like the poetry, New England regional prose is haunted by the sense of the cultural landscape that it portrays as an absence, and its authors typically desire both to exploit that absence and to transform it into its opposite. This aspect of regional prose is so complex in its sources and manifestations that it will take the remaining chapters to begin unfolding them. Here are some preliminary generalizations.

First, any sense of absence imputed to the New England landscape in the works cited in this chapter is partly to be understood in relation to another sort of absence: the departure of sizable segments of the rural population (like Tenty's errant lover) to frontiers both western and maritime, and to the city. The New England literature of place, as defined in this chapter, is inherently conservative. It is literature, for the most part, written from the standpoint of the ones who stayed behind. It is by no means always inclined to be defensive about staying put, the way Dwight, Emerson, and Thoreau are about the frivolity of footloose traveling. More often, as in Whittier, the acknowledgment of self-limitation takes the form of a sober, even mellow resoluteness tinged with a bit of melancholy. But in either case the sense of being at least nominally committed to roots in an age of rootlessness is implicit.

Particularly striking is the comparative exclusion of the city and the marks of industrialization from New England literature of place through the Civil War, especially since New England was the nation's first region to industrialize; it was economically distinct among all American culture regions precisely by reason of that development, and it was known to be such by all New England writers. Yet the preferred settings are small towns, villages, and the countryside. The rusticity of period writing, altogether, was markedly greater than that of the writers who produced it, as the analysis of residence and migration patterns in the Appendix confirms and as this chapter's second epigraph confesses. It pleased the self-rusticized Channing to stick to the fields. It pleased Hawthorne to write about Boston as premodern village, about modern Salem from the perspective not of the marketplace but of a haunted chamber. It pleased Emerson, and especially Thoreau, both of whom were living in one of the satellite towns of Boston, with the city's conveniences (such as the Harvard library and faculty) near at hand when they wanted them, to stress the pastoral seclusion of their lives.

New England literature of the period does, of course, take some account of urbanization and industrialization. In addition to famous canonical examples such as the railroad passages in *Walden* and *The House of the Seven Gables,* the Boston sequence in *The Blithedale Romance,* and the like, antebellum New England produced at the "subliterary" level a great deal of work in such urban modes as Dickensian gothic – the earlier sections of Maria Cummins' *The Lamplighter,* for example, and Harriet E. Wilson's recently discovered *Our Nig.* Their comparative absence from my book is one of its acts of repression, since to most New England imaginations during the early nineteenth century the saga of the Lowell textile mills was certainly as enthralling as the saga of Natty Bumppo.[35] Even the caustic Thoreau was not immune to its allure. Still, it is fair to say that in New England literature of the most sophisticated kind, as in British Romanticism to an even greater degree, urban settings and industrial images are conspicuous mainly through their minimization and through the tardiness with which they become a central issue for major writers (in England, with Carlyle and Dickens; in New England, with Emerson's essays of the 1850s and in Holmes's *Autocrat* prose). Up until that point, technology and the city exist mostly in parentheses, as a symbol of the social reality that Clifford and Hepzibah abortively venture into in *The House of the Seven Gables,* or as the briefly glimpsed end of the road where Stowe characters seeking to escape from provincial narrowness go to contract storybook marriages. Until that point, and indeed well beyond that, the more usual approaches to dealing with the manifest symptoms of technological and social change are either to imply them, through references to stagnation of traditional provincial culture (celebration of pastoral utopia being the opposite side of the same coin), or to exercise the same sort of sorcery on them as Wordsworth did in his Westminster Bridge sonnet, which captures London at the one moment in the day (dawn) when the city could be convincingly pastoralized.

Another challenge posed by the theme of cultural absence is the problem of determining the extent to which impoverishment can be called the heart of regional representation. As regards women local colorists, Ann Douglas has vigorously pressed this case on both textual and biographical levels, arguing that the writers' vision constitutes a retreat into privatism

and aestheticism, an acknowledgment of the defeat of feminist expectations that the sentimentalists had sought more aggressively to impose on
male-dominated society, despite their ostensible conservatism. Against
this it has been urged by Josephine Donovan that the aesthetic sophistication of the local colorists rests on a feminist vision of a realm in which
women achieve self-sufficiency and often also social control.[36] Douglas
and Donovan reason on the basis of the same literary images: a provincial
setting marked by the lack of acceptable work options, by internalized
codes of gentility, and by the dearth of men. But where Douglas looks at
this scenario and sees terminal fantasy, Donovan sees victories wrung
from defeat by a series of small-scale but heroic acts of coping.[37]

Both interpretations seem supported by a story like "'Tenty Scran,'"
which can be read either as a last-ditch attempt to salvage some consolation in a world without attractive options or as an exaltation of humble
rootedness as the basis of true "Content" (Tenty's actual name).[38] Between the early and the late nineteenth century, New England rural representation unquestionably shifted toward more overt acknowledgment
of the bucolic as backwater or cul-de-sac, yet in a sense that recognition
is there from the start, as Dwight reveals:

> Yes! let the proud despise, the rich deride,
> These humble joys, to Competence allied:
> To me, they bloom, all fragrant to my heart,
> Nor ask the pomp of wealth, nor gloss of art.[39]

That is Cooke's overt position too. Perhaps the best way to characterize
the regional position, then, is not to identify it in terms of its extremes of
celebration or defeatedness but to see it as operating out of a mediatorial
or self-divided interplay – not always at the conscious level – between
these images, and as having been stimulated most especially by the sense
of polarity. Our next analysis, of village iconography, should bear this
diagnosis out.

Finally, a few words on the larger tendency of the feminist revisionary
scholarship to which the studies of Douglas and Donovan both belong.
Both scholars concentrate on the experience of women as it bears on literary production and representation. They thereby encourage readers to
think of regional realism, and particularly local color fiction, as "A
Women's Tradition" (Donovan's subtitle) and raise the question as to
whether gender differentiations should figure more prominently than
they have done in this chapter. Perhaps they should have. It is true that
the "overwhelming majority" of the "recorders of the New England ebb-
tide were women," and likewise true that in our own day feminist scholars have been largely responsible for the rehabilitation of local colorism,
and of nineteenth-century regionalism generally, from critical neglect
through their analyses of the links among women practitioners and

through single-text explications of the more traditional sort.[40] Yet the tradition was not so overwhelmingly the domain of female writers as that of antebellum domestic fiction; the local color story represents one among various interrelated modes of regional representation, a field that looks considerably more androgynous once we survey the whole panoply; the predominance of women as producers of the best regional sketches and tales became clear-cut only after 1860. Even in late-century New England there were some first-rate male local colorists (Rowland Robinson most notably), and some of the characteristic "female" motifs of local colorism (such as the emphasis on the problem of coping with emotional isolation in the context of economic, physical, or psychic entrapment) have male counterparts.[41] Clifford Pyncheon is just as typical a product of the New England regional vision as his sister Hepzibah, even though the Hepzibahs outnumbered the Cliffords in both literature and life. So although I agree that the conception of social reality that underlay New England regional poetry and prose lent itself to feminist appropriation and became, in the postwar era, increasingly a women's construct, the next chapters will treat provincial literary iconography as a project in which writers of the two sexes participated together.

13

The Village as Icon

> in every village, smil'd
> The heav'n-inviting church, and every town
> A world within itself . . .
> Timothy Dwight, *Greenfield Hill* (1794)

> The charming thing – if that be the best way to take it – is that the scene is everywhere the same. . . . These communities stray so little from the type, that you often ask yourself by what sign or difference you know one from the other.
> Henry James, *The American Scene* (1907)

When New Englanders of our period pictured the cultural geography of their region in their mind's eye, the first thing they thought they saw was a patchwork of largely rural "towns" (i.e., townships) – small, self-contained, preindustrial districts, agricultural or maritime, dotted with hamlets and with a central village as the social and economic hub. The following portrait, from Harriet Beecher Stowe's first important publication, is one of many:

> Did you ever see the little village of Newbury, in New England? I dare say you never did; for it was just one of those out of the way places where nobody came unless they came on purpose: a green little hollow, wedged like a bird's nest between half a dozen high hills, that kept off the wind and kept out foreigners; so that the little place was as straitly *sui generis* as if there were not another in the world. The inhabitants were all of that respectable old standfast family who make it a point to be born, bred, married, to die, and be buried all in the selfsame spot. There were just so many houses, and just so many people lived in them; and nobody ever seemed to be sick, or to die either, at least while I was there. The natives grew old till they could not grow any older, and then they stood still, and *lasted* from generation to generation. There was, too, an unchangeability about all the externals of Newbury. Here was

a red house, and there was a brown house, and across the way was a yellow house; and there was a straggling rail fence or a tribe of mullein stalks between. The minister lived here, and 'Squire Moses lived there, and Deacon Hart lived under the hill, and Messrs. Nadab and Abihu Peters lived by the crossroad, and the old "widder" Smith lived by the meeting house, and Ebenezer Camp kept a shoemaker's shop on one side, and Patience Mosely kept a milliner's shop in front; and there was old Comfort Scran, who kept store for the whole town, and sold axe heads, brass thimbles, licorice balls, fancy handkerchiefs, and everything else you can think of. Here, too, was the general post office, where you might see letters marvellously folded, directed wrong side upward, stamped with a thimble, and superscribed to some of the Dollys, or Pollys, or Peters, or Moseses aforenamed or not named.

For the rest, as to manners, morals, arts, and sciences, the people in Newbury always went to their parties at three o'clock in the afternoon, and came home before dark; always stopped all work the minute the sun was down on Saturday night; always went to meeting on Sunday; had a school house with all the ordinary inconveniences; were in neighborly charity with each other; read in their Bibles, feared their God, and were content with such things as they had – the best philosophy, after all.[1]

Its modern editor rightly calls the piece from which this passage comes (originally titled "A New England Sketch") the "foundation of Mrs. Stowe's literary career."[2] Essentially the same image is rerun as Oldtown and Poganuc. Indeed, it appears throughout New England literature, from Dwight's *Greenfield Hill* through Thornton Wilder's *Our Town* and beyond.[3] Although Stowe had much to do with its perpetuation, there is no question of originality here. The landscape described, as in most of the best New England village literature, was based partly on life models that the author had intimately experienced and to which she gave some original twists, but it was, by the same token, a communal product – a product of village culture, on the one hand, and of Anglo-American literary imagings of that culture, on the other. We understand literary depictions of the New England village best if we approach them at once semiologically, as a codification of a repertoire of motifs built up over time, and mimetically, as referring to a historical reality, however transmuted that reality may have been in the process of literary embodiment. Likewise, the broadest significance of Stowe's New England village iconography lies in the twin facts of the persistence and dissemination of the small town as a social model and as a literary and mythic image – thanks partly to New England influence, in each case – throughout much of America as a whole.[4] To study the cult of the New England village is to study the most distinctively New Englandish contribution to the American social ideal.

The salient features of Stowe's fictional community seem to be these. The village is a self-contained unit, sheltered from the outside world and organically interdependent: a bird's nest shielded from wind and "foreigners." That is why it can seem sui geueris even while being patently generic. It is ethnically homogeneous and institutionally stable: the population stays the same; the houses stay the same color; nobody leaves; nobody even dies. The social structure is simple, headed by the minister (always mentioned first in such catalogs, just as sabbath keeping is one of the main cultural activities mentioned and most of the characters are given scriptural names.) The list of personages is short and humble; one store sells everything; town industry is limited to a few traditional trades. The social life is innocent and low-key. The town closes up at night. The conventionalism of these traits is suggested by their presence in the texts cited in Chapter 12, especially Cooke's "'Tenty Scran,'" in which the main thing to be said about the village where the action "happens" is that nothing happens there.

Stowe's bird's-eye view in her sketch of the New England village is too hasty to include the entire roster of conventional motifs. Had it been extended, as it is in her novels, the meetinghouse and school would have been described in detail, along with the local minister and schoolmaster, life in a representative village home (gentry or prosperous farmers preferred), and such communal rituals as sabbath observance and Thanksgiving, possibly also Independence Day and Election Day celebrations. The manners of the rural inhabitants would have been described, with emphasis on their simple, thrifty industriousness, as well as their piety and its secularized mutations (for better and for worse) into conscientious do-gooderism and pig-headed willfulness. A quilting, a tea party, a husking bee, or a dance might have been shown. Some further attention would also have been given to the physical environment, particularly the hills and local river (if the town were inland), the seacoast (if the town were a port), and the changing of the seasons. But the traits Stowe emphasizes of smallness, isolation, cohesiveness, innocence, and unchangingness are central, and understandably so. For these traits constituted those actual elements of traditional village life that lent themselves most readily to the pastoralizing tendency that affected almost all literary portrayals in different degrees and for different reasons (the main ones being nostalgia, fear that the village system might change, and awareness that it was in the process of changing) and that was the primary source of difference between literary image and actual model.

A bare catalog of motifs conveys neither the litanylike mesmeric effect of their reiteration in New England writing nor the subtlety of the variations. As an example, consider the motif of the great, ancient tree that functions as a community's spiritual center. Like all other obsessive motifs in village portraiture, this tree figure involves both a codification of social reality and the reincarnation of archetypal symbolism, in this case the symbol of the tree of life. The first historical marker that caught my eye upon moving years ago to Oberlin, Ohio, a "classic example of the transplanted New England community,"[5] was a plaque on a small, circular, fenced-in plot at the exact center of the town commemorating the "Oberlin Elm," the site of the first dwelling and the symbol of local prosperity and cohesiveness – until Dutch elm blight caught up with it in the 1960s. The same iconography had been at work for more than a century in New England topographical writing. Sometimes the subject is a chestnut tree, like the one in Longfellow's "Village Blacksmith" or Royall Tyler's most ambitious poem, "The Chestnut Tree," a visionary sketch of Brattleboro East Village down to about A.D. 2000, that uses the tree image as a metaphor of communal growth from a "misshapen seed" planted by the poet himself to a developed community where the literal tree becomes a favorite place of resort. Children climb it; courtships take place there; the sick sit by it for refreshment. As the poem unfolds, the tree becomes temporarily eclipsed by the poet's interest in the social scene, but he returns to it at last with new eyes, praying that he himself may, "like that tree of Life Divine," grow in grace and "bloom in Immortal verdure" in the hereafter.[6]

Elsewhere, oak trees, like Connecticut's Charter Oak or the oak under which Puritan missionary John Eliot supposedly preached to the Indians, are given similar mythic significance. But most often the totem tree is an elm, elms being above all other trees the "peculiar glory of New England," in the opinion of most self-appointed judges of the matter. "Nobody knows New England," says the omniscient narrator of Holmes's *Elsie Venner*, "who is not on terms of intimacy with one of its elms. The elm comes nearer to having a soul than any other vegetable creature among us."[7] The elm tree lyric was a flourishing branch of nineteenth-century New England descriptive verse. The most famous subject was the Cambridge Elm, under which Washington took command of the Revolutionary forces. Lydia Sigourney personified it as a "vigorous heart" with "sleepless memories of the days that were," "giving utterance to the mighty past" in a monitory speech to future generations; James Russell Lowell made the incident the subject of his centennial poem "Under the Old Elm"; Oliver Wendell Holmes invoked it in 1861 as a rallying cry for the Union cause.[8] But the Cambridge Elm was by no means unique in its filiopietistic resonances. No less important was the "sacred elm" on the Boston Common, which, during the Revolution, as Catherine Albanese remarks, "became a kind of transcendent cosmo-historical tree around which the other Liberty Trees and liberty signs of the colonies took root."[9] Another was the "Old Elm of Newbury," praised by local poet Hannah Gould.[10] Still another was the fictional "vast elm" of Henry Ward Beecher's *Norwood*. Beecher begins and ends his novel with reference to New England elm trees – "As much a part of her beauty as the columns of the Parthenon were the glory of its architecture," and emblematic as well:

> Their towering trunks, whose massiveness well symbolizes Puritan inflexibility; their over-arching tops, facile, wind-borne and elastic, hint the endless plasticity and adaptableness of this people; – and both united, form a type of all true manhood, broad at the root, firm in the trunk, and yielding at the top, yet returning again, after every impulse, into position and symmetry.[11]

This passage shows the ripening of several generations of patriotic geography into a more fully developed myth of place. Note that Beecher assumes both the regional particularity and the prototypical quality of the traits that the elm and the region have in common: The trees "form a type of all true manhood," not just that of the Puritan and Yankee. So too his sister, in the earlier passage, stresses that the Newburyites have the "best philosophy, after all." This confidence of centrality within the cosmos is one of the distinctive marks of the New England brand of regionalism.

Contemporary local historians made the same appraisal – a correspondence that can be taken either as an argument for the historical accuracy of the literature or for the susceptibility of both genres to deformation under ideological pressure. A good example, for comparative purposes, is the southern Connecticut town of Ridgefield, for which we have an old-style late nineteenth-century antiquarian documentary history by Daniel W. Teller, as well as two other detailed accounts dating from 1800 (by the Reverend Samuel Goodrich, the Congregational minister there) and from 1855–6 (by his son, Samuel Griswold Goodrich ["Peter Parley"]), the latter including both a boyhood reminiscence and impressions of an 1855 visit to his hometown.[12] This material suggests that the conventional descriptive motifs of village literature were grounded in a late eighteenth-century preindustrial reality that changed significantly during the nineteenth century but at a pace that was in many communities sufficiently gradual to permit the onlooker to picture them in terms of the old order that was passing, rather than the new order that was coming to pass.[13]

In most details, the Ridgefield of Teller and the Goodriches conforms to Stowe's fictional Newbury, though the Goodriches are less glowing ("Our little town has not much to boast of superior genius or intellects") and have much more to say about the community's agricultural base.[14] Ridgefield, a township of approximately 2,000 souls, contained only three foreigners and two nonwhites at the start of the nineteenth century; none of the inhabitants, reports the senior Goodrich, has ever committed a capital crime; the town poor "do not exceed 10 or 12"; the climate is "exceedingly salubrious," the town being on high ground in hilly country, if not exactly a bird's nest among mountain peaks; the meetinghouse is the most prominent building; two sects, the Episcopalians and the Methodists, compete with the Congregationalists, but both are puny by comparison. Local manners, the younger Goodrich recollected, were marked by piety, "homeliness[,] and simplicity."[15]

Returning in 1855, Samuel Griswold Goodrich found Rigefield considerably beautified and modernized: "In all parts of the town I was struck with the evidences of change," so that the visit reinforced his prior conviction that the "inherent tendency of our New England society is to improvement." At the same time, despite his desire to emphasize the "tide of progress" theme, Goodrich noted no basic institutional changes except the rise of Methodism. The population was about the same; the ethnic composition was apparently about the same; the village was still a country town, which the railroad had not yet reached; the local tavern served blackberry and huckleberry pies "just such as our mother made fifty years ago," while in the Congregational church the Confession and Covenant of 1750 were "still in force, just as our father left them." The changes that the younger Goodrich reports are uniformly in the direction of consolidating what were already New England values in 1800: moral respectability (drunkenness, sabbath breaking, and swearing, once "common, are now almost wholly unknown"), better education, financial independence, and prosperity (many fewer farmers in debt). The official town historian likewise sees little change during the period.[16]

The younger Goodrich's testimony as to the condition of Ridgefield in 1855 is especially arresting because his explicit theme is change, rather than continuity (with much wry emphasis on his Rip Van Winkleish disorientation at the sight of new faces, new buildings, a remodeled church, and other innovations), and yet it is clear that the greatest pleasure he takes in the town's prosperity arises from being able to conclude that it consists in preservation and purification of traditional institutions and values. This, of course, is wishful thinking, a substitution of the part for the whole. Goodrich sees and approves, for instance, the moral reforms that occurred throughout New England in the years after his father's sketch was written (the temperance movement made great gains against the problem of alcoholism, and church attendance greatly increased), but he omits mention of the economic shifts (e.g., the revolution in transportation that gave Ridgefield farmers better access to markets) that were more fundamentally responsible for material prosperity and that in the long run threatened village integrity. Thus Goodrich is able to proclaim the enduringness of the village as a sociocultural unit and moral institution, as well as his progressivism, consigning all significant elements of change to the moral rather than the socioeconomic sphere. Goodrich re-writes as history the same scenario that Sylvester Judd, in *Margaret,* pre-sents as utopian fantasy: transformation by moral regeneration and intel-lectual enlightment within the limits of a very traditional vision of preindustrial village society that the author desires to purify but not to scrap.

Stowe's Newbury, then, corresponds to a perceived social reality for which there was enough empirical evidence and consensus acceptance to sustain belief throughout our period, not only for fictional purposes but for purposes of documentary prose as well. On the other hand, both Newbury and the Goodriches' Ridgefield are compensatory mythic im-ages. As Stowe herself clearly realizes,

> There were just so many houses, and just so many people lived in them; and nobody ever seemed to be sick, or to die either, at least while I was there. The natives grew old till they could not grow any older, and then they stood still, and *lasted* from generation to generation.

Particularly in the second sentence, the passage uses a playfully exagger-ated, tall-tale manner, calling attention to the fact that what is being im-aged is not the village itself but the cosmopolitan visitor's sense of the town as peculiarly stable. The description of Newbury most obviously calls attention to itself as a fantasy construct, interestingly, at the point where Stowe most obviously suppresses key historical information sup-plied in more factual accounts such as those of the Goodriches. The issue in question is population mobility, the high rate of out-migration. That is what kept the population from increasing in Ridgefield and other iso-lated upland communities in Connecticut, as Stowe well knew, having been, not so long before, an emigrant from Newbury's prototype, Litch-field. Her sketch shows the emigrant's need to believe in the existence of a constant reference point, as does the younger Goodrich's sketch of Ridgefield, although in his case this need is subordinated to the equally strong American impulse to associate one's hometown with the great ideal of progress (which Goodrich saw himself as having furthered). He too signals that there is an element of fictionality in his verbal recreation of the "'sweet Auburn' of my young fancy."[17]

This metafictional dimension in Stowe and Goodrich reflects a prob-lem of split allegiance. They are charmed by the village ideal and their memories of life there; but they themselves have outgrown it and belong to a larger world, although they find it pleasant to imagine the possibility of returning to it at last. Two of Hawthorne's minor tales in the same vein feature a narrator who finds his stuffy, boorish native village suddenly beautiful when he contemplates it from a distance: "'Why have I never loved my home before?' thought I, as my spirit reposed itself on the quiet beauty of the scene."[18] Up close it is not so attractive. Indeed Hawthorne first broke into print with a sketch of the Stowe-Goodrich type of village that exhibited this same sort of ambivalence. Here is his description of the setting of Harley College, in *Fanshawe:*

> The local situation of the College, so far secluded from the sight and sound of the busy world, is peculiarly favorable to the moral, if not to the literary habits of its students; and this advantage probably caused the founders to overlook the inconveniences that were inseparably connected with it. The humber edifices rear themselves almost at the farthest extremity of a narrow vale, which, winding through a long extent of hill-country, is well-nigh as inaccessible, except at one point, as the Happy Valley of Abyssinia. A stream, that farther on becomes a considerable river, takes its rise at a short distance above the college, and affords, along its wood-fringed banks, many shady retreats, where even study is pleasant, and idleness delicious. The neighborhood of the institution is not quite a solitude, though the few habitations scarcely constitute a village. . . . The character of the inhabitants does not seem . . . to be in any degree influenced by the atmosphere of Harley College. They are a set of rough and hardy yeoman, much inferior, as respects refinement, to the corresponding classes in most other parts of the country. This is the more remarkable, as there is scarcely a family in the vicinity that has not provided, for at least one of its sons, the advantages of a "liberal education." [*HW* 3:334]

Like the young Stowe, the young Hawthorne runs down the repertoire of already familiar motifs, with special emphasis, in this case, on the contrast between educational goals, supposedly prized in New England, and their actual embodiment in both college and community. Hawthorne's sketch, like those of Stowe and Goodrich, mixes the affectionate and the ironic but is more bittersweet overall. The seclusion of this Happy Valley (a common analogy, during the period, between the New England town and Johnson's *Rasselas*) is idyllic yet confining, like the Johnsonian original. The rural atmosphere is pleasant, but more conducive to idleness than to study; the cultural life is nil; the pretensions of the small college community are gently travestied in this first among American academic novels.

The examples cited so far begin to suggest the wide range of tones with which the New England community was depicted during our period. These vary from the eulogistic to the witheringly satirical. At the one extreme we have Dwight's Greenfield; at the other, Elizabeth Stoddard's New Bedford ("The literary miasma in the atmosphere . . . is never powerful enough to agitate the brains of its natives" [*MOW* 319–20]) or the Hanover of the following anonymous Federalist era poem:

> A CHAPEL, meetinghouse, and college,
> Crammed with every thing – but knowledge;
> . . . .

A crazy academick dome,
That painted will be time to come;
An Indian school and printing press,
For making news and novices;
One money catching tavern keeper,
Another without meat or liquor;
. . . .
One poet, quondam priest, and proctor,
One wooden legged trepanning doctor;
One painter, one apothecary;
A dozen girls who *long to marry;*
Two lawyers who bewrack their wits,
To swell their purse by drawing writs;
Three pious justices to sign 'em,
Three barbers, shops – with blockheads in 'em;
. . . .
Say is this Boston, York or Rome?
No faith, I guess tis nearer home.[19]

Sometimes the same author uses the two wavelengths in alternation or even within the same work. Thus Royall Tyler fulsomely eulogizes Brattleboro in one poem ("Of all New England's lovely spots, the loveliest, I ween") and in another spoofs small-town boorishness,[20] whereas in *The Contrast* the provincial as gentleman (Colonel Manly) is juxtaposed with the provincial as bumpkin (his servant Jonathan). This two-track approach, artificial in itself, is not simply a reflection of Neoclassical decorum, which routinely called for sharp tonal distinctions according to genre (pastoral lyric versus hudibrastic genre sketch) or character type (gentry versus plebeian); it also indicates the writers' ambivalent attitude toward the village as an institution, which on the one hand appealed to Yankee sensibilities as a utopian model of millennial promise yet, partly by reason of the mood of expectancy that this created, lent itself to satirical exposés of the unattractiveness of actual villages and the ease with which second-rate minds could slip into confusing the ideal with actuality.

An especially good example of the complex mentality that I am describing is New England's first distinguished historian of the period, Jeremy Belknap. At the end of his *History of New-Hampshire* is a well-known passage painting a "picture of happy society," an idealized Yankee village *à la* Stowe:

> . . . a town consisting of a due mixture of hills, valleys and streams of water: The land well fenced and cultivated. . . . The inhabitants mostly husbandmen; their wives and daughters domestic manufacturers; a suitable proportion of handicraft workmen, and two or three traders; a physician and a lawyer. . . . A clergyman of any denomination, which

should be agreeable to the majority. . . . A school master. . . . A social library. . . . A club of sensible men, seeking mutual improvement.[21]

Belknap's actual experience of living in a New Hampshire town, however, had been quite the reverse. His pastorate in Dover (from whence he had recently fled to Boston) was one long exile for him, relieved by his capacity for grim amusement at local small-mindedness. He conceived it "one of the greatest misfortunes of my life to be obliged to rear a family of children in a place and among a people where insensibility to the interests of the rising generation, and an inveterate antipathy to literature, are to be reckoned among the prevailing vices; where there is not so much public spirit as to build a school-house; where men of the first rank let their children grow up uncultivated as weeds on the highway."[22] Even Timothy Dwight, ordinarily a booster of small New England towns, thought Dover a dreary-looking place (*DT* 1:305). Belknap held to the village ideal, then, in spite of actuality and indeed might have been all the more inclined to be severe on the latter because of its betrayal of the ideal. The natural result was that Belknap, like Tyler, wrote at different times on quite different mimetic levels. We see the same thing a generation later in another depiction of a New Hampshire town by another refugee who fled to Boston, Sarah Hale, whose novel *Northwood* starts by insisting that Belknap might have cited her imaginary town as an illustration of his happy society,[23] although later she chides the stinginess of the local deacon and the perfidy of the postmaster.

When New England writers juxtaposed images of the real and ideal, the effect was not, however, always to critique the former in the name of the latter. The relationship was more complicated than that. Take, for instance, Sylvester Judd's minor classic *Margaret: A Tale of the Real and the Ideal* (1845), considered in its own day the best fictional portrait of rural New England manners to date. On one level, the book has a tractarian purpose: to portray the moral reform wrought by liberal religion in a New England village between the end of the eighteenth century (which Judd's contemporaries often viewed as a moral and spiritual low point in New England) and Judd's own time. Yet Judd also clearly relishes the spectacle of the town of Livingston (modeled on his native Westhampton, Massachusetts) in its unregenerate state: its drinking bouts, sabbath breakings, and petty squabbles. In one amusing scene, a preacher tries unsuccessfully to break up a Thanksgiving Day dance:

> "Thus saith the Lord God, thy pomp shall be brought down to the grave, and the noise of thy viols!"
>
> "A sermon! a sermon!" cried Abel Wilcox.
>
> *Preacher.* "You look fair and seemly, but you are stench in the nostrils of the Almighty."

Crowd. "Another set, who'll lead off?"

Preacher. "The Lord will take the bravery of your tinkling ornaments, your cauls and round tires [tiaras] like the moon, your chains and bracelets and mufflers."

Pluck [Margaret's father]. "Let us praise God in the dance, praise him with the stringed instrument. Let us, as David did, dance before the Lord."

Preacher. "This place shall be as God overthrew Sodom and Gomorrah; owls shall dwell here, and satyrs shall dance here."

Crowd. "Peggy and Molly!" "The Haymakers," "Here's Zenas Joy and Delinda Hoag want 'Come haste to the Wedding!'"

Preacher. "You stand on slippery places, your feet shall stumble on the dark mountains."

Crowd. "Chorus Jig! Hoa!" [24]

Conceivably some readers might have taken this passage as serious satire against doctrinaire Calvinism, here shown as provoking the populace to further mindlessness and blasphemy in what would otherwise be an innocent if frivolous amusement. But surely this is not so much satire as a comedy of cross-purposes more amusing than judgmental. Such is the first two-thirds of *Margaret,* for the most part: a series of colorful genre sketches, often with comic heightening of the contrast between pious cant and lay rowdiness to increase our sense of the ludicrous. As a *minister*-author, Judd's literary aim was didactic; as a minister-*author* his chief delight was in the recreation of "primitive" New England manners. Richard Hathaway is correct in asserting that Judd was "uncertain whether he was writing an attack on the Calvinistic village of his boyhood or a nostalgic reminiscence." [25] The conclusion toward which the book works – the regeneration of the community through the enlightened gospel of Mr. Evelyn – seems to define *Margaret* as committed to the conception of the New England village as millennial utopia attainable through the purgation of local vices created by the corrupt and obsolete Calvinist ideology. But the novel takes and imparts such delight in this local rowdiness as to make the ideal toward which it eventually works seem as restrictive and effete, in its own way, as that of the Calvinist preacher in the dance scene. *Margaret* is reduced to an aesthetic muddle because Judd's literary and doctrinal bents were not fully in touch with each other. Stylistically speaking, the source of energy in Judd's prose (like that in Emerson's as appraised in Chapter 6), lies in the interplay of speech levels (which may also be the reason why it delighted James Russell Lowell), and this in turn connotes a larger ideological conflict between the earthy real and the polite ideal. [26] Judd finally capitalizes on this when juxtaposing Calvinist dogmatics and popular behavior, but he has less tolerance than Emerson – not to mention Thoreau – for discourse and ideology in which the real remains incompletely assimilated into the ideal. So, in the end, he must betray the impulse that led him to seek the natural as distinct from the dogmatic by reidealizing it, on both the linguistic and the doctrinal levels, into a new vision of village order. The vision, for all its loving-kindness, seems, after the sprightliness of what has come before, an even more primly totalitarian imposition than the old order, which for all its brimstone – or, indeed, because of it – was so delightfully vivid and ungenteel.

In Oliver Wendell Holmes's regional fiction, the contrast and interplay of mimetic levels are handled with less force than in *Margaret* but also with more subtlety and control. Anyone familiar with such works as Teller's *History of Ridgefield* will appreciate the cleverness of this passage from *Elsie Venner* (1861). It begins with a "quotation" from the imaginary history of Pigwacket, by the Reverend Jabez Grubb.

> "The situation of Pigwacket is eminently beautiful, looking down the lovely valley of Mink River, a tributary of the Musquash. The air is salubrious, and many of the inhabitants have attained great age, several having passed the allotted period of 'threescore years and ten' before succumbing to any of the various 'ills that flesh is heir to.' Widow Comfort Leevins died in 1836, Aet. LXXXVII. years. Venus, an African, died in 1841, supposed to be C. years old. The people are distinguished for intelligence, as has been frequently remarked by eminent lyceum-lecturers, who have invariably spoken in the highest terms of a Pigwacket audience. There is a public library, containing nearly a hundred volumes, free to all subscribers. The preached word is well attended, there is a flourishing temperance society, and the schools are excellent. It is a residence admirably adapted to refined families who relish the beauties of Nature and the charms of society. . . ."
>
> That is the way they all talk. After all, it is probably pretty much like other inland New England towns in point of "salubrity," – that is, gives people their choice of dysentery or fever every autumn, with a season-ticket for consumption, good all the year round. And so of the other pretenses. "Pigwacket audience," forsooth! Was there ever an audience anywhere, though there was n't a pair of eyes in it brighter than pickled oysters, that did n't think it was "distinguished for intelligence"? – "The preachèd word"! That means the Rev. Jabez Grubb's sermons.[27]

This genial bluffness partly conceals, partly suggests the fact that Holmes himself was quite capable of invoking hoary New England stereotypes when the time came to write Civil War battle hymns or celebrate Whittier's birthday. Holmes was both a cosmopolitan urbanite who surveyed the quaintness of provincial manners from the safe distance of Cambridge and a dyed-in-the-wool New England ethnic, who, never having been trapped in late eighteenth-century Dover, New Hampshire, could not only take for granted the longevity of village institutions but regard them with amused indulgence rather than antipathy. Although *Elsie Venner* serves, like *Margaret,* as a vehicle for liberal consciousness raising (the target in this case being not simply Calvinism but theological frameworks in general), Holmes is not so rash as to attempt to transform the flesh-and-blood community into mere utopia. The reason for the difference may be partly that Holmes is more realistic, less susceptible to the vision of New England village life as a possible ideal; but also it may be partly that, in another sense, he has seen the village as a sort of utopia all along – as a realm unalterably innocent by reason of its very small-mindedness. The Reverend Jabez Grubb's prose, for instance, is charming, rather than obnoxious, because it is totally unaware of its own banality. This urbane indulgence of the village mentality as deliciously lilliputian shows that Holmes takes the village as prospective social model much less seriously than does Judd. The two villages of the novel, Pigwacket and Rockland, finally interest Holmes not as subjects but as backcountry settings into which his Harvard medical student hero – ultimately destined for much bigger things – ventures in an archetypal pattern of exile and return, in order to encounter nineteenth-century equivalents of the traditional epic military and amatory ordeals.

The contrast between Judd and Holmes is another instance of the contrast noted in Chapter 11 between the culture of Connecticut Valley Congregationalism and that of the Arminian coastal enclaves. From the perspective of the latter, urbanization and industrialization had advanced so far by midcentury that backcountry villages were reduced to the status of literary games or summer retreats. The contrast also suggests the directions that New England regionalism was to take in the late nineteenth century. Like Judd, Jewett, and Freeman, Rowland and Edwin Arlington Robinson were products of village culture; but like Holmes they saw village life as existing outside the cultural mainstream in an autumnal state that excluded, for better and for worse, the possibility of social transformation. Stimulated by this conception, their work carries to new heights of sophistication such devices as the cosmopolitan observer figure (especially well exemplified by the device of the narrator in Jewett's *Country of the Pointed Firs,* with her bewitchment by the world of Dunnet's Landing and by her hostess, Mrs. Todd) and the ritualization of community life (increasingly seen as decadent or entrapping but all the more fascinating thereby for its intricacy and the tortuous emotional blocks and complications it creates for those dwelling within it.)

Such achievements of late-century regionalism are, as noted earlier, most obviously explainable in terms of shifts in the economic and cultural milieu of late nineteenth-century rural New England.[28] Yet the image of the village as cultural wasteland existed before the full development of the image of the ideal village, as Sedgwick's aggressively antiprovincial *New-England Tale* makes clear. The dark pastoral of much regional realism was not simply a revolt against the by-and-large more idealizing portraiture of earlier eras but a highlighting of an element that had been part of the repertoire of village iconography almost from the start, thanks to Neoclassical, and later to anti-Calvinist, urbanity.

Indeed, at one time or another every cherished New England village trait celebrated in silver-tongued oratory had been exposed elsewhere as euphemistic. Take the supposed egalitarianism of the New England village, often celebrated as a "more perfect democracy than ever existed at Athens." "You would hardly have noticed there was a higher and a lower class," declared Samuel G. Goodrich of turn-of-the-century Ridgefield. Yet Dwight, in *Greenfield Hill,* had made clear that Connecticut's social stability was built on patterns of deference, patterns that Stowe later spelled out. The reputation of the village for egalitarianism, like the reputation of the Puritans as harbingers of civil and religious liberty, quickly led to a debunking tradition that focused on harsh treatment of the town poor and other marginal folk. As one poet bitterly wrote:

> Bury him there –
> No matter where!
> None by his death are bereft;
> Stopping to pray?
> Shovel away!
> We still have enough of them left.[29]

Again, take the theme of schooling. No regional piety led to a richer vein of satirical undercutting than the supposed value of education in New England. New Englanders loved to boast about the latter. "Literature," affirmed Sarah Hale, "is the star and garter of a Yankee." "The nearest approach to a line drawn between the common people and an aristocratic class in New England is that which education furnishes," declared Henry Ward Beecher. At least ideally, and sometimes even in practice, the schoolmaster was an important and respected local figure, part of the town gentry:

> His useful days in learning's toil were spent,
> And all his mind to youth's improvement lent.
> His scholars loved him for his gentle skill,
> And their soft minds were moulded to his will.[30]

Such a figure was Master James Benton, the hero of Stowe's "Uncle Lot"; such a figure, if tradition does not lie, was Henry Thoreau's brother John; to such a role Bronson Alcott aspired. Yet New Englanders were also quite sensitive to the fact that district schoolhouses were apt to be "little, mean shanties, built in the cheapest possible manner"; that schoolteachers were apt either to be mediocre charlatans like Irving's Ichabod Crane or Judd's bibulous Bartholomew Elliman, or incompetents like Royall Tyler's Updike Underhill, whose main qualification for his job was an inordinate love of Greek that made him give "Greek names to all our farming tools, and cheer the cattle with hexameter verse." Even Dwight equipped his nearly utopian Greenfield with a lackluster pedagogue: "Little he knew, though much he wish'd to know"; "Many his faults; his virtues small, and few; / Some little good he did, or strove to do."[31]

As a result of this double vision, New England village iconography illustrates Emerson's advice to the aspiring stylist: "Everything has two handles" (i.e., is susceptible to stylized overstatement and stylized understatement), and the effective rhetorician makes full use of both (*EW* 12:300). The conceptualizations of the village as utopia and the village as backwater developed symbiotically during our period, the balance finally shifting decisively from the first to the second not simply as a function of economic and cultural change but also as a result of the fact that village culture had been "done" to the point of cliché. The theme of enclosure in late-century regional realism probably arose from a sense of a literary as well as a cultural déjà vu about the patterning of the behavior depicted. At the same time, late-century regionalism found in this very patterning – in one respect the sign of cultural stagnation – a sort of compensation for the loss of the utopian spirit, insofar as it could bring itself to see ritual behavior as sacred, not just stultifying, or insofar as extreme ritualization could be seen as giving even tiny acts of rebelliousness or deviation (such as the flight of an old woman from the town poorhouse) a kind of heroic grandeur. These resources too preexisted in regionalist tradition, as we shall see in the next chapter: The steadiness of New England habits was for Dwight one of the great incentives to think of the village as utopia, and the symbolic importance of small forms of dissent was one of the consolations of village life for Thoreau. Approached as a matched pair, Dwight and Thoreau, as the chief Neoclassical and Romantic expositor-critics of New England village culture, will give us a better idea of both the directional movement of village iconography and its constants.

14

Lococentrism from Dwight to Thoreau

> What are the rivers around Damascus to this river sleeping around Concord? Are not the Musketaquid and the Assabet, rivers of Concord, fairer than the rivers of the plain?
>
> > Henry David Thoreau, *Journal* (1853)

> I believe that some of our New England villages within thirty miles of Boston are as boorish and barbarous communities as there are on the face of the earth.
>
> > Henry David Thoreau, *Journal* (1851)

The most extensive literary accounts of the New England landscape produced during our period were those of Timothy Dwight and Henry Thoreau. Dwight's poem *Greenfield Hill* celebrates his parish as the prototypical New England town; his posthumously published *Travels in New-England and New-York* (4 vols., 1821–2) moves from microcosm to macrocosm, recording some eighteen thousand miles of vacation journeys and semisystematic background reading undertaken over a twenty-year period (1796–1815) when Dwight was president of Yale. Thoreau's even more prolific contribution consists, in addition to his multivolume *Journal,* of five more specialized books of travels both literal and metaphorical, as well as sundry essays on excursions and natural-history topics.[1]

The apparent irreconcilability of their visions of New England makes Dwight and Thoreau an especially interesting pair. If Dwight has a unifying theme in his *Travels,* that theme is the nobility and soundness of the beliefs and institutions established by the Puritan saints and bequeathed to their progeny with minor modifications. If Dwight has a plot, that plot is the astonishingly rapid triumph of the civilizing process, which he rightly insists is a "novelty in the history of man. The colonization of a wilderness by civilized men, where a regular government, mild manners,

319

arts, learning, science, and Christianity have been interwoven in its progress from the beginning, is a state of things of which . . . the records of
past ages furnish neither an example, nor a resemblance" (*DT* 1:6). Thoreau, by contrast, delighted in what Joan Burbick aptly calls "counter-
history," which "breaks the mold of civilized time" and exposes the
parochial quality of New England filiopietism by putting the Indians on
the same footing of respect as the Pilgrims and by playing off the Hindu
scriptures against the Bible.[2] He was resolutely anticlerical, if not anti-
religious. Thoreau instinctively satirizes the march of progress, despite
occasional tributes to commerce and typically American gestures of
trying to accommodate the machine by naturalizing it.[3] "Convinced that
my genius dates from an older era than the agricultural,"[4] Thoreau spe-
cializes in describing those tracts of New England where civilization has
not reached, which time has passed by, or where something like wilderness can be found within the boundaries of settled society. Dwight likes
to portray leading citizens in his character sketches; Thoreau favors socially marginal types: woodchoppers, Indian guides, retired oystermen.

Such differences correlate with the writers' real and perceived social
status (Dwight the establishmentarian, Thoreau the maverick who refused to assume the occupational and social responsibilities expected of a
Harvard graduate) and with the difference between Neoclassical and Romantic ethos (Dwight, the public spokesman, for whom civilization and
order are inherently superior to the state of nature, however picturesque;
Thoreau, the visionary, for whom the values of civilization are inherently
problematic and the state of nature a standard against which to measure
them). These ideological contrasts make the two writers seem even more
different than they actually were. We have seen, for example, that Dwight
had considerable sensitivity to landscape but that his sense of propriety
kept him from doing much more than pile up interchangeable banalities
like "The valley is every where romantic" and "I saw here a beautiful
object" (*DT* 2:260, 279).[5]

Thoreau's impatience with this approach comes out in a passage in
Cape Cod where he snorts at an unnamed Dwight-like characterization of
Sandwich as a beautiful village:

> Our villages will bear to be contrasted only with one another, not with
> nature. I have no great respect for the writer's taste, who talks easily
> about *beautiful* villages, embellished perchance, with a "fulling-mill,"
> "a handsome academy," or a meeting-house, and "a number of shops
> for the different mechanic arts;" where the green and white houses of
> the gentry, drawn up in rows, front on a street of which it would be
> difficult to tell whether it is most like a desert or a long stable-yard.[6]

Yet Thoreau did use Dwight's *Travels* and lesser such compendiums as his
travel guides, and apart from that we can detect a number of resemblances

in their manner of conceptualizing the New England geo-cultural landscape.

Both, in the first place, were compulsive data gatherers. "In no country, probably," says Dwight, "are the inhabitants more inquisitive than in New England" (*DT* 1:296). He and Thoreau were prime examples of the truth of this cliché. We do not leave Thoreau's Cape Cod without finding out how far clams spit (with a tail wind) and how much lobsters cost in Provincetown (three cents). The metaphorical structure of *Walden* turns, surveyorlike, on a problem of mensuration: Thoreau discovering the depths of the supposedly bottomless pond and the fact that its deepest point coincides, symbolically, with the intersection of the points of greatest breadth and length.[7] Thoreau's Indian guide in "Chesuncook" came to rely on him for the measurement of distances. Dwight was also an ardent, if less profound, student of natural philosophy who kept statistics about rainfalls, snowfalls, and temperatures, who took pleasure in speculating about why New England's winters are colder than Britain's, in observing that barberry bushes blast wheat and rye, in testing experimentally whether vegetable putrefaction increases disease, and in discerning the process by which forests grew – also one of Thoreau's major interests in his later years. How many tons of timber went into the bridge over the Piscataqua? How many duels were fought in early New England? Read Dwight.

Dwight is more content to remain on the level of raw data. Whereas Thoreau asserts that the value of facts comes when they flower into truths, Dwight often piles up facts as if they are ends in themselves. At the end of *Walden,* Thoreau uses the image of the beautiful bug emerging from the table as an emblem of spiritual metamorphosis, whereas Dwight, one of his sources for this anecdote, tells it dryly by comparison, taking pains to report the length of the bug, the size and shape of the cavity from which it emerged ("about two inches in length, nearly horizontal, and inclining upward very little except at the mouth"), and the precise age of the tree. Still, Thoreau too is quite capable of such statistical overkill; and Dwight, conversely, seldom refrains from didacticism after laying such extensive groundwork. The anecdote of the bug leads by analogy to meditation on the "vivacious nature of seeds," and thence to meditation on the long cycles of the locust and the palmer worm, and thence to a pious reverence and wonder that is really the orthodox precursor of Thoreau's mood at the end of *Walden:* "Who can fail to admire the wisdom and goodness displayed in this conduct of Providence?" (*DT* 2:276–8). Ultimately the two approaches to natural phenomena converge as variants of the same Yankee syndrome: a strongly utilitarian aesthetic in which the poetic element flourishes within an even more fundamental commitment to edification, be it in the form of data or inspirational philosophizing. In Thoreau, of course, the poetical element is more obviously struggling to transform information and precept into art; but if that element were to break away completely from its ethical and utilitarian commitments, the authority of the speaker would be so compromised that Thoreau would cease to be Thoreau.

The reflections of Dwight and Thoreau, furthermore, were often directed toward similar ends. Both distrusted newfangledness and prized simplicity. Dwight's satirical chapter on fashionable education in Boston (*DT* 1:370–5) could almost have been written by Thoreau. Thoreau is, of course, more extreme in his economic pronouncements, such as his boast that he could live in a coffinlike toolbox that he saw by the railroad, and in his tributes to the precivilized state. Dwight would have thought him a crank and would, if transported to nineteenth-century Concord, surely have preferred to consort with Judge Hoar and Parson Frost. Thoreau might have found the steadiness that Dwight continually praises in Connecticut society its most objectionable feature. Yet Dwight's grounds of praise sound in some ways like Thoreau's. Connecticut's chief glory, for Dwight, lies in its combination of unprecedented stability with unprecedented freedom: "There is not a spot on the globe where so little is done to govern the inhabitants, nor a spot where the inhabitants are so well governed" – that is, "so peaceable, orderly, and happy" (*DT* 4:236). To the extent that the sense of freedom becomes Dwight's key test of the health of the social order and the latter is seen as dependent upon the nature of the inhabitants rather than upon political structures themselves, Dwight's vision is the germ of Thoreau's radically open-ended no-government individualism. Transcendentalist "anarchism" is conceivable only in peaceable kingdoms, only against a secure background of a long history (or myth) of effective self-government, at least at the local level, which would permit even someone as suspicious of human nature as Dwight to boast that in all his travels he never saw "two men employed in fighting" (*DT* 1:123). Thoreau was antagonistic to the restraining social institutions that Dwight praised; yet in a not too well-defined way Thoreau also believed that freedom should arise *from* mental and moral discipline, although in his case it was always a discipline voluntarily assumed. In *Walden,* for instance, retrenchment ("Economy"), farming ("The Bean Field"), asceticism ("Higher Laws"), and surveying ("The Pond in Winter") are all seen as at least potentially bearing spiritual fruit. Steady habits, then, were crucial to Thoreau as a means if not as an end, though at times he found them constricting.

They were a means rather than an end to him partly because steadiness was more a felt social reality for Thoreau than for Dwight. Dwight wrote when civil war in New England (Shay's Rebellion), Indian attacks, and European invasion were still living memories. Under such conditions it was natural for Dwight, whose family had been broken up by the social upheavals of the Revolution, to celebrate stability as an end. For Thoreau, despite (and also because of) elements of social change in nineteenth-century Concord to be noted later, organized society seemed a more dominant, long-standing, hence potentially oppressive fact.[8] In all of his books, not only does Thoreau never see men fighting – he rarely sees respectable people doing anything of interest. Just as Stowe took the myth of "steady habits" and turned it into whimsical fantasy in "Uncle Lot," so Thoreau portrays his respectable folks in light of the counter-myth of conformity, presenting us with a New England populated by hidebound farmers, creedbound ministers, and gentility-bound gentry, with only the very old, the very young, and the very unsocialized exempt from the onus of steadiness. At the same time, Thoreau does not come out flatly against steadiness but combines a deliberate whimsicality and irreverence with a "steadier-than-thou" posture ("I have always endeavored to acquire strict business habits" [*Wa* 20]). Partly as a result, "Pope" Dwight and antiestablishment Thoreau project, for all their differences, somewhat similar personae: staunch, opinionated, probing, overbearing, impatient, sardonic: speakers who stand firm and put their readers on the spot.

Equally notable for present purposes is the way these personae come to terms, throughout their observations, with the concept of the New England town. This form of social organization dictates, for one thing, the most basic narrative unit in Dwight's *Travels* and in Thoreau's travels through the region's settled parts, in that the travelers chart their progress through the countryside township-by-township, typically pausing to characterize the communities through which they move and report selected local memorabilia: natural disasters, historical events, and the like. That they should have organized their books in terms of their itineraries is, in itself, hardly surprising. The more significant point is their shared acceptance of the principle of the "village manner" of settlement in New England. Overtly, Dwight always speaks as a booster of the system, Thoreau as a critic of its results; yet it never occurs to Thoreau, any more than to Dwight, to doubt that the system is established for all time. Both writers are full of admonitions concerning the status of the social order, Dwight for the sake of preserving it and Thoreau for the sake of reforming it; but they worry about the problem of the debasement rather than the obliteration of New England social institutions as they know them. Both contemplated with a grim relish the possibility that the American union might dissolve, and they were emboldened to do so because they believed that New England's moral fiber and institutions were sounder than those of the other regions. Thoreau on the necessity of keeping Massachusetts free from the slaveholding influence is a reincarnation of Dwight on keeping Connecticut free of Jeffersonianism.

✓ The nature and strength of their commitment to a town-centered view of the cultural landscape is best seen in Dwight's *Greenfield Hill* and Thoreau's *Walden,* each of which shapes the author's observations and experiences within a self-contained community – his community – into a model of how the good life should be. In *Greenfield Hill,* this means running through a standard literary agenda in a public voice, to the end of presenting "my" township and "my" experience as everybody's; first the poem paints the landscape, then the rise of the village, then episodes from the two key historical epochs (Puritan and Revolutionary), then two exemplary local figures (minister and farmer), then an Augustan vision of the rosy future predictable from the sociocultural base that has been described. "I" merges into "we"; "Greenfield," into "everytown."

Walden seems initially to take its strength from its dissent from Dwight's programmatic complacency. It is an escape from the town norms, not a celebration of them, an escape that involves at least a symbolic flight into the wilderness. Yet Thoreau, as is well known, was no primitivist, although he did have leanings in that direction.[9] The best analyses of his "passion for pristine wildness" recognize his antithetical desire for "reclamation" (intellectual as well as agricultural).[10] The best characterizations of the setting of Thoreau's Walden hut, such as Leo Marx's, place it "at the center of a symbolic landscape in which the village of Concord appears on one side and a vast reach of unmodified nature on the other."[11] Indeed one could go a step farther even than this in qualifying Thoreau's primitivism: Any images of "unmodified nature" to the thither side of Thoreau's hut are stylizations of a conventional feature of the layout of New England towns – the fringe of unsettled tracts on the periphery.[12] Any rhetorical erasure of civilized markers in *Walden* has to be understood in relation to the speaker's voluntary self-confinement within the jurisdictional unit. From the time the speaker tells us, in the first sentence, that his experiment was carried out "in Concord," the boundaries of this "wilderness" are fairly announced. The careful reader will note that the Hallowell farm, which the speaker says he almost bought (*Wa* 83), is in some ways more secluded than his hut itself and that, conversely, the privacy he seeks and finds is a privacy within an established settlement that might not be as hard to come by as his rhetoric sometimes suggests, since the most distant traveling he speaks of is between souls rather than between places. This is what makes his exaggerations of the remoteness and wildness of his retreat something more than mere hyperbole. The paradox of "traveling" in Concord registers the fact that significant physical distance from society is achievable even within the limits of New England's oldest inland town and, more important, that intellectually the speaker has achieved thereby a degree of disengagement that makes his townsmen as foreign as superstitious Brahmins with their thousand penances (*Wa* 4). And vice versa: Any such stylization is not just a matter of the experiencer's personal recoil but also, and maybe more profoundly, a rendering of his fellow citizens' fantasies of him, at least as he perceives them; for Thoreau continually notes how conventional people who visited the cabin were obsessed by the "great distance at which I dwelt from something or other" (*Wa* 153), meaning that they were the ones who exaggerated.

Thoreau's "subjective" romanticization of distances, then, is partly an "objective" mirror of how he saw his solitude as being publicly perceived. Consequently we should be alert to the possible element of satire ✓ in such passages as "Where I lived was as far off as many a region viewed nightly by astronomers" (*Wa* 87–8); for although the speaker does take pleasure in the fancifulness of this notion, he is also amused and sometimes scornful at the denseness of the popular perception of his retreat, according to which its strangeness and deviance are exaggerated. Thus _Walden_ becomes at the same time a process of mystification of an experience that was actually much tamer than that of more thoroughgoing "wilderness people" like John Muir, whom we tend to align with Thoreau, and a process of demystification, whereby, through a detailed description of and apologia for the author's life-style, including budget and balance sheet, the case is made for the practicability of the experiment as a business enterprise on a par with that of any Concordian. Dwight holds to the ordinary and tries to romanticize it; Thoreau deviates willfully from the ordinary partly to argue that the extravagance of literary and behavioral expression for which he has contended is not so extraordinary after all.

Thoreau therefore goes out of his way to remind us continually of how his Walden life is a part of his relationship to the town of Concord, even as the former seems ostensibly a retreat from the latter. The book began, says the speaker, in answer to "very particular inquiries" by "my townsmen concerning my mode of life" (*Wa* 3). Although he envisions other, wider audiences ("poor students" and "you . . . who are said to live in New England" [*Wa* 4]), his agenda is set as a partial reply to local questioners. More frequently than one at first notices, the reference point for ✓ the ensuing discourse is "my townsmen," "my neighbors," "my neighborhood," "my fellow citizens," "this town," "my neighbors, the farmers of Concord" (*Wa* 5, 10, 19, 28–9, 32). A sizable list might be made of seemingly gratuitous local references that help site the book not merely at Walden Pond and environs but in Concord township: the annual Middlesex Cattle Show; Edward Johnson's account of Concord's settlement in his *Wonder-Working Providence* (Stanley Cavell suggests that the speaker presents himself as reenacting the original settlement of the town);[13] the Concord trader with a salt fish for a sign; "our Circulating Library"; the "half-starved" village lyceum; the new town hall; the poet "who came through the village to my house from the other side of town" (*Wa* 33, 38–9, 104, 108–9, 223). This of course does not begin to cover the full roster of local place references: Pleasant Meadow, Brister's Hill, Fair Haven Ledges, and so forth.

Such references do not, of course, add up to anything like the conventional schematic view of the town and its people and institutions that Dwight gives in *Greenfield Hill* and his *Travels*. Thoreau deliberately rejects the normative and central for the marginal or eccentric – the view, as he sees it, from

> . . . the shore of a small pond, about a mile and a half south of the village of Concord and somewhat higher than it, in the midst of an extensive wood between that town and Lincoln, and about two miles south of that our only field known to fame, Concord Battle Ground. [*Wa* 86]

This is the book's only direct reference to the detail to which Dwight gives primary attention on his visit to Concord – and understandably, given the public voice of the *Travels*. Otherwise, Concord's Revolutionary heritage, in the literal sense, is present in *Walden* by its conspicuous absence. "Of historical facts of the more commonly valued sort," as a recent critic puts it, "Walden Pond is blessedly innocent."[14] One suspects, however, that the "innocence" of the passage just quoted reflects a studied casualness, given the fanfare with which the same historical fight is paraded before the reader in *A Week on the Concord and Merrimack Rivers*.[15]

A similar effect is created by the chapter called "The Village," which is the book's shortest and even at that, less about the village itself than about the speaker's relief at being free of it. Ostensibly the village is described only to be put in its place, so that the speaker can relegate it to the same obscurity to which the villagers have relegated him. That would be in keeping with the view from the woods of south Concord on the border of Lincoln: From this vantage point, the village itself is peripheral, and vice versa. But in the process, "The Village" also reasserts the author's tie with the town not just negatively (his arrest for civil disobedience) but in a somewhat grudgingly positive sense (he admits that he went there "every day or two . . . to hear some of the gossip which is incessantly going on there" [*Wa* 167]). The villagers are part of the local phenomena that he has charged himself to record ("I went there frequently to observe their habits, . . . as if they had been prairie dogs" [*Wa* 167]), and the village life-style, as always, is the norm used to define his own. The chapter ends, for example, by contrasting the village's compulsive need for security – evinced by its jailing of him – with his lack of need for locks and bolts at Walden. Here and elsewhere the details of the Walden experiment take on meaning by reference to how they do not fit the village.

The most important sense in which *Walden* is a local work is, of course, its lovingly attentive recreation of the rural landscape of "my lake country" (*Wa* 197). The largest additions to the original text during the later drafts were extensions of the description of natural phenomena (thanks to years of further walks and *Journal* data) and the subsumption of these into the seasonal myth that became the book's dominant metaphor.[16] In particular, the six chapters starting with "Brute Neighbors," in contrast to the preceding, are organized less in topical fashion than in terms of such individual sightings and events as chestnut gathering in the Lincoln woods; the discovery of the groundnut, "the potato of the aborigines," which Thoreau had thought lost (*Wa* 239); the turning of the leaves of the maples by the first of September; the hibernation of wasps in October; and so forth. Such data, though loosely arranged in a seasonal order that suggests in turn the idea of spiritual metamorphosis, cannot be wholly rationalized in terms of any ulterior metaphorical or rhetorical purpose; in the first instance, and sometimes in the last instance too, the details are there because they are in Concord and this is a book about Thoreau's Concord travels.[17] This commitment to realizing the Walden environment in its minute particulars looks forward to the posthumously published travel books, which are more resolutely literal. To some readers, and sometimes to the author himself, the dwindling of the transcendental element is a telltale symptom of failing visionary powers. Although that is probably true, Thoreau might not have turned his Walden hawk into a magical symbol of spiritual freedom had he not first observed it "on the 29th of April, as I was fishing from the bank of the river near the Nine-Acre-Corner bridge" (*Wa* 316). Not only at his most boring but also at his best, Thoreau is an even more local writer than Dwight, *Walden* providing a much fuller record of what it is possible to experience in one's own backyard. The beautiful bug that emerges from the table at the end astonishes because it comes unexpectedly "forth from amidst society's most trivial and unhandselled furniture" (*Wa* 333).

Such metamorphic images, so abundant in *Walden,* sanctify the experience of the speaker and the place where they occurred. *Walden* is a book about spiritual renewal at a sacred place, which modern pilgrims still perceive as sacred on account of Thoreau's memorialization of it. By achieving this sanctification through a self-devised ritual of repossession and by making the desert places his shrine, rather than the village center, Thoreau inverted what would have seemed the proper order of things to Dwight, for whom the New England town was sacred in its institutionalization and for whom the town center rather than the unsettled periphery was the sanctum. Thoreau takes the forest that any good Puritan or pioneer regarded as "desert," if not as the abode of the devil, and places it at the center of the town experience.[18] Taking a longer view, however, we can see Thoreau's work as an elaboration rather than as a denial of Dwight's lococentrism, aptly summarized by Kenneth Silverman's adage, "Love of place unexpectedly imbues the banal with life."[19] Dwight's defense of lococentrism also applies to Thoreau. Local attachment, says Dwight, "contributes both to fix and to fasten man" – a vital function, given the "fierce and the roving spirit of our race" (DT 3:73). To read between the lines: Local attachments discourage frivolous pioneering, which breeds social and moral anarchy. Dwight's defense of emotional bonding to place as a means of social control would have seemed small-minded to Thoreau, yet Thoreau actually follows Dwight closely in prescribing a closer rapport with one's immediate surroundings as a better antidote to the spirit of restlessness than indulgence of wanderlust. Why pan gold in California, why "count the cats in Zanzibar" (Wa 322), when so much richer a journey is possible near at hand? On this level, both Dwight and Thoreau belong to a tradition of antiemigration propaganda literature that deserves a chapter as a New England genre in itself.

√   To endow a place with the sense of the sacred requires not simply fine powers of observation but immersion in local history and tradition as well. Here is another way in which Thoreau shows up as a revisionist successor to Dwight. Both approach new places with book in hand. Thoreau makes a joke of this in *Cape Cod*, representing himself and his companion as reading a volume of the Massachusetts Historical Society *Collections* under their umbrella as they hike over the Plains of Nauset in the rain. Dwight's *Travels* intersperse references to virtually all significant Indian and Revolutionary War battles that occurred in the spots the author visits and to sundry other happenings of local note, both historical and apocryphal. Thoreau habitually does the same, although he is apt to ridicule as well as filiopietize. Dwight lovingly but sadly chronicles the failure of missionary efforts on Cape Cod (DT 3:53–4); Thoreau chuckles over Eastham's ancient regulation that beached whales are to go to the support of the ministry. But both relish the minutiae of local history; both, for instance, regard Truro's ordinance that every inhabitant must annually plant beach grass as a remarkable and important fact.[20]

The basis of Dwight's valuation of history and tradition is clear-cut: As a traditionalist, he regards an assimilation of its past as part of one's total rapport with the cultural landscape. Thoreau's position is not so clear-cut. "He is characteristically direct in announcing his refusal to pay attention to the past and indeed to anything second-hand," yet "equally direct in his use of an astonishing range of second-hand accounts, historical and otherwise."[21] And when he does use such lore, it is hard to predict whether he will take it seriously ("for I love to quote so good author-ity")[22] or parodistically ("Farther in the woods than any of these . . . Wy-man the potter squatted, and furnished his townsmen with earthen ware, and left descendants to succeed him" *Wa* 261). Of course, any historiciz-ing, solemn or droll, has the effect of evoking a fourth dimension to the landscape, regardless.

The main difference between Thoreau and Dwight on this point seems to be that the epic of settlement has an immediacy for Dwight that it does not have for Thoreau. Thoreau distances himself from the claims of that history, just as he has distanced himself from the claims of his townsmen. "These battles," he says with reference to Lovewell's Fight,

> sound incredible to us. I think that posterity will doubt if such things ever were; if our bold ancestors who settled this land were not strug-gling rather with the forest shadows, and not with a copper colored race of men. They were vapors, fever and ague of the unsettled woods. Now, only a few arrow-heads are turned up by the plow.[23]

For Dwight, on the other hand, an event such as the Deerfield Massacre of 1675, though just as remote from his time of writing as Lovewell's Fight was from Thoreau's, still lives in the mind:

> The very tradition which conveyed it down to succeeding generations was, for ninety years at least, attended with peculiar gloom and horror. I remember it perfectly as one of the most awful and melancholy tales of childhood; and, when I first passed by the spot, could not refrain from shuddering at the sight of this scene of woe. [*DT* 2:40]

References here and elsewhere to his having imbibed the history that he describes not just from books but, as it were, from the cradle, are de-signed to dramatize the idea of participation in and celebration of a con-tinuous tradition, the saga of the New England "race." The sense of ur-gency is all the greater because of Dwight's awareness that the continuity of tradition is threatened. "This kind of knowledge," he says, again refer-ring to the Indian wars, "is daily becoming less, and will soon be lost. It is much to be wished that inquisitive men throughout this country would glean and preserve the little which is left" (*DT* 1:296). Actually, at the moment Dwight wrote, regional historiography, commemorative ora-tory, and other such enterprises were starting to do just that. By the time Hawthorne, Emerson, and Thoreau began their literary careers, the writ-ten sources of early New England history were far more copious and thorough, in comparison to oral sources, than in Dwight's day. This may help explain the comparatively alienated view of history in their work. So much sepulcher-building had gone on in the interim that the sense of a living bond with colonial and even with Revolutionary history had be-come irretrievably attenuated.

The mediation of print accounts only in part for this alienation, however. Other factors certainly include the Unitarian-Transcendentalist tendency to resist the authority of "Puritan" values, the Romanticist tendency to portray the past as exotically distant, and the social changes that gave momentum and credibility to such portrayals – for example, the virtual eradication of Indian civilization in the Northeast and the transformation of traditional town life wrought during the nineteenth century by the interrelated impact of technological advance, urbanization, immigration, and the rise of entrepreneurial capitalism. One of the most interesting breakthroughs in recent Thoreau criticism has been the intensive study of Concord social history vis-à-vis *Walden*. The last word on the subject may not be said for some time, but what has emerged so far suggests a picture of Thoreau's Concord as a place where property and wealth were becoming increasingly concentrated, where mobility and foreign immigration rates were at levels typical of the region's larger cities, where a new spirit of entrepreneurship and tangible signs of economic development coexisted with a new malaise, with growing economic inequality, with frustration for many. Thoreau's Concord was in the process of being transformed from a preindustrial village, to a hive of agricultural enterprise, to a satellite suburb of Boston. Robert Gross, who has charted these changes carefully, suggests a link between Concord's development and Thoreau's

> . . . underlying sense of isolation, a feeling that the inner selves of men may be irremediably separate. Perhaps in the simpler past direct, spontaneous contact could arise among men organically rooted in Nature, but in his Concord, Thoreau was compelled to ask, "Could a greater miracle take place than for us to look through each other's eyes for an instant?"[24]

Gross's approach to Thoreau builds to some extent on the Leo Marxian notion that Romantic pastoralism represents an attempt to compensate for future shock by resort to an ethos of economic and spiritual simplicity that reincarnates the vision of a "simpler past." Thoreau's appeal, as the passage just quoted implies, was necessarily different in its starting point from Dwight's, since it had to be made from a sense of isolation (rather than as an appeal to preserve a corporate solidarity still perceived as intact, however threatened), and it was necessarily different in tone, because of its greater anxiety that the ethos of spiritual, social, and economic oneness might be irretrievable and because of its insistence on the need to preserve individual integrity against the bogus individualism of emergent capitalism. Thus Thoreau's social ideas were bound to be more conflicted than Dwight's, since Thoreau envisaged a model of human community that was a purified version of a social order that as a historical entity he was inclined to satirize for inertia and traditionalism, invoking for that purpose a spirit of enterprise that Gross shrewdly interprets as a purified version of the new, economically aggressive order that in its normal manifestations Thoreau was also inclined to indict for compulsive materialism and overreaching.[25] Yet Thoreau is still readable here as successor to Dwight, who was himself caught between his enthusiasm for economic development and his idyllicization of the small, stable, consensual agrarian community, which late eighteenth-century economic change was already starting to threaten. The ideal communities of both Dwight and Thoreau, in other words, are retrospections arising from ideological self-division, from the sense that the aggressive drive for improvement (in whatever sense) to which one is fundamentally committed must also be kept in check.

These reflections may convey an exaggerated impression of the extent to which the frustration or breakup of human community surfaces as an overt subject in *Walden*. But its presence behind the speaker's bluffness is strongly suggested throughout by his reliance on homily and apologia, which give the book its public dimension. In his manner of presenting the history of his antisocial secession, the exhermit reestablishes his tie with society. Insofar as it converts the Walden event from private experience to shareable exemplum, the book reintegrates the persona into the life of the community of his readers, who, as we have seen, are in the first instance considered to be his townsmen.

In emphasizing the problems of economic stagnation and spiritual isolation within the village life that he would like to reenchant into pastoral utopia, Thoreau looks forward to postwar regionalism. In local color prose, the basic sources of local deprivation are the same, and the remedy, to the extent that remedy seems possible, again is seen to consist largely in spartan economic and spiritual self-sufficiency, although most of the regionalists also give far more emphasis to the presence and sustaining power of mundane social relationships than Thoreau does. They share with him the dual impulse to cry out against intellectual and social stagnation and to retrieve the utopian vision that itself ironically entails a sort of submission to the very limitations that are bewailed. Despite its liability to syrupiness, local colorism, at least in the hands of its more jaundiced practitioners like Mary Wilkins Freeman and Edith Wharton, is indeed even more conscious of this irony than Thoreau – one of the mixed blessings of being born later, when the idyllic vision of the small town was even harder to sustain, since the actual old-fashioned communities were much fewer and their old-fashionedness was normally a mark of depression or decay.

To be sure, in *Walden* irony is always and inevitably present, if only because of the gap between the experiment and the literary record of it. "His problem," Stanley Cavell states with reference to the theme of personal metamorphosis, "is that every line of his account is cause for despair, because each is an expression he was waited for, and yet with each he is not transformed."[26] But surely the speaker does not always remain conscious of this: He wavers between trust in the ability of the experiment to bring about the personal and social transformations he desires and an ironic awareness that he may not be acting for anyone's benefit – not even his own.

A sequence that illustrates this perceptual vacillation beautifully is the rumination on the former inhabitants of Walden woods. "For human society I was obliged to conjure up the former occupants of these woods," the speaker says (*Wa* 256). He proceeds to recall Cato, Zilpha, Brister Freeman, Breed, Quoil, and others – a "small village" of social deviants like himself, consisting of blacks, Irish, poor whites – all vanished since. "Why did it fail while Concord keeps its ground?" he muses (*Wa* 264). The overt device here is mock elegy, seriocomic imitation of the plot that thousands of earlier Romantic graveyard and ruin set pieces had made stereotypical. The conclusion toward which the meditation works is a contrast between these unfruitful precedents and the speaker's own experiment: "Again, perhaps, Nature will try, with me for a first settler, and my house raised last spring to be the oldest in the hamlet" (*Wa* 264). The terms of the contrast suggest that the speaker desires not simply to be an *isolato* but for his experiment to be the start of a new community. They confirm, rather than deny, that the fantasy of former settlers was conjured up to compensate for an excess of the isolation he supposedly wanted when he retreated to the woods. And they suggest, through the wistfulness of the "perhaps," his uncertainty lest his fancy of himself as founder prove insubstantial. The passage as a whole might be regarded as the climax of a familiar and important device used throughout *Walden,* that of populating solitude with images of sociability (usually drawn from nature), in order to ward off loneliness and alienation. This device first is underscored at the point in "Solitude" when the speaker admits that once (but only once) he felt lonesome. What enabled him to recover his spirits was the sudden awareness of "such sweet and beneficent society in Nature, in the very pattering of the drops, and in every sound and sight around my house, an infinite and unaccountable friendliness all at once like an atmosphere sustaining me" (*Wa* 132). This is his usual consolation: to reinvent nature as society. But in winter, when his capacity for solitude is put fully to the test, there is a corresponding proliferation in the images of sociability, the text supplying us not only with a bestiary of friends but also with a range of real and imaginary human companions, such as the former inhabitants. In this situation, even the commercial ice farmers are a welcome diversion.

What remains unclear about these images of sociability in the woods is the extent to which Thoreau realizes that the speaker is engaging in compensatory fantasy.[27] Is the ghost-town sequence really written with double meaning, not only as a humorous sketch of how not to be a creative homesteader but also as a parody, in advance, of the speaker's aspirations to found a new and more utopian hamlet? And in that statement of aspiration, does the telltale "perhaps" suggest an awareness not only of the precariousness of the dream but also of its appearance of comic inconsistency with the speaker's manifest desire to withdraw from society? Although no contemporary writer was more self-consciously alert for signs of rhetorical posturing in others and in himself than was Thoreau, I am not confident that his text goes that far down the road to self-deconstruction here. Thoreau certainly realizes the fantasticalness of the meditation on the former inhabitants; that is the fun of it. He also realizes (in the phrase "obliged to conjure up") that the meditation results from cabin fever. But he probably does not realize that the ghost town, as an act of private fantasy, might serve as a monitory image of the social consequences of willful individualism, which might not be able to replace the literal Concord (spectral as he is pleased to regard it) with anything more substantial than another abandoned cabin. On the contrary, the inmost layer of the ruminations here seems not to be this ironic self-consciousness but the intensity of the speaker's continuing desire – partly concealed from himself through the air of playful sketchery – to rebuild town society on his own terms.

If we want to be severe on Thoreau, then, we can diagnose him as having shortsightedly opted for a rarefied version of the bourgeois individualism that he opposed in its grosser forms, in order naively to embrace a perverse variant of the old-fashioned village pastoralism that had already been rendered unworkable by the forces he thought he was opposing, and producing thereby a classic American reaction formation that ever since has deluded readers with similar susceptibilities.

Yet we can also see Thoreau's achievement more positively by crediting him with having effected a timely and fruitful translation of the old-fashioned village ideal *à la* Dwight into Romantic terms, penetrating much more deeply into the local landscape by subjecting its received stereotypes to criticism in light of an ostensibly antiestablishment individualism, while at the same time reanimating the local objects within his field of vision with an unprecedented reach and luminousness of personal knowledge. Seen this way, Thoreau seems to have taken the best possible literary advantage of the moment in history when the village ideal could still be entertained, but no longer with the old naïveté. As an exemplum of how to resist what geographer David Lowenthal calls the American "cult of bigness"[28] – of how to be content with what Dwight liked to call a "modest competence" and of how to compensate for any such self-imposed restrictions by exploring what Thoreau called one's "higher latitudes" – *Walden* belongs in the mainstream of New England village iconography.

It contributed to that tradition, however, mainly by unsettling it. The terms under which Thoreau was prepared to envisage literary recuperation of utopia at the village level were so eccentric as to make *Walden* look, in retrospect, like a further blow to the weakening civic solidarity on which the village ideal had been based. From the standpoint of Thoreau's impact on American thought and writing, we cannot quarrel with those who place his late essay "Walking," with its celebration of an idealized wildness identified with an archetypal West, at the center of his imagination and define Thoreau's vicarious wandering as a more fundamental trait than his homing instinct – even though in "Walking" itself he finally draws back and domesticates wildness by stressing how it can be found near home.[29] At bottom, Thoreau on the New England village is rather like the Arminian romance of Puritanism. Both place their center of values on the social margin and, in the Romantic manner, use instances of deviance to critique the establishment. Even where an author's political instincts are rather conservative, as are Longfellow and Eliza Lee, for instance, the effect of this mode of envisioning is to elevate personal integrity above social order and to produce not so much "anatomies" as "pathographies" of the societies depicted. The late-century regionalists continued this practice of imaging regional society as grotesque, despite their more objectified style of representation and their more thoroughly domestic, stay-at-home ideology. And in this respect New England writing set an example that later regionalisms have followed. The next two chapters will examine some of the characteristic forms of regional grotesque and undertake a rough classification of its modes.

15

Comic Grotesque

> We all grew in those days like the apple-trees in our back lot. Every
> man had his own quirks and twists, and threw himself out freely in the
> line of his own individuality; and so a rather jerky, curious original set
> of us there was.
>
> Harriet Beecher Stowe, *Oldtown Folks* (1869)

> The perpetual game of humor is to look with considerate good nature
> at every object in existence, *aloof,* as a man might look at a mouse,
> comparing it with the eternal Whole.
>
> Ralph Waldo Emerson, "The Comic" (1843)

In depictions of regional manners, it seems impossible to resist condescension. Whatever his or her degree of sympathy with the culture depicted, the observer writes as a sort of anthropologist on whom a higher
knowledge has been conferred than on those described. When Timothy
Dwight, from Greenfield Hill, sings how

> in rural pride
> The village spreads its tidy, snug retreats,
> That speak the industry of every hand

he seeks to glorify the enchanting scene spread out before him by contrast
to the more storied landscapes of the Old World.[1] But the effect is to
miniaturize the objects beneath the superiority (both spatial and intellectual) of the speaker's gaze. More often than not, furthermore, the literary
anthropologist of regional manners overtly regards them as either cute or
benighted, as touchingly passé or stultifyingly circumscribed. Regional
literature, as a result, usually winds up divided between the impulse nos-
talgically to identify with the bygone or simplified life-style depicted and
the cosmopolitan impulse to mock it as clownish or repressive.
    This spectrum of responses is already present in the work of the most

335

influential early regionalist in the English-speaking world, Walter Scott. Consider the central character configuration in *Old Mortality* (1816), a romance about an abortive late seventeenth-century revolt of Scottish Covenanters. Scott's hero, Henry Morton, torn between respect for legitimate authority and sympathy for the wrongs of the people, temporarily and reluctantly becomes a rebel chieftain. As such he is used both as Scott's means of dramatizing the revolt's more noble, chivalrous side without falling into an irretrievably traitorous opposition to the Crown and also as a means of highlighting, by contrast, the rebellion's more absurd and sordid aspects. These are exemplified particularly by two of the characters by whom Morton is flanked. On the one side he is accompanied by a Sancho Panza, Cuddie Headrigg, Morton's bumpkin servant, who suggests the well-meaning thickheadedness and resiliency of the common people. On the other side, he is shadowed by the sinister John Balfour of Burley, a dark double figure (bonded to Morton partly by a quasi-familial tie of friendship with Morton's father), who becomes the chief representative of the ruthless, fanatical side of the revolt. The novel's denouement completes Scott's critique of the rebellion by purging the fanatics, dispensing comic justice to the bumpkins, and placing them under the rule of enlightened (and therefore forgiven) patriots like the Mortons. Scotland's dignity is thereby reaffirmed, at the expense of repressing what is ethnically most peculiar and recessive – after, of course, we have fully enjoyed the sensation of its release.

For present purposes, Cuddie and Burley may be seen as the polar extremes of the grotesque toward which depictions of provincial manners are typically attracted and that normally account, as in Scott, for more of the dramatic interest and local color than does the comparatively insipid protagonist. In the discourse of literary regionalism, comic grotesque and provincial gothic (as I shall call them) are inseparable. They comprise the same Janus-faced identity as Emerson's lectures on comedy and tragedy. These lectures amount to a unified field theory of the grotesque, for Emerson defines both comic and tragic visions in terms of the discrepancy between what is represented and some implied norm or ideal.[2] My split discussion in this chapter and the next is a similar hypostasization of categories for convenience's sake. Yet individual texts do tend to revolve more around one of these poles than the other and, as they sort themselves out, to develop conventions more or less peculiar to it. Of the two, provincial gothic is the richer and more interesting vein of the grotesque in New England writing, I think – a judgment that may be tinctured with fashionable modernism, though I believe it reflects an authentic regional perception that Puritanism at bottom is no laughing matter. But let us start with the comic.

I

To tell the story of New England comic grotesque between the
Revolution and the Civil War at first seems an easy task. One need not
look far to find either a plot or a hero. The story, ably documented by a
number of scholars, is a tale of the rise of the "Yankee" or "Jonathan"
from Neoclassical bumpkinhood to Romantic heroism.[3] Let us review
the tale briefly, then tackle two thorny problems that it poses.

Comic regional representation in New England writing begins as a
large-scale project under the aegis of neoclassical cosmopolitanism, according to whose norms the writer looks upon provincial manners with
a condescending eye while traveling, like the witty and observant Sarah
Kemble Knight, from Boston to New York, or the equivalents. Thus
eighteenth-century New England produced an increasing number of literary hits on provincial backwardness, of which Knight's *Journal* (1704)
is the first significant example and Hawthorne's portrait of Robin Molineux is a belated reflection. Titles like these – "An Affecting Eclogue, in
the Style of Gay, between Clodpole and Dobbin" and "Phelim O'Bluff's
Epistle to Miss Betty Broadface" – suggest the combination of urbanity
and ethnocentrism underlying such works.[4] They may, of course, be affectionate even when savage; the Sheridan-like tendency to temper satire
with sentimentalism helps account for the popularity of Royall Tyler's
Jonathan in *The Contrast* (1787), the first really impressive and influential
literary representation of the true-blue rustic Yankee. Although Tyler certainly intended him as a comic subordinate, a caricature of the idealized
American Colonel Manly, Jonathan threatens to upstage the priggish
nominal hero.[5] Conceived as a playful hit on the "democracy," Jonathan
contains the seeds of transformation into a bona fide folk hero in his exuberance, his innocence, his indestructibility, and his pithy vernacular
speech. Over the next half century this transformation took place, a symbolic turning point being Samuel Woodworth's drama *The Forest Rose*
(1825), in which the bumpkin, Jonathan Ploughboy, not only provokes
humor but also frustrates the villain and precipitates the denouement.[6]
This shift reflects something closer to a Jacksonian conception of ordinary people and a Romantic conception of the rustic as opposed to the
urban. Even under these new auspices, the rustic generally remains a folk
hero rather than a full hero – remains, that is, in the comic mode; the
heroes and heroines in Stowe's regional fiction, for example, talk in standard English and are in other respects as well a step removed from the
villagers among whom they live. Even in late-century regional prose,
where the protagonists themselves are more fully rusticized, they rarely
escape the narrator's condescension. The visitor-narrator's self-
subordination to the local matriarch Mrs. Todd, in Jewett's *Country of the*

Pointed Firs, is an exceptional case (exceptional even within that text: The narrator views other local figures with the customary distancing).

The assumption of a rustic mask to critique an effete establishment was, however, from the start of New England writing a viable option that could be used to valorize provincialism as honest bluntness. Such was the approach of New England's first comic work, Nathaniel Ward's *Simple Cobbler of Aggawam* (1647). Later the same approach was used in Revolutionary satires and again in postcolonial and antebellum political and religious controversy, such as Theodore Parker's assumption of the persona of Levi Blodgett in his pro-Transcendentalist pamphlet on the Unitarian controversy.[7] One might, in fact, read not only the text of *Walden* but the entire text of Thoreau's public life in this way, as a highly sophisticated man's bumpkinization of himself for the sake of delivering wry rebukes to the "civilized." Altogether it is a fair guess (although for substantiation more research would be needed, to sort out truth from wish fulfillment) that American literature was from the start, because of its self-conscious provincialism, more predisposed than English literature to use the provincial mask as a defensive weapon and thereby to ease the transition from a condescending to a comparatively affectionate comedy of provincial manners.

So much for basic generalizations about the movement of provincial comic representation in New England writing. At this point the troubles begin. One is the difficulty of sorting out what differentiates Yankee provincialism from bumpkinism or folk heroism in general. Constance Rourke's seminal work *American Humor* introduces this problem by presenting "the Yankee" as the first avatar of the American folk consciousness, who then, in some way only vaguely hinted at, metamorphoses into "the frontiersman."[8] We are left with the impression of analogy without causality or clear differentiation. And this is understandable, because the confrontation between provincial and cosmopolitan manners is by no means a peculiarly regional or even national theme. We isolate a Yankee element at our peril. When the attempt has been made, however, the conclusions have been reassuringly similar, at least up to a point. The first peculiarity usually isolated is shrewdness: the Yankee as a wily, close-to-the-vest, sharp dealer with an eye on the main chance. This deduction, too, is understandable. It reflects, for one thing, the outlander's stereotypical image of the New Englander, as in Washington Irving's comic account of how the Puritans outreached the feckless Dutch in Connecticut (*Knickerbocker's History of New York*) or Cooper's depiction, in *The Pioneers,* of how Richard Jones and Hiram Doolittle twisted the law for their own ends. This trait is also inscribed in some of the most memorable Yankee figures created by New Englanders themselves. For ex-

ample, Major Jack Downing, created by Portlandite Seba Smith as a vehicle for satirizing Jacksonianism in its own vernacular terms, is not
simply a Down East equivalent of the frontiersman, although he is shown
as besting such people at their own feats of ring-tailed roarerdum.[9]
Downing is also the Yankee trickster, intriguing to become the next president instead of "little Van." His letters report him matching Van Buren
(who, as one of America's first great machine politicians, was notorious
for chicanery) trick for trick, presenting himself meanwhile, with the
frontiersman's "naive" braggadocio, as the people's choice. Although
stock frontier heroes like Davy Crockett are also shown as having a resourceful mother wit, it tends to be pictured more as the spontaneous
effusion of high-spiritedness than as a result of careful strategy. The stock
Yankee is a more cerebral creature. The difference appears more pointedly in Downing's most immediate successor in the tradition of comic
Yankee prose, Sam Slick, the clockmaker created by Nova Scotia judge
T. C. Halliburton. But Downing's is the more interesting case, because
of his having preserved his Yankee credentials even though he was created
in the image of the frontiersman.[10]

Some classic American autobiographies also feature personae of the
Yankee type. Benjamin Franklin's and, especially, P. T. Barnum's are obvious cases. Barnum, for example, shows that his future career as show-
man originated in the small-town Connecticut culture of his boyhood,
where, it seems, the life of the community was built on the rituals of
tricking or being tricked. But I waive detailed treatment of these famous
figures for the sake of an equally quintessential but more neglected Yankee autobiography, the *Memoirs of the Notorious Stephen Burroughs* (1794?),
which Robert Frost once said belongs "on the same shelf with Benjamin
Franklin and Jonathan Edwards (grandfather of Aaron Burr)."[11] A Hanover, New Hampshire, minister's son and Dartmouth College dropout,
Burroughs, by the age of thirty-five, had been a soldier, sailor, schoolmaster, ministerial impersonator, counterfeiter, surveyor, land specula-
tor, convict, and escapee. So great was his fame – or so he says – that
strangers regaled him with apocryphal stories of his own exploits. Burroughs was careful to gild his lively picaresque narrative with respectable
moralizing (e.g., on the right way to bring up young people) and self-
justification (portraying himself as suffering far more than his due), but
the vital ingredient is the persona's protean resourcefulness in the face of
emergency. A hilarious example is his improvisation of a sermon on
Joshua 9:5 ("old shoes and clouted on their feet"), given to satisfy the
people of Pelham, Massachusetts, where he is masquerading as a
preacher, that the sermons he has hitherto preached from pilfered manu-
scripts of his father's are really his own.

I truly felt somewhat blanked, at the nature of the passage I had [been requested] to discourse upon. However . . . I had not thought long on it, before the matter opened to my mind, in such a manner, as to give me much satisfaction. . . .

The exordium consisted of a description of the Gibeonites; the duplicity which they practiced upon the Jews; the nature and general tendency of deceit, etc. After I had gone through with the introduction, I divided my discourse into three general heads, viz. to consider in the first place of shoes; secondly, of old shoes; and thirdly, of clouted shoes. In treating of the first general head, viz. shoes, I considered them in a metaphorical sense, as showing our mode of conduct in life. We are all, said I, sojourners in this world but for a season, travelling to another country. . . .

In treating the second head, viz. old shoes, I endeavored to show, that . . . the old shoes represent old sins, which mankind have made use of from old times, down to the present day. . . .

In considering the last general head, viz. of clouted shoes, I observed, that those, who wore those old shoes, and practiced upon a system of jealousy, were sensible of its odious and hateful nature, and of consequence, ashamed to be seen by God, man, or the devil; nay, they were ashamed to be seen by themselves, therefore, they had recourse to patching and clouting themselves over with false and feigned pretenses, to hide their shame and disgrace.[12]

In the remainder, Burroughs applied this doctrine to the congregation, using hellfire rhetoric interlarded with scriptural tags, to the end of shaming them into charity (i.e., toward him). The result was a homily in the approved Puritan-style three-part form (text, doctrine, application) that cleverly turned the tables on the parish – for the moment. Not bad for a nineteen-year-old. The twenty-five or more printings that the autobiography went through by 1840 suggest that Burroughs was even better as a literary con artist than he was in person. The artistry consists in his success at making us see his roguery as a blend of the outrageous, the magical, and the innocent.

Burroughs's witty manipulation of abstruse learning deserves underscoring as a Yankee tactic. The mental alertness of the stereotypical Yankee might be regarded as a folk counterpart of the comparatively "learned" or "scholarly" cast of New England culture, with its early institutionalization of education and its pride in its literacy, but as antagonistic to the establishment conception of what counts as intellectual prowess. Underlying the young Burroughs's adeptness is a contempt for formal learning, represented by his father and the ministerial establishment generally, as superflous pedantry. In this the *Memoirs* looks forward to a series of New England texts in which the stock character of the humorous pedant whose learning interferes with effective functioning in

daily life is contrasted with characters free of such encumbrances: Hawthorne's Dr. Melmoth, in *Fanshawe;* Lowell's Parson Wilbur, in *The Biglow Papers;* Hawthorne's Dimmesdale; and Stowe's Samuel Hopkins.
This was also the mold in which Federalist satire cast Thomas Jefferson's
"philosophical" researches, in which Unitarianism cast Calvinist theology, and in which Theodore Parker cast scholastic divinity in general.
The Unitarian caricature of Cotton Mather as a Puritan Quixote become
purblind through too much reading and the imitation *Dunciads* of literary
Federalism are other typical literary results. The stereotype of the humorous pedant is, of course, a European import (cf. Shakespeare's Polon-
ius, Fielding's Parson Adams, Scott's Domine Sampson) and, in its importation, hardly confined to New England (cf. Cooper's Obed Bat in
The Prairie and the nationwide ground swell of opposition to a classically
based curriculum that started in the late eighteenth century). The New
England strain seems distinct mainly in its prominence and in its tendency to represent the unpedantic opposite as credentialed in its own
right. Hester Prynne is said to have thought her way into the thickets of
theology during her years of ostracism; Mary Scudder writes an epistolary rebuttal of Hopkins's doctrine of unconditional submission; and the
mind of Judd's Margaret must be refined by Mr. Evelyn before she can
qualify as the completely satisfactory alternative to Calvinist dogma.
Sometimes the New England satirist of pedantry reveals, as Burroughs
does, a considerable relish at being able to play the intellectual game dismissed as useless. An excellent example is James Russell Lowell's *Biglow
Papers,* as can be seen by comparing Parson Wilbur's short disquisition on
the Yankee dialect in *Biglow,* first series, with Lowell's much longer essay
that prefaces the second series. Wilbur proves to be a stalking horse for
Lowell. Initially the poet seems to have used him as a device to disarm the
polite reader impatient with dialect experimentation by presenting it as
the parson's antiquarian crotchet. But Lowell takes seriously the underlying argument that Yankee English is closer to the language of Shakespeare than is that of modern England, and so in the later preface Lowell
drops the mask and soars far beyond Wilbur's rather modest seven rules
of pronunciation ("7. To the dish thus seasoned add a drawl *ad libitum*")
into a much more elaborate flight of unconscious pedantry on the same
and related topics ("I will take first those cases in which something like
the French sound has been preserved in certain single letters and diph-
thongs" etc.) (*LoW* 8:39, 167).

The prime example of the Yankee wit who unsettles all pedantry ✓
through intellectual suppleness, while demonstrating in the process an
array of learning that rivals any pedantic adversary's, is of course Emerson. The great texts here are the Divinity School Address, "Circles,"
"New England Reformers," and "Illusions." I quote from the second:

> We can never see christianity from the catechism: – from the pastures, from a boat in the pond, from amidst the songs of wood-birds, we possibly may. Cleansed by the elemental light and wind, steeped in the sea of beautiful forms which the field offers us, we may chance to cast a right glance back upon biography. Christianity is rightly dear to the best of mankind; yet was there never a young philosopher whose breeding had fallen into the christian church, by whom that brave text of Paul's, was not specially prized: – "Then shall also the Son be subject unto Him who put all things under him, that God may be all in all." Let the claims and virtues of persons be never so great and welcome, the instinct of man presses eagerly onward to the impersonal and illimitable, and gladly arms itself against the dogmatism of bigots with this generous word, out of the book itself. [*EW* 2:185–6]

This is not comic, like Burroughs, but it too turns on a trick – almost a joke – of learning. The argument against scholastic bigotry in the name of nature or the illimitable is clinched by appeal to the "book itself," whose authority we are tempted to see as having been undermined by the initial antithesis of catechism versus nature. The text – in this respect, incidentally, quite in line with Unitarian anti-Calvinist polemics – dangles the specter of a total naturalism in front of the reader (with nothing left of Christianity, demystified into "biography" [of Jesus], but the sentiment of dearness) just long enough to make the reader cheer or fume, then proceeds to demonstrate that either reaction was premature. Ultimately the text shows that simply to oppose nature and learning is not enough. They must be put in opposition, yes, but the achievement of superiority over the pedantic necessitates being able to redigest the realm of learning from the standpoint of the larger universe of which it gives fitful and imperfect glimpses. In this, of course, Emerson anticipates Thoreau's intellectual attack by withdrawal-plus-absorption-of-civilization in *Walden*.

In our progression of examples from Downing to Burroughs to Emerson, we may seem to have strayed from the comic grotesque, since Emerson's Yankee voice does not present itself as a deformation in the same sense as Downing's or even Burroughs' persona. There is a connection, nonetheless.[13] The final secret the persona in "Circles" discloses is that "I am only an experimenter"; "I unsettle all things"; "I am not careful to justify myself" (*EW* 2:188): In other words, "I decline to be held responsible for my previous arguments" – although, he appears to add, in a characteristically Emersonian gesture, "I trust that they are somehow solidly grounded after all." The persona emerges from the disclosure scene as a kind of rueful trickster. He is more high-minded than a Jack Downing or a Stephen Burroughs, to be sure, but he cannot see any modus operandi other than a kind of tricksterhood, because the nature of the experience that he has pledged himself to record involves a continual pro-

cess of being overtaken by the mood of the moment. As essayist, he cannot help but replicate this process and inflict it on the reader. The persona,
then, is not simply a grotesque, like Jack Downing, but rather like a composite of Burroughs as actor and Burroughs as narrator. He is a figure
who both reveals and partially atones for the trickery that he practices as
a condition of his nature through those moments of "omniscience" in
which he disarmingly knows himself to be a trickster, although by the
same token he also achieves at such moments what might be regarded as
another form of trickery by seeming to reestablish himself as an authority
on a higher plane.

It is not altogether wordplay, then, to characterize Emerson as a Yankee
peddler of intellectual notions, resembling the wandering traders who
inspired the popular American conception of Yankee shrewdness. Indeed,
as peripatetic lecturer, Emerson was a true equivalent, the lyceum being
as much an exported article of New England commerce as the clocks,
cutlery, textiles, and wooden nutmegs of popular Yankee peddler stories.

II

It would be pleasant to end the chapter at this point, with the
tidy correlation between New England comic grotesque and the motif of
Yankee shrewdness, but that would be to suppress the existence of contrary motifs at least as stereotypical of the New England character, and at
least as productive of the comic grotesque. The one I especially have in
mind is the reputation of New Englanders for laconic stolidity. This trait
can coexist with tricksterhood, for Yankee shrewdness can take the form
of cautious reserve. Yet they also tend to work against each other, the
trickster tending toward loquacity and dominance, the stolid Yankee toward taciturnity and defensiveness. Let us inspect some cases of the second motif and then try to reconcile it with the first as best we can.

A convenient vantage point is the sizable body of stories about rustic ✓
courting rituals generated between the late 1700s and late 1800s, and in
particular the way these stories turn on the difficulty that the lovers (especially the male figure) have in coming to the point of declaring their
love. The subject may have had a special interest for post–Puritan New
England because of the comparatively sharp restraints imposed by the
proverbial New England reticence, on the one hand, and the importance
attached by the community to at least the appearance of moral propriety.
Such givens inhibited overt expression of feelings and increased the potential for comic misunderstanding.

Thomas Green Fessenden's poem "The Country Lovers, or Mr. Jonathan Jolthead's Courtship with Miss Sally Snapper" (1795?) is a typical
Federalist portrayal.[14] Jonathan is a clotpoll prodded by his mother into
courting Sal for her money. She sees this at once and decides to have some

fun with him. He is first terrified, then overbold, and in either case gauche. The climax comes when Jonathan absurdly promises her his father's bull calf as a marriage present, to which Sal replies that his father must have been quite a joker "to send his *fav'rite calf* to me, / His nice bull calf a courting." Whereat Jonathan is so taken aback that he starts to shake all over. Sal, alarmed, douses him with a bucket of water to restore his senses. Jonathan then decamps, ironically relieved that "though the jade did wet him some, / He didn't get the bag, sir!" End of farce.

Lowell's "Courtin'" (1857) (*LoW* 8:211–14) recasts the awkward swain in a more sentimental-Romantic manner.

> He stood a spell on one foot fust,
>   Then stood a spell on t'other,
> An' on which one he felt the wust
>   He could n't ha' told ye nuther.

Both poems are comic exploitations of the awkwardness radiating from the man's inexperience and the women's initial coyness. But Lowell's lovers are idealized: Zekle is "six foot o'man, A 1," the heroine sweet rather than manipulative, the setting idyllic ("Moonshine an' snow on field an' hill, / All silence an' all glisten"), the outcome predictable. He finally kisses her; it is clear that she consents (though her speech is never reported – Lowell's imitation of New England reticence); and their banns "was cried / In meetin' come nex' Sunday." End of sentimental comedy.

Although these Federalist and Romantic period pieces differ in both tone and linguistic realism, the difference is hardly clear-cut. Both start with an act of poetic condescension. Lowell's comparative ennoblement of the scene nevertheless announces itself as the report of a person of superior culture, good-naturedly observing the uncouth. It is notable that although Lowell was much concerned to demonstrate that "high and even refined sentiment may coexist with the shrewder and more comic elements of the Yankee character," he was uncomfortable about remaining on the "level of mere *patois*" (*LoW* 8:207, 156). Thus it is that the accentuation of the grotesque that especially marks the Neoclassical treatment of provincial manners persisted long after the vogue of Neoclassicism as an ideology had declined.[15] Most antebellum versions of the "courtin'" motif, in fact, read more like Jonathan and Sal than like Zekle and Huldy. In one, the hero staggers his way to unexpected success despite the fact that a pot on the stove explodes in his face when he tries to steal a kiss. We never learn whether the saucy heroine really loves him or just tolerates him. In another, the inarticulate hero is abetted by the canny girl, but only because she knows she can control his thereafter. In another, after overcoming shyness, the tongue-tied hero becomes so physical that he starts a knock-down, drag-out wrestling match with the heroine in quest of a kiss. He succeeds, but despite this daring, even after twenty visits he still cannot get up the nerve to pop the question. In another, the hero cannot make the deaf father understand that he wants to marry the daughter – not borrow a halter – so the poor girl dies unwed.[16]

Toward the end of the nineteenth century, the motif of the courting protracted by awkwardness or passivity at least becomes partially disengaged from the limitations of the comic genre sketch and is elaborated in a more sensitive yet even more obsessive and equally grotesque and formulaic way. One Mary Wilkins Freeman tale tells the pathetic story of "Two Old Lovers" who have been "courting" for twenty-five years or more, during which time he "had never reely come to the p'int." On his deathbed, he looks up at her "with a strange wonder in his glazing eyes" and stammers out at last "I allers meant to – have asked you – to – marry me." In Freeman's "New England Nun," her version of Cooke's "Tenty Scran" (discussed in Chapter 12), Joe Daggett and Louisa Ellis are engaged for fifteen years while he makes his fortune in Australia, but when it comes to the point of marriage, she finds that she fears his intrusion on her calm, secure privacy and is relieved to release him to another woman. In another of Freeman's tales, "In Butterfly Time," because Adoniram perceives his sweetheart's mother's disapproval he conscientiously refrains from proposing for forty years, until the couple's ancient mothers prepare the way.[17] In a tale inserted into *The Country of the Pointed Firs*, Sarah Orne Jewett tells of another forty-year courtship, between William Blackett and Esther Hight, happily consummated when her mother finally dies.

Although up to a point some of these stories could be regarded as exempla of laudatory self-sacrifice, <u>what primarily stands out is the extreme restraint and passivity of the lovers</u>. The aging William and Adoniram are both described as preserving remarkably youthful, even boyish, appearances during (and perhaps because of) their enforced long-term chastity; this is seen as beautiful, but also as pathetic and strange. Overall, Jewett and Freeman might be said to have combined the comic plot of ineffectual courtship with the more deeply serious treatment of the theme of the union perpetually deferred by character flaw or moral scruple that one finds in such works as Hawthorne's "Minister's Black Veil" and Dickinson's "There Came a Day at Summer's Full." "In Butterfly Time," for example, has, superficially, a jokeloric quality like the tale of the poor girl condemned to celibacy by her father's deafness. Forty years of sequestration because of her mother's jibe about the hero's fondness for butterflies: The conceit seems outlandish. But on closer inspection, the butterfly issue is seen to epitomize a larger contrast between the sensitivity and spirituality of the lovers' relationship as opposed to the mother's pragmatic desire for an advantageous match.

The device of protracted courtship owing to passivity or awkwardness by no means originated in New England writing; it goes back to Shakespeare and Chaucer. What makes it of special interest here is its prominence as a motif, its spectacular elaboration as New England regionalism unfolds, and the tendency of its perpetrators to see it as culturally symptomatic. As Longfellow's *Courtship of Miles Standish* suggests, the idea of the difficulty of broaching one's love came increasingly to be seen by New England writers as built into the historic decorums of the New England way. *The Scarlet Letter* is the most distinguished elaboration, though the theme of adultery rather than courtship proper makes it an eccentric example. What makes it possible for this romance to sustain itself through two hundred pages is the discipline imposed on the expression of love, owing to public decree and the lovers' internalization of that decree, partially in Hester's case, more thoroughly in Dimmesdale's. Few previous long fictions with love as a key concern have been so laconic in their portrayals of interaction between the main figures and so largely given over to interior action. But within this design, as in Hawthorne's other romances, perhaps the most remarkable element is one that later regional writers, especially woman writers, subject to even more subtle analysis: namely, the suggestion that the blockage of courtship, for whatever reason, may signify that the desire for celibacy is stronger than the desire for love. Dimmesdale's theology would make even a heavenly reunion with Hester unlikely; Parson Hooper's vow calls him away from Elizabeth; the calculus of love in Dickinson calls for the denial of love ("Dont you know you are happiest while I withhold and not confer –" she writes the one man with whom we know she had an affair; "dont you know that 'No' is the wildest word we consign to Language?") (*DL* 2:617). Freeman's Louisa Ellis's self-enclosure is, to her at any rate, preferable to the normality of marriage. If she had "sold her birthright," the narrator comments noncommitally, "she did not know it, the taste of the pottage was so delicious, and had been her sole satisfaction for so long. Serenity and placid narrowness had become to her as the birthright itself."[18] New England writing about the deferral of desire is at its richest and its most suggestive when it labors over the question of whether chastity, as Thoreau averred in *Walden*, might not be the "flowering of man" after all (*Wa* 219–20), whether the "grotesque" is only in the reader's imagination of it.

III

The difficulty of resolving the two stereotypes defined in this chapter into a single image of the "comic Yankee" is evident from those instances where the antithesis gets converted into literary capital. In Lowell's *Biglow Papers,* for example, the two main actors, Hosea Biglow and Birdofredum Sawin, represent the staunch and the entrepreneurial im-

ages of the Yankee rustic in conflict with each other on the question of
southern threats to Yankee integrity. Hosea, representing New England's
"homely common-sense vivified and heated by conscience" (*LoW* 8:156)
is shown as standing firm in honorable, simpleminded, principled resistance to fast-talking recruiting officers and legislative rodomontades in defense of Manifest Destiny and the Mexican War. Sawin opportunistically
enlists for the war and when wounded turns politician, as the obvious
alternative channel of self-aggrandizement. In Mary Wilkins Freeman's
"Humble Romance," the contrast presents Yankee wiliness in a more favorable light. A fast-talking but kindly peddler persuades a dutiful but
oppressed country Cinderella to elope with him. She immediately trans-
fers her total loyalty to him and becomes equally docile in her new role.
When, very soon after, he deserts her, leaving a mysterious note, the tale
raises the question of whether the one moment of her life in which she
violated her stereotype will turn out to be tragic because the peddler was,
after all, only too true to *his* stereotype. But the tale ends happily when
the husband returns to disclose that he left only because his first wife,
whom he thought dead, and who now really *is* dead, had suddenly turned
up. The spirit of enterprise turns out to be benevolent after all.

Freeman's desire quite literally to marry her stereotypical opposites en-
courages us also to seek a reconciliation. Her story provides only a factitious answer; indeed it does not try very hard: Its dramatic effect lies more
in its playful execution of a union we know to be fabulous than in making
that fabulousness plausible. But better clues may be found elsewhere.
The following shard of folklore, for example, suggests the idea that stolid
reserve may be a characteristic vehicle for Yankee shrewdness. In this anecdote, a Bostonian traveling in Vermont accosts a passing boy:

> "Jack! Jack! I want to know which is the way to Chesterfield?"
> "How did you know my name was Jack?" responded the youth.
> "Why, I guessed it," replied the traveller.
> "Oh, then you may guess your way to Chesterfield!"[19]

The sense of being patronized drives the yokel into laconic standoffish-
ness, from which stronghold he outwits the urbanite by the notorious
Yankee device of answering a question with another question.

To jump abruptly from the most rudimentary to the most sophisticated level of literary achievement, consider also the self-presentation of
the persona in *Walden*. As one of the best discussions of the subject points
out, the speaker-audience relationship in *Walden* can be seen in terms of
the traditional comic antithesis of *eiron* versus *alazon*.

> The narrator is the *Eiron*, the virtuous or witty character whose actions
> are directed toward the establishment of an ideal order. The audience
> and hecklers, who take for granted "what are deemed 'the most sacred
> laws of society,'" serve as the *Alazon* or impostor. This comic type is a

braggart, misanthrope, or other mean-spirited figure, usually an older man, who resists the hero's efforts to establish harmony but who is often welcomed into the ideal order when the hero succeeds.[20]

This type of rhetorical opposition characterizes not only the speaker-listener relationship in the book's more homiletic sections but also a number of the confrontations between the persona and various characters, such as the Irish laborer John Field and the farmer-neighbor who insists that people cannot survive on a vegetable diet. To a considerable extent the contrast involves a recasting of the shrewd trickster stereotype, sympathetically conceived in this instance, and the stolid stereotype, conceived here as obtuse – a correspondence, incidentally, that reinforces the point that formulations of quintessential New England stereotypes are pages in the much longer text of Western comedy. Yet the Thoreauvian persona also includes the opposite role of the stolid resister, sympathetically viewed as the taciturn, encastled opponent of newfangled schemes of less admirable tricksters – reformers, fashionmongers, entrepreneurs in a strictly commercial sense – who seek to bring about bogus millennia of their own envisioning. This side of Thoreau becomes the basis of Emerson's (and posterity's) conception of the contrast between them: Emerson, in his "eulogy" to his friend, inclined to criticize him for an excess of stoic reserve and a failure of enterprise, posterity inclined to turn the charge back on Emerson and cast him in the role of Transcendentalist turncoat who exchanged integrity for shrewdness, pastoral non-conformity for solidarity with bourgeois capitalism. In any case, to the extent that so complex an artifact as the Thoreauvian persona can be seen in terms of comic stereotypes, nimble shrewdness and laconic stolidity seem to apply almost equally well.

Nor, I expect, are most readers at all conscious of a conflict between these roles. The reason is partly that the roles are implanted at distinct levels of the narrative, the former more or less characterizing Thoreau as rhetor, the latter Thoreau as actor. The loquacity of the diatribe against philanthropy, for example, contrasts with the author's sullen behavior in the presence of aggressive do-gooders. Yet even at that, one must strain to represent the rhetoric as conflicting with the behavior. Really, the two are in keeping with each other. Both identities suggest reserve, repression, and redirection of impulse and emotion into solitary thought and into guarded, modulated, intellectualized forms of expression. The restless, loquacious peripatetics that mark the extreme of the trickster figure and the catatonic inertness that marks the extreme of Yankee stolidness both reflect a high degree of sublimation and internalization. Yankee comic grotesque might in this respect be compared to Yankee poetry, in which, as we saw in Chapter 5, self-imposed formal and rhetorical constraints conduce to a poetics of stylized abstraction rather than lyric immediacy.

The dependence of apparently disparate forms of Yankee comic grotesque upon the constraint of sublimation is especially well illustrated by the function of Harriet Beecher Stowe's most famous comic character, village n'er-do-well Sam Lawson, who became such a "household familiar,"[21] on the basis of his peripheral role in *Oldtown Folks,* as to precipitate a later volume devoted entirely to *Sam Lawson's Oldtown Fireside Stories.* Up to a point, Sam is a Rip Van Winkle type whose presence in the text creates humor by the contrast between his casualness and the town's bustle ("he never had anything more pressing to do than croon and gossip with us") and by the comic run-ins between him and his sharp-tongued wife. In these respects, the contrast between him and the villagers looks like a version of the contrast between the stereotypes of Yankee sharpness and Yankee stolidity, between the neighbors' briskness and Sam's refusal to be "druv" – a contrast that in this case validates the second at the expense of the first. A couple of other features, however, add some interesting overtones. One is Stowe's clear sense of the importance of this apparently unproductive creature within the social order ("Society would burn itself out with intense friction were there not interposed here and there the lubricating power of a decided do-nothing," who, among other things, provides a haven of friendly cheer for local children who might otherwise be overwhelmed by the relentless industry of respectable life).[22] Thus the communal welfare depends on "worthless" Sam.

Even more significant for our purposes, however, is the way in which Sam's character, despite its deviance, mirrors that of the community. He, too, was "always rigidly moral and instructive in his turn of mind," although he had "that fellow-feeling for transgressors which is characteristic of the loose-jointed, easy-going style of his individuality."[23] His tales and his companionableness provide a sort of safety valve for village children, not an avenue into delinquency; his role as model is to help them grow up unscarred but entirely responsible. Likewise, Sam is not really so much a "do-nothing" as a jack-of-all-trades, who, like Thoreau, becomes a kind of alternative model of village enterprise in his desultory but very competent work as handyman, mechanic, undertaker, and dispenser of charity (to all but his immediate family). Once we see that Sam does not so much oppose village norms as transmute them, the comic antithesis drawn by the narrator of *Oldtown Folks,* Horace Holyoke, seems superficial. On the surface Stowe exploits the sense of incongruity between inertia and enterprise, personified by Sam and the villagers. But beyond this, the text explores their interaction within the town community and within Sam, who in this respect is a microcosm. In Sam's apparent opposite, Horace's superconscientious Aunt Lois, the traits of stubbornness and mental vivacity create an energy-producing machine that threatens to burn out those around it, and ultimately the machine itself. Sam's more casual life-style makes fun of this not so much by any rejection of Lois as by the great difference resulting from the modification of essentially similar traits. Sam and Lois become exempla of parallel modes of channeling vital energy, parallel modes of sublimation.

Stowe does not make the clandestine intimacy between Lawson and the respectable folks explicit, although she repeatedly hints at it, as when Sam becomes the person to urge (over Aunt Lois's financial objections) that Horace "ought to have a liberal education."[24] The text's silence at this point is both strategic – if Sam's bondage to Oldtownism were flaunted, he would no longer look like a comic alternative – and substantive, for one of Stowe's favorite contentions about traditional New England life (see the epigraph to Chapter 11) is that it preserves itself through its blindness to the implications of the values to which it nominally adheres. This point gets addressed very directly in the portrait of Horace's Hopkinsian but warmhearted grandmother, who "theoretically . . . was an ardent disciple of the sharpest and severest Calvinism" yet "practically" was the most kindly, "easy-to-be-entreated old mortal on earth." In this disquisition also, although it is billed as a "serious chapter," the text shies away from the lower depths of the first side of this schizoid mentality (out of reluctance to reopen the past? or to avoid depressing the reader? or to suggest that the practical denial of Calvinist gloom was a more authentic aspect of village life than the theoretical gloom itself?). Yet the narrator also openly acknowledges that the "underlying foundation of life . . . in New England," as a consequence of its post-Puritan value system, "was one of profound, unutterable, and therefore unuttered, melancholy, which regarded human existence itself as a ghastly risk, and, in the case of the vast majority of human beings, an inconceivable misfortune."[25]

This passage bears out the Emersonian dictum that the "Comic . . . has its own speedy limits" (EW 8:173–4), implying, as Stowe does, that the New England provincial vision was at bottom somber and blighting, however brisk and cheery it may have seemed. As a mode of representation committed to depicting repressed forms of behavior, in a style that itself represses full exploration of the causes of that behavior, New England comic grotesque can do no more than throw out hints of ulterior depths. In provincial gothic, the costs of the repression that turns Sam Lawson and Henry Thoreau into village characters are more fully weighed.

16

Provincial Gothic: Hawthorne, Stoddard, and Others

> The world is so sad and solemn, that things meant in jest are liable, by an overpowering influence, to become dreadful earnest, – gayly dressed fantasies turning to ghostly and black-clad images of themselves.
>
> Nathaniel Hawthorne, *American Notebooks* (1835)

> The music of all barbarous nations is said to be in the minor key, and there is in its dark combinations something that gives piercing utterance to that undertone of doubt, mystery, and sorrow by which a sensitive spirit always is encompassed in this life.
>
> Harriet Beecher Stowe, *Oldtown Folks* (1869)

By "provincial gothic," I mean the use of gothic conventions to anatomize the pathology of regional culture.[1] Although the phrase is uncommon, most readers will immediately and rightly associate it with such works as Emily Brontë's *Wuthering Heights*, Edwin Arlington Robinson's Tilbury Town poems, Edgar Lee Masters's *Spoon River Anthology*, Sherwood Anderson's *Winesburg, Ohio*, and the "southern gothic" tradition exemplified by the fiction of William Faulkner, Carson McCullers, and Flannery O'Connor. The student who wishes to understand New England's place in American literary history as a whole will have a special interest in such writing, since New Englanders produced the first sizable body of it in this country and since provincial gothic constitutes America's most distinctive contribution to the gothic tradition as a whole.[2]

It did not, of course, originate in this country but among Anglo-Scottish and Anglo-Irish writers such as Maria Edgeworth, Walter Scott, John Galt, and James Hogg, whose sensitivity to provincial difference from English norms led them to invest the former with an atmosphere of romantic otherness and grotesquerie (qualified by post-Augustan satirical distancing) that looks forward to the great American practitioners,[3] whose similar doubleness of vision, as cosmopolitanized provincials, led them to carry on work in the same vein.

351

Delineators of a gothic mainstream, from its origins in Horace Walpole's *Castle of Otranto* (1764), through the novels of Ann Radcliffe and Matthew G. Lewis, and on to Edgar Allan Poe's "Fall of the House of Usher," Robert Louis Stevenson's *Doctor Jekyll and Mr. Hyde,* and Bram Stoker's *Dracula,* tend to relegate to the periphery works like the two on which this chapter primarily concentrates and to define as paradigmatic depictions of nightmare fantasy realms in which the representational element is less pronounced. One critic goes so far as to suggest that the stimulus that gothic fiction gave to sociohistorical mimesis was "essentially accidental" and that the earliest gothic fiction showed "no serious interest in veracity of fact or atmosphere."[4] This is useful as a corrective to such crudities as the argument that gothic, by undermining Neoclassical decorums, struck the first blow of the French Revolution against the ancien régime;[5] but it understates the significance of gothic fiction as a historical symptom expressive of the limits of human order and rationality at the very moment when these were being most aggressively promoted as values, and the potential inherent in gothic, from the start, to give this irrationalist vision a social ground. By the 1790s, the gothic, as David Morse points out, had become a "field of discourse saturated with political connotations."[6] The precedent for this was in fact set by the first gothic novels, which we soon come to expect will set their chronicles of perversity in aristocratic circles of southern and central Europe, during the era of medieval (and specifically Catholic) superstition. To be sure, this exoticism is not quite the same thing as "social context." As William Patrick Day wittily remarks, "In the world of cardboard battlements and mock-monasteries which dot the landscape of the early Gothic novels, the past vanishes into an aspect of the mind, a projection of fantasy."[7] From such reifications, however, it was an easy step for William Godwin to write a political novel depicting all of late eighteenth-century England as a sort of medieval prison for Caleb Williams. And it was equally predictable that the literary explorers of the remote corners of Great Britain should have adapted, as vehicles for analysis of provincial manners, the central gothic motifs of terror, entrapment (typically localized in an isolated mansion over which there is a fight for ownership or control), the supernatural (or appearance of same), and the melodramatic struggle between male villain and female victim (with purity, power, and property usually all at stake). In such works as Edgeworth's *Castle Rackrent,* Scott's *Bride of Lammermoor,* and Hogg's *Private Memoirs and Confessions of a Justified Sinner,* Anglo-American provincial gothic was born.

I

Perhaps because New England's aesthetic utilitarianism tended to encourage its writers to naturalize gothic as moral parable or sociocultural analysis, rather than simply as psychological thriller; perhaps because New England fiction matured during an age when regional consciousness was on the upswing at home and realist aesthetics were pressing in from abroad; perhaps because New Englanders found it just as easy to gothicize their regional heritage by invoking Puritan superstition as Southerners later did by invoking the curse of slavery – perhaps for all these reasons the gothic element became a conspicuous ingredient in depictions of New England manners within a generation of Sarah Wood's first Yankee experiments with Radcliffean formulas. The earliest important texts are William Austin's "Peter Rugg, the Missing Man" (1824), an Irvingesque story about a traveler who is perpetually unable to make his way to Boston, and Catherine Sedgwick's *New-England Tale* (1822), which depicts heroine Jane Elton as trapped in a miasma of Calvinist bigotry that has warped her relatives (also her captors) into an embracement of perversity as their norm. In this way the motif of entrapment within the province was introduced, the province was associated with the uncanny, and the uncanny was tied to Puritanism. Within another decade, John Neal, Nathaniel Hawthorne, and others had fully institutionalized New England gothic, which throve even more vigorously after the Civil War as the more mordant regional writers – Freeman, Edwin A. Robinson, and Edith Wharton, particularly – elaborated further, between the late 1880s and World War I, on the theme of backcountry ingrownness and decadence. Whereas Hawthorne and Neal had been inspired mostly by European models, the late-century regionalists looked back increasingly to their compatriots, Stowe and Hawthorne especially, and in this way New England gothic became self-sustaining. Down to the present the same vein has continued to be mined by Robert Frost (in *North of Boston*), Robert Lowell, Shirley Jackson, John Cheever, and others. A complete survey of the unfolding conventions of New England gothic from Sedgwick through Cheever (in whom it softens back toward comic grotesque) is much to be desired, but for present purposes its range and possibilities may be suggested by centering on comparable work by two of its greatest practitioners, Hawthorne and Elizabeth Barstow Stoddard.

Hawthorne is an obvious choice, since more than any other writer, he was responsible for crystallizing the image of New England strangeness, and his *House of the Seven Gables* is an equally obvious focal point, relying most heavily of all his major works on traditional gothic devices. Stoddard, known even to specialists mainly as the spouse of anthologist and fifth-rate genteel poetaster Richard Henry Stoddard, is not so obvious a choice. Although her three novels of the 1860s and her best tales won the praise of Hawthorne and Howells and comparisons of her work to that of Balzac, Turgenev, the Brontës, and Thomas Hardy, Stoddard today is absurdly undervalued. Those who trouble to read her are in for the treat of finding a genuinely first-rate talent as yet virtually unrediscovered, for whose best work absolutely no apology is needed to place it alongside that of Melville, Hawthorne, and Poe. Stoddard converted her home-town of Mattapoisett, Massachusetts, a small seaport near New Bedford, into a country of the mind that for resonance and complexity can be matched in mid–nineteenth-century New England fiction only by Haw-thorne's tales and patches of Stowe.[8]

Stoddard's first and best novel, her semiautobiographical *The Morge-sons* (1862), one of the few major female bildungsromane of the nine-teenth century,[9] dramatizes the attempts of a more aggressive woman than Hepzibah or Phoebe Pyncheon (who might be seen as parody and counterfeit, respectively, of the traditional gothic heroine) to resist the dead weight of provincial culture that threatens to imprison her, in an emotional if not a physical sense. *The Morgesons* and *The House of the Seven Gables* are family romances – tales of two families whose fates turn out to be both opposed and inextricable (in *The Morgesons* the two clans are even genealogically interlinked), families that function in their pair-ings as epitomes of both social stratification (the pedigreed Pyncheons and the Pickersgill Somerses versus the plebeian Maules and Morgesons) and cultural inbreeding. In both texts what is dramatically most at stake is the question of whether the central characters will be delivered from these webs of circumstance that are symptomatic of cultural inertia, and in both cases the deliverance is executed with an ambivalence and a pre-cipitousness that, as often in gothic, suggests a stronger imaginative al-legiance to the haunted and deformed world in which the inheritors ini-tially find themselves than to the rectification nominally achieved on their behalf in the end. Finally, the contrasts between the two texts also make comparative discussion helpful, the main contrast for our purposes being in the different statuses of these books as belated exercises in gothicism. *The House of the Seven Gables* is one of the last and most self-conscious nineteenth-century Anglo-American examples of a thoroughgoing gothic plot, replete with all the usual appurtenances. *The Morgesons,* like Charlotte Brontë's *Jane Eyre* and Dickens' *Great Expectations,* is a more typical mid–nineteenth-century example of the commingling of gothic devices with representational realism.[10]

But rather than dwell on such relationships in the abstract, it will be more useful to anchor for a time in two luminous passages and move outward from that center. The first, from *The House of the Seven Gables,* presents the failure of Clifford's and Hepzibah's abortive impulse to ven-ture out to church; the second, from *The Morgesons,* is a vignette of the maternal grandfather of protagonist-narrator Cassandra Morgeson, as seen in retrospect through her eyes.

First the Hawthorne:

"Dear Brother," said she, earnestly, "let us go! We belong nowhere. We have not a foot of space, in any church, to kneel upon; but let us go to some place of worship, even if we stand in the broad aisle. Poor and forsaken as we are, some pew-door will be opened to us!"

So Hepzibah and her brother made themselves ready – as ready as they could, in the best of their old-fashioned garments, which had hung on pegs, or been laid away in trunks, so long that the dampness and mouldy smell of the past was on them – made themselves ready, in their faded bettermost, to go to church. They descended the staircase together, gaunt, sallow Hepzibah, and pale, emaciated, age-stricken Clifford! They pulled open the front-door, and stept across the threshold, and felt, both of them, as if they were standing in the presence of the whole world, and with mankind's great and terrible eye on them alone. The eye of their Father seemed to be withdrawn, and gave them no encouragement. The warm, sunny air of the street made them shiver. Their hearts quaked within them, at the idea of taking one step further.

"It cannot be, Hepzibah! – it is too late," said Clifford with deep sadness. – "We are ghosts! We have no right among human beings – no right anywhere, but in this old house, which has a curse on it, and which therefore we are doomed to haunt. And, besides," he continued, with a fastidious sensibility, inalienably characteristic of the man, "it would not be fit nor beautiful, to go! It is an ugly thought, that I should be frightful to my fellow-beings, and that children would cling to their mothers' gowns, at sight of me!"

They shrank back into the dusky passage-way, and closed the door. But, going up the staircase again, they found the whole interior of the house tenfold more dismal, and the air closer and heavier, for the glimpse and breath of freedom which they had just snatched. They could not flee; their jailor had but left the door ajar, in mockery, and stood behind it, to watch them stealing out. At the threshold, they felt his pitiless gripe upon them. For, what other dungeon is so dark as one's own heart! What jailor so inexorable as one's self! [*HW* 2:168–9]

And now the Stoddard passage:

Grandfather Warren was a little, lean, leather-colored man. His head was habitually bent, his eyes cast down; but when he raised them to peer about, their sharpness and clear intelligence gave his face a wonderful vitality. He chafed his small, well-shaped hands continually; his long polished nails clicked together with a shelly noise, like that which beetles make flying against the ceiling. His features were delicate and handsome; gentle blood ran in his veins, as I have said. All classes in Barmouth treated him with invariable courtesy. He was aboriginal in character, not to be moved by antecedent or changed by innovation – a Puritan, without gentleness or tenderness. He scarcely concealed his contempt for the emollients of life, or for those who needed them. He whined over no misfortune, pined for no pleasure. His two sons, who broke loose from him, went into the world, lived a wild, merry life, and died there, he never named. He found his wife dead by his side one morning. He did not go frantic, but selected a text for the funeral sermon; and when he stood by the uncovered grave, took off his hat and thanked his friends for their kindness with a loud, steady voice. Aunt Mercy told me that after her mother's death his habit of chafing his hands commenced; it was all the difference she saw in him, for he never spoke of his trouble or acknowledged his grief by sign or word. [*MOW* 28–9]

In each passage, the figures described are established as symptomatic grotesques through a combination of direct portrayal ("gaunt, sallow Hepzibah"; the beetlelike clicking of Warren's nails) and the contrast, not fully dramatized, between their vanishing, ghostly world and the modern mundane world to which they cannot or will not adapt. This is the most common way in which the light irony of comic grotesque shades into the pathos and eeriness of provincial gothic: The representation of broadly typical figures frozen in cultural contexts that are seen as blighted by unbreakable habits, ancestral obsessions, ancient grievances, and restrictive codes that unsuit their inhabitants from entering the modern world even when they are so inclined, as many (like Grandfather Warren) are not. The sense of psychological repression and the climate of economic and cultural scarcity that have been identified in the preceding chapters of Part IV as prime ingredients of grotesquification in portrayals of the New England cultural landscape are here accentuated to an extreme degree and capped by the metaphor, explicit or implied, of self-imprisonment.

The ambience of the self-imprisoning provincial culture so pervades each passage that the mundane surrounding world remains as much a mystery as the strangeness of the gothic realm itself. The modern mundane world is the place where the Warren boys vanish, never to be named again, and is also the realm of the imaginary ogres of Hepzibah's and Clifford's invention. We realize, well before Holgrave tells Hepzibah, that her ancient gentility has rendered her helpless in democratic America; but although we may judge her from that standpoint, we are not allowed to settle there, because the narrator keeps us almost entirely within the precincts of the house. The reader must make a concerted effort to keep in mind that these works presuppose a historical context of modernization and that whatever devices may be attributed to purely literary borrowings (such as the enchanted-mansion motif so thoroughly picked over by Hawthorne), the conception of the grotesque in both of the passages arises just as powerfully from the impact of contemporary social reality that presses upon the milieus depicted here and brackets them as obsolete and grotesque. This impact is suggested both through the occasional portrayal of technological innovations like the railroad, in *The House of the Seven Gables,* and through such internal erosions as Cassandra's refusal to suppress her drive for self-realization by accepting Warren's post-Puritan austerity and moralism, as her mother had done. Although provincial gothic fixes its sights ostensibly on the archaic, the consciousness of what is going on in the largely invisible urban centers is what permits the identification of the obsolete as such.[11] Hence, in part, its extreme fondness both for portraying ancient characters like the ones in these two passages and for juxtaposing these with youthful figures in counterpoint: Warren and Cassandra; the Pyncheon siblings and Holgrave/Phoebe; Rosa Coldfield and Quentin Compson; the two Tarwaters, in Flannery O'Connor's *The Violent Bear It Away;* Tom Scanlon and the two boys, Gordon and Calvin, in Wright Morris' *Ceremony at Lone Tree;* the gerontocracy and the young Miranda and Maria, in Katherine Anne Porter's "Old Mortality." The young people function, so to speak, as reader surrogates mirroring the possible range of responses evoked by the old order: recoil, surrender, usurpation, sometimes all three. The presence, in any case, of the prospective but usually reluctant inheritor of the obsolescent ethos is a typical means of bracketing that ethos as gothic and dramatizing its characteristic mixture of repulsiveness and charm.

In both of the passages quoted, time is in a sense arrested. Hepzibah and Clifford end where they started; Warren is pulled out of time altogether and encapsulated in a cameo portrait that starts and ends with the hand-chafing image. This static quality is not genre-specific. We have noted it before as a sign of the unusual faintness of the distinction between fiction and nonfiction in the writing of our period, suggesting that it is symptomatic of contemporary distrust of narrative invention as against informational or moralistic content. The analytical (and in Hawthorne overtly judgmental) approach of the narration seems to corroborate that. But in provincial gothic there seems to be an additional pertinence to resisting a strong linear narrative, with its implied affirmation of the importance of temporal development in shaping human experience. Provincial gothic fictions usually do employ some sort of linear plot, including change of fortunes and even personality change in the younger and less acculturated characters. But those characters shown to be products of context and tradition do not essentially alter; nor is there social transformation, except symbolically, as in *The House of the Seven Gables,* where the union of Holgrave and Phoebe "transfigured the earth, and made it Eden again, and themselves the two first dwellers in it" (*HW* 2:307). But this is a transformation that most readers have understandably either found unconvincing or defensible only by the rather shaky argument that the metaphysical or fairy-tale element of the romance is somehow extricable from its sociohistorical matrix. Certainly the latter does not change. Hepzibah, Clifford, and Uncle Venner will remain themselves, even if in new surroundings; property law does not change as a result of the judge's accidental death; and the immobility of Salem culture in general is thrust home by the closing dialogue between the two stereotypical locals, who exchange a slightly altered version of the same fatuities about the Pyncheons that we have heard several times before. There may be escape from Salem, but for Salem and for Salemites there is no escape.[12]

In *The Morgesons,* the disparity between progress and stasis is even more striking. In the bildungsroman manner, the novel is more a chronicle of initiatives than of defenses, presumably somewhat as *The House of the Seven Gables* would have been had Holgrave been the chief protagonist. The aggressive and impetuous Cassandra, who combines the passion of Catherine Earnshaw with the survival skills of Jane Eyre, deviates markedly from standard sentimental, gothic, and domestic heroines in the directness with which she confronts the sexual and economic barriers that threaten to keep her subordinate: patriarchal conditioning, encountered especially on her first journey to be educated in the Puritan regime of her maternal grandfather; male sexual domination, faced during her second journey, in which she makes an extended visit to her Byronic cousin Charles, whose lust she excites (and reciprocates) but keeps at bay; and social ineligibility, which threatens to intimidate her during her third visit, to the elegant home of the two brothers who later marry her and her sister and alter ego, Veronica. Gathering strength and confidence through these tests, Cassandra eventually gains control of the family mansion and marries the husband of her choice. Yet so much emphasis is put on the scenes of combat, and so sudden are the final reversals (of property transfer and of the reform of Cassandra's dissipated fiancé, Desmond Somers), that at first sight *The Morgesons* looks like another case of the forced ending. Stoddard, however, manages such things somewhat better than Hawthorne in *The House of the Seven Gables. The Morgesons* makes it clear that Cassandra's "liberation" has not been accompanied by any fundamental change in the status quo (which she has merely turned to her advantage) and that genuine fulfillment continues to elude her. In the process of achieving what she wants – economic control and enlightened marriage – she seems only to add to her original alienation the ethic of submission to domestic responsibility that she despised in her mother. In woman's fiction, this translation into the sphere of adult responsibility is celebrated; here it is a dimunition. In symbolic terms, Cassandra both slays and becomes her parents. She takes possession at the price of accepting confinement within the house of Morgeson, inaugurating what would seem to be a new cycle – not a new era.

Provincial gothic, then, takes impetus from the awareness of social change but is grounded in the premise that institutions and values resist change. This insight, in turn, supplies the ideological foundation for pro-

vincial gothic's assimilation of the standard theme of entrapment (typically imaged by symbolic houses that function as extensions of familial
and cultural constraints) and for the standard plot elements of ordeal by
immurement, suffering, resistance, and escape. Yet the sense of cultural
inertia as the basis of the gothic effect makes any attempt at closure of the
standard liberation plot much more risky than in mainstream gothic
works such as *The Castle of Otranto, The Mysteries of Udolpho,* and *Dracula,* whose more explicit fantasticalness permits not only a more thoroughgoing evocation of the demonic but also its exorcism. In provincial
gothic, any attempt at exorcism of the dead hand of the past that is not at
least partially self-undermining, as in *The Morgesons,* will seem forced. In
Holgrave's sudden comic-embarrassed gesture of conservatism at the end
of Hawthorne's novel, that text too shows at least a partial awareness of
the betrayal of its original premises involved in the capitulation to readerly (and writerly) wish fulfillment.[13]

In New England gothic, the most distinctive thematic ingredient is the
perception of Puritan culture as inherently grotesque. Catherine Maria
Sedgwick's *New-England Tale* makes this diagnosis explicit from the start.
The wicked-stepmother figure, Jane's Aunt Wilson, having "fancied herself one of the subjects of an awakening at an early period of her life, had
passed through the ordeal of a church-examination with great credit" and
"thus assumed the form of godliness without feeling its power."[14] As a
visible saint, she feels free both to spoil and to bully her children, who
sink into total depravity as a result, and to despise her niece, whose goodness the aunt sees as meaningless because it has not been accompanied by
the forms of conversion. Grotesquification here is essentially the consequence of mistaking form for substance, which is seen as a typically Calvinist failing: Calvinism leads to phariseeism, which distorts the whole
social environment. Actually this insight is just as Puritan as it is anti-
Puritan, since the devout Puritan's intense concern for distinguishing authentic from simulated conversion was precisely what first implanted
within New England thought an intense suspicion of mere formalism, as
well as the paradoxically opposite compulsion to formalize by testing experience against an accepted paradigm of grace. Anti-Calvinist polemics
like Sedgwick's and anti-Unitarian polemics like Lyman Beecher's are in
this sense mirror images, each accusing the other of reducing sanctification to externals. But in practice, New England gothic, like the overlapping genre of historical romances about Puritanism, was usually produced by Arminian apologists (Sedgwick), renegade Congregationalists
(Freeman), or relatively secularized liberals (Hawthorne, Stoddard) – in
recoil against, or fascination with, the mystique of the old-time, preindustrial village and town life and of their forebears, which had been

marked by a degree of pious observance, moralism, and social stratification from which the authors saw the more advanced minds of their own day as having at least partially broken.

One of the most popular vehicles in New England writing for transmuting Puritanism into the stuff of gothic is the evocation of witchcraft as a theme.[15] We owe the fact that the Salem delusion is the best-known episode of early New England history next to the voyage of the Mayflower largely to Hawthorne and fellow gothicizers of his era, to whom witchcraft appealed, as we began to see in Part III, for a mixture of reasons: as an opportunity for proxy war against religious conservatives, as that instance from the regional past that resonated most strongly with the supernaturalism of traditional Gothic, and as a proof that New England culture was not so humdrum as early national critics had feared. These themes appear to have been highbrow translations of themes from folk culture. One of Stowe's narrators, for instance, taking note of the pervasiveness of satanic names in local topography (every village seems to have its "Devil's Pulpit" or "Devil's Punchbowl"), recalls how the "very idea of going to the Devil's Den was full of a pleasing horror. . . . This spirit land was my only refuge from the dry details of a hard, prosaic life."[16] The suggestion made here of old-style supernaturalism as culturally close enough to supply the thrill and creepiness of the mysterious yet far enough away to be encountered without any real risk (even the child senses that it is mere superstition) helps explain such initially strange and touching period paradoxes as the spectacle of Whittier, a confirmed opponent of theological bigotry, devoting his spare time to the collection of regional superstitions, which he cherished as an endangered species in need of preservation, though at the same time he did not fail to turn them into monitory exempla: "All this is pleasant enough now; we can laugh at the Doctor [Mather] and his demons: but little matter of laughter was it to the victims on Salem hill" – and so forth.[17] Such twistings and turnings make it easier to point to the presence of witchcraft as a source of gothicization in such literary works as *The House of the Seven Gables* and *The Morgesons* than to unpack their ideological ramifications. But let us try.

In *The House of the Seven Gables,* witchcraft is the most obvious means used to give mystical potency to the theme that the sins of the fathers are visited on the children. "God will give him blood to drink!" prophesies wizard Maule (*HW* 2:8), and so it is, down to the *n*th generation. In *The Morgesons,* witchcraft is a less explicitly central means of dramatizing the protagonist's perceived strangeness. "That child is possessed," is the novel's opening statement, spoken by Cassandra's maternal aunt, who, despite a natural kindliness, has been programmed by her Puritan father (Grandt'her Warren) to misread Cassandra's obstreperousness as demonic

(*MOW* 5). Images of witchcraft and demonism are interspersed throughout and, of course, encoded in Cassandra's name, given her in deliberate
violation of the custom of baptizing local children with "scriptur'"
names. On one level, her intellectual maturity can be seen as hinging on
the discovery of what her name means. (She knows nothing of her namesake until she grows up.) Her fate is to understand and to make effective
use of the charisma and penetration that others see in her much more
quickly than she sees in herself, but finally to feel the same impotence as
her prototype.[18]

Each text plays a triple game with witchcraft. Witchcraft, in the first
instance, is what defines the social order as oppressive, insofar as it is a
kind of unavoidable extreme to which the "witch" has been driven out of
desperation and the need for self-protection by norms we thereby recognize as grotesque. Yet at the same time witchcraft, rather than the provincial gothic society that gives rise to it, thus becomes the carrier and
perpetuator of the uncanny. Thus the most dangerous moment in *The
House of the Seven Gables* is not when Judge Pyncheon threatens to force
his way to Clifford but when Holgrave is tempted to do to Phoebe what
his ancestor did to Alice Pynchon. Cassandra's more innocent yet ultimately more lethal witchery is to become a kind of femme fatale in relation to her potential seducer, Cousin Charles (who is symbolically destroyed by the passion for her that she incites even as she resists). "What
do you think of those scenes in Jane Eyre," Stoddard once asked James
Russell Lowell, "where she watches with a professional eye the rising of
[Rochester's] passional emotions, and skilfully prevents any culmination
of feeling by changing her manner?"[19] Stoddard's variation on this is to
make Cassandra a half-ingenuous, half-deliberate provoker of the emotions from whose intensity she backs away into reserve. Here, for instance, is how she handles Ben Somers' brotherly/loverly admonitions
against Charles. Cassandra's provocations prompt Ben to blurt out:

> "I do not like him. He is a savage. . . . He has never seen a woman like
> you; who has? Forgive me, but I watch you both."
> "I have perceived it."
> "I suppose so, and it makes you more willful."
> "You said you were but a boy."
> "Yes, but I have had one or two manly wickednesses. I have done
> with them, I hope."
> "So that you have leisure to pry into those of others."
> "You do not forgive me."
> "I like you; but what can I do?"
> "Keep up your sophistry to the last."[*MOW* 102]

Cassandra's probing yet guarded ironic manner (replicated in the whole
style of narration) is the basis of her power as an enchantress, telegraph-

ing to the men around her a tantalizing mixture of audacity and reserve yet also serving as a defense against the advances that her boldness might provoke. Whatever Ben means by his last comment, it testifies that her "sophistry" gives her an eerie charm that attracts men of "manly wickednesses" (especially the book's two "devils," Charles and Desmond), and vice versa ("I like devils," she later tells a friend [MOW 110]). But what gives her the balance of power is her resistance to her own "devilishness." That keeps her from yielding to what she regards as an illicit passion for Charles (even as she lingers temptingly, and tempted, in his neighborhood until he meets with an accident that symbolizes death by excess of repressed lust).[20] Indispensable to the happy ending of Hawthorne's novel is exorcism of sorcery, as well as retribution for the offense that called it into being: Holgrave must submit to Phoebe's sway. The Morgesons provides a sort of equivalent to his Prospero-like wand breaking in Cassandra's acceptance of responsible domestic matronhood.

So witchcraft is linked, in both texts, to social and personal derangement in ways that differ sharply but point in each case to a world in need of exorcism. Yet with exorcism comes not simply rescue but also disenchantment. There is an anticlimactic, even self-emasculating aspect to Holgrave's embracement of Phoebe's sunny normality, as in Hawthorne's own life at those moments when he compared artistry to prying or murder and protested that his Phoebe (one of his pet names for his wife, Sophia) kept him from morbidness. The indulgence of the role of Holgrave or Maule, the artist-mesmerist, is as indispensable a part of Hawthorne's curve of imagination as his final retreat from that role.[21] On one level, Holgrave, Maule, Rappaccini, Chillingsworth, and all the rest of Hawthorne's quasi-artist figures are dreams of power, deeply exciting even as they horrify. The clear desire to play the sorcerer-artist, even as another side of him disowns the role, is present from the start of his career, as in "Alice Doane's Appeal," where the narrator builds a tale of witchcraft and interrupts his illusion with commentary in which he presents himself first as failing to impress his female auditors with his manuscript, then as manipulating their emotions overweeningly.

The coda to The Morgesons presents the anticlimactic nature of disenchantment more baldly than the end of The House of the Seven Gables, which whips up the counterenchantment of domestic romance. Ben has died of alcoholism; his widow, Cassandra's Pre-Raphaelitish, Emily Dickinson-like sister, has withdrawn into a state of seeming immobility. Cassandra herself is listless. The sea, which has functioned throughout the book as Lawrentian emblem of her passionate desire, "wears a relentless aspect to me now; its eternal monotone expresses no pity, no compassion" (MOW 252). Unlike woman's fiction, of which The Morgesons is in some respects a sophisticated parody,[22] the ending of The Morgesons makes the reader wish for the return of an unregenerated Cassandra and for a resuscitated Charles with whom she could engage in the old sexual combat. It is worth noting that Stoddard herself diagnosed the failure of Cassandra and Charles to consummate their affair as a failure of nerve rather than a triumph of restraint. "With the capacity between them of a magnetic and profound passion," she wrote in late life to a publisher friend, "the pressure of generations of Puritan teachings and examples, prevented it from being in result nothing [*sic;* anything?] more than nebulous particles striving in the universe to come together and make a new world." [23] This statement is disingenuous, a refusal to acknowledge any prudential motivation for the novel's strategic retreat from adultery with Charles to a socially acceptable marriage with the reformed rake, Desmond. Yet the necessity of this repression, this settling for the second-best thrill, exists not just as a concession to readerly expectation but as the logical, if initially unexpected, expression of Cassandra's character, whose witchcraft is always exercised behind self-imposed bars. What is most piquant about Stoddard's distinctive, dryly incisive narrative voice (a trademark that establishes her, along with Emerson, Thoreau, Hawthorne, and Dickinson, as a master of tone) is that its reserve ultimately forces us to reread its ironies not just as astringencies directed against Ben, Grandfather Warren, or provincial stupidity but as the self-recoil of a disenchanted mind that in retrospect perceives but stubbornly clings to its own dissatisfied self-constraint by striking a posture of ironic reserve.

One final passage will help us here. It describes Cassandra's feelings after she returns home from her visit to Charles.

> I had a comfortable sense of property, when I took possession of my own room. It was better, after all, to live with a father and mother, who would adopt my ideas. Even the sea might be mine. I asked father the next morning, at breakfast, how far out at sea his property extended.
>
> "I trust, Cassandra, you will now stay at home," said mother; "I am tired of table duty; you must pour the coffee and tea, for I wish to sit beside your father."
>
> "You and Aunt Merce have settled down into a venerable condition. You wear caps, too! What a stage forward!"
>
> "The cap is not ugly, like Aunt Merce's; I made it," Veronica called, sipping from a great glass.
>
> "Gothic pattern, isn't it?" father asked, "with a tower, and a bridge at the back of the neck?" [*MOW* 129]

As always in vintage Stoddard, this is rich in innuendo but stingy in disclosure. The typical nonconversation among family members who talk past each other (the kind of scene that made Thomas Wentworth Higginson compare the disconcerting autonomy of the Dickinson family members to Stoddard's people [*DL* 2:473]) is the complement of the narrator's posture of holding her own feelings in suspension. The sense of Cassandra's vulnerability and self-contradiction (as she is torn between the regressive embracement of domestic security and the aggressive desire for ownership) is shown only through the amusing hyperbole of her question to her father. That her homing instinct (however we interpret it) may betray her even as it promises fulfillment is foreshadowed by the exchange with her mother, from whose demand she scornfully draws back, and is obliquely clinched by the father's gloss on the matronly cap as of "gothic pattern." The desire to "take possession" of her inheritance, the passage hints, will in the long run cause her to become repossessed herself. But the text's refusal to make all of this explicit frees us both to relish Cassandra the heroine for her wry thoughts and acerbic manner and to appreciate, as we read on, that Cassandra the narrator has directed the wryness and acerbity more against herself than we thought. Hawthorne achieves a similar doubleness through Coverdale in *The Blithedale Romance*.

This discussion of various kinds of witchcraft is one illustration among many of how provincial gothic, like traditional gothic, is built upon the ambivalence of clinging to and exploiting the eeriness that it somehow also feels compelled to exorcise. It lingers in the shadow land of Hepzibah and Clifford while complaining about the dead hand of the past; it gets its most memorable effects from the grotesquerie that it feels obliged to kill off or tame down. Like Quentin Compson and his roommate Shreve, in Faulkner's *Absalom, Absalom!*, it lives a double existence in the modernity of a Harvard dormitory and in the obsolescence of the old order; and, indeed, it is most alive when in the process of imaginatively embracing the strangeness of the latter. Quentin's "*I dont hate it*" is provincial gothic's secret motto – uttered in the "iron New England dark."[24]

II

The treatment of the witchcraft theme in our two texts also makes clear the importance of putting them in a sequence of development in several respects. First, both novels show the drift toward secularization in New England gothic. Up to a point, Hawthorne, like Sedgwick, seems to have created a fictional world governed by the Calvinist premise of imputed sin, the mutual transgressions of the first Pynchon and the first Maule having been bequeathed to their descendants until a new Adam and Eve expiate the curse. The persistence of sorcery among the Maules and of avarice, apoplexy, and hypocrisy among the Pynchons creates an aura of preternatural fatality and threatens to turn history into allegorical nightmare. Stoddard, however, portrays a setting in which theology is reduced to parlor conversation and the supernatural resolves itself into a combination of offbeat bohemian charm and scattered instances of rather hackneyed psychic communication between the Morge-son sisters and their beaux. It should be added that Stoddard provides far more circumstantial theological contexting than Hawthorne usually does and thereby reveals her genealogy as a "moderate" Calvinist descended from the Old Light faction opposed by the Edwardsean New Divinity camp to which the Beechers belonged. Cassandra's emancipation from childhood restraints, for example, is expedited by trips to communities of increasing theological liberalism. The ecclesiastical politics of Cassandra's hometown parish are also intermittently detailed. Yet such details are treated as interesting only to pious elders against whom she has defined herself. ("When I was young," Stoddard once noted, "I was fed on the strong dish of New England polemics"; as an adult, "sinner that I am, I confess to secular habits entirely" [*MOW* 315]). *The Morgesons* pseudonymously invokes none other than Reverend Thomas Robbins, the early nineteenth-century orthodox historian and editor of Cotton Mather's *Magnalia* (cf. Chapter 9), as Cassandra's intellectual mentor – as he was Stoddard's in real life; however, he appears not in his role as theologue but simply as a nice old gentleman who lets Cassandra read the eighteenth-century secular classics in his well-stocked library.[25]

This process of secularization is not a simple progression. In Hawthorne, the "Calvinist" aspect of the fictional world is put under question from the start with the Preface's self-consciousness about the choice of moral. The world turns out not to be depraved and predestinated after all – at least not if the narrator can help it; he wants finally to suggest that any impression of human nature and history as inexorably fallen was a mistaken hypostasis of the evil side of human nature, the effects of which can be offset by generosity. The narrator, in other words, wants to suggest not only that sunny virtue can triumph over gothic gloom – a standard Radcliffean ploy – but that the gothic gloom in a sense need never have existed. It was more a false consciousness than the more literally demonic iniquity personified by gothic villains like *Udolpho*'s Montoni, of whom that portly burgher Jaffrey Pyncheon is a faint replica, droll by comparison. Nevertheless, until its denouement, *The House of the Seven Gables* effectively masquerades as one of those texts that lend support to Joel Porte's argument that Anglo-American gothic takes its chief energy from the Calvinist imagination, whereas Stoddard points more directly to Mary Wilkins Freeman's fully secularized way of aligning Puritan and grotesque by reducing Puritan twistedness to an excess of secular will.

Perry Westbrook exaggerates only a little, if at all, in claiming that Freeman "among American writers is the supreme analyst of the Puritan will."[26] Her most powerful work deals with characters whose fixed obsessions turn them into grotesques. But there is very little specifically Puritan in her case studies. Will, as a category, is divested of theological rhetoric even more thoroughly than the theological issues treated in *The Scarlet Letter,* manifesting itself simply as a behavioral trait, though with moral overtones to be sure. Take the familiar case of "A New England Nun." Freeman could easily have written this story in such a way as to correlate Louisa Ellis' inertia and sublimation of sexuality with Puritan ideology. But she chose not to, despite the clear sense (evident from the title) of the story as a typical New England portrait, and despite the fact that fellow writers like Dickinson were, almost at the same moment, grounding symbolic nunhood in an elaborate post-Calvinist religious framework. Instead Freeman writes an everyday fable of spinsterly entrenchment that might be transferable to a number of other American regions. The reason for the contrast between Freeman and Dickinson was not so much one of temperament (both were intense, somewhat neurotic quasi Congregationalists) but probably that, in the first place, Freeman was portraying a nonelite figure unlikely to be interested in or deft at doctrinal intellectualizations and that, second, Freeman would have recognized the anachronism of the latter in the 1880s and 1890s. Several decades earlier, when *A New-England Tale* was republished (1852), Sedgwick had taken care to emphasize that liberalization had made her story obsolete: "A pharisaical, canting bigot, of the old orthodoxy of New-England, like the Dame Wilson of our story, would talk an unknown tongue to a sister in the communion of the new school, albeit evangelical."[27] Still burning at the memory of the hard-shell Hopkinsianism under which her family had suffered during her childhood, Sedgwick cannot resist one or two kicks at the dead horse, but the message is clear: The hegemony is over; the Calvinist bogeyman is no longer in evidence; Puritanism, in the sense of theologically based intimidation, is no longer going to be an effectual source of gothic terror for the New England artist. Dickinson's poetry, still to come, shows that Sedgwick's epitaph was premature. But Sedgwick has accurately predicted the secularization of gothic in Stoddard and later New England practitioners. Henceforth the source of gothic will be seen increasingly in the residue left behind by the decay or evaporation of aggressive Calvinism, rather than in Puritan ideology as such: in the "corpse-coldness" that Emerson saw in Unitarianism; in the obstinate inertia of Freeman's figures; and in the elder Morgesons' dogged adherence to the idea that "existing Institutions should not be disturbed" (*MOW* 20), leading to an intellectual passivity that abets willful self-assertion on their children's part and retards the formation of distinct values of their own through its mushy vagueness. The end of the road is Edith Wharton's hapless ménage à trois in *Ethan Frome,* who are unable to do anything but marginally survive as moral and physical invalids, in torpor and mutual resentment.

    The shift just described is related to the mimetic shift from romance to regional realism. Hawthorne defined himself as a romancer; so did Stoddard, but more ambivalently, and she was quick to defend the mimetic accuracy of her portrayals.[28] The difference in posture is important. To return to our pair of original passages: Stoddard shows Warren mainly from the outside, in terms of his social relationships; Hawthorne is more concerned with the inner life. His narrative voice also is more subjectified, despite the fact that it is undramatized and therefore potentially less so. The ruminations of the narrator shift the passage from the level of descriptive vignette to that of mood piece, so that the subjective orientation in the definition of character (the Pyncheons' inner compulsions being seen as dominating their external lives and rendering them immobile) is paralleled by the introspective mode of narration.

Stoddard, in her own way, also gives a very filtered glimpse of Grandfather Warren. The passage announces itself as an orderly character sketch: "Grandfather Warren was a little, lean, leather-colored man," and so forth. But Stoddard plays down narrative voice as such in order to let dialogue and image stand more on their own. In fact, as we saw a moment ago, one of the most haunting traits of her narrative style is that she plays narrative voice down so much that the reader is constantly prodded, as in Emerson's densest essays, into inferential leaps. What, for instance, are we to make of the last two sentences of the Stoddard passage? Do they mask admiration, horror, bitterness, contempt – or all of these? Freeman brought regional realism to a higher pitch of descriptive precision, but Stoddard's laconic mode of rendering significant detail was richer in its power of insinuation than her successors', whose commitment to representing social texture divests their portrayals of New England idiosyncrasy of some of its elliptical magic.

All of this suggests that provincial gothic is potentially most powerful when operating somewhere in between the imaginary poles of romance and realism, interfusing both approaches. When portraying character, for instance, the writer must at once present the figure as arising from some authentic sociohistorical matrix and yet also as weird or dreamlike by reason of having been warped (from a "normal" outsider's standpoint) by the conditioning of that matrix. Flannery O'Connor was getting at this mimetic duality when she called the novelist of southern grotesque a "realist of distances" who depicts social reality from the perspective of a "prophetic vision" that sees it as skewed.[29] O'Connor's formulation, imputing to the artist an unscarred detachment from the agonies portrayed, reflects her commitment to a more fixed dogmatic position (Catholic) than we find in either Hawthorne or Stoddard. This keeps O'Connor from noting, at least in the statement just quoted, one of the most poignant features of provincial gothic, the doppelgänger quality of the skewed world depicted or invented by the realist of distances. The concluding reflections of the Hawthorne passage ("What other dungeon is so dark as one's own heart! What jailor so inexorable as one's self!") acknowledge just such a bond between the created world and the "detached" narrator, who significantly emphasizes at the book's start that "on my occasional visits to the town aforesaid, I seldom fail to turn down Pyncheon-street" (*HW* 2:5). Perhaps such scandalous acknowledgments of self-implication may have had something to do with the fact that O'Connor had trouble reading Hawthorne, even though she said that she felt "more of a kinship with him than with any other American." But, in fairness of O'Connor, it should be added that the relationship between the observer and the observed in her work is more complex than her formulation suggests,[30] and that her repression of her affinity for the grotesque is simply the opposite pole from Hawthorne's shuddering empathy of the provincial gothicist's ambivalence toward his or her created world. Presentations of that created world as alien other clandestinely acknowledge its status as personal obsession; that is the "realistic" approach. Presentations of that world as an internalized reality distance it by representing it as alien other; that is the Romantic approach.

Perhaps the most decisive shift suggested by the contrast between Hawthorne's romance and Stoddard's realism is neither the theological nor the mimetic shift but the withering away of the fourth dimension, the disappearance of historical consciousness itself, such as we noted at the end of Part III. Consider the focal characters: In *The House of the Seven Gables,* whichever one regards as the "principal character" to whom Hawthorne so mysteriously alludes (*HW* 16:406), the emphasis is clearly much more on those who live in the past than in *The Morgesons,* whose protagonist is a would-be Holgrave. Consider too the use of duplicate characters as mirror images, in which both works abound. In Hawthorne, this is done in order to show history as a "series of echoes and reflections," although there are, of course, also contrasts between prototype and successor.[31] In Stoddard, however, there is no *historical* significance in Desmond's resemblance to Charles, and there is at most a psychosocial significance in Cassandra's becoming a duplicate of her mother. The Morgesons, like the Pyncheons, are a dynasty that has asserted power over rivals on the strength of entrepreneurial aggressiveness, but in Stoddard this is pictured not as the burden of history but as a break from history – a supplanting of the more pedigreed New England families such as the Warrens (descended from the Plymouth Pilgrims) – rather than as the start of New England civilization. Although Cassandra experiences repression and inertia from both sides of the family, her struggle for self-realization is in a sense also a continuation of her father's line, an equivalent of Transcendentalist radicalism succeeding Unitarian liberalism. Above all, the past that haunts Cassandra is much more her personal past than the historical, institutional past evoked in *The House of the Seven Gables,* Hawthorne's most ambitious dramatization of the impress of history on the contemporary world.[32]

It is tempting to read the shrinkage of the historical consciousness in *The Morgesons* as a form of dramatic irony – as evidence of intention to portray, by banishing history to the subconscious, a further degree of cultural impoverishment than is envisaged in Hawthorne's romance. In *The House of the Seven Gables,* the hand of the past warps those who live in the past, but characters without a past (as Holgrave initially tries to be) are also stunted by comparison with those who are in touch with the right kind of past, like Phoebe, who personifies the New England village ideal.[33] In any event, the disappearance of the historical consciousness is typical of late-century New England gothic fiction, which increasingly focuses on cultural inertia as it obtains at a particular (usually contemporary) moment and does not depict the remote origins of that inertia prior to the life-spans of the family or local circle being depicted. We are shown their rootedness but not their roots; we are apprised that this is a state of decay much more often than we are shown the state from which they have declined.

Indeed, these late-century characters (with such exceptions as Sarah Orne Jewett's "Dulham Ladies") seem less and less aware that they represent a state of decline – a fact that of course confirms and reinforces their bondage to that state. Whether we criticize Hawthorne's thinking about history for self-contradictoriness or try to find in it a deeper consistency, it is clear that his ability to contemplate the flow of history to begin with (and the similar ability of such "emancipated" Hawthorne characters as Holgrave) depended on his having felt, however erroneously, a contemplative distance from it and at least a qualified faith in being able to redirect its course. The disappearance of this historical self-consciousness from late-century New England gothic as an element in character psychology and in narrative voice betokens a loss of vision in keeping with the economic and cultural decline that rural New England experienced after the Civil War.[34] Freeman's "Puritans" have lost the intellectual and spiritual benefits of Puritanism by having fallen out of touch with its traditions. What is left is the hard shell. Stoddard's characters are on their way to this conclusion. On the other hand, its own declension was an explicit theme within Puritanism almost from the start. Perhaps that is why New England gothic has continued vigorously after Hawthorne, even after Freeman's terminal visions: The creative powers of the post-Puritan mind, if not those of the figures it depicts, have always thrived on the vision of decay.

Before closing, we should linger a moment on that scholarly common-place. How curious a thought it is, really! How curious that the "notion that the New England way of life has decayed" should be the "liveliest tradition" in its literary history, as Howard Mumford Jones once re-marked.[35] This testifies most obviously to New England's heavy dose of moral idealism, measured against which actual civilization always seems to be on the wane. Such is the burden of the jeremiad. But an additional testimony seems concealed here. The vision of decay also points to a problem of envisionment and representation only half acknowledged – not just a moral reservation about the health of the represented world but a doubt as to whether that world has any sort of substantial existence at all. Hawthorne may have been more candid than we have realized when he suggested that *The House of the Seven Gables* depicts cloudland rather than Essex County (*HW* 2:3). Not that he or Stoddard wished us to infer that Salem and Surrey have no reference to actual New England. The point is, rather, that in their depictions of New England, it exists only as a distorted image of itself, like the reflection of Hester Prynne's letter in Governor Bellingham's mirror. Indeed provincial gothic, in this respect, is only the most striking instance of all of the types of regional writing that we have surveyed in the last nine chapters. It is the magnifying mir-ror in which we see a crucial aspect – maybe *the* crucial aspect – of the provincial imagination writ large. Puritan romance, village iconography, comic and gothic grotesque – all portray half-worlds kept remote or di-minished through the selective exclusion of memory and through the condescensions of authorial urbanity. Even encomiastic genres like Fore-fathers' Day orations and the locodescriptive verse for town centennials acknowledge this, as we have seen, indirectly through the element of role playing involved in their production and directly through scattered tex-tual clues. Provincial representation may be entered into with zest and reverence or with malice and intent to expose, but in either case its ma-terials have clearly been "put in perspective" through an imaginative re-possession that appropriates them as vehicles for a statement that they are incapable of making on their own. In this sense, provincial gothic is ar-guably the quintessential mode of regional writing, because of the clarity with which it reveals the superiority of the act of repossession to the ob-jects represented and the insubstantiality and bleakness of those objects when not suffused by that power of imagination. At the heart of the pro-vincial vision is always the intimation that it is less than what is capable of being envisioned. Of that intimation, provincial gothic is the most conspicuous mark.

Postscript

The literary elaborations of the myths of place and history explored in Parts III and IV mark New England's coming of age as a literary culture region, yet confirm that the "regional impulse" is only part of the explanation for that flowering. The conventions of regional portrayal were themselves adapted from Anglo-European models. All of the major New England writers, from Barlow through Emerson, were international in the scope of their reading and the literary sources they appropriated. Loyal though they usually were to their New England roots, they would have objected strenuously to being classified as the exponents of a merely provincial culture. Indeed the consciousness of wider affinities ran stronger in Transcendentalist Concord and Brahmin Cambridge than it did in the Charleston of William Gilmore Simms or the literary nationalism of the Young America movement in New York.

Thus the agenda of the New England Renaissance ranged far beyond the codification of regional manners and values. This we have seen most clearly in our analyses of the three modes dealt with in Part II, all of which were widely favored by New England writers but used only intermittently as vehicles of provincial depiction. A cosmopolitanism of perspective also marks most of the important literary treatments of the New England experience per se, which, as we have seen, tend to view with considerable ambivalence the stereotypical images and consensus values that they dramatize. At the same time, the nineteenth century's intensive exploitation of New England materials, like the tradition of providential history during the Puritan era, does bespeak a distinct – and growing – ethnocentricity of perspective.[1] In this sense, what commentators have normally been pleased to consider the narrowness of late-century local colorism is diagnosable as an outgrowth of the work of antebellum figures like Hawthorne and Thoreau, whom scholars have normally sought to exempt from the category of "regionalist."[2] Yet none of the major fictions of New England life discussed here, even such affectionately filiopietistic tributes as the sketch by Stowe with which Chapter 13 began, is uncritical in its ethnic loyalty. Indeed, to provincialize, it seems, is ultimately to gothicize. Whether the artist of the provincial writes in affection or in scorn, the text tends to reflect a sense of the smallness of the depicted world. Whether that realm is a happy valley or a prisonlike enclosure, it is less than the full range of human possibility. Even though it may seem the most important place on earth, the text rarely avoids intimating at some level that this is not quite all the world. Europe, the West, the city are all conspicuously missing or suppressed.

The ambivalence that our writers display toward their created images of New England life is not to be understood merely as a symptom of resistance to provincialism, however. That point too was underscored by the first half of this study, where the period's creative achievement was seen as arising from a dialogue between ethical and stylistic norms and the authors' will to detach themselves from those norms even while speaking through them. Our authors' handling of provincial stereotypes was consistent with their response to the poetic tradition of bound accentual-syllabic forms, to the conventions of classical rhetoric, and to the status of Scripture as a doctrinal and literary model. Both the attachment to norms and the will to flout those norms to which, in an attenuated way, they continued to defer seem to have run strong in the New England imagination of our period, whatever the genre or subject matter.

Hence the incipient metaliterary character of even the more pedestrian literature cited in Chapters 3 and 4. If for example, one's patriotic impulses were, like John Trumbull's, not quite strong enough to prod one into forgoing one's elitist hauteur, one at least had the recourse of presenting the epic of the Revolution as a literary game. Even if one were nothing more than a hack imitator of Irving and Hawthorne, like Donald T. Mitchell, one could not help expressing the same complicated epistemological questions concerning the authority of poetic vision that better writers were exploring with greater sophistication. Such metaliterary tendencies were prompted, as we have seen, by elements within Neoclassicism and Romanticism, both of which acknowledged (on different grounds) the status of art as artifice. Further reinforcement came from the increasing ferment of the period (religious, social, economic) as it unfolded within a culture that expected the artist to function as a public guardian. The tendency of the major writers to temper any impulses to iconoclasm or prophetic self-assertiveness with complicated, self-dismantling ironies suggests a hesitation to assume the monitorial role that for whatever combination of social pressure and personal aspiration they also felt driven to assume.

The status of writing as an emerging profession was also crucial here. From the practicing artist's pragmatic standpoint, a story pitting Quakers against Puritans loomed most significantly not as an "authentic passage from history" or as a vehicle for enforcing consensus ideology but as artistic fodder: one possible option in a bag of assorted literary tricks. Hawthorne's peculiar narrative self-consciousness – his almost obsessive sense of his characters as mere figures, his plots as contrivances – may reflect his awareness of having to confront the expectations of a utilitarian society whose crude sense of the artist as purveyor of useful precepts and information he seeks to resist as faulty aesthetics and as a crushing spiritual burden, yet at the same time to propitiate through acknowledgment of delinquency and dutiful (indeed quite sincere) moral drawing about the perils of art as free-floating fancy.

Consequently, the literature of the New England Renaissance sometimes presents an appealingly "modern" face – its provincial mythography, for example, leaning not only in the direction of regional self-criticism but even toward fabulation, an awareness of its conventions as counters of the imagination inhabiting either a never-never land of romance or a grotesque world that advertises itself as a travesty of what reality ought to be. Yet New England poetics of our period cannot be reduced to this tendency alone. For one thing, it is not equally present in all writers. In Stowe, for instance, doubts about the New England way may lead to fascinatingly self-divided forms of regional mimesis but not to doubts about the capacity to render a mimesis. N. P. Willis and the ruck of literary scripturists betray no sense whatsoever of the possibility that their narratives, let alone Scripture itself, might be conceived as mere story. Nor does the "modernism" of the period's more sophisticated writing reflect the same ideological commitments to the autonomy or nonreferentiality of discourse that underlie both the formalist and the structuralist traditions in modern critical thought. When Emerson, Thoreau, Hawthorne, and Dickinson decenter language through puns, paradox, multiplication of symbolic implications, and the like, they usually aim either to use problematization as a homiletic tool for consciousness-raising or (more neutrally) to dramatize subjectivity of perception, not to proclaim the nonreferentiality of discourse as such. When they do suggest the possibility of the latter, it is generally in the context of contrasting art disparagingly with "vision" or of confessing that the inner logic of artistry is at odds with the philistine expectation that art shall play a monitorial role.

All of this is not to say that the great New England Romantics should not in some sense be regarded as precursors of modernism, which, in the broadest sense, is diagnosable as one end result of the Kantian epistemology that was instrumental in shaping Romantic critical thought to begin with. But that the line of descent is neither regular nor even predictable, except by hindsight, is shown by the waning of the New England Renaissance in the late nineteenth century, when the more radical innovativeness of the major figures became largely neutralized and crystallized into a genteel orthodoxy, through voluntary revision (the later Emerson and the later Elizabeth Stoddard), selective interpretation (Hawthorne enshrined on Longfellow's rather than on Melville's terms; Longfellow's notes of quiet desperation ignored), banishment from the canon (Lowell's strictures on Thoreau and Percival), self-exile (Dickinson's decision not to publish), and the conventionalism reinforced by the fully emergent publishing industry. That the Victorian ethos of the artist as moral guardian, even more hegemonic than its Neoclassical precursor, was able to reassert itself after the comparatively individualistic ferment of the antebellum years and that it was able to claim such figures as Emerson and Hawthorne as its heroes are historical facts that testify not simply to the willful blindness of late nineteenth-century editors and readers but also to the soundness of the principle that the whole history of a text's interpretation is pertinent to the process of its recovery. The writers we have examined in this book *are* our contemporaries; to write a long book about them is a statement of faith in that proposition. But to see them as ours alone is to fall into the same error for which we so complacently roast Dickinson's "preceptor" Thomas Wentworth Higginson, and other likeminded late-Victorian guardians of New England taste. We see some things that they missed, but they were not wholly wrong.[3] On the contrary, they were arguably more attuned than we to the web of societal and internalized assumptions about the moral responsibility of art – maintained surprisingly intact from Pope to Arnold – within which the thematic and linguistic dissents of the major New England Renaissance writers were contained. For a full understanding of literary ideology as it operated in even the most antinomian of these writers, the essentially utilitarian conception of art's moral purpose is at least as important as the phenomenon of authorial resistance to it. If this book has maintained a similar double vision, it will have fulfilled its primary aim.

Appendix

Vital Statistics: A Quantitative Analysis of Authorship as a Profession in New England

It is remarkable how the American mind runs to statistics.

Henry David Thoreau, *Journal* (1854)

I let nothing slip, however small; and feel myself actuated by the same motive which has prompted many worthy old chroniclers, to set down the merest trifles concerning things . . . which, if not preserved in the nick of time, must infallibly perish from the memories of man.

Herman Melville, *White-Jacket* (1850)

The generalizations made in Chapters 2 and 3 about the rise of literary professionalism in New England were based on study of the lives and careers of several hundred authors, examined with a special eye to career patterns, according to period (early national versus antebellum), gender, class, and literary stature ("major" versus "minor" authors). This Appendix presents my findings more systematically than has been done so far in this book, by means of an adaptation of some of the more elementary quantitative methods of recent social history, whose unfamiliarity to many literary scholars will, I hope, prove stimulating rather than repellent.

To study authorial careers in the aggregate tells one little about the aesthetic individuality of literary texts. Such study can be valuable, however, in preventing naive judgments about the uniqueness or typicality of the handful of writers and works in each period on which literary scholarship naturally concentrates. The work summarized in this Appendix has in that sense helped me greatly in understanding the period's mountain peaks of achievement, and I hope that it will also help others to attain a firmer grasp of the relationships between major and minor talents, as well as the place of such controversial factors as class, gender, and ethnicity in New England and, by extension, American literary history.

The 276 authors listed at the end of this Appendix have been selected as follows.

1. They must have reached literary maturity between 1770 and 1865.
2. They must have been reared primarily in New England or have resided there for at least half of their working careers.
3. They must have published in book or pamphlet form at least one work of creative literature (poetry, fiction, drama, literary prose), although the works need not have been published during their lifetimes.

For present purposes, I was stringent in defining "literary prose," disallowing some aesthetically influential figures (e.g., Fisher Ames and Daniel Webster) on the ground of insufficient belletristic output. I also excluded authors of juvenile literature who did not at some point try to reach the adult market too.

4. The authors must have received a biographical notice in at least one of the following: the Duyckinck brothers' *Cyclopedia of American Literature* (1856); *Appleton's Cyclopedia of American Biography* (1886–9); *The Dictionary of American Biography* (1928–36); Kunitz and Haycraft, ed., *American Authors, 1660–1900* (1938); Edward James, ed., *Notable American Women* (1971); Lina Mainiero, ed., *American Women Writers* (1979–82); and the *Dictionary of Literary Biography* (1978–   ).

These criteria did not, of course, eliminate subjective judgment, nor are they above criticism. Criterion 2, for instance, rules out the Transcendentalist poet Christopher Cranch, and the combination of criteria 3 and 4 rules in some very marginal "literary" figures such as Amherst geology professor and president Edward Hitchcock, who in his youth published a tragedy (performed by his students with considerable success), then veered completely away from belles lettres. In addition to my final group of 276, some 300 authors whom I discovered in the course of my investigations who were ruled out by criterion 4 as insignificant include a few whom I believe to have written works of real merit. But the roster surely encompasses the overwhelming majority of New England writers who produced work of even passing literary interest between the Revolution and the Civil War.

My criterion for identifying "major" figures within this group was that, in addition to meeting the first four tests,

5. They must either have been assigned an individual bibliography in the *Literary History of the United States* (1948) or have been the subject of an article or book as reported in at least five of the annual Modern Language Association bibliographies from 1970 to 1982.[1]

This stipulation was designed to factor in the judgments of both traditional and recent scholarship. Again, objections can be raised. My short list omits one figure whom I have accorded major status in this book, Elizabeth Stoddard, and includes some, like David Humphreys and N. P. Willis, whom I consider trivial compared to many who are left out. But again, the roster has at least the merit of excluding no figures whom the majority of scholars today would regard as being of the first significance.

The work of approximately one-fifth (55) of the authors falls mainly within the time span of the Revolutionary and early national periods (1770–1820); that of the remainder (221), within the antebellum period and Civil War years.[2] For the sake of convenience, I shall refer to these as the "first" and "second" eras. The group consists of 209 men and 67 women, with men outnumbering women by a ratio of 3:1, less skewed than the 4.8:1.0 ratio for the 35 major figures, who include 29 men and only 6 women. As might be expected, the gender ratio for the second era is less skewed than that for the first percent (26.6 percent women authors as opposed to 14.5 percent), reflecting a rise of an acknowledged role for literary women construable in a variety of ways: as a sign of increased respect for their intellectual prowess; as a symptom of the restrictions placed on women's sphere in Victorian America (authorship being one of those enterprises that could be pursued in the privacy of the home and perceived as so marginal as not to challenge male dominance); or as part of the systematic exploitation of the female reader's market by the publishing industry.[3]

As might be expected, the 276 authors were socially unrepresentative with respect to class and ethnicity as well as gender. The list includes only one member of a racial minority, Phillis Wheatley. In both eras, 94 percent of the authors for whom the necessary information could be obtained (259) had parents who were both native-born New Englanders. This accords with the general population during the first era but not during the second era, at the end of which only 85 percent of all New England residents were native-born. Nearly 30 percent of the writers' fathers attended college, as did 71 percent of the male writers themselves – a strikingly high percentage, even for the best-educated region in America,[4] and higher also than for their British counterparts.[5] The fathers of nearly one-half of the writers appear to have been ministers, lawyers, physicians, or merchants, as against no more than about one-fifth who made their income mainly from farming.[6] With regard to religion, the information available (for about half the writers) suggests that more than three-fourths, to the extent that they can be associated with any sect, came from the wealthiest and socially most elite sects – the Episcopalian and the Congregational churches (the latter including both Orthodox and

Unitarian). We find only a smattering of Baptists, Universalists, and Quakers; one or two Methodists at most; and a single practicing Catholic: the convert Orestes Brownson.[7]

By any standard, then, the 276 authors look genteel as compared with New Englanders at large. They had to be. Literature appears to have become the primary income source for at most one-fifth, all during the second era.[8] For at least two-thirds of the writers in the first era and one-third in the second era, literary income was surely close to zero.

Breaking down these data further, we find interesting contrasts between the two eras. Insofar as college attendance can be taken as an index of gentry status, the writers of the first era were a more select group. Although the regionwide rate of college attendance greatly increased between the Revolution and the Civil War, among our authors and their families the reverse was true. One-third of the fathers of the authors in the first era are known to have attended college, as against 27 percent of those in the second era; for the male writers themselves the rates are 74.5 percent versus 70.9 percent.[9] The latter figure suggests, correctly, that a classical education continued to be a normal preface to male authorship, but a more complicated picture is revealed by the fact that only one-half of the men for whom literature proved to be the primary income source (13 of 28) ever attended college. Increasing commercial opportunity, in other words, caused a predictable diversification among the ranks of authors.

Women writers seem especially to have gained from the professionalization of writing. The percentage of them who depended mainly on literary income during the second era was double that for men (34 percent versus 17 percent. The women writers of the second era, however – not only the more commercial writers but the entire group – tended to come from more genteel backgrounds, the percentage of professional and merchant fathers in the second era being about 55 percent for women, as opposed to 40 percent for men.[10] Literature was, it would seem, a more respectable vocational choice for a woman than for a man in antebellum New England, relative to other vocational options. More on this later, when we turn to the subject of vocational development.

One might expect a higher percentage of women writers to have remained unmarried, and so it was (22 percent versus 19 percent).[11] It is hard to find a significant pattern here, however, contrary to what one might think from concentrating on the 6 "major" literary women, who included Alcott, Dickinson, and Fuller (the others being Stowe, Warren, and Wheatley). During the first era the marital pattern is skewed in the opposite direction (24 percent bachelors as against no spinsters), and for only 4 of the 15 unmarried women from the second era does it seem very plausible to argue that they refrained from marriage for the sake of pursuing their careers.[12] The criterion of marriage, though, is too crude an index to use for measuring the tension between domestic and literary spheres for women. The writing of at least 6 additional women during the second era was either terminated by marriage or quickened by widowhood or divorce.[13] On the other hand, these cases were outnumbered by the instances of literary partnership between spouses, among the 48 married women (about one-third by my count), husband's and wife's work reinforcing each other in some way.[14] Ann Stephens' husband was sometimes her publisher; poet-anthologist Richard Henry Stoddard helped to get his wife's work placed and reviewed; Mercy Otis Warren attempted to further through her writing the same causes for which her husband worked politically; Elizabeth Payson Prentiss supplemented the evangelism of her minister-husband with highly successful didactic fiction. Rarely did such partnerships lead to serious disputes or jealousy, although the wife's creativity was sometimes hampered by her spouse's kindly patronizing or by her own sense of domestic dutifulness.

By what paths did writers become writers? Among the men, the commonest approaches were to begin as collegians and/or in connection with a career in divinity, law, or journalism.

Divinity and law were each pursued, for varying lengths of time, by about one-quarter of the male writers.[15] Those who chose divinity were far less likely to give it up, perhaps because the ministry, seen as the less lucrative and prestigious career by most genteel young men throughout both eras, tended to attract a more self-selected and committed group of novices than did the law. In any event, of the 55 men who studied divinity, 33 remained career ministers;[16] another 12 held regular pastorates for varying lengths of time;[17] and probably not more than 4 ever relied on literature as their primary income source.[18] Law, on the other hand, was more apt to be studied transiently by authors to start with and to become a springboard for a literary career. Twenty-four of the 57 law students moved within a few years or less from law to journalism (usually newspaper editing) as their primary occupations, and for only 22 did law (including politics) remain the chief professional field.[19] The careers of William Cullen Bryant and James Russell Lowell, then, were more typical of the period than that of Ralph Waldo Emerson.

Journalism, however, was the commonest professional refuge for eking out a literary existence. At least 35 percent of the male authors (76) engaged in it for at least a year as a primary means of livelihood, working as newspaper or magazine editors or as staff writers, and for close to half of these (31) journalism could be regarded as the main profession of their working lives.[20] Unlike law and the ministry, however, journalism was not a common initial choice of career (only one-fourth of the 76 chose it originally), and the ranks of journalists were much more socially diverse.

Those who went into newspaper or magazine work initially fell into equal and distinct categories: those who began as printers, none of whom attended college and almost all of whom were poor,[21] and those who started as editors or staff writers, a slight majority of whom had been collegians.[22] At the opposite extreme from the printer-journalists, 21 of the 24 who moved from law to journalism had attended college.[23] Well-known examples from these three categories were William Lloyd Garrison, an orphan who worked his way up to editor from printer's apprentice; N. P. Willis, the son of a prosperous Boston journalist who, after graduating from Yale, started his own career as an editor and a writer for periodicals in the same city; and Bryant, who after experimenting with law and creative writing as possible careers sublimated both interests in his highly successful editorship of the *New York Evening Post*.[24] This flow of energy from the occupation of relatively high status to that of relatively low status did not produce instant benefits either for journalism or for literature, but in the long run the journalists from the gentry class, with the assistance of self-made editors of acquired sophistication, such as Fields, helped, as we saw in Chapter 2, both to raise the tone of American publishing (e.g., Dennie's editorship of the *Port Folio* and Lowell's of the *Atlantic*) and to institutionalize traditions of popular as distinct from serious writing (e.g., Willis's development of the "correspondent's letter" as a remunerative form of newspaper literature).

The groups that I have identified as consisting primarily of ministers, lawyers, and journalists, together with those who made their living from a combination of these roles, account for roughly two-thirds of those male writers who can be said to have pursued a career at all. The next most popular vocational choices were those of educator (schoolmaster, college professor, administrator) and physician, the chief occupation of 10 to 15 men for each of these categories. Beyond that, we find a sprinkling of civil servants, merchants, booksellers and publishers, ship's captains, artists, actors, and military officers (3 to 6 men for each category). What is especially striking about this picture is that so few writers chose to enter the business world, except through journalism and publishing. Thoreau's distaste for the family pencil-making concern seems to have been typical, and the career of pioneer manufacturer-poet David Humphreys is a great anomaly. Although New England writers before the Civil War by no means evinced the degree of anticapitalist feeling common among literary people today (even Thoreau intermittently praised commerce, in *A Week on the Concord and Merrimack Rivers* and *Walden*), so far as their own vocational preferences were concerned, it is clear from the very start of American literary professionalism that writers felt their roles as writers to be less compatible with commerce than with professions to which verbal artistry was more clearly central. They agreed in spirit with the young Hawthorne's insistence that "no man can be a Poet & a Book-Keeper at the same time" – a view, incidentally, that their British and French counterparts seem to have shared.[25]

The main differences between the professional lives of men and women writers were, of course, that the "learned" professions of law, medicine, and the ministry were virtually closed to women, as was commerce, and that the majority of literary women were not their families' chief breadwinners. Almost none of the 67 women in our study tried the four professions just named,[26] and relatively few (less than one-third, by my count) were at any time in their lives *required* to be their family's chief, let alone sole, means of support – although some were so successful as to assume this role.[27] Nor, of course, were women generally encouraged to pursue careers of any sort unless forced to do so for economic reasons. This situation had interesting implications for authorship. On the one hand, women were more likely than men to start writing for purely recreative or cathartic reasons, with no particular design of converting this activity into a marketable skill. Probably that is how Emily Dickinson began composing, for instance, as opposed to, say, Emerson and Thoreau, whose juvenile compositions already show the assumption that something portentous, directly related to their future professional lives, is at stake in how they wield their pens. On the other hand, women writers, insofar as they developed a conception of themselves as having identities independent of their domestic roles, were probably more ready than their male counterparts to define their professional selves in terms of their writing, despite the widespread perception, as Lydia Child was once admonished, that "no woman could expect to be regarded as a *lady* after she had written a book."[28] This outcome resulted from a combination of personal interest and a paucity of vocational alternatives. Probably a rather small minority of the 209 male writers would have responded to the question "How would you describe your professional identity?" by saying, "I see myself primarily as a writer," but more than half of the women writers might well have felt so, whatever they might have seen fit to declare publicly.

Perhaps as many as a dozen of the women writers pursued careers as teachers or lecturers at some point in their lives. A roughly equal number tried journalism, as editors of periodicals or gift books or as columnists and reporters.[29] Most, however, stayed at home and wrote. In some cases their work remained on the level of sporadic recreation. Roughly one-fifth of our writers seem to fall into this category.[30] More often, though, the woman writer working from the basic situation of housewife or dependent daughter was prompted to go beyond this level by some chance event. Julia Dorr, for instance, might not have gone further than clandestine scribbling had her enthusiastic husband not published her fugitive pieces without her consent or knowledge. But the commonest stimulus was financial. In at least 10 cases, there seems to be clear evidence that the sense of family financial emergency was a crucial factor in professionalizing what might not have become more than recreative writing; in several other cases, it hastened the professionalization of writers who had previously evinced literary aspirations; in several others, need was apparently not so much a factor as the astonishing success of the author's first experiment in publication.[31] The profit motive, however, is an inadequate explanation of the literary drive, even for most of these women. The need for literary income was cited in the prefaces of some of them, for example, as a way of placating real or imagined public objections to the impropriety of women venturing into the marketplace. Probably an even larger group than those who wrote for profit were those inspired by the same combination of motives that we like (sometimes naively) to impute to all writing that we honor as "serious": interest in one's medium, the hope of fame, the desire to say something important to the world. Only these can explain, for example, why Mercy Otis Warren spent twenty years writing a history of the American Revolution, why Louisa Park Hall wrote biblical drama, why Lydia Child persisted in her literary radicalism at great economic risk. Altogether, the percentage of literary women for whom writing was a passion as well as an enterprise was probably at least as high as was the case for men, and the percentage of women who had the opportunity to indulge this passion without (at least in theory) having to worry about turning it into something commercially viable was probably higher.

The overall professional picture for women writers, then, looks more polarized than for men. It follows the same general pattern of increased professionalism as we move from the first to the second era, and it exhibits the same sharp contrast between writers of both sexes at one end of the spectrum who were able to dabble or immerse themselves in writing because they were financially secure (e.g., Emily Dickinson and William Hickling Prescott) and writers at the other end who were thrust completely into the marketplace. This contrast, however, was more extreme among women writers, owing to the fact that middle-class women both were shielded in larger numbers from the necessity of making a living yet, when they were under such pressure, depended more frequently than male writers on literature as a primary income source. This latter contrast may have had something to do with the overrepresentation of women as authors of best-selling fiction, of which more later on.

Where did New England writers come from? The overwhelming majority grew up within the region itself (96 percent) and in the state where they had been born (89 percent). Generally speaking, the chances of becoming a recognized writer increased according to the nearness of one's

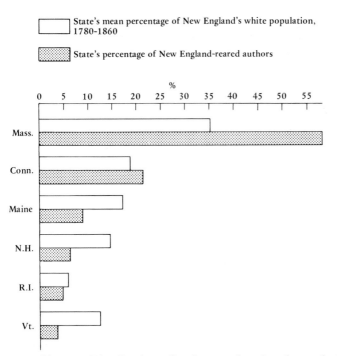

□ State's mean percentage of New England's white population, 1780-1860

▦ State's percentage of New England-reared authors

Chart 1. Distribution of authors and regional population.

home to Boston. Altogether, 134 of the 276 authors grew up in Massachusetts east of the Connecticut Valley, and Massachusetts as a whole was the home of 57 percent of all authors who are known to have grown up in New England (266). This statistic can be put in context by comparing the fraction of New England's entire white population in each state with the percentage of New England – reared authors produced by each (Chart 1).[32] In this as well as in absolute numbers Massachusetts comes out far ahead of the other states, with upper New England lagging substantially behind its population share.

The demographic distribution helps to explain such other factors as the record of colleges with the largest shares of graduates among the authors (Chart 2), Harvard being by far the most popular alma mater (for nearly half of the 148 college-attending authors), with Yale a distant second and Bowdoin, Dartmouth, and Brown well behind it.

The geographical imbalance is actually even more pronounced than the figures suggest. For one thing, it is more skewed for the second era than for the first, given that the authors we are dealing with were almost wholly of native Yankee stock whereas the populations of the three lower

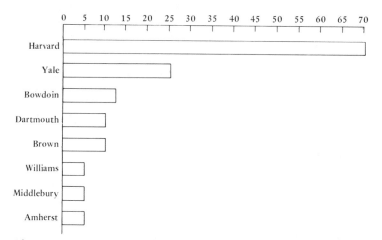

Chart 2. Colleges attended by three or more authors.

New England states, particularly eastern Massachusetts, included an increasingly large fraction of immigrants during the antebellum years.[33] In 1860 the four Massachusetts counties that throughout both eras were by far the largest producers of authors – Essex, Middlesex, Suffolk, and Norfolk – had an average immigrant population of 33 percent. Reckoning only American-born residents of these counties and New England as a whole, their share of the region's total native white population was 19 percent, as against an almost double portion (35 percent) of authors in the second era.

Beyond this, migration of authors has to be considered. As we saw in Chapter 2, the rate of emigration of literati from New England was fairly high: 30 percent of the 276 authors left the region during their careers, either not to return or to return only upon retirement. The figures nearly double from the first era to the second (18 to 32 percent), and they are much higher for northern New England and central and western Massachusetts (43 percent) than for the region's hub in eastern Massachusetts (29 percent).[34] This difference is in keeping with the general trend in migration from New England to New York and the Midwest, the preferred destinations for authors as well as for the population at large.[35] But the demographic shift looks even more lopsided when internal migration is taken into account. Eastern Massachusetts north of the old Plymouth Colony actually realized a net gain from antebellum authorial mobility. Although it lost by far the greatest number of native-reared authors of any of New England's subregions (24 of the 71 expatriates during the second era), it gained an even greater number (25) of literary people who came, mostly from other parts of New England, to settle in and around Boston. William Ellery Channing, from Newport; Henry Wadsworth Longfellow, from Portland; James A. Fields, from Portsmouth; Samuel G. Goodrich, from Hartford; Bronson Alcott, from rural Connecticut – these are well-known examples. Conversely, through a combination of external and internal migration, the three northern New England states lost 30 of the 41 authors who had grown up there, and gained only one (Sylvester Judd, Unitarian minister and novelist, who settled in Augusta, Maine). Connecticut, as well as central and western Massachusetts also suffered net losses of 50 percent of their local authors. Even by 1865, in other words, the mid- to late-century redistribution of notable literary talent among the more provincial parts of the region noted at the end of Chapter 2 had not had much impact on the overall statistics.

Combining the statistics with the fact that more than 90 percent of the authors were of old Anglo-Saxon New England stock, born there, and reared there, we come up with a clear substantiation of the picture presented in Chapter 2 of New England, between the Revolution and the Civil War, as a culture region where literary activity became increasingly centralized under the custodianship of an increasingly small ethnic majority that rarely absorbed ethnic or regional outsiders. New England exported 8 authors for every literary immigrant it gained who had been reared elsewhere, and almost all of the latter were likewise white Protestants. Such figures do not tell the whole story about cultural inbreeding, to be sure. Such factors as breadth of reading and extensiveness of travel are also important, and by these indices New England culture looks more cosmopolitan. (Probably fewer than 10 percent of our authors lived their entire lives without traveling out of the region, and the majority resided outside of it for periods of at least a year.) Nevertheless, the demographic picture may be helpful in explaining the intellectual centripetalism we encountered in Parts III and IV.

One further set of figures suggests some largely but not entirely predictable inferences about the status value of different literary genres. If one of the male authors in the group wrote a book of poems during either era, the odds were 3:1 that he had attended college, which was about the average rate of attendance. During the first era, a book of fiction suggested much the same (7 of the 8 men in question attended college). But in the second era, the chances were only 2:1 that the author had been a collegian. In drama, the shift was even more pronounced: 3:1 in favor during the first era, only fifty-fifty in the second era – probably a reflection of the revulsion against drama on both aesthetic and moral grounds once it became clear that the polite element in society was not going to control the behavior of the theater.[36] Perhaps the most striking correlation between genre and gentility, for male writers, was in the field of historiography, where the chances were 5:1 that a male historian had attended college.

The genre breakdown becomes additionally intriguing when one compares male and female writers. Among the women who can be said to have had a preferred genre, 43 percent (27 of 63) were writers of fiction, as against only 18 percent of the men (37 of 204), whereas for nonfictional prose the percentages are the reverse (more than one-quarter of the men, fewer than one-eighth of the women) and for poetry identical (43 percent for both sexes). Women, then, were far less hesitant to venture into the less prestigious genre of prose fiction. This may partly have been because fiction had always been regarded as a woman's genre; partly it may have reflected a realistic appraisal of marketplace rewards: 8 of the 27 women novelists met Frank Luther Mott's somewhat questionable test for best-selling fiction, as against only 3 of the men.[37]

The typical New England author, then, was a male of the second era, born during the first two decades of the nineteenth century to new England-born parents distinctly more affluent and better educated than the average. The author was a native of northeastern Massachusetts (most likely Boston, Cambridge, Salem, or Newburyport) who had been reared in the place where he was born. He matriculated at Harvard. After college he tried his hand at one of the learned professions (law or the ministry, most likely), with perhaps a stint of schoolteaching during or immediately after college. At some point he involved himself in editing a periodical or in writing for one regularly. Poetry was his preferred genre, but he also experimented with at least one other, probably nonfictional prose. He did not depend on literature as his primary source of income, but he entertained the dream of literary distinction much more seriously than the literati of his father's generation, and he was more likely to have been paid for his writing. He married, had children, and was not divorced. He probably resided for most of his life within forty miles of Boston, and if he left the region he did not move to a less cosmopolitan community than the one in which he had been brought up. With respect to politics, he was a middle-of-the-road Whig, perhaps a bit on the liberal side, who voted for Harrison and Taylor; he opposed slavery in principle but doubted that much could be done about it. He became a Republican in the mid-1850s and was a staunch unionist during the Civil War, but he was not as active or as prominent politically as his literary forebears. In religion, he was a loyal Protestant of Congregational stamp – if not Unitarian, probably not very evangelical. His writings were largely forgotten within a generation of his death, but his career was well enough regarded to merit a page in the *DAB,* as much on the strength of his civic virtues as on that of anything he wrote.

Few actual figures, of course, match these criteria exactly. For examples of some who come close, the reader may wish to scan the *DAB* entries for Unitarian minister-poet Nathaniel L. Frothingham, Episcopalian lawyer-editor-poet-fictionist George Lunt, and dentist-poet-translator Thomas W. Parsons.

The typical female writer would have resembled the above profile in parental background, place of nativity and residence, socioeconomic status, and political and religious affiliation. Her formal education would have been much more limited, although she would have been as likely as her male counterpart to have received the best education conventionally available to her sex. She would have been more likely to write fiction, and more likely to devote her main energies to writing when she stepped beyond her domestic role, although she would have been less likely to be regularly employed. She would have been less likely to live outside the region during her lifetime but more likely than the average male author's wife to contribute to the economic support of the household, and more likely to demand a marriage that would be a partnership rather than a hierarchy, if her husband (usually more enlightened than the average) were not disposed to offer it. Perhaps because of this, she would have been more likely than the average male writer to have a spouse who actively shared her literary or other professional interests (more than 40 percent of cases).

Some representative instances (again, consult the *DAB* or *Notable American Women*) of this profile would be Maria Cummins, Eliza Cabot Follen, and Sarah Edgarton Mayo.

Turning now to our 35 "major" authors, let us see what can be gained by looking at them in the context just established.

In a number of ways, they are indistinguishable from the larger group. All but 1 grew up in New England; all but 2 were born in New England; all but 1 were children of New Englanders. The geographical distribution of home regions is comparable: 19 grew up in eastern Massachusetts; 8, in Connecticut.[38] Also in keeping with overall residence patterns was their rate of emigration from the region (7 of the 35) and their tendency not to move to less cosmopolitan locations than those where they grew up (only 3 cases).[39] Allowing for the fact that my selection criteria for the larger group were somewhat biased against writers of nonfictional prose, the spread of genres practiced by the major authors is probably also comparable, although historians are overrepresented (Bancroft, Motley, Parkman, Prescott) and novelists somewhat underrepresented (L. M. Alcott, De Forest, Hawthorne, Neal, Stowe). The major authors were somewhat more versatile than the overall group average, at least 6 having tried drama, 14 having written book-length fictions, and 24 having composed a significant body of poems.

The statistics for major authors start to diverge noticeably from their lesser contemporaries when we look at social and educational background. The percentage of college attendance for the men is slightly higher (79 percent versus 71 percent overall). The institutions attended by all but 4 of the men were Harvard (14) and Yale (5), a much heavier weighting in favor of the most established, academically and socially prestigious colleges than even for the 276 authors as a whole (see Chart 2). The major writers' fathers also attended at a higher rate than average (50 percent, as opposed to 32 percent for all authors) and were more likely to be merchants or members of the three learned professions (60 percent versus 40 percent).

These differences accord with the fact that the major writers were even more likely than the larger group to belong to gentry churches, particularly to churches of a liberal cast. The major authors' denominational affiliations, prior to lapses and conversions, was entirely Congregational/Presbyterian and Episcopalian (in about a 5:1 ratio), except for two birthright Quakers (Neal and Whittier). Half the group were Unitarians for most of their lives, and the group as a whole was far less inclined toward evangelicalism than the minor authors.[40] This greater degree of religious liberalism may have helped to create a more than ordinarily supportive atmosphere for the development of these authors' talents. Such counterevidence as Squire Edward Dickinson's supposed crotchetiness about his daughter's secular reading probably conveys an exaggerated picture of the "Puritan" restraints with which the major authors, relative to the average case, had to cope.

Even more important than any intellectual support that these writers' families might have given them on principle were the economic advantages. A large minority of the major authors received significant financial support from their families that allowed them, at crucial periods (sometimes with a little scrimping) to concentrate on authorship. Three of the 4 historians (Motley, Parkman, Prescott) were subsidized by parental wealth, as was the poet Tuckerman; Emerson was aided by money from his first wife's estate, Hawthorne by his mother's family, De Forest by investment income from the sale of the family business, Longfellow and Lowell by their fathers and also by marrying money. Dickinson was supported by her family throughout her life; Jones Very was put through Harvard by an uncle and apparently supported thereafter mainly on his siblings' income. If we add to these Emerson's periodic assistance of Bronson Alcott and Thoreau and the accommodations in work schedule made by Phillis Wheatley's masters so as to permit her to write, nearly half of the major authors – including all those who today are most respected – qualify as recipients of major subsidies. Although specific information is hard to come by, this rate certainly is greater than the rate for minor authors.[41] Altogether it seems that the major writers of the age were an unusually privileged lot.

The major writers also appear to have been advantaged by family background in the sense of having had "literary" relatives. Parents of about one-third either published in various genres (L. M. Alcott, Beecher and Stowe, Emerson, Fuller, Holmes, Lowell, Parkman, Willis) or wrote manuscript poetry (Bryant, Hawthorne, Very). In addition to this group, Dickinson and Warren had older brothers who took an active interest in their intellectual and literary development, as did Hawthorne's older sister. It is interesting, whatever the significance, that the 35 authors include at least 13 cases of significant sibling literary activity: In addition to Nathaniel and Elizabeth Hawthorne, there were Harriet Beecher Stowe and Henry Ward Beecher; William Cullen Bryant and his younger brother John; William Ellery Channing and his brother Edward (Harvard professor of rhetoric and *North American Review* critic), Emerson and his two younger brothers; Henry Wadsworth Longfellow and his brother Samuel; James Russell Lowell and two younger siblings; Jones and Lydia Very; Nathaniel and Sarah Willis; Mercy Otis Warren and James Otis; John Greenleaf and Elizabeth Whittier. Counting all cases mentioned in this paragraph, more than one-half of the major writers might be described as coming from literary families, a rate probably twice that for minor authors.[42]

Perhaps partly as a consequence, the major authors might have been more ready to consider themselves as in some sense literary people, even though creative writing was a primary means of livelihood for only one-third at most. It seems likely that well over one-half of the major writers would have accepted a designation such as "poet," "novelist," or "man/woman of letters" as a summary of their professional identity, though they might have preferred another term such as Emerson's "scholar." Or, to put it another way, it seems unlikely that more than a few, had they spoken honestly, would have declared that literature was merely an ancillary outlet for them. For the minor writers, the proportions would have been closer to the reverse, at least among the men.

In view of their socioeconomic advantages, one might expect the major writers to be politically more conservative than their lesser colleagues. Such was not the case. The 8 figures from the first era seem to have been about average among New England intellectuals of the era with respect to political slant (7 patriots and 1 Loyalist, Joseph Dennie; 4 Federalists and 2 Jeffersonians, Barlow and Warren).[43] This subgroup stands out instead for its political prominence, 5 of the 6 men holding major governmental offices and Warren, the spouse of a Revolutionary leader, serving as an important literary spokesperson for patriot, and later for Republican, views.[44] For the second era, party identifications are vaguer. The ratio of approximately 3 Whig-Republicans to 1 Democrat again looks about average for New England literati. More striking is again the degree of political involvement, Bancroft and Bryant being Democrats of national visibility; Brownson and Hawthorne intermittently prominent in the same party; and the largest single contingent, reform-minded literati at least loosely associated with Conscience Whig, Free Soil, and radical Republican circles, including a number of people who engaged in significant political activity either at the rhetorical or the organizational level, starting as early as Channing's and Whittier's efforts in the 1830s. (Some other notable cases included the Alcotts, the Beechers, De Forest, Emerson, Parker, and Thoreau.) The number of bona fide reactionaries among major authors is very small (Halleck and Prescott). Transcendentalist scholars may chide Emerson for pusillanimousness compared to Thoreau, but compared to the average New England author of the era, Emerson and the major writers as a group look distinctly progressive and *engagé*.[45]

It should be added, however, that the most radical ideology was not espoused by the most genteel element. All but 1 of the 6 merchant-manufacturer scions (Dennie, Dwight, Halleck, Motley, Tuckerman – De Forest the exception) were conservative or apolitical, whereas the children of farmers tended to be strongly antiestablishmentarian (Barlow, Warren, Bronson Alcott, Brownson, Parker, Whittier). Among the cases that have been cited earlier of writers supported by family money, only Lowell and Emerson became in any real sense radicalized.

The major New England writers, all told, were by no means a breed apart from their less talented cohorts, although they did stand out in certain respects. They were similar in ethnicity, residence, mobility, degree of education if not particular alma mater, and generic preference but exceptional in socioeconomic status and cultural advantages, in the literary bent of their families, in religious liberalism, in political visibility, and (during the second era) also in political liberalism – although, as just noted, these various points of differentiation did not always correlate mutually. These indices suggest that the common image of classic American authors as distinctly at odds with their society is not without basis, particularly insofar as the political orientation of the antebellum contingent is concerned, but that the image is exaggerated and misdirected in that the single most conspicuous point of quantifiable differentiation lay in the socioeconomic and cultural advantages that the major authors enjoyed. They look more like society's elite than society's fringe.

Before jumping unreservedly to this revisionary conclusion, however, we must take closer note of what these major authors did with their economic and cultural advantages. A number of them, including the best, clearly felt it necessary at some point to reject the proffered advantages in order to develop as authors. Emerson, thanks more to his connections than to his abilities, was very nicely started on his way to becoming a pillar of the Boston Unitarian establishment when he abruptly resigned his pulpit. Bancroft, son of the first president of the American Unitarian Association, could probably have entrenched himself at Harvard if he had behaved more prudently. Channing was a Brahmin of impeccable credentials whose sense of social justice caused his hero-worshipping congregation to turn against him. Hawthorne could have found a reasonably secure post in his uncle's business instead of flapping about in literary limbo for a dozen years; Longfellow and Lowell could easily have become well-to-do attorneys; Thoreau could have earned an adequate living as schoolmaster and perhaps a very tidy one in pencil making – and been a respected figure in the village under either condition. Dickinson probably had ample opportunity not only to submit to Christianity but to snag an eligible beau as well. If Parker had not been so perverse, he could have been accepted into the Unitarian establishment and become another Algeresque case of a poor boy making good. If Bronson Alcott had kept the Gospels out of his lesson plans, he might have become a prophet of educational reform with honor in his own day.

Altogether, in the careers of nearly half of our major figures we find the author rejecting the easy career path, for which the way had typically been prepared by the influence of family or friends, for the sake of doing things the hard way. This does not necessarily show, of course, that social and cultural advantages have no positive value in nurturing literary genius. It seems doubtful whether people like Dickinson and Thoreau would have been able to exercise their cantankerousness productively without such genteel aids (e.g., leisure to write, the presence of at least a minimal intellectual community to serve as a creative irritant, and so forth), which our elite group of 35 enjoyed to a greater extent than the average writer of the period, who was a female dependent or middling merchant's son.

The origins of authorial cantankerousness, furthermore, also remain to be explicated. I once felt more confident about that matter than I now do. When I began this study, I was much taken by David Donald's controversial theory of the abolitionists as displaced gentry of Puritan descent, Federalist parentage, and Congregational/Presbyterian or Quaker stock, who turned to abolitionism in compensation for a felt loss of economic and political power that their families and class had sustained during the early 1800s.[46] Donald's thesis has, in fact, been applied to New England literary history,[47] and I would agree that in some cases it seems to fit. Among these would certainly be Bancroft, the son of a prominent Unitarian minister but relegated to a tutorship at Harvard after his splendid academic training in Germany; Emerson, the impoverished son of a succession of ministers, who attempted to fill a liberal pulpit right after the period when Unitarianism had made its greatest gains and Boston's religious orientation was shifting to the right (or, for many others, into total indifference); Fuller, the daughter of a disappointed Harvard-educated politician who expected great intellectual feats of her but died suddenly without leaving her much to live on; and Stowe, who had to contend with the fame of one parent and the reputed sainthood of the other, with the frustrations of the domestic role her culture expected of her, with acute financial distress as a young wife, and with erosion of her father's prestige after midcareer. Prescott and Parkman, who turned to letters because their health did not permit the vocations usual to their class, are a simple variation of the type. But there are enough cases of writers making a relatively easy full- or part-time commitment to letters as an alternative form of public service or appropriate gentlemanly pursuit (e.g., Halleck, Holmes, Longfellow, Lowell, Tuckerman) to show that the displaced-gentry theory is no more sufficient as a total explanation of the course of literary history than it has proved to be in the realm of politics – indeed probably less so. Even those for whom a writing career meant a marked deviation from what was perceived by both themselves and others as a more respectable path (Emerson, Hawthorne, and Thoreau, for instance) did not encounter anything like the obloquy that was heaped on Wendell Phillips and Charles Sumner. To become a writer in nineteenth-century New England did involve social and economic risk taking, but it was not nearly so provocative a step as political radicalism. Indeed, literary pioneering was, as we have seen, in principle if not in practice considered laudable. Artistic innovation during our period was certainly in a sense a countercultural force, but in another sense it reflected the national aspiration.

Table of Authors Surveyed

Note: Listed below are the 276 authors surveyed in the Appendix. Names of authors from the first (early national) era are asterisked (★); those of "major" authors are italicized. For each author the source containing the most useful short biographical sketch (or sketches, where none is clearly preferable) is cited in parentheses. The following abbreviations are used:

AA   *American Authors, 1660–1900.* Ed. Stanley J. Kunitz and Howard Haycraft. New York: Wilson, 1938.

AW   *American Writers before 1800.* Ed. James A. Levernier and Douglas R. Wilmes. 3 vols. Westport; Conn.: Greenwood Press, 1983.

AWW   *American Women Writers.* Ed. Linda Mainero. 4 vols. New York: Ungar, 1979–82.

CAB   *Appleton's Cyclopedia of American Biography.* Ed. James Grant Wilson and John Fiske. 6 vols. New York: Appleton, 1886–9.

CAL   *Cyclopaedia of American Literature.* Ed. Evert Duyckinck and Augustus Duyckinck. 2 vols. New York: Scribner, 1856.

DAB   *Dictionary of American Biography.* Ed. Allen Johnson and Dumas Malone. 20 vols., with 7 supplements. New York: Scribner, 1928–36 *et seq.*

DLB   *Dictionary of Literary Biography.* Vols. 1 and 3, ed. Joel Myerson; vol. 12, ed. Donald Pizer and Earl N. Harbert. Detroit: Gale, 1978–82.

NAW   *Notable American Women.* Ed. Edward T. James. 3 vols., with supplement. Cambridge, Mass.: Harvard Univ. Press, 1971 *et seq.*

1.   ABBOTT, Jacob (*DAB*)
2.   *ADAMS, John Quincy (*DAB*)
3.   AIKEN, George (*DAB*)
4.   *ALCOTT, Amos Bronson (DLB)*
5.   *ALCOTT, Louisa May (NAW)*
6.   *ALLEN, Paul (*DAB, AW*)
7.   *ALLEN, William (*DAB*)
8.   ALLSTON, Washington (*DAB*)
9.   *ALSOP, Richard (*DAB*)
10.   *ARNOLD, Josias Lyndon (*CAL*)
11.   AUSTIN, William (*DAB*)
12.   BACON, Delia (*AWW, DAB*)
13.   BALDWIN, John Denison (*DAB*)
14.   BALLOU, Maturin (*DAB*)
15.   *BANCROFT, George (DAB, DLB)*
16.   BANVARD, Joseph (*DAB*)
17.   *BARLOW, Joel (AW, DAB)*
18.   *BARTLETT, Joseph (*DAB*)
19.   BARTOL, Cyrus (*DAB*)
20.   *BEECHER, Henry Ward (DAB)*
21.   *BELKNAP, Jeremy (*DAB, AW*)
22.   BENJAMIN, Park (*DLB*)
23.   BENNETT, Emerson (*DAB*)
24.   BIGELOW, Jacob (*DAB*)
25.   *BIGLOW, William (*CAL*)
26.   *BINGHAM, Caleb (*DAB*)
27.   BOLTON, Sarah Knowles (*AWW*)
28.   BOTTA, Anne Lynch (*NAW*)
29.   BOUTON, John Bell (*DAB*)
30.   BRACE, John Pierce (*DAB*)
31.   BRACKETT, Edward (*DAB*)
32.   BRAINARD, John Gardiner Calkins (*DAB*)
33.   BRIGGS, Charles (*DLB*)
34.   BROOKS, Charles T. (*DAB*)
35.   BROOKS, Maria Gowen (*NAW*)
36.   BROWN, John Newton (*DAB*)
37.   BROWN, Solyman (*DAB*)
38.   *BROWN, William Hill (*AW, DAB*)
39.   BROWNELL, Henry Howard (*DAB*)
40.   *BROWNSON, Orestes Augustus (DLB)*
41.   *BRYANT, John Howard (DAB)*
42.   *BRYANT, William Cullen (DLB)*
43.   BULFINCH, Stephen Greenleaf (*DAB*)

44. BURGESS, George (*DAB*)
45. BURLEIGH, George Shepard (*DAB*)
46. BURLEIGH, William Henry (*DAB*)
47. BURTON, Warren (*DAB*)
48. CALDWELL, William W. (*CAL*)
49. CALVERT, George Henry (*DAB*)
50. CARTER, Nathaniel H. (*CAL, CAB*)
51. *CHANNING, William Ellery* (*DAB, DLB*)
52. CHANNING, William Ellery, II (*DAB*)
53. CHEEVER, George Barrell (*DAB*)
54. CHILD, Lydia Francis (*NAW*)
55. CLAPP, Henry, Jr. (*AA*)
56. CLAPP, William Warland (*DAB*)
57. CLARKE, James Freeman (*DLB, DAB*)
58. CLARKE, McDonald (*DAB*)
59. COBB, Sylvanus (*DAB*)
60. CODMAN, John (*DAB*)
61. COFFIN, Charles Carleton (*DAB*)
62. COFFIN, Robert Stevenson (*CAL*)
63. COGGESHALL, George (*DAB*)
64. COLTON, Calvin (*DAB*)
65. COLTON, Walter (*DAB*)
66. CONGDON, Charles Tabor (*DAB*)
67. COOKE, Rose Terry (*NAW*)
68. CROSWELL, William (*CAL*)
69. CUMMINS, Maria (*NAW*)
70. CURTIS, George William (*DAB*)
71. DANA, Richard Henry (*DLB, DAB*)
72. DANA, Richard Henry, Jr. (*DAB*)
73. DAWES, Rufus (*CAL, CAB*)
74. DAY, Martha (*CAB*)
75. ★DEANE, Samuel (*DAB*)
76. DEERING, Nathaniel (*DAB*)
77. *DE FOREST, John W.* (*DLB*)
78. ★*DENNIE, Joseph* (*AW*)
79. DERBY, George Horatio (*DAB*)
80. *DICKINSON, Emily* (*DLB*)
81. ★DINSMOOR, Robert (*DAB*)
82. DODD, Mary Ann Hanmer (*CAB*)
83. DORR, Julia Ripley (*AWW, DAB*)
84. DUGANNE, Augustine Joseph Hickey (*DAB*)
85. DURFEE, Job (*DAB*)
86. DURIVAGE, Francis Alexander (*DAB*)
87. ★*DWIGHT, Timothy* (*AW, DAB*)
88. EASTMAN, George (*DAB*)
89. ★ELLIOT, James (*AW, DAB*)
90. ELLSWORTH, Erastus (*CAB*)
91. *EMERSON, Ralph Waldo* (*DLB*)
92. EVERETT, Alexander Hill (*DAB*)
93. ★EVERETT, David (*AW, DAB*)
94. EVERETT, Edward (*DAB*)
95. FAIRFIELD, Sumner Lincoln (*DAB*)
96. FARLEY, Harriet (*NAW*)
97. ★FESSENDEN, Thomas Green (*DAB*)
98. FIELDS, James T. (*DAB*)
99. FINN, Henry (*DAB*)
100. ★FITCH, Elijah (*AW*)
101. FLAGG, Edmund (*DAB*)
102. FLAGG, Thomas Wilson (*DAB*)

103. FLINT, Timothy (*DAB*)
104. FOLLEN, Eliza Cabot (*NAW*)
105. ★FOSTER, Hannah (*NAW*)
106. FROTHINGHAM, Nathaniel Langdon (*DAB*)
107. *FULLER, Sarah Margaret* (*DLB*)
108. ★GARDINER, John Sylvester John (*DAB*)
109. GARRISON, William Lloyd (*DAB*)
110. GILMAN, Caroline (*NAW*)
111. GILMAN, Samuel (*DAB*)
112. GOODRICH, Frank Boott (*DAB*)
113. GOODRICH, Samuel Griswold (*DAB*)
114. GOULD, Edward (*DAB*)
115. GOULD, Hannah (*AWW*)
116. GOULD, John (*CAL*)
117. GREENE, Albert Gorton (*DAB*)
118. GREENE, Asa (*DAB*)
119. GREENOUGH, Henry (*DAB*)
120. HALE, Edward Everett (*DAB*)
121. HALE, Lucretia Peabody (*NAW*)
122. HALE, Sarah Josepha (*NAW*)
123. HALL, Louisa J. Park (*AWW*)
124. *HALLECK, Fitz-Greene* (*DLB, DAB*)
125. HANAFORD, Phebe (*NAW*)
126. ★HARRIS, Thaddeus Mason (*DAB*)
127. *HAWTHORNE, Nathaniel* (*DLB*)
128. HENTZ, Caroline Lee (*NAW*)
129. HEWITT, Mary E. (*AWW*)
130. HIGGINSON, Thomas Wentworth (*DLB, DAB*)
131. HILDRETH, Richard (*DAB*)

132. HILL, Frederic Stanhope (*DAB*)
133. HILL, Thomas (*DAB*)
134. HILLHOUSE, James Abraham (*DAB*)
135. ★HITCHCOCK, David (*CAL*)
136. ★HITCHCOCK, Edward (*DAB*)
137. ★HITCHCOCK, Enos (*AW, DAB*)
138. HOLLAND, Josiah Gilbert (*DAB*)
139. HOLLISTER, Gideon (*DAB*)
140. HOLMES, Mary Jane (*NAW*)
141. *HOLMES, Oliver Wendell* (*DLB*)
142. ★HONEYWOOD, St. John (*CAL*)
143. HOOKER, Herman (*CAB*)
144. HOOPER, Ellen Sturgis (*NAW*)
145. HOOPER, Lucy (*AWW*)
146. ★HOPKINS, Lemuel (*AW, DAB*)
147. HOWE, Julia Ward (*NAW*)
148. ★*HUMPHREYS, David* (*AW, DAB*)
149. INGRAHAM, Joseph Holt (*DLB*)
150. ★JENKS, William (*DAB*)
151. JONES, Joseph S. (*DAB*)
152. JUDD, Sylvester (*DAB*)
153. KETTELL, Samuel (*DAB*)
154. KIMBALL, Richard Burleigh (*DAB*)
155. ★KNAPP, Samuel Lorenzo (*DAB*)
156. KNIGHT, Henry C. (*DAB*)
157. ★LADD, Joseph Brown (*AW, DAB*)
158. LARCOM, Lucy (*NAW*)
159. ★LATHROP, John (*DAB*)
160. LEE, Eliza Buckminster (*DAB*)
161. LEE, Hannah Farnham Sawyer (*AWW*)

162. *LINCOLN, Enoch (*DAB*)
163. LOCKWOOD, Ralph Ingersoll (*DAB*)
164. *LONGFELLOW, Henry Wadsworth* (*DLB, DAB*)
165. LONGFELLOW, Samuel (*DAB*)
166. *LOWELL, James Russell* (*DLB, DAB*)
167. LOWELL, Maria White (*CAL*)
168. LOWELL, Robert Traill Spence (*DAB*)
169. LUNT, George (*DAB*)
170. McDOUGALL, Frances Harriet Green (*DAB*)
171. McLELLAN, Isaac (*DAB*)
172. MAYO, Sarah Edgarton (*AWW*)
173. MELLEN, Grenville (*DAB*)
174. MITCHELL, Donald Grant (*DAB*)
175. *MORTON, Sarah Wentworth (*NAW*)
176. *MOTLEY, John Lothrop* (*DAB*)
177. MOULTON, Louise Chandler (*NAW*)
178. *MURRAY, Judith Sargent (*NAW*)
179. *NEAL, John* (*DAB*)
180. NICHOLS, Mary Sargent (*NAW*)
181. NORTON, Andrews (*DAB*)
182. O'CONNOR, William Douglas (*DAB*)
183. *OSBORN, Selleck (*DAB*)
184. OSGOOD, Frances Sargent (*NAW*)
185. *PAINE, Robert Treat (*DAB*)
186. PALFREY, Sarah (*CAB*)
187. *PARKER, Theodore* (*DLB*)
188. *PARKMAN, Francis* (*DAB*)
189. PARSONS, Thomas William (*DAB*)
190. PARTON, Sarah Payson Willis (*NAW*)
191. PECK, George Mason (*DAB*)
192. PEIRSON, Lydia (*CAB*)
193. PERCIVAL, James Gates (*DAB*)
194. PHELPS, Elizabeth Stuart (*AWW*)
195. PICKERING, Henry (*DAB*)
196. PIERPONT, John (*DAB*)
197. PIKE, Albert (*DAB*)
198. PIKE, Mary Hayden (*NAW*)
199. *PLUMMER, Jonathan (*DAB*)
200. PRAY, Isaac (*DAB*)
201. PRENTICE, George (*DAB*)
202. *PRENTISS, Charles (*CAL*)
203. PRENTISS, Elizabeth Payson (*NAW*)
204. *PRESCOTT, William Hickling* (*DAB*)
205. QUINCY, Edmund (*DAB*)
206. QUINCY, Josiah (*DAB*)
207. *RANDALL, Samuel (*DAB*)
208. RICKETSON, Daniel (*DAB*)
209. ROBINSON, Solon (*DAB*)
210. *ROWSON, Susannah Haswell (*NAW*)
211. SARGENT, Epes (*DAB*)
212. SARGENT, Lucius Manlius (*DAB*)
213. SAWYER, Caroline (*NAW*)
214. SAXE, John G. (*DAB*)
215. SEARS, Edmund Hamilton (*DAB*)
216. SEDGWICK, Catherine Maria (*NAW*)
217. *SEWALL, Jonathan Mitchell (*AW*)
218. SHAW, Henry Wheeler (*DAB*)
219. SHILLABER, Benjamin Penhallow (*DAB*)
220. SIGOURNEY, Lydia Huntley (*NAW*)
221. *SILLIMAN, Benjamin (*DAB*)

222. ★SMITH, Elihu Hubbard (*AW*)
223. SMITH, Elizabeth Oakes (*NAW*)
224. SMITH, Samuel Francis (*DAB*)
225. SMITH, Seba (*DAB*)
226. SNELLING, William Joseph (*DAB*)
227. ★SOUTHWICK, Solomon (*DAB*)
228. SPOFFORD, Harriet Prescott (*NAW*)
229. SPRAGUE, Charles (*DAB*)
230. STEPHENS, Ann (*NAW*)
231. ★STILES, Ezra (*DAB*)
232. STIMSON, Alexander (*DAB*)
233. STODDARD, Elizabeth Barstow (*DAB*)
234. STONE, John Augustus (*DAB*)
235. ★STORY, Isaac (*AW, DAB*)
236. ★STORY, Joseph (*DAB*)
237. STORY, WIlliam Wetmore (*DAB*)
238. *STOWE, Harriet Beecher* (*DAB*)
239. TAGGART, Cynthia (*CAL*)
240. TAPPAN, William Bingham (*CAB*)
241. ★TENNEY, Tabitha (*NAW*)
242. THATCHER, Benjamin B. (*DAB*)
243. THOMES, William Henry (*DAB*)
244. THOMPSON, Daniel Pierce (*DAB*)
245. *THOREAU, Henry David* (*DLB*)
246. TICKNOR, George (*DAB*)
247. TOWNSEND, Eliza (*AA*)
248. TROWBRIDGE, John Townsend (*DAB*)

249. ★*TRUMBULL, John* (*AW, DAB*)
250. *TUCKERMAN, Frederick Goddard* (*DAB*)
251. TUCKERMAN, Henry (*DAB*)
252. TUDOR, William (*DAB*)
253. TUTHILL, Louisa C. (*NAW*)
254. ★*TYLER, Royall* (*AW, DAB*)
255. UPHAM, Thomas C. (*DAB*)
256. *VERY, Jones* (*DLB*)
257. VERY, Lydia (*DAB*)
258. WALTER, William B. (*CAL*)
259. WARE, Henry, Jr. (*DAB*)
260. WARE, Katherine Augusta (*CAL*)
261. WARE, William (*DAB*)
262. ★*WARREN, Mercy Otis* (*NAW*)
263. WELLS, Anna Maria (*CAL*)
264. ★*WHEATLEY, Phillis* (*NAW*)
265. WHIPPLE, Edwin Percy (*DAB*)
266. WHITMAN, Sarah Helen (*NAW*)
267. *WHITTIER, John Greenleaf* (*DLB*)
268. WILCOX, Carlos (*AA*)
269. WILLARD, Emma (*NAW*)
270. WILLIAMS, Catherine Read Arnold (*AWW*)
271. *WILLIS, Nathaniel Parker* (*DAB*)
272. ★WINCHESTER, Elhanan (*DAB*)
273. WINTER, William (*DAB*)
274. WINTHROP, Theodore (*DAB*)
275. ★WOOD, Sarah Keating (*NAW*)
276. WOODWORTH, Samuel (*DAB*)

Notes

Part I: Four Overviews

CHAPTER 1: THEORETICAL PREMISES

1 Geoffrey Hartman, *Beyond Formalism* (New Haven: Yale Univ. Press, 1970), p. 356.

2 Paul de Man, *Blindness and Insight,* 2nd ed. (Minneapolis: Univ. of Minnesota Press, 1983), p. 35.

3 Energy, of course, does not always lead to accuracy, and any sort of extrinsic criticism, feminist or otherwise, is at its best when it recognizes that social reality and its textualizations are two different domains. Jonathan Culler makes this point with reference to feminist interpretation when he notes that "for a woman to read as a woman is not to repeat an identity or an experience that is given but to play a role she constructs with reference to her identity as a woman, which is also a construct" (*On Deconstruction* [Ithaca: Cornell Univ. Press, 1982], p. 64). This is a useful corrective to naive historicism. A sophisticated historicism, however, will then want to attempt to reconstruct the contextual as well as textual factors that prompt the construction of the particular identity that the woman reader assumes as a woman reader. Kenneth Burke's characterization of both "critical and imaginative works" as stylized "strategies for the encompassing of situations" still seems an admirably comprehensive and exact summation of the contextual versus textual, idiosyncratic versus conventionally determined elements of discourse, elements that historicists, and structuralists, and poststructuralists are, each in their own ways, often too quick to pull apart (*The Philosophy of Literary Form*, 3rd ed. [Berkeley and Los Angeles: Univ. of California Press, 1973], p. 1).

4 René Wellek and Austin Warren, *Theory of Literature* (New York: Harcourt, Brace, 1949), p. 280.

5 Umberto Eco, *A Theory of Semiotics* (Bloomington: Indiana Univ. Press, 1979), p. 66.

6 Wellek and Warren, *Theory of Literature*, p. 282: Hartman, *Beyond Formalism*, pp. 356–86; Jonathan Culler, *The Pursuit of Signs* (Ithaca: Cornell Univ. Press, 1981), p. 13.

7 De Man, *Blindness and Insight,* p. 165.

8 Two major collaborative efforts are now under way: a one-volume *Columbia History of American Literature,* under the general editorship of Emory Elliott, and a five-volume *Cambridge History of American Literature,* general editor Sacvan Bercovitch.

9 Culler, *Pursuit of Signs,* p. 6.

10 Clifford Geertz, *The Interpretation of Cultures* (New York: Basic Books, 1973), p. 30.

11 I have in mind especially William Charvat's *Literary Publishing in America, 1790–1850* (Philadelphia: Univ. of Pennsylvania Press, 1959); Matthew J. Bruccoli, ed., *The Profession of Authorship in America* (Columbus: Ohio State Univ. Press, 1968); and Charvat and Warren S. Tryon, eds., *The Cost Books of Ticknor and Fields and Their Predecessors, 1832–1858* (New York: Bibliographical Society of America, 1949). Charvat's *Origins of American Critical Thought, 1810–1835* (Philadelphia: Univ. of Pennsylvania Press, 1936) is another classic of empirical literary research.

12 For a convenient introduction to this historiographical debate, see Robert William Fogel and G. R. Elton, *Which Road to the Past?: Two Views of History* (New Haven: Yale Univ. Press, 1983), especially Fogel's "'Scientific' History and Traditional History."

13 Geertz, *Interpretation of Cultures,* p. 15.

14 Hans Robert Jauss, *Toward an Aesthetic of Reception,* trans. Timothy Bahti (Minneapolis: Univ. of Minnesota Press, 1982), p. 65. Cf. Robert C. Holub's overview, *Reception Theory* (London: Methuen, 1984).

15 Natalie Zemon Davis, *The Return of Martin Guerre* (Cambridge, Mass.: Harvard Univ. Press, 1983), p. 5.

16 See especially "'Reception Aesthetics,' and the Crisis in Literary History," *Clio,* 5 (1975), 3–35, by East German scholar Robert Weimann, who deserves to become much better known to Americanists. The third section of his *Structure and Society in Literary History* (Charlottesville: Univ. Press of Virginia, 1976), provides, in my judgment, the most penetrating critique of American literary historiography ever written.

17 Raymond Williams, *Marxism and Literature* (Oxford: Oxford Univ. Press, 1977), p. 38.

18 Frederic Jameson, *The Political Unconscious* (Ithaca: Cornell Univ. Press, 1981), pp. 34–5.

19 Michel Foucault, *The Archaeology of Knowledge,* trans. A. M. Sheridan Smith (New York: Harper & Row, 1972), p. 148.

20 Wellek and Warren, *Theory of Literature,* p. 277. Cf. Walter F. Eggers, Jr., "The Idea of Literary Periods," *Comparative Literature Studies,* 17 (1980), 1–15. Both discussions stress period style at the expense of periodization as a function of literary institutions.

21 I venture this definition hesitantly in view of the large number of earlier attempts, most of which stress the difficulty of the task, the irony of our inability to say what it is we are studying, and so forth. The troubles arise mainly from the fact that the word *literature* is used both descriptively and honorifically, that it is sometimes extended to oral performances, and that it can be defined in terms of at least four criteria: its innate qualities, its intentionality, its status in relation to the object-world, and reader expectation. See especially Paul Hernadi, ed., *What Is Literature* (Bloomington: Indiana Univ. Press, 1978), in which the essays by Sparshott, Wellek, Hirsch, and Scholes have helped me the most.

22 De Man, *Blindness and Insight*, p. 18.

23 Jeffrey Sammons, *Literary Sociology and Practical Criticism* (Bloomington: Indiana Univ. Press, 1977), p. 55. For a more cautious definition of the "object stratum" of literature, which establishes its presence while insisting more vigorously on the difference between aesthetic and extrinsic domains, see Roman Ingarden, *The Literary Work of Art*, 3rd ed., trans. George G. Grabowicz (Evanston: Northwestern Univ. Press, 1973), pp. 288–304.

24 George Levine, "Books," *College English*, 43 (1981), 146.

25 Two of the most penetrating statements of the problem of traditional ethnic and gender constraints in determining the American literary canon are Nina Baym, "Melodramas of Beset Manhood: How Theories of American Fiction Exclude Women Authors," *American Quarterly*, 33 (1981), 123–39, and Paul Lauter, "Race and Gender in the Shaping of the American Literary Canon," *Feminist Studies*, 9 (1983), 435–63. For the period covered by this study, see also Jane Tompkins, *Sensational Designs: The Cultural Work of American Fiction, 1790–1860* (New York: Oxford Univ. Press, 1985).

26 R. S. Crane, "Critical and Historical Principles of Literary History," in *The Idea of the Humanities* (Chicago: Univ. of Chicago Press, 1967), 2:92–3; T. S. Eliot, "Tradition and the Individual Talent," in *Selected Essays* (New York: Harcourt, Brace, 1950), p. 5. It is a telling commentary on the underdevelopment of the field that Crane's "uncompleted short monograph" of 1950 (2:45n) was the most sophisticated treatise on doing literary history that had been written in the English-speaking world up to that time.

27 Roy Harvey Pearce, *The Continuity of American Poetry* (Princeton: Princeton Univ. Press, 1961); Michael Bell, *The Development of American Romance* (Chicago: Univ. of Chicago Press, 1980); Ann Douglas, *The Feminization of American Culture* (New York: Knopf, 1977); and Leo Marx, *The Machine in the Garden: Technology and the Pastoral Ideal in American Culture* (New York: Oxford Univ. Press, 1964). I deliberately limit myself here to distinguished works from which I have learned a great deal.

28 Claudio Guillén, *Literature as System* (Princeton: Princeton Univ. Press, 1971), p. 376.

29 Crane, *The Idea of the Humanities*, 2:46.

30 Ralph Cohen, "A Propadeutic for Literary Change," *Critical Exchange*, 13 (1983), 3; Guillén, *Literature as System*, pp. 131–2. Cohen's paper argues for a redefined "genre" as the key to understanding literary change but without proposing the radical reconception that he invokes when he accepts the criticism of antigenre theorists; cf. Gregory S. Jay's comment on Cohen's paper, *Critical Exchange*, 13 (1983), 70. Jameson, in *Political Unconscious*, also engages in genre criticism after finding it "thoroughly discredited by modern literary theory and practice" (p. 105), reanimating it with a brilliant analysis of genre (illustrated by what he calls "magical narratives") as ideological vehicle.

31 A checklist of the way genre concepts have historically been misused through excess of precision is given in Adrian Marino, "Toward a Definition of

Literary Genres," in *Theories of Literary Genre,* ed. Joseph P. Strelka (University Park: Pennsylvania State Univ. Press, 1978), p. 50.

32 Alistair Fowler, *Kinds of Literature* (Cambridge, Mass.: Harvard Univ. Press, 1982), p. 32. Jacques Derrida aptly sums up the problematics of genre classification in "The Law of Genre" (*Glyph,* 7 [1980]): "A text cannot belong to no genre, it cannot be without or less a genre. Every text participates in one or several genres, there is no genreless text; there is always a genre and genres, yet participation never amounts to belonging" (p. 212).

33 Maria Corti, *An Introduction to Literary Semiotics,* trans. Margherita Bogat and Allen Mandelbaum (Bloomington: Univ. of Indiana Press, 1978), p. 115.

34 Thomas Metscher, "Literature and Art as Ideological Form," *New Literary History,* 11 (1979), 33, 27.

35 Pierre Macherey, *A Theory of Literary Production* (1966), trans. Geoffrey Wall (London: Routledge & Kegan Paul, 1978), p. 76. Macherey's line of thinking is reworked in Terry Eagleton's *Criticism and Ideology* (London: Verso, 1978), especially Chap. 3, "Towards a Science of the Text."

36 Carolyn Porter, *Seeing and Being: The Plight of the Participant Observer in Emerson, James, Adams, and Faulkner* (Middletown, Conn.: Wesleyan Univ. Press, 1981).

37 Machercy, *Theory of Literary Production,* p. 91.

38 A good example of the position whose one-sidedness I am criticizing is Michel Foucault, "What Is an Author," in *Textual Strategies: Perspectives in Post-Structuralist Criticism* ed. Josué V. Harari (Ithaca: Cornell Univ. Press, 1979), pp. 141-60.

CHAPTER 2: A NARRATIVE OVERVIEW OF NEW ENGLAND'S LITERARY
DEVELOPMENT

1 Among previous studies of broad scope like the present chapter, see especially the following. Among memoirs: Joseph T. Buckingham, *Personal Memoirs and Recollections of Editorial Life* (Boston: Ticknor, Reed, & Fields, 1852); Ralph Waldo Emerson, "Historic Notes of Life and Letters in New England," *EW* 10:323-70; Samuel G. Goodrich, *Recollections of a Lifetime* (New York and Auburn: Miller, Orton & Mulligan, 1856). Among previous literary and cultural histories: Van Wyck Brooks, *The Flowering of New England, 1815-1865* (New York: Dutton, 1936); Russel Nye, *The Cultural Life of the New Nation, 1776-1830* (New York: Harper & Row, 1960), and Nye, *Society and Culture in America, 1830-1860* (New York: Harper & Row, 1974). Among histories of literary institutions: Frank Luther Mott, *History of American Magazines, 1741-1850* (New York: Appleton, 1930) and ibid., *1850-1865* (Cambridge, Mass.: Harvard Univ. Press, 1938); William Charvat, *Literary Publishing in America, 1790-1860* (Philadelphia: Univ. of Pennsylvania Press, 1959); and John Tebbel, *A History of Book Publishing in the United States* (New York: Bowker, 1972), vol. 1.

2 For overviews of this generation, see Leon Howard, *The Connecticut Wits* (Chicago: Univ. of Chicago Press, 1943); Kenneth Silverman, *A Cultural History of the American Revolution* (New York: Crowell, 1976); and Emory Elliott, *Revolutionary Writers: Literature and Authority in the New Republic, 1725-1810* (New York: Oxford Univ. Press, 1982).

3 Especially valuable for information on writers of this era has been the research of Milton Ellis and his students, including numerous *DAB* biographies, Ellis' *Joseph Dennie and His Circle* (Austin: Univ. of Texas, 1915), and the *University of Maine Studies* monographs on other early national figures (N. Deering, T. G. Fessenden, S. W. Morton, J. S. Murray); Lewis Simpson's studies of the literary culture of the second and third generation in Boston, especially *The Federalist Literary Mind* (Baton Rouge: Louisiana State Univ. Press, 1962), *The Man of Letters in New England and the South* (Baton Rouge: Louisiana State Univ. Press, 1973), and "Literary Ecumenicalism of the American Enlightenment," in *The Ibero-American Enlightenment,* ed. A. Owen Aldridge (Urbana: Univ. of Illinois Press, 1971), pp. 317–32; and Lewis Leary's studies of individual figures in *Soundings* (Athens: Univ. of Georgia Press, 1975), and elsewhere.

4 For the Massachusetts Historical Society and the historical society movement, see Leslie W. Dunlap, *American Historical Societies, 1790–1860* (Madison: pvt., 1944), and Stephen Riley, *The Massachusetts Historical Society 1791–1959* (Boston: Massachusetts Historical Society, 1959). For the *Massachusetts Magazine,* see Mott, *American Magazines.* For the first stages of American fiction, see especially Henri Petter, *The Early American Novel* (Columbus: Ohio State Univ. Press, 1971), which includes discussions and plot summaries of all the examples mentioned here.

5 For the early history of the New England theater, see William Warland Clapp, *A Record of the Boston Stage* (Boston and Cambridge, Mass.: Munroe, 1853); George O. Willard, *History of the Providence Stage* (Providence: Rhode Island News Co., 1891); Arthur Hobson Quinn, *A History of the American Drama from the Beginning to the Civil War,* 2nd ed. (New York: Crofts, 1943); and Walter J. Meserve, *An Emerging Entertainment: The Drama of the American People to 1828* (Bloomington: Indiana Univ. Press, 1977). These sources show that the battle to legalize theater in Boston during the 1790s was anomalous in its acrimony but typical in the issues polarizing the disputants.

6 Robert B. Winans, "The Growth of a Novel-Reading Public in Late Eighteenth-century America," *Early American Literature,* 9 (1975), 267–75. Among "significant" writers of New England (see Appendix for criteria) who were still alive in the 1790s and who were to reach literary maturity by 1815, at least fourteen (of fifty-one) wrote plays or poetic fore and after pieces (P. Allen, Bartlett, Brown, D. Everett, Edward Hitchcock, Humphreys, Murray, Paine, Randall, Rowson, Sewall, Smith, Tyler, Warren), as against eleven who wrote prose fiction (Belknap, Bingham, Brown, Foster, Enos Hitchcock, Knapp, Rowson, Silliman, Tenney, Tyler, Wood). Fiction was not seen as the likelier field of literary accomplishment until the vogue of Walter Scott. The interest in theater on the part of Federalist era writers, at least half of whom were interested spectators if not composers of drama, is another index of their unrepresentativeness of the population at large.

7 Quoted in G. Thomas Tanselle, *Royall Tyler* (Cambridge, Mass.: Harvard Univ. Press, 1967), p. 26.

8 Jeremiah Mason, *Memoirs* (1873; rpt. Boston: Law Book Co., 1917), p. 29; Ellis, *Dennie,* pp. 84–109.

9 Laura G. Pedder, ed., *The Letters of Joseph Dennie* (Orono: Univ. of Maine Press, 1936), p. 165.

10 William Charvat, outlines the situation lucidly in *Literary Publishing,* Chap. 1, and in Charvat, *The Profession of Authorship in America,* ed. Matthew J. Bruccoli (Columbus: Ohio State Univ. Press, 1968), pp. 29–48.

11 Note the space Griswold accorded in *The Poets and Poetry of America* (1842) to New England poets, the ones with copious selections being almost all New Englanders.

12 For the New England conception of woman's sphere, see especially Nancy F. Cott, *The Bonds of Womanhood: "Woman's Sphere" in New England, 1780–1835* (New Haven: Yale Univ. Press, 1977). For Sarah Hale, see Ruth Finley, *The Lady of Godey's* (Philadelphia: Lippincott, 1931); Ernest Earnest, *The American Eve in Fact and Fiction, 1775–1914* (Urbana: Univ. of Illinois Press, 1974), pp. 93–98; and Cott, *Bonds of Womanhood,* pp. 95–100. Hale played a major part in getting New England's favorite festival, Thanksgiving, approved as a national holiday. For Catherine Sedgwick and Caroline Gilman, see Nina Baym, *Woman's Fiction* (Ithaca: Cornell Univ. Press, 1978), pp. 53–71, and Mary Kelley, *Private Woman, Public Stage: Literary Domesticity in Nineteenth-century America* (New York: Oxford Univ. Press, 1984). To call Sedgwick an expatriate is perhaps stretching a point, since the Berkshires remained for her a part-time residence.

13 Significant sources of information on the literary history of Litchfield during the period under review include Samuel G. Goodrich, *Recollections; The Diary of Elihu Hubbard Smith,* ed. James Cronin (Philadelphia: American Philosophical Society, 1973); *The Autobiography of Lyman Beecher,* ed. Barbara Cross (Cambridge, Mass.: Harvard Univ. Press, 1961); Samuel Herbert Fisher, *The Litchfield Law School, 1775–1833* (New Haven: Yale Univ. Press, 1933); and Emily Noyes Vanderpoel, *Chronicles of a Pioneer School from 1792 to 1833, being the History of Miss Sarah Pierce and her Litchfield School* (Cambridge: Cambridge Univ. Press, 1903). See also the autobiographical novels of Harriet Beecher Stowe, *Poganuc People* (1878), and her brother Henry Ward Beecher, *Norwood* (1867).

14 Goodrich, *Recollections,* 2:94.

15 For Portland's literary history during the period reviewed here, see Frederick Gardiner Fassett, Jr., *A History of Newspapers in the District of Maine, 1785–1820* (Orono: Univ. of Maine Press, 1932); William Willis, *The History of Portland, from 1632 to 1864* (Portland: Bailey & Noyes, 1865); John Neal, *Wandering Recollections of a Somewhat Busy Life* (Boston: Roberts, 1869); Benjamin Lease, *That Wild Fellow John Neal* (Chicago: Univ. of Chicago Press, 1972); Leola Bowie Chaplin, *The Life and Works of Nathaniel Deering* (Orono: Univ. of Maine Press, 1934); Mary Alice Wyman, *Two American Pioneers, Seba Smith and Elizabeth Oakes Smith* (New York: Columbia Univ. Press, 1927); Bertha Monica Sterns, "New England Magazines for Ladies, 1830–1860," *New England Quarterly,* 3 (1930), 635–9.

16 Aspects of Boston literary and social life treated in this paragraph are discussed in Mott, *American Magazines,* Silverman, *Cultural History of the American Revolution,* Buckingham, *Personal Memoirs,* and M. Ellis, *Dennie;* in Josiah Phillips Quincy, "Social Life in Boston: From the Adoption of the Federal Constitution to the Granting of the City Charter," in *Memorial History of Boston,* ed.

Justin Winsor (Boston: Ticknor, 1880–1), 4:1–24; Charles Warren, "Samuel Adams and the Sans Souci Club," *Proceedings of the Massachusetts Historical Society,* 60 (1927), 318–44; Lewis P. Simpson, "'The Intercommunity of the Learned': Boston and Cambridge in 1800," *New England Quarterly,* 23 (1950), 491–503; Sidney Willard, *Memories of Youth and Manhood* (Cambridge, Mass.: Bartlett, 1855); Buckingham, *Specimens of Newspaper Literature* (Boston: Little, Brown, 1850); Lewis Leary, "John Lathrop, Jr.: The Quiet Poet of Federalist Boston," *Proceedings of the American Antiquarian Society,* 19 (1981), 39–89; Charles Prentiss, ed., *The Works, in Verse and Prose, of the Late Robert Treat Paine, Jun.* (Boston: Belcher, 1812).

17 Vose to Dennie, September 28, 1790, in grudging praise of Warren's *Poems,* in Ellis, *Dennie,* p. 43.

18 Dennie, *Letters,* p. 164.

19 For a short account of the Anthology Club, its magazine, and their significance, see Simpson, *Federalist Literary Mind;* also M. A. DeWolfe Howe, ed., *Journal of the Proceedings of the Society which Conducts the Monthly Anthology* (Boston: Boston Athenaeum, 1910); and Josiah Quincy, *History of the Boston Athenaeum, with Biographical Notices of Its Deceased Founders* (Cambridge, Mass.: Metcalf, 1851). The long-range significance of the Anthologists' varied enterprises in bringing about the nineteenth-century consolidation of the Boston elite is meticulously demonstrated in Ronald Story's "Class and Culture in Boston: The Athenaeum, 1807–1860," *American Quarterly,* 27 (1975), 178–99.

20 *DT* 1:365–6; this from one not predisposed to admire Boston.

21 Robert Hallowell Gardiner, *Early Recollections* (Hallowell, Ma.: White & Horne, 1936), p. 93.

22 The dispute is summarized by Simpson, *Federalist Literary Mind,* p. 26, and documented by *Anthology* excerpts, ibid., pp. 196–207. This exchange has understandably been seen as a harbinger of New England Romanticism. As with other Federalist era "literary" discussions, however, the literary issue was partly a pretext for skirmishing, motivated by touchier disagreements – in this case, theology (Gardiner's Episcopalianism versus the younger Anthologists' drift toward Unitarianism; v. Simpson, *Federalist Literary Mind,* p. 27), and morals (the unpublished Buckminster–A. M. Walter correspondence in the Boston Athenaeum reveals that the younger Anthologists considered Gardiner's life-style unclerically frivolous.)

23 Josiah (?) Quincy, "Works of Fisher Ames," *Monthly Anthology,* 7 (1809), 323; Andrews Norton, "Character of Rev. Joseph Stevens Buckminster" (1812), rpt. in *The Works of Joseph Stevens Buckminster* (Boston: Munroe, 1839), 1:50. For an analysis of Boston Federalist hagiography as a collegial product, see Lawrence Buell, "Joseph Stevens Buckminster: The Making of a New England Saint," *Canadian Review of American Studies,* 10 (1979), 1–29.

24 J. S. J. Gardiner, "Remarker No. 44," *Monthly Anthology,* 7 (1809), 37.

25 For the anthology, see Elihu Hubbard Smith, ed., *American Poems* (Litchfield, Conn.: Collier & Buel, 1793). Smith's articles on the four major Wits plus Hopkins were published in the *Monthly Magazine and British Register* and reprinted, along with a sketch of Smith (a correspondent of Joseph Dennie's), in the *Farmer's Weekly Museum* (April and September, 1799), which also published a nine-part, sympathetic critique of Dwight's *Conquest of Canaan* between February and August of the same year.

26 Beecher, *Autobiography* 1:240.

27 Alsop, "The Charms of Fancy," in *The Poetry of the Minor Connecticut Wits,* ed. Benjamin Franklin V (Gainesville, Fla.: Scholars' Facsimiles and Reprints, 1970), p. 433; John Adams, *Diary and Autobiography,* ed. L. H. Butterfield (Cambridge, Mass.: Harvard Univ. Press, 1961), 3:189; John Quincy Adams, *Diary,* ed. David Grayson Allen (Cambridge, Mass.: Harvard Univ. Press, 1981), 1:375; Solyman Brown, *An Essay on American Poetry* (New Haven: Howe, Flagg, & Gray, 1818), p. 134. For Trumbull on Dwight's *Conquest,* see Victor Gimmestad, *John Trumbull* (Boston: Twayne, 1974), p. 142.

28 William Cullen Bryant, "American Poetry," *North American Review,* 7 (1818), 198–211.

29 F. Sheldon, "The Pleiades of Connecticut," *Atlantic,* 15 (1865), 198.

30 *Monthly Anthology,* 1 (1804), 507–11; 4 (1807), 274–5; 5 (1808), 684–5.

31 Gimmestad, *John Trumbull,* p. 143; Charles T. Hazelrigg, *American Literary Pioneer: A Biographical Study of James A. Hillhouse* (New York: Bookman, 1953), p. 65: "Hillhouse never published a drama without first heeding the detailed advice of this aging 'Connecticut Wit.'" Sigourney and Hillhouse might have done better to go their own ways. They were essentially grave poets, and Trumbull's own gift was for burlesque. When he tried to be solemn, he fell into Johnsonian ponderousness, as did his protégés.

32 Quoted by Hazelrigg, *American Literary Pioneer,* p. 137.

33 Julius H. Ward, *The Life and Letters of James Gates Percival* (Boston: Ticknor & Fields, 1866), pp. 77, 117; see Chaps. 3–12 for the history of various efforts to befriend Percival; also Goodrich, *Recollections,* 2:129–41.

34 Sheldon, "Pleiades," p. 187; *LoW* 2:140–61. To date, the most generous attempt to give the Connecticut Romantics their due – generous perhaps because of the nature of the occasion – has been Stanley T. Williams' state-commissioned pamphlet, *The Literature of Connecticut* (New Haven: Yale Univ. Press, 1936).

35 Jarvis Means Morse, *A Neglected Period of Connecticut's History, 1818–1850* (New Haven: Yale Univ. Press, 1933), p. 171.

36 Ward, *Life and Letters of Percival,* pp. 68–72, 135–7, makes clear that when Tuthill shifted posts he had to become "officially" less cordial to Percival (because of the latter's heterodoxy), although he continued to be friendly on a personal level and apparently even encouraged Percival to contribute to the *Spectator* at the same time as Tuthill was depicting Percival's work in that journal as "hostile to the influence of the Gospel" (v. *Christian Spectator,* 4 [1822], 643–56). Cf. James Kingsley Blake, "*The Microscope* and James Gates Percival," *New Haven Historical Society Papers,* 8 (1914), 215–37.

37 Whittier, *Letters,* ed. John P. Pickard (Cambridge, Mass.: Harvard Univ. Press, 1975) 1:117; Goodrich, *Recollections,* 2:252.

38 See Appendix for statistics on authorial mobility.

39 Edward Everett Hale, *Memories of a Hundred Years* (London: Macmillan, 1902) 2:236; Charvat, *Literary Publishing in America,* esp. pp. 37, 27, and Charvat, *Profession of Authorship,* pp. 168–89.

40 See Appendix for criteria defining "major" authors and for discussion of their careers.

41 This bears out Charvat's claim that a Boston imprint was considered a status symbol for a book of poems throughout the period (*Literary Publishing*, p. 34).

42 W. S. Tryon, *Parnassus Corner: A Life of James T. Fields* (Boston: Houghton, Mifflin, 1963), esp. pp. 93–111, tells the story. As was his general practice, Fields both cultivated Longfellow's friendship and helped see to it that the firm offered him favorable terms. For *Evangeline* (1847), Longfellow's first book of poems originally published by Ticknor & Fields, the poet was given the best royalty arrangement ever accorded an American poet (ibid., p. 111, and W. S. Tryon and William Charvat, eds., *The Cost Books of Ticknor and Fields and Their Predecessors* [New York: Bibliographical Society of America, 1949], p. 111) – a bargain that turned out well for both sides, for *Evangeline* far outsold any previous book of American poems. It is interesting that the alternative that Longfellow was apparently most seriously considering when Fields bagged him was his struggling Cambridge publisher John Owen, not the New York and Philadelphia houses that had turned larger profits for him (Tryon, *Parnassus Corner*, p. 109).

43 The people in question were, respectively, George Ripley, Horace Greeley, Charles A. Dana, and Daniel Appleton.

44 Oliver Wendell Holmes, *The Autocrat of the Breakfast-Table* (Boston: Houghton Mifflin, 1891), 1:127.

45 For Buckminster's European gleanings, see Jerry Wayne Brown, *The Rise of Biblical Criticism in America, 1810–1870* (Middletown, Conn.: Wesleyan Univ. Press, 1969), pp. 10–26. For the others, see Orie W. Long, *Literary Pioneers: Early American Explorers of European Culture* (Cambridge, Mass.: Harvard Univ. Press, 1935). For the general situation at Harvard, see Samuel Eliot Morison, *Three Centuries of Harvard, 1636–1936* (Cambridge, Mass.: Harvard Univ. Press, 1936), pp. 195–272. For the intellectual impact of the higher criticism, see especially Brown, *Rise of Biblical Criticism*, and Philip Gura, *The Wisdom of Words* (Middletown, Conn.: Wesleyan Univ. Press, 1981), pp. 15–31, as well as Chap. 7 of the present volume.

46 Harvard's growth and consolidation during the nineteenth century is documented in Ronald Story, *The Forging of an Aristocracy: Harvard and the Boston Upper Class, 1800–1870* (Middletown, Conn.: Wesleyan Univ. Press, 1980). Story's representation of Harvard as an increasingly organized force in the service of Boston's cultured elite squares with my own account in this chapter of the centralization of regional literary institutions, although I agree with Richard D. Brown's review of Story (*Reviews in American History*, 9 [1981], 58–61) that Story has depicted the rise to hegemony as a more conspiratorial process than it actually was. In any case, as the example of Emerson shows, Harvard became a significant weapon used for purposes of both exclusion and cooptation of literary deviants. For a more speculative but also penetrating analysis of Boston's rise and decline as a cultural center, see Martin Green, *The Problem of Boston* (New York: Norton, 1966).

47 For the rise and ideology of Unitarianism, see especially Conrad Wright, *The Beginnings of Unitarianism in America* (Boston: Starr King Press, 1955); Daniel Walker Howe, *The Unitarian Conscience* (Cambridge, Mass.: Harvard Univ.

Press, 1970); and Conrad Wright, "The Early Period (1811–1840)," in *The Harvard Divinity School: Its Place in Harvard University and in American Culture*, ed. George Hunston Williams (Boston: Beacon Press, 1954).

48   For the basis of Unitarianism's special encouragement of creative expression, see Howe, *Unitarian Conscience*, pp. 174–204; Buell, "The Unitarian Movement and the Art of Preaching in 19th Century America," *American Quarterly*, 24 (1972), 166–90, and *Literary Transcendentalism* (Ithaca: Cornell Univ. Press, 1973), pp. 21–54; also David Robinson, *Apostle of Culture: Emerson as Preacher and Lecturer* (Philadelphia: Univ. of Pennsylvania Press, 1982), pp. 7–29.

49   For the compatibility of Dana's Romanticism with his Calvinism, see Doreen Hunter, "America's First Romantics," *New England Quarterly*, 45 (1972), 11–20.

50   Charles Feidelson, *Symbolism and American Literature* (Chicago: Univ. of Chicago Press, 1953), p. 158. See also Randall Stewart, "Regional Characteristics in the Literature of New England," *College English*, 3 (1941), 130–2, for reflections on its scholarly cast.

51   See Winans, "Growth of a Novel-Reading Public" (note 6 above) and the narrator's preface to Tyler's *Algerine Captive*, remarking on the upsurge of popular fiction in the 1790s.

52   Karl Harrington, *Richard Alsop: "A Hartford Wit"* (Middletown, Conn.: Mattabesett Press, 1939), pp. 117–38; James D. Hart, *The Popular Book: A History of America's Literary Taste* (Berkeley and Los Angeles: Univ. of California Press, 1963), pp. 51–66; Herbert Ross Brown, *The Sentimental Novel in America, 1789–1860* (Durham: Duke Univ. Press, 1940), pp. 3–27; "Jonathan Plummer," *DAB*.

53   All the major pioneer American authors of juvenile fiction discussed in Anne Scott MacLeod, *A Moral Tale: Children's Fiction and American Culture, 1820–1860* (Hamden, Conn.: Archon, 1975), were New England natives (pp. 32–40).

54   Buckingham relates the history of the *Galaxy*, with information about contributors, in *Personal Memoirs*, 1:93ff. For the vogue of annuals, see Ralph Thompson, *American Literary Annuals and Gift Books, 1825–1865* (New York: Wilson, 1936), and Goodrich, *Recollections*, 2:259–75. For magazines, see Mott, *American Magazines*.

55   For Lewis, see the biographical sketch by his son in Lewis' *Poetical Works* (Boston: Williams, 1883); for Gould, see *DAB;* for Tappan, see William Allen, *The American Biographical Dictionary*, 3rd ed. (Boston: Jewett, 1857), p. 778.

56   On Sumner Lincoln Fairfield, see *DAB;* and Jane Fairfield, *The Life of Sumner Lincoln Fairfield* (New York: the author, 1847).

57   *A Mortal Antipathy* (Boston: Houghton Mifflin, 1891), p. 6.

58   Ungraciously, because Snelling (as Holmes well remembered) had praised him as "the muses' youngest son, / Equall'd by few, surpass'd by none" (*Truth*, 2nd ed. [Boston: Mussey, 1832], p. 70). That, of course, *was* confirmation of Snelling's provincialism.

59   Even more pathetic than Fairfield's, the life of Coffin, product of a broken albeit genteel home (the father a Harvard-educated Congregational minister, the mother "nurtured in the lap of luxury") is told in his own *Life of the Boston Bard*

(Mount Pleasant, N.Y.: Marshall, 1825), a tortured and ineffectual self-advertisement.

60 Ann Stephens, *High Life in New York, by Jonathan Slick, Esq.* (New York: Stephens, 1843); Frances Whitcher, *Widow Bedott Papers* (New York: Derby, 1856). Walter Blair, in *Native American Humor* (1937; rpt. San Francisco: Chandler, 1960), pp. 38–62, briefly discusses Stephens and Whitcher in a general section entitled "Down East Humor." For the other figures, see Arthur Lachlan Reed, "Asa Greene, New England Publisher, New York Editor and Humorist, 1789–1838," Ph.D. thesis, Univ. of Minnesota, 1953; Chaplin, *Deering.* For Nathaniel Deering's "Mrs. Sykes," see the *Portland Sketch Book* (Portland: Colman & Chisholm, 1836), pp. 102–14. In Deering's tale, characteristically told by a pedantic but drolly witty gentleman narrator, Dr. Tonic's patient, Mrs. Sykes, revives from apparent death to find her husband being consoled by an attractive widow.

61 See especially W. B. O. Peabody, "The Decline of Poetry," *North American Review,* 28 (1829), 1–18.

62 For the *North American Review* on Scott see esp. 5 (1817), 257; 7 (1818), 149; 32 (1831), 386. On Wordsworth, see 18 (1824), 356, and 59 (1844), 352. On Edgeworth, see 6 (1818), 153; 17 (1823), 383; 32 (1831), 449; 41 (1835), 437. On Hemans, see 24 (1827), 443. On Bryant, see 13 (1821), 380; 22 (1826), 432; 34 (1832), 502; 35 (1832), 181. On Sedgwick, see 20 (1825), 245; 23 (1826), 212; 26 (1828), 403; 41 (1835), 444. For synopses, see Harry Hayden Clark, "Literary Criticism in the *North American Review,* 1815–1835," *Transactions of the Wisconsin Academy of Sciences, Arts, and Letters,* 32 (1940), 299–350. Many of the same texts were also reviewed in the *Christian Examiner.* By 1840, Brahmin reviewers had begun to respond positively to Victorian literary influences, recognizing Dickens as the most important figure in fiction and Tennyson in poetry. For Dickens, see *North American Review,* 69 (1849), 383. Also see ibid., 56 (1843), 212, and *Christian Examiner,* 27 (1839), 161, and 32 (1842), 1. For Tennyson, see *Examiner,* 23 (1838), 305, and *North American Review,* 90 (1860), 1. Dickens was given the ultimate compliment of being credited with having "acted with incalculable effect upon the principles which the late Dr. Channing carried out so nobly in another form" (*North American Review,* 56 [1843], 221) and was commended for his realism and inventiveness, but Scott was still revered as the model novelist (*North American Review,* 69 [1849], 385), and Dickens drew some criticism for sloppy craftsmanship (*North American Review,* 77 [1853], 409). Tennyson was often seen as being exquisitely graceful but not "prophet-eyed" (*Christian Examiner,* 23 [1838], 324); James Russell Lowell summed up the reservation when he described Tennyson as belonging to the "highest order of minor poets" (*North American Review,* 99 [1864], 626). Orthodox Congregational reviewers continued also to admire the art and the moral (if not theological) tendency of Scott and Wordsworth but showed more interest in Tennyson than in Dickens, perhaps because of reservations about fiction, on the one hand, and appreciation of the Christian dimension of Tennyson's work on the other (v. *New Englander,* 8 [1850], 613; 18 [1860], 1; 1 [1843], 64).

If Victorian era models did not greatly diminish the prestige of earlier literary eminences such as Scott and Wordsworth, the reason may have been that these authors were always valued by New England readers for their proto-Victorian character: Scott as the father of the modern novel (for having introduced a new standard of mimetic and historical fidelity), Wordsworth as a Victorian sage, and both for the purity of their morals.

63 An excellent group study of the four great Brahmin historians is David Levin, *History as Romantic Art* (Stanford: Stanford Univ. Press, 1959), which is particularly detailed on the subject of their Anglo-Saxon orientation (pp. 74–159) and which rightly stresses their ideological and collegial compatibility despite Bancroft's "lapse" into Jacksonianism (pp. 5–6, 49–50). Cf. also Prescott's correspondence with Bancroft in *The Papers of William Hickling Prescott*, ed. C. Harvey Gardiner (Urbana: Univ. of Illinois Press, 1964). As Gardiner says, "WHP, although he detested George's politics, was Bancroft's friend for life" (p. 89n).

64 Edward W. Emerson, comp., *The Early Years of the Saturday Club, 1855–1870,* (Boston: Houghton Mifflin, 1918), p. 120. This book is full of insights (many of them unintentional) into the inner workings of the Boston literary elite.

65 Compare Longfellow's review in *North American Review*, 45 (1837), 59–73, with Melville's review of *Mosses from an Old Manse,* "Hawthorne and His Mosses" (1850) in *The Norton Anthology of American Literature,* 2nd ed., ed. Hershel Parker (New York: Norton, 1985), 1:2160–74.

66 James T. Fields, "Hawthorne," in *Yesterdays with Authors* (Boston: Houghton Mifflin, 1871), p. 41. It is clear from this chapter, as from the Hawthorne-Longfellow correspondence (and indeed Hawthorne's correspondence in general), that Hawthorne did homage to the ideal of literary normality in the presence of those whom he regarded as members of the literary establishment. Indeed, there is no reason to doubt the entire sincerity of his 1860 declaration to Fields that "my own individual taste is for quite another class of works than those which I myself am able to write" (ibid., pp. 87–8).

67 "I cannot for a moment think of entering the political arena," replied the horrified Longfellow (*LL* 3:44).

68 "He had fought the 'Cotton Whigs' of State Street too bitterly to stretch his legs under respectable Boston mahogany and feel quite at easy in Zion" (Bliss Perry, memoir of Whittier, in Emerson, *Early Years of the Saturday Club,* p. 189). Edward Emerson, ibid., p. 208, tells the amusing story of Holmes's badgering Hawthorne into attending meetings of the club. For a summary of Whittier's views on the poetry of his great American contemporaries (toward whom he was almost invariably kind so long as they stayed within the boundaries of ethical idealism), see Edward Wagenknecht, *John Greenleaf Whittier: A Portrait in Paradox* (New York: Oxford Univ. Press, 1967), pp. 111–17. For evidence of establishment reservations about Whittier's prosodic crudity and mild antiestablishmentarianism, see James Russell Lowell's "Whittier's *In War Time,*" *North American,* 98 (1864), 290–2.

69 Studies of the various aspects of the Transcendentalist movement are so numerous as to have elicited a book-length study in themselves: Joel Myerson, ed., *The Transcendentalist Movement: A Review of Research and Criticism* (New York: Modern Language Association, 1984). The best concise scholarly introduction is still Alexander Kern, "The Rise of Transcendentalism, 1815–1860," in *Transitions* *in American Literary History,* ed. Harry Hayden Clark (Durham: Duke Univ. Press, 1954), pp. 245–314. For religious, social, and literary aspects, see especially William R. Hutchison, *The Transcendentalist Ministers* (New Haven: Yale Univ. Press, 1959); Anne C. Rose, *Transcendentalism as a Social Movement, 1830–1850* (New Haven: Yale Univ. Press, 1981); Lawrence Buell, *Literary Transcendentalism;* Perry Miller, ed., *The Transcendentalists: An Anthology* (Cambridge, Mass.: Harvard Univ. Press, 1950); and the references cited in the next note.

70 Emerson, *Letters,* ed. Ralph L. Rusk (New York: Columbia Univ. Press, 1939), 2:29. For details on the club's history, see Joel Myerson, "A History of the Transcendental Club," *ESQ,* 23 (1977), 27–35. Myerson, in *The New England Transcendentalists and the Dial* (Rutherford, N.J.: Fairleigh Dickinson Univ. Press, 1980), discusses the evolution of the informal club into the Transcendentalists' most important collective literary experiment, the *Dial* (1840–4), the most distinguished among several Transcendentalist literary periodicals, for which Myerson supplies an authoritative history. For short accounts of the others, see Clarence Gohdes, *The Periodicals of American Transcendentalism* (Durham: Duke Univ. Press, 1931).

71 The two novelists most often acclaimed as Transcendentalist, Sylvester Judd and Lydia Child, would have been uncomfortable with such praise.

72 The following progression in the *Christian Examiner* tells the story: *Nature,* reviewed acerbically by Francis Bowen, 21 (1837), 371–85; *Essays, First Series,* reviewed condescendingly by C. C. Felton, 30 (1841), 253–62; *Essays, Second Series, Poems,* and *Representative Men,* reviewed with increasing appreciation by Emerson's friends, the Transcendentalist ministers Frederic H. Hedge (the first work) and Cyrus Bartol (the latter two), 38 (1845), 87–106; 42 (1847), 255–63; and 48 (1850), 314–18. The objections to Emerson's heterodoxy become increasingly pro forma. By 1856, even fuddy-duddy Felton is making polite verbal gestures of alignment with the Emersonian camp (v. Emerson, *Early Years of the Saturday Club,* p. 15).

73 *JMN* 15:344, 440, makes plain Emerson's lukewarm view of Holmes, Lowell, Longfellow, and Whittier as poets. A charming example is Emerson's response to receipt of a copy of *The Song of Hiawatha* (1855): "I have always one foremost satisfaction in reading your books, – that I am safe. I am in variously skilful hands, but first of all they are safe hands. However, I find this Indian poem very wholesome; sweet and wholesome as maize; very proper and pertinent for us to read, and showing a kind of manly sense of duty in the poet to write" (Samuel Longfellow, *Life of Henry Wadsworth Longfellow* [Boston: Ticknor, 1886], 2:265–66). Freely translated: "Your poem is glib and insipid, but at least it is harmless, and I like you too well to say anything mean." Longfellow seems not to have been deceived but, characteristically, he was not at all hurt and continued to admire Emerson both as writer and as person.

74 William Dean Howells, *Literary Friends and Acquaintance,* ed. David F. Hiatt and Edwin H. Cady (Bloomington: Indiana Univ. Press, 1968), p. 100.

75 Boston's decline in literary leadership after the Civil War is chronicled elegiacally in Van Wyck Brooks's *New England: Indian Summer, 1865–1915* (New York: Dutton, 1940), anatomized by Martin Green in *The Problem of Boston,* and disputed by Howard Mumford Jones in "The Unity of New England Culture,"

Proceedings of the Massachusetts Historical Society, 79 (1967), 74-88; cf. also his "Literature and Orthodoxy in Boston after the Civil War," *American Quarterly,* 1 (1949), 149-65. To a considerable extent, Jones and Green are looking at the same symptoms, only where Jones sees a harmonious network of fully developed and productive cultural institutions, as opposed to the factionalism and growth pangs that marked the antebellum period, Green sees timorous, conformist gentility. Neither observer is wrong; but on the whole, Green, despite overkill (notably his attack on Hawthorne) is more correct than Jones in stressing the danger that cultural conformism posed for literary rigor and quality. For a case study of an important instance, the calculated genteel circumspection in literary reviews of the late nineteenth century, see Leonard Lutwack's perceptive "New England Hierarchy," *New England Quarterly,* 28 (1955), 164-85.

76 Less eminent but also significant literary products of late Calvinist Connecticut Valley culture include lecturer and Shakespearean scholar Delia Bacon, author of historical fiction and drama as well; Stowe's teacher John P. Brace, author of several novels; Dickinson's editor friend Josiah G. Holland – historian of western Massachusetts, author of a historical romance about the founding of Springfield, poet of the best-selling *Bitter-Sweet* (1858), which focuses on questions of sin and conversion in typical late Calvinist ways; Gideon Hollister of Litchfield – attorney, historian of Connecticut, author of a historical romance about Puritans and Indians; essayist Donald G. Mitchell; and apostate to Unitarianism Sylvester Judd. See also Charles W. Everest, ed., *The Poets of Connecticut* (Hartford: Case, Tiffany & Burnham, 1843).

77 See especially Ann Douglas, *The Feminization of American Culture* (New York: Knopf, 1977); Richard Isaac Rabinowitz, "Soul, Character, and Personality: The Transformation of Personal Religious Experience in New England, 1790–1860," Ph.D. thesis, 1977; Bruce Kuklick, *Churchmen and Philosophers* (New Haven: Yale Univ. Press, 1981); David W. Reynolds, *Faith in Fiction* (Cambridge, Mass.: Harvard Univ. Press, 1981); George Whicher, *This Was a Poet: A Critical Biography of Emily Dickinson* (1938; rpt. Ann Arbor: Univ. of Michigan Press, 1957), pp. 153–205; Albert J. Gelpi, *Emily Dickinson: The Mind of the Poet* (Cambridge, Mass.: Harvard Univ. Press, 1965), pp. 55–93; Richard B. Sewall, *The Life of Emily Dickinson* (New York: Farrar, Straus & Giroux, 1974), esp. 1:17–27 and 2:668–705; Karl Keller, *The Only Kangaroo among the Beauty: Emily Dickinson and America* (Baltimore: Johns Hopkins Univ. Press, 1979), Chaps. 2–4, 8; Barton Levi St. Armand, *Emily Dickinson and Her Culture* (Cambridge: Cambridge Univ. Press, 1984); Rowena Revis Jones, "The Preparation of a Poet: Puritan Directions in Emily Dickinson's Education," *Studies in the American Renaissance, 1982,* ed. Joel Myerson (Boston: Twayne, 1982), 285–324; Charles Foster, *The Rungless Ladder: Harriet Beecher Stowe and New England Puritanism* (Durham: Duke Univ. Press, 1954); Kathryn Kish Sklar, *Catherine Beecher* (New Haven: Yale Univ. Press, 1973); Marie Caskey, *Chariot of Fire: Religion and the Beecher Family* (New Haven: Yale Univ. Press, 1978); and Lawrence Buell, "Calvinism Romanticized: Harriet Beecher Stowe, Samuel Hopkins, and *The Minister's Wooing," ESQ,* 24 (1978), 119–32.

78 John T. Morse, Jr., *Life and Letters of Oliver Wendell Holmes* (Boston: Houghton Mifflin, 1897), esp. 2:246 and 223–55. Personal relations between Stowe and

Holmes were cordial, but she was somewhat distressed by his greater flipness toward old-fashioned orthodox culture; v. Forrest Wilson, *Crusader in Crinoline: The Life of Harriet Beecher Stowe* (Philadelphia: Lippincott, 1941), pp. 466, 530–1, 598, 612–15, 635–6.

79 See, e.g., Henry B. Parkes's "Emerson," reprinted from *The Pragmatic Test,* in Milton Konvitz and Stephen Whicher, eds., *Emerson: A Collection of Critical Essays* (Englewood Cliffs, N.J.: Prentice-Hall, 1962), pp. 121–35.

80 Feidelson, *Symbolism and American Literature,* pp. 151–7; Gura, *Wisdom of Words,* pp. 51–71; Donald A. Crosby, *Horace Bushnell's Theory of Language* (The Hague: Mouton, 1975).

81 For Dickinson's reading of Mitchell, see Sewall, *Life of Emily Dickinson,* 2:678–83, which notices the absence of any conspicuous religious element in Mitchell's essays.

82 For histories of the movement, see especially Perry D. Westbrook, *Acres of Flint,* rev. ed. (Metuchen, N.J.: Scarecrow Press, 1981), and Josephine Donovan, *New England Local Color Literature: A Woman's Tradition* (New York: Ungar, 1983).

83 For regional realism as a women's tradition, see especially Donovan, *New England Local Color Literature;* the third chapter ("Annie Adams Fields and Her Network of Influence") is especially interesting both for its substantiation of the idea of women regionalists as a community and for its identification of Boston as the hub of that community. See also Annie Fields, *Authors and Friends* (Boston: Houghton Mifflin, 1896) (on Stowe and Thaxter); Annie Fields, ed., *The Letters of Sarah Orne Jewett* (Boston: Houghton Mifflin, 1911); *Sarah Orne Jewett, Letters,* ed. Richard Cary (Waterville, Me.: Colby College Press, 1956); as well as Cheryl Walker's discussion of the Dickinson–Helen Hunt Jackson relationship in *The Nightingale's Burden* (Bloomington: Indiana Univ. Press, 1982).

84 See, e.g., Richard D. Birdsall, *Berkshire County: A Cultural History* (New Haven: Yale Univ. Press, 1959).

85 Cf. such literary organs of these three denominations as *Brownson's Quarterly Review,* the *Universalist Quarterly,* and the *Christian Review.*

86 E.g., consider Elizabeth Stoddard's expatriation to New York and the presence of outstanding male local colorist Rowland Robinson in Vermont.

CHAPTER 3: MARKETPLACE, ETHOS, PRACTICE

1 See especially Burton J. Bledstein, *The Culture of Professionalism* (New York: Norton, 1976); Daniel Calhoun, *Professional Lives in America: Structure and Aspiration, 1750–1850* (Cambridge, Mass.: Harvard Univ. Press, 1965); Donald M. Scott, *From Office to Profession: The New England Ministry, 1750–1850* (Philadelphia: Univ. of Pennsylvania Press, 1978); Bruce Kuklick, *Churchmen and Philosophers* (New Haven: Yale Univ. Press, 1985); Anton Hermann Chroust, *The Rise of the Legal Profession in America* (Norman: Univ. of Oklahoma Press, 1965), vol. 2; and Robert Ferguson, *Law and Letters in American Culture* (Cambridge, Mass.: Harvard Univ. Press, 1984).

2 For Longfellow, see William Charvat, *The Profession of Authorship in America, 1800–1870,* ed. Matthew J. Bruccoli (Columbus: Ohio State Univ. Press, 1968), pp. 106–67; for Stowe, see Mary Kelley, *Private Woman, Public Stage:* (New York:

Oxford Univ. Press, 1984), p. 169; for Emerson, see Ralph Leslie Rusk, *The Life of Ralph Waldo Emerson* (New York: Columbia Univ. Press, 1949), esp. pp. 391–2. For information on journalistic compensation, see Frank Luther Mott, *A History of American Magazines, 1741–1850* (New York: Appleton, 1930), pp. 504–12; ibid., *1850–1865* (Cambridge, Mass.: Harvard Univ. Press, 1938), pp. 19–25; Merle Hoover, *Park Benjamin* (New York: Columbia Univ. Press, 1948), p. 64; Charles T. Congdon, *Reminiscences of a Journalist* (Boston: Osgood, 1880), p. 127. For general background, see especially William Charvat, *Literary Publishing in America* (Philadelphia: Univ. of Pennsylvania Press, 1959), and Neil Harris, *The Artist in American Society: The Formative Years, 1790–1860* (New York: Braziller, 1966).

3 Raymond Williams, *The Sociology of Culture* (New York: Schocken Books, 1982), pp. 44–51.

4 William Charvat, *The Origins of American Critical Thought, 1810–1835* (Philadelphia: Univ. of Pennsylvania Press, 1936), p. 5.

5 Joseph Story, *The Power of Solitude* (1804); William Wetmore Story, *Life and Letters of Joseph Story* (Boston: Little, Brown, 1851), 1:107–9; David Robinson and Lawrence Buell, "The Poems of Joseph Stevens Buckminster," *Resources for American Literary Study,* 7 (1977), 41–52; "Eliza B. Lee," *DAB;* Lawrance Thompson, *Young Longfellow* (New York: Macmillan, 1938), pp. 59–60, 74–7.

6 Robert Ferguson, "The Emulation of Sir William Jones in the Early Republic," *New England Quarterly,* 52 (1979), 3–26.

7 Benjamin Spencer, *The Quest for Nationality: An American Literary Campaign* (Syracuse: Syracuse Univ. Press, 1957), p. 65 (for Adams); Samuel G. Goodrich, *Recollections of a Lifetime* (New York and Auburn: Miller, Orton, & Mulligan, 1856) 2:132 (for Percival).

8 As the Appendix shows, literary commercialism was not only more prevalent among women writers than among men during the antebellum period but also more respectable as an overt intention. In fact, female writers such as Hale and Sigourney would have felt pressured to resort to the profit motive as a justification for entering the literary arena (made respectable by their lack of appropriate male sources of support), whereas in a male writer such overt avowals of commercialism would have been seen as in questionable taste. Hale's preface to *Northwood* was done for the second edition (1852).

9 Ferguson, "Sir William Jones," p. 26.

10 Thoreau, *Early Essays and Miscellanies,* ed. Joseph J. Moldenhauer and Edwin Moser (Princeton: Princeton Univ. Press, 1975), p. 195.

11 Lydia Sigourney, *Letters of Life* (New York: Appleton, 1866), p. 324; Gordon Haight, *Mrs. Sigourney: The Sweet Singer of Hartford* (New Haven: Yale Univ. Press, 1930), pp. 33, 36.

12 Goodrich, *Recollections* 2:321: "It is true that I have written openly, avowedly, to attract and to please children; yet it has been my design at the same time to enlarge the circle of knowledge, to invigorate the understanding, to strengthen the moral nerve, to purify and exalt the imagination."

13 Quoted in Mark A. DeWolfe Howe's memoir of Fields in Edward Emerson, comp., *The Early Years of the Saturday Club, 1855–1870* (Boston: Houghton Mifflin, 1981), pp. 379–80.

14 Nina Baym, *Novels, Readers, and Reviewers: Responses to Fiction in Antebellum America* (Ithaca: Cornell Univ. Press, 1984), p. 174. Cf. Charvat, *Origins of American Critical Thought*, pp. 13–17.

15 Thoreau, *A Week on the Concord and Merrimack Rivers*, ed. Carl F. Hovde, William L. Howarth, and Elizabeth Hall Witherell (Princeton: Princeton Univ. Press, 1980), p. 151.

16 The politics of Transcendentalist rhetoric were in part suggested by the Unitarians' strategic redefinitions of Calvinist terms, on which point see Lawrence Buell, *Literary Transcendentalism* (Ithaca: Cornell Univ. Press, 1973), pp. 114–8. This Arminian penchant for metaphorizing theological categories reflected in part its engagement with the higher criticism, although Unitarian exegetes tended to cling to a rationalist rather than a poetic mode of analysis, as noted by Philip Gura in *The Wisdom of Words* (Middletown, Conn.: Wesleyan Univ. Press, 1981), pp. 15–31. It was finally the influence of Coleridge and Carlyle, both in themselves and as purveyors of German Romanticism, along with the mysticism of Swedenborg, that drove Emerson and fellow Transcendentalists interested in the issue toward a theory of the inevitable metaphoricity of discourse, first expounded in Emerson's *Nature*. The outrage provoked by this "obscurantism" has understandably tempted some to see the contrast between Transcendentalism and Unitarianism as "merely" rhetorical (Mary W. Edrich, "The Rhetoric of Apostasy," *Texas Studies in Literature and Language* 8 [1967], 547–60), although it would be truer to say that the quarrel over language, though significant in itself, became (like the modern quarrel between old-fashioned new-critical formalism and new-fashioned post structuralism) as heated as it did because of the underlying epistemological issue. The Transcendentalists precipitated a crisis over the authority of the biblical text that they showed was a necessary outcome of the intuitionalism that lay at the heart of Unitarian "empirical" scholarship, hitherto unrecognized by it. Likewise, contemporary deconstructionism has challenged new-critical epistemology by taking its text-centeredness to the logical conclusion that new-critical close readings are critical fictions based on naive assumptions about the determinacy of text and meaning.

17 Susan Geary, "The Domestic Novel as a Commercial Commodity: Making a Best Seller in the 1850s," *Publications of the Bibliographical Society of America,* 70 (1976), 365–93. Stowe's spectacular sales are compelling testimony to the importance of moral and religious considerations for the American antebellum reader, a point also made by Lewis O. Saum, *The Popular Mood of Pre–Civil War America* (Westport, Conn.: Greenwood Press, 1980), which conclusively demonstrates the moral seriousness of the plain people of America at this time.

18 For an extended analysis of the ambivalent responses of Emerson, Thoreau, Hawthorne, and Melville to the rise of literary commercialism, see Michael T. Gilmore, *American Romanticism and the Marketplace* (Chicago: Univ. of Chicago Press, 1985).

19 Congdon, *Reminiscences*, p. 12.

20 For a collection of key primary documents, see Robert E. Spiller, ed., *The American Literary Revolution, 1783–1837* (Garden City, N.Y.: Doubleday, 1967); for an analysis, see Spencer, *Quest for Nationality*.

21 *The Letters of William Cullen Bryant*, ed. William Cullen Bryant II and

Thomas G. Voss (New York: Fordham Univ. Press, 1975), 1:380; James Russell Lowell, "Nationality in Literature," *North American Review,* 69 (1849), 199.

22   Adams *apud* Gordon Bigelow, *Rhetoric and American Poetry of the Early National Period* (Gainesville: Univ. of Florida Press, 1960), p. 45 (a monograph that deals intensively with this theme); Selleck Osborn, *Poems, Moral, Sentimental and Satirical* (Boston: Orcutt, 1823), p. x; Barlow, preface to the *Columbiad,* in *Works,* ed. William K. Bottorff and Arthur L. Ford (Gainesville, Fla.: Scholars' Facsimiles and Reprints, 1970), 2:378, 381–2, 389.

23   Charvat, *Origins of American Critical Thought,* p. 15.

24   For analysis of Poe's assimilation of Coleridge, by contrast to other American critics and particularly the Transcendentalists, see Edward H. Davidson, *Poe: A Critical Study* (Cambridge, Mass.: Harvard Univ. Press, 1957), esp. pp. 43–75; and Alexander Kern, "Coleridge and American Romanticism: The Transcendentalists and Poe," in Donald Sultana, ed., *New Approaches to Coleridge* (New York: Barnes & Noble Books, 1981), pp. 113–36.

25   The fullest discussion of Emerson's theories of the creative process and of aesthetic reception is Vivian Hopkins, *Spires of Form* (Cambridge, Mass.: Harvard Univ. Press, 1951).

26   Buell, *Literary Transcendentalism,* p. 42.

27   *The Works in Verse and Prose, of the Late Robert Treat Paine* (Boston: Belcher, 1812); Henry J. Finn, ed., *American Comic Annual* (Boston: Richardson, Lord, & Holbrook, 1831); Henry Finn, *Finn's Comic Almanac* (Boston: Marsh, Capen & Lyon, 1835); *The Poetry of Royall Tyler,* ed. Marius Péladeau (Charlottesville: Univ. of Virginia Press, 1968), pp. 10–15. G. Thomas Tanselle notes that the attribution to Tyler is not certain, though likely, in *Royall Tyler* (Cambridge, Mass.: Harvard Univ. Press, 1967), p. 135.

28   Baym makes this point in *Novels, Readers, and Reviewers,* pp. 124–8. I trust that it was not simply obtuseness that caused reviewers to interpret Hawthorne's preface as an invitation to read the romance as a moral exemplum: e.g., *North American Review,* 76 (1853), 233 (A. P. Peabody); *Universalist Quarterly,* 8 (1851), 291 (A. D. M.).

29   Baym, *Novels, Readers, and Reviewers,* p. 173.

30   Willis' dandyism was the butt of satire by some Boston literary people whose standards were hardly Puritanical, e.g., William Joseph Snelling, *Truth,* 2nd ed. (Boston: Mussey, 1832), p. 34; Oliver Wendell Holmes, *A Mortal Antipathy* (Boston: Houghton Mifflin, 1891), p. 4. For more on New York as a haven for New England expatriates seeking a freer atmosphere, see Perry Miller, *The Raven and the Whale* (New York: Harcourt, Brace, 1956), esp. pp. 36–58. Miller's study, however, is full of dubious impressionistic generalizations about the cultural "differences" between New York and Boston: e.g., "For some reason it was more difficult in New York than in Boston to be so cheerfully urban, to be unimpressed by the Mississippi" (p. 33). Somewhat more circumspect is John Paul Pritchard, *Literary Wise Men of Gotham: Criticism in New York, 1815–1860* (Baton Rouge: Louisiana State Univ. Press, 1963), pp. 92, 155–8. The generalizations about the difference between New York and New England literary ethos that I feel secure about venturing are these: (1) In New England, the moral dimension of literary works was more stringently insisted upon and practiced. (2)

In New England, the literary avant-garde was associated with the radical (Conscience) Whigs, whereas in New York it was associated with the reform (Locofoco) "Young America" Democrats: cf. John Stafford, *The Literary Criticism of "Young America"* (New York: Russell & Russell, 1952). (3) In New York, literary activity was somewhat more openly recognized as a commercial pursuit.

31 George Bancroft, "Mrs. Hemans' Poems," *North American Review*, 24 (1827), 446. Bancroft was always impetuous, both in conformity and in dissent.

32 *The Instructed Vision: Scottish Common Sense Philosophy and the Origins of American Fiction* (Bloomington: Indiana Univ. Press, 1961). Martin ascribes the aesthetic of veracity to the influence of Scottish realism, with which I would in part concur, though such other sources as Puritan distrust for profane images and the pragmatism of a frontier culture might be proposed. In any case, Martin does a masterful job of summing up the early-American aesthetic of fiction, even if the causal explanation that he proposes leaves some factors out of account. Michael Bell, in *The Development of American Romance* (Chicago: Univ. of Chicago Press, 1980), does an equally masterful job of showing how the concern for the disjunction between the realms of imagination and reality became an important issue within American romance theory itself. Bell argues that this concern led to a mainstream "conservative" theory of romance, still tied to the associationist aesthetics of Scottish realism, in which the romancer was seen as "'mingling' imaginary ideas with 'real' materials" and thereby overcoming the "essential disrelation of romance" (p. 18). But the more independent-minded major writers (Brown, Irving, Poe, Hawthorne, and Melville, in Bell's view) recognized and exploited the sense of the fictionality of romance, although, having internalized the norms of conservative romancing, they did so with a somewhat guilty and self-conscious awareness of their deviationism. My thinking has been stimulated greatly by Bell, from whom I dissent only in believing that his list of aesthetically self-conscious romancers is too limited and that his method of analysis, despite his sensitivity to the hazard, leads him to hypostasize romance as a coherent generic category to a greater extent than did the writers of the period. On this last point, see Nina Baym, "Concepts of the Romance in Hawthorne's America," *Nineteenth-Century Fiction*, 38 (1984), 426–44, which points out that Hawthorne's clear-cut distinction between novel and romance was atypical.

33 On this point, see especially Raymond Williams, *Culture and Society, 1780–1850* (New York: Harper & Row, 1958), pp. 30–48.

34 Sacvan Bercovitch, *The Puritan Origins of the American Self* (New Haven: Yale Univ. Press, 1975), pp. 136–86. That a concern for a corporate dimension to Romantic individualism is inherent in the European as well as the American strain is pointed out in James D. Wilson, *The Romantic Heroic Ideal* (Baton Rouge: Louisiana State Univ. Press, 1982), pp. 51–78. See Wordsworth's "Prospectus" to *The Recluse, Poems,* ed. John O. Hayden (New Haven: Yale Univ. Press, 1981), 2:39–40, particularly lines 94–9. For Wordsworth as for Emerson, the subject of "the Mind and Man / Contemplating" was "lowly matter," compared to "the thing / Contemplated."

35 Strictly speaking, it is neologistic to speak of Anglo-American "Romantic irony." The term was coined in Germany, and it was never absorbed by Anglo-American Romantic criticism. Perhaps because critics who invoke the concept with reference to Anglo-American Romanticism must perforce detach it from its original context, they seem to want to broaden its meaning, using it to refer to the idea of inner dialectic or indeterminacy; see, for instance, Anne K. Mellor, *English Romantic Irony* (Cambridge, Mass.: Harvard Univ. Press, 1980), discussed in Jerome McGann, *The Romantic Ideology* (Chicago: Univ. of Chicago Press, 1983), and Stuart Sperry, "Toward a Definition of Romantic Irony in English Literature," in *Romantic and Modern: Revaluations of Literary Tradition,* ed. George Bornstein (Pittsburgh: Univ. of Pittsburgh Press, 1977), pp. 3–28. I have probably drifted somewhat in that direction too, although I have tried to use the term in what I take to be the original sense, which is formulated helpfully by D. C. Muecke, *The Compass of Irony* (London: Methuen, 1969), pp. 159–215.

36 The most suggestive recent study of phases of English Romanticism is McGann, *Romantic Ideology* (just cited in n. 35), especially pp. 95–160. Whereas I have described these attitudes as characterizing the first and second generations of major English Romantic poets, McGann locates this contrast within individual careers, an approach with which I have considerable sympathy. Each of the two phases that I have described as successive has been proposed as a normative definition of Romantic epistemology. This issue, indeed, has been a major point of debate in recent scholarship. M. H. Abrams, in *Natural Supernaturalism* (New York: Norton, 1971), taking *The Prelude* as the central Romantic document, sees the goal of Romanticism as the reconciliation of humanity and nature through the agency of the poetic imagination (designed as a substitute for prophecy in a secularized age). On the other hand, for Paul de Man and J. Hillis Miller, who wrote the most influential early critiques of the Abrams position, the "dialectical relationship between subject and object" is to be understood rather as a "defensive strategy that tries to hide from [the] negative self-knowledge" that the subject-object relationship is only a pseudo dialectic, located, in fact, "within a system of allegorical signs." In this view, the essence of Romanticism consists in its reluctant intimations not of immortality but of ironic difference between its own discourse and the object of desire (Paul de Man, "The Rhetoric of Temporality" [1969], in *Blindness and Insight,* 2nd ed. [Minneapolis: Univ. of Minnesota Press, 1983], p. 208; cf. J. Hillis Miller, "Tradition and Difference," *Diacritics,* 2 [1972], 6–13). It seems to me that in effect Abrams has described the initial hope, De Man and Miller the increasingly suspected reality of the dialectical process as the major Anglo-Americans saw it, but also that neither of the two positions can be regarded unequivocally as *the* Romantic norm, either in Britain or America, except by critical fiat.

37 Harold Bloom, "Bacchus and Merlin: The Dialectic of Romantic Poetry in America," in *Ringers in the Tower* (Chicago: Univ. of Chicago Press, 1971), p. 301. Bloom's later criticism stresses the distinctiveness of the "native strain" of "Orphism" that he sees Emerson as having started: "He committed [his successors] to an enterprise that British High Romanticism was either too commonsensical or too repressed to attempt, an enterprise that can be summed up in the single word 'divination'" (*Figures of Capable Imagination* [New York: Seabury Press, 1976], p. 75). Again, however, the idea seems to be that Emerson outBlaked the English Romantics.

38 R. A. Yoder's searching and elegant essay "The Equilibrist Perspective: Toward a Theory of American Romanticism," *Studies in Romanticism*, 12 (1973), 705–40, helped me formulate this paragraph, as did Harold Bloom's essays on poetic influence in America in *Ringers in the Tower; Figures of Capable Imagination; and Poetry and Repression* (New Haven: Yale Univ. Press, 1976).

39 Two thoughtful essays that interrelate Hawthorne and Emerson are R. A. Yoder, "Transcendental Conservatism and *The House of the Seven Gables*," *Georgia Review*, 28 (1974), 33–51, and James M. Cox, "Emerson and Hawthorne," *Virginia Quarterly Review*, 45 (1969), 88–107, which makes the key point that both writers "conducted their revolts" against traditional allegory and homily "not by evolving a new language, but by involving the language which they inherited in narrative and logical actions largely counter to the sentiments, forms, and rituals which had conditioned and were still attached to it" (p. 101) – and to which they themselves were lingeringly attached, I would add. The essays of Cox and Yoder are more sophisticated than Marjorie Elder's full-length study, *Nathaniel Hawthorne: Transcendental Symbolist* (Athens: Ohio Univ. Press, 1969). See also R. A. Yoder, "Hawthorne and His Artist," *Studies in Romanticism*, 7 (1968), 193–206.

40 I have in mind, for example, Barbara Packer, *Emerson's Fall* (New York: Continuum Press, 1982), which argues for the inherence of "late" Emerson in the Emerson of the Transcendentalist phase, an interpretation that may help shift the focus of Emerson studies away from concentrating (as in my own past work) on the side of him most opposed to Hawthorne, to the later, more compatibly ironic Emerson whom recent scholars have not taken so seriously. (In corroboration of Packer's argument I have chosen my first example from one of Emerson's most Transcendentalist essays.) The only major comprehensive study of antebellum literature so far to rely on a poststructuralist conception of language, however, tends to reinforce the old light versus dark dichotomy: John T. Irwin, *American Hieroglyphics* (New Haven: Yale Univ. Press, 1980), although it is iconoclastic in its aggressive presentation of Poe as the central American Romantic. But see also the theory-oriented Emerson studies listed in n. 47. Other recent work of a more traditional kind of scholarship that will contribute further toward the blurring of an Emerson-Hawthorne polarization includes the biocritical studies of Joel Porte, *Representative Man* (New York: Oxford Univ. Press, 1979), and Leonard Neufeldt, *The House of Emerson* (Lincoln: Univ. of Nebraska Press, 1982) (see especially Neufeldt's discussion of the Emersonian speaker); also R. A. Yoder, *Emerson and the Orphic Poet in America* (Berkeley: Univ. of California Press, 1978), pp. 134–69.

41 D. H. Lawrence, *Studies in Classic American Literature* (1923; rpt. New York: Viking Press, 1951), pp. 92–3; Jonathan Bishop, *Emerson on the Soul* (Cambridge, Mass.: Harvard Univ. Press, 1964), pp. 128–43. See also Barbara Packer, "Uriel's Cloud: Emerson's Rhetoric," *Georgia Review*, 31 (1977), 322–42.

42 Michael Colacurcio, *The Province of Piety: Moral History in Hawthorne's Early Tales* (Cambridge, Mass.: Harvard Univ. Press, 1984), pp. 283–313, which also makes clear that the tale is hardly a piece of naive realism.

43 In the appropriation of Wordsworth, Emerson's actual position, contrary to what the quotation insinuates, is of course an extension of Wordsworth rather than a correction, an aporia that suggests a further complication in the relation of ego to history for Emerson.

44 See Chap. 3 of Charles Feidelson, *Symbolism and American Literature* (Chicago: Univ. of Chicago Press, 1953); "From Hermeneutics to Symbolism" is the title of Chap. 4 of Bercovitch's *Puritan Origins*.

45 For studies of the historical kind, see especially Gura, *Wisdom of Words*, and Robert D. Richardson, Jr., *Myth and Literature in the American Renaissance* (Bloomington: Indiana Univ. Press, 1978). For the theoretical, see, e.g., Irwin's treatment of Poe, Hawthorne, and Melville in *American Hieroglyphics*.

46 The self-referentiality of *The Scarlet Letter* was pointed out well before the vogue of theory-oriented criticism, in such readings as Joel Porte, *The Romance in America* (Middletown, Conn.: Wesleyan Univ. Press, 1969), pp. 98–115, which interprets this and several of Hawthorne's other fictions as aesthetic allegories. For a helpful recent discussion of the problematics of signification in Hawthorne's masterpiece, see Millicent Bell, "The Obliquity of Signs: *The Scarlet Letter*," *Massachusetts Review*, 23 (1982), 9–26.

47 I refer especially to Joseph Riddel, "Decentering the Image: The 'Project' of 'American' Poetics?" *Textual Strategies: Perspectives in Post-structuralist Criticism,* ed. Josué V. Harari (Ithaca: Cornell Univ. Press, 1979), pp. 322–58, and Riddel's paper, presented at the annual meeting of the Modern Language Association, on "Emerson and the 'American Signature'" (Los Angeles, December, 1982), the first of which stresses "Emersonian logocentrism" (p. 328) as the target of subsequent deconstruction, the second of which sees in Emerson's "Quotation and Originality" (*EW* 8:175–204) something of a model for such a deconstructive effort and presses the notion of an affinity between Emerson and Nietzsche. See also Joseph Kronick, *American Poetics of History* (Baton Rouge: Louisiana State Univ. Press, 1984), esp. pp. 85–9; and Donald Pease, "Emerson, *Nature,* and the Sovereignty of Influence," *Boundary 2,* 8, iii (1980), 43–74.

48 Henry Nash Smith, *Democracy and the Novel* (New York: Oxford Univ. Press, 1978), pp. 56, 74. A now classic article that to some extent exhibits this problem yet also shows the way to transcend it is Bernard Bowron, Leo Marx, Arnold Rose, "Literature and Covert Culture," *American Quarterly,* 9 (1957), 377–86, an essay of special interest as foreshadowing the methodology of Marx's landmark study of "technology and the pastoral ideal in America," *The Machine in the Garden* (1964). The authors argue that high literature articulates self-consciously the disaffection with official norms reinforced naively by popular culture. This argument is self-limiting in its tendency to define the role of high literature simply as a mode of dissent, but commendable in its attempt to put high and popular writing on some sort of continuum.

49 The foregoing represents an attempt to steer between two opposing views, on a course closer to, but not completely identified with, the second of them. The first is the reading of American high literary culture as markedly solipsistic, as exemplified by Quentin Anderson's *The Imperial Self* (New York: Knopf, 1971). The second is the strongly consensual reading exemplified by Sacvan Bercovitch, "The Rites of Assent: Rhetoric, Ritual, and the Ideology of American Consensus," in *The American Self,* ed. Sam B. Girgus (Albuquerque: Univ. of New Mexico Press, 1981), pp. 5–42, and "The Ideological Context of the American Renaissance," in *Forms and Functions of History in American Literature,* ed. Winifred Fluck, Jürgen Peper, and Willi Paul Adams (Berlin: Erich Schmidt, 1981), pp. 1–20. The need for a middle course can easily be shown, in Emerson's case, through comparison with a fellow-Transcendentalist such as Orestes Brownson, who represents the extreme "collectivist" pole of Transcendentalist thinking yet was inspired by Emerson in a number of ways. Cf. Girgus' comparison of the two figures in Chap. 3 of *The Law of the Heart* (Austin: Univ. of Texas Press, 1979).

50 *Reveries of a Bachelor,* vol. 2 of *The Works of Donald G. Mitchell* (New York: Scribner, 1907), 2:83–4.

51 *"Tempest and Sunshine" and "The Lamplighter,"* ed. Donald A. Koch (New York: Odyssey Press, 1968), p. 458.

52 Ibid., pp. 517, 528.

53 Cf. Nina Baym, *Woman's Fiction* (Ithaca: Cornell Univ. Press, 1978), pp. 22–50, 165–70, for the conventions of the genre and for a discussion of *The Lamplighter*. Mary Kelley, in *Private Woman, Public Stage* (cited in n. 2), esp. p. 189, makes clear that the ideology of Cummins and other "literary domestics" was complicated and conflicted, involving resistance within conformity to socially mandated gender expectations.

CHAPTER 4: NEOCLASSICAL CONTINUITIES

1 Eliza Buckminster Lee, ed., *Memoirs of Rev. Joseph Buckminster, D.D., and of His Son, Rev. Joseph Stevens Buckminster,* 2nd ed. (Boston: Ticknor & Fields, 1851), p. 15.

2 Lewis Simpson, ed., *The Federalist Literary Mind* (Baton Rouge: Louisiana State Univ. Press, 1962), pp. 3–9. Emerson's remark is quoted approvingly by Vernon L. Parrington in *Main Currents of American Thought* (New York: Harcourt Brace, 1927), 2:317, following an indictment of turn-of-the-century New England literati as "blind sailors navigating the Dead Sea of Federalist Pessimism" (p. 278). Parrington's viewpoint has precedents in two important turn-of-the-century studies: Barrett Wendell, *A Literary History of America* (New York: Scribner, 1901), pp. 117–36, and Henry Adams, *History of the United States, 1801–1817* (New York: Scribner, 1889–91), vol. 1, Chap. 3. In our time the myth has proven more durable than most other aspects of Parrington's scholarship. Russel B. Nye noted in 1960 that early national literature was commonly thought of "as a sort of blank space between the Revolution and the mature work of Irving, Bryant, and Cooper" (*The Cultural Life of the New Nation* [New York: Harper & Row, 1960]), p. 251, and even today one finds such sweeping dismissals: e.g., Emily Stipes Watts, *The Poetry of American Women from 1632 to 1945* (Austin: Univ. of Texas Press, 1977), p. 29: "The literary output of [the last half of the eighteenth century] is a national embarrassment." To the extent that the persistence of this view can be traced to the authority of any one scholar, Robert E. Spiller stands out especially. Cf. his reference, in his discussion in *Literary History of the United Sates* (New York: Macmillan, 1948) to the "false literary dawn of the nineties and the 'dark ages' that followed" (1:129–30), as well as in *The Cycle of American Literature* (New York: Macmillan, 1955), pp. 27–9, and *The American Literary Revolution* (Garden City, N.Y.: Doubleday, 1967), p. 4.

3 I have in mind especially Kenneth Silverman, *A Cultural History of the American Revolution* (New York: Crowell, 1976); Joseph Ellis, *After the Revolution: Profiles of Early American Culture* (New York: Norton, 1979); Jay Fliegelman, *Prodigals and Pilgrims: The American Revolution against Patriarchal Authority, 1750–1800* (Cambridge: Cambridge Univ. Press, 1982); Emory Elliott, *Revolutionary Writers: Literature and Authority in the New Republic, 1725–1810* (New York: Oxford Univ. Press, 1982); and Robert Ferguson, *Law and Letters in American Culture* (Cambridge, Mass.: Harvard Univ. Press, 1984). No less important, however, has been the scholarship, extending over a longer period of time, of Lewis Simpson and William Hedges. See especially Simpson's "Satiric Mode: The Early National Wits," in Louis Rubin, ed., *The Comic Imagination in American Literature* (New Brunswick, N.J.: Rutgers Univ. Press, 1973), pp. 49–61; and "Literary Ecumenicalism of the American Enlightenment," in A. Owen Aldridge, ed., *The Ibero-American Enlightenment* (Urbana: Univ. of Illinois Press, 1971), pp. 317–32, as well as the sources cited in n. 2 above; William Hedges, "Toward a Theory of American Literature, 1765–1800," *Early American Literature,* 4 (1969), 5–14, and "The Myth of the Republic and the Theory of American Literature," *Prospects,* 4 (1979), 101–20, as well as the sources cited in nn. 7 and 34 below. None of the above studies deal exclusively with New England, but taken together they help provide a corrective to the myth of New England's intellectual lapse.

4 Of the people listed in the *DAB* index as "authors" born between 1740 and 1799, 53 percent were native New Englanders, whereas the mean percentage of New Englanders in the total American white population during the same six decades was only 36 percent. For the category "poets," the gap is even more striking: 64 percent of the listed American poets born during the six decades were New England natives. Only in one genre did New England underproduce: drama. These percentages are in keeping with those of the more inclusive *American Writers before 1900: A Biographical and Critical Dictionary,* ed. James A. Levernier and Douglas R. Wilmes (Westport, Conn.: Greenwood Press, 1983). Slightly over 50 percent of all writers listed in vol. 1 who flourished in the eighteenth century were New England–born.

5 Spiller, for example, argues that the "whole concept of romanticism as a revolt against neoclassicism is invalid for our literature" because American literature never had a bona fide Neoclassical literary establishment ("Critical Standards in the American Romantic Movement," *College English,* 8 [1947], 345). This is half shrewd, half wrongheaded: right in surmising that American Romanticism reacted against British rather than American Neoclassicism, wrong in denying the entrenchment of Neoclassical aesthetics in America. An eloquent demonstration of the contrary is Howard Mumford Jones, *O Strange New World: American Culture: The Formative Years* (New York: Viking, 1967), pp. 227–72.

6 For the fullest presentation of this view, see Benjamin T. Spencer, *The Quest for Nationality: An American Literary Campaign* (Syracuse: Syracuse Univ. Press, 1957).

7 Perry Miller's essay, "From Edwards to Emerson," *New England Quarterly,* 13 (1940), 589–617, is sensitively critiqued by William Hedges, in "From Franklin to Emerson," in *The Oldest Revolutionary: Essays on Benjamin Franklin,* ed.

J. A. O. Leo Lemay (Philadelphia: Univ. of Pennsylvania Press, 1976), pp. 139–56.

8 See especially Sacvan Bercovitch, *The Puritan Origins of the American Self* (New Haven: Yale Univ. Press, 1975), and *The American Jeremiad* (Madison: Univ. of Wisconsin Press, 1978).

9 Henry F. May, *The Enlightenment in America* (New York: Oxford Univ. Press, 1976), pp. 358–62. May is right, I think, in his view of the more scholarly and secularized modes of Enlightenment thinking as elitist phenomena that never fully penetrated popular thought, but his notion of the passing of the Enlightenment applies less self-evidently to belles lettres, a more or less elitist phenomenon to start with.

10 Two discussions by feminist scholars are Linda K. Kerber, *Women of the Republic: Intellect and Ideology in Revolutionary America* (Chapel Hill: Univ. of North Carolina Press, 1980), pp. 243–4, and Josephine Donovan, *New England Local Color Literature: A Women's Tradition* (New York: Ungar, 1983), pp. 26–7. See also Henri Petter, *The Early American Novel* (Columbus: Ohio State Univ. Press, 1971), pp. 46–55, which rightly presents *Female Quixoticism* as one of the best early American fictions.

11 Leon Howard's pioneering study, *The Connecticut Wits* (Chicago: Univ. of Chicago Press, 1943), pp. 212–30, set the tone for subsequent evaluation of these two poems. For a recent critique along similar lines, see Elliott, *Revolutionary Writers*, pp. 69–88. A more sympathetic analysis of Dwight's *Triumph* is Jack Stillinger, "Dwight's *Triumph of Infidelity:* Text and Interpretation," *Studies in Bibliography*, 15 (1961), 259–66, though the interpretation of the poem's conclusion is forced. The most detailed and accurate reading is Kenneth Silverman's *Timothy Dwight* (New York: Twayne, 1969), pp. 82–93, which, however, finds the poem wanting for lack of pastoral spirit: "He failed to make clear that behind his hatred of Chauncy . . . was a love not of correct doctrine but of the peace and quiet of Greenfield Hill" (p. 93). Yet the point of *Triumph,* in the context of Dwight's work as a whole, is that correctness of doctrine is a *prerequisite* to the peace and quiet of the more engaging *Greenfield Hill* and the descriptive passages of *Travels in New-England and New-York.* The strength of Dwight's "pre-Romantic" pastoral-agrarian vision of New England really arises from his self-appointed role of prescriptive *defensor fidei,* which comes out in *Triumph* most quintessentially when he is being most defensive. To my knowledge, among Dwight's previous critics only Lewis Leary has taken the position that "he is strongest in protest, as in *The Triumph of Infidelity*" (*Literary History of the United States*, 1:166).

12 For an appraisal of the historiography, see David Hackett Fischer's landmark revisionist study, *The Revolution of American Conservatism* (New York: Harper & Row, 1965), pp. xvi–xviii. For examples of minimization of the enduring importance of Federalist culture, see John C. Miller, *The Federalist Era, 1789–1801* (New York: Harper & Row, 1960), p. 276; and Nye, *Cultural Life of the New Nation*, pp. 110–11. I deliberately cite works of solid scholarship rather than melodramatic treatments like Parrington's.

13 See especially Lewis Simpson, "Federalism and the Crisis of Literary Order," *American Literature*, 32 (1960), 253–66; Jones, *O Strange New World*; Simpson, *The Federalist Literary Mind,* and Hedges "Toward a Theory of American Literature" and "The Myth of the Republic" (note 3 above).

14 "Caricature and Satire in Old and New England before the American Revolution," *Proceedings of the Massachusetts Historical Society,* 88 (1976), 19–34.

15 Jonathan Mitchell Sewall, *Miscellaneous Poems* (Portsmouth, N.H.: Treadwell, 1801), p. 66.

16 *The Satiric Poems of John Trumbull,* ed. Edwin Bowden (Austin: Univ. of Texas Press, 1962), p. 40; Joel Barlow, "The Prospects of Peace," in *Works,* ed. William K. Bottorff and Arthur L. Ford (Gainesville, Fla.: Scholars' Facsimiles and Reprints, 1970) 2:5.

17 Elliott, *Revolutionary Writers,* pp. 114–16, points out that Barlow's cosmopolitanization did not result in a superior poem.

18 Robert Arner, "The Connecticut Wits," in *American Literature, 1764–1789: The Revolutionary Years,* ed. Everett Emerson (Madison: Univ. of Wisconsin Press, 1977), p. 251.

19 Silverman, *Cultural History of the American Revolution,* p. 491. See William Hedges' comments on this subject in his review in *Early American Literature,* 13 (1978), 137, which also justly praises Silverman's overall achievement.

20 I have in mind here especially the difference between M. H. Abrams's accounts of the history of Romanticist thinking, in *The Mirror and the Lamp* (New York: Oxford Univ. Press, 1953) and *Natural Supernaturalism* (New York: Norton, 1971) and those of the Harvard literary historians Walter Jackson Bate, in *From Classic to Romantic* (Cambridge, Mass.: Harvard Univ. Press, 1946), and James Engell, in *The Creative Imagination* (Cambridge, Mass.: Harvard Univ. Press, 1981). Although all see Romanticism as having emerged from trends in eighteenth-century thought, Abrams (particularly in his second book) emphasizes the idea of paradigm *shift* more strongly than the other two.

21 Paul Allen, *Original Poems, Serious and Entertaining* (Salem, Mass.: Cushing, 1801), pp. 110, 133; Milton Ellis, *Joseph Dennie and His Circle* (Austin: Univ. of Texas, 1915), 146–7; Eliza Townsend, *Poems and Miscellanies* (Boston: Rand & Avery, 1856), pp. 1, 106–9.

22 *LoW* 4:25. On one occasion, the young Lowell fell back on Pope when trying self-consciously to demonstrate to a conservative peer his resistance to Emersonian influence: v. Joel Myerson, "Lowell on Emerson," *New England Quarterly,* 44 (1971), 650–1.

23 *HW* 5:121–2; E. L. Chandler, ed., "Hawthorne's Spectator," *New England Quarterly,* 4 (1931), 288–330.

24 Fisher Ames, "American Literature" (about 1800) reprinted in Spiller, *American Literary Revolution,* p. 86.

25 Linda Kerber, *Federalists in Dissent: Imagery and Ideology in Jeffersonian America* (Ithaca: Cornell Univ. Press, 1970), pp. 62–3.

26 Thoreau, "A Plea for Captain John Brown," *Reform Papers,* ed. Wendell Glick (Princeton: Princeton Univ. Press 1973), p. 129.

27 Fisher Ames, "The Republican, No. 1," in *Works,* ed. Seth Ames (Boston: Little, Brown, 1854), 2:251–2.

28 A provocative and explicit nineteenth-century formulation of this kind is the 1841 Yale valedictory oration of young Donald G. Mitchell ("Ik Marvell"), who declared that "the dignity of American learning must rest in a great measure on its restraint and modification of public sentiment. . . . Public opinion in America needs the constant, efficient, renovating action of learning, in view of her political institutions. . . . Classic learning must modify and should chastise American letters" (quoted in Waldo H. Dunn, *The Life of Donald G. Mitchell* [New York: Scribner, 1922], pp. 68–9). This formulation, from a minister's son who was soon (like Emerson) to turn Romantic essayist, is interesting because of its obvious linkage of classicism and anti-Jacksonian Whiggery, and of literary and social control.

29 For an overview of American Neoclassical satire, in addition to the works mentioned earlier, see the following articles by George L. Roth: "New England Satire on Religion, 1790–1820," *New England Quarterly*, 28 (1955), 246–54; "American Theory of Satire, 1790–1820," *American Literature*, 29 (1958), 339–407; and "Verse Satire on 'Faction,' 1790–1815," *William and Mary Quarterly*, 3rd ser., 17 (1960), 473–85.

30 *Poems by St. John Honeywood* (New York: Swords, 1801), pp. 57, 59.

31 Spencer, *Quest for Nationality*, p. 39.

32 Quoted (from a 1776 speech of Perez Morton) by editor James Spear Loring in *The Hundred Boston Orators*, 2nd ed. (Boston: Jewett, 1853), p. 129.

33 Cf. Randall Stewart, "Regional Characteristics in the Literature of New England," *College English*, 3 (1941), 130–5.

34 Stow Persons, "The Cyclical Theory of History in Eighteenth Century America," *American Quarterly*, 6 (1954), 147–63, explains the assumptions about history that led the post-Revolutionary generation to entertain rival theories of progress and decay. James W. Davidson, *The Logic of Millennial Thought: Eighteenth Century New England* (New Haven: Yale Univ. Press, 1977), gives a learned and persuasive account of the juxtaposition of utopian and holocaust motifs in the religious thought of the period. For some literary applications, see, e.g., Simpson, "Satiric Mode," and Hedges, "Toward a Theory of American Literature, 1765–1800" (cited in note 3), and Hedges, "The Old World Yet: Writers and Writing in Post-Revolutionary America," *Early American Literature*, 16 (1981), 3–18.

35 See especially Bercovitch, *American Jeremiad*, pp. 3–30, which makes explicit his points of dissent from Perry Miller, *The New England Mind: From Colony to Province* (Cambridge, Mass.: Harvard Univ. Press, 1953), pp. 27–39.

36 For the relation between millennialism and American nationalism, see especially Ernest Lee Tuveson, *Redeemer Nation: The Idea of America's Millennial Role* (Chicago: Univ. of Chicago Press, 1968). For literary continuities between early national and later periods (using Barlow as chief exemplar of the former), see Roy Harvey Pearce, *The Continuity of American Poetry* (Princeton: Princeton Univ. Press, 1961), pp. 59–136, and especially Cecelia Tichi, *New World, New Earth: Environmental Reform in American Literature from the Puritans through Whitman* (New Haven: Yale Univ. Press, 1979).

37 John R. May, *Toward a New Earth: Apocalypse in the American Novel* (Notre Dame: Notre Dame Univ. Press, 1972), remarks with pardonable exaggeration that "almost all [contemporary] American literature has an apocalyptic tone" (p. 202). The immediate stimuli may differ (e.g., today, the threat of nuclear holocaust), but the gesture is quite traditional in a literature whose classic works end with such pronouncements as "The angel and apostle of the coming revelation must be a woman" (Hawthorne, *Scarlet Letter*); "Not surer is the eternal law by which the millstone sinks in the ocean, than that stronger law, by which injustice and cruelty shall bring on nations the wrath of Almighty God!" (Stowe, *Uncle Tom's Cabin*); and "The kingdom of man over nature, which cometh not with observation . . . he shall enter without more wonder than the blind man feels who is gradually restored to perfect sight" (Emerson, *Nature*).

38 Trumbull, *Satiric Poems*, p. 108.

39 Wayne Booth, *A Rhetoric of Irony* (Chicago: Univ. of Chicago Press, 1974), pp. 3–7.

Part II: Three Representative Genres

CHAPTER 5: NEW ENGLAND POETICS

1 Roy Harvey Pearce, *The Continuity of American Poetry* (Princeton: Princeton Univ. Press, 1961), esp. p. 5; Hyatt Waggoner, *American Poets: From the Puritans to the Present* (New York: Dell, 1968), esp. p. xv; Harold Bloom, *Figures of Capable Imagination* (New York: Seabury Press, 1976), p. 73. In addition to his essay entitled "The Native Strain: American Orphism," see also Bloom's "The Central Man" and "Bacchus and Merlin," in *The Ringers in the Tower* (Chicago: Univ. of Chicago Press, 1971); "Emerson and Influence" and "In the Shadow of Emerson," in *A Map of Misreading* (New York: Oxford Univ. Press, 1975); "Emerson and Whitman: The American Sublime," in *Poetry and Repression* (New Haven: Yale Univ. Press, 1976); Chap. 1 of *Wallace Stevens: The Poems of Our Climate* (Ithaca: Cornell Univ. Press, 1977); and "Whitman's Image of Voice," in *Agon: Towards a Theory of Revisionism* (New York: Oxford Univ. Press, 1982). The prosodic and linguistic dimensions of American poetic distinctiveness are given special emphasis in Paul Fussell's *Lucifer in Harness* (Princeton: Princeton Univ. Press, 1973). Pearce, Waggoner, Bloom, and Fussell I take to be among the half-dozen scholars who have theorized most comprehensively about American poetic distinctiveness to date, the others being Albert Gelpi, who integrates the perspectives of Pearce and Waggoner in his semi-Jungian study of Taylor, Emerson, Poe, Whitman, and Dickinson, *The Tenth Muse* (Cambridge, Mass.: Harvard Univ. Press, 1975), and Bernard Duffey, whose *Poetry in America* (Durham: Duke Univ. Press, 1978) I shall later discuss.

2 An example of critical dissonance would be that although Pearce and Bloom are both interested in defining the American poetic impulse as a desire to transcend limits, Pearce tends to see these limits in cultural-historical terms (e.g., Puritan dogma and culture); Bloom in psychological terms (e.g., the relation of poet to precursor in America, as opposed to Britain). Bloom's American Orphism is to a considerable extent, however, a reinvention of Pearce's polarity of antinomian versus mythic as it applies to the sensibilities of Bloom's chosen poets (cf. Pearce, *Continuity*, pp. 420–2).

3 Waggoner, *American Poets*, p. 180.

4 Cf. Bloom, "The mind of Emerson is the mind of America," in *Agon*, p. 145.

5 Hyatt Waggoner is typical of the older criticism in stating that "from Emerson, Dickinson got not only a religious alternative to late Calvinism but a conception of the proper role of the poet," *American Poets*, p. 192, although there is a prefeminist tradition of dissent from this: e.g., James Mulqueen, "Is Emerson's Work Central to the Poetry of Emily Dickinson?" *Emily Dickinson Bulletin*, 24 (1973), 211–20. The feminist approach, by and large, has been not so much to dismiss Emerson's influence as to put it at one side for the sake of concentrating on Dickinson's links with other women writers in America and in England: Cf. Cheryl Walker, *The Nightingale's Burden: Women Poets and American Culture Before 1900* (Bloomington: Indiana Univ. Press, 1982), pp. 87–116. A more directly critical reappraisal is made in Margaret Homans, *Women Writers and Poetic Identity* (Princeton: Princeton Univ. Press, 1980), which categorizes the Romantic conception of the poet-prophet (of which Emerson is seen as the most extreme expositor) as a patriarchal myth that Dickinson could not accept (pp. 31–2). Homans' point, however, is not that Emerson had no impact on Dickinson but to object to the oversimplification of the disciple metaphor. Altogether, the effect of feminist criticism has been to convey, through its principles of selection, an underestimate of the importance of the Emerson-Dickinson connection, but, when the subject is broached seriously, to treat that connection with greater sophistication than earlier criticism did.

6 See especially Waggoner, *American Poets*, Pearce, *Continuity*, and Gelpi, *Tenth Muse*. Even Bloom, most of whose work gives the impression that American poetry sprang miraculously from Emerson's head, notes (*Agon*, p. 179) that the "voice of an American poetry goes back before Bryant, and can be heard in Bradstreet."

7 The poets treated in this chapter, for example, take up substantial portions of five (of twelve) chapters in Donald Barlow Stauffer's descriptive *Short History of American Poetry* (New York: Dutton, 1974).

8 Duffey, *Poetry in America*, p. 42. Duffey's one significant mistake, I think, is the exclusion of Lowell from the group. Among earlier overviews, the best is George Arms, *The Fields Were Green* (Stanford: Stanford Univ. Press, 1953).

9 Gelpi, *Tenth Muse*, pp. 63–5, contrasts Bryant and Wordsworth along these lines. See also Robert A. Ferguson's perceptive chapter on Bryant in *Law and Letters in American Culture* (Cambridge, Mass.: Harvard Univ. Press, 1984), pp. 173–95.

10 For documentation of how Bryant's process of composition reflects shifting views of death, see Tremaine McDowell, "Bryant's Practice in Composition and Revision," *PMLA*, 52 (1937), 474–502, and William Cullen Bryant II, "The Genesis of 'Thanatopsis,'" *New England Quarterly*, 21 (1948), 163–84.

11 The context is a comparison of Very and Ellery Channing, in Emerson, *Letters*, ed. Ralph L. Rusk (New York: Columbia Univ. Press, 1949), 2:331.

12 Jones Very, *Poems and Essays*, ed. James Freeman Clarke (Boston: Houghton Mifflin, 1886), p. 73.

13 Very, "The Promise," in William Bartlett, *Jones Very* (Durham, N.C.: Duke Univ. Press, 1942), p. 168. For discussion of Very's Transcendentalist egoism as a rhetorical and thematic device, see my *Literary Transcendentalism* (Ithaca: Cornell Univ. Press, 1973), pp. 312–24, and especially David Robinson, "The Exemplary Self and the Transcendent Self in the Poetry of Jones Very," *ESQ*, 24 (1978), 206-14.

14 *The Satiric Poems of John Trumbull,* ed. Edwin T. Bowden (Austin: Univ. of Texas Press, 1962), p. 85 (lines 283-90).

15 Hyatt Waggoner, *Emerson as Poet* (Princeton: Princeton Univ. Press, 1974); David Porter, *Emerson and Literary Change* (Cambridge, Mass.: Harvard Univ. Press, 1978); and R. A. Yoder, *Emerson and the Orphic Poet in America* (Berkeley: Univ. of California Press, 1978). To this roster should be added Bloom's essays and the reappraisals by Gelpi and Duffey.

16 Porter, *Emerson and Literary Change,* pp. 23-4, and Yoder, *Emerson and the Orphic Poet,* p. 168. Both are correct.

17 Gelpi, *Tenth Muse,* pp. 91, 85.

18 Porter, *Emerson and Literary Change,* p. 39. His entire second chapter is devoted to the limitations of "Threnody."

19 Although Emerson argues that "it is not metres, but a metre-making argument, that makes a poem" (*EW* 3:6) and defends the legitimacy of prose poetry (8:50), he also tends to celebrate rhyme as an ennoblement ("You shall not speak ideal truth in prose uncontradicted: you may in verse," 8:52) and as an inherent principle in Nature ("For Nature beats in perfect tune, / And rounds with rhyme her every rune," 9:54).

20 The most sound and thorough discussion of the Emerson–Dickinson relation to date, Karl Keller's *The Only Kangaroo among the Beauty* (Baltimore: Johns Hopkins Univ. Press, 1979), pp. 148-83, emphasizes both that Dickinson "was enlarged" by Emerson (p. 166) and that she was as much his parodist as his disciple. Keller likewise finds their penchant for "gnomic generalization" a major ground of similarity (p. 171). In his insightful "Sign and Process: The Concept of Language in Emerson and Dickinson," *ESQ,* 25 (1979), 137-55, Roland Hagenbüchle points out that Dickinson's implicit theory of language is contrary to Emerson's, he stressing nature as a model for language and discourse, she stressing the gap between nature and perception, signifier and signified. In practice, Emerson and Dickinson look more similar on account of their common tendency to turn external stimuli into conceptual abstractions.

21 Robert Weisbuch, *Emily Dickinson's Poetry* (Chicago: Univ. of Chicago Press, 1975), esp. p. 16. Weisbuch has been taken to task for characterizing Dickinson as a solipsistic modernist and thereby failing to recognize her rootedness in Connecticut Valley culture (August Fry, "Writing New Englandly," in *From Cooper to Philip Roth,* ed. J. Bakker and D. R. M. Wilkinson [Amsterdam: Rodolpi, 1980], pp. 21-31), but it seems to me that "solipsism," as Weisbuch treats it, is arguably an aspect of Dickinson's rootedness.

22 David Porter, *Dickinson: The Modern Idiom* (Cambridge, Mass.: Harvard Univ. Press, 1981), p. 31. Porter's sense of the affinity between Dickinson and modern nonobjective painting leads him to make claims about the "subjectlessness" of Dickinson's art to which feminist critic Suzanne Juhasz has understandably objected on the ground that they deny "experiential status to the events that Dickinson's poems so obviously are about" (Juhasz, ed., *Feminist Critics Read Emily Dickinson* [Bloomington: Indiana Univ. Press, 1983], introduction, p.8). Porter has, however, given a brilliant and thorough demonstration of Dickinson's textual practices, an account that in itself squares rather well with the feminist conception of the biography-to-text process, as Porter suggests in his final chapter. See also Roland Hagenbüchle, "Precision and Indeterminacy in the Poetry of Emily Dickinson," *ESQ,* 20 (1974), 33–56, an excellent article on which Porter draws.

23 The poem is "Success is counted sweetest" (*DP* 67). See *DL* 2:626–7. The first quatrain reads, "Success is counted sweetest / By those who ne'er succeed. / To comprehend a nectar / Requires sorest need."

24 Sandra Gilbert and Susan Gubar, *The Madwoman in the Attic* (New Haven: Yale Univ. Press, 1979), pp. 539–650, has been the single most influential discussion. The consensus emerging from it and its immediate successors is summed up in Suzanne Juhasz, *The Undiscovered Continent: Emily Dickinson and the Space of the Mind* (Bloomington: Indiana Univ. Press, 1983), pp. 4–14.

25 Terence Diggory, "Armored Women, Naked Men: Dickinson, Whitman, and Their Successors," in *Shakespeare's Sisters,* ed. Sandra Gilbert and Susan Gubar (Bloomington: Indiana Univ. Press, 1979), pp. 140–1.

26 Homans, *Women Writers,* p. 173. Weisbuch, the most sophisticated of the critics whom I have called "religiocentric," comes to a similar conclusion.

27 "Of course, it is not a question of 'rejecting' these notions [having to do with the myth of an absolute logos]; they are necessary and, at least at present, nothing is conceivable for us without them. . . . The age of the sign is essentially theological. Perhaps it will never *end.* Its historical *closure* is, however, outlined" (Jacques Derrida, *Of Grammatology,* trans. Gayatri Spivak [Baltimore: Johns Hopkins Univ. Press, 1976], pp. 13–14).

28 The strong ties between Dickinson and the dominant American Victorian culture of her day have been documented most extensively by Barton Levi St. Armand, *Emily Dickinson and Her Culture* (Cambridge: Cambridge Univ. Press, 1984), chiefly with regard to religion, nature, and the visual arts. I take a somewhat similar contextual approach to Dickinson's poetic method.

29 Susan Juhasz, "The Double Bind of the Woman Poet," in Juhasz, ed., *Naked and Fiery Forms: Modern American Poetry by Woman: A New Tradition* (New York: Harper & Row, 1976), pp. 1–6.

30 My thinking on this subject has been stimulated by Ann Douglas, *The Feminization of American Culture* (New York: Knopf, 1977). Whatever one thinks of Douglas' Perry Milleresque admiration for patriarchal Calvinism as opposed to nineteenth-century sentimentalism, she has done a splendid job of dramatizing the relationship between literary women and nonevangelical ministers, describing them both as marginalized groups that sought to compensate for a loss of political power by imposing social control through the ethos of feminization that the dominant culture had itself invoked as an ultimate value while using it to circumscribe woman's sphere. Much the same generalization can be made, I think, about writers of both sexes, and particularly about the more capable writers' manipulation of received forms and themes. Emory Elliott suggests that the conception of authorship as a feminine pursuit entered into American thinking as a consequence of a cult of "republican manliness, which flourished just after the Revolution" (*Revolutionary Writers: Literature and Authority in the New Republic, 1725–1810* [New York: Oxford Univ. Press, 1982] p. 46–7). The full history of the image of an interconnection between authorship and symbolic femininity, entrenched in American thought by the era of Emerson and Hawthorne, has yet to be traced. Obviously, male and female authors were not equally marginalized: Men did not need to contend against the argument that their gender disqualified them from writing. The similarities lay in the inhibition against speaking in a voice of one's own and in the split image of writer and woman as simultaneously central and subordinate.

31   The antisocial melancholy in Longfellow's subtext was perceived by (among other readers) Charles Baudelaire, who borrowed a significant image from the poem ("Our hearts, though stout and brave, / Still, like muffled drums, are beating / Funeral marches to the grave") in *Fleurs du mal*. See Alfred G. Engstrom, "Baudelaire and Longfellow's 'Hymn to the Night,'" *Modern Language Notes*, 74 (1959), 695–8, and Robert T. Cargo, "Baudelaire, Longfellow, and 'A Psalm of Life,'" *Revue de Littérature Comparée*, 54 (1980), 196–201. Longfellow had, as his editor Andrew Hilen remarks, a "Childe Harold complex". that he never fully outgrew (*LL* 1:151).

32   Yoder, *Emerson and the Orphic Poet*, p. 109, comments sensitively on this point.

33   Only partly, since "priest" and "Pentecost" still have, to say the least, an Anglican tinge to them.

34   Adrienne Rich, "Vesuvius at Home: The Power of Emily Dickinson," *Parnassus*, 5, i (1976), 49–74.

35   William L. Hedges, "Towards a Theory of American Literature, 1765–1800," *Early American Literature*, 4 (1969), 5–14. Early national writers and orators used classical modes of expression both to express their anxiety and, at the same time, to contain it.

36   *The Works, in Verse and Prose, of the Late Robert Treat Paine, Jun.* (Boston: Belcher, 1812), 178–9. Cf. Marshall Smelser, "The Federalist Period as an Age of Passion," *American Quarterly*, 10 (1958), 391–419, for discussion of the issue of expression versus control of emotion during the period.

37   Longfellow noted in 1832 that every "village had its little Byron, its self-tormenting scoffer at morality, its gloomy misanthropist in song" (*North American Review*, 34 [1832], 76). The New England sensibility had been amply prepared for Byron's cosmic gloom by pre-Romantic mortuary poetry from Robert Blair through Henry Kirke White (cf. Bryant's "The Ages"). Cheryl Walker, in *Nightingale's Burden*, p. 88, points to a common motif of the "secret sorrow" in period poetry by women. This might be considered the female counterpart. Its chief British source was probably Felicia Hemans ("Hast thou some grief that none may know, / Some lonely, secret, silent woe?" – "Lines Written in a Hermitage on the Seashore"). William Ellery Leonard, *Byron and Byronism in America* (1907; rpt. New York: Gordian, 1965), the one book-length survey – readable but dated – sets the high-water mark of American Byronism at 1815–30.

38   Ellen Hooper, *Poems* (n.p.: pvt., n.d.), unpaged. The sole copy cited in the *National Union Catalog* is in the Boston Public Library.

39   Cf. Buell, *Literary Transcendentalism*, pp. 115–24.

40   *The Complete Poems of Frederick Goddard Tuckerman*, ed. N. Scott Momaday (New York: Oxford Univ. Press, 1965), p. 22, sonnet 7 in Second Series.

41 Tuckerman's most ardent admirer, Yvor Winters, claims that Tuckerman's sensibility is not that of New or old England but "that of the gentler French symbolism" ("Foreword" to Tuckerman, *Complete Poems,* p. xi). Stauffer, *Short History of American Poetry,* correctly observing that Tuckerman's poems had "no influence whatever on the development of American poetry," concurs that his verse is "strangely modern" (p. 114). "He is still eluding categorization," agrees Samuel A. Golden in *Frederick Goddard Tuckerman* (New York: Twayne, 1966), p. 127. Much of the perplexity arises, I take it, from Tuckerman's isolation from his American contemporaries and the anomaly of a superior American craftsman whose preferred form (the sonnet) and themes are not manifestly indigenous, except in their sensitivity to environmental detail.

42 For a good overview of this issue, see Edward Wagenknecht, *John Greenleaf Whittier: A Portrait in Paradox* (New York: Oxford Univ. Press, 1967), pp. 81–90.

43 Frances Osgood, *Poems* (New York: Clark & Austin, 1846), pp. 67–8. See also "To Sybil," p. 29; "The Fetter 'Neath the Flowers," p. 68; and "She Says She Loves Me Dearly," p. 250. Literary historians have generally tended to reduce Osgood to a flat character in Poe's life drama, but feminist criticism is changing this situation. See Emily Stipes Watts, *The Poetry of American Women from 1632 to 1945* (Austin: Univ. of Texas Press, 1977), pp. 105–20, the first work to make a claim for Osgood's importance, and Walker, *Nightingale's Burden,* pp. 28–42, which takes a different view of Osgood's posture of invulnerability from mine.

44 See Porter, *Dickinson: The Modern Idiom,* pp. 19–24, and Sharon Cameron, *Lyric Time: Dickinson and the Limits of Genre* (Baltimore: Johns Hopkins Univ. Press, 1979), esp. pp. 136–200. Actually Cameron, and especially Porter, might question whether in view of the antireferential bent of Dickinson's language her poetry can be said to be about any specific "state of experience" at all.

45 My thinking about this poem has been stimulated by Robert Arner, "The Smooth and Emblematic Song," *Early American Literature,* 7 (1972), 76–91, and J. A. O. Leo Lemay, "The Contexts and Themes of 'The Hasty-Pudding,'" *Early American Literature,* 17 (1982), 3–23, both of which discuss the poem's regional ideology, although their lines of argument differ from mine.

46 For the text of the poem, see *The Works of Joel Barlow,* ed. William K. Bottorff and Arthur L. Ford (Gainesville, Fla.: Scholars' Facsimiles and Reprints, 1970), vol. 2; quotes from pp. 97, 89. Vernon Louis Parrington, ed., *The Connecticut Wits* (New York: Harcourt, Brace, 1926), pp. 329–30, prints Barlow's prefatory epistle.

47 Albert J. von Frank, in *The Sacred Game: Provincialism and Frontier Consciousness in American Literature, 1630–1860* (Cambridge: Cambridge Univ. Press, 1985), points, as the foregoing discussion does, to a link between jeremiad tradition and the sense of cultural attenuation in early national and conservative nineteenth-century writers, explaining this link in terms of the provincial mind's fear of cultural deterioration when situated far from the literal or metaphorical center of civilization. This explanation fits these cases well.

48 George Orwell, "Rudyard Kipling," in *Collected Essays, Journalism and Letters,* ed. Sonia Orwell and Ian Angus (New York: Harcourt, Brace & World, 1968), 3:195.

49   *The Poetical Works of Oliver Wendell Holmes* (Boston: Houghton Mifflin, 1908), 2:108; Whitman, "Passage to India," line 254.

50   Duffey, *Poetry in America*, p. 36.

51   Townsend, who contributed a number of pieces to the *Port Folio* in its later years, was the author of the first Greater Romantic Lyric in America ("A Fragment," 1817) and of a defense of the character of Lady Macbeth, as well as of "Incomprehensibility" (*Poems and Miscellanies* [Boston: Rand & Avery, 1856], pp. 106–9, 261–71, 80–2.

52   See Nina Baym, *Woman's Fiction* (Ithaca: Cornell Univ. Press, 1978). Walker has made a good beginning in *Nightingale's Burden*, Chaps. 2 and 3.

53   Lydia Sigourney, *Select Poems* (Philadelphia: Parry & McMillan, 1854), pp. 160, 230, 310, 57–60.

54   Bryant, *Poetical Works*, 1:46, 51–2.

55   Arms, *The Fields They Were Green*, p. 124.

56   *The Verse of Royall Tyler*, ed. Marius B. Péladeau (Charlottesville: Univ. of Virginia Press, 1968), p. 47.

57   I draw here on my discussion in *Literary Transcendentalism*, pp. 182–3, and adduce as a collateral witness Melvin G. Storm, Jr., "The Riddle of 'The Sphinx': Another Approach," *ESQ*, 62 (1971), 44–8, which argues that the poet has "failed by presuming to explain the world before even explaining himself" (p. 47), noting Emerson's aphorism that history is a sphinx that is "all to be explained from individual experience" (*EW* 2:3).

58   Even more egregiously, because "Each and All" is supposed to come to an affirmative close ("I yielded myself to the perfect whole") (*EW* 9:6) as a consequence of the speaker's turn from an analytical and dissecting mood to a sensuous and affective one; yet this shift on the narrative level is betrayed by the summary fashion in which it is rendered, using the language of the Understanding rather than the language of Reason. This is a poem that at least in its denouement, fully warrants Porter's strictures.

59   *The Poetry of Robert Frost* (New York: Holt, Rinehart & Winston, 1975), pp. 33–4.

60   Bryant, "On Originality and Imitation," in *Prose Writings*, 1:41.

61   John C. Kemp, *Robert Frost and New England: The Poet as Regionalist* (Princeton: Princeton Univ. Press, 1979). Frost's most extended tribute to Emerson is "On Emerson" (1959), reprinted in Milton R. Konvitz and Stephen E. Whicher, eds., *Emerson: A Collection of Criticism* (Englewood Cliffs, N.J.: Prentice-Hall, 1962), pp. 12–17. Frost's Emersonianism is discussed from a generally skeptical point of view by Alvan S. Ryan, "Frost and Emerson: Voice and Vision," *Massachusetts Review*, 1 (1959), 5–23, and from an affirmative point of view in Yoder, *Emerson and the Orphic Poet*, esp. pp. 168–9 and 194–7. The grounds of divergence are basically these: If one concentrates on Emerson's Transcendentalist prose, from *Nature* through "The Poet," the case for Frost as Emersonian is shaky; if one concentrates on the later, "skeptical" Emerson (both the essays and the poems), the two sensibilities seem more akin. Yoder is quite correct that "much of 'Hamatreya' and a poem like 'The Titmouse' are the essence of Frost" (p. 168). What Yoder calls the "Titmouse Dimension" of Emerson's most typical poetic achievement synchronizes closely with Frost as well as with Emily Dickinson.

62 Yoder, *Emerson and the Orphic Poet,* p. 192.

63 Flannery O'Connor, *Wise Blood* (New York: Farrar, Straus & Giroux, 1962), p. 224.

64 Francis's (sometimes irreverent) devotion to Emerson, Thoreau, Dickinson, and especially Frost is documented in his autobiography, *The Trouble with Francis* (Amherst: Univ. of Massachusetts Press, 1971), his *Collected Poems, 1936–1976* (Amherst: Univ. of Massachusetts Press, 1976), and his criticism. His observations in *The Satirical Rogue on Poetry* (Amherst: Univ. of Massachusetts Press, 1968), pp. 41, 57, 73, are especially good examples of this New Jersey–born, Amherst-dwelling New England adoptee's alignment with the aesthetic described in this chapter. I single out Francis only as the most conspicuous case of New England traditionism among contemporary poets of high excellence. (Anyone skeptical of the latter claim should consult the Francis number of *Field,* No. 25 [1981].) All this is not to say that Francis' philosophical values are the same as Emerson's, any more than Emerson's are the same as Frost's or – for that matter, Dickinson's or Longfellow's. As one would expect, the specific cast of the moral and spiritual vision becomes more "pessimistic" as one moves from Romantic, to modern, to contemporary. Cf. the final chapter of *The Trouble with Francis.*

CHAPTER 6: NEW ENGLAND ORATORY FROM EVERETT TO EMERSON

1 The title of a detailed study of period oratory by Edward G. Parker: *The Golden Age of American Oratory* (Boston: Whittmore, Niles, & Hall, 1854). In Parker's judgment, the Revolutionary era orators ushered in the golden age that had reached its apogee during the previous two decades. A compendium of examples (mostly of ceremonial oratory) that I have found particularly useful is James Spear Loring, *The Hundred Boston Orators,* 2nd ed. (Boston: Jewett, 1853), which includes biographical sketches. For the best modern general study of American oratory, with individual chapters on selected major figures, see William Norman Brigance, ed., *A History and Criticism of American Public Address* (New York: McGraw-Hill, 1943). See also Warren Choate Shaw, *History of American Oratory* (Indianapolis: Bobbs-Merrill, 1928). For searching discussions of several key orators and for valuable reflections on the cultural significance of oratory during the period, I am much indebted to Daniel Walker Howe, *The Political Culture of the American Whigs* (Chicago: Univ. of Chicago Press, 1979), although I do not see oratory, classicism, and Whiggery as quite so tightly interdependent as he does.

2 See especially Gordon E. Bigelow's monograph, *Rhetoric and American Poetry of the Early National Period* (Gainesville: Univ. of Florida Press, 1960) for the situation at the turn of the nineteenth century. A brief study of the Romantic critics tells the rest of the story. To Bryant, "Eloquence is the poetry of prose; poetry is the eloquence of verse." By "eloquence" he means "those appeals to our moral perceptions that produce emotion as soon as they are uttered" ("On the Nature of Poetry," in Bryant, *Prose Works,* ed. Parke Godwin [New York: Appleton, 1884], 1:13). For Emerson, the visionary conception of the poet as

free-lance articulator of the secrets of the universe was circumscribed by imposing as the test of legitimacy the poet's ability to move his auditor.

3   F. O. Matthiessen, *American Renaissance* (New York: Oxford Univ. Press,
1941), p. 18.

4   Samuel L. Knapp, *Lectures on American Literature* (1829; rpt. 1961 as *American
Cultural History, 1607–1829;* Gainesville, Fla.: Scholars' Facsimiles and Reprints),
p. 227.

5   There was some dissent. John Quincy Adams, holder of America's first
chair of rhetoric (Harvard, 1806–9), claimed that modern eloquence fell below
the ancients', that the "spirit of Washington must have nauseated at some of the
reeking honors, which have issued from his tomb" (*Lectures on Rhetoric and Oratory* [Cambridge, Mass.: Hilliard & Metcalf, 1810], 1:22, 236). Thomas Wentworth Higginson, however, expressed the majority view in claiming that "no
one can deny that the proportion of oratory furnished from this side the water
has been for at least three centuries greater than that from the other" (*American
Orators and Oratory* [Cleveland: Imperial Press, 1901], p. 7).

6   *DT* 4:313; John G. Palfrey, "Pulpit Eloquence," *North American Review*, 10,
(1820), 204; James D. Knowles, "American Literature," *Christian Review*, 1
(1836), 583.

7   Carl Bode, *The American Lyceum: Town Meeting of the Mind* (New York:
Oxford Univ. Press, 1956), pp. 41–98.

8   Bingham's text went through many editions after its first publication in
1797. The one to which I refer below is the Boston edition of 1817 published by
Bingham. Frederick Douglass tells the story of its impact on him in his *Narrative,*
ed. Benjamin Quarles (Cambridge, Mass.: Harvard Univ. Press, 1960), p. 66.

9   Knapp, *Lectures,* p. 218.

10   Adams, *Lectures,* 1:72.

11   Hugh Blair, *Lectures on Rhetoric and Belles Lettres* (1783; rpt. Carbondale:
Southern Illinois Univ. Press, 1965), 2:11, 34. Adams' professorial career is appraised in Donald M. Goodfellow, "The First Boylston Professor of Rhetoric
and Oratory," *New England Quarterly,* 19 (1946), 372–89.

12   Adams, *Lectures,* 1:28; 1:46; 1:179–81, 229–52.

13   Bingham, *Columbian Orator,* p. 32; extract from a 1794 oration on eloquence.

14   *Life and Letters of George Ticknor* (Boston: Houghton Mifflin, 1876), 1:330.

15   Quoted in George V. Bohman, "The Colonial Period," in Brigance, *History
of American Public Address,* 1:36.

16   *The Diary and Autobiography of John Adams,* ed. L. H. Butterfield (Cambridge, Mass.: Harvard Univ. Press, 1961), 3:336.

17   Daniel Webster, *Works* (Boston: Little, Brown, 1860), 1:133–6. Richard
Rush told Webster that reading it "made my hair rise. . . . Nothing of Livys ever
moved me so much" (*Papers of Daniel Webster: Correspondence,* ed. Charles M.
Wiltse [Hanover, N.H.: University Press of New England, 1976], 2:129.

18   Adams, *Diary and Autobiography* 3:396–7. "Technical competence tri-
umphed over general learning and philosophical discourse as case law accumu-
lated," observes Robert Ferguson of the antebellum period, in *Law and Letters in
American Culture* (Cambridge, Mass.: Harvard Univ. Press, 1984), p. 200. The

main theme of Ferguson's final section is the divergence of the two domains as legal institutions became more specialized.

19 Rufus Choate, "Eulogy on Daniel Webster," in Choate, *Works* (Boston: Little, Brown, 1862), 1:516–17. Webster's parting shot was reported to Choate by eyewitness Chauncey A. Goodrich, whose letter to Choate, along with Choate's manuscript, is in the Boston Public Library. Perhaps the best authority on the subject, Maurice G. Baxter, *Daniel Webster and the Supreme Court* (Amherst: Univ. of Massachusetts Press, 1966), p. 84, reports the anecdote as a characteristic example of the Websterian aura without explicitly endorsing its authenticity, noting also that Choate's exact language is unreliable.

20 Shaw, *History of American Oratory*, p. 54; Loring, *Hundred Boston Orators*, p. 238. Richard Buel, Jr., *Securing the Revolution: Ideology in American Politics, 1789–1815* (Ithaca: Cornell Univ. Press, 1972), p. 54–71, looks at the Jay Treaty episode as a more hardheaded political struggle but reinforces the impression that this was in fact a critical moment in early national history.

21 Young William Croswell, later a minister and minor poet, described the effect of his first playgoing experience (*Macbeth*) as follows: "The house was thin, and the actors, as I was informed, were not first rate. With me, however, the performance excited a deep interest, which was probably heightened by the novelty of the splendid decorations and dresses, and the beauty of the building" (Harry Croswell, *A Memoir of the Late William Croswell, D.D.* [New York: Appleton, 1854], p. 22). Nathaniel Deering, of Portland – attorney, playwright, and short-fiction writer, a Yankee gentleman of culture if ever there was one – became, late in life, so excited by a performance of *Uncle Tom's Cabin* that he reportedly sprang onto the stage to outbid the cruel master during a slave auction scene, crying "Six thousand!" (Leola Bowie Chaplin, *The Life and Works of Nathaniel Deering* [Orono: Univ. of Maine Press, 1934], p. 128).

22 Loring, *Hundred Boston Orators*, p. 352.

23 Edward Everett, *Orations and Speeches on Various Occasions* (Boston: Little, Brown, 1879), 4:622.

24 Blair, *Lectures on Rhetoric and Belles Lettres*, 1:206.

25 John Thornton Kirkland, "Life of Fisher Ames," in Ames, *Works*, ed. Seth Ames (Boston: Little, Brown, 1854), 1:19; Loring, *Hundred Boston Orators*, pp. 289–90.

26 Lawrence Buell, "The Unitarian Movement and the Art of Preaching in 19th Century America," *American Quarterly*, 24 (1972), 179–80.

27 William Ellery Channing, "The Demands of the Age on the Ministry," *Works* (Boston: Channing, 1843), 3:146–7.

28 For an early statement and exemplification of this view, see Eliphalet Porter, *The Simplicity That Is Christ* (Boston: Eliot, 1810).

29 See George Ripley's *Discourses on the Philosophy of Religion* (Boston: Munroe, 1836), as well as Margaret Fuller's allusions to the limitations of his powers as a speaker, in *The Letters of Margaret Fuller*, ed. Robert Hudspeth (Ithaca: Cornell Univ. Press, 1983), 2:135.

30 Theodore Parker, *Theism, Atheism and the Popular Theology*, ed. Charles Wendte (Boston: American Unitarian Association, n.d.), p. 109.

31 Sumner was not a Channing Unitarian but was an admirer of Channing and a legatee of the Conscience Whig tradition that Channing helped inspire.

32 Loring, *Hundred Boston Orators,* p. 626.

33 Charles Sumner, *Works* (Boston: Lee & Shepard, 1875), 4:144-5.

34 Ibid., p. 151.

35 Adams, *Lectures,* 1:397.

36 Edward T. Channing, *Lectures Read to the Seniors in Harvard College* (Boston: Ticknor & Fields, 1856), p. 70.

37 Ibid., pp. 220-32. Henry S. Canby, *Thoreau* (Boston: Houghton Mifflin, 1939), pp. 51-4, points out that Channing did not give any real encouragement to stylistic innovation. Canby is fighting such oversimplifications as Edward Everett Hale's claim that Channing "deserves the credit of the English of Emerson, Holmes, Sumner, Clarke, Bellows, Lowell, Higginson" (*James Russell Lowell and His Friends* [Boston: Houghton Mifflin, 1899], p. 19).

38 Ibid., pp. 126, 129-30.

39 Austin Phelps, *Theory of Preaching* (New York: Scribner, 1881).

40 Henry Ward Beecher, *Yale Lectures on Preaching* (New York: Ford, 1872), p. 229.

41 Webster, *Works,* 1:188; 5:329. Helpful earlier treatments of Webster as orator include Wilbur S. Howell and Hoyt H. Hudson, "Daniel Webster," in Brigance, *History and Criticism,* 2:665-733; Irving Bartlett, "Daniel Webster as Symbolic Hero," *New England Quarterly,* 45 (1972), 484-507; Daniel Walker Howe, *Political Culture of the American Whigs,* pp.211-25, which suggests that "Webster's chief contribution was to American literature" (p. 212); and especially Ferguson, *Law and Letters in American Culture,* pp. 207-40, a discussion valuable both for its analysis of Webster's rhetorical strategies and for placing these in the context of the development of the legal profession and the political vicissitudes of nineteenth-century America.

42 Everett, *Orations and Speeches,* 1:526-7.

43 Webster, *Works,* 1:64.

44 Edwin Percy Whipple, "Daniel Webster as a Master of English Style," in Whipple's Preface to *The Great Speeches and Orations of Daniel Webster* (Boston: Little, Brown, 1879), pp. xiii-xviii.

45 Webster, *Works* 3:342; Whipple, *Great Speeches,* p. xiii. Bartlett and Ferguson note the care with which Webster crafted and revised his speeches.

46 Theodore Parker, "Discourse on the Death of Daniel Webster," in *Autobiographical and Miscellaneous Pieces,* ed. Frances P. Cobbe (London: Trübner, 1865), p. 89.

47 Webster, *Works,* 5:333-4.

48 Ibid., p. 357; Wendell Phillips, *Speeches, Lectures, and Letters* (Boston: Lee & Shepard, 1870), p. 248; Thoreau, "Slavery in Massachusetts," in *Reform Papers,* ed. Wendell Glick (Princeton: Princeton Univ. Press, 1973), p. 103.

49 Eliza A. Dana, "Webster," in *The Poets and Poetry of Vermont,* ed. Abby M. Hemenway (Rutland, Vt.: Tuttle, 1858), p. 295.

50 The New England penchant for engaging in such mystification of Webster is especially remarkable in view of Webster's venial private life. "Daniel Webster drinks, and is notoriously immoral; he is enormously in debt . . . and altogether a disreputable character," Hawthorne writes his sister in 1836 (*HW* 15:230) – a piece of Jacksonian scandal-mongering, to be sure, but not without basis.

51 Donald M. Scott, "The Popular Lecture and the Creation of a Public in Mid-Nineteenth-century America," *Journal of American History*, 66 (1980), 793.

52 Josiah G. Holland, "The Popular Lecture," *Atlantic*, 15 (1865), 370.

53 Bode, *American Lyceum*, p. 206; Scott, "The Popular Lecture," p. 797.

54 One statement drawn up by the father of the American lyceum movement, Josiah Holbrook – *American Lyceum, or Society for the Improvement of Schools and Diffusion of Useful Knowledge* (Boston: Marvin, 1829) – listed as the first two advantages of the lyceum the "improvement of conversation" and "directing amusements" (p. 5). The lyceum was later reluctantly commended by New England's leading Baptist journal partly on the ground that it offset the lure of the theater "because it works something in the same line" ("Popular Lecturing," *Christian Review*, 15 [1850], 243).

55 *Historical Sketch of the Salem Lyceum* (1879); rpt. Kenneth W. Cameron, ed., *The Massachusetts Lyceum during the American Renaissance* [Hartford, Conn.: Transcendental Books, 1969], p. 20. This volume is a valuable collection of lyceum records.

56 See, e.g., Sarah J. Hale's gruesome monitory tale, *The Lecturess; Or, Woman's Sphere* (Boston: Whipple & Damrell, 1839), about a woman who comes to grief by refusing to defer to her husband's objections to women lecturers. The feminist lecturer Elizabeth Oakes Smith reports a run-in with the influential Hale on this issue (*Selections from the Autobiography of Elizabeth Oakes Smith,* ed. Mary Alice Wyman [New York: Columbia Univ. Press, 1924], pp. 97–8).

57 Lawrence Buell, *Literary Transcendentalism* (Ithaca: Cornell Univ. Press, 1973), pp. 75–92, discusses the art of the Transcendentalist conversation.

58 Merle Hoover, *Park Benjamin* (New York: Columbia Univ. Press, 1948), pp. 168–74.

59 For Thoreau's revisions, see J. Lyndon Shanley, *The Making of Walden* (Chicago: Univ. of Chicago Press, 1957), and Ronald Clapper, "The Development of *Walden*: A Genetic Text," Ph.D. thesis, UCLA, 1967.

60 Taylor Stoehr, *Nay-Saying in Concord* (Hamden, Conn.: Archon Books, 1979), pp. 25–66. This book is one of the most thoughtful studies ever written of the Concord Transcendentalists' conception of themselves in relation to their times. See also Alfred Rosa, *Salem, Transcendentalism, and Hawthorne* (Rutherford, N.J.: Fairleigh Dickinson Univ. Press, 1980), Chaps. 2–3, for further insights on the Transcendentalists as lyceum performers.

61 Bingham, *Columbian Orator*, pp. 20, 19.

62 For testimony as to Emerson's peculiarly compelling voice, see Charles T. Congdon, *Reminiscences of a Journalist* (Boston: Osgood, 1880), pp. 33–4; Oliver Wendell Holmes, *Ralph Waldo Emerson; John Lothrop Motley* (Boston: Houghton Mifflin, 1892), pp. 292–3; Samuel Longfellow, *Life of Henry Wadsworth Longfellow* (Boston: Ticknor, 1886), 2:32; Bode, *American Lyceum*, p. 223; and Herbert A. Wichelns, "Ralph Waldo Emerson," in Brigance, *History and Criticism*, 2:518. "Don't fail," Longfellow wrote a friend in 1840, "to hear Emerson's lectures. The difference between him and most other lecturers is this. From Emerson you go away and remember nothing save that you have been much delighted, you have had a pleasant dream in which angelic voices spoke. From most other lecturers you go away and remember nothing save that you have been lamentably *bored*" (*LL* 2:215). Longfellow was an inveterate attender of Emerson's lectures, even though he sometimes came away feeling "I had not the most remote idea . . . what he was driving at in particular" (3:325).

63 Not that Thoreau was a "failure" as a public speaker. See Walter Harding, "Thoreau on the Lecture Platform," *New England Quarterly*, 24 (1951), 365–74, which concludes that he was "both a success and a failure as a lecturer. He could amuse his audiences and they enjoyed him thoroughly. But he did not have sufficient platform appeal to get across his more abstruse thoughts unless he was roused enough to forget all self-consciousness and deliver a ringing address" (p. 374). For a sampling of Thoreau's other comments on the lyceum, both enthusiastic and skittish, see *TJ* 2:141–2; 4:324; 12:9–11.

64 And to a considerable extent the third as well: "metonymy," which Emerson defines in this context (*EW* 12:299–300) as the capacity to subject the same topic, in alternation, to earthy understatement and rhetorical hyperbole.

65 Ralph Waldo Emerson, "Duty," in *The Early Lectures of Ralph Waldo Emerson*, ed. Robert Spiller and Wallace Williams (Cambridge, Mass.: Harvard Univ. Press, 1972), 3:147.

66 *The Journals of Bronson Alcott,* ed. Odell Shepard (Boston: Little, Brown, 1938), p. 338.

67 Quotations from M. M. Bakhtin, *The Dialogic Imagination,* ed. Michael Holquist, trans. Caryl Emerson and Holquist (Austin: Univ. of Texas Press, 1981), pp. 61, 62–63. See the entire chapter "From the Prehistory of Novelistic Discourse," as well as Bakhtin's *Rabelais and His World,* trans. Helene Iswolsky (Cambridge, Mass.: MIT Press, 1968), pp. 1–144, in which the concept and history of medieval carnivalization is spelled out. For earlier discussion of the transitional state of antebellum literary language, see especially Richard Bridgman, *The Colloquial Style in America* (New York: Oxford Univ. Press, 1966), pp. 3–77. My appraisal of the same evidence differs a good deal, Bridgman's emphasis being on the elements of colloquialization in period literature as an anticipation of what was later developed more fully and mine being on the aesthetic and thematic possibilities inherent in the intermixture of colloquial and formal rhetoric.

68 Ellery Channing, *Thoreau the Poet-Naturalist,* ed. F. B. Sanborn (Boston: Goodspeed, 1902), p. 58.

69 Barbara Packer, *Emerson's Fall* (New York: Continuum Press, 1982), p. 27.

70 M. M. Bakhtin, *Problems of Dostoyevsky's Poetics,* ed. and trans. Caryl Emerson (Minneapolis: Univ. of Minnesota Press, 1984), pp. 5–46.

71 Harold Bloom remarks that "deconstructing Emerson is . . . impossible, since no discourse ever has been so overtly aware of its own status as rhetoricity" (*Wallace Stevens* [Ithaca: Cornell Univ. Press, 1977], p. 12). To this Joseph Riddel is justified in replying that Emerson's theory of language is "pneumatological" rather than "grammatological" (i.e., based on the assumption of a natural and spiritual ground to language rather than on the notion of language as a human fabrication and imposition) ("Decentering the Image," in *Textual Strategies,* ed. Josué V. Harari [Ithaca: Cornell Univ. Press, 1979], p. 335). In this respect Emerson belongs squarely in the Rousseauvian logocentric tradition defined by Jacques Derrida in *Of Grammatology,* trans. Gayatri Spivak (Baltimore: Johns Hopkins Univ. Press, 1976). Bloom is also correct, however, in suggesting that Emerson's sense of the rhetoricity of language-as-text anticipates the modern sense of the rhetoricity of discourse; it is a step in the direction of detaching all conceptions of language from the kind of natural and spiritual ground for which Emerson argued in *Nature.* (Derrida's approach to Saussure in *Of Grammatology,* where he exposed Saussure as a member of Rousseau's camp, made it inevitable that his work would understate transitional gradations of the kind Emerson represents.) In any case, it is probable that Emerson's experience of the gap between text and performance, public address and written essay, contributed, along with such influences as British Romantic literary theory and the higher criticism, to his sense of the arbitrariness of language as writing.

72   Harriet Beecher Stowe, *Uncle Tom's Cabin,* ed. Ann Douglas (New York: Penguin Books, 1981), p. 618.

73   Bigelow, *Rhetoric and American Poetry,* p. 60.

74   Howe, *Political Culture of the American Whigs,* p. 303; M. F. Heiser, "The Decline of Neoclassicism, 1810–1848," in *Transitions in American Literary History,* ed. Harry Hayden Clark (Durham: Duke Univ. Press, 1953), pp. 93–159; Kenneth G. Hance, H. O. Hendrickson, and Edwin W. Schoenberger, "The Later National Period, 1860–1930," in Brigance, *History and Criticism of American Public Address,* 1:137–8; Edwin A. Miles, "The Young American Nation and the Classical World," *Journal of the History of Ideas,* 36 (1974), 259–74.

75   The landmark event was the 1828 Yale University report on curriculum; see Meyer Reinhold, "The Silver Age of Classical Studies in America, 1790–1830," in *Ancient and Modern,* ed. John H. D'Arms and John W. Eadie (Ann Arbor: Univ. of Michigan, 1977), pp. 210–11, for a discussion of the impact. In Reinhold's view, nevertheless, "All the indicators reveal that pervading the first four decades of the national period there was an awareness of marked deterioration of classical studies in America" (p. 206).

76   See Anthony John Harding, "Thoreau and the Adequacy of Homer," *Studies in Romanticism,* 20 (1981), 317–32; Ethel Seybold, *Thoreau: The Quest and the Classics* (New Haven: Yale Univ. Press, 1951); Margaret Fuller, *Woman in the Nineteenth Century,* in *Essays on American Life and Letters,* ed. Joel Myerson (New Haven: College and Univ. Press, 1978), pp. 111–15; Edward W. Emerson, comp., *The Early Years of the Saturday Club, 1855–1870* (Boston: Houghton Mifflin, 1918), pp. 151–2.

77   Hance, Hendrickson, and Schoenberger, "Later National Period," esp. pp. 111–50 and 151; Edgar DeWitt Jones, *The Royalty of the Pulpit* (New York: Harper, 1951), pp. 3–56.

CHAPTER 7: LITERARY SCRIPTURISM

1   Richard B. Davis, *Intellectual Life in the Colonial South* (Knoxville: Univ. of Tennessee Press, 1978), 2:705 and 703–800, and Lewis O. Saum, *The Popular Mood of Pre–Civil War America* (Westport, Conn.: Greenwood Press, 1980), pp. 3–104, 234–5, suggest that overall sectional differences in religious writing and expression were smaller than have been supposed. The period's literature, however, seems to support the traditional view (reinforced by popular stereotypes) of New England's greater religiocentrism.

2 Northrop Frye, *Anatomy of Criticism* (Princeton: Princeton Univ. Press, 1957), pp. 315–7. Frye extends his analysis in *The Great Code: The Bible and Literature* (New York: Harcourt Brace Jovanovitch, 1982).

3 Laurence Veysey, "Intellectual History and the New Social History," in *New Directions in American Intellectual History,* ed. John Higham and Paul K. Conkin (Baltimore: Johns Hopkins Univ. Press, 1979), p. 17.

4 See, e.g., Darrett B. Rutman's appraisal of John Winthrop's motives for emigrating, in *Winthrop's Boston* (Chapel Hill: Univ. of North Carolina Press, 1965), p. 21.

5 Daniel Boorstin, *The Americans: The Colonial Experience* (New York: Random House [Vintage Books], 1958), p. 5.

6 James Davison Hunter, in *American Evangelicalism* (New Brunswick, N.J.: Rutgers Univ. Press, 1983), p. 49, estimates, on the basis of his survey of 1,553 randomly selected cases, that the percentage of evangelicals in America is 22 percent, with a weighting toward the older, the less affluent, the less well educated, and the rural.

7 This seems clear from the many studies of American civil religion, of which Sacvan Bercovitch, *The Puritan Origins of the American Self* (New Haven: Yale Univ. Press, 1975), and Robert Bellah, *The Broken Covenant: American Civil Religion in Time of Trial* (New York: Seabury Press, 1975), have perhaps been the most seminal. Such studies, however, must resist the temptation to subsume all American cultural phenomena under the rubric of "post-Puritan." Daniel Walker Howe, for instance, points out in his review of Bercovitch's *American Jeremiad* that the book "never conveys any sense of what the non-Puritan groups in America were, or how a false consciousness was imposed upon them through Puritan hegemony over them" (*American Quarterly,* 34 [1982], 92) – a timely reminder for the reader of my somewhat Bercovitchian analysis.

8 For general background on biblical criticism from the Reformation to the nineteenth century, I am especially indebted to Hans Frei, *The Eclipse of Biblical Narrative* (New Haven: Yale Univ. Press, 1974), and Jack B. Rogers and Donald K. McKim, *The Authority and Interpretation of the Bible* (New York: Harper & Row, 1979), pp. 73–405. Frei concentrates on England and Germany; Rogers emphasizes the rise of reformed scholasticism in Europe and later in America at Princeton. For the American, and specifically the New England background, see Nathan O. Hatch and Mark A. Noll, eds., *The Bible in America* (New York: Oxford Univ. Press, 1982), and Jerry Wayne Brown, *The Rise of Biblical Criticism in America, 1800–1870* (Middletown, Conn.: Wesleyan Univ. Press, 1969). A helpful recent genre study of the aesthetic and religious dimensions of American writing between the Revolution and the Civil War is David W. Reynolds, *Faith in Fiction* (Cambridge, Mass.: Harvard Univ. Press, 1981), whose bibliography, pp. 219–25, provides a good guide to further investigation. For discussions of the relation between religious liberalism and the rise of literary culture in New England, see Lawrence Buell, *Literary Transcendentalism* (Ithaca: Cornell Univ. Press, 1973), pp. 23–54; Philip Gura, *The Wisdom of Words: Language, Theology, and Literature in the New England Renaissance* (Middletown, Conn.: Wesleyan

Univ. Press, 1981); and David Robinson, *Apostle of Culture: Emerson as Preacher and Lecturer* (Philadelphia: Univ. of Pennsylvania Press, 1982), pp.7–29. I have been helped additionally by E. S. Shaffer's study *"Kubla Khan" and the Fall of Jerusalem: The Mythological School in Biblical Criticism and Secular Literature, 1770–1880* (Cambridge: Cambridge Univ. Press, 1975). See also the essays by Herbert Schneidau and Edwin Cady in *The Bible and American Arts and Letters,* ed. Giles Gunn (Philadelphia: Fortress Press, 1983).

9   Robert D. Richardson, Jr., *Myth and Literature in the American Renaissance* (Bloomington: Indiana Univ. Press, 1978), is an excellent study of the origins and American Romanticist manifestations of both the affirmative approach to myth as a model of creativity and the debunking approach to myth as falsehood. Richardson relates these developments to the rise of the higher criticism, pp. 9–64.

10   David Reynolds, "From Doctrine to Narrative: The Rise of Pulpit Story-telling in America," *American Quarterly,* 32 (1980), 479–98; Lawrence Buell, "The Unitarian Movement and the Art of Preaching," *American Quarterly,* 24 (1972), 166–90.

11   Horace Bushnell, *God in Christ* (Hartford: Hamersley, 1852), p. 73.

12   Frank Kermode, *The Genesis of Secrecy* (Cambridge, Mass.: Harvard Univ. Press, 1979), p. 123.

13   *The Major Poems of Timothy Dwight,* ed. William J. McTaggart and William K. Bottorff (Gainesville, Fla.: Scholars' Facsimiles & Reprints, 1969), p. 545.

14   Barbara Lewalski, *Milton's Brief Epic: The Genre, Meaning, and Art of Paradise Regained* (Providence: Brown Univ. Press, 1966), Chaps. 1–2, 5. The germ of Dwight's dissertation may well have been a passage from Milton's *Reason of Church Government* (quoted by Lewalski, p. 7) noting the use of diverse classical genres in Scripture. Vincent Freimarck, "Timothy Dwight's *Dissertation* on the Bible," *American Literature,* 24 (1952), 73–6, points out the indebtedness of Dwight's oration to British sources.

15   Robert Lowth, *Lectures on the Sacred Poetry of the Hebrews,* trans. G. Gregory (Boston: Buckingham, 1815), 1:76–87.

16   See, for instance, the selections by Dwight in *American Poems,* ed. Elihu Hubbard Smith (1793), reedited by William K. Bottorff (Gainesville, Fla.: Scholars' Facsimiles & Reprints, 1966), pp. 33n and 33–54.

17   For the Miltonic background, see George Sensabaugh, *Milton in Early America* (Princeton: Princeton Univ. Press, 1964), pp. 158, 166–83. One index of cultural lag in the production of literary adaptations of Scripture in New England is the fact that a century intervened between Milton's *Paradise Regained* (1671) and Samuel Wesley's *Life of Christ* (1694) and the first American Christ epic, Thomas Brockway's *Gospel Tragedy* (1795).

18   Dwight, *Major Poems,* pp. 17–18.

19   For examples of parallels, see Dwight, *Conquest,* 1:76, 3:758, 7:410, 8:433. For Dwight's intentions, see Theodore A. Zunder, "Noah Webster and *The Conquest of Canaan,*" *American Literature,* 1 (1929), 200–2. Dwight claimed that the epic was substantially finished before the war began, but he granted that the representation of Israel's suffering under Egypt's yoke might have been influenced by his sense of Britain's mistreatment of America.

20   Frei, *Eclipse of Biblical Narrative,* p. 130.

21   Timothy Dwight, "On the Manner in Which the Scriptures Are to Be Understood," *Panoplist,* 12 (1816), 193–203, 249–56, esp. p. 256. This two-part article summarizes Dwight's and the contemporary strict (New Light) Calvinist principles of scriptural interpretation. Dwight stresses the reliability, systematic coherence, and inspired character of Scripture at the literal level; ascribes its apparent obscurities, contradictions, and errors to the reader's clouded vision; and implies a doctrine of verbal inerrancy. "If we allow the Scriptures to be the Word of God our only duty is to inquire what they say, and to receive it with implicit confidence. What God has said must be true" (p. 256). This was the position of antebellum Calvinist theologians generally.

22   Dwight, *Conquest* 4:51, 75; cf. Josh. 7:10–15, 25.

23   Hannah More, *Complete Works* (New York: Derby, 1856), 1:75.

24   Ursula Brumm, *American Thought and Religious Typology,* trans. John Hoaglund (New Brunswick, N.J.: Rutgers Univ. Press, 1970), pp. 92–3, notes how the analogy between the conquest of Canaan and the nation building of America conforms to Puritan typological practice. On the general subject of Puritan typology as a mode of conceptualizing and stimulating the rise of American nationlism, see especially Sacvan Bercovitch, *Puritan Origins,* and "How the Puritans Won the American Revolution," *Massachusetts Review,* 17 (1976), 597–630. For a history of typological thinking in New England, see Mason I. Lowance, *The Language of Canaan* (Cambridge, Mass.: Harvard Univ. Press, 1980).

25   On the drift toward "improving" the Bible, see Reynolds, *Faith in Fiction,* pp. 128–32. On the mutation of typology from exegetical principle to literary device, see Karl Keller, "Alephs, Zahirs, and the Triumph of Ambiguity: Typology in Nineteenth-Century American Literature," in Earl Miner, ed., *Literary Uses of Typology from the Late Middle Ages to the Present* (Princeton: Princeton Univ. Press, 1977), pp. 274–314. On Dwight's own practice, see also his expanded edition of his translation of the Psalms, *The Psalms of David* (1801), which went through many editions. Dwight not only translates very freely but also makes some notable changes, for patriotic reasons, in those texts that he takes from Isaac Watts. Compare, e.g., these two versions of Ps. 147:12.

Let Zion praise the mighty God	Bless, O thou western world, thy God,
And make his honours known abroad:	And make his honours known abroad;
For sweet the joy – our songs to raise;	He bids the sea before thee flow:
And glorious is the work of praise.	Not bars of brass could guard thee so.
(Watts)	(Dwight)

The adaptation is partly licensed by verses 18–20, but the fact remains that Dwight's text exhibits two marked deviations simultaneously: from Scripture, and from the translation nominally followed here. The conventions of psalmic translation were flexible, however: Dwight pleads Watts's "free example" as justification for his own practice ("Advertisement").

26 Barrett Wendell, *A Literary History of America* (New York: Scribner, 1901), pp. 224–5.

27 On this point, see especially Ann Douglas, *The Feminization of American Culture* (New York: Knopf, 1977).

28 Nathaniel Parker Willis, *Poems* (New York: Clark, Austin & Smith, 1856), p. 18.

29 Lydia Sigourney, *Select Poems* (Philadelphia: Parry & McMillan, 1841), p. 117.

30 Henry Knight, *Poems* (Boston: Wells & Lilly, 1821), 1:116–17.

31 Despite this poem's bitterness, it is clear that Dickinson was sometimes sincerely moved by sentimental retellings of biblical narrative. "The loveliest sermon I ever heard," she writes in 1873, "was the disappointment of Jesus in Judas. It was told like a mortal story of intimate young men" (*DL* 2:502–3). For an excellent study relating Dickinson to the mainstream of mid-nineteenth-century sentimental piety, see Barton Levi St. Armand, *Emily Dickinson and Her Culture* (Cambridge: Cambridge Univ. Press, 1984), esp. Chaps. 2, 4, and 5.

32 With the partial exception of Jones Very's dramatic sonnets: e.g., "The Kingdom of God Is Within You," "My Church," "Come unto Me," in William Irving Bartlett, *Jones Very: Emerson's Brave Saint* (Durham: Duke Univ. Press, 1942), pp. 154, 160.

33 William Cullen Bryant, who defended the use of scriptural narrative for dramatic poetry, acknowledged that the "dread of taking improper liberties with his subject, and the fear of offending the scruples of others, act as shackles upon the invention of the writer" (*Prose Writings,* ed. Parke Godwin [New York: Appleton, 1884], 2:362–3). This is certainly one reason why Byron's example inspired no first-rate New England work in the same genre, as can be seen by perusal of the best of the imitations, James A. Hillhouse's *Hadad* (1825), which occasioned Bryant's too charitable review.

34 The textual background of this poem mirrors the interpretative problem. The poem exists in two manuscript versions. The one conjecturally dated later (c. 1862), the Johnson text printed here, is addressed to "Sue," Dickinson's sister-in-law and next-door neighbor. This supports the first interpretation proposed. The version conjecturally dated c. 1861 is one of a packet of manuscript poems. Among other variants, it has "hiding" for "lady's" in line 6, universalizing the reference. This, plus its position in the context of the packet, assembled by Dickinson presumably with some conception of interrelationship in mind, suggests the second reading. Cf. R. W. Franklin, ed., *The Manuscript Books of Emily Dickinson* (Cambridge, Mass.: Harvard Univ. Press, 1981), 1:214.

35 John Pierpont, *The Airs of Palestine and Other Poems* (Boston: Munroe, 1840) is the text used here; the quotations are from pp. 4–5. For Pierpont's reputation, see Rufus Griswold, ed., *Poets and Poetry of America* (Philadelphia: Carey & Hart, 1847), p. 79. The witticism is from W. J. Snelling, *Truth,* 2nd ed. (Boston: Mussey, 1832), p. 23.

36 On the Unitarians' unintentional anticipations of Transcendentalist intuitionalism, see Buell, *Literary Transcendentalism,* pp. 34–5, 39, 128–35.

37 For Ware's significance, see Reynolds, *Faith in Fiction,* pp. 139–44; Willard Thorp, "The Religious Novel as Best Seller in America," in *Religious Perspectives* *in American Culture,* ed. James Ward Smith and A. Leland Jamison (Princeton: Princeton Univ. Press, 1961), 2:196–200; Curtis Dahl, "New England Unitarianism in Fictional Antiquity: The Romances of William Ware," *New England Quarterly,* 48 (1975), 104–15.

38 Thorp, "Religious Novel," p. 200.

39 In what follows I rely both on my own researches into Unitarian literature, theology, and historiography and on those of Dahl, "New England Unitarianism in Fictional Antiquity," and Reynolds, *Faith in Fiction.*

40 Brown, *Rise of Biblical Criticism,* pp. 18–26, 75–93, 129–49, provides a convenient overview of these trends.

41 Theodore Parker, *A Discourse of Matters Pertaining to Religion,* 4th ed. (Boston: Little, Brown, 1856), p. 308.

42 See especially Richardson, *Myth and Literature,* pp. 12–21, and Henry F. May, *The Enlightenment in America* (New York: Oxford Univ. Press, 1976), pp. 116–32, as well as Millicent Bell, "Pierre Bayle and *Moby-Dick*," *PMLA,* 66 (1951), 626–48.

43 For example: their post-Calvinist orientation, their anatomization of a society sub specie aeternatis, the gothic villain stereotype, the motif of the journey, the voyage into the vortex, the theme of racial and cultural contrast and conflict. For the "Puritan" roots of the two works, the courts of first resort are Charles Foster, *The Rungless Ladder: Harriet Beecher Stowe and New England Puritanism* (Durham: Duke Univ. Press, 1954), pp. 29–63, and T. Walter Herbert, *Moby-Dick and Calvinism* (New Brunswick, N.J.: Rutgers Univ. Press, 1977). My thoughts about the affinities between Stowe and Melville and on the Jonah story in *Moby-Dick* have been greatly stimulated by Oberlin's students of American Romanticism, particularly by Andrew Lewis and G. Emory Valliant.

44 On this point, see especially Edgar Dryden, *Melville's Thematics of Form* (Baltimore: Johns Hopkins Univ. Press, 1968), pp. 83–5; A. Robert Lee, "*Moby-Dick:* The Tale and the Telling," in *New Perspectives on Melville,* ed. Faith Pullin (Kent, Ohio: Kent State Univ. Press, 1978), pp.95–102; John T. Irwin, *American Hieroglyphics* (New Haven: Yale Univ Press, 1980), pp. 285–309.

45 For earlier analyses of the pertinence of the Jonah analogy in *Moby-Dick,* see especially Nathalia Wright, *Melville's Use of the Bible* (Durham: Duke Univ. Press, 1949), pp. 78–91; Daniel G. Hoffman, "Moby-Dick: Jonah's Whale or Job's?", *Sewanee Review,* 69 (1961), 205–24, incorporated in revised form into *Form and Fable in American Fiction,* rev. ed. (1965; rpt. New York: Norton, 1973), pp. 236, 256–62, 271–2; Nathalia Wright, "Moby-Dick: Jonah's or Job's Whale?" *American Literature,* 37 (1965), 190–5. Viola Sachs, *The Game of Creation: The Primeval Unlettered Language of Moby-Dick* (Paris: Editions de la Maison des Sciences de l'Homme, 1982), is an occasionally brilliant interpretation of *Moby-Dick* as "counter-scripture" that therefore, on the highest level of abstraction, resonates with my own; but her commitment to reading the text cryptographically leads to willful obscurantism and reductionism. The text is opened up, only to be closed off into the hideous and intolerable allegory that Ishmael/Melville said he feared. For Melville's use of commentaries on the book of Jonah, Pierre Bayle's *Dictionary* and John Kitto's *Cyclopedia of Biblical Literature,* see Bell,

"Pierre Bayle and *Moby-Dick*," and Luther S. Mansfield and Howard P. Vincent, eds., *Moby-Dick* (New York: Hendricks House, 1952), pp. 617, 779–82.

46 See, for example, Calvin Stowe, "The Prophet Jonah," *Bibliotheca Sacra*, 10 (1853), 739–64, which gamely attempts to defend not only the theological and moral but also the historical reliability of the Jonah narrative. Melville's chapter reads like a parody in advance of Stowe's defense, published in the New England Calvinists' most scholarly periodical.

47 Hoffman, *Form and Fable*, p. 236. Hoffman later qualifies this to the extent of noting that "Father Mapple's Christianity is meaningless in a world of sharks" (p. 269).

48 Melville, *Moby-Dick*, ed. Harrison Hayford and Hershel Parker (New York: Norton, 1967), pp. 53, 50.

49 See Parker's review, "Strauss's Life of Jesus," in *Critical Writings*, vol. 1, ed. Frances Power Cobbe (London: Trübner, 1864); also his *Discourse*, Book IV. Richardson, *Myth and Literature*, pp. 34–48, summarizes Parker's public position and gives evidence that his private views might have been more radical than he indicated. My own conjecture is that the core of pietistic feeling underlying Parker's erudition and forensic rationalism would have kept him from full agreement with Strauss. Brown is right, however, in calling Parker the "most radical critic in America" (p. 170) and in noting that "Parker's popular writing made the Bible seem unnecessary" (p. 169).

50 For an authoritative account of the controversy, see William R. Hutchison, *The Transcendentalist Ministers* (New Haven: Yale Univ. Press, 1959), pp. 52–97. The exegesis discussed here is given in Andrews Norton, *A Translation of the Gospels* (Boston: Little, Brown, 1856), 2:31–54. Brown discusses Norton's biblical criticism, *Rise of Biblical Criticism*, pp. 75–93.

51 Norton, *Translation*, 2:33–4, 44.

52 Previous critics have made nothing of this analogy, which reinforces both the idea of Ahab as false prophet and the discreditable aspect of the biblical Jonah. The silence is owing to Melville's lack of explicitness. Yet to deny a possible parallel here is to disregard what commentators, then and now, have often seen as the central importance of the Jonah story: namely, the correction of the ethnocentric view that God is concerned only with Israel's welfare. Cf. Wilhelm M. L. De Wette, *A Critical and Historical Introduction to the Canonical Scriptures of the Old Testament*, rev. ed., trans. and ed. Theodore Parker (Boston: Little, Brown, 1850), 2:453–4.

53 Brumm, *American Thought and Religious Typology*, pp. 162–97, discusses Melville's use of typological motif, noting correctly that Melville does not use the word *type* in its original religious sense but unmistakably reflects typological thinking in certain instances – e.g., the linkage between Adam and Christ in the characterization of Billy Budd. The idea of Jonah as another type of Christ, which originates in the Gospels themselves (Matt. 12:39; Luke 11:29), is not made explicit in *Moby-Dick*. Possibly the Ahab-Christ parallels are meant to suggest it ironically; perhaps the omission of the reference is meant to suggest that there is no typical Jonah. Or perhaps Melville simply neglected to capitalize. See also Keller "Alephs, Zahirs," for a survey of the fuzzy use of typology in nineteenth-century American writing.

54 Cf. Buell, *Literary Transcendentalism,* esp. pp. 135–6, as well as Charles Foster, "Emerson as American Scripture," *New England Quarterly,* 16 (1943), 91–105.

55 *EW,* 2:10, 3. Despite this universalism, however, Emerson continued to think at least intermittently in Christocentric terms, as in his observation that "in order to present the bare idea of virtue it is necessary that we should go quite out of our circumstance and custom, else it will be instantly confounded with the poor decency & inanition, the poor ghost that wears its name in good society. Therefore it is that we fly to the pagans & use the name & relations of Socrates, of Confucius, Menu, Zoroaster; not that these are better or as good as Jesus & Paul (for they have not uttered so deep moralities), but because they are good algebraic terms not liable to confusion of thought like those we habitually use" (*JMN* 7:104).

56 For the sources of Emerson's idea of the mystical correspondence of nature and spirit, see Sherman Paul, *Emerson's Angle of Vision* (Cambridge, Mass.: Harvard Univ. Press, 1952), pp. 27–70. See also Michel Beaujour, "Genus Universum," *Glyph,* 7 (1980), 15–31, for a penetrating meditation on the ideological implications of a version of Emersonian literary scripturism in the new age of print during the Renaissance: "The poet had to reclaim a specific, exceptional science: this visionary understanding of the ancient gods' meanings was qualitatively incommensurable with the inferior knowledge which any reader could now acquire through easily available books. This was the poet's first attempt to rise above the unhappy choices that now faced him in the age of print culture" (p. 25). The American Romantics seeking to find their place in an emerging mass society can be described in similar terms.

57 The first and pithiest is Emerson's statement to his fiancée that "I am a poet in the sense of a perceiver & dear lover of the harmonies that are in the soul & matter, & specially of the correspondences between these & those" (*Letters,* ed. Ralph L. Rusk [New York: Columbia University Press, 1939], 1:435).

58 *Wa* 327. On *Walden* as scripture, see especially Stanley Cavell, *The Senses of Walden,* rev. ed. (San Francisco: North Point Press, 1981),pp. 14–20. Larry R. Long, "The Bible and the Composition of *Walden,*" *Studies in the American Renaissance, 1979,* ed. Joel Myerson (Boston: Twayne, 1979), pp. 309–53, notes that Thoreau "more than tripled the amount of biblical material while only doubling the size of the text" (p. 312), sacramentalizing natural processes by the addition of such key phrases as "Walden was dead and is alive again" (*Wa* 311; Luke 15:24) and "O Death, where was thy sting? O Grave, where was thy victory, then?" (*Wa* 317; 1 Cor. 15:55).

59 Roger Asselineau, *The Evolution of Walt Whitman,* trans. Asselineau and Burton L. Cooper (Cambridge, Mass.: Harvard Univ. Press, 1962), 2:92–5; "Song of Myself," line 98. "Starting from Paumanok" affirms that "solely to drop in the earth the germs of a greater religion, / The following chants each for its kind I sing" (lines 129–30). In a later essay, however, Whitman declared that "no true bard will ever contravene the Bible" (*Prose Works, 1892,* ed. Floyd Stovall [New York: New York Univ. Press, 1964], 2:548). This balancing act was typical of American literary scripturism.

60 See *DP* 569, especially ("I reckon – when I count at all – / First – Poets – Then the Sun –"). In another group, related to this one by a logic of inversion, the poet-seer records natural symbols of ultimate despair (e.g., *DP* 258: "There's a certain Slant of light").

61 Carlyle, *Two Note Books,* ed. Charles Eliot Norton (New York: Grolier, 1898), p. 264.

62 The poems are from William I. Bartlett, *Jones Very: Emerson's "Brave Saint"* (Durham: Duke Univ. Press, 1942), p. 154, and Jones Very, *Poems and Essays,* ed. James Freeman Clarke (Boston: Houghton Mifflin, 1886), p. 87. For discussion of this aspect of Very, see the works cited in Chap. 5, n. 13, especially Robinson, p. 211 (on the former poem).

63 The two classic studies of Emerson's shift in intellectual emphasis are Stephen E. Whicher, *Freedom and Fate: An Inner Life of Ralph Waldo Emerson* (Philadelphia: Univ. of Pennsylvania Press, 1953), and Jonathan Bishop, *Emerson on the Soul* (Cambridge, Mass.: Harvard Univ. Press, 1964), pp. 165–215. The concept of an early Transcendentalist Emerson giving way to a later stoical Emerson has been complicated, by more recent studies, among which see especially Barbara Packer, *Emerson's Fall* (New York: Continuum, 1982), and Gertrude Hughes, *Emerson's Demanding Optimism* (Baton Rouge: Louisiana State Univ. Press, 1984).

64 Thomas McFarland, *Romanticism and the Forms of Ruin* (Princeton: Princeton Univ. Press, 1981), p. 28. See also Julie Ellison's analysis of the link in Emerson's thinking and style between discontinuity and power, *Emerson's Romantic Style* (Princeton: Princeton Univ. Press, 1984), esp. Chap. 8.

65 On this point, see especially Rodolpe Gasché's reading of *Moby-Dick* with the "Cetology" chapter as its center, "The Scene of Writing: A Deferred Outset," *Glyph,* 1 (1977), 150–71.

66 Wright, *Melville's Use of the Bible,* pp. 61–5, notes the correspondence between the dualities of Melville's Ahab and his biblical antecedent. For modern scholarly discoveries concerning Ahab's portrayal in 1 Kings, see Robert Pfeiffer, *Introduction to the Old Testament* (New York: Harper & Brothers, 1940), pp. 403–4, and John Gray, *I and II Kings: A Commentary* (Philadelphia: Westminster Press, 1963), pp. 369–70.

67 I would paraphrase the second quatrain as follows: "Each one of us has tasted, with furtive exhilaration, the very food under discussion and been strengthened as a result."

68 I here depart from most of those earlier readings of this poem to which I am indebted, which either seem to overlook the conditional "if" or to depict the Logos-Eucharist-Resurrection cluster as mere metaphorical vehicle: Charles Anderson, *Emily Dickinson's Poetry: Stairway of Surprise* (New York: Holt, Rinehart & Winston, 1960), pp. 40–1; Albert Gelpi, *Emily Dickinson: The Mind of the Poet* (Cambridge, Mass.: Harvard Univ. Press, 1965), p. 144; Sharon Cameron, *Lyric Time: Dickinson and the Limits of Genre* (Baltimore: Johns Hopkins Univ. Press, 1979), pp. 189–92; and Joanne Feit Diehl, "'Ransom in a Voice': Language as Defense in Dickinson's Poetry," in *Feminist Critics Read Emily Dickinson,* ed. Suzanne Juhasz (Bloomington: Indiana Univ. Press, 1983), p. 158. Closest to my own reading is Shira Wolosky, *Emily Dickinson: A Voice of War* (New Haven: Yale Univ. Press, 1984), pp. 145–9. Although this book overstates the extent to which Dickinson's poems respond directly to current events, it provides the most scrupulous treatment to date of Dickinson's conflicted theocentrism.

69 See John Cline, "Hawthorne and the Bible," Ph.D. thesis, Duke University, 1948, for a competent analysis of Hawthorne's knowledge and use of Scripture, stronger in the area of biography than in literary criticism. His publisher Fields claimed that "Hawthorne was a diligent reader of the Bible" (*Yesterdays with Authors* [Boston: Houghton, 1871], p. 94), whereas his son Julian remembered him as a nonchurchgoer (*Nathaniel Hawthorne and His Wife* [Boston: Osgood, 1885], 2:22).

70 Susan Geary, "The Domestic Novel as a Commercial Commodity: Making a Best Seller in the 1850s," *Publications of the Bibliographical Society of America,* 70 (1976), 370. By 1858, *Uncle Tom's Cabin* had sold 310,000 copies; *The Lamplighter,* the number two fiction best-seller, had sold 90,000.

71 See, for example, Winthrop S. Hudson, *Religion in America* (New York: Scribner, 1965), pp. 109–203, and Sydney E. Ahlstrom, *A Religious History of the American People* (New Haven: Yale Univ. Press, 1972), pp. 385–509. Bruce Kuklick, *Churchmen and Philosophers* (New Haven: Yale Univ. Press, 1985), demonstrates beyond dispute the continuing vigor of the Edwardsean tradition in New England theology ("the most sustained intellectual tradition the United States has produced," p. 222) until well after the Civil War.

72 A number of recent scholars have commented astutely on the evangelical-activist underpinnings of *Uncle Tom's Cabin.* See, in addition to studies cited below, Cushing Strout, "*Uncle Tom's Cabin* and the Portent of Millennium," in *The Veracious Imagination* (Middletown, Conn.: Wesleyan Univ. Press, 1981), pp. 59–69, and Ann Douglas' Introduction to the Penguin edition of the novel (New York, 1981).

73 See the chapter of that title in Amanda Porterfield, *Feminine Spirituality in America* (Philadelphia: Temple Univ. Press, 1980); also, for a fuller though less sympathetic account, Douglas, *Feminization of American Culture,* Parts I–II.

74 Jane P. Tompkins, *Sensational Designs: The Cultural Work of American Fiction, 1790–1860* (New York: Oxford Univ. Press, 1985), p. 125. The more usual approach to Stowe's renderings of Christian themes (cf. Keller, "Alephs, Zahirs") is to stress their traditionalness, and by contrast to such other major writers as Dickinson and Melville that makes sense. But feminist criticism has shown that there is also a revisionary impulse behind Stowe's scripturism, though one may argue as to the degree.

75 Tompkins, *Sensational Designs,* p. 134.

76 Theodore Ziolkowski, *Fictional Transfigurations of Jesus* (Princeton: Princeton Univ. Press, 1972), argues that the first bona fide examples were products of the Christian Socialist movement of the late nineteenth century (pp. 58–9). Ziolkowski would perhaps class *Uncle Tom's Cabin,* which he does not discuss, as a transitional work of the same character as, say, Jacques Louis David's painting "The Death of Socrates" (1787), depicting a "remarkably Jesus-like Socrates, with index-finger raised, preparing to drink his last cup in the midst of precisely twelve disciples" (p. 11).

77 Elizabeth Ammons, "Heroines in *Uncle Tom's Cabin,*" in Ammons, *Critical Essays on Harriet Beecher Stowe,* p. 159.

78 *Uncle Tom's Cabin,* ed. Douglas, p. 624.

79 Joseph Allen, *Our Liberal Movement in Theology* (Boston: Roberts, 1882), p. 87.

Part III: Reinventing Puritanism

CHAPTER 8: THE CONCEPT OF PURITAN ANCESTRY

1 *The Poems of Celia Thaxter* (Boston: Houghton Mifflin, 1896), pp. 59–61.

2 George Callcott, *History in the United States, 1800–1860: Its Practice and Its Purpose* (Baltimore: Johns Hopkins Univ. Press, 1970), p.25.

3 The most important discussions of early national histories of the Revolution are William Raymond Smith, *History as Argument: Three Patriot Historians of the American Revolution* (The Hague: Mouton, 1966); Arthur H. Shaffer, *The Politics of History: Writing the History of the American Revolution, 1783–1815* (Chicago: Precedent, 1975); and especially Lester H. Cohen, *The Revolutionary Histories: Contemporary Narratives of the American Revolution* (Ithaca: Cornell Univ. Press, 1980).

4 For background on the historical-society movement, see Leslie W. Dunlap, *American Historical Societies, 1790–1860* (Madison: pvt., 1944), as well as Walter Muir Whitehill, *Independent Historical Societies* (Boston: Boston Athenaeum, 1962).

5 Callcott, *History in the United States*, p. 33. For other helpful works dealing with the historiography of this period, see especially David D. Van Tassel, *Recording America's Past* (Chicago: Univ. of Chicago Press, 1960), as well as David Levin, *History as Romantic Art: Bancroft, Prescott, Motley, and Parkman* (Stanford: Stanford Univ. Press, 1959), which along with Cohen, *Revolutionary Histories,* is the most sophisticated study of the literary qualities of historiography between the Revolution and the Civil War.

6 The only general survey is Peter Gay's relatively superficial *Loss of Mastery: Puritan Historians in Colonial America* (Berkeley and Los Angeles: Univ. of California Press, 1966).

7 Van Tassel, *Recording America's Past,* pp. 181–2, which comments further on New England leadership in state and local history, pp. 56–7.

8 Callcott, *History in the United States,* p. 68, notes that New England overproduced historians, relative to its share of the U.S. population, by a ratio of 4.8 to 1.0.

9 For Connecticut, Benjamin Trumbull, *A Complete History of Connecticut,* 2 vols. (1818); for Maine, William D. Williamson, *The History of the State of Maine,* 2 vols. (1832); for Rhode Island, Samuel G. Arnold, *History of Rhode Island,* 2 vols. (1859–60); for Vermont, Samuel Williams, *The Natural and Civil History of Vermont* (2 vols., 1809). Thomas Hutchinson had already writen a serviceable *History of the Colony and Province of Massachusetts Bay* (1760–8, third vol. published 1828), and in general the field of Massachusetts historiography became specialized at an early date, so that the bulk of the important contributions between the Revolution and the Civil War were on a regional or local scale, like Josiah G. Holland's *History of Western Massachusetts* (2 vols., 1855) and Lemuel Shattuck's *History of Town of Concord to 1832* (1835). By the end of our period the same was true of other states as well.

10 "Historical Novels," *Harvard Lyceum* (1811), pp. 364–9.

11 Wesley Frank Craven, *The Legend of the Founding Fathers* (New York: New York Univ. Press, 1956), p. 19. This is an excellent study of the development of the New England–oriented myth of American origins as a national symbol from the Revolution to the present. Equally valuable is Sacvan Bercovitch's study *The American Jeremiad* (Madison: Univ. of Wisconsin Press, 1978), which examines the development of that form from tribal ritual to national consensus myth. John F. Berens, *Providence and Patriotism in Early America, 1640–1815* (Charlottesville: Univ. Press of Virginia, 1978), is particularly helpful for its analysis of the nationlization of New England premises during the mid-eighteenth century. The Puritan, if not the Arminian, contribution to American Revolutionary thought is profoundly assessed in Alan Heimert, *Religion and the American Mind* (Cambridge, Mass.: Harvard Univ. Press, 1966). For the importance of the notion of Puritan origins in shaping the Revolutionary historians' conceptualization of American nationality, see Shaffer, *Politics of History*, p. 57, Smith, *History as Argument*, p. 49, and both works in general. Among documents of the 1760s that anticipate the Puritan–Revolutionary linkage that later propagandists and historians institutionalized, the most notable are John Adams' *Dissertation on the Canon and Feudal Law* (1765), in *Works of John Adams,* ed. Charles Francis Adams (Boston: Little, Brown, 1851), 3:451), and Amos Adams, *A Concise Historical View of . . . New-England* (Boston: Kneeland & Adams, 1769), pp. 51–2: "This country was at first sought and settled as an Assylum for liberty, civil and religious: And it is worthy of observation, that the abettors of arbitrary power, and ecclesiastical tyranny, have, all along, been the enemies of New-England."

12 See E. Digby Baltzell, *Puritan Boston and Quaker Philadelphia* (Boston: Beacon Press, 1979), for the most extensive work of comparative historical sociology yet undertaken on the subject of Puritan influence in American culture, attempting to explain that influence (relative to Quakerism) in terms of differences in group behavior arising from differences in ethos.

13 Alexander Cowie, *John Trumbull, Connecticut Wit* (Chapel Hill: Univ. of North Carolina Press, 1936), p. 3.

14 George E. Ellis, "Oliver's *Puritan Commonwealth,*" *North American Review,* 84 (1857), 427.

15 For a history of the New England societies, see Pershing Vartanian, "The Puritan as a Symbol in American Thought: A Study of the New England Societies," Ph.D. thesis, Univ. of Michigan, 1971. For a valuable collection of orations, see Cephas Brainerd and Eveline Warber Brainerd, ed., *The New England Society Orations: Addresses Sermons and Poems Delivered before the New England Society in the City of New York, 1820–1885,* 2 vols. (New York: Century, 1901), abbreviated as *Orations* below. Also very helpful is Craven, *Legend.*

16 In some other contexts, however, the differentiation between *Pilgrim* (introduced into common usage about 1800: see n. 23 below) assumed great importance in New England historical discourse. *Pilgrim* had a more favorable connotation than *Puritan,* and was used increasingly during the nineteenth century, except by religious conservatives, as the honorific term of preference; cf. Craven, *Legend,* especially pp. 81–2; Vartanian, "Puritan as a Symbol," esp. pp. 90–102. Cf. Catherine Sedgwick's remark, in *Hope Leslie,* one of the first important New England historical romances: "Never was a name more befitting the condition of a people, than 'Pilgrim' that of our forefathers. It should be redeemed from the puritanical and ludicrous associations which have degraded it, in most men's minds" (*Hope Leslie: or, Early Times in the Massachusetts* [1826; rpt. New York: Garrett, 1969], 1:31). Liberal historians typically liked to distinguish between the rigidity of "Puritan" Massachusetts Bay and the comparative liberalism of the Plymouth "Pilgrims," whereas orthodox historians tended to minimize differences and to stress the much greater historical impact of Massachusetts Bay.

17 Horace Bushnell, "The Founders, Great in Their Unconsciousness" (1849), in *Orations*, 2:96. Evangelical orators like Lyman Beecher, however, felt that such discourses tended to eulogize the Fathers as the "apostles of civil liberty" and to treat "their doctrines, their piety, their church order, and the other peculiarities of their religious institutions . . . with cold commendations" or excuses ("The Memory of Our Fathers" [1827 discourse at Plymouth], in *Sermons Delivered on Various Occasions* [New York: Saxton & Miles, 1842], pp. 310–11n).

18 Leonard Bacon, "Address" (1838), in *Orations*, 1:180; Daniel Webster, "First Settlement of New England" (1820), in *The Works of Daniel Webster* (Boston: Little, Brown, 1851), 1:13–22.

19 Webster, "First Settlement," in *Works*, p. 12; William M. Evarts, "Oration" (1854), in *Orations*, 2:245; George S. Hilliard, "The Past and the Future" (1851), in *Orations*, 2:151; Webster, "The Constitution and the Union," in *Orations*, 1:355.

20 Charles B. Hadduck, "The Elements of National Greatness" (1841), in *Orations*, 1:272; Winthrop, "Address" (1839), in ibid., p. 248; Upham, "The Spirit of the Day and Its Lessons" (1846), in ibid., p. 461; Emerson, "Oration and Response" (1870), in ibid., 2:379.

21 Philip M. Whepley, "The Memory of the Just Is Blessed," (1822), in ibid., 1:122.

22 On this point, see J. V. Matthews, " 'Whig History': The New England Whigs and a Usable Past," *New England Quarterly*, 51 (1978), 193–208, and Daniel Walker Howe, *The Political Culture of the American Whigs* (Chicago: Univ. of Chicago Press, 1979), pp. 69–95. Both argue that the orators' emphasis on Puritan determination of American history bespeaks a Burkean conservatism on the Whigs' part that contrasts with the Democrats' location of authority in popular will rather than in the historical continuity of institutions. As this and the next chapter show, I partly agree and partly dissent. My research convinces me that although New England conservatives (Federalists and Whigs) were especially keen celebrators of institutional continuity, when it came to representations of Puritanism differential party allegiances were, for New Englanders, less important variables than the common bond of New England ancestry, on the one hand, and the divisive influences of ethnicity and religion on the other. To take a simple example, the Universalists were one of the most Democratically oriented of the New England Protestant denominations (cf. Ronald Formisano, *The Transformation of Political Culture: Massachusetts Parties, 1790s–1840s* [New York: Oxford Univ. Press, 1983], pp. 292–4), yet in an article entitled "The Intolerance of the Puritan Church of New England," the *Universalist Quarterly*, 15 (1858), 158–79, took a position that could scarcely be distinguished from that of the overwhelmingly Whiggish Unitarians (cf. Formisano, *Transformation*, pp. 295–

6, for Unitarian political allegiances). In this case the common denominator of religious liberalism was the crucial factor. The obloquy cast on Universalism by New England's other post-Puritan sects did not prevent it from defining itself as an enlightened offshoot of Calvinism – the same strategy used by the Unitarians, as we shall see in Chap. 9.

23 Albert Matthews, "The Term Pilgrim Fathers and Early Celebrations of Forefathers' Day," *Publications of the Colonial Society of Massachusetts*, 17 (1914), 333–4.

24 Vartanian, "Puritan as a Symbol," pp. 16–17, 48; cf. the speech of New Hampshire–born Democratic presidential candidate Lewis Cass, *Address Delivered before the New England Society of Michigan, December 22, 1848* (Detroit: Markham, 1849): "They left behind them the institutions they founded, and these have come down to us, gaining in strength as they gained in years, till time has made them bone of our bone, and flesh of our flesh" (p. 26).

25 Russel Nye, *George Bancroft: Brahmin Rebel* (New York: Knopf, 1944), p. 188. Of Bancroft's two modern biographers, Nye is stronger on Bancroft as historian, Lilian Handlin on the complex mixture of idealistic and political motives that underlay all that Bancroft wrote (*George Bancroft: The Intellectual as Democrat* [New York: Harper & Row, 1984]). The basic ideological stance of Bancroft's *History* is summarized in Richard C. Vitzthum, "Theme and Method in Bancroft's *History of the United States*," *New England Quarterly*, 41 (1968), 362–80.

26 For a sampling of Arminian reviews, mostly quite favorable, see *North American Review*, 40 (1835), 99–122; 52 (1841), 75–103; 74 (1852), 507–14; and 87 (1858), 449–81 (by Edward Everett, W. H. Prescott, Francis Bowen, and George E. Ellis, respectively). For more conservative denominational opinion, see *American Biblical Repository*, 5 (1835), 479; 2nd ser. 5 (1841), 246–7; *Christian Review*, 17 (1852), 470–1. For the reaction to Hildreth, see Chap. 9, nn. 64, 67.

27 George Bancroft, *History of the United States* (Boston: Little, Brown, 1852), 5:6.

28 Ibid., 1:460–9, 2:440–66.

29 Ibid., 2:452. Orestes Brownson, "Bancroft's *History of the United States*," *Brownson's Quarterly Review*, n.s. 6 (1852), 450–9, exposes Bancroft's religious and cultural biases from an ideological viewpoint that is the mirror image of Bancroft's own.

30 Levin, *History as Romantic Art*, p. 74.

31 Ronald G. Walters, *The Antislavery Appeal* (Baltimore: Johns Hopkins Univ. Press, 1976), pp. 56–9, notes these two cases, emphasizing also that even prejudiced abolitionists, though racist by present-day standards, were "considerably less malignantly racist than their white contemporaries" (p. 57).

32 Bancroft, *History*, 1:463; cf. 1:449, 461. For this line of argument Bancroft drew a rebuke from his friend and political opposite, William H. Prescott, in an 1841 review (rpt. in Prescott, *Biographical and Critical Miscellanies* [New York: Harper & Brothers, 1845], pp. 315–16).

33 George Bancroft, *Oration* (Springfield, Mass.: Meriam, 1836), pp. 7, 11.

34 Sacvan Bercovitch, "How the Puritans Won the American Revolution," *Massachusetts Review*, 17 (1976), 602. The generalizing force of this very thoughtful essay is weakened by its concentration on the single example of Bancroft, but Bercovitch is certainly right that Bancroft's history had a bipartisan appeal that is an important fact of antebellum intellectual history. Rush Welter's analysis of the distinctions, and blurring of distinctions, between Whig and Democratic Fourth of July rhetoric, in *The Mind of America, 1820–1860* (New York: Columbia Univ. Press, 1975), also suggests the risks of insisting on party allegiance as a major differential on most public issues. Welter unfortunately comments only in passing on colonial history as a point of debate.

35 Julia Ward Howe, "Our Country," *Atlantic Monthly,* 8 (1861), 506; Edward Everett, "The Circumstances Favorable to the Progress of Literature in America" (1824), in *Orations and Speeches* (Boston: Little, Brown, 1853), 1:39.

36 William R. Taylor, *Cavalier and Yankee* (Garden City, N.Y.: Doubleday, 1963), p. 304.

37 Leonard Neufeldt sensitively discusses Emerson's bond to Concord in "'The Fields of My Fathers' and Emerson's Literary Vocation," *American Transcendental Quarterly,* 31, suppl. 1 (1976), 5–9.

38 For Augustan historical thinking, see, for example, James W. Johnson, *The Formation of Neo-Classical Thought* (Princeton: Princeton Univ. Press, 1967), pp. 31–68, which notes that history was valued for the "concrete embodiment of general truths applicable to all mankind" (p. 33). Bolingbroke's maxim (echoing Aristotle and Sydney) that "history is philosophy teaching by examples" leads easily into the antihistoricism of Emerson's "History," once we add to Bolingbroke the mystical concept of the universal mind.

39 Emerson, "Introductory," in *Early Lectures of Ralph Waldo Emerson,* ed. Stephen Whicher, Robert Spiller, Wallace Williams (Cambridge, Mass.: Harvard Univ. Press, 1964), 2:13. For discussions of Emerson's Transcendentalist position on history, see Jonathan Bishop, *Emerson on the Soul* (Cambridge, Mass.: Harvard Univ. Press, 1964), pp. 59–66, and Robert D. Richardson, Jr., "Emerson on History," in *Emerson: Prospect and Retrospect,* ed. Joel Porte (Cambridge, Mass.: Harvard Univ. Press, 1982), pp. 49–64; Joseph Kronick, *American Poetics of History* (Baton Rouge: Louisiana State Univ. Press, 1984), Chaps. 1–2; and Julie Ellison, *Emerson's Romantic Style* (Princeton: Princeton Univ. Press, 1984), pp. 64–5. Not all Transcendentalists subscribed to the premises of "History." Cf. A. Robert Caponigri, "Emerson and Brownson: Nature and History," *New England Quarterly,* 18 (1945), 368–90, and John B. Wilson, "Elizabeth Peabody and Other Transcendentalists on History and Historians," *Historian,* 30 (1967), 72–86. Emerson himself modified his early view in *English Traits* (1856).

40 Quoted in George Ticknor, *Life of William Hickling Prescott* (Boston: Ticknor & Fields, 1866), p. 272.

41 Levin, *History as Romantic Art,* p. 24, and pp. 24–45.

42 In contrast to Levin, R. W. B. Lewis, *The American Adam* (Chicago: Univ. of Chicago Press, 1955), pp. 159–73, and Harry Henderson, *Versions of the Past* (New York: Oxford Univ. Press, 1974), pp. 16–49, are inclined to disassociate Parkman, and especially Prescott, from the myth of progressive history. I agree that there are differences in emphasis (mostly also noted by Levin) but fail to see a sharp distinction of categories such as Henderson draws between the "progressive" history of Bancroft and Motley and the "holistic" history of Prescott and

Parkman, "characterized by a relativistic view of time-bound man and by a belief that historical change is not measurable except *in terms of the period under consideration*" (p. 14). See, for example, Theodore Parker's scathing reviews of Prescott (*Critical Writings,* ed. Frances Power Cobbe [London: Trübner, 1865], 2:81–153). Parker chides Prescott for attending too much of narrative and description while ignoring "philosophy," by which Parker refers partly to Prescott's ignorance of social science but mostly to a failure to take what Parker considers a strong enough stand against King Ferdinand, the Inquisition, Cortez's butchery, and other symptoms of despotism. Here we might seem to have a marked difference between a judgmental, progressivist approach to history and a holistic re-creation. But ultimately what Parker dislikes is not so much the absence of progressive assumptions about history as the incorrect identification of good and bad forces: e.g., Parker complains about *The Conquest of Mexico* (p. 153) that "all this providential action is in behalf of the invaders."

43 George Bancroft, *Literary and Historical Miscellanies* (New York: Harper & Brothers, 1857), p. 517.

44 See especially Philip L. Nicoloff, *Emerson on Race and History* (New York: Columbia Univ. Press, 1961), pp. 45–96.

45 Robert Treat Paine, *Works* (Boston: Belcher, 1812), p. lxxi; Matthews, "The Term Pilgrim Fathers," pp. 326–8.

46 *Federal Orrery,* December 25, 1794 (p. 78), March 12, 1795 (p. 166).

47 State historian Samuel Greene Arnold, for example, addressed the state historical society in 1853 as follows: "The cause of the Pilgrim [and Puritan] emigration was . . . the desire, not of religious freedom, but of freedom to enjoy their own religion"; Rhode Island, in contrast, owes "its foundation alone to the spirit of liberty, which elsewhere could find no congenial home" (*The Spirit of Rhode Island History* [Providence: Whitney, 1853], p. 10). "The influence of our example has extended far beyond our narrow borders," affirmed Arnold in his peroration, "and has already made the American Union one vast Rhode Island in principle and feeling. What we must require, is, that other States should know and bear in mind, whence sprang the seed of all their greatness; that HERE, on this spot, was the hallowed ground, and the fathers of Rhode Island were the husbandmen" (p. 32). Arnold's monumental two-volume *History of the State of Rhode Island and Providence Plantations* (New York: Appleton, 1859), 1:10–46, presented a toned-down version of this doctrine. For the predictable controversy with Massachusetts antiquarians that ensued, see George E. Ellis, "Palfrey's and Arnold's Histories," *Atlantic,* 3 (1859), 441–5, and Charles T. Brooks, "The Old Rhode Island Question," *Christian Examiner,* 66 (1859), 274–85.

48 George Richards Minot, *Continuation of the History of the Province of Massachusetts Bay, from the year 1748* (Boston: Manning & Loring, 1798), 1:vii.

49 James Russell Lowell, "Reviews and Literary Notices," *Atlantic Monthly,* 4 (1859), 645.

50 James Russell Lowell, "Recent American Publications," *Atlantic Monthly,* 6 (1860), 638.

51 Anonymous review of Theodore Winthrop's oration before the New England Society of New York, "Winthrop's Address," *New York Review,* 6 (1840), 488.

52   Webster, "The Constitution and the Union," in *Orations* 2:125.

53   Thoreau, "A Plea for Captain John Brown," in *Reform Papers,* ed. Wendell Glick (Princeton: Princeton Univ. Press, 1973), p. 113: "He was one of that class of whom we hear a great deal, but, for the most part, see nothing at all – the Puritans. He died lately in the time of Cromwell, but he reappeared here. Why should he not? Some of the Puritan stock are said to have come over and settled in New England. They were a class that did something else than celebrate their forefathers' day." Thoreau is daring fellow New Englanders to have the courage to recognize the reality to which their rhetoric supposedly refers.

54   See the very similar statements in the introduction to Beecher's *Norwood* (1867) and the preface to Stowe's *Oldtown Folks* (1869).

55   Lyman Beecher, *Spirit of the Pilgrims,* vol. 1 (1828), p. 8; cf. ibid., pp. 337–43.

56   For Gardiner Spring's address and the response, see *Orations,* 1:9–72.

57   On Scott's breadth of international appeal, see especially Donald Davie, *The Heyday of Sir Walter Scott* (London: Routledge & Kegan Paul, 1961). On Scott's American impact, the standard brief overview is G. Harrison Orians, "The Romance Ferment after *Waverley,*" *American Literature,* 3 (1932), 408–31. For more particulars, see George Dekker, *James Fenimore Cooper* (London: Routledge & Kegan Paul, 1967); Rollin G. Osterweis' somewhat overdramatized *Romanticism and Nationalism in the Old South* (New Haven: Yale Univ. Press, 1949); and especially (on New England) Neal Frank Doubleday, *Hawthorne's Early Tales* (Durham: Duke Univ. Press, 1972).

58   William H. Gardiner, "*The Spy,*" *North American Review,* 15 (1822), 255.

59   Rufus Choate, "The Importance of Illustrating New-England History by a Series of Romances Like the Waverley Novels," in *Works,* ed. Samuel Gilman Brown (Boston: Little, Brown, 1862), 1:333; Leonard Withington, *Puritan Morals Defended* (Salem, Mass.: Palfray, 1832), pp. 6, 11.

60   Cf. John G. Palfrey, "*Tales of My Landlord,*" *North American Review,* 5 (1817), 285, and "Review of Imitation Waverley Novels," *Christian Spectator,* 7 (1825), 84–7. One finds exceptions on both sides, of course: e.g., A. P. Peabody, "Philosophy of Fiction," *Christian Examiner,* 32 (1842), 11, a Unitarian review that objected to anti-Covenanter bias.

61   This point is noted in David S. Reynolds, *Faith in Fiction: The Emergence of Religious Literature in America* (Cambridge, Mass.: Harvard Univ. Press, 1981), p. 106.

62   Leo Braudy, *Narrative Form in History and Fiction* (Princeton: Princeton Univ. Press, 1970).

63   For the tendency in historiography to move toward more professional research methods and a stronger documentary base, see Thomas Preston Peardon, *The Transition in English Historical Writing, 1760–1830* (New York: Columbia Univ. Press, 1933); Michael Kraus, *The Writing of American History* (Norman: Univ. of Oklahoma Press, 1953), pp. 57–114; Denys Hay, *Annalists and Historians: Western Historiography from the Eighth to the Eighteenth Centuries* (London: Methuen, 1977), pp. 169–85; and Callcott, *History in the United States,* pp. 121–50. Lester Cohen does an admirable job of charting the historiographical shift from providential toward secular causality, *Revolutionary Histories,* Chaps. 1–4.

For the dependence of early American fiction on genre-specific fictive conventions, see Henri Petter, *The Early American Novel* (Columbus: Ohio State Univ. Press, 1971), which concludes that these authors generally relied on the "patterns of the conventional story of love, adventure, and mystery" (p. 400).

64 Jeremy Belknap, *The History of New-Hampshire,* ed. John Kirtland Wright (New York: Johnson, 1970), 1:vii–viii.

65 Michael Colacurcio, *The Province of Piety: Moral History in Hawthorne's Early Tales* (Cambridge, Mass.: Harvard Univ. Press, 1984), demonstrates with subtlety and erudition that Hawthorne's New England tales "constitute as intractably historical a body of literature as it has been possible for anyone in America to produce" (pp. 520–1). Colacurcio persuasively reconstructs Hawthorne's "conversion" to historicism, pp. 39–98.

66 On this last point, see, for instance, W. H. Prescott's discussion of the breakthrough from eighteenth-century rationalistic history to modern narrative history, "Historical Composition," *North American Review,* 29 (1829), 293–305, and Charles W. Upham's appraisal of "Prescott as an Historian," *North American Review,* 83 (1856), 97. Shrewder critics like Parker were much less ready than Upham to identify narration with objectivity, however (see Parker, *Critical Writings,* 2:81–153). On the Romantic historians' general valuation of the literary dimension of historical writing, see especially Levin, *History as Romantic Art,* pp. 3–23. For an example of the Romantic narrative historian attempting to be fair to less speculative compilers like Belknap, whose work they considered inferior, see George Bancroft, "Documentary History of the Revolution," *North American Review,* 46 (1838), 475–87.

67 See Hayden White, *Metahistory* (Baltimore: Johns Hopkins Univ. Press, 1973), esp. pp. 1–42, and the essays by White, Lionel Grossman, and Louis O. Mink in Robert H. Canary and Henry Kozicki, eds., *The Writing of History: Literary Form and Historical Understanding* (Madison: Univ. of Wisconsin Press, 1978). Grossman argues, I think correctly, that although "many modern historians . . . have repudiated the goals and premises of historical realism," nonetheless "there seems to have been no radical reform of the historian's mode of writing comparable with the changes that have affected literary writing and fiction in the last half-century," namely the reaction against narrative realism (p. 36).

68 For example, Francis Parkman, "James Fenimore Cooper," *North American Review,* 74 (1852), esp. 148–9, praises Cooper particularly for narrative realism and chides him for historical inaccuracy, yet classes Cooper's achievement entirely with other historical romances.

69 Choate, "The Importance of Illustrating New England History," in *Works,* 1:324.

70 Ibid., pp. 339–40.

71 Colacurcio, *Province of Piety,* pp. 251–82, provides a more detailed reading of the tale as an exercise in manipulation of reader expectation. He argues, however, that what's being undermined is the Puritans' self-serving and confessedly fabricated version of the incident. I would agree that to convey the awareness of the Puritans' version as distorted is part of the tale's intent, but it seems to me that the tale's ultimate thrust is to suggest that the reader must confront the Puritans as something more profound and portentous than "dismal wretches," rather than merely to expose the Merry Mount story as chimerical in the Puritan retelling. The difference between my reading and Colacurcio's here stems partly from my belief that Puritan history, rather than Puritan historiography, is Hawthorne's central theme here.

72 Robert H.Gardiner, "*The Spy*," *North American Review*, 15 (1822), 255–59.

73 Michael Kammen, *A Season of Youth: The American Revolution and the Historical Imagination* (New York: Knopf, 1978), surveying romances of the Revolution, pp. 145–85, calls attention to the overwhelmingly nationalistic sentiments in antebellum examples (pp. 161–71).

CHAPTER 9: THE POLITICS OF HISTORIOGRAPHY

1 On the principles and historical emergence of Unitarianism, see especially Conrad Wright, *The Beginnings of Unitarianism in America* (Boston: Starr King Press, 1955), and Daniel Walker Howe, *The Unitarian Conscience* (Cambridge, Mass.: Harvard Univ. Press, 1970). For the mutations of Calvinism, see especially Sydney E. Ahlstrom, "Theology in America," in *The Shaping of American Religion*, ed. James Ward Smith and A. Leland Jameson (Princeton: Princeton Univ. Press, 1961), 1:232–321; Frank Hugh Foster, *A Genetic History of the New England Theology* (Chicago: Univ. of Chicago Press, 1907); Joseph Haroutunian, *Piety versus Moralism: The Passing of the New England Theology* (New York: Henry Holt, 1932); and Richard Isaac Rabinowitz, "Soul, Character, and Personality: The Transformation of Personal Religious Experience in New England, 1790–1860," Ph.D. thesis, Harvard Univ., 1977.

2 For Belknap's life and career, see Jane Belknap Marcou, *Life of Jeremy Belknap* (New York: Harper & Brothers, 1847), and George B. Kirsch, *Jeremy Belknap* (New York: Arno Press, 1982). For his character as a historian, see also Jere Daniell, "Jeremy Belknap and the *History of New Hampshire*," in *The Colonial Legacy*, ed. Lawrence Leder (New York: Harper & Row, 1973), 4:241–64, and Sidney Kaplan, "*The History of New-Hampshire*: Jeremy Belknap as Literary Craftsman," *William and Mary Quarterly*, 3rd ser., 21 (1964), 18–39. For his character as a minister, see also John Eliot, "Sketch of the Life and Writings of the Rev. Jeremy Belknap, D.D.," *Polyanthos*, 1 (1805), 5–13.

3 Belknap, April 11, 1784, to Ebenezer Hazard, *Collections of the Massachusetts Historical Society*, 5th ser., 2 (1877), 326.

4 Jeremy Belknap, *The History of New-Hampshire*, ed. John Kirtland Wright (New York: Johnson Rpt. Corp., 1970), 1:37, 52, 67.

5 On the establishment and early history of the Massachusetts Historical Society, see *Proceedings of the Massachusetts Historical Society*, 1 (1791–1835); Stephen Riley, *The Massachusetts Historical Society, 1791–1959* (Boston: Massachusetts Historical Society, 1959); and Kirsch, *Jeremy Belknap*, pp. 133–40.

6 Joseph W. Phillips, *Jedidiah Morse and New England Congregationalism* (New Brunswick, N.J.: Rutgers Univ. Press, 1983), by far the best of the three biographies of Morse, suggests Belknap's role in the procurement of Morse (p. 25). For more details, see the Belknap–Hazard correspondence in *Collections of the Massachusetts Historical Society*, 5th ser., vol. 2.

7 For Morse's significance as a theorist of regionalism, see Fulmer Mood, "The Origin, Evolution, and Application of the Sectional Concept, 1750–1900," in *Regionalism in America,* ed. Merrill Jensen (Madison: Univ. of Wisconsin Press, 1951), pp.38–46.

8 Jedidiah Morse, *The American Geography* (1789; rpt. London: Stockdale, 1792), p. 212. Until well into the nineteenth century, Rhode Island's neighbors – particularly conservative religionists like Dwight (see *DT* 3:40–2), though also some comparative moderates like Belknap (May 7, 1790 to Hazard, *Collections of the Massachusetts Historical Society,* 5th ser., 3 [1877], 220) – tended to disparage it as a poorly managed and unruly place. Charity toward Rhode Island is generally, however, a rather accurate barometer of a New Englander's religious liberalism during our period.

9 Jedidiah Morse, *The American Universal Geography* (Boston: Thomas & Andrews, 1793), was a revised version of the 1789 edition of Morse's *American Geography,* with a second volume on the geography of the Eastern Hemisphere. For the Morse–Freeman dispute, see Phillips, *Jedidiah Morse,* pp. 36–7, and especially Conrad Wright, "The Controversial Career of Jedidiah Morse," *Harvard Library Bulletin,* 31 (1983), 64–87, which does a splendid job of tracing and appraising Morse's disputes with Boston liberals.

10 James Freeman, *Remarks on the American Universal Geography* (Boston: Belknap & Hall, 1793), p. 25. See Morse, *American Universal Geography,* 1:253, 315. It should be emphasized that although Morse was unquestionably *the* evangelical troublemaker among the otherwise harmonious and more liberal knot of turn-of-the-century Boston historians, he was neither the only nor the best orthodox-leaning New England historian of the time. The first section of Mercy Otis Warren's *History of the Rise, Progress, and Termination of the American Revolution* (Boston: Larkin, 1805) gives a pious and distinctly pro-Puritan account of early New England, and it was partly on the strength of this that she received, despite her Jeffersonianism, a not unfavorable review in Morse's *Panoplist,* 2 (1807), 380–4, 429–32. Another Morse friend and fellow Boston-area minister, moderate Calvinist Abiel Holmes (father of Oliver Wendell Holmes), was respected by both conservatives and liberals because of the conscientious avoidance of sectarian bias in his *American Annals* (Cambridge, Mass.: Hilliard, 1805). Even around Boston, then, American historiography was not the exclusive territory of Arminians. In fact, before Bancroft, the authoritative American history was the distinctly pro-Puritan *History of the United States* (vol. 1–2, 1827) by the Scotsman James Grahame, who "once said that 'the depths of my heart are with the primitive Puritans and the Scottish Covenanters'" (quoted in Michael Kraus, *The Writing of American History* [Norman: Univ. of Oklahoma Press, 1953], p. 106.

11 William Allen, *American Biographical Dictionary,* 3rd ed. (Boston: Jewett, 1857), p. 459; William Emerson, *An Historical Sketch of the First Church in Boston* (Boston: Munroe, Francis, 1812), pp. 41, 52.

12 See Chap. 8, n. 47; James Savage, editor of John Winthrop's *History of New England from 1630 to 1649* (Boston: Phelps & Farnham, 1825), 1:41n, and especially George Bancroft, *History of the United States* (Boston: Little, Brown, 1850), which argues that "Roger Williams asserted the great doctrine of intellectual liberty" (1:375).

13 Sacvan Bercovitch, *The Puritan Origins of the American Self* (New Haven: Yale Univ. Press, 1975), turns to the *Magnalia* as the paradigmatic expression of the Puritan-American ethos; for recent biographies, see David Levin, *Cotton Mather: The Young Life of the Lord's Remembrancer* (Cambridge, Mass.: Harvard Univ. Press, 1978), and Kenneth Silverman, *The Life and Times of Cotton Mather* (New York: Harper & Row, 1984).

14 Belknap to Hazard, October 22, 1789, *Collections of the Massachusetts Historical Society*, 5th ser., 3 (1877), 198; William Tudor, "Books Relating to America," *North American Review*, 6 (1818), 256; James Russell Lowell, "Recent American Publications," *Atlantic*, 6 (1860), 639.

15 Belknap, *History of New-Hampshire*, 1:43; Robbins, *An Historical View of the First Planters of New-England* (Hartford: Gleason, 1815), pp. 266–7.

16 James Savage, ed. *The History of New England . . . by John Winthrop* (Boston: T. B. Wait, 1825–6), 2:24n.

17 Charles Wentworth Upham, *Lectures on Witchcraft* (Boston: Carter, Hendee & Babcock, 1831), pp. 114, 107; cf. Upham, *Salem Witchcraft* (1867; rpt. Williamstown, Mass.: Corner House, 1971), 2:366–9.

18 Francis Parkman, "Salem Witchcraft," *Christian Examiner*, 11 (1831), 251.

19 Josiah Quincy, *History* (Cambridge, Mass.: Owen, 1840), 1:65, 62–3, 88, 47–9, 132.

20 William Allen, *An American Biographical and Historical Dictionary*, 3rd ed. (Boston: Jewett, 1857), p.559.

21 Enoch Pond, *The Lives of Increase Mather and Sir William Phips* (Boston: Massachusetts Sabbath School Society, 1847). Pond's review is in *American Biblical Repository*, 2nd ser., 7 (1842), 89–145, 254–328; see especially pp. 122–45, 254–78. Another article, "Review of Quincy's History of Harvard University," by an anonymous Yale professor, is in ibid., 2nd ser., 6 (1841), 177–95, 384–403; 7 (1842), 175–207. See also R. D. C. Robbins, "Cotton Mather and the Witchcraft Delusion," *Bibliotheca Sacra*, 34 (1877), 473–513, and Alonzo H. Quint, "Cotton Mather," *Congregational Quarterly*, 1 (1859), 234–64.

22 Pond, "Examination," pp. 129–45; *Lives*, pp. 153–7.

23 Quint, "Cotton Mather," p. 257; Pond, "Examination," pp. 273, 277.

24 For a detailed account, see Conrad Wright, "The Election of Henry Ware: Two Contemporary Accounts Edited with Commentary," *Harvard Library Bulletin*, 17 (1969), 245–78.

25 Edward Everett Hale, "Our First Fathers, and Their First Children," *Christian Examiner*, 63 (1857), 267–70.

26 Pond, "Examination," pp. 273–8; Quint, "Cotton Mather," pp. 254–7; Pond, *Lives*, pp. 171–82. For the Unitarian view, see Upham, *Salem Witchcraft*, 2:433–5; George E. Ellis, "The Fathers of New England," *North American Review*, 68 (1849), 92–5.

27 G. W. Haven, "Cotton Mather," *North American Review*, 51 (1840), 21. Cf. J. G. Palfrey and C. C. Felton, *North American Review*, 43 (1836), 519.

28 W. B. O. Peabody, "Life of Cotton Mather," in *The Library of American Biography*, ed. Jared Sparks (Boston: Hilliard, Gray, 1839), 6:211, 187, 167 (for criticisms); 6:345–50 (general estimate of character); 6:212–13, 223–5, 251, 346 (Mather and the witchcraft delusion).

29 W. B. O. Peabody, "Diary of Cotton Mather," *Knickerbocker*, 8 (1836), 196–201; Peabody, "Life of Cotton Mather," pp. 343, 269.

30 Chandler Robbins, *History of the Second Church* (Boston: Wilson, 1852), pp. 68, 80, 83, 75, 97.

31 For Orthodox and Unitarian reviews of Robbins, see *New Englander*, 10 (1852), 483–4; *North American Review*, 76 (1853), 249–52; *Christian Examiner*, 52 (1852), 151–2.

32 William Poole, "Cotton Mather and Salem Witchcraft," *North American Review*, 108 (1869), 342, 357. Lowell's notice of Upham is in *North American Review*, 106 (1868), 226–32.

33 Charles Wentworth Upham, *Salem Witchcraft and Cotton Mather: A Reply* (Morrisania, N.Y.: n.p., 1869). The rebuttal originally appeared in the *Historical Magazine.*

34 William Poole, "Witchcraft in Boston," in *The Memorial History of Boston*, ed. Justin Winsor (Boston: Ticknor & Fields, 1881), 2:131–72.

35 Z. Swift Holbrook, "Dr. Poole and the New England Clergy," *Bibliotheca Sacra*, 57 (1900), 297. Holbrook also surveys later disputes between Poole and liberal historians.

36 James Duncan Phillips, *Salem in the Seventeenth Century* (Boston: Houghton Mifflin, 1933), p. 303.

37 Perry Miller, *The New England Mind: From Colony to Province* (Cambridge, Mass.: Harvard Univ. Press, 1953), p. 204. David Levin reflects shrewdly on the problems of combating the bogeyman myth of Mather in "Trying to Make a Monster Human: Judgment in the Biography of Cotton Mather," *Yale Review*, 73 (1984), 210–29; see pp. 227–9 for reflections on Mather's role in witchcraft cases. In his "Witchcraft and the Limits of Interpretation," *New England Quarterly*, 58 (1985), 262–3, David D. Hall notes that "debate continues on the attitude and role of Cotton Mather" during the Salem affair, citing the discrepancy between Levin's relatively charitable assessment in *Cotton Mather* and Silverman's more astringent diagnosis in *The Life and Times of Cotton Mather.*

38 See William Emerson's comments on Adams' *Abridgment* in *Monthly Anthology*, 2 (1805), 538–41 ("We know of no work of the kind deserving equal praise," p. 540), and on Morse-Parish, *Monthly Anthology*, 2 (1805), 541–9. For accounts of the controversy between Morse and Adams, see Phillips, *Jedidiah Morse*, pp. 151–6, and especially Wright, "Controversial Career of Jedidiah Morse," pp. 77–85.

39 Jedidiah Morse, *An Appeal to the Public* (Charlestown, Mass.: pvt., 1814), which was countered by Hannah Adams, *A Narrative of the Controversy between the Rev. Jedidiah Morse, D.D., and the Author* (Boston: Eliot, 1814).

40 Hannah Adams, *A Summary History of New England* (Dedham, Mass.: Mann & Adams, 1799), p. 102; Jedidiah Morse and Elijah Parish, *A Compendious History of New England* (Charlestown, Mass.: Etheridge, 1804), p. 237 (on Quakers); Adams, *Summary History*, p. 23 (on Plymouth versus Massachusetts Bay); ibid., pp. 55–7, versus Morse-Parish, pp. 163–5 (on Rhode Island).

41 Adams, *Summary History*, pp. 72–3, versus Morse-Parish, p. 191 (on the founding of Harvard); Adams, *Summary History*, p. 513, versus Morse-Parish, pp. vii, 290. See William Gribben, "A Mirror to New England: The *Compendious History* of Jedidiah Morse and Elijah Parish," *New England Quarterly*, 45 (1972), 340–54, for further discussion of the argumentative strategies in Morse-Parish and how they altered in succeeding editions. Owing in good part to the fact that the orthodox considerably outnumbered the Arminians, notwithstanding the hegemony of the latter in eastern Massachusetts, Morse-Parish consistently outsold Adams by a large margin.

42 William Allen, *An American Biographical and Historical Dictionary* (Cambridge, Mass.: Hilliard, 1809); John Eliot, *A Biographical Dictionary* (Salem, Mass.: Cushing & Appleton, 1809; and Boston: Oliver, 1809). For reviews, see *Monthly Anthology*, 8 (1810), 321–35; 9 (1810), 116–28 (two-part review by J. T. Kirkland); and *Panoplist*, 5 (1809–10), 225–32, 370–3 (anon.)

43 Jedidiah Morse, "Biographical Sketch of the Rev. William Cooper," *Panoplist*, 2 (1807), 538.

44 *Anthology*, 5 (1808), 167–72 (on Callender); 6 (1809), 341–7 (on Ward); 7 (1809), 346–51, 414–21 (on Neal); 8 (1810), 420–5; 9 (1810), 49–55 (on Morton). All but the review of Ward were by John Eliot, Jeremy Belknap's protégé and ministerial colleague. It is much to Eliot's credit that he was even aware of the very rare and almost unknown *New English Canaan*.

45 Bancroft, *History* 3:398–9.

46 John Gorham Palfrey, *History of New England* (Boston: Little, Brown, 1876), 1:xv, 406–20; 2:453–85; 1:300–1.

47 Ibid., 1:101, 254.

48 Gribben, "A Mirror to New England," pp. 344–6. Gribben also argues, however, that the *Compendious History* was revised in such a way as to make it even more filiopietistic (p. 344).

49 Bancroft treats the Salem witchcraft episode as a tragic drama illustrating the death throes of Puritan theocracy, with Mather and the clergy at large as the villains, hoodwinking a well-meaning populace in order to maintain their eroding power (*History*, 3:73–7). Palfrey, much less tied than Bancroft to Unitarian progress theory, flatly rejects the hypothesis of Puritan declension in the seventeenth century, advances no such argument of arrogant priestcraft, yet makes an exception in the case of Mather, whom Palfrey depicts as conceited, credulous, "always infallible in his own eyes" (4:100, 114). Why? Certainly in part because Palfrey, by his own admission, relied heavily on Upham; also, perhaps, because Palfrey was a former pastor and historian of Brattle Street Church, whose founding Mather had opposed. Palfrey's memorial address, *Sermon Preached to the Church in Brattle Square* (Boston: Greenleaf, 1825) described Mather as "a man . . . whose character, intellectual and moral, has been sometimes astonishingly overrated" (p. 12).

50 See especially Samuel Middlebrook, "Samuel Peters: A Yankee Munchausen," *New England Quarterly*, 20 (1947), 75–87.

51 The *Anthology*, for example, did not deign to grace Backus' *History* with a retrospective review, nor did the Massachusetts Historical Society invite Backus to become a member, though it purchased at least one volume of his work (*Proceedings of the Massachusetts Historical Society*, 1 [1791–1835], 36) and accepted his donations from time to time.

52 Isaac Backus, *A History of New-England with Particular Reference to the Denomination of Christians Called Baptists* (rpt. New York: Arno, 1969), 2:231–2.

53 Universalism, the most recent and least reputable of the major Protestant

New England sects, was the most striking instance of this; see Chap. 8, n. 22. In his monumental study of *New England Dissent, 1630–1833* (Cambridge, Mass.: Harvard Univ. Press, 1971), William G. McLoughlin rightly claims that "essentially, the dissenters and the defenders of the establishment had . . . a far greater harmony of interest than they had in opposition" (2:1280).

54 Joseph S. Clark, *A Historical Sketch of the Congregational Churches in Massachusetts* (Boston: Congregational Board of Publication, 1858), pp. 226, 282.

55 See, for example, Orestes Brownson, "Protestantism Ends in Transcendentalism," *Brownson's Quarterly Review*, 3 (1846), 369–99; "Bancroft's *History of the United States*," *Brownson's Quarterly Review*, n.s., 6 (1852), esp. 421–58; C. Carroll Hollis, "Brownson on Native New England," *New England Quarterly*, 40 (1967), 212–26; Leonard Gilhooley, *Contradiction and Dilemma: Orestes Brownson and the American Idea* (New York: Fordham Univ. Press, 1972), pp. 179–84. In late life, Brownson renewed his friendship with fellow Democrat and quasi-Transcendentalist Bancroft, dedicating his *American Republic* (1866) to Bancroft as a "sort of public atonement" (Theodore Maynard, *Orestes Brownson: Yankee, Radical, Catholic* [New York, Macmillan, 1943], p. 341). Bancroft and Brownson shared what might loosely be called a Transcendentalist theory of social history, but Brownson came to locate the principle of authority in the institutional church rather than in the people.

56 Peter Oliver, *The Puritan Commonwealth* (Boston: Little, Brown, 1856), pp. 1, 332.

57 Ibid., pp. 73–4.

58 Ibid., pp. 167, 191.

59 Ibid., p. 151.

60 George E. Ellis, "Oliver's *Puritan Commonwealth*," *North American Review*, 84 (1857), 427, 432–3, 429, 431–2. For Ellis's anti-Matherism, see *North American Review*, 68 (1849), 92–3. For other Unitarian criticisms of Oliver, see Edward Everett Hale, "Our First Fathers, and Their First Children," *Christian Examiner*, 63 (1857), 259, and Palfrey, *History of New England*, 1:470n.

61 Oliver's thesis, however, as he was no doubt aware, was only an exaggerated version of a disdain for Puritanism that New England Episcopalians of the period tended to evince as a group. See, for example, William Tudor, *Letters on the Eastern States*, 2nd ed. (Boston: Wells & Lilly, 1821), p. 76, which discusses the "cruel character and appalling ferocity of this religious creed" (i.e., Puritan Calvinism). Tudor later prophesies that Episcopalianism will become increasingly popular in New England as a denominational alternative (p. 103). Coming from such a prominent man of letters as the founder of the *North American Review*, such anti-Puritan, pro-Anglican sentiments would have been much more familiar to Unitarian intellectuals than the shocked reviewers of Oliver suggest.

62 Francis Bowen, "Hildreth's *History*," *North American Review*, 73 [1851], 445. For the quotations, see Richard Hildreth, *History of the United States*, rev. ed. (New York: Harper & Brothers, 1880), 1:vii, 81; Bancroft, *History*, 1:93. Arthur Schlesinger, Jr., argues that it is doubtful whether Hildreth saw Bancroft as part and parcel of the sentimental school he was attacking: "The Problem of Richard Hildreth," *New England Quarterly*, 13 (1940), 226–9. Hildreth in fact acknowledged Bancroft as a scholarly source in the preface to his revised edition of vols.

1–3 (1:ix). Nevertheless, Hildreth certainly can be seen as putting himself in opposition to Bancroft's Romantic tone, even though he quite properly differentiated Bancroft from Forefathers' Day oratory.

63 Hildreth, *History*, 1:191–2, 282, 475–6, 492.

64 Bowen, "Hildreth's *History*," p. 411. Donald E. Emerson, *Richard Hildreth* (Baltimore: Johns Hopkins Univ. Press, 1946), summarizes a cross-section of reviews (pp. 131–4): "He was too devoted to his idea that history should be written as an undecorated account of the ascertainable facts" to satisfy Bostonians; at the same time, "He was too convinced of the errors of religious orthodoxy to keep his opinions of the colonial theocracy from showing through his austere, restrained account" (p. 139). This formulation rightly suggests that Hildreth's Olympian "objectivity" of perspective served, in his historical circumstances, as an instrument for satirical corrective.

65 W. F. Poole, "Hildreth's History of the United States," *Dial*, 1 (1880), 1–3.

66 Schlesinger, "Problem of Richard Hildreth," p. 224; Emerson presents a more plausibly complex picture, *Hildreth*, pp. 143–62.

67 *Christian Review*, 15 (1850), 193–202; *Universalist Quarterly*, 12 (1855), 344–64; *American Biblical Repository*, 3rd ser. 6, (1850), 376; *Christian Examiner*, 53 (1852), 306 (by George E. Ellis); Theodore Parker, "Hildreth's *History of the United States*," in *Critical Writings*, ed. Frances Power Cobbe (London: Trübner, 1865), 2:254–96. Emerson, *Hildreth*, pp. 167–8, points out that Hildreth became *the* standard in American history that the next generation (James F. Rhodes, Edward Channing, etc.) sought to rival.

68 Bowen, "Hildreth's *History*," p. 438. Hildreth's abolitionism might have been the reason why he was twice denied an appointment to Harvard's chair of history (losing out the first time to Francis Bowen). But as Emerson points out, abolitionism was only one of many points that Harvard would have been inclined to hold against an acerbic boat-rocker like Hildreth (*Hildreth*, p. 138), dominated as the institution was by the spirit of President Quincy's 1840 admonition to a young faculty member that "every officer of the Institution" should "abstain from any act tending to bring within its walls discussions upon questions on which the passions and interests of the community are divided, and warmly engaged" (quoted in Ronald Story, *The Forging of an Aristocracy: Harvard and the Boston Upper Class, 1800–1870* [Middletown, Conn.: Wesleyan Univ. Press, 1980], p. 76). When Charles Sumner tried to take up a collection for Hildreth in the 1860s, Edward Everett wrote him that Bostonians were reluctant to donate because of Hildreth's "unsympathizing account of the Pilgrim Fathers" (quoted in Schlesinger, "Problem of Richard Hildreth," p. 225).

69 *HW* 6:94; 11:279. Hawthorne took a Bancroftian view of the witchcraft delusion: "The ministers and wise men were more deluded than the illiterate people" (*HW* 6:78).

70 Harriet Beecher Stowe, *Poganuc People* (1878; rpt. Hartford: Stowe-Day, 1977), p. 174. For the contrast between Edwards and Mather, see Stowe, *Oldtown Folks*, ed. Henry F. May (Cambridge, Mass.: Harvard Univ. Press, 1966), p. 416.

71 Michael Bell, *Hawthorne and the Historical Romance of New England* (Princeton: Princeton Univ. Press, 1971), esp. pp. 34, 161–2. Two other studies shed additional light on antebellum fictions of Puritanism: Adelheid Staehlin-Wackernagel, *The Puritan Settler in the American Novel before the Civil War* (Bern: Francke, 1961), which discusses a few works not in Bell's useful bibliography, and John Caldwell Stubbs, *The Pursuit of Form: A Study of Hawthorne and the Romance* (Urbana: Univ. of Illinois Press, 1970), which, like Bell, treats Hawthorne in relation to the subgenre of Puritan historical romance. Bell, in particular, is required reading for a full understanding of the genre's conventions. Although all three of these works concentrate solely on fiction, much of what they say is also applicable to poetry and drama about Puritanism.

72 Sedgwick's earlier fictions were the trenchantly anti-Calvinist *New-England Tale* (1822), discussed in Chap. 16, and *Redwood: A Tale* (1824), where the effects of religious bigotry are satirized using the much safer example of Shakerism. For biographical background, see Mary E. Dewey, *Life and Letters of Catherine M. Sedgwick* (New York: Harper & Brothers, 1871) and Mary Kelley, *Private Woman, Public Stage* (New York: Oxford Univ. Press, 1984); for critical discussion of Sedgwick's historical themes, see Michael Bell, "History and Romance Convention in Catherine Sedgwick's *Hope Leslie*," *American Quarterly,* 22 (1970), 213–21.

73 Lydia Child, *The First Settlers of New-England* (Boston: Munroe & Francis, n.d.), p. 66: "Whatever objections there may be for people of different colors to unite," says the didactic mother-narrator to her children, "it would doubtless abundantly diminish the amount of crime, and we might thus testify our obedience to the will of our heavenly Father, who has made of one blood all the nations of men, that they may dwell together."

74 Lydia Child, *Hobomok* (1824; rpt. New York: Garrett, 1970), quotation from p. 187.

75 John P. Brace, *Fawn of the Pale Faces* (New York: Appleton, 1853), p. 9.

76 Review of Imitation Waverley Novels," *Christian Spectator,* 7 (1825), 90.

77 Thomas Robbins, *An Historical View of the First Planters of New-England*, p. 85.

78 See John P. McWilliams, "Fictions of Merry Mount," *American Quarterly,* 29 (1977), 3–30.

CHAPTER 10: FICTIONALIZING PURITAN HISTORY

1 See especially the critique of George Lukács' *Historical Novel* (1937) and Avrom Fleishman's *English Historical Novel* (1971) in Harry E. Shaw, *The Forms of Historical Fiction* (Ithaca: Cornell Univ. Press, 1983), pp. 19–30. See also Richard Waswo, "Story as Historiography in the Waverley Novels," *ELH,* 47 (1980), 304–30, for an ingenious if not wholly convincing inversion of the metahistorical argument that narrative history is a form of fiction: "If formal history can be constituted by literature, so literature can constitute an historiography" (304). Ursula Brumm's "Thoughts on History and the Novel," *Comparative Literature Studies,* 6 (1969), 317–30, lends support to Waswo's position that historical knowledge is conveyed in fiction through imaginative realization rather than through facticity.

2 Michael Colacurcio, "Footsteps of Ann Hutchinson: The Context of *The Scarlet Letter*," *ELH,* 39 (1972), 459–94; Colacurcio, *The Province of Piety: Moral*

History in Hawthorne's Early Tales (Cambridge, Mass.: Harvard Univ. Press, 1984), esp. "Prologue," "Polemical Introduction," "Problematic Conclusions"; Colacurcio, "The Sense of an Author: The Familiar Life and Strange Imaginings of Nathaniel Hawthorne," *ESQ,* 27 (1981), 118–19; Nina Baym, *The Shape of Hawthorne's Career* (Ithaca: Cornell Univ. Press, 1974), esp. pp. 31–2, 37; "Hawthorne," in *American Literary Scholarship, 1974,* ed. James Woodress (Durham: Duke Univ. Press, 1976), p. 25.

3 Catherine Maria Sedgwick, *Hope Leslie* (1826; rpt. New York: Garrett, 1969), 1:v; Eliza Buckminster Lee, *Naomi; or Boston Two Hundred Years Ago* (Boston: Crosby & Nichols, 1848), p. 85. Both authors, it should be added, issue qualifications on the other side.

4 Compare, for example, the treatments of Scott in Robert Kiely, *The Romantic Novel in England* (Cambridge, Mass.: Harvard Univ. Press, 1972), pp. 136–54, and George Levine, *The Realistic Imagination: English Fiction from Frankenstein to Lady Chatterley* (Chicago: Univ. of Chicago Press, 1981), pp. 81–106. By and large, Scott criticism since Georg Lukács's characterization of him as the father of bourgeois realism, in *The Historical Novel,* trans. Hannah Mitchell and Stanley Mitchell (1937, 1962; rpt. Lincoln: Univ. of Nebraska Press, 1983), pp. 30–63, has inclined more toward Levine's position. This view has been obliquely reinforced by those Americanists who, conceiving the difference between British and American fiction in terms of novel versus romance, tend to view the Americans as having pushed the romance beyond Scott; cf. Richard Chase, *The American Novel and Its Tradition* (Garden City, N.Y.: Doubleday, 1957), pp. 14–15, and Leslie Fielder, *Love and Death in the American Novel,* rev. ed. (New York: Dell, 1966), esp. Chap. 7.

5 See especially Scott's 1829 "General Preface" to the Waverley novels, the 1814 "Introductory" essay to *Waverley,* and the "Dedicatory Epistle" to *Ivanhoe,* in Mark A. Weinstein, ed., *The Prefaces to the Waverley Novels* (Lincoln: Univ. of Nebraska Press, 1978).

6 Mary Lascelles, *The Story-Teller Retrieves the Past: Historical and Fictitious History in the Art of Scott, Stevenson, Kipling, and Some Others* (Oxford: Oxford Univ. Press, 1980), pp. 2–14.

7 Levine, *Realistic Imagination,* pp. 93–4.

8 See particularly Terence Martin, *The Instructed Vision: Scottish Common Sense Philosophy and the Origins of American Fiction* (Bloomington: Indiana Univ. Press, 1965).

9 Andrew Peabody, "Philosophy of Fiction," *Christian Examiner,* 32 (1842), 10.

10 W. B. O. Peabody, "Waverley Novels," *North American Review,* 32 (1831), 387, 391.

11 *Christian Review,* 14 (1849), 212. This Baptist journal was understandably more convinced of Whittier's accuracy than the ultra-Calvinist *Christian Observatory,* 3 (1849), 187.

12 On this point, see Michael Bell, *Hawthorne and the Historical Romance* (Princeton: Princeton Univ. Press, 1971), pp. 149–90.

13 For a modern appraisal stressing the use of Margaret's point of view as unifying device, see Donald Ringe, "The Artistry of Whittier's *Margaret Smith's Journal*," *Essex Institute Historical Collections*, 108 (1972), 235–43.

14 Job Durfee, *Complete Works*, ed. Thomas Durfee (Providence: Gladding & Proud, 1849), pp. 5, 36. For information about Durfee, see *DAB*; Rowland Hazard, *Essay on Language, and Other Papers*, ed. Elizabeth Peabody (Boston: Phillips, Sampson, 1857), pp. 203–55; and Marvin E. Gettleman, *The Dorr Rebellion* (New York: Random House, 1973), pp. 74–7. For the pedagogical adaptation of *Whatcheer*, see Anne P. Child, *Whatcheer, A Story of Olden Times* (Providence: Knowles, Anthony, 1857). In fact the first well-researched biography of Williams, published two years after *Whatcheer*, differs from it only in a few particulars: James D. Knowles, *Memoir of Roger Williams* (Boston: Lincoln, Edmonds, 1834).

15 Scott, "Introductory," p. 10. The resemblance between the two passages was first noted by John C. Stubbs, "A Note on the Source of Hawthorne's Heraldic Device in *The Scarlet Letter*," *Notes & Queries*, 213 (1968), 175–6. The best general study of the Scott-Hawthorne relationship is Neal Frank Doubleday, *Hawthorne's Early Tales* (Durham: Duke Univ. Press, 1972), Chaps. 2–3. What allows Doubleday to perceive "how much Hawthorne was working in the tradition of Scott" (p. 49) is his recognition of the "gothic" element in Scott himself (p. 54). Cf. also Donald A. Ringe, *American Gothic: Imagination and Reason in Nineteenth-century Fiction* (Lexington: Univ. Press of Kentucky, 1982), pp. 78–9. With this recognition, and the resistance it provides to full acceptance of the Lukács tradition of placing Scott in the realist camp and the Trilling-Chase tradition of polarizing British and American fiction in terms of realism and romance, it becomes possible to align Scott and Hawthorne as practitioners of a mixed mode of fictional historicizing and to identify the Hawthornian emphasis on the symbolic as opposed to the mimetic as a variation within this mixed mode. The two parallel passages quoted here help to establish, both in stylistic level and in the symbolic contrast they draw between sable (prosaic) and gules (passional), the borderline quality of Scott's and Hawothorne's art.

16 As Michael Bell points out in *Hawthorne and the Historical Romance of New England*, pp. 17–81, the romancers' imaging of "the Puritan" was not monolithic but marked by polarization of moral opposites, the Puritan as hero versus the Puritan as bigot. In both roles, however, Puritanism was associated with the inauguration and consolidation of the social order, the preservation of which as an end in itself was seen by the romancers as assuming increasingly higher priority with the succession of generations – the major symptom of "declension" being perceived as this lapse into formalism. In that respect, the romancers of course reflected the Puritan-inaugurated tradition of the jeremiad, which in turn reflected the seventeenth century's own myth of declension.

17 Most readers have found the ending of *Seven Gables* abrupt and inconsistent with the preestablished givens of the romance. Perhaps the best defenses have been Francis Joseph Battaglia, "*The House of the Seven Gables:* New Light on Old Problems," *PMLA*, 82 (1967), 579–90, and John Gatta, Jr., "Progress and Providence in *The House of the Seven Gables*," *American Literature*, 50 (1978), 37–48. Both of these critics say that internal and external evidence shows Hawthorne did not consider humankind irredeemably fallen but instead was a cosmic optimist, albeit of a conservative sort. (Cf. also R. A. Yoder's article, "Transcendental Conservatism and *The House of the Seven Gables*," *Georgia Review*, 28 [1974], 33–51). Gatta, however, points out that this vision is not really dramatized on the social level: "It is only at the level of sacred or visionary history . . . that the teleological progress of the race is assured" (p. 45). Translating this into stylistic terms, we might say that the redemptive ending will convince readers intellectually to the extent that the narrative voice has previously been interpreted as signaling, through its tone of ironic detachment, a reservation about the predestinarian framework that has been invoked but such detachment tends to create a problem on another level by its contrast to the more sentimental tone of the ending.

18 The one significant critical discussion is Bell, *Hawthorne and the Historical Romance*, pp. 95–9; the standard biographical account is *DAB*, although further biographical information is extractable from Eliza Buckminster Lee's *Memoirs of Rev. Joseph Buckminster, D.D., and of His Son, Rev. Joseph Stevens Buckminster*, 2nd ed. (Boston: Ticknor & Fields, 1851), and *Sketches of a New-England Village* (Boston: Munroe, 1838). For further family background, see Lawrence Buell, "Joseph Stevens Buckminster: The Making of a New England Saint," *Canadian Review of American Studies*, 10 (1979), 1–29.

19 Lee, *Sketches*, pp. 4–6, 33, 22–3.

20 Lee, *Memoirs*, pp. 152, 190, 189, 145, 327, 25, 66.

21 Lee, *Naomi*, pp. 336; Bell, *Hawthorne and the Historical Romance*, pp. 97–8, 162, 176. The adjectives are Lee's.

22 Lee, *Naomi*, pp. 336, 410. For the text's summary appraisal of Hutchinson, see pp. 42–3.

23 Harry Houston Peckham, *Josiah Gilbert Holland in Relation to His Times* (Philadelphia: Univ. of Pennsylvania Press, 1940), pp. 1, 60, 70. For further biographical information, presented with more sympathy but less discrimination, see Mrs. H. M. Plunkett, *Josiah Gilbert Holland* (New York: Scribner, 1894). For the Holland-Dickinson relationship, see Richard Sewall, *The Life of Emily Dickinson* (New York: Farrar, Straus & Giroux, 1974), 2:593–625. To some extent, Holland figured in Dickinson's world as a lesser Higginson (i.e., as one of those male guardians of taste whose solidity and denseness were both important to her), although she was closer to Holland's wife than to Holland himelf.

24 Josiah Holland, *The Bay-Path: A Tale of New England Colonial Life* (1857; rpt. New York: Scribner, 1872) went through at least fifteen editions between 1857 and 1914. For Holland's treatment of the same material historiographically, see his *History of Western Massachusetts* (Springfield: Bowles, 1855), 1:21–44. For further historical information about the events of the book, I have relied on Mason A. Green, *Springfield, 1636–1886* (Springfield, Mass.: Nichols, 1888); *Colonial Justice in Western Massachusetts, 1639–1702: The Pynchon Court Record*, ed. Joseph H. Smith (Cambridge, Mass.: Harvard Univ. Press, 1961); Samuel G. Drake, *Annals of Witchcraft* (1869; rpt. New York: Blom, 1967), pp. 64–72, 219–58; Samuel Eliot Morison, "William Pynchon: The Founder of Springfield," *Proceedings of the Massachusetts Historical Society*, 64 (1931), 67–107; and Philip Gura, *A Glimpse of Sion's Glory* (Middletown, Conn.: Wesleyan Univ. Press, 1984), pp. 304–22.

25 The book was Holland's etiquette manual, *Titcomb's Letters to Young People* (1858). As the leader of a "Bible class of young men" during Porter's pastorate in Springfield, Holland had been accused of doctrinal laxity and insufficient reverence for the Old Testament (Plunkett, *Holland*, pp. 110–11). These, however, were simply symptoms of Holland's lifelong tendency to follow in the wake of conservative liberalization.

26 Holland, *Bay-Path*, p. 375.

27 See Kai Erikson, *Wayward Puritans: A Study in the Sociology of Deviance* (New York: Wiley, 1966), for a piece of historical sociology that in its pursuit (both theoretically and through illustration) of the thesis that a society is defined by the way it defines its deviants articulates the implicit premise of Holland's and many other antebellum fictional treatments of Puritanism.

28 See especially Robert S. Ward, "Longfellow's Roots in Yankee Soil," *New England Quarterly*, 41 (1968), 180–92.

29 Newton Arvin, *Longfellow* (Boston: Little, Brown, 1962), pp.86–99, 258–79. The best pertinent textual study, Edward L. Tucker's *The Shaping of Longfellow's "John Endicott"* (Charlottesville: Univ. Press of Virginia, 1985), tends, like Arvin, to see the unity of the overall trilogy as factitious but entertains a higher opinion of the merits of *The New England Tragedies* and demonstrates that "John Endicott" was meditated and composed with care.

30 Samuel Longfellow, *Final Memorials of Henry Wadsworth Longfellow* (Boston: Ticknor, 1887), p. 112; Edward Wagenknecht, *Longfellow: A Full-length Portrait* (London: Longman Group, 1955), p. 152.

31 Tucker, *Shaping of Longfellow's "John Endicott,"* pp. xlvi–l, summarizes the critical reaction. Also note Samuel Longfellow's insistence that *The New England Tragedies* "did not altogether satisfy" their author, "and with reason, as representing the modern phase of Christianity" (*Life of Henry Wadsworth Longfellow* [Boston: Ticknor, 1886], 2:458). Longfellow thought in 1871 of adding a "third play, to complete the third part of Christus," that would be "set among the Moravians at Bethlehem, Pennsylvania" (*Final Memorials*, p. 159), but this was never written. As Longfellow's editor, Horace Scudder, says, "It is most probable that Mr. Longfellow finally regarded the *Tragedies* as satisfying the requirements of the Trilogy" (*LW* 5:15), and even if that were not wholly the case it is interesting that Longfellow had to think of going outside the New England tradition in order to give the saga of Protestantism a happier ending. It is also worth noting that both Scudder and Longfellow's best early biographer, Thomas Wentworth Higginson (*Henry Wadsworth Longfellow* [Boston: Houghton Mifflin, 1902], pp. 236–47) took *Christus* very seriously, although Higginson did not care for *The New England Tragedies*.

32 Arvin, *Longfellow*, p. 277.

33 Quoted in Samuel Longfellow, *Life*, 2:151–2.

34 Samuel Longfellow, *Final Memorials*, 2:150. For the progress of *Christus*, see Tucker, *Shaping of Longfellow's "John Endicott,"* and Samuel Longfellow, *Life*, 2:171, 183, 191–2, 275–6, 285, 289, 325–7; *Final Memorials*, pp. 104–5, 112, 148–51, 153, 158–9, 171–3; *LL* 5:213, 217, 237, 547, 663. One point that is unclear is precisely when Longfellow began to conceive of *The New England Tragedies* as a part of *Christus*. The germ of the former (the "John Endicott" portion) Longfellow recorded in 1856 as a promising suggestion by a literary friend rather than as a premeditated part of the trilogy (Samuel Longfellow, *Life*, 2:275). Initially Longfellow seems to have had some doubt as to whether *The New England Trag-edies* should be published (*LL* 5:217, 237). We are left, finally, with Longfellow's ex post facto declaration on two occasions that the plan was a long-standing one.

35 Quoted in Samuel Longfellow, *Life*, 2:310.

36 Z. Swift Holbrook, "W. F. Poole and the New England Clergy," *Bibliotheca Sacra*, 57 (1900), 285–6. Longfellow also consulted Upham's work (*LL* 5:210).

37 Arvin, *Longfellow*, p. 275; Samuel Longfellow, *Final Memorials*, p. 104. Longfellow did not altogether avoid bombast. The use of Tituba as a *Macbeth*-like witch is an example.

CHAPTER 11: HAWTHORNE AND STOWE AS RIVAL INTERPRETERS OF NEW
ENGLAND PURITANISM

1 For the theological context of each work, see especially Michael Colacurcio, "Footsteps of Ann Hutchinson: The Context of *The Scarlet Letter*," *ELH*, 39 (1972), 459–94, and Lawrence Buell, "Calvinism Romanticized: Harriet Beecher Stowe, Samuel Hopkins, and *The Minister's Wooing*," *ESQ*, 24 (1978), 119–32. Sarah I. Davis, "Another View of Hester and the Antinomians," *Studies in Amer-ican Fiction*, 12 (1984), 189–98, adds some details to Colacurcio's account but is less careful in its inferences.

2 Michael Davitt Bell, *Hawthorne and the Historical Romance of New England* (Princeton: Princeton Univ. Press, 1971), pp. 149–90, discusses Hester (but not Mary) very shrewdly in relation to this tradition. For Mary's status as romance heroine, see Paul John Eakin, *The New England Girl* (Athens: Univ. of Georgia Press, 1976), pp. 27–48.

3 In taking this position I see myself not as repudiating but as supplementing, and thereby partially redirecting, the lines of thought pursued in previous studies of Hawthorne's relationship to Puritanism, all of which recognize an intimacy-distance, attraction–repulsion syndrome. Some studies of help to me in clarify-ing the general question of Hawthorne's rapport with Puritanism have been those of Colacurcio, "Footsteps of Ann Hutchinson," and *The Province of Piety: Moral History in Hawthorne's Early Tales* (Cambridge, Mass.: Harvard Univ. Press, 1984); Larzer Ziff, "The Artist and Puritanism," in *Hawthorne Centenary Essays*, ed. Roy Harvey Pearce (Columbus: Ohio State Univ. Press, 1964), pp. 245–69; Ursula Brumm, "Hawthorne's 'The Custom-House' and the Problem of Point of View in Historical Fiction," *Anglia*, 93 (1975), 391–412 (which calls attention to Hawthorne's "peculiar American selfconsciousness" in reconstructing the past, aggravated by the sense of Puritanism as an embarrassment); Paula K. White, "Puritan Theories of History in Hawthorne's Fiction," *Canadian Review of American Studies*, 9 (1978), 135–53 (which relates Hawthornian narratology to "providential" and "redemptive" modes of historical discourse); and William H. Shurr, "Eve's Bower: Hawthorne's Transition from Public Doctrines to Private Truths," in *Ruined Eden of the Present*, ed. G. R. Thompson and Virgil L. Lokke (West Lafayette, Ind.: Purdue Univ. Press, 1981), pp. 143–69 (which defines Hawthorne in terms of a Puritan-Transcendentalist polarity).

4 Harriet Beecher Stowe, *The Minister's Wooing* (Boston: Houghton Mifflin, 1896), p. 17.

5 Harriet Beecher Stowe, *Oldtown Folks*, ed. Henry F. May (Cambridge, Mass.: Harvard Univ. Press, 1966), p. 47.

6 Hawthorne's tendency to treat the typologically oriented Puritanism-to-Revolution consensus saga, as mediated by Bancroft and other early nineteenth-century historians, in varying but for the most part ironic lights is well demonstrated by John P. McWilliams, Jr., *Hawthorne, Melville and the American Character* (Cambridge: Cambridge Univ. Press, 1984), esp. Chap. 3; and by Michael Colacurcio, *Province of Piety*, esp. Chaps. 7–10.

7 Frederick Crews, *The Sins of the Fathers: Hawthorne's Psychological Themes* (New York: Oxford Univ. Press, 1965).

8 For this aspect of Stowe, see especially Charles Foster, *The Rungless Ladder: Harriet Beecher Stowe and American Puritanism* (Durham: Duke Univ. Press, 1954), as well as Marie Caskey, *Chariot of Fire: Religion and the Beecher Family* (New Haven: Yale Univ. Press, 1978), both of which discuss *The Minister's Wooing*, among other works, as coded autobiography. For a broad overview of Stowe's New England fictional vision, see Chap. 4 of Alice Crozier, *The Novels of Harriet Beecher Stowe* (New York: Oxford Univ. Press, 1964).

9 Foster, *Rungless Ladder*, pp. 91ff.

10 Quoted in Gloria C. Erlich, "The Paradox of Benevolence: Hawthorne and the Mannings," Ph.D. thesis, Princeton University, 1978, p. 9.

11 Charles Feidelson, "*The Scarlet Letter*," in Pearce, *Hawthorne Centenary Essays*, p. 32. In venturing to agree with Feidelson on this point I may risk overstating the psychological and epistemological as opposed to the moral and religious attraction of Puritanism for Hawthorne. This is a matter on which every reader must form an independent judgment. It does seem indisputable, however, that (1) Hawthorne was not reared as a Puritan, although his pious mother at one time apparently hoped he would become a minister; and (2) his mature faith, to the extent that a coherent picture can be reconstructed, seems to have incorporated distinctively Puritan elements very sparingly. For the most careful study of Hawthorne's theology, see Leonard J. Fick, *The Light Beyond* (Westminster, Md.: Newman, 1955). For biographical background, see Arlin Turner, *Nathaniel Hawthorne: A Biography* (New York: Oxford Univ. Press, 1980); James R. Mellow, *Nathaniel Hawthorne in His Times* (Boston: Houghton Mifflin, 1980); the sources mentioned in n. 12 below; and particularly Colacurcio, *Province of Piety*, pp. 21–8, which carefully argues from a review of the biographical evidence that "Hawthorne's natal mind and early sympathies were formed at a considerable distance from the various Calvinisms of his remote Puritan ancestors" (p. 24).

12 See Erlich, "Paradox of Benevolence"; her article "Hawthorne and the Mannings," in *Studies in the American Renaissance, 1980*, ed. Joel Myerson (Boston: Twayne, 1980) pp. 97–117, and her book *Family Themes and Hawthorne's Fiction* (New Brunswick, N.J.: Rutgers Univ. Press, 1984). Erlich's appraisal of the contrast in ostensible piety between the aunts and the uncles suggests that their proximity would have reinforced the young Hawthorne's suspicions as to the bankruptcy of Puritan theology. For additional information on family background, see also *HW* 15 (Hawthorne's early letters), Vernon Loggins, *The Hawthornes:*

The Story of Seven Generations of an American Family (New York: Columbia Univ. Press, 1951), and the following articles by Manning Hawthorne: "Parental and Family Influences on Hawthorne," *Essex Institute Historical Collections,* 76 (1940), 1–13; "Hawthorne's Early Years," *Essex Institute Historical Collections,* 74 (1938), 1–21; "Nathaniel Hawthorne Prepares for College," *New England Quarterly,* 11 (1938), 66–88; and "Nathaniel Hawthorne at Bowdoin," *New England Quarterly,* 13 (1940), 246–79.

13 See *EW* 10:397–433 for Emerson's public appraisal. Recent studies of Mary Emerson tend to stress her influence on her nephew; see Phyllis Cole, "The Advantage of Loneliness," in *Emerson: Prospect and Retrospect,* ed. Joel Porte (Cambridge, Mass.: Harvard Univ. Press, 1982), pp. 1–32, and Evelyn Barish, "Emerson and the Angel of Midnight: the Legacy of Mary Moody Emerson," in *Mothering the Mind,* ed. Ruth Perry and Martine Watson Brownley (New York: Holmes & Meier, 1984), pp. 219–37. Mary Emerson's influence probably had more to do with character than with creed, however. Albert J. von Frank, "Emerson's Unpublished Boyhood and Collegiate Verse," in *Studies in the American Renaissance, 1983,* ed. Joel Myerson (Charlottesville: Univ. Press of Virginia, 1983), notes that "Emerson may have reached the zenith of his orthodoxy before the age of ten" (p. 3).

14 To grant that Hawthorne was interested in Puritan history for family reasons does not necessarily mean, of course, that he identified with his patriarchal ancestors, as Nina Baym shows in "Nathaniel Hawthorne and His Mother," *American Literature,* 54 (1982), 1–27. Whether or not one accepts Baym's view that the "Puritans versus a defenseless woman equalled the Hawthornes versus his mother" (p. 10), the essay, along with Erlich's work, must be regarded as a significant challenge to the assumption that Hawthorne's ancestral identification was patrilineal.

15 No comprehensive scholarly study exists that speaks directly to this point, but it can readily be established by noting the relative absence of direct reference to the Edwardseans in the writings of the major Unitarians and Transcendentalists. References to Edwards are generally of a perfunctory, grudgingly respectful nature. References to his disciples are generally few and disparaging. Hawthorne's 1852 comment on Emmons (d. 1840) is entirely characteristic: Hawthorne refers to Emmons simply as an "old Orthodox minister" of whom he has heard only at second hand and whom he understands to have been a fusty anachronism (*American Notebooks, HW* 8:314). The most conspicuous exception to Unitarian-Transcendentalist lack of interest in Edwardseanism is William Ellery Channing's tribute to Samuel Hopkins (*Works* [Boston: Channing, 1841], 4:342–5), which, however, is hedged about with considerable qualification and is more accurately read as an index of Channing's generous spirit toward Hopkins, and toward Channing's Newport audience, than as an indication of significant Hopkinsian influence on Channing. For a scholarly appraisal of the relationship, see Conrad Wright, *The Liberal Christians* (Boston: Beacon Press, 1970), pp. 23–9.

16 A complete analysis of the fragmentation of Calvinism in the late eighteenth century would also take into account the intermediate category of Old Light or "moderate" Calvinists, who were the dominant conservative force within eastern Massachusetts Congregationalism until early in the nineteenth century. Several important contemporaries of Stowe and Hawthorne were descended from this background – e.g., Oliver Wendell Holmes and Elizabeth Barstow Stoddard.

17 Hawthorne, *American Notebooks, HW* 8:351–2, 323, 339. Hawthorne deals with the decline of piety under liberalism in several tales, e.g., "The Celestial Railroad" and "Passages from a Relinquished Work." The theological overtones of the latter are discussed in James Duban, "The Triumph of Infidelity in Hawthorne's *The Story Teller,*" *Studies in American Fiction,* 7 (1979), 49–60. One must appreciate, however, that criticism of religious liberalism was itself a tradition within liberalism (cf. Lawrence Buell, *Literary Transcendentalism* [Ithaca: Cornell Univ. Press, 1973], pp. 48–9). Thus Emerson, in a famous passage in "The Method of Nature," waxed wistful about the decline of "that old religion which, in the childhood of most of us, still dwelt like a sabbath morning in the country of New England," yet noted in his journal that "Calvinism suited Ptolemaism" (*EW* 1:135; *JMN* 4:26). In "Passages from a Relinquished Work," the doctrinally disparate alter egos, the storyteller and the evangelist, are both presented as rather pathetic characters. When Hawthorne contrasts the "cold, lifeless, vaguely liberal clergyman of our own day" with the "narrow but earnest cushion-thumper of puritanical times" and declares a preference for the latter (*HW* 8:339), one must appreciate that he has in fact disassociated himself from each. The patronizing tone here bespeaks not a neo-Calvinist commitment but rather a secularized sensibility, which, in the security of its own detachment from the rigors of the doctrinal system by which it was never personally oppressed, can indulge the luxury of looking back on the old ways with nostalgia. The passage just quoted, significantly, occurs in the context of a sustained Adamic-Transcendentalist reverie.

18 I.e., in "Mrs. Hutchinson," *Grandfather's Chair, The Scarlet Letter,* and "Main-Street."

19 S. W. S. Dutton, "Nathaniel Hawthorne," *New Englander,* 5 (1847), 61–7, excerpted in J. Donald Crowley, ed., *Hawthorne: The Critical Heritage* (London: Routledge & Kegan Paul, 1970), pp. 135–40. Dutton was not the only nineteenth-century Calvinist to read Hawthorne as a fellow traveler; see also Austin Phelps, "The Theology of 'The Marble Faun,'" in *My Portfolio* (New York: Scribner, 1882), pp. 130–9. However, Calvinist reviewers also expressed discomfort with Hawthorne's views (see Crowley, *Hawthorne,* pp. 138–40, and Martha Gale, "*The Marble Faun,*" (New Englander, 19 [1861], 860), and in general it is fair to say that the liberal Arminian critics of the *North American Review* and the *Christian Examiner* were definitely Hawthorne's most vigorous promoters among New England reviewers. See Crowley, *Hawthorne,* pp. 55, 64, 80, 86, 164, 250, 390, 412. Concerning "The Celestial Railroad," it might be noted that the attentiveness with which Bronson Alcott read and commended *Pilgrim's Progress* to his children is evidence that admiration of Bunyan did not necessarily correlate with theological orthodoxy (David E. Smith, *John Bunyan in America* [Bloomington: Indiana Univ. Press, 1966], esp. p. 95). Hawthorne's tale should be read more as an affectionate tour de force in reminiscence of a loved Protestant classic than as a serious warning against backsliding from Calvinism.

20 See Chap. 10, n. 2.

21 This is not to deny the very real possibility that Hawthorne may have been driven toward what comes across finally as a bogus concept because of a fascination that runs deeper than he chooses to acknowledge and that the sudden deliverance at the end represents the censorship of psychological inhibition, intertextual pressure from romance stereotypes, marketplace considerations, or some other motive. More on that below and in Chap. 16.

22 Charles Ryskamp, "The New England Sources of *The Scarlet Letter*," *American Literature*, 31 (1959), 265.

23 Colacurcio, "Footsteps," p. 476; *HW* 1:99.

24 Colacurcio, "Footsteps," pp. 486–93.

25 A particularly searching interpretation in this vein is Dennis Foster's "The Embroidered Sin: Confessional Evasion in *The Scarlet Letter*," *Criticism*, 25 (1983), 141–63; Foster observes that "Dimmesdale is careful never to confess any specific act which might interfere with his role as signifier of the divine" (p. 150) and that "by assuming the role of a *pharmakos*, the ritualistic victim who will carry the sins out of the community, he represents his sin as the preservation of the society" (p. 151). The latter point seems rather to describe the structure than the intent of Dimmesdale's confession, but some desire to maintain a position of spiritual centrality and leadership indeed seems manifest.

26 Fick, *Light Beyond*, p. 132, puts the problem correctly, if too judgmentally, when he observes that Hawthorne fails "to consider sin as primarily an offense against an all-good God," that "such penitence as he demands" seems to be a matter of reconciliation with fellow men rather than with God. This may not be an accurate statement of Hawthorne's private opinion on the issue, but it makes a valid point about Hawthorne's dramatic emphasis. Those critics who argue that the final scaffold scene undercuts Dimmesdale – Frederic I. Carpenter, e.g., in "Scarlet A Minus," *College English*, 5 (1944), 173–80 – tend to do so primarily in sympathy with Hester Prynne, but their position seems cogent in proportion to the doubts they are able to raise as to whether Dimmesdale's repentance is shown to be authentic and endorsed by the narrator. Conversely, those who defend Dimmesdale, like John Caldwell Stubbs in *The Pursuit of Form* (Urbana: Univ. of Illinois Press, 1970), pp. 81–102, succeed only to the extent that they can refute Fick's objection and make the case that Dimmesdale in fact "throws himself repentant before God."

27 For the orthodox view, see Jedidiah Morse and Elijah Parish, *A Compendious History of New England* (Charlestown, Mass.: Etheridge, 1804), pp. 165–6; Thomas Robbins, *An Historical View of the First Planters of New England* (Hartford: Gleason, 1815), pp. 114–5; and William Allen, *The American Biographical Dictionary*, 3d ed. (Boston: Jewett, 1857), p. 459. For the liberal view, see Hannah Adams, *A Summary History of New England* (Dedham, Mass.: Mann & Adams, 1799), pp. 58–61, and John Winthrop, *The History of New England from 1630 to 1649*, rev. ed., ed. James Savage (Boston: Little, Brown, 1853), 1:257n, 295n. The Arminian William Emerson, in *An Historical Sketch of the First Church in Boston* (Boston: Munroe, Francis, 1812), pp. 31–60, gives the most detailed early account. It is characteristic of the liberal line, though on the conservative side of it, in recognizing the Puritans' need to preserve law and order but sympathizing with Hutchinson's plight and noting that she was simply exercising the "rights of conscience" for the sake of which New England was originally settled (p. 58).

28 See Bell, *Hawthorne and the Historical Romance of New England*, pp. 149–90.

29 *HW* 1:195–6, 202. The most explicit Transcendentalist statement of the Hutchinson-Transcendentalist connection, linking Hutchinson with Fuller, is Caroline H. Dall, *Transcendentalism in New England: A Lecture* (Boston: Roberts, 1897), esp. pp. 6–7. Fuller herself appeals in passing to Hutchinson as a spiritual progenitor in *Woman in the Nineteenth Century,* Joel Myerson, ed., *Margaret Fuller: Essays on American Life and Letters* (New Haven: College and Univ. Press, 1978), p. 199.

30 Two reviewers were working toward this perception from an obtuse angle when they described the romance's denouement as a corrective to French libertinism à la George Sand (Crowley, *Hawthorne*, pp. 156–7, 162).

31 Stowe, *Minister's Wooing*, pp. 193–4; cf. *Poganuc People* (1878; rpt. Hartford: Stowe-Day, 1977), p. 255.

32 This process is traced in Amanda Porterfield, *Feminine Spirituality in America from Sarah Edwards to Martha Graham* (Philadelphia: Temple Univ. Press, 1980), which discusses Stowe, esp. pp. 71–6, in relation to *Uncle Tom's Cabin* and *Oldtown Folks*. See also Julie Ellison, "The Sociology of Holy Indifference: Sarah Edwards' Narrative," *American Literature,* 56 (1984), 479–95.

33 See Harriet Beecher Stowe, "Old Father Morris," in *Regional Sketches*, ed. John R. Adams (New Haven: College and University Press, 1972), pp. 75–80, and her "New England Ministers," *Atlantic,* 1 (1858), 485–92. Cf. Daniel Howe, *The Unitarian Conscience* (Cambridge, Mass.: Harvard Univ. Press, 1970), pp. 151–60. To some extent such differentiations were at cross-purposes with the tendency among both liberal and orthodox to picture the present generation as more refined than the preceding one; cf. Stowe, "Uncle Lot," in *Regional Sketches,* pp. 31–55, versus Emerson, "Ezra Ripley" (*EW* 10:379–95).

34 For studies applying Puritan typology to nineteenth-century literary practice, see especially Ursula Brumm, *American Thought and Religious Typology,* trans. John Hoaglund (New Brunswick, N.J.: Rutgers Univ. Press, 1970), which has a chapter on Hawthorne; Sacvan Bercovitch, *The Puritan Origins of the American Self* (New Haven: Yale Univ. Press, 1975); Mason Lowance, *The Language of Canaan* (Cambridge, Mass.: Harvard Univ. Press, 1980); and Karl Keller, "Alephs, Zahirs, and the Triumph of Ambiguity: Typology in Nineteenth-century American Literature," in Earl Miner, ed., *Literary Uses of Typology from the Late Middle Ages to the Present* (Princeton: Princeton Univ. Press, 1977), pp. 274–314. Keller rightly points out the looseness of most American Romantic typological thinking and rightly places Stowe closer to the Puritans in this respect. As regards Hawthorne, this diagnosis is confirmed by Brumm and by John E. Becker, *Hawthorne's Historical Allegory* (Port Washington, N.Y.: Kennikat, 1971), pp. 155–79, although see also n. 39 below.

35 For the typological interpretation of Canticles, see Lowance, *Language of Canaan,* pp. 41–54. The complex ironic links between the earthly union of Hopkins and Mary Scudder, the typological marriage figure, and the millennium are established by a series of passages scattered throughout the book; see esp. pp. 109, 148, 178, 299, 312–15.

36 *HW* 1:70, 143. For the exegetical–representative distinction, see Lowance, *Language of Canaan,* p. 4.

37 See Sacvan Bercovitch, "Endicott's Breastplate," *Studies in Short Fiction,* 4 (1967), 289–99, for a typological reading of "Endicott and the Red Cross" of a traditional kind.

38 See, for instance, the following treatments of the figure of John Endicott: Frederick H. Newberry, "The Demonic in 'Endicott and the Red Cross,'" *Papers on Language and Literature,* 13 (1977), 251–9; McWilliams, *Hawthorne, Melville, and the American Character,* pp. 25–48; and Colacurcio, *Province of Piety,* esp. pp. 221–38, 265–9.

39 Sacvan Bercovitch, *The American Jeremiad* (Madison: Univ. of Wisconsin Press, 1978), pp. 206–10, takes account of the ironic dimension of the scene while arguing that the irony does not undermine the "symbolic configuration" (208n). If by that is meant that, irony or no, we must interpret the scene using typological categories, I would unhesitatingly agree. Hawthorne surely raises the question, however, as to whether Dimmesdale's homiletic ritual may be nothing more than an empty sign. See Foster, "Confessional Evasion," and Millicent Bell, "The Obliquity of Signs: *The Scarlet Letter,*" *Massachusetts Review,* 23 (1982), esp. pp. 25–6.

40 Michael Bell, *The Development of the American Romance* (Chicago: Univ. of Chicago Press, 1980), p. 140. Bell's interpretation seems to have been inspired by Angus Fletcher's theory of allegory as daimonism, in *Allegory: The Theory of a Symbolic Mode* (Ithaca: Cornell Univ. Press, 1964), a notion that may not be quite so broadly applicable as Fletcher suggests but that Bell shows to be rooted in Hawthornian thinking.

41 See especially Michael Bell, *Development of the American Romance,* esp. pp. 140–2; Millicent Bell, "Obliquity of Signs," and Foster "Confessional Evasion"; Joel Porte, *The Romance in America* (Middletown, Conn.: Wesleyan Univ. Press, 1969), pp. 98–151; and William C. Spengemann's creatively eccentric reading of *The Scarlet Letter* in *The Forms of Autobiography* (New Haven: Yale Univ. Press, 1980), pp. 132–69.

42 James McIntosh, "The Instability of Belief in *The Blithedale Romance,*" *Prospects,* 9 (1984), 72.

43 Charles Edward Stowe, *Life of Harriet Beecher Stowe* (Boston: Houghton Mifflin, 1889), pp. 414–15. It has been argued that Stowe's regression began with her switch from slavery to New England history as her main fictional topic; see, for instance, James M. Cox, "Harriet Beecher Stowe: From Sectionalism to Regionalism," *Nineteenth-Century Fiction,* 38 (1984), esp. pp. 464–5.

44 Elizabeth Stuart Phelps, *Austin Phelps: A Memoir* (New York: Scribner, 1892), p. 206; Martha Gale, "*Marble Faun,*" p. 860.

45 On American detachment from and recoil against Puritan history in the later nineteenth century, see Jan C. Dawson's survey *The Unusable Past: America's Puritan Tradition, 1830 to 1930* (Chico, Calif.: Scholars Press, 1984).

Part IV: New England as a Country of the Imagination

CHAPTER 12: THE CULTURAL LANDSCAPE IN REGIONAL POETRY AND PROSE

1 Cecelia Tichi, *New World, New Earth: Environmental Reform in American*

Literature from the Puritans to the Present (New Haven: Yale Univ. Press, 1979), p. 81.

2 "Salmon River," in *The Literary Remains of John G. C. Brainard* (Hartford: Goodsell, 1832), p. 141.

3 Alexander Pope, *Windsor Forest* (1713), lines 1–2.

4 Larzer Ziff, *Literary Democracy: The Declaration of Cultural Independence in America* (New York: Viking Press, 1981), p. 195.

5 The standard history of the genre is Robert Arnold Aubin, *Topographical Poetry in XVIII-Century in England* (New York: Modern Language Association, 1936), which also includes the nineteenth century and considers American as well as British examples. See also Eugene L. Huddleston, "Topographical Poetry in the Early National Period," *American Literature,* 38 (1966), 303–22.

6 On this point see especially Earl Wasserman's discussion of *Cooper's Hill* in *The Subtler Language* (Baltimore: Johns Hopkins Univ. Press, 1959), pp. 53–88.

7 Timothy Dwight, *Greenfield Hill* (1794; rpt. New York: AMS, 1970), 2:166; Samuel Deane, *The Populous Village* (Providence: Miller & Grattan, 1826), p. 9.

8 Sarah Wentworth Morton, *Beacon Hill* (Boston: Manning & Loring, 1797), pp. 13–14.

9 Dwight, *Greenfield Hill,* 1:12–13.

10 Wordsworth, "The River Duddon," Sonnet iii, lines 8, 10; John Dyer, "Grongar Hill," lines 16–18, 1761 text, ed. Richard C. Boys (Baltimore: Johns Hopkins Univ. Press, 1941). Ultimately this motif has its sources in the theme of rural retirement in classical literature. In early national verse it may reflect that influence rather than any special association between America and romantic obscurity. Such is clearly the case, for instance, in "Pitch-wood Hill," by Samuel Deane the elder, a close imitation of Dyer's poem written in 1780 and published in 1785 (*Massachusetts Centinel,* March 16, p. 4). For Deane, the Americanization of landscape means the loss of obscurity (associated with privatistic, meditative retirement), because the forests have been cut for firewood and to permit more cultivation by the "peasants." Deane's patrician grumblings anticipate Thoreau, but only dimly.

11 *The Complete Poems of Frederick Goddard Tuckerman,* ed. N. Scott Momaday (New York: Oxford Univ. Press, 1965), p. 28.

12 The quotations represent a collage of four sources: Josiah Canning, "Poem Delivered at the Field Meeting, Bicentennial Celebration of the Turners Falls Fight," in *Connecticut River Weeds* (Boston: Cupples, 1892), pp. 24–5; S. D. Phelps, "Poem," in *Celebration of the Bi-Centennial Anniversary of the Town of Suffield, Conn.* (Hartford: Wiley, Waterman, & Eaton, 1871), p. 66; Charles Brimblecom, "Poem," in *A Memorial of the One Hundredth Anniversary of the Town of Barre* (Cambridge, Mass.: Wilson, 1875), pp. 185, 190; John Pierpont, "Poem," in *Litchfield County Centennial Celebration* (Hartford: Hunt, 1851), pp. 74–5, 99.

13 Jedidiah Morse, *The American Geography* (1789; rpt. London: Stockdale, 1792), p. 141; cf. *DT* 1:18.

14 Quotations from Thomas C. Upham, *American Cottage Life,* 3rd ed. (Portland: Sanborn & Carter, 1852), p. 65; Canning, *Connecticut River Weeds,* p. 4; and Lydia Sigourney, "The Connecticut River," in *Select Poems* (Philadelphia: Parry & McMillan, 1854), p. 17. Cf. also *DT* 2:220, 233; Brainard's "To the Connecticut River," in *Literary Remains*, pp. 58–65; and sundry fluvial tributes by Fitz-Greene Halleck and others, conveniently anthologized in Charles W. Everest, ed., *The Poets of Connecticut* (Hartford: Case, Tiffany, & Burnham, 1843). In sharp contrast to these purling lucubrations is A. A. Earle, "By the Connecticut," in *Green Mountain Poets*, ed. Albert J. Sanborn (Claremont, N.H.: Claremont Mfg. Co., 1872), pp. 297–9, which sees in the stream of time only the memory of the genocidal ferocity that began when the "despot band" from the "treach'rous Mayflower" turned its energies against the Indians immediately after giving thanks for a safe arrival. This poem represents a striking assimilation of one subgenre to another: The conventions of locodescriptive commemoration of the agrarian legacy of Puritanism are evoked and reappropriated in the service of a noble-savagist tribute to King Philip, Earle's hero here.

15 Quotations from Keats, "To Autumn," line 1; N. P. Willis, "The Cherokee's Threat," in *Portland Sketch Book*. ed. Ann Stephens (Portland: Colman & Chisholm, 1836), p. 252; P. H. Greenleaf, "Autumnal Days," in ibid., p. 120; "Wachusett," in *The Collected Poems of Ellery Channing the Younger*, ed. Walter Harding (Gainesville, Fla.: Scholars' Facsimiles and Reprints, 1967), p. 255–6.

16 Isaac McLellan, "Autumn," in *The Native Poets of Maine*, ed. S. Herbert Lancey (Bangor: Bugbee, 1854), p. 125; *LW* 1:332; G. N. Brigham, "Closing Seasons," in *Poets and Poetry of Vermont*, ed. Abby Maria Hemenway (Rutland: Tuttle, 1858), p. 190; James Thomson, *The Seasons:* "Autumn," lines 1321–2; Robert Lowell, "Mr. Edwards and the Spider," in *Lord Weary's Castle* (New York: Harcourt, Brace, 1946), p. 58.

17 Wallace Stevens, "Sunday Morning," *Collected Poems* (New York: Knopf, 1954), p.69.

18 Christopher P. Cranch, "Summer Dawn," in *Ariel and Caliban* (New York: Houghton Mifflin, 1887), p. 109; Channing, "New England," in *Collected Poems*, p. 160; Stevens, "Like Decorations in a Nigger Cemetery," in *Collected Poems*, p. 152.

19 Channing, "New England," pp. 170–1.

20 Among earlier studies that deal with aspects of regional prose in nineteenth-century New England, the following general works have been most helpful: Babette May Levy, "Mutations in New England Local Color," *New England Quarterly*, 19 (1946), 338–58; Benjamin Spencer, "Regionalism in American Literature," in *Regionalism in America*, ed. Merrill Jensen (Madison: Univ. of Wisconsin Press, 1951), pp. 219–60; Robert L. Russell, "The Background of the New England Local Color Movement," Ph.D. thesis, Univ. of North Carolina, 1968; Ann Douglas Wood, "The Literature of Impoverishment: The Women Local Colorists in America, 1865–1914," *Women's Studies*, 1 (1972), 3–45; Robert D. Rhode, *Setting in the American Short Story of Local Color, 1865–1900* (The Hague: Mouton, 1975); Alice Hall Petry, "Universal and Particular: The Local Color Phenomenon Reconsidered," *American Literary Realism*, 12 (1979), 111–26; Perry D. Westbrook, *Acres of Flint: Writers of Rural New England*, rev. ed. (Metuchen, N.J.: Scarecrow Press, 1981); and Josephine Donovan, *New England Local Color Literature: A Women's Tradition* (New York: Ungar, 1983).

21 For indications as to how these three genres developed in more "literary" directions, see Wayne Franklin, *Discoverers, Explorers, Settlers: The Diligent Writ-

ers of Early America (Chicago: Univ. of Chicago Press, 1979) (for travel writing); Philip Marshall Hicks, *The Development of the Natural History Essay in American Literature* (Philadelphia: Univ. of Pennsylvania, 1924); and Richard Slotkin, *Regeneration through Violence* (Middletown, Conn.: Wesleyan Univ. Press, 1973) (for the captivity narrative).

22 For testimony and discussion of the relationship of *The Sketch Book* to Hawthorne, Longfellow, and Whittier, see, for example, William Hedges, *Washington Irving* (Baltimore: Johns Hopkins Univ. Press, 1965), esp. Chap. 6; Newton Arvin, *Longfellow: His Life and Work* (Boston: Little, Brown, 1963), pp. 17–18; Edward Wagenknecht, *John Greenleaf Whittier: A Portrait in Paradox* (New York: Oxford Univ. Press, 1967), p. 129; and Neal Frank Doubleday, *Hawthorne's Early Tales* (Durham: Duke Univ. Press, 1972), esp. pp. 13–20, 51–72.

23 For discussion of Mitford's style and significance, see especially W. J. Keith, *The Rural Tradition: A Study of the Non-fiction Prose Writers of the English Countryside* (Toronto: Univ. of Toronto Press, 1974), pp. 83–103, the best study of the prose tradition equivalent to the topographical poetry tradition treated in its Neoclassical phase in Aubin, *Topographical Poetry*. Keith also has a chapter on Gilbert White (pp. 39–59). Mitford was probably the single British writer of this tradition who most strongly influenced American literature, particularly women writers; cf. Donovan, *New England Local Color Literature*, pp. 23, 32–8, and John L. Idol, Jr., "Mary Russell Mitford: Champion of American Literature," in *Studies in the American Renaissance, 1983*, ed. Joel Myerson (Charlottesville: Univ. Press of Virginia, 1983), pp. 313–34.

24 William Cullen Bryant, in his review of *Redwood* in *North American Review*, 20 (1825), 245–72, rightly saw it as setting a new standard of realistic mimesis.

25 Hale's regional myth making and cross-sectional comparatism is extensively and penetratingly discussed in William R. Taylor's *Cavalier and Yankee* (New York: Braziller, 1961). *Redwood* and *Northwood* may be said to have invented the structural device of fictive cross-sectional comparison through Yankee eyes. The device reached its antebellum culmination in Stowe's *Uncle Tom's Cabin* and its war era apogee in John W. De Forest's *Miss Ravenel's Conversion from Secession to Loyalty* (1867).

26 Richard D. Hathaway, *Sylvester Judd's New England* (University Park: Pennsylvania State Univ. Press, 1981), pp. 12–13.

27 John Neal, "New England as It Was," in *The Yankee* (1829), pp. 83, 146.

28 Warner Berthoff, *The Ferment of Realism* (New York: Free Press, 1965), p. 100.

29 Sylvester Judd, *Margaret: A Tale of the Real and the Ideal,* rev. ed. (1851; rpt. Boston: Roberts, 1891), p. 92–3.

30 Bernard R. Bowron, Jr., "Realism in America," *Comparative Literature,* 3 (1951), 274.

31 Rose Terry Cooke, "'Tenty Scran,'" *Atlantic Monthly,* 6 (1860), 591.

32 Ibid., pp. 600, 590–1.

33 F. O. Matthiessen, "New England Stories," in *American Writers on American Literature,* ed. John Macy (New York: Liveright, 1931), p. 411; Perry D. Westbrook, *Mary Wilkins Freeman* (New Haven: College and Univ. Press, 1967), p. 15.

34 Cooke, "'Tenty Scran,'" p. 591.

35 In this regard, see especially Thomas Bender, *Toward an Urban Vision: Ideas and Institutions in Nineteenth-century America* (Lexington: Univ. Press of Kentucky, 1975), and Bernard Rosenthal, *City of Nature: Journeys to Nature in the Age of Romanticism* (Newark: Univ. of Delaware Press, 1980). The first, stressing the example of Lowell, Massachusetts, emphasizes the nineteenth-century romance of technology; the second stresses the American enthusiasm for civilizing nature literally and metaphorically.

36 See n. 20 for citations.

37 Donovan, *New England Local Color,* plausibly discusses the story as an example of local colorist demolition of the "Cinderella Myth" (p. 72). Douglas, "The Literature of Impoverishment," does not deal directly with this work but could plausibly have appropriated it as an exemplum of psychological entrapment within provincialism. The manifest tone supports Donovan; Douglas might wish to demystify it as a defense mechanism.

38 Cf. the title story in Rose Terry Cooke's *Root-Bound* (1885).

39 Dwight, *Greenfield Hill,* 2:49–52.

40 Matthiessen, "New England Stories," p. 399. Some obvious signs of the influence of feminist scholarship in reviving interest in local colorism – in addition to the works by Donovan, Douglas, and Petry cited above – have been Leonore Hoffmann and Deborah Rosenfelt, ed., *Teaching Women's Literature from a Regional Perspective* (New York: Modern Language Association, 1982), and Emily Toth, ed., *Regionalism and the Female Imagination* (New York: Human Sciences Press, 1985).

41 For example, Donovan's characterization of "'Tenty Scran'" as an "unromantic look at a failed courtship" (p. 73) keys in on a crucial aspect, but the significance of the story as a literary and cultural document goes beyond this feminist nexus, important though that nexus is. The scholarship of Perry D. Westbrook is closer to my own approach of dealing with women authors in the context of general patterns of regional iconography to whose development writers of both sexes contributed. Westbrook too, however, has revised his work so as to take account of the "feminine domination" of local colorism (*Acres,* pp. viii and 8–10).

CHAPTER 13: THE VILLAGE AS ICON

1 Stowe, "Uncle Lot" (orig. "A New England Sketch," (1834), in *Regional Sketches,* ed. John R. Adams (New Haven: College and Univ. Press, 1972), pp. 31–2.

2 Ibid., p. 10.

3 For previous work on the relationship between literary depictions of New England towns and their social history, the court of first resort is Perry Westbrook, *The New England Town in Fact and Fiction* (Rutherford, N.J.: Fairleigh Dickinson Univ. Press, 1982), which also contains useful bibliographical notes, pp. 272–9. See also Ima Honaker Herron, *The Small Town in American Literature* (Durham: Duke Univ. Press, 1939), esp. pp. 28–145.

4 For historical background on New England towns and their development, see Michael Zuckerman, *Peaceable Kingdoms: New England Towns in the Eighteenth Century* (New York: Knopf, 1970); Percy Wells Bidwell, "Rural Economy in

New England at the Beginning of the Nineteenth Century," *Transactions of the Connecticut Academy of Arts and Sciences*, 20 (1916), 241–399; Joseph S. Wood, "The Origin of the New England Village," Ph.D. thesis, Pennsylvania State Univ., 1978; Percy Bidwell, "The Agricultural Revolution in New England," *American Historical Review*, 26 (1921), 683–702; Richard D. Brown, "The Emergence of Urban Society in Rural Massachusetts, 1760–1820," *Journal of American History*, 61 (1974), 29–51; Edward Chase Kirkland, *Men, Cities and Transportation: A Study in New England History, 1820–1900*, 2 vols. (Cambridge, Mass.: Harvard Univ. Press, 1948); Robert Doherty, *Society and Power: Five New England Towns, 1800–1860* (Amherst: Univ. of Massachusetts Press, 1977); Jack Larkin, "The View from New England: Notes on Everyday Life in Rural America to 1850," *American Quarterly*, 34 (1982), 244–61; Harold F. Wilson, *The Hill Country of Northern New England* (New York: Columbia Univ. Press, 1936); and Hal S. Barron, *Those Who Stayed Behind* (Cambridge: Cambridge Univ. Press, 1984). For background on the transplantation of the New England town model, see Lois Kimball Mathews, *The Expansion of New England* (Boston: Houghton Mifflin, 1909); Page Smith, *As a City upon a Hill: The Town in American History* (New York: Knopf, 1966); and Richard Lingeman, *Small Town America* (New York: Putnam, 1980).

5   Smith, *City upon a Hill*, p. 47.

6   *The Verse of Royall Tyler*, ed. Marius Péladeau (Charlottesville: Univ. Press of Virginia, 1968), pp. 194, 216.

7   Henry Ward Beecher, *Norwood: or, Village Life in New England* (1867; rpt. New York: Fords, Howard & Hulbert, 1890), p. 4; Lydia Sigourney, *Letters of Life* (New York: Appleton, 1866), p. 147; Oliver Wendell Holmes, *Elsie Venner* (Boston: Houghton Mifflin, 1891), p. 56.

8   Lydia Sigourney, "The Washington Elm," in Samuel Adams Drake, *A Book of New England Legends and Folklore* (Boston: Roberts, 1884), p. 117; *LoW* 10:74.

9   Catherine Albanese, *Sons of the Fathers: The Civil Religion of the American Revolution* (Philadelphia: Temple Univ. Press, 1976), p. 17.

10   Hannah Gould, "The Old Elm of Newbury," in Drake, *New England Legends*, p. 303.

11   Beecher, *Norwood*, p. 5.

12   Daniel W. Teller, *The History of Ridgefield, Conn.* (Danbury, Conn.: Donovan, 1878), pp. 165–79, prints Rev. Samuel Goodrich's description. For Samuel Griswold Goodrich's, see *Recollections of a Lifetime* (New York and Auburn: Miller, Orton, & Mulligan, 1856), 1:15–323. Also cf. Daniel Roselle, *Samuel Griswold Goodrich, Creator of Peter Parley* (Albany: State Univ. of New York Press, 1968), pp. 3–24.

13   Contemporary social historians tend to stress the gap between the pastoral literary image of small-town New England life in the nineteenth century and the actual facts of socioeconomic change. See, for instance, Robert Gross, "Lonesome in Eden: Dickinson, Thoreau, and the Problem of Community in Nineteenth-century New England," *Canadian Review of American Studies*, 14 (1983), 1–17, and other essays by Gross cited in Chap. 14, n. 24, for a salutary jolt to the standard impression among literary scholars that mid-nineteenth-century Concord and Amherst were actually such self-contained country villages as a casual

reading of Dickinson and Thoreau might suggest. On the other hand, Perry Westbrook, *The New England Town in Fact and Fiction* (n. 3), also seems correct in arguing for at least a vestigial persistence to this day, in the remoter districts of New England, of the institutions celebrated in Dwight's *Greenfield Hill*.

14 Goodrich, Sr., *apud* Teller, *History of Ridgefield*, p. 179.

15 Ibid., pp. 176–7; Goodrich, Jr., *Recollections*, 1:83.

16 Goodrich, *Recollections*, 1:312, 317, 305, 309; Teller, *History of Ridgefield*, p. 240.

17 Goodrich, *Recollections*, 1:13.

18 Hawthorne, "My Home Return," from "Fragments of the Journal of a Solitary Man," *HW*, 11:323; see also "Passages from a Relinquished Work," *HW*, 10:405–21.

19 "A Town, to Those Who Dwell Therein, Well Known," *Farmer's Weekly Museum*, August 21, 1797, p. 4.

20 *Verse of Royall Tyler*, p. 116.

21 Jeremy Belknap, *The History of New-Hampshire* (1792; rpt. New York: Johnson Reprints, 1970), 3:251.

22 Belknap to Ebenezer Hazard, December 21, 1783, *Collections of the Massachusetts Historical Society*, ser. 5, 2 (1877), 287–88.

23 Sarah J. Hale, *Northwood; or, Life North and South* (1827; New York: Long, 1852), p.8.

24 Sylvester Judd, *Margaret: A Tale of the Real and the Ideal*, rev. ed. (1851; rpt. Boston: Roberts, 1891), pp. 55–6.

25 Richard Hathaway, *Sylvester Judd's New England* (University Park: Pennsylvania State University Press, 1981), p. 62. This is an exceptionally sensitive study of the relationship between village experience and its literary embodiment.

26 In *A Fable for Critics*, Lowell called *Margaret* "the first Yankee book / With the *soul* of Down East in 't" (*LoW* 9:80). Margaret Fuller had praised it in somewhat similar terms (*Papers on Literature and Art* [New York: Wiley, 1846], 2:137), though overstressing its natural piety and idealizing elements.

27 Holmes, *Elsie Venner*, pp. 23–4.

28 On this point, see especially Perry D. Westbrook, *Acres of Flint*, rev. ed. (Metuchen, N.J.: Scarecrow Press, 1981), and Wilson, *Hill Country of Northern New England* (n. 4).

29 "Some Recollections of a Village," *New England Magazine*, 2 (1832), 192; Goodrich, *Recollections*, 1:88; Charles Eastman, "The Town Pauper's Burial," in *Poems* (Montpelier: Eastman & Danforth, 1848), pp. 24–5; cf. William Ray, "Village Greatness," in Charles W. Everest, ed., *The Poets of Connecticut* (Hartford: Case, Tiffany, & Burnham, 1843), pp. 121–2. The plight of the town poor, at the mercy of local miserliness, is an increasingly insistent theme in local color writing.

30 Hale, *Northwood*, p. 11; Beecher, *Norwood*, p. 181; Alonzo Lewis, "The Schoolmaster," in *Poetical Works*, ed. Ion Lewis (Boston: Williams, 1883), pp. 58–9.

31 Harriet Beecher Stowe, *Poganuc People* (1878; rpt. Hartford: Stowe-Day, 1977), p. 151; Royall Tyler, *The Algerine Captive*, ed. Don L. Cook (New Haven: College & Univ. Press, 1970), p. 50; Dwight, *Greenfield Hill*, 2:372, 381–2.

CHAPTER 14: LOCOCENTRISM FROM DWIGHT TO THOREAU

1 Little work has been done on Dwight-Thoreau affinities apart from Walter Harding's "Thoreau and Timothy Dwight," *Boston Public Library Quarterly,* 10 (1958), 109–15. Kathryn Whitford, "Excursions into Romanticism: Timothy Dwight's *Travels,"* *Papers on Language and Literature,* 2 (1966), 225–33, suggests the possibility of further parallels on the basis of Dwight's crypto-Romanticism, though she overemphasizes the latter.

2 Joan Burbick, "Henry David Thoreau: The Uncivil Historian," in *The American Renaissance: New Dimensions,* ed. Harry R. Garvin and Peter C. Carafiol (Lewisburg, Pa.: Bucknell Univ. Press, 1983), p. 83. It should be added, however, that this "uncivility" involves an extension of a kindred sense of wonder and interest in curious local fact and legend displayed by more conventional New England historicizers, both Puritan and early national, including Dwight. On this point, see especially Philip Gura, "Thoreau and John Josselyn," *New England Quarterly,* 48 (1975), 505–18, and Eugene Green, "Reading Local History: Shattuck's *History,* Emerson's *Discourse,* and Thoreau's *Walden,"* *New England Quarterly,* 50 (1977), 303–14.

3 See especially Leo Marx, *The Machine in the Garden: Technology and the Pastoral Ideal in America* (New York: Oxford Univ. Press, 1964), pp. 242–65, which traces the tortuousness with which the speaker in *Walden* attempts to assimilate such technological incursions as the railroad by transmuting them into natural imagery, a tactic that, as Marx points out, in effect removes the "pastoral hope. . . . from history, where it is manifestly unrealizable, and relocates it in literature," which, after all was "its traditional location" (p. 265).

4 Thoreau, *A Week on the Concord and Merrimack Rivers,* ed. Carl F. Hovde, William L. Howarth, and Elizabeth Hall Witherill (Princeton: Princeton Univ. Press, 1980), p. 54. Dwight, by contrast, "prefers civilized landscapes that display evidences of economic prosperity and order" (John Sears, "Timothy Dwight and the American Landscape," *Early American Literature,* 11 [1977], 316).

5 See Chap. 4, pp. 92–3.

6 Thoreau, *Cape Cod and Miscellanies* (Boston: Houghton Mifflin, 1906), p. 21.

7 Thoreau's passion for limits, as a concomitant of his poeticizing, is discussed in Lewis H. Miller, Jr., "The Artist as Surveyor in *Walden* and *The Maine Woods,"* *ESQ,* 21 (1975), 76–81. William Howarth, *The Book of Concord* (New York: Viking Press, 1982), makes plain the strength of Thoreau's interest in "natural philosophy" on the literal level.

8 Thoreau's sense of oppression by the town establishment has been remarked by all of his biographers. See especially Richard Lebeaux's Eriksonian study *Young Man Thoreau* (Amherst: Univ. of Massachusetts Press, 1977), and its sequel, *Thoreau's Seasons* (Amherst: Univ. of Massachusetts Press, 1984). For the larger psychohistorical significance of this biographical difference from Dwight, see especially George Forgie, *Patricide in the House Divided: A Psychological Interpretation of Lincoln and His Age* (New York: Norton, 1979), which reflects shrewdly in Chapter 1 and elsewhere on early nineteenth-century disaffection with having been born in a postheroic age, which saw the Revolutionary fathers

as having "end[ed] history and replace[d] it with a kind of domestic timelessness" (p. 49).

9 The limits of Thoreau's relish for actual wilderness is best illustrated by "Ktaadn." For discussions, see James McIntosh, *Thoreau as Romantic Naturalist* (Ithaca: Cornell Univ. Press, 1974), pp. 188–215, and Ronald Wesley Hoag, "The Mark on the Wilderness: Thoreau's Contact with Ktaadn," *Texas Studies in Literature and Language*, 24 (1982), 23–46.

10 Frederick Garber, *Thoreau's Redemptive Imagination* (New York: New York Univ. Press, 1977), p. 45. The discussions I especially have in mind are those of Garber and McIntosh, *Thoreau as Romantic Naturalist*. McIntosh characterizes Thoreau as a "mugwump, sitting resolutely on the fence between mind and nature" (pp. 20–1).

11 Marx, *Machine in the Garden*, p. 245, which discusses *Walden* as a version of pastoral.

12 John R. Stilgoe, *Common Landscape of America, 1580–1845* (New Haven: Yale Univ. Press, 1982), pp. 51–2.

13 Stanely Cavell, *The Senses of Walden*, rev. ed. (San Francisco: North Point Press, 1981), pp. 8–10.

14 John Hildebidle, *Thoreau: A Naturalist's Liberty* (Cambridge, Mass.: Harvard Univ. Press, 1983), p. 122.

15 Thoreau, *Week*, pp. 17–18.

16 J. Lyndon Shanley, *The Making of "Walden"* (Chicago: Univ. of Chicago Press, 1957), pp. 55–101. For the seasonal metaphor in *Walden*, see especially Sherman Paul, *The Shores of America: Thoreau's Inward Exploration* (Urbana: Univ. of Illinois Press, 1958), pp. 293–353.

17 The surviving *Journal* material from Thoreau's first summer at Walden (*TJ* 2:155–79) shows that his first formulation of the experience was aggressively universalized (in terms of Homeric epic) rather than local. As a result of his expanded particularization of the experience, however, the metaphorical and mythic overtones found their place in the final version as symbolic extensions or ultimate implications of the local, rather than as the predetermined schema in terms of which the local is viewed.

18 For the traditional "sacral" ordering of New England space, see Stilgoe, *Common Landscape;* D. W. Meinig, "Symbolic Landscapes: Some Idealizations of American Communities," in Meinig, ed., *The Interpretation of Ordinary Landscapes* (New York: Oxford Univ. Press, 1979), pp. 165–7; Peter N. Carroll, *Puritanism and the Wilderness* (New York: Columbia Univ. Press, 1969); and Perry D. Westbrook, *The New England Town in Fact and Fiction* (Rutherford, N.J.: Fairleigh Dickinson Univ. Press, 1982), pp. 15–25, which uses *Greenfield Hill* as its paradigm case from literature. For the best discussion of the lengths to which Thoreau went in constructing an alternative, personalized symbolic geography of Concord, see William L. Howarth, "Travelling in Concord: The World of Thoreau's Journal," in *Puritan Influences in American Literature*, ed. Emory Elliott (Urbana: Univ. of Illinois Press, 1979), pp. 143–66. See also Reginald Cook, "Ancient Rites at Walden," *ESQ*, 39 (1965), 52–6. An interesting parallel between Thoreauvian decentering and Second Awakening camp-meeting–style revivalism suggests itself when one reads J. B. Jackson, "The Sacred Grove in

America," in *The Necessity for Ruins and Other Topics* (Amherst: Univ. of Massachusetts Press, 1980): "Whenever the existing spatial order proves too restrictive, new sacred groves or their equivalent will be discovered and used" (p. 88).

19 Kenneth Silverman, *Timothy Dwight* (New York: Twayne, 1969), p. 118. The chapter where this remark appears provides (pp. 114-36) one of the two best critical appraisals of Dwight's *Travels*, the other being Barbara Solomon's introduction to her John Harvard Library edition of *The Travels*.

20 Thoreau, *Cape Cod*, pp. 60, 51-2, 249; *DT* 3:60.

21 Hildebidle, *Thoreau*, p. 5.

22 Thoreau, *Week*, p. 5.

23 Ibid., pp. 168-9.

24 Robert Gross, "'The Most Estimable Place in All the World': A Debate on Progress in Nineteenth-Century Concord," *Studies in the American Renaissance, 1978*, ed. Joel Myerson (Boston: Twayne, 1978), p. 9. See also Gross, "Agriculture and Society in Thoreau's Concord," *Journal of American History*, 69 (1982), 42-61, and Philip R. Yannella, "Socio-Economic Disarray and Literary Response: Concord and *Walden*," *Mosaic*, 14 (1981), 1-24.

25 Gross extends his analysis of Thoreau's response to Concord in a most interesting comparative study, "Lonesome in Eden: Dickinson, Thoreau, and the Problem of Community in Nineteenth-century New England," *Canadian Review of American Studies*, 14 (1983), 1-17, which relates the isolation of the two authors to the rise of privatism that accompanied the economic transformations of village life in nineteenth-century New England. For a complementary approach to Thoreau's ambivalence toward enterprise, see Michael Gilmore's diagnosis of the composition and text of *Walden* as responses to the pressure of literary commercialism, in "*Walden* and the Curse of Trade," in *The American Writer and the Marketplace* (Chicago: Univ. of Chicago Press, 1985), pp. 35-51.

26 Stanley Cavell, *Senses of Walden*, p. 60. Among Thoreau's commentators, Cavell is particularly astute in sensing how the speaker's aesthetic and temporal distance from the experiment becomes written into the text of *Walden*.

27 Richard Bridgman, in *Dark Thoreau* (Lincoln: Univ. of Nebraska Press, 1982), pp. 130-4, the best recent discussion, seems likewise of the opinion that Thoreau was not fully in control of his connotations.

28 David Lowenthal, "The American Scene," *Geographical Review*, 58 (1968), 65.

29 Cf. McIntosh, *Thoreau as Romantic Naturalist*, pp. 285-8; Garber, *Thoreau's Redemptive Imagination*, pp. 38-46.

CHAPTER 15: COMIC GROTESQUE

1 Timothy Dwight, *Greenfield Hill* (1794; rpt. New York: AMS Press, 1970), 1:39-41.

2 *EW* 8:155-74; 12:405-17.

3 The following studies have been especially helpful. Among general works on American humor, see Constance Rourke, *American Humor* (New York: Harcourt, Brace, 1931); Walter Blair, *Native American Humor* (1937; rpt. San Francisco: Chandler, 1960); Jesse Bier, *The Rise and Fall of American Humor* (New York: Holt, Rinehart and Winston, 1968); Walter Blair and Hamlin Hill, *Ameri-*

ca's Humor from Poor Richard to Doonesbury (New York: Oxford Univ. Press, 1978). Among studies of New England humor, comic folklore, and its literary applications, see Richard Dorson, "The Yankee on Stage: A Folk Hero of American Drama," *New England Quarterly,* 13 (1940), 467–93; Dorson, *Jonathan Draws the Long Bow* (Cambridge, Mass.: Harvard Univ. Press, 1946); Ben A. Botkin, ed., *A Treasury of New England Folklore,* rev. ed. (New York: Bonanza, 1955); Laurence P. Springarn, "The Yankee in Early American Fiction," *New England Quarterly,* 31 (1958), 484–95; Daniel Hoffman, *Form and Fable in American Fiction,* rev. ed. (1965; rpt. New York: Norton, 1973), esp. pp. 33–82; Cecil D. Eby, "Yankee Humor," in Louis D. Rubin, ed., *The Comic Imagination in American Literature* (New Brunswick, N.J.: Rutgers Univ. Press, 1973), pp. 77–84.

4 Poem titles from Paul Allen, *Original Poems* (Salem, Mass.: Cushing, 1801), p. 64; *Farmer's Weekly Museum,* August 16, 1796.

5 On the subject of Manly's priggishness, see Donald T. Siebert, Jr., "Royall Tyler's 'Bold Example': *The Contrast* and the English Comedy of Manners," *Early American Literature,* 13 (1978), 3–11, which overstates the case against Manly but raises serious questions about the legitimacy of taking him as a center of values.

6 Dorson, "Yankee on Stage," pp. 479–83. In Woodworth's melodrama involving two affairs between city men and country girls (the virtuous man succeeds, the foppish seducer is repulsed), there are actually two leading male rustics. William, an idealized farmer (to whom the fop is an antagonist) speaks standard English; Jonathan, a more fully Yankeeized figure, speaks in dialect. William is a democratized version of Colonel Manly; Jonathan represents a partial sentimentalization of two stereotypes – that of the rustic bumpkin (underlying Tyler's Jonathan) and that of the sharp-dealing Yankee (see below). Jonathan has enough keen wit and canniness to be above the bumpkin level, but he is too ineffectual and good-hearted to be a real trickster.

7 During the Neoclassical period, when it was more fashionable to mock the untutored voice than to assume it, writers who did the latter underwent some interesting contortions. Charles Prentiss' "Sailor's Description of a Modern Newlight Preacher," for example (in *A Collection of Fugitive Pieces* [Leominster, Mass.: pvt., 1797], pp. 77–8), uses one provincial voice to undercut another:

> A damned saucy fellow, with a damned ugly face,
> First gave us a damned long account of the place
> Created for those poor damned souls who've no grace:
> Told what a damned parcel of brimstone was there;
> How damned hot the country, damned filthy the air;
> How the damned fires would burn, and the damned devils stare,
> How the damned smoke would roll, and the damned pitchforks fly –
> And when some old women set up a damned cry,
> He dropt the damned sermon – and damned glad was I.

A more typical, less oblique contemporary mode of this kind was Federalist anti-Jefferson satire. For a notable example, see John Quincy Adams, "The Discoveries of Captain Lewis," *Monthly Anthology* (1807), reprinted in Lewis P. Simpson, ed., *The Federalist Literary Mind* (Baton Rouge: Louisiana State Univ. Press,

1962), pp. 58–62. For discussion of the underlying Federalist position, see Linda Kerber, *Federalists in Dissent* (Ithaca: Cornell Univ. Press, 1970), pp. 67–94.

8   Rourke, *American Humor,* p. 31: "But again the character of the legendary Yankee was altered. The backwoodsman, rising in the West, was also destined to command the national horizon."

9   For instance, Major Jack responds thus to the boasting of a Georgia Jacksonian: "Says he, 'can you shoot a rifle, Major?' 'Pretty considerable,' said I. 'I can hit a chip in the air,' says he, 'five times out of six shots.' Says I, 'well I can beat that I guess, for I can hit one seven times in four shots.' 'Well,' says he, 'that's enuf, we won't waste powder, and I knock under'" (*Letters Written during the President's Tour 'Down East'* [1833; rpt. Freeport, N.Y.: Books for Libraries, 1969], p. 37).

10   Milton Rickels and Patricia Rickels aptly describe Downing as a mixture of "sentimental and comic versions of pastoral" but treated more with condenscension than idealization (*Seba Smith* [Boston: Twayne, 1977], p. 27). Pp. 24–71 of their study has the fullest analysis of the Downing letters, an illuminating one although it overplays the anti-Jacksonian implications. More balanced in this respect is Walter Blair, *Horse Sense in American Humor* (Chicago: Univ. of Chicago Press, 1942), pp. 51–76. For comments on Downing's later adventures when the series was revived in the 1840s, see John H. Schroeder, "Major Jack Downing and American Expansionism," *New England Quarterly,* 50 (1977), 214–33.

11   Robert Frost, preface to Stephen Burroughs, *Memoirs of the Notorious Stephen Burroughs* (New York: Dial Press, 1924), p. vii.

12   Burroughs, *Memoirs,* pp. 55–7.

13   The possibility of a connection linking Emerson and American humor generally was first called to my attention by Joel Porte's stimulating essay, "Transcendental Antics," in *Veins of Humor,* ed. Harry Levin (Cambridge, Mass.: Harvard Univ. Press, 1972), pp. 167–73.

14   For both original and revised versions (the latter less colloquial), see Porter Gale Perrin, *Thomas Green Fessenden* (Orono: Univ. of Maine Press, 1925), pp. 186–92.

15   Blair and Hill, *America's Humor,* pp. 172–9, emphasize this point about literary New England humor from the Connecticut Wits through Lowell and Holmes.

16   Samuel Kettell, "Josh Beanpole's Courtship," in *Yankee Notions* (Boston: Otis, Broadus, 1838), pp. 119–35; Asa Greene, *The Life and Adventures of Dr. Dodimus Duckworth* (New York: Hill, 1833); William L. McClintock, "Courtship," in *The New Hampshire Book* (Nashua, N.H.: Marshall, 1842), pp. 152–8; "A Love Story," *Yankee Blade* (1851), in Dorson, *Jonathan Draws the Long Bow,* pp. 98–9.

17   These works are to be found in Mary Wilkins Freeman's first two collections, *A Humble Romance and Other Stories* (New York: Harper & Brothers, 1887) and *A New England Nun and Other Stories* (New York: Harper & Brothers, 1891). Quotations from *Humble Romance,* pp. 31, 36.

18   Freeman, *New England Nun,* p. 17.

19   Botkin, *Treasury,* p. 10.

20   Joseph Moldenhauer, "Paradox in Walden" (1964; rpt. in *The Recognition of*

Henry David Thoreau, ed. Wendell Glick [Ann Arbor: Univ. of Michigan Press, 1969]), pp. 358-9. Charles R. Anderson extends this line of discussion in *The Magic Circle of Walden* (New York: Holt, Rinehart & Winston, 1968), pp. 47-56.

21 Forrest Wilson, *Crusader in Crinoline: The Life of Harriet Beecher Stowe* (Philadelphia: Lippincott, 1941), p. 531.

22 Harriet Beecher Stowe, *Oldtown Folks*, ed. Henry F. May (Cambridge, Mass.: Harvard Univ. Press, 1966), p. 74.

23 Harriet Beecher Stowe, *Sam Lawson's Oldtown Fireside Stories* (1892; rpt. Ridgewood, N.J.: Gregg Press, 1967), pp. 205-6.

24 Stowe, *Oldtown Folks*, p. 283.

25 Ibid., pp. 391-2.

CHAPTER 16: PROVINCIAL GOTHIC

1 In this chapter the terms *gothic* and *grotesque* are used in overlapping senses – *gothic* to denote a more or less specific cluster of conventions that emanate originally from the English gothic novel but become much more loose and various over the course of time, and *grotesque* to denote what I take to be the primary gothic effect of stylized distortion.

2 The American mutations of provincial gothic have so far been studied piecemeal. The most ambitious work on gothicism in American literature, Leslie A. Fiedler, *Love and Death in the American Novel*, rev. ed. (New York: Dell, 1966), does not concentrate on its regional aspect, which students of southern writing have been quickest to identify: e.g., William Van O'Connor, "The Grotesque in Modern American Fiction," *College English*, 20 (1959), 342-6, and Frederick J. Hoffman, *The Art of Southern Fiction* (Carbondale: Southern Illinois Univ. Press, 1967), pp. 115-43. Among New England writers, the gothicism of Hawthorne has of course been most closely examined; see especially Jane Lundblad, *Nathaniel Hawthorne and European Literary Tradition* (Cambridge, Mass.: Harvard Univ. Press, 1947), which correlates standard gothic motifs and Hawthornian practice in a literal-minded way useful to the beginning student; Taylor Stoehr, *Hawthorne's Mad Scientists* (Hamden, Conn.: Archon, 1978), pp. 252-75; Donald A. Ringe, *American Gothic* (Lexington: Univ. Press of Kentucky, 1982), pp. 152-76; and Ronald R. Curran, "'Yankee Gothic': Hawthorne's 'Castle of Pyncheon,'" *Studies in the Novel*, 8 (1976), 69-80. For those seeking to connect gothic practice among different regional cultures, the most helpful study to date is William H. Shurr's monograph on American literary Calvinism, *Rappaccini's Children* (Lexington: Univ. Press of Kentucky, 1981). That the strong interest in gothicism on the part of American writers is not simply a function of regional interest is quite clear from such works as Fiedler, *Love and Death*, Ringe, *American Gothic,* and especially Irving Malin, *New American Gothic* (Carbondale: Southern Illinois Univ. Press, 1962), which groups Truman Capote, James Purdy, Flannery O'Connor, John Hawkes, Carson McCullers, and J. D. Salinger with hardly any reference to cultural context. Nor have the leading practitioners of what I call provincial gothic always recognized the provincial element as a key ingredient in their writing. Cf. Sherwood Anderson's preamble to *Winesburg, Ohio:* "It was the truths that made the people grotesques. . . . The moment one of the people [observed by the "old man" writer, Anderson's surrogate,] took one of the truths

to himself, called it his truth, and tried to live his life by it, he became a grotesque and the truth he embraced became a falsehood" [1919; rpt. New York: Viking Press, 1958], p. 25). My analysis then, in stressing the correlation between gothic style and provincial culture, risks an Andersonian grotesqueness by concentrating on one component of that style.

3   The best short discussion of early provincial gothic that I have seen is Francis R. Hart, "Limits of the Gothic: The Scottish Example," in *Racism in the Eighteenth Century*, ed. Harold E. Pagliaro (Cleveland: Case-Western Reserve Univ. Press, 1973), pp. 137–53. See also Hart's *Scottish Novel* Cambridge, Mass.: Harvard Univ. Press, 1978), pp. 13–30.

4   Robert D. Hume, "Gothic versus Romance: A Revaluation of the Gothic Novel," *PMLA*, 84 (1969), 283.

5   For a good critique of such thinking, see Maurice Lévy, *Le Roman 'Gothique' Anglais, 1764–1824* (Toulouse: Association des Publications de la Faculté de Lettres et Sciences Humaines de Toulouse, 1968), p. 606.

6   David Morse, *Romanticism: A Structural Analysis* (New York: Barnes & Noble Books, 1982), p. 3. Like Hart, *Scottish Novel*, Morse, *Romanticism*, the concluding chapter to David Punter, *The Literature of Terror* (London: Longman, 1980), and William Patrick Day, *In the Circles of Fear and Desire* (Chicago: Univ. of Chicago Press, 1985), put more emphasis on the sociopolitical dimension of the gothic than Hume and most of his predecessors do, while acknowledging the "Gothic's general opposition to realist aesthetics" (Punter, *Literature of Terror*, p. 405). Those studies that tend to show the fullest appreciation of the potential of gothic as an instrument of social vision are, however, those that concentrate on the persistence of gothic in the Victorian era: e.g., Masao Miyoshi, *The Divided Self: A Perspective on the Literature of the Victorians* (New York: New York Univ. Press, 1969); James Hunt Maddox, Jr., "The Survival of Gothic Romance in the Nineteenth-century Novel: A Study of Scott, Charlotte Brontë, and Dickens," Ph.D. thesis, Yale University, 1971; Ellen Moers's chapter on "Female Gothic," in *Literary Women* (Garden City, N.Y.: Doubleday, 1977); and Judith Wilt, *Ghosts of the Gothic: Austen, Eliot, and Lawrence* (Princeton: Princeton Univ. Press, 1980).

7   Day, *In the Circles of Fear and Desire*, p. 33.

8   The best extended biocritical study is James H. Matlack, "The Literary Career of Elizabeth Barstow Stoddard," Ph.D. thesis, Yale University, 1967, a remarkably fine piece of pioneering. Shorter overviews are the critical introductions to Richard Foster, ed., *The Morgesons* (New York: Johnson Reprints, 1971), and *MOW*.

9   Two ground-breaking critical analyses are Sybil Weir, "*The Morgesons*: A Neglected Feminist *Bildungsroman*," *New England Quarterly*, 49 (1976), 427–39; and James Matlack, "Hawthorne and Elizabeth Barstow Stoddard," *New England Quarterly*, 50 (1977), 278–302, the latter especially valuable for discussion of the biographical relationships. I am even more indebted to my colleague Sandra Zagarell's essay "The (Re)possession of a Heritage: Reading Elizabeth Stoddard's *The Morgesons*," *Studies in American Fiction*, 13 (1985), 45–56. Since *The Morgesons* will be unfamiliar to many readers, here is a plot summary. The novel depicts the maturation of its narrator-protagonist Cassandra from approximately age ten

to her midtwenties, as she develops into a self-controlled young woman from a willful and somewhat spoiled child of a New England family that is old, but distinguished (like Stoddard's own) only for its recent successes in the shipbuilding industry. Cassandra's progress is marked by three significant journeys: to her maternal grandfather's home, where she is briefly and unsuccessfully subjected to an old-fashioned post-Puritan system of education; to the home of her cousin Charles Morgeson, a factory owner, where her experiences with peers at a more enlightened school and an intense but unconsummated flirtation with Charles (a married man with children) initiate her into sexual combat; and to the sumptuous home of her new friend Ben Somers, where she meets his brother, her future husband, Desmond (a rakish alcoholic who later reforms), and their formidable and disapproving matriarch, Bellevue Pickersgill Somers, who in her elegance and imposingness functions both as an antagonist and as a model in Cassandra's development. She returns home to find that her mother has suddenly died and soon thereafter takes command of the household, with an assurance and a sense of responsibility that she had lacked before. This sets the stage for the bittersweet ending to be discussed later in the chapter.

10   Among many specific examples of this contrast, a good one with which to start is Hawthorne's broodingly self-conscious elaboration of the central house as a "great human heart, with a life of its own" (*HW* 2:27), in contrast to Stoddard's much greater degree of literalism in the depiction of her houses (the Morgesons', Grandfather Warren's, Cousin Charles's, Bellevue Somers'), in which, however, Cassandra experiences quasi-gothic confinements analogous to those of Hepzibah, Phoebe, Clifford, and Holgrave.

11   This line of analysis is both a reaffirmation of and a dissent from the familiar critical argument that *Seven Gables* "constitutes Hawthorne's most forthright use of American democratic philosophy as a basis for a social ethic" (Lawrence Hall, *Hawthorne: Critic of Society* [New Haven: Yale Univ. Press, 1944], p. 160). Like Curran, "Yankee Gothic," pp. 76–7, I agree that a key source of gothic effect – e.g., in the long passage from *The House of the Seven Gables* quoted earlier – is the objective of depicting the anachronism of "aristocrats in a democratic society," but it is important to stress that the presentation of a democratic gospel is hardly an end in itself here.

12   Note my earlier overview of the ending of *The House of the Seven Gables* and the scholarship concerning it, in Chap. 10, n. 17.

13   Richard Gray, whose "Hawthorne: A Problem" adeptly summarizes the book's most important cruxes, suggests that in the ending Hawthorne is attempting a fictive commemoration of his "own earlier departure from what he called the 'haunted chamber' of his youth – or trying, by a process of sympathetic magic, to engineer his release from that feeling of self-imprisonment which he tended to associate with the figure of the house" (in *Nathaniel Hawthorne: New Critical Essays*, ed. A. Robert Lee [London: Vision Press, 1982], p. 100). Nina Baym, in *The Shape of Hawthorne's Career* (Ithaca: Cornell Univ. Press, 1976), p. 171, puts her finger squarely on the public motive: "He wanted to be a writer of happy books."

14   Catherine Maria Sedgwick, *A New-England Tale, and Miscellanies* (New York: Putnam, 1852), p. 39. Here and later in this chapter I have been stimulated

by Joel Porte, "In the Hands of an Angry God: Religious Terror in Gothic Fiction," in *The Gothic Imagination,* ed. G. Richard Thompson (Pullman: Washington State Univ. Press, 1974), pp. 42–63, which argues that "Gothic mystery" should be regarded as a "substitute for discredited religious mystery" (p. 43), and in particular as a secularization of nightmares provoked by the Calvinist imagination. I have two reservations about this view, namely, that it is too much a single-thesis argument and that even where it applies (as in New England) the gothic dimension may often more plausibly be seen as a defense against Calvinism than a transposition of a Calvinist sensibility into the aesthetic sphere. Despite any such refinements that need to be made in the Porte thesis, however, the analogy between Calvinist ideology and gothic taste is unquestionably important in New England literary history.

15 For background, see G. Harrison Orians, "New England Witchcraft in Fiction," *American Literature,* 2 (1930), 54–71; David Levin, "Historical Fact in Fiction and Drama: The Salem Witchcraft Trials," in *In Defense of Historical Literature* (New York: Hill & Wang, 1967), pp. 77–97; and Michael Bell, *Hawthorne and the Historical Romance of New England* (Princeton: Princeton Univ. Press, 1971).

16 Harriet Beecher Stowe, *Sam Lawson's Oldtown Fireside Stories* (1892; rpt. Ridgewood, N.J.: Gregg Press, 1967), p. 191.

17 John Greenleaf Whittier, *The Supernaturalism of New England* (1847), ed. Edward Wagenknecht (Norman: Univ. of Oklahoma Press, 1969), p. 79.

18 Cassandra does not fit easily into stereotypical mid-nineteenth-century images of uncanny women. She is distantly related to the Judith figure discussed by John R. Reed (*Victorian Conventions* [Athens: Univ. of Ohio Press, 1975], pp. 44–58), still more tenuously to the queenly and demonic configurations defined by Nina Auerbach (*Woman and the Demon: The Life of a Victorian Myth* [Cambridge, Mass.: Harvard Univ. Press, 1982], Chaps. 2–3), and not at all to the lamia figures analyzed by James B. Twitchell (*The Living Dead: A Study of the Vampire in Romantic Literature* [Durham: Duke Univ. Press, 1981], pp. 39–73). Where there is common ground, its basis is in the link between the female character's nonconforming willfulness and her perceived strangeness, as also with Pearl and Hester in *The Scarlet Letter,* for example.

19 Stoddard to J. R. Lowell, May 5, 1860, manuscript, Houghton Library, Harvard.

20 Charles dies in a carriage accident when the latest and most vicious of the unmanageable horses that he loves to collect has an inexplicable fit. As in many Western texts, from Chaucer's "Reeve's Tale" to D. H. Lawrence's "St. Mawr," Charles's horses are emblems of passion. After Charles's death, Cassandra, who accompanied him on his last ride and, in a certain sense even dared him to take it with the dangerous animal, mourns for the "kiss he never gave me" (*MOW,* 123).

21 The most extensive treatment of this frequently discussed paradox in Hawthorne is Millicent Bell, *Hawthorne's View of the Artist* (Albany: State Univ. of New York Press, 1962).

22 For an analysis of "The Forms and Ideology of Woman's Fiction," see Nina Baym, *Woman's Fiction* (Ithaca: Cornell Univ. Press, 1978), Chap. 2. For its bearing on Stoddard, see Susan K. Harris, "Stoddard's *The Morgesons:* A Contextual Evaluation," *ESQ,* 31 (1985), 11–22.

23 Stoddard to John Bowen, October 19, 1889, manuscript, American Antiquarian Society, Worcester, Mass.

24 William Faulkner, *Absalom, Absalom!* (1936; rpt. New York: Random House, 1964), p. 378.

25 For the Stoddard-Robbins relationship, see Matlack, "Literary Career of Stoddard," pp. 31–5.

26 Perry D. Westbrook, *Mary Wilkins Freeman* (New Haven: College and Univ. Press, 1967), p. 81.

27 Sedgwick, *New-England Tale,* p. 15. For Sedgwick's early experiences, see especially Mary E. Dewey, *Life and Letters of Catherine M. Sedgwick* (New York: Harper & Brothers, 1871).

28 For a summary of Stoddard's somewhat contradictory pronouncements, see *MOW* xxii.

29 Flannery O'Connor, *Mystery and Manners,* ed. Sally Fitzgerald and Robert Fitzgerald (New York: Farrar, Straus, 1962), p. 44.

30 Flannery O'Connor, *The Habit of Being: Letters,* ed. Sally Fitzgerald (New York: Vintage Press, 1980), pp. 457, 343.

31 Gray, "'Hawthorne: A Problem,'" p. 101.

32 Roy Harvey Pearce, "Romance and the Vision of History," in Pearce, ed., *Hawthorne Centenary Essays* (Columbus: Ohio State Univ. Press, 1964), pp. 238–43.

33 "A girl learns many things in a New England village," Phoebe tells Hepzibah (*HW* 2:74). For Phoebe's status as romanticized New England ideal, see Paul John Eakin, *The New England Girl* (Athens: Univ. of Georgia Press, 1976), pp. 74–5. The sense of Phoebe as representing the best of tradition – tradition kept up-to-date – justifies the description of her temperament as containing the "stern old stuff of Puritanism, with a gold thread in the web" (*HW* 2:76).

34 See especially Rollin Lynde Hartt, "A New England Hill Town," *Atlantic Monthly,* 83 (1899), 561–74, 712–20, and Harold F. Wilson, *The Hill Country of Northern New England* (New York: Columbia Univ. Press, 1936). Hal S. Barron, *Those Who Stayed Behind* (Cambridge: Cambridge Univ. Press, 1984), esp. pp. 31–50, argues that the decline has been overstated but ends up confirming that some sort of stagnation did in fact occur.

35 Howard Mumford Jones, "New England Dilemma," in *Ideas in America* (Cambridge, Mass.: Harvard Univ. Press, 1944), p. 211.

POSTSCRIPT

1 Different aspects of this point are covered thoughtfully in David Levin, *History as Romantic Art* (Stanford: Stanford Univ. Press, 1959); Barbara Miller Solomon, *Ancestors and Immigrants: A Changing New England Tradition* (Cambridge, Mass.: Harvard Univ. Press, 1956); Jay B. Hubbell, *Who Are the Major American Writers?* (Durham: Duke Univ. Press, 1972), pp. 75–114; and Howard Mumford Jones, *The Theory of American Literature* (1948; rev. ed., Ithaca: Cornell Univ. Press, 1965), pp. 79–117.

2 See, in this regard, the most authoritative studies of American literary regionalism and American literary nationalism, both by Benjamin Spencer: "Regionalism in American Literature," in *Regionalism in America,* ed. Merrill Jensen (Madison: Univ. of Wisconsin Press, 1951), esp. p. 224, and *The Quest for Nationality: An American Literary Campaign* (Syracuse: Syracuse Univ. Press, 1957), esp. p. 264.

3 For a superb case study of the contrast and complementarity of late Victorian and modernist critical perspectives, see Lionel Trilling, "Our Hawthorne," in *Hawthorne Centenary Essays,* ed. Roy Harvey Pearce (Columbus: Ohio State Univ. Press, 1964), pp. 429–58. The modernism that Trilling has in mind is existentialist (Hawthorne envisaged as a nineteenth-century Kafkaesque sensibility) rather than poststructuralist, and the "old-fashioned" Jamesean reading that Trilling pits against the former actually resonates rather well with the latter ideology. This suggests that the ideological contrasts that one posits between eras are just as apt to be artifacts of the critic's present-minded concerns as are single-thesis interpretations. That, however, does not invalidate Trilling's eloquent testimony in support of a historical approach to interpretation.

APPENDIX: VITAL STATISTICS

1 Major figures so identified include A. Bronson Alcott, Louisa May Alcott, George Bancroft, Joel Barlow, Henry Ward Beecher, Orestes Brownson, William Cullen Bryant, William Ellery Channing, Joseph Dennie, John W. De Forest, Emily Dickinson, Timothy Dwight, Ralph Waldo Emerson, Margaret Fuller, Fitz-Greene Halleck, Nathaniel Hawthorne, Oliver Wendell Holmes, David Humphreys, Henry Wadsworth Longfellow, James Russell Lowell, John Lothrop Motley, John Neal, Theodore Parker, Francis Parkman, William Hickling Prescott, Harriet Beecher Stowe, Henry David Thoreau, Frederick Goddard Tuckerman, John Trumbull, Royall Tyler, Jones Very, Mercy Otis Warren, Phillis Wheatley, John Greenleaf Whittier, and Nathaniel Parker Willis.

2 In doubtful cases, I was influenced by whether the author's work seemed predominantly Neoclassical or Romantic in temper. Most authors proved easy to classify. Designations are given in the Table of Authors Surveyed.

3 In this regard, see Elisabeth Williams Dexter, *Career Women of America, 1776–1840* (Francestown, N.H.: Jones, 1950), pp. 90–115; Ann Douglas, *The Feminization of American Culture* (New York: Knopf, 1977), and especially Mary Kelley, *Private Woman, Public Stage; Literary Domesticity in Nineteenth-century America* (New York: Oxford Univ. Press, 1984), of particular value in pointing up the constraints placed on the professionalism of literary women by the cult of domesticity. It might be noted that the percentage of women among New England authors of the second era was higher than for British writers of the same period. Richard D. Altick, "The Sociology of Authorship: The Social Origins, Education, and Occupation of 1,100 British Writers, 1800–1935," *Bulletin of the New York Public Library,* 66 (1962), 392, records a decrease in the percentage of women authors from 20.9 percent in 1800–35 to 16.1 percent in 1835–70, with a return to slightly more than 20 percent thereafter. It would seem, however, that New England and British women writers encountered similar prejudices when they entered the literary marketplace. Elaine Showalter, *A Literature of Their Own*

(Princeton: Princeton Univ. Press, 1977), esp. pp. 3–72, describes the problems faced by Victorian women writers.

4 Note that my definition of "college" is broad, including post–secondary school programs leading to degrees of certification other than the A.B. (e.g., theological seminaries, to name the commonest alternative). But the overwhelming majority of cases involve enrollment in liberal arts programs. My percentages are based on the assumption that none of the unknown cases (2 writers, 25 fathers) attended. At least 50 percent of the male writers completed A.B. requirements. This compares with a rate of graduation that by the most generous estimate must have been less than 1 in every 130 white males, at the start of the period, and no more than 1 in 90 at the end – calculations arrived at by comparing census data for white New England males in 1800, 1820, and 1860 with the numbers of graduates of New England colleges given by David I. Allmendinger, Jr., *Paupers and Scholars: The Transformation of Student Life in Nineteenth-century New England* (New York: St. Martin's Press, 1975), p. 10, and making the very generous assumption that the number of graduates in the regional population was equal to the number of New England college graduates for the previous fifty years.

5 Altick, "The Sociology of Authorship," p. 395, gives the following percentages for university attendance by male writers: 52.5 percent (for 1800–35), 66.2 percent (for 1835–70). After 1870, however, the British figures reached and remained at the 70-percent level; and even for our period, if Altick is correct, it would seem that the British literary establishment was at least as socially elite as their New England counterparts, with more than 95 percent of writers coming from the top 25 percent of the social hierarchy (nobility and middle class) (ibid., p. 394).

6 Of the 232 cases where information is available on fathers, 52 percent were in the former four occupational categories; 15 percent were farmers (34 cases, as compared to 37 ministers, 30 lawyers, 43 merchants, 16 physicians). The unknown cases probably include a high percentage of lower-status individuals. If all 43 unknown cases were farmers, the total percentage of farmers would be 28 percent, and that of merchants and learned professionals 44 percent. In all cases, information is based on my sense of the parent's primary occupation, a point sometimes hard to judge.

7 As an index of the increasing denominational unrepresentativeness of the authors: According to one historian's estimate, in 1800, Massachusetts churches were 72 percent Congregational and Episcopalian (as compared with 19 in 20 of the denominationally identifiable Massachusetts writers who reached adulthood around 1800), whereas in 1857 these elite churches comprised only 44.6 percent of the total number (Joseph S. Clark, *A Historical Sketch of the Congregational Churches in Massachusetts* [Boston: Congregational Board of Publication, 1858], pp. 226, 282).

8 This estimate is based on inferences from biographical data gathered from a wide array of sources. Since there have been very few specialized studies of authors' incomes like William Charvat's studies of Longfellow and Melville in *The Profession of Authorship in America,* ed. Matthew J. Bruccoli (Columbus: Ohio State Univ. Press, 1968), and Wayne Allen Jones's of Hawthorne, in "Hawthorne's 'Slender Means,'" *Nathaniel Hawthorne Journal, 1977,* ed. C. E. Clark, Jr. (Detroit: Gale, 1980), 1–34, I would expect to be proved wrong in some cases. My overall estimate of 17 percent is probably generous in overlooking hidden subsidies and investment income. On the other hand, I have restricted the list by excluding those who seem to have depended on creative writing (including literary lecturing) for a period of less than three years (this excludes, for instance, the elder Elizabeth Stuart Phelps, enormously successful at the very end of her life). Here, in any case, is the list. Men: Abbott, Benjamin, Bennett, Briggs, Cobb, Congdon, Curtis, Duganne, Emerson, S. Goodrich, E. Gould, Hawthorne, Higginson, Holland, Holmes, Ingraham, Kettell, Longfellow, Mitchell, Neal, Shaw ("Josh Billings"), Shillaber, Seba Smith, Thomes, Trowbridge, Whipple, Whittier, Willis, Winter. Women: Alcott, Child, Cooke, Cummins, Farley, Follen, Fuller, L. Hale, S. Hale, Hentz, Holmes, H. Lee, Parton, Prentiss, Sigourney, E. Smith, Stephens, Stowe, Tuthill, Williams.

9 Allmendinger, *Paupers and Scholars,* p. 5n, calculates that in the 1780s New England produced 1 graduate in every 6,495 persons, as against 1 in every 2,560 in the 1830s.

10 Among writers for whom literature was the primary source of income and where parental occupation was known, 11 of 19 women and 10 of 23 men came from backgrounds that I have defined as genteel.

11 The one ambiguous case, Margaret Fuller, I have reckoned as unmarried.

12 L. M. Alcott, Dickinson, Larcom, and Sedgwick.

13 Farley, Follen, S. Hale, Nichols, Tuthill, Wheatley.

14 Bolton, Child, Follen, Gilman, Lowell, Mayo, Murray, Nichols (second husband), Parton (second husband), Prentiss, Smith, Stephens, Stoddard, Tuthill, Warren, Whitman.

15 In all, 112 cases with an overlap of 2.

16 Beecher, Belknap, Brooks, J. N. Brown, Bulfinch, Burgess, Channing, Cheever, Clarke, W. Colton, Croswell, Deane, Dwight, Fitch, Frothingham, Gardiner, S. Gilman, E. Hale, Harris, Enos Hitchcock, Hooker, Ingraham, Judd, S. Longfellow, R. Lowell, Norton, Parker, Pierpont, Sears, H. Ware, W. Ware, Wilcox, Winchester.

17 W. Allen, Baldwin, S. Brown, Brownson, Burton, Emerson, E. Everett, Flint, Higginson, Hill, Knight, Upham.

18 Abbott, Emerson, Higginson, Ingraham.

19 Adams, Austin, the younger Dana, Deering, Durfee, Elliot, A. Everett, A. G. Greene, Hollister, Honeywood, Kimball, Lincoln, Lockwood, Lunt, Randall, Saxe, Sewall, I. Story, J. Story, Thompson, Trumbull, Tyler. Fourteen others practiced more or less seriously at different points in their lives: Bartlett, the elder Dana, D. Everett, Fessenden, Lathrop, McLellan, Mellen, Neal, Paine, Peck, Pike, Pierpont, W. Story, Thatcher. The percentage of serious pursuers of law remains, however, considerably lower than the percentage of serious pursuers of the ministry (60 percent, versus 80 percent). Very likely the relative prestige of law had something to do with attracting a greater number of people who proved marginally committed to it.

20 P. Allen, Benjamin, Bouton, Brainard, Bryant, W. Burleigh, H. Clapp, W. Clapp, Cobb, C. Coffin, R. Coffin, Congdon, Dawes, Dennie, Durivage, Eastman, Fessenden, E. Flagg, Garrison, Hildreth, Knapp, Osborn, Pray, Prentice, C. Prentiss, E. Sargent, Shillaber, Southwick, Thomes, Winter, Woodworth.

21 W. Burleigh, Cobb, R. Coffin (who never rose above printer), Garrison, Osborn, Shillaber, Southwick, Thomes, Woodworth.

22 Beecher*, H. Clapp, W. Clapp, C. Coffin, Congdon*, Durivage, Eastman*, Pray*, Prentiss*, Whittier, Willis*. (Asterisks here indicate those who attended college.)

23 P. Allen*, Benjamin*, Bouton*, Brainard*, Bryant*, the elder Dana*, Dawes*, Dennie*, D. Everett*, Fessenden*, E. Flagg, Hildreth*, F. Hill, Knapp*, J. R. Lowell*, McLellan*, Mellen*, Neal, Peck*, Prentice*, J. Quincy*, Stimson, Thatcher*, Winter*. (Asterisks here indicates college attendance.)

24 Bryant was atypical in not having completed college. In family background, however, he was like most other law students-turned-journalists in being of gentry extraction. In 13 of the 22 cases for which information is available, the fathers were ministers, lawyers, or doctors (like Peter Bryant) who had attended Harvard or Yale.

25 *HW* 15:132; cf. Altick, "The Sociology of Authorship," p. 401, and Robert Escarpit, *Sociology of Literature,* trans. Ernest Pick (Painesville, Ohio: Lake Erie College Press, 1965), p. 36, give occupational categories for selected late nineteenth-century British and French writers and their fathers.

26 The exceptions were Universalist minister Phebe Hanaford; Elizabeth Oakes Smith, briefly a Congregational pastor; and water-cure apostle Mary Gove Nichols, who might be called a sort of physician.

27 L. M. Alcott, Bacon, Child, Cooke, Farley, Fuller, S. Hale, Larcom, H. Lee, McDougall, Mayo, Nichols, Parton, Rowson, Stephens, Stowe, Tuthill, Wheatley, Willard, Williams.

28 Quoted in Patricia G. Holland, "Lydia Maria Child as a Nineteenth-century Professional Author," in *Studies in the American Renaissance, 1981,* ed. Joel Myerson (Boston: Twayne, 1981), p. 163.

29 In the first category belong Bacon, Bolton, Botta, Howe, Larcom, Nichols, Rowson, Smith, Ware, and Willard; in the second, Botta, Child, Farley, S. Hale, Larcom, Mayo, Parton, Stephens, Stoddard, and Ware.

30 Some examples appear to have been E. Hooper, M. Lowell, Peirson, Tenney, and Wells, all but one of whom published in their lifetimes but apparently without thought of a career as such.

31 In the first category belong S. Hale, Hanaford, Hentz, H. Lee, Parton, Rowson, Smith, Spofford, and Tuthill; in the second, Sigourney, Stephens, Stoddard, and Stowe; in the third, Cummins, Holmes, and Phelps.

32 Between 1780 and 1860, the balance of population within New England fluctuated considerably. Whereas that of Massachusetts, New Hampshire, and Rhode Island remained relatively stable (ranging from 31 percent to 39 percent, 11 percent to 16 percent, and 4 percent to 7 percent of the region's total white population), in Connecticut the percentage dropped from 29 percent, in 1780, to between 14 percent and 15 percent after 1840; in Maine it increased from 7 percent to 21 percent; and in Vermont it rose from 7 percent to nearly 15 percent in 1830, before subsiding to 11 percent in 1860. The averages for the period, however, give an accurate indication of the relationship between population share and percentage of native-reared authors in each era.

33 According to the 1860 census, 21 percent of the Massachusetts population was comprised of immigrants, on a par with Connecticut and Rhode Island but far below northern New England, where the percentage stood between 5 percent and 10 percent. The contrast reflected the differing degrees of urbanization and industrialization in lower and upper New England.

34 Here and below I calculate migration statistics on the basis of where an author grew up, rather than on the basis of where that author resided at the time of departure.

35 Lois Kimball Mathews, *The Expansion of New England* (Boston: Houghton Mifflin, 1909), pp. 193–4, 139–70; Lewis D. Stilwell, "Migration from Vermont (1776–1850)," *Proceedings of the Vermont Historical Society*, n.s., 5 (1937), 63–245; U.S. Bureau of the Census, *Population of the United States in 1860* (Washington, D.C.: Government Printing Office, 1864), p. xxxiii.

36 In keeping with this speculation would be these facts: Drama was the main field of literary distinction for two major writers of the first era (Warren and Tyler) but of none in the second era; and drama was attempted by roughly one-fifth of the writers in the first era (11) as against roughly one-eighth (about 25) in the second era.

37 Frank Luther Mott, *Golden Multitudes: The Story of Best Sellers in the United States* (New York: Macmillan, 1947), pp. 304–9. The authors are L. M. Alcott, Cummins, Foster, Holmes, H. Lee, Rowson, Stephens, and Stowe. Among the 33 male novelists, only Hawthorne, Ingraham, and Thompson are listed; and Hawthorne should probably be excluded, since Mott counts all-time sales, not just sales within the period.

38 Stowe and Beecher are regarded as having been brought up in Connecticut (which they left for Boston at the ages of fifteen and thirteen, respectively) on the basis of autobiographical self-appraisal. By the same token, Hawthorne is not counted as having grown up in Massachusetts, since as a teenager he thought of Maine as his home.

39 Barlow, Beecher, Brownson, Bryant, Dennie, Fuller, and Willis moved away from the region permanently while still in their prime. The rest, despite prolonged periods of absence, in some cases, remained New Englanders – as did some of the emigrants. Only Emerson, Tuckerman, and Tyler chose more rustic homes than those where they had grown up. Not more than a score of the minor authors did the same. Emerson's retreat to Concord, then, was decidedly atypical.

40 Among the major authors, Beecher, Dwight, Stowe, Very, and Wheatley might be reckoned as evangelicals. Dickinson and De Forest intermittently leaned that way. Among the first 35 minor authors (in alphabetical order), on the other hand, I count at least 9 evangelicals in the two dozen or so whose orientation I can identify, 2 Baptists, and the rest Congregationalists: Abbott, W. Allen, Bacon, Banvard, Bingham, Bolton, Bouton, Brace, J. N. Brown.

41 Among the first 35 minor authors, the following seem to be the only cases: Allston, Alsop, Benjamin, Botta, Brainard, M. Brooks, Brown, Brownell.

42 The following among the first 35 minor authors (in alphabetical order) seem to be the only ones to meet the "literary family" test (parent or sibling as writer): Abbott, Adams, W. Allen, Alsop, Bacon, Ballou, Banvard, Bryant.

43 Among the 32 (of 46) minor writers of the first era whose political orientation I can positively identify, I count 22 Federalists and 10 Jeffersonians.

44 Among the 41 minor male writers, only 6 held state or national office.

45 Among the first 35 minor second-era writers (in alphabetical order) only a few associated themselves in any sense with radical social and political reform measures. Baldwin, Bolton, Cheever, and the two Burleigh brothers are the only clear-cut cases.

46 David Donald, "Toward a Reconsideration of Abolitionists," *Lincoln Reconsidered* (New York: Knopf, 1956), pp. 19–36. For criticism of Donald's methodology, see Robert Skotheim, "A Note on Historical Method: David Donald's 'Toward a Reconsideration of Abolitionists,'" *Journal of Southern History*, 25 (1959), 356–65. For substantive weaknesses in Donald's evidence, see Chapter 5 of Leonard Richards, *"Gentlemen of Property and Standing": Anti-abolition Mobs in Jacksonian America* (New York: Oxford Univ. Press, 1970); Gerald Sorin, *The New York Abolitionists* (Westport, Conn.: Greenwood Press, 1971), esp. Chap. 4, which argues (p. 119) in direct contradiction to Donald that the abolitionist leaders surveyed "generally seem to have had higher status in their respective communities than their fathers had in theirs"; and the essays by Alan M. Kraut and Bertram Wyatt-Brown in Lewis Perry and Michael Fellman, eds., *Antislavery Reconsidered* (Baton Rouge: Louisiana State Univ. Press, 1979). For qualified endorsement of Donald, see James Brewer Stewart, *Holy Warriors* (New York: Hill & Wang, 1967), pp. 37–8.

47 E.g., Doreen Hunter, "America's First Romantics: Richard Henry Dana, Sr., and Washington Allston," *New England Quarterly*, 45 (1972), 3–30.

Index

Trumbull, John (*cont.*)
tioned, 90, 107, 108, 372, 397, 406, 424, 426, 428, 450, 492, 494
Tuckerman, Frederick Goddard: as neglected figure, 52, 123; poetry discussed, **122–3,** 288, **431;** mentioned, 107, 124, 289, 388, 390, 392, 397, 430, 476, 492, 496
Tudor, William, 31, 397, 459, 462
Tuthill, Cornelius, 35, 406
Tuthill, Louisa, 397, 494, 495
Twain, Mark, 34, 96, 99, 164
Tyler, Royall: *Algerine Captive,* 25, 27, 317–18; *Contrast, The,* 26, 86, 88, 97, 312, **337–8,** 485; poetry discussed, 65, 132, 307; on village ideal, 307, 312, 313; mentioned, 26, 27, 35, 107, 160, 397, 403, 416, 432, 480, 481, 494, 496
Typology and New England literary culture, 126–7, 171, **201, 276–7,** 442, 445, 474; *see also* Jeremiad tradition; Puritan antecedence, myth of; Puritanism

Unitarianism: and (Congregationalist) orthodoxy, 52, **215,** 295; and historical literature, 208, **232–7, 247–50, 254–60, 262–76,** 334; and historiography, 207, **214–28, 230–2,** 455; and literary scripturism, **175–7, 180–1;** in oratory, 138, **143–5,** 146–7; in poetry, 44–5, 116, 129–30, **254–60;** prevalence among antebellum literati, **44–9,** 378, **388;** and provincial gothic, 359, 365–6; supportive of literary culture, **38–9;** and Transcendentalism, 16, **46–8,** 62, 180; and Whiggery, 41, 44, 451
United States Literary Gazette, 31, 58
Universalist literary culture, 25, 30, 54, 232, 451–2, 461–2, 495
Unraveling, poems of, **131–4**
Upham, Charles Wentworth: on Puritan fathers, 199; on Salem witchcraft and Cotton Mather, 219, 222–4, 232; mentioned, 456, 459, 460
Upham, Thomas C., 397, 476, 494
Urbanization: as backdrop to portrayal of New England village life, **283, 300–1,** 315, 330, **480–1,** 484; metropolitan migration of authors, 383–4, 386–7

Vermont, literary life of, 26–7, 204
Very, Jones: career, 46, 47, 135, 388, 389; poetry discussed, 109, 183, 443; mentioned, 36, 52, 72, 77, 107, 116, 153, 397, 427, 428, 447, 492, 496
Very, Lydia, 389, 397
Voltaire, 178, 209

Walpole, Horace, 352, 359
Walpole, New Hampshire, as literary center, **27–8**
Walter, William B., 397
Ward, Elizabeth Phelps, *see* Phelps (Ward), Elizabeth Stuart
Ward, Nathaniel, 226, 338, 461
Ware, Henry, Jr., 269, 397, 459, 494
Ware, Katharine, 397, 495
Ware, William, **176–7,** 397, 443–4, 494
Warren, Austin, 6, 11, 399, 400
Warren, Mercy Otis, 25, 30, 382, 389, 390, 397, 403, 458, 492, 494, 496
Washington, George, 32, 170, 204, 225, 230, 434
Watts, Isaac, 120, 170, 442
Webster, Daniel: on New England fathers, 198–9, 205, 280; as oratorical model, 138, **140–1, 147–52,** 158, 163, 434, **436;** personal life, 436–7; mentioned, 59, 65, 137, 154, 163, 376, 435, 451, 455
Webster, Noah, 37, 40
Wellek, René, 6, 11, 399, 400, 401
Wells, Anna Maria, 397, 495
Wharton, Edith, 353, 367
Wheatley, Phillis, 25, 377, 388, 397, 492, 494, 495, 496
Whig Party: and antebellum cultural establishment, 41, 44, 94–6, 207, 232, 386, 390; and classicism, 425, 433; and intellectual avant-garde, 95, 417, 436; and oratory, 138; and Puritan antecedence myth, **199–201,** 227, 451–3; mentioned, 52, 152; *see also* Democratic Party; Federalist literary culture; Jacksonianism and New England literary culture; Jeffersonianism and New England literary culture
Whipple, Edwin Percy, 45, 48, 149, 397, 436, 494
Whitcher, Frances, 44, 409
Whitman, Sarah Helen, 135, 395, 494
Whitman, Walt: and American poetic tradition, 88, 91, **106,** 135–36; and Dickinson, 114; and Emerson, 106, 112, 135–6; and literary language, 159–60; and oratory, 146, 163; prophetic strain in, 183, 446; mentioned, 20, 47, 96, 99, 108, 129, 134, 426, 429
Whittier, John Greenleaf: antiestablishment tendencies, 46, 390, **410;** "Last Walk in Autumn, The," **286–7,** 289, 291; literary relationships, 34, 42, 46, 135, 315, 389; *Margaret Smith's Journal,* **242,** 247, 465–6; as recorder of regional culture, 40, 127, 212, 242, 286–8, 292, 294, 300, 360; *Snow-Bound,* 127–8; stature as poet, 42, 43, 107, 196; "Telling the Bees," **123–4,**